ANCIENT INK

Ancient Ink
THE ARCHAEOLOGY OF TATTOOING

EDITED BY

LARS KRUTAK

AND

AARON DETER-WOLF

A McLellan Book

UNIVERSITY OF WASHINGTON PRESS
Seattle & London

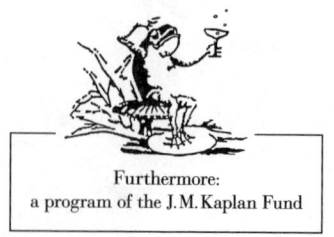

Furthermore:
a program of the J.M. Kaplan Fund

Ancient Ink was made possible in part by a grant from Furthermore, a program of the J. M. Kaplan Fund.

Additional support was provided by the McLellan Endowment, established through the generosity of Martha McCleary McLellan and Mary McLellan Williams.

Copyright © 2017 by the University of Washington Press
Paperback edition 2020
Printed and bound in the United States of America
Design by Katrina Noble
Layout by Jennifer Shontz, www.redshoedesign.com
24 23 22   5 4 3 2

All rights reserved. No part of this publication may be reproduced or transmitted in any form or by any means, electronic or mechanical, including photocopy, recording, or any information storage or retrieval system, without permission in writing from the publisher.

UNIVERSITY OF WASHINGTON PRESS
uwapress.uw.edu

LIBRARY OF CONGRESS CATALOGING-IN-PUBLICATION DATA ON FILE
ISBN (hardcover): 978-0-295-74282-3
ISBN (paperback): 978-0-295-74283-0
ISBN (ebook): 978-0-295-74284-7

Front cover: Egyptian faience figurine with tattoos on truncated legs (ca. 1980–1800 BCE); not to scale. Photograph by Renée Friedman. British Museum, London (EA52863)

The paper used in this publication is acid-free and meets the minimum requirements of American National Standard for Information Sciences—Permanence of Paper for Printed Library Materials, ANSI z39.48–1984. ∞

To the memory of

PAUL R. KRUTAK (1934–2016),
DANIEL R. DETER (1948–2015),

and

LEONID T. YABLONSKY (1950–2016)

I suppose . . . that the value of these artifacts lies in how one looks at them.

—SUSIE SILOOK, *St. Lawrence Island Yupik artist (2009)*

CONTENTS

Acknowledgments xi

Introduction
AARON DETER-WOLF AND LARS KRUTAK 3

Part 1: Skin

1   New Tattoos from Ancient Egypt: Defining Marks of Culture
    RENÉE FRIEDMAN 11

2   *Burik*: Tattoos of the Ibaloy Mummies of Benguet, North Luzon, Philippines
    ANALYN SALVADOR-AMORES 37

3   Reviving Tribal Tattoo Traditions of the Philippines
    LARS KRUTAK 56

4   The Mummification Process among the "Fire Mummies" of Kabayan:
    A Paleohistological Note
    DARIO PIOMBINO-MASCALI, RONALD G. BECKETT,
    ORLANDO V. ABINION, AND DONG HOON SHIN 62

5   Identifications of Iron Age Tattoos from the Altai-Sayan Mountains in Russia
    SVETLANA PANKOVA 66

6   Neo-Pazyryk Tattoos: A Modern Revival
    COLIN DALE AND LARS KRUTAK 99

7   Recovering the Nineteenth-Century European Tattoo:
    Collections, Contexts, and Techniques
    GEMMA ANGEL 107

8   After You Die: Preserving Tattooed Skin
    AARON DETER-WOLF AND LARS KRUTAK 130

Part 2: Tools

9   The Antiquity of Tattooing in Southeastern Europe
       PETAR N. ZIDAROV 137

10   Balkan Ink: Europe's Oldest Living Tattoo Tradition
       LARS KRUTAK 150

11   Archaeological Evidence for Tattooing in Polynesia and Micronesia
       LOUISE FUREY 159

12   Reading Between Our Lines: Tattooing in Papua New Guinea
       LARS KRUTAK 185

13   Scratching the Surface: Mistaken Identifications of
       Tattoo Tools from Eastern North America
       AARON DETER-WOLF, BENOÎT ROBITAILLE, AND ISAAC WALTERS 193

14   Native North American Tattoo Revival
       LARS KRUTAK 210

15   The Discovery of a Sarmatian Tattoo Toolkit in Russia
       LEONID T. YABLONSKY 215

16   Further Evaluation of Tattooing Use-Wear on Bone Tools
       AARON DETER-WOLF AND TARA NICOLE CLARK 231

Part 3: Art

17   What to Make of the Prehistory of Tattooing in Europe?
       LUC RENAUT 243

18   Sacrificing the Sacred: Tattooed Prehistoric Ivory Figures of
       St. Lawrence Island, Alaska
       LARS KRUTAK 262

19   A Long Sleep: Reawakening Tattoo Traditions in Alaska
       LARS KRUTAK 286

References 295
Contributors 339
Index 341

Color plates follow page 180.

ACKNOWLEDGMENTS

This volume is intended as a modest contribution to the study of ancient tattooing practices and technology. The collection of essays is the outcome of many conversations over the years, including those held at international conferences: European Association of Archaeologists Annual Meetings (2010/2011, The Hague and Oslo); "Into the Skin: Identity, Symbols and History of Permanent Body Marks" conference (2011, Vatican City); 7th World Congress on Mummy Studies (2011, San Diego); and Musée du Quai Branly conference "Tattooed Images" (2015, Paris).

As a collaborative project, this book would not have been possible without the support of numerous individuals who provided guidance, contacts, imagery, stories, and tattoo knowledge, as well as humor when we needed it most. In this regard, we extend our appreciation to the St. Lawrence Island (Alaska) elders; Kalinga master tattooist Whang-Od; Elle Festin; Tina Astudillo-Ash; Mark of the Four Waves; Marjorie Tahbone; Qaiyaan and Jana Harcharek; Dave Mazierski; Alexander Yablonsky; Orlando Abinion; Art Tibaldo; Colin Dale of Skin & Bone Tattoo; Peter van der Helm; Tsvetan Chetashki; Ivan Vajsov; Svend Hansen; Cristina Georgescu; Zele of Zagreb Tattoo; Sasha Aleksandar of Orca Sun Tattoo; Carol Diaz-Granados; Jim Duncan; Johann Sawyer; Heidi Altman; Tanya Kanceljak; Tea Turalija Mihaljevic; Wal Ambrose; Julia Mage'au Gray, Nata Richards, and Ranu James (www.teptok.com); Ade Baroa; Vali Kolou; Taitá Koroka; Dion Kaszas of Vertigo Tattoo; Carla Wells-Listener; Alan White; Michael Galban; Kiano Zamani; Anna Felicity Friedman; Ethan Freeman; Matt Lodder; Sébastien Galliot; Francesco d'Errico; Gerhard Bosinski; Magda Lazarovici; Camilla Norman; Claire Alix; Owen Mason; Dave Hunt; Chris Dudar, and the two anonymous reviewers who offered critiques of the draft manuscript.

Documenting the antiquity, significance, and meaning of ancient tattooing would have been quite difficult without the assistance of the collectors, photographers, galleries, archives, museums, publishers, and institutional staff who provided permission to reproduce written documents, publications, objects of material culture, and photography. Our gratitude goes out to the Petrie Museum of Egyptian Archaeology, University College London; the British Museum; Sudan National Museum; the Oriental Institute; Ashmolean Museum of Art and Archaeology, Oxford University; The State Hermitage Museum; Regional Historical Museum Veliko Turnovo; the National Archaeological Institute with Museum at the Bulgarian Academy of Sciences; Auckland Museum; Orenburg Governor's Museum of Local Lore and History; Editions Ophrys; Cotsen

Institute of Archaeology Press, UCLA; Institute for Prehistoric Archaeology, Free University Berlin; The American School of Classical Studies at Athens; Association Hellas et Roma; Donald Ellis Gallery; Angela Linn and Scott Shirar, of the University of Alaska Museum of the North; Dave Rosenthal and National Museum of Natural History; Sean Mooney, of the Rock Foundation Collection; National Museum of the American Indian; Daisy Njoku and the National Anthropological Archives; American Museum of Natural History Special Collections and Department of Anthropology; Bryan Just and Princeton University Art Museum; Bill and Carol Wolf Collection; Perry and Basha Lewis Collection; Anna Cannizzo and the Oshkosh Public Museum; Steve Davis and the Research Laboratories of Archaeology, University of North Carolina; Neal Oshima and En Barong, Inc.; Joe Ash Photography; Kalynna Ashley Photography; Cora DeVos / Little Inuk Photography; and Charles Hamm and the National Association for the Preservation of Skin Art.

We gratefully acknowledge the financial support of a generous subvention grant and research grant from Flavia Robinson and the Daniele Agostino Derossi Foundation (Torino, Italy) for the senior editor's travel to Papua New Guinea. We would also like to give special recognition to Lorri Hagman and her staff at the University of Washington Press for supporting the publication of this book, and to Ellen Wheat for copyediting the manuscript. Numerous others also assisted us during the course of writing and editing this book, and we thank you all for your invaluable support.

ANCIENT INK

Introduction

Aaron Deter-Wolf and Lars Krutak

THE DESIRE TO ALTER, DECORATE, AND ADORN THE HUMAN BODY IS A cultural universal. While specific forms of body decoration and the underlying motivations vary according to region, culture, and era, human societies from the past and present have engaged in practices designed to enhance their natural appearance. Tattooing—the process of inserting pigment into the skin to create permanent designs and patterns—as a form of body decoration has been practiced by cultures around the globe and throughout human history. Preserved tattoos on mummified human remains demonstrate that the practice extends back to at least the fourth millennium BCE (Deter-Wolf et al. 2016). However, the exact antiquity and archaeological footprint of tattooing remain poorly understood, and it was not until recently that the various pieces of archaeological evidence for tattooing have been seriously or systematically evaluated by qualified scholars.

Over the past two decades there has been a surge in interest among both academics and the general public in learning more about ancient and historic tattooing. Researchers studying past societies have begun to recognize the importance of tattooing in both social and ritual contexts. Professional tattoo artists are increasingly interested in learning more about the history of their profession, about authentic ancient and historical motifs, and about the techniques involved in applying tattoos in the pre-electric era. The ever-growing population of tattooed individuals (as well as those aspiring to become tattooed) are similarly intrigued by traditional tattoo methods, and by the designs and meanings of ancient and historic body art. Members of Indigenous cultures worldwide are actively seeking out information regarding the tattoo tools, symbols, and significance associated with their unique cultural traditions, which were historically suppressed by colonial, missionary, and other acculturative agents.

Despite this growing interest, there are few solidly researched volumes examining ancient tattoo traditions. Those works are generally region specific (e.g., Deter-Wolf and Diaz-Granados 2013; Krutak 2014a), contain dated or suspect scholarship (e.g., Hambly 1925; van Dinter 2005), are generalist texts that do not contain in-depth or specific archaeological information, or are overly academic and unapproachable for the general public. In the absence of definitive source material, scholars, tattoo artists, and the interested public rely instead on questionable sources, including the fountain of readily accessible but often inaccurate information on the internet, to learn about the history and archaeology of tattooing. As a result, myths and misunderstandings are being perpetuated regarding the historical scope of tattooing, the historic and Indigenous tools, methods, and meanings, and the available archaeological evidence.

Ancient Ink is the first book dedicated to the archaeological study of tattooing. In the volume, we present essays by international researchers working to understand our shared human past through examination of the principal lines of archaeological evidence used to examine ancient and historic tattooing: preserved human skin, tattoo tools, and the artistic record. These studies contribute to our understanding of the antiquity, durability, and significance of tattooing and human body decoration by illuminating how different societies of the past have employed their skin in the construction of their identities. Moreover, they illustrate how ancient body art traditions connect to our modern culture through Indigenous tattoo revitalization efforts and the recontextualization of tattoo meanings and praxis through the work of contemporary artists. To this end, chapters alternate analyses of the archaeological record with descriptions of contemporary work by tattoo artists who employ historic and traditional techniques and/or imagery, thereby demonstrating the persistence of traditions discussed in the preceding chapter. When possible, the chapter authors draw parallels between modern and historic or Indigenous traditions.

Part 1: Skin

The first part of this volume addresses topics related to naturally and deliberately preserved tattooed human remains, which constitute the most spectacular and direct form of archaeological evidence of tattooing in ancient and historic societies. Hundreds of human mummies with tattooed skin have been recovered from archaeological settings around the globe, including in Europe, South America, Central America, North Africa, Western Asia, Siberia, the Philippines, and the Arctic (Deter-Wolf et al. 2016: table 1). Most of these finds were historically regarded as curiosities for collection and exhibition, but prior to the past decade—with the notable exception of the Tyrolean mummy known as Ötzi—only a few have undergone substantive documentation or analysis. In some cases, natural darkening of preserved skin as a result of age and weathering obscured tattoos, and only with the application of new imaging technologies have these marks been discovered (e.g., Samadelli et al. 2015). Today, recognition of the cultural importance of tattooing combined with advances in imaging and detection technology facilitate new examinations and identifications of preserved tattooed remains both in the archaeological record and in museum collections. The authors in the first part describe new finds of preserved, tattooed skin, as well as new discoveries and analysis of previously recorded examples.

In chapter 1, Renée Freidman discusses recent identifications of preserved tattoos on Egyptian and Nubian C-Group mummies from the sites of Gebelein and Hierakonpolis. Freidman also marshals comparative evidence to identify a possible tattoo toolkit from Hierakonpolis Cemetery HK43, and reassesses the tattooed mummies discovered at Deir el Bahari in 1891. Altogether, these various lines of evidence engage tattoo traditions spanning the Predynastic period (ca. 3900–3100 BCE) through the New Kingdom (1550–1069 BCE), demonstrate the presence of separate and distinctive tattoo traditions in Egypt and Nubia, and entirely reframe our understanding of tattooing in the region. In addition, radiocarbon analysis reveals that the Gebelein mummies are the oldest tattooed remains yet discovered in Africa.

On the island of Luzon, Philippines, the *burik* (tattoo) tradition of the Indigenous Ibaloy people increasingly constitutes a significant aspect of historical and contemporary identity. In chapter 2, Analyn Salvador-Amores describes these *burik* practices as they appear in historical records, on the bodies of the Kabayan mummies, and as they are manifested in contemporary culture. In chapter 3, Lars Krutak describes the revival of Ibaloy and Filipino tattoo traditions through the work of the Kalinga tattooist Whang-Od and the Mark of the Four Waves Tribe. Finally, Dario Piombino-Mascali, Ronald G. Beckett, Orlando V. Albinion, and Dong Hoon Shin provide a formal histiological analysis of a Kabayan mummy in chapter 4. This study results in new insights concerning the substances and techniques used in local Filipino mummification practices.

The elaborate animal tattoos on the mummies of the Iron Age Pazyryk culture of Siberia regularly make their way through the news cycle and various social media feeds. However, reliable information on these finds has not—until now—been widely available to English-speaking audiences. In chapter 5, Svetlana Pankova describes preserved tattoos from both the Pazyryk and Tashtyk cultures of the Altai-Sayan region, spanning the period between approximately 300 BCE and 400 CE. Following this discussion, Colin Dale and Krutak explore the resurrection of Pazyryk tattoo motifs by Danish archaeologist Søren Nancke-Krogh, Canadian tattooist Steve Gilbert, and Canadian artist Dave Mazierksi.

In chapter 7, Gemma Angel turns our focus away from ancient mummies to examine early twentieth century specimens of tattooed human skin from the Wellcome Collection in London. This collection was originally purchased in 1929 for inclusion in a medical museum, and contains little contextual information regarding the individuals from whom the specimens were obtained. Angel provides a wealth of information about historic European tattooing, including data on the methods and tools used, the iconography, and where tattooing and tattooed bodies fit into the early twentieth century European cultural milieu.

The preservation of tattooed human flesh has historically occurred mainly as a byproduct of either unintentional or deliberate mummification, or as a result of anatomical and medical studies. Today, tattooed individuals have the agency to intentionally preserve their own tattoos, with the assistance of several foundations. As described by Deter-Wolf and Krutak in chapter 8, the Foundation for the Art and Science of Tattooing and Save My Ink Forever will work with individuals to posthumously collect and protect their tattoos for posterity.

Part 2: Tools

Although tattooing has been practiced for millennia by cultures around the world, there have until recently been relatively few archaeological identifications of tattoo tools outside of Oceania (Deter-Wolf 2013a). This lack of identification is due to various factors, including the rapid historic abandonment of Indigenous tools in favor of European metal needles, the suppression of Indigenous tattoo traditions under colonial rule, and misunderstandings of tattoo techniques and technologies. Contributors to this part of the volume focus on the archaeological identification of tattoo implements, how these tools may be distinguished from other visually similar artifacts, and what they reveal about cultural development, change, and migration within past societies. In their efforts to identify and understand these artifacts, the authors employ a variety of lines of evidence, including human figural art, historic and ethnographic accounts, and both cross-cultural and use-wear analysis.

In chapter 9, Petar Zidarov uses art historical, historical, and archaeological evidence to suggest that tattooing in southeastern Europe existed as early as the sixth millennium BCE. Toward this end, he discusses the archaeological identification of bone tools from the Copper Age site of Pietrele, Romania, which may have functioned as tattoo implements. In a subsequent discussion in chapter 10, Krutak describes contemporary efforts to document historic tattoo traditions of the Balkans through the ethnographic work of Bosnian researcher Tea Mihaljevic and Croatian artists Zele and Sasha Aleksandar who incorporate traditional imagery into their modern tattoo work.

To the east in Polynesia, Louise Furey examines the distribution of Indigenous tattooing across Oceania in chapter 11. Her presentation of an island-by-island overview of archaeological materials demonstrates that while tattooing practices in the region share a common ancestry, the technology used to mark the body was quite diversified and functions as an important indicator of the settlement history of Oceania. In chapter 12, Krutak writes about the revival of Indigenous tattooing practices in coastal Papua New Guinea through the journey of four women of Papuan and Australian descent who traveled across Polynesia to resurrect them.

Turning to North America, in chapter 13 Aaron Deter-Wolf, Benoît Robitaille, and Isaac Walters examine issues surrounding the archaeological identification of ancient Native American tattoo tools from the Eastern Woodlands. The authors use a combination of archaeological, ethnographic, and historical data, including identification of rare surviving toolkits, to reiterate the ritual and technological differences between Native American tattooing, scarification, and scratching practices, and to address mistaken archaeological identifications of tattoo tools from the region.

Just as tattoos were closely linked to identity in ancient North America, today they testify to the resilience of Indigenous cultures and peoples. In chapter 14, Krutak probes the meanings of tattooing for contemporary Native tattoo bearers in Canada and the eastern United States, underscoring the role that tattoo revival efforts have had on the process of decolonization.

In chapter 15, Leonid Yablonsky expands our knowledge of the nomadic, early Iron Age Sarmatian people of Eurasia through recent discoveries of their tattooing material culture, the oldest evidence from this region. This long-awaited, but sadly posthumous, study of tattooing tools and related objects has an important role to play in reconstructing the tattoo history of these ancient nomadic people and their neighbors.

Deter-Wolf and Tara Nicole Clark address the task of developing use-wear analysis as a tool to identify tattoo tools in archaeological and museum collections in chapter 16. After creating a set of bone tools using prehistoric techniques, they then use those implements to tattoo both pig skin and human skin. Deter-Wolf and Clark then examine the microwear patterns created during the tattooing process in an attempt to both refine our understanding of the use-wear signature of tattooing, and assess the suitability of pig skin as a surrogate for human skin in future experimental studies.

Part 3: Art

Possible representations of human body decoration appear on anthropomorphic figurines and art dating back to at least 35,000 years ago. Although the artists who created these images intended to show alteration of the human skin, it is challenging for modern scholars to establish the specific type and permanence of the body decoration(s) in question. Some examples may represent clothing, while others may indicate tattooing, body paint, scarification, or something else altogether. Identifying the symbolic significance and ideological roles of these ancient objects can also be difficult. To address these problems, the final part of the book examines the artistic, ethnographic, and archaeological record of ancient and historic cultures from Europe and the Arctic in order to assess how members of those societies projected their decorated bodies onto their material culture.

In chapter 17, Luc Renaut turns a skeptical eye toward artistic depictions of possible ancient European tattooing. His examination spans the Upper Paleolithic through the Bronze Age, and describes anthropomorphic art recovered from numerous sites across the continent in an effort to differentiate likely depictions of tattooing from works depicting other forms of body decoration.

The final chapters focus on the American Arctic, as Lars Krutak examines the prehistoric and historic use of decorated anthropomorphic dolls from Bering Strait. These religious objects, usually carved of walrus ivory, were employed in various rituals for more than two millennia, but the question of their tattoos has always remained a mystery. This study serves as a companion piece to Krutak's subsequent brief survey of contemporary Indigenous tattooing in Alaska. Motivated by ancestral traditions, spiritual beliefs, and contemporary cultural values, a new generation of tattoo bearers has reawakened tattooing customs that were once in danger of disappearing forever.

The studies presented here are pioneering efforts in the analysis, recognition, and interpretation of tattooing instruments and practices worldwide. Indeed, tattooing is an almost universal human tradition that embodies an astonishing range of cultural meanings articulated through performance and permanent symbols. For millennia, tattooing has been more than mere ornamentation. Instead, the practice has been integral to the social fabric of community and religious life, and has anchored societal values on the skin for most everyone to see. Seen in this light, tattooing was, and continues to be, a system of knowledge transmission, a visual language of the skin whereby culture is inscribed, experienced, and preserved in myriad specific ways.

Part 1

Skin

1

New Tattoos from Ancient Egypt

DEFINING MARKS OF CULTURE

Renée Friedman

INTERPRETATIONS OF THE ARTISTIC RECORD AND CERTAIN TOOL SETS SUGGEST that body modification, and especially tattooing, was practiced by diverse cultures reaching back into remote antiquity (Deter-Wolf 2013a). Not surprisingly, given the nature of the medium—human skin—examples of actual tattoos are hard to come by in the archaeological record. Until recent discoveries in Europe and South America (see Deter-Wolf et al. 2016: table 1), Egypt's Nile Valley provided the earliest actual evidence of the practice. The tattoos visible on three well-preserved individuals buried at Deir el Bahari in Thebes during the early Middle Kingdom (ca. 2004 BCE[1]) (map 1.1), and the more fragmentary remains from Kubban in Nubia, have long been known and widely reviewed.[2] However, new observations using infrared imaging now extend the temporal range of known examples in Egypt from within the Predynastic (ca. 3900–3100 BCE) into the New Kingdom (1550–1069 BCE) (see table 1.1, which augments and updates Deter-Wolf et al. 2016: table 1). These recent discoveries not only allow ancient Egypt to regain its position among the earliest entries in the chronological table, but also, and more importantly, provide further information with which to reconsider the use of tattoos in the ancient Nile Valley by the various cultures living there and to identify artifacts related to the practice.

Five tattooed individuals from ancient Egypt discussed here were observed by the author in 2014–2016 using a Panasonic Lumix DMC ZS19 camera, preconverted by the sellers, Kolari Vision, to 720 nm infrared.[3] While all were found on (and in) Egyptian soil, three can be identified as ethnically Nubian. These remains range in date from the

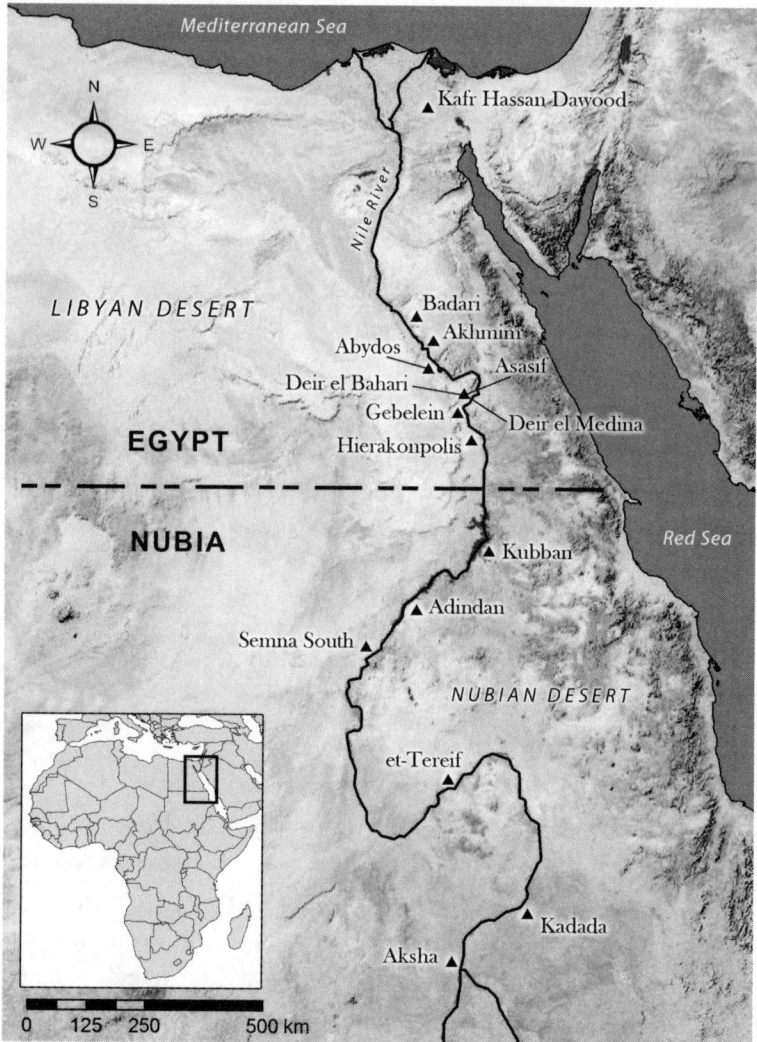

Map 1.1. Ancient Egypt and Nubia, showing sites discussed in this chapter.

latter part of the Predynastic period to the Middle Kingdom, and the new evidence they preserve can now help us to distinguish more clearly enduring tattooing traditions both in Egypt and Nubia that were culturally specific with regard to both motifs and techniques.

Predynastic Tattoos

Infrared examination of the six naturally preserved Predynastic mummies obtained by the British Museum in 1899 from Gebelein in Upper Egypt (see map 1.1) revealed the presence of tattoos on the body of one female (BM EA32752) and one male (BM

1

New Tattoos from Ancient Egypt

DEFINING MARKS OF CULTURE

Renée Friedman

INTERPRETATIONS OF THE ARTISTIC RECORD AND CERTAIN TOOL SETS SUGGEST that body modification, and especially tattooing, was practiced by diverse cultures reaching back into remote antiquity (Deter-Wolf 2013a). Not surprisingly, given the nature of the medium—human skin—examples of actual tattoos are hard to come by in the archaeological record. Until recent discoveries in Europe and South America (see Deter-Wolf et al. 2016: table 1), Egypt's Nile Valley provided the earliest actual evidence of the practice. The tattoos visible on three well-preserved individuals buried at Deir el Bahari in Thebes during the early Middle Kingdom (ca. 2004 BCE[1]) (map 1.1), and the more fragmentary remains from Kubban in Nubia, have long been known and widely reviewed.[2] However, new observations using infrared imaging now extend the temporal range of known examples in Egypt from within the Predynastic (ca. 3900–3100 BCE) into the New Kingdom (1550–1069 BCE) (see table 1.1, which augments and updates Deter-Wolf et al. 2016: table 1). These recent discoveries not only allow ancient Egypt to regain its position among the earliest entries in the chronological table, but also, and more importantly, provide further information with which to reconsider the use of tattoos in the ancient Nile Valley by the various cultures living there and to identify artifacts related to the practice.

Five tattooed individuals from ancient Egypt discussed here were observed by the author in 2014–2016 using a Panasonic Lumix DMC ZS19 camera, preconverted by the sellers, Kolari Vision, to 720 nm infrared.[3] While all were found on (and in) Egyptian soil, three can be identified as ethnically Nubian. These remains range in date from the

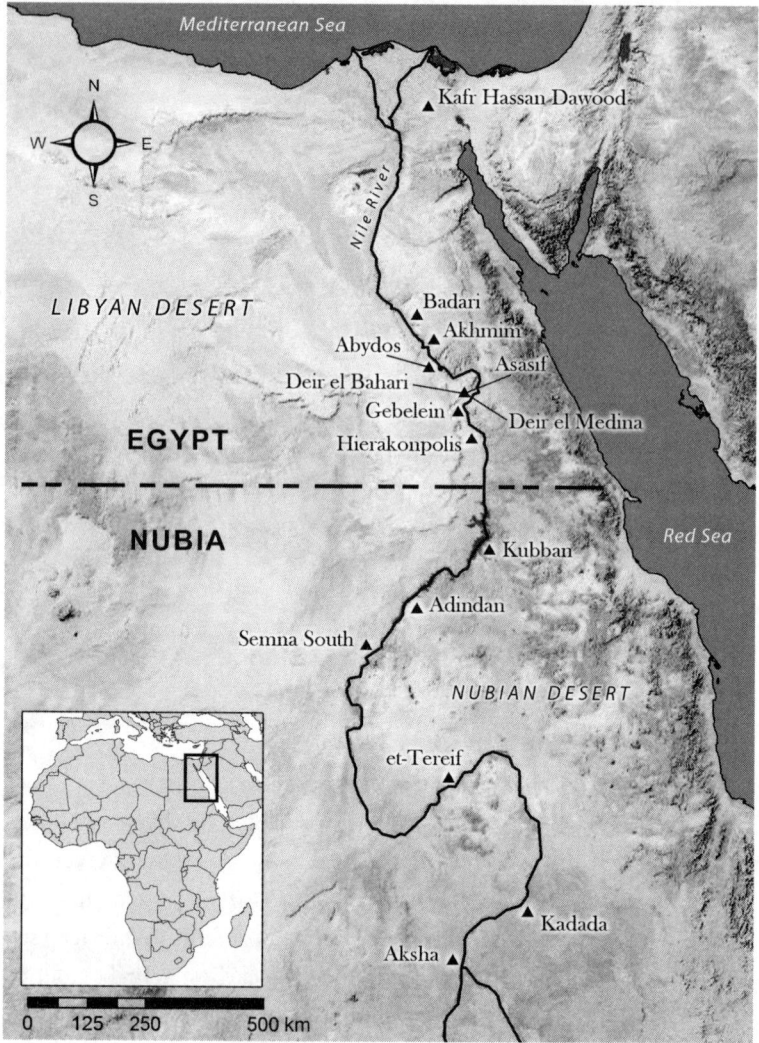

Map 1.1. Ancient Egypt and Nubia, showing sites discussed in this chapter.

latter part of the Predynastic period to the Middle Kingdom, and the new evidence they preserve can now help us to distinguish more clearly enduring tattooing traditions both in Egypt and Nubia that were culturally specific with regard to both motifs and techniques.

Predynastic Tattoos

Infrared examination of the six naturally preserved Predynastic mummies obtained by the British Museum in 1899 from Gebelein in Upper Egypt (see map 1.1) revealed the presence of tattoos on the body of one female (BM EA32752) and one male (BM

Table 1.1. Summary of tattooed mummies from Egypt and Nubia.

Date	Relative date	Site	Identifier	Sex	Comments	Source
3349–3093 BCE	Predynastic	Gebelein, Egypt	BM EA32752	F		Discussed herein.
3340–3018 BCE	Predynastic	Gebelein, Egypt	BM EA32751	M		Discussed herein.
2055–2004 BCE	Dynasty XI (Nebhepetre Mentuhotep II)	Deir el Bahari, Thebes, Egypt.	Amunet	F		Fouquet 1898; Keimer 1948.
2055–2004 BCE	Dynasty XI (Nebhepetre Mentuhotep II)	Deir el Bahari, Thebes, Egypt.	Pits 23 and 26	F	2 individuals	Keimer 1948; Winlock 1923.
1985–1955 BCE	Dynasty XII (Amenemhet I?)	Asasif, Thebes, Egypt.	Asasif 1008	F		Morris 2011: fig. 5.
1985–1855 BCE	C-Group Nubia (first half of Dynasty XII)	Hierakonpolis, Egypt, Cemetery HK27C.	Tombs 9, 10, 36	F	3 individuals	Friedman 2004; Pieri and Antoine 2014; discussed herein.
1750–1500 BCE	C-Group, Nubia Phase III	Kubban, Nubia Cemetery 110.	Grave 271	F		Firth 1927.
ca. 1750 BCE	Pan Grave	Hierakonpolis, Egypt, Cemetery HK47.	Burial 12	M		Friedman 2016; discussed herein.
1295–1069 BCE	New Kingdom, Egypt (Ramesside)	Deir el Medina, Thebes, Egypt.		F	3 individuals	Anne Austin, pers. comm.*; Watson 2016.
ca. 1000 BCE	Late Period?	Egypt			Private collection, Perth, Australia.	Poon 2008.
332 BCE–395 CE	Graeco-Roman Period	Akhmim, Egypt.		F	Unconfirmed**	Strouhal 1992.
100 BCE–150 CE	Meroitic Period, Nubia.	Semna South, Sudan.	N-247	F?	Possibly 2 individuals	Alvrus et al. 2001.
100 BCE–150 CE	Meroitic Period, Nubia.	Aksha, Sudan.	AM 4,12,32,36,43, 45,62,65,77,81.	7F; 1M; 2U	10 tattooed individuals	Vila 1967.
350–550 CE	X Group, Nubia			M		Armelagos 1969.
700 CE	Christian Period, Nubia.	et-Tereif, Sudan Site 3-J-23.	Grave 50	F		Vandenbeusch and Antoine 2015.

*Personal communication, January 27, 2016.
**Indirect identification, based on marks from mummy masks.

EA32751; Antoine and Ambers 2014: 26–28; Dawson and Gray 1968).[4] On the female, these tattoos appear as very faint green marks under natural lighting conditions, but can be clearly distinguished in infrared. A mark present on the upper right arm is a linear motif bending nearly 90 degrees toward the front of the body (fig. 1.1a). On the right shoulder there is a series of four S-shaped motifs running vertically over the joint of the humerus and the shoulder (fig. 1.1b). At both ends of each S-motif the line appears to widen and terminate with a short perpendicular stroke. An irregular line was also detected running horizontally across the lower abdomen at approximately the level of the navel (see fig. 1.1c, marked by arrow), but the nature and origin of this particular mark remains unclear since the tight contraction of the legs hinders full view.[5] Corresponding tattoos were not found on the left side, and no other markings were detected elsewhere on the body.

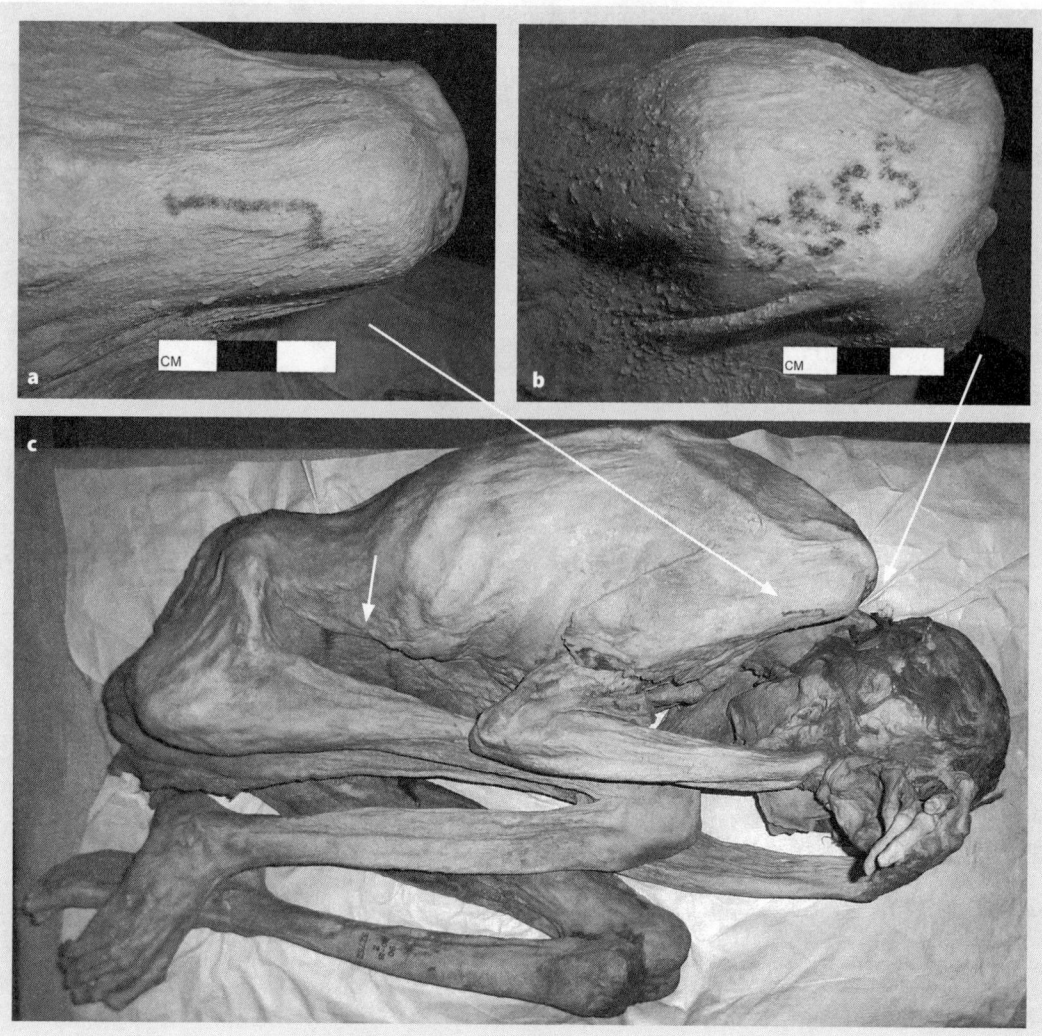

Fig. 1.1. Infrared image of the Predynastic female mummy from Gebelein (3349–3018 cal BCE) and details of the tattoos observed on the (a) right shoulder and (b) upper right arm. The tattoos on this individual appear as faint green marks under natural lighting conditions, but can be clearly distinguished in infrared (c). Photographs by Renée Friedman. British Museum, London (EA32752).

The male body (Gebelein Man A) is the best preserved natural mummy known from Predynastic Egypt, and also bears tattoos on his upper right arm (fig. 1.2a). The marks appear as dark smudges in natural light (figs 1.2b, 1.2c), but under infrared can be identified as two horned animals facing toward the front of the body. One is placed below and in front of the other, which it slightly overlaps. No marks are present on the shoulder and no further indications of tattooing could be detected on the portions of the body currently visible in the museum display.

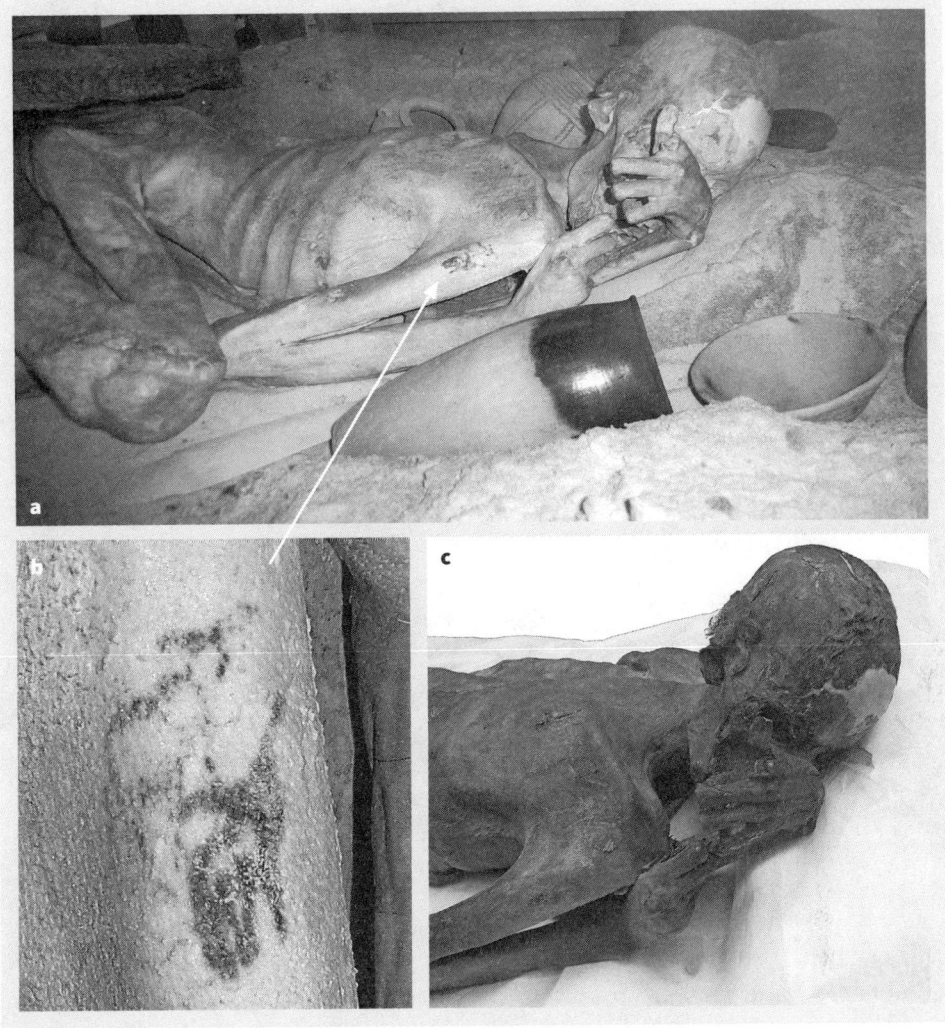

Fig. 1.2. (a) Infrared image of the Predynastic male mummy from Gebelein (3349–3018 cal BCE) and details of the tattoos observed on the (b) upper right arm under infrared lighting and (c) natural lighting. These marks appear as dark smudges in natural light, but under infrared they resolve into two horned animals facing toward the front of the body. Photographs by Renée Friedman. British Museum, London (EA32751).

Recent accelerator mass spectrometry (AMS) radiocarbon testing has dated both of these bodies from Gebelein to 3349–3018 cal BCE (with 95.4 percent confidence).[6] Stylistic comparison of the tattoos with elements of material culture place them within the late and terminal phases of the Predynastic period[7] and point to the earlier part of the broad dating range.[8] Roughly contemporary with the Alpine mummy known as Ötzi (see Deter-Wolf et al. 2016), the Gebelein mummies have the oldest preserved tattoos in Africa, and are the second and third oldest tattooed mummies in the world.

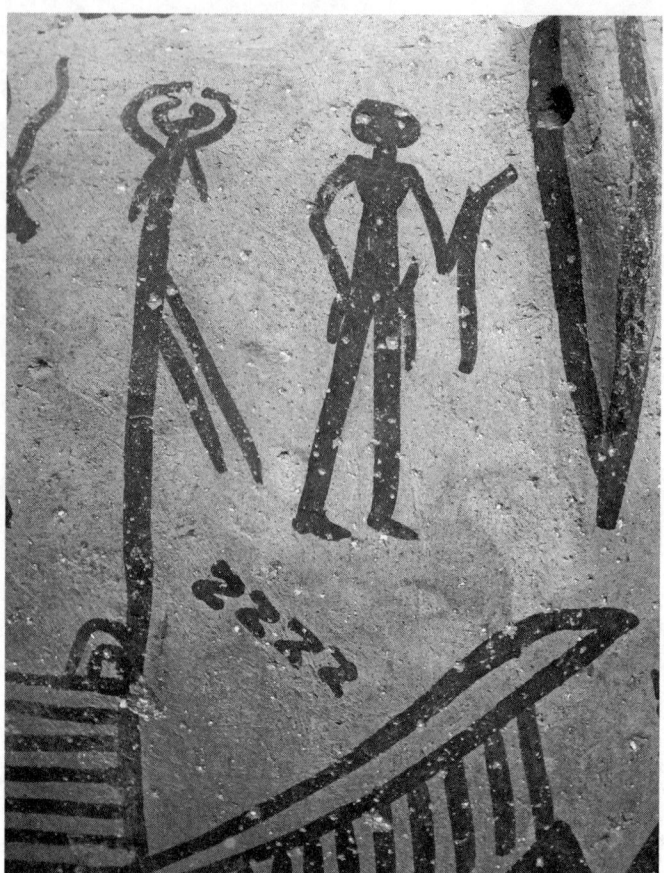

Fig. 1.3. Detail of Predynastic pottery (ca. 3500 BCE) exhibiting S-motifs similar to the tattoos on the right shoulder of the female mummy from Gebelein. The specific meaning of this design is not known. Photograph by Renée Friedman. British Museum, London (EA49570).

The female mummy is the earlier of the two examples from Gebelein. Both of her figural tattoos have parallels specifically in the material culture of the late Predynastic period (ca. 3450–3300 BCE). The S-motif is well known in pottery decoration of this period, where it occurs in multiples (fig. 1.3), like in the tattoo. To date we have no satisfactory explanation for the meaning of this motif, which has been identified as schematic birds in flight, and most recently as an indicator of emphasis or connection with other elements in a composition (Graff 2009:78, motif NI 35), a reading that is perhaps not out of place given the tattoo's position on the shoulder.

The linear motif on the woman's arm may be compared with the crooked staves carried as symbols of power and status, or the batons and/or clappers seen in the hands of mainly male figures in scenes depicting ceremonial activity and ritual dance, especially on pottery (Graff 2009:71 motif BT1-3). Such objects, as either symbols of status or implements of ritual performance, were no doubt redolent with power; however, neither they nor the S-motifs is ever the main focus of the compositions of scenes on pottery. Instead, their ancillary use on painted ceramics suggests that these tattoos are not directly related to the restricted vocabulary of pottery design, which was mainly focused on mortuary concerns at this time. Potential parallels in other media are neither common nor especially compelling, leaving little to help us establish the meanings or purposes these tattoos might possess. It is perhaps especially notable that similar motifs are absent on the decorated figurines that have hitherto been central to discussions of tattooing in early Egypt.

The tattooed animal images on Gebelein Man A are more familiar from Predynastic art, where horned animals frequently appear but identification of the species is not straightforward (cf. Graff 2009:31–33, 58–60). The downward curving horns and the humped shoulder of the upper creature suggest a representation of a Barbary sheep, although the characteristic chest mane is absent (see Hendrickx et al. 2009). The lower animal, by virtue of the extravagant horns and long tail, is probably bovine and more specifically a depiction of extinct wild cattle (aurochs). Both animals are known from datable art of the earlier Predynastic period, where they generally appear in a more stylized form (see, for example, fig. 1.5). They become rare later on in the Predynastic period, but re-emerge more naturalistically portrayed on carved ivories and in potmarks of the terminal portion of the period. It is with these later forms that the tattoos find their closest parallels (see e.g., Churcher 1984; Patch 2011: cat. 5, cat. 178; Petrie 1896:plate LI.14;).[9] Both species also appear in rock art, where they are often the subject of the desert hunt (Hendrickx et al. 2009; Judd 2009:20–25).

Hunting at this time was not critical for subsistence and had instead become a symbolic activity demonstrating the imposition of order over the chaos of nature, while also allowing men to practice with weapons and show their prowess. Its main goal was not to kill the animals but rather to capture them for ritual slaughter in the socially sanctioned setting of a temple or shrine (Hendrickx et al. 2009:231). Within this context, it is possible that the tattoos on the man from Gebelein represent triumphs during the hunt and commemorate bravery. The difference in line weight between the two tattoos and the fact that they slightly overlap may indicate that the images were applied at different times, reflecting different events.

Such a specific interpretation is admittedly speculative and more general concerns may have also motivated the application of the tattoos. Although the Barbary sheep disappears from the iconography by the beginning of the Dynastic period, the wild bull endures as a symbol of male power and virility, especially that of the king, throughout ancient Egyptian civilization (Hendrickx 2002). This may suggest that the tattoos in some way conveyed power or strength to the wearer or provided protection from the disorder inherent in the wild.

With only two tattooed individuals of this period known to date, each bearing different types of imagery, it is difficult to distinguish among myriad meanings these tattoos may have held for the bearer and the viewer. The preservation of these tattoos, however, demonstrates that tattooing was an established procedure by the end of the Predynastic period and lends support to interpretations of the artistic record that suggests the practice is far older.

Predynastic Figurines

Scholars have long debated the question of whether tattooing existed in Predynastic Egypt based on the evidence of ceramic female figurines ornamented with a variety of geometric and figural motifs. Anthropomorphic ceramic figurines are not especially prevalent in the Predynastic record, and of the roughly 250 examples, those with body decoration (excluding that around the eyes) are limited to only about sixteen examples. Of those, less than half have known excavated contexts (Patch 2011; Stevenson 2017; Ucko 1968).

The earliest figurine showing body decoration was found in a grave dating to the Neolithic Badarian period (4500–3900 BCE) (fig. 1.4). One of only five figurines known from that period, it depicts a female schematically rendered without arms (fig. 1.4a). Four incised lines running down the back of each shoulder are possibly meant to represent hair. Between these lines in the middle of the back are three incised chevrons (Brunton and Caton-Thompson 1928:plate 24.3). Incised decoration is known on only two other excavated pieces of Predynastic date. One is a partially preserved figurine again with omitted arms, which is similarly decorated only on the back with an incised motif resembling a fan (Brunton and Caton-Thompson 1928:plates 36.6 and 53.48)

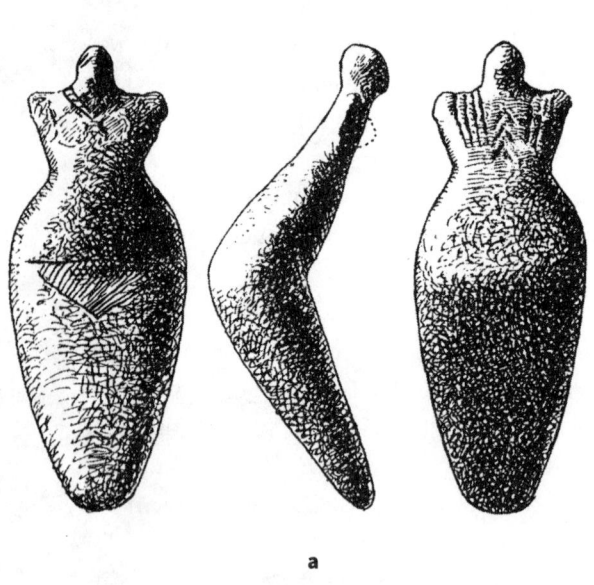
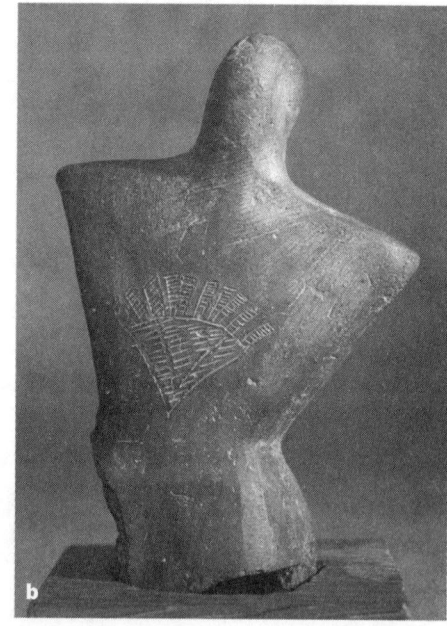

Fig. 1.4. Badarian (4500–3900 BCE) and Predynastic Egyptian (ca. 3600 BCE) ceramic figurines with incised designs in a figural style probably reflecting tattoos: (a) Badarian figurine, showing a female with incised lines and chevrons down her back; vertical lines may represent hair (drawing after Brunton and Caton-Thompson 1928: plate 24.3). (b) Rear view of Predynastic figurine, showing incised fan-like motif. Photograph courtesy of the Petrie Museum of Egyptian Archaeology, University College London, London (UC 9601).

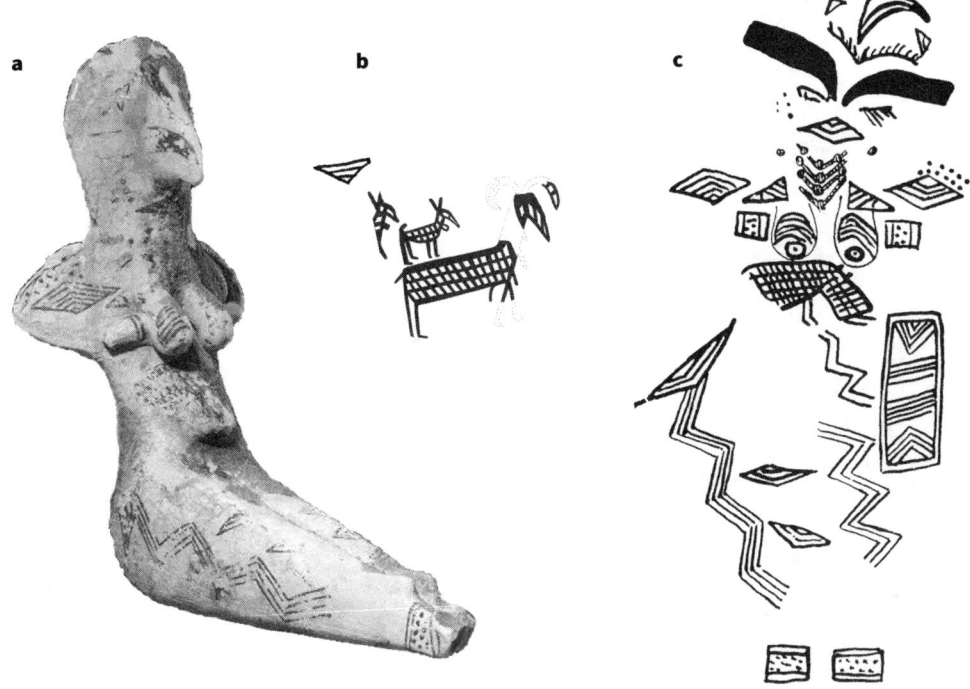

Fig. 1.5. Predynastic Egyptian (ca. 3700–3500 BCE) ceramic figurine with details of designs painted over the front and back of the body. It is not clear whether these designs were intended to represent tattoos or some other form of body decoration. Photograph © the Trustees of British Museum (EA58064). Drawings after Hornblower (1929) and revised by Claire Thorne.

(fig. 1.4b). The other is the lower part of a seated female figurine with an incised zigzag design across one thigh accompanied by a curvilinear motif (Anderson 2011:fig. 10). The figural nature and limited extent of the motifs, which seem to correspond with that observed on the tattooed woman from Gebelein, and the incised method with which they were applied to the figurine speak in favor of them representing tattoos. From their rarity we can conclude that either tattooing was not a widespread phenomenon within Predynastic society or (more likely) that such potentially personal marks were not relevant within the context for which such figurines were made or used.

More controversial are the Predynastic figurines with elaborately painted decoration (fig. 1.5), which are more often illustrated in historical surveys of tattooing (e.g., Keimer 1948:figs. 1–5). These figures bear extensive markings on both the front and back of the body, the legs, and sometimes also the face, and include scenes of hunting Barbary sheep, vegetal motifs, and various geometric symbols. Only one fragmentary example has a known excavated context, and although the authenticity of this group of figurines has been called into question (Ucko and Hodges 1963), a growing body of analysis suggests that several may be considered authentic (Friedman and Ambers

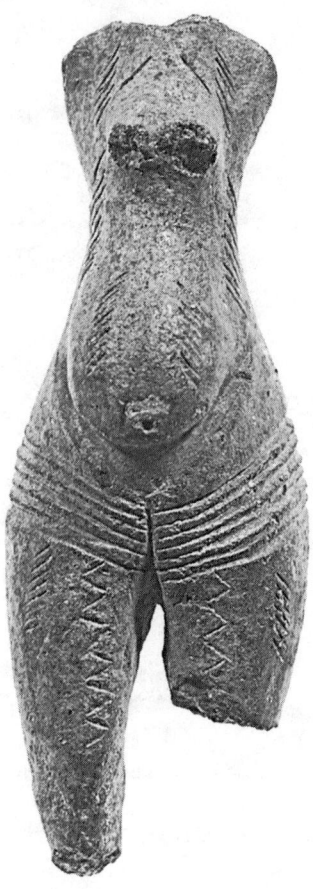

Fig. 1.6. Neolithic figurine (ca. 3600 BCE) with incised body markings from the site of Kadada in Upper Nubia. These designs may indicate either tattooing or scarification. Photograph courtesy of the Sudan National Museum, Khartoum (SNM 26969).

2016). While at least three of these figures have wavy lines on or near the shoulder, the resemblance to the S-motif of the Gebelein tattoo is not close.

It has long been debated whether the painted designs on these figurines represent tattoos or body paint. Confirmation that tattooing was practiced does little to resolve the issue, given the obvious importance of pigments and pigment preparation in Predynastic Egypt as attested by numerous palettes of specially obtained greywacke,[10] grinding pebbles, and the remains of pigment ores (malachite, galena, and ochre) in graves and settlement contexts (Baduel 2008). While such figurines have generally been regarded within the realm of fertility magic, based on later evidence (discussion following), it has been suggested that they instead represent the practitioners of this magic: the musicians and dancers who performed at ritual hunting and butchery events that took place in conjunction with various other ceremonies, including those surrounding funerals and births (Hendrickx et al. 2009:212–19). Once embellished with images of Nilotic vegetation on their front and the desert hunt on their back, such performers may have embodied and mediated the dualities of the fertile river and dangerous desert, celebration and sacrifice, and life and death (Hendrickx et al. 2009:215). If this is indeed the case, it now requires us to contemplate several possibilities within the context of Predynastic society. First, whether the elaborate and extensive imagery associated with such a potent ceremonial role would be permanently inscribed as tattoos, indelibly marking group affiliation and knowledge of sacred rites; or whether these marks were instead donned with temporary pigments more like a mask, to channel the powers at the appropriate time and place, allowing for wider participation. We must await further finds for confirmation.

Whether permanent or transitory, the figural motifs visible on the Predynastic figurines as well as on the Gebelein individuals indicate a specific tradition of body ornamentation, which becomes especially clear when contrasted to the markings found incised on figurines of contemporary but distinct cultures in Nubia. Here, a limited but evocative number of clay female figurines have been uncovered incised with dots and dashes which depended on arrangement and patterning to convey their meaning (Caneva 1988; Reinold 2000) (fig. 1.6). Whether these designs reflect scarification or tattoos, figural motifs are absent in this Nubian tradition and continue to be absent into the Meroitic period (300 BCE–400 CE) (cf. Vila 1967). While the Nubian character of the dot-and-dash technique has long been recognized (Bianchi 1988), though sometimes questioned (Tassie 2003), the preserved tattoos from Gebelein provide evidence for a parallel tradition in Egypt going back to prehistory. These traditions differed both in technique and vocabulary, as do many other aspects of the respective material cultures.

Predynastic Toolkits

With the practice of tattooing in Predynastic Egypt now proven, it is possible to examine elements of material culture to assess their relationship to the practice. Previously Tassie (2003) tentatively suggested that a set of five copper rods found in the grave of a woman in the Early Dynastic (ca. 3000 BCE) cemetery at Kafr Hassan Dawood (see map 1.1) may have been used for tattooing. He also stressed that any number of other pointed implements, such as the bone awls prevalent at this time, could have been utilized for this purpose, and that context was all important for determining their function. More recently Deter-Wolf (2013a) has described the sort of context or "toolkit" that one might seek to identify tattoo implements in the archaeological record. Suggested components include one or more tattooing tools, pigment remains, and materials of use in the preparation and/or maintenance of the tools, along with culturally specific items associated with the ritual aspects of the tattooing process.

With this contextual approach in mind, it is interesting to reconsider a "toolkit" found within an intact grave of an older (40 to 50 years) woman of the Predynastic period (ca. 3600 BCE) at Hierakonpolis in cemetery HK43 (plate 1). Burial 333 was one of the richest in this nonelite cemetery, indicating the woman was of some standing in her community. From the initial study of the grave contents it had already been proposed that she was a magico-medical practitioner (Friedman 2003). Reassessment of the assemblage now suggests tattooing may have been among her skills. By her elbow was a basket. Leaning against it, there was a bird-shaped palette of greywacke. This artifact was used for grinding cosmetic ores (such as galena and ochre) with rounded pebbles, all of which were found in the basket. The basket also included stone pendants, a human-headed amulet, an ivory comb, three fine flint bladelets, five awls made from sheep and pig metatarsals, charred material wrapped in a linen parcel, and the remains of a leather bag containing chunks of resin, a mixture of plant remains, and slivers of an aromatic, exotic wood (juniper or cypress). The plant remains were preliminarily identified as an incense mixture (Fahmy 2005), but some of the fruits and tubers, found whole, also have medicinal and antiseptic qualities as emollients and unguents.

Seemingly out of place within this collection of special materials were the bone awls, a tool commonly found in settlement debris. However, recent experimental work on the efficacy of various natural materials for tattooing has shown that tools of polished bone produced among the best results (Deter-Wolf and Peres 2013). Use of these carefully split and polished awls as tattooing instruments fits the context well,[11] and it is not hard to imagine tattooing being undertaken in an atmosphere of aromatic incense surrounded by resins, unguents, and amuletic devices.[12]

Whether Predynastic tattoos were applied for therapeutic, protective, or transformative (among many other) reasons, we cannot know, but it is unlikely that one explanation will suffice. That two individuals within a restricted collection from Gebelein bear tattoos is remarkable and that both sexes are represented is significant, but whether they reflect a local predilection for the practice at Gebelein or indicate a wider spread use of tattoos remains to be determined. It is hoped that further examination of the artifactual record and preserved bodies surviving from this time will help to illuminate the purpose and prevalence of tattoos in Predynastic Egypt.[13]

Middle Kingdom Tattoos

Despite their former fame as bearing the oldest preserved tattoos, the three mummies from Deir el Bahari are still inadequately published and have become the subject of some confusion in the secondary literature. To quickly clarify and review: The first of these mummies, that of a woman named Amunet, was discovered in 1891 in an intact tomb with rich grave goods buried within the funerary complex of King Nebhepetre Mentuhotep II (ca. 2055–2004 BCE), who reigned during the XI Dynasty at the beginning of Egypt's Middle Kingdom (see Keimer 1948:8). This burial was located in the area of ancient Thebes known by the modern name Deir el Bahari (see map 1.1).

Amunet's titles indicate she was a Priestess of Hathor and "Chief Royal Ornament," a title formerly translated as "concubine" but now better understood as "Chief Lady in Waiting" in attendance to the queen (see discussion in Tooley 1989:324). Shortly after her discovery, on October 8, 1891, the mummy was unwrapped and found to bear tattoos. These were briefly described and accompanied by a sketch in an article

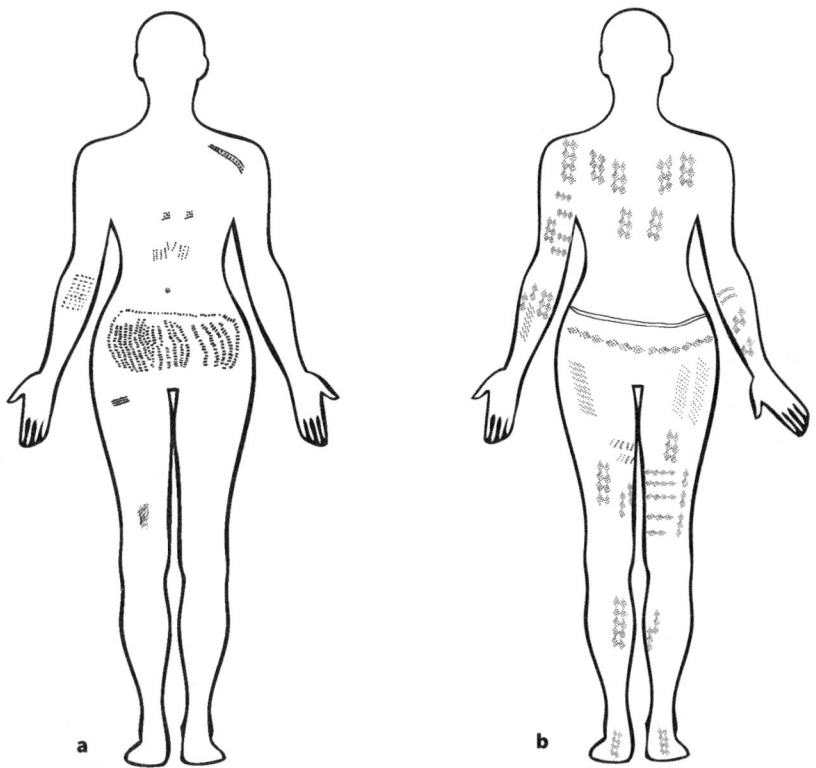

Fig. 1.7. Distribution of dot-and-dash tattoos on the mummified bodies of the Middle Kingdom women from Deir el Bahari (2055–2004 BCE): (a) Tattoos of Amunet, priestess of Hathor and "Chief Royal Ornament." (b) Woman from Pit 23, recreated from photographs and drawings in Keimer (1948: plates 2–9) and Roehrig (2015: figs. 1 and 4).

mainly concerned with the medicinal use of tattooing in nineteenth century CE Egypt (Fouquet 1898:fig. 1). In 1938, Ludwig Keimer re-examined the mummy and found Fouquet's description and sketch to be both incomplete and erroneous. While Keimer published a new account of the tattoos and provided photographs and rough sketches to substantiate his observations (Keimer 1948:8–13, plates 1–5), Fouquet's drawing continues to be reproduced in the literature (e.g., Bianchi 1988:fig. 2; Gilbert 2000a:12; Poon and Quickenden 2006:fig. 2), although its origin has not always been correctly recognized.[14] While a new drawing based entirely on the photographs and sketches of Keimer is provided in fig. 1.7a, further investigation is required.[15] Tattoos were observed on the left upper chest as a band of large dots encased by two lines; in two groupings on the upper abdomen as a series of dotted lines; and across the lower abdomen as a dense array of dashes. Dotted patterns appear on the right lower arm and also on the lower right thigh, where they were possibly arranged in lozenges, while three parallel lines composed of pointillist dots were present on the upper thigh. The body was examined while on its side, so the full extent of the tattooing has not been determined.

Two more tattooed bodies were discovered at Deir el Bahari in 1923 in the same king's funerary complex (Keimer 1948:13–15). Both burial pits (Pits 23 and 26) were heavily disturbed and the names and titles of these women are unknown. Winlock (1923:26) states that drawings were carefully made of their tattoos, but these have only recently been published (Roehrig 2015). Photographs of the full body from Pit 23 provided to Keimer (1948:plates 6–9) have long been available.

Figure 1.7b shows the approximate arrangement of the tattoos on the body from Pit 23 at Deir el Bahari, based on those visible in the photographs with additions adapted from the drawings (Roehrig 2015:figs. 1 and 4). The tattoos mainly appear to be composed of lozenge shapes made up of sixteen dots (four rows of four dots each, set diagonally) arranged in various combinations, often creating a lattice or checkerboard pattern. These marks appear on both sides of the chest, shoulder, upper abdomen, and dorsum of the feet, while a string of single lozenges runs across the suprapubic region. Rows and lattices of dotted lozenges also adorn the thighs and arms, along with vertical sets of lines composed of four, five, or ten dots per line. In addition, a linear scar, or cicatrix, that crosses the abdomen below the navel is reported to terminate in leaf-shaped scars at the back of the hip. Further small scarifications were documented in the gluteal region on the right side (Derry 1942, as cited in Keimer 1948:13–14).

The woman from Pit 26, described as short and middle aged, was less well preserved and seems to have been less extensively tattooed. According to the recently published drawing, her tattoos are almost exclusively composed of dotted lozenges arranged in horizontal or diagonal rows on her upper chest, shoulder, arms, hand, and thighs. She also had a cicatrix across her abdomen below which was a string of tattooed lozenges running from hip to hip. Further scarification consisting of a number of short diagonal lines is reported present between the shoulder blades and on the buttocks (Derry 1942:253; Roehrig 2015: 528–29; fig. 2). These later scars are similar to the ones seen in the gluteal region of the body from Pit 23.

While Amunet was apparently a lady of some standing, historic scholarly comparisons with other aspects of the material culture in both Egypt and Nubia led to the unnamed tattooed women from Deir el Bahari being identified as Nubian dancing girls,[16] a designation carrying salacious connotations (cf. Bianchi 1988:22–23; Keimer 1948:100–105). This moniker was based on the resemblance of the tattoos to marks found on Middle Kingdom figurines depicting generally nude or scantily clad women, often called "Brides of the Dead" (plate 2a). Depictions of tattoos on underdressed acrobats and musicians in later times and a misunderstanding of Amunet's titles also influenced the interpretation.

Further study of the Middle Kingdom "bride" figurines has refuted their identification as "concubines" and places their use within the realm of magico-medical rites (Pinch 1993:211–25; Waraksa 2008). Other scholars (e.g., Morris 2011; Tooley 1989:305–25) make an interesting case for both the tattooed women and certain types of figurines to be seen not simply as erotic entertainers, present solely for the pleasure

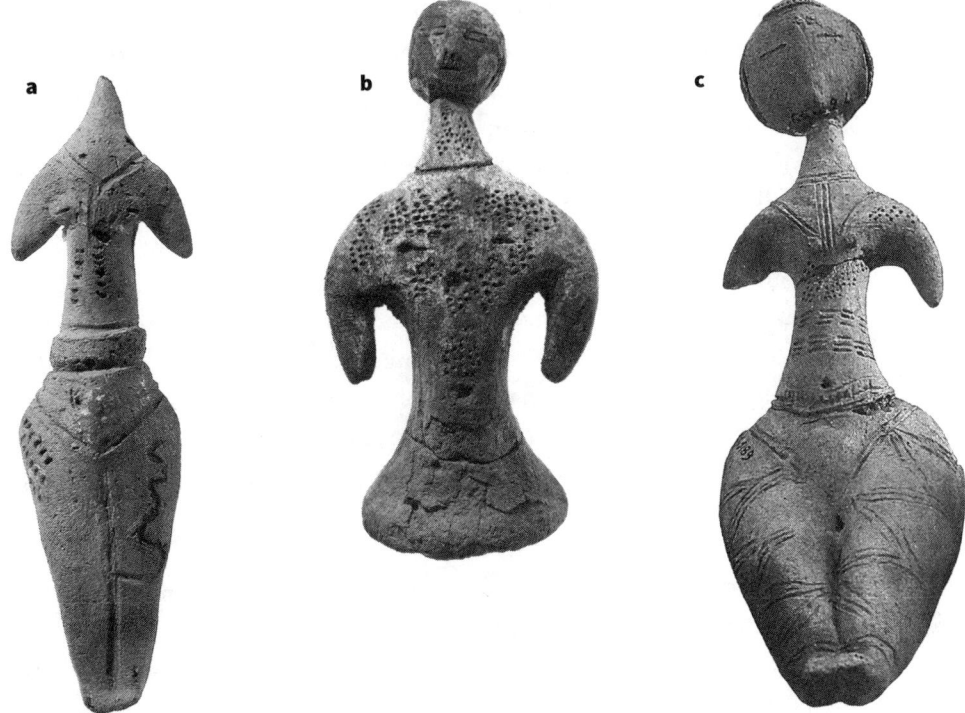

Fig. 1.8. Nubian C-Group ceramic figurines (ca. 2050–1600 BCE), bearing incised lines and dot-and-dash designs representing tattoos: (a) Clay figurine with head modeled separately, showing tattoos on torso and thighs. Photograph courtesy of the Sudan National Museum, Khartoum (SNM 61266). (b) Upper part of figurine with tattoos on the torso. Photograph courtesy of the Oriental Institute of the University of Chicago (OI 23202). (c) Seated figure with tattoos on legs and body. Photography by Renée Friedman, Egyptian Museum Cairo (10862). Not to scale.

of the king or deceased, but rather as ritual performers in the service of Hathor, the goddess of music, beauty, sexuality, and its attendant fertility in this world and the next. Recently Tooley (2017) has further demonstrated that the predominantly faience figurines, many with lozenge-shaped markings that can be equated with tattoos on their truncated legs, embodied the specific social persona of a sacred dancer in early Middle Kingdom Egypt. Because figures of this specific type (Pinch 1993:type 1) are found almost exclusively in graves, they are proposed to have served as vehicles for the revivification of the dead through dance and ritually sanctioned exotic display. With time, the function of female figurines shifted to include the world of the living, suggesting that they, as well as the women they represent, assisted people with issues such as fertility during their lifetimes through performances that focused on the power of the goddess. In this way, the tattoos may have expressed initiation in the cult of Hathor and knowledge of the associated rites, as well as perhaps augmenting the wearer's beauty and effectiveness.

The question of Nubian ethnicity for the Deir el Bahari women remains a more contentious issue (e.g., Meurer 1996; Pinch 1993; Renaut 2014). The un-Egyptian nature of the dot-and-dash tattoos and their resemblance to the incised decoration on female figurines of the contemporaneous Nubian C-Group culture (fig. 1.8) has been long recognized, and is reinforced by the find of preserved tattooed skin at Kubban in Nubia explored in the following discussion (cf. Firth 1927:54, plate 25d; Keimer 1948:16–17). In combination with other lines of evidence pointing to the presence of Nubians in the court of Mentuhotep II at Deir el Bahari, the tattooed women (and the Egyptian tattooed figurines[17]) were therefore identified as Nubian. This hypothesis remains controversial. Since clear evidence of earlier tattoos in Egypt was unknown to mid-twentieth-century scholars, some argued that this method of tattooing may have been introduced into Egypt by Nubians during the increased interaction between the two cultures in the Middle Kingdom (Bianchi 1988:22–24), but its presence did not imply the ethnicity of the bearer (e.g., Pinch 1993:211–14).

It now seems likely that dot-and-dash was not the only style of tattoo available in Egypt during the Middle Kingdom. Recent publication of a previously unknown tattoo on a Middle Kingdom woman buried near Deir el Bahari (see map 1.1) in another unfinished royal tomb complex in Asasif (also found by Winlock) suggests the figural tradition of tattooing known from the Predynastic period was still alive and well. The tattoo, present on the upper arm, shows two facing birds (see Morris 2011:fig. 5). Based on this discovery, a convincing case can be made for identifying tattoos in the figural motifs painted on another class of Egyptian figurines, the so-called paddle dolls, dating from the early Middle Kingdom when intensive contact with Nubia was just beginning (see plate 2b). The animals and symbols on these figurines recall motifs known from the Predynastic period, but most popular was the Egyptian goddess of fertility and protection, Ipet-Tawaret (Keimer 1948:figs. 17–26; Morris 2011:79–90). Therefore it seems likely that these marks represent the reappearance or perseverance of a practice that had remained in Egypt since the Predynastic period and was quite distinctly their own.

CEMETERY HK27C AT HIERAKONPOLIS

The distinction between the tattooing traditions of Egypt and Nubia during the Middle Kingdom is further supported by new discoveries at Hierakonpolis in cemetery HK27C of the remains of three women whose burials display their clear Nubian ethnic affiliation and whose dot-and-dash tattoos are strongly similar in patterning, placement, and technique to those seen on the Deir el Bahari women. The evidence from Hierakonpolis not only makes it highly likely that such tattoos were important markers of ethnicity and were recognized as such among cultures, but that they were also associated with only selected women who may well have been involved in ritual performance.

Hierakonpolis Locality HK27C is a cemetery of ethnic Nubians resident at this Egyptian site during the Middle Kingdom (XI–mid XII Dynasty; see map 1.1). The reason for the presence of these C-Group Nubians is still unclear, but it seems likely they formed part of the retinue of the local governors near whom they were buried (Friedman 2007). The site was excavated over the course of four seasons and revealed sixty-four graves containing sixty-nine individuals: fifteen male, twenty-six female, eleven indeterminate adults; thirteen juveniles, and four infants under one year of age (Dougherty and Pieri 2015). All of the burials were disturbed to some extent, yet all but the most plundered provided clear evidence for the Nubian cultural affiliation of their owners, including the presence of culturally specific pottery, distinctive architectural features, characteristic ritual practices, and traditional leather garments, jewelry, and hairstyles. The finds show that, at least in death, the occupants of cemetery HK27C proudly displayed their cultural links (Friedman 2001, 2004, 2007).

Despite anthropogenic disturbance, organic preservation in the cemetery was good and three individuals bearing tattoos were observed. All were older women, who share an intriguing number of common traits. The remains were fragmentary but in many cases it was possible to distinguish the parts of the body from which the tattooed skin originated and reconstruct at least partial designs.

Tomb 9. The best preserved example was found in Tomb 9 (Friedman 2003). The single occupant was a woman aged over fifty years, with extensive ante mortem tooth loss (Pieri and Antoine 2014). The tattoos are visible to the naked eye and appear blue or greenish, but understanding of their design was greatly enhanced with infrared imaging (Paulson 2012) (fig. 1.9).

The majority of the tattoos are composed of a quadrilinear sixteen-dot lozenge, as known from Deir el Bahari. Although detached, skin probably from the area of the shoulder indicated a pattern of dotted lozenges accompanied by three rows of heavier dashes on the upper chest (fig. 1.9a). From the left side of the torso, a large section of skin preserves a zigzag design of dots (six per side) running diagonally down along the edge of the lower ribs. Over the ribs themselves are the remains of at least seven stepped lines, composed mainly of five or six dots per line (fig. 1.9b). Skin on the right side of the body did not survive, so it cannot be determined whether the designs were symmetrically arranged. A single lozenge appears on the top of the left hand (over the second metacarpal), while similar lozenges arranged in a row run along the back of the lower arm of the same side (figs. 1.9c–d). Similarities in size and shape suggest that marks in both areas were made at the same time using a four-pronged instrument. The skin of the upper arms was not preserved, but that present on the lower right arm showed no tattoos.

The most elaborate tattoos on the woman from Tomb 9 occur on the lower abdomen, where skin still adhering to the pelvic bones provides information about their arrangement (fig. 1.9e–f). Here it was possible to reconstruct a lattice pattern composed of at least three rows of quadrilinear dotted lozenges placed along the side of the abdomen, while over the hip was a series of short parallel lines of four dots each. Other detached fragments of tattooed skin suggest the lower abdomen was highly decorated. Among them is an intriguing arrangement of curvilinear dots flanked by dashes,

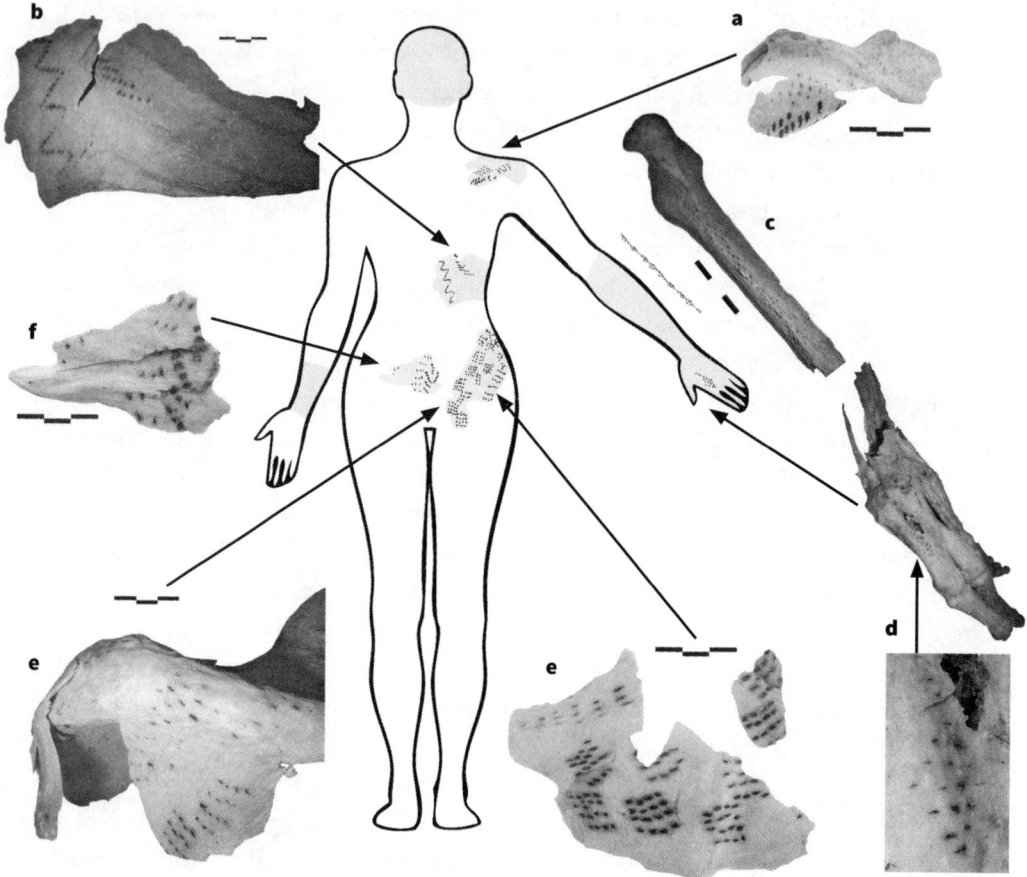

Fig. 1.9. Tattoos of the Nubian C-Group woman from Hierakonpolis, Egypt, cemetery HK27C, Tomb 9 (1985–1855 BCE). Areas of preserved skin are shaded, with details of tattoos shown in infrared photographs. Photographs by Renée Friedman, Joel Paulson, and James Rossiter. Graphics by Xavier Droux. Courtesy of the Hierakonpolis Expedition.

perhaps coming from the center, which suggests that the design here was carefully composed (fig. 1.9f).

Skin is present on her face but it displays no marks, nor does the skin still adhering at the mid back and back shoulder. So it seems likely that the tattoos were limited to her front side. The legs were not present in the grave because of plundering.

In addition to human skin, leather preservation in Tomb 9 was also very good. Like most of the women in this cemetery, she had a long skirt of patchwork leather (Skinner and Veldmeijer 2015). A similar garment is seen in depictions of Nubian women in ancient Egyptian tomb paintings. More notable were fragments of intricately pierced or punched leather. One item has been identified as a leather loincloth. The other, which exhibits even finer perforations, appears to be a form of headgear based on the impressions evident on the skin of the ear and jaw (Friedman 2004:47–50; plates 1–3, fig. 3).

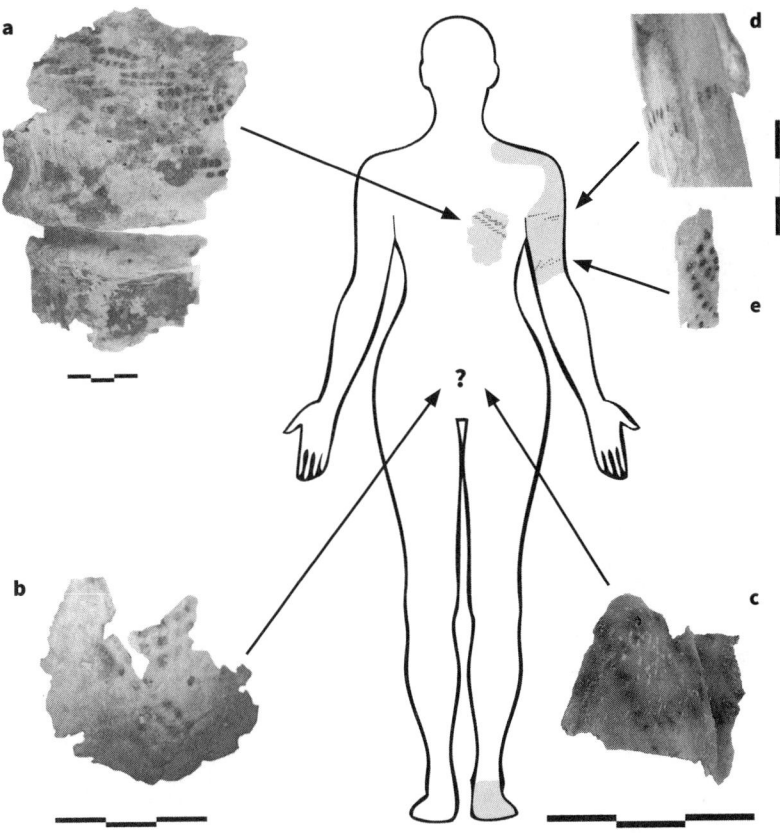

Fig. 1.10. Tattoos of the Nubian C-Group woman from Hierakonpolis, Egypt, cemetery HK27C, Tomb 10 (1985–1855 BCE). Areas of preserved skin are shaded. The tattoos on this individual were invisible to the naked eye, and were only revealed by infrared photography. Photographs by Renée Friedman, Joel Paulson, and James Rossiter. Graphics by Xavier Droux. Courtesy of the Hierakonpolis Expedition.

Tomb 10. Another tattooed woman was found in the adjacent Tomb 10. Although the investigators were already aware of the possible presence of tattoos, and had examined the remains closely during the 2003 excavations, the markings on this individual only became visible under infrared (Friedman and Paulson 2013). The remains in Tomb 10 had been disturbed by looting. The rib cage, held together by tendons and muscles, was displaced against the tomb wall and the lower body was jumbled on the tomb floor. Her head was not recovered.

Tattoos observed on one piece of skin from the chest of the woman in Tomb 10 (ribs still adhering) (fig. 1.10) were composed of linear segments of six dots each arranged in a stepped pattern (fig. 1.10a). Other pieces collected with the ribcage had networks of dotted lozenges, again made up of sixteen points set in four lines (fig. 1.10b). An isolated fragment appears to have lines of dots arranged in a cross-hatched pattern similar

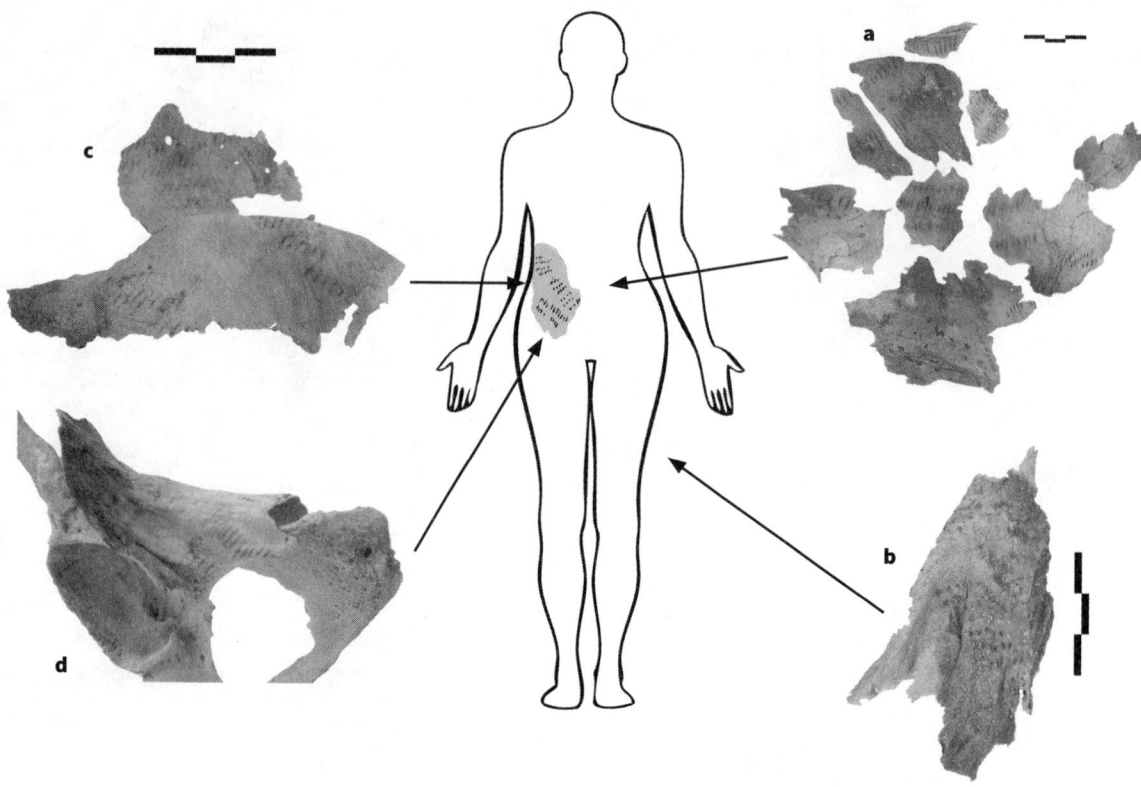

Fig. 1.11. Tattoos of the Nubian C-Group woman from Hierakonpolis, Egypt, cemetery HK27C, Tomb 36 (1985–1855 BCE). Areas of preserved skin are shaded. The tattoos on this individual were invisible to the naked eye, and were only revealed by infrared photography. Photographs by Renée Friedman, Joel Paulson, and James Rossiter. Graphics by Xavier Droux. Courtesy of the Hierakonpolis Expedition.

to that seen on the example from Kubban in Nubia (see below). It is presumably from the abdominal area, but cannot be placed with certainty (fig. 1.10c).

A series of diagonal dashes were found around the upper arm, possibly encircling it two or three times, but the skin on the inner arm has been lost (fig. 1.10d). No skin was preserved on the lower arm, but a fragment probably from that region has a line of dotted lozenges similar to those from Tomb 9, though again with larger dots (fig. 1.10e). Skin present on one foot, the back of the shoulder and the sternum showed no tattoos. Due to the disturbance of the grave, the presence of tattoos on the lower abdomen cannot be confirmed. Leather preservation within the tomb was also fairly poor, precluding other comparisons. However, it is perhaps significant that this woman shared with her slightly older neighbor in Tomb 9 the trait of having a sixth lumbar vertebra, which together with the proximity of the graves may suggest they were genetically related (Pieri and Antoine 2014).

Tomb 36. The third example from Hierakonpolis cemetery HK27C was recovered from Tomb 36, located a short distance away from Tombs 9 and 10. This small oval grave contained the body of a woman, over fifty years of age at time of death. Her legs, still in situ, show that she had been laid on her right side in a tightly flexed position. Tattoos were observed through infrared imaging seven years after the excavation on collected pieces of skin, some of which could be replaced on the chest and the pelvis (fig. 1.11). These indicate a continuous line of long dashes, up to 1 cm in length, running diagonally down over the abdomen from the hip (fig. 1.11a). An isolated piece with a dotted lozenge pattern, composed this time of three lines of six dots each, may be from the upper leg (fig. 1.11b). A series of shorter dashes set in staggered lines runs more or less perpendicular up the side of the waist, the mid-abdominal region, and ribs (fig. 1.11c–d). No regularity in the number of dashes per line could be determined; they range between five and thirteen. These marks are highly reminiscent of those on the lower abdomen of Amunet at Deir el Bahari. Skin, but mainly sinew, was preserved at places on the lower legs and arms, back left shoulder and right foot, but no further tattoos were observed.

Like her companions in the cemetery, the woman in Tomb 36 also had a patchwork leather skirt, but she together with the occupant of Tomb 9 are the only women to wear fine cutwork leather head coverings (which left distinctive impressions on her ear, cheek, and jaw) and perforated leather loincloths. Remnants of the loincloth in Tomb 36 were discovered mixed with leather fragments above the legs, and it was apparently worn under her skirt (Skinner and Rogge 2016). Osteological examination of this individual also revealed healed fractures of the arm and fingers, possibly suggesting an active lifestyle. Like the woman in Tomb 9, she also suffered from poor dental health as indicated by extensive ante mortem tooth loss (Pieri and Antoine 2014).

Discussion

A certain amount of skin was found in almost every tomb at HK27C, and the preservation in eight other tombs was equally as good or better (in two cases the body was almost complete). However, thorough examination under infrared of all skin remains revealed no other tattooed individuals. While it is possible that tattoos at that time were accrued over the course of a lifetime, and therefore the marks on younger individuals were less extensive and less likely to be preserved, this can only be conjectured. The evidence from HK27C indicates that not everyone, or more specifically not every woman, was tattooed.

It has generally been reported that tattooed remains were frequent in C-Group Nubia, based on a remark made by Grafton Elliot Smith (1923:63), claiming that a number of marked bodies had been found by Cecil Firth during his excavations in 1910–11. This claim remains unsubstantiated, since Firth himself mentions only one example, the cross-hatched design on the abdomen of a woman buried at Kubban.[18] The reason for this discrepancy may be that Smith was extrapolating from the clay figurines of the C-Group culture, about half of which are incised with dot-and-dash patterns on

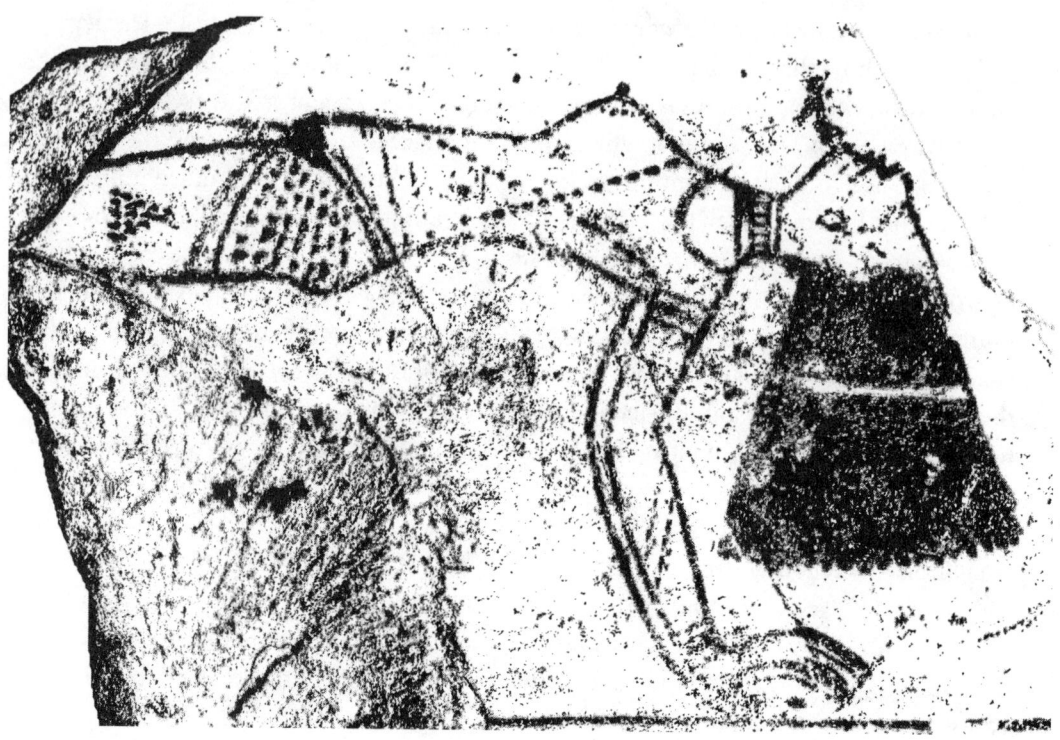

Fig. 1.12. Detail of a New Kingdom ostracon (ca. 1250–1100 BCE) depicting an acrobatic dancer wearing a perforated leather loincloth. Dashes on her thigh and arm likely represent tattoos. After Peck (1978:139; IFAO 3779).

their torso and legs (see fig. 1.8), which were believed to represent the individual with whom they were buried (cf. Säve-Söderbergh 1989:146). Although these figurines—almost exclusively female, often nude—are sometimes found in association with graves containing bodies of the same sex and age, this is far from a rule. The high number of these objects found in settlements (e.g., MacIver and Woolley 1909; Steindorff 1935) suggests instead that such representations are apersonal and, like nude female figurines the world over, should broadly be understood within the general realm of fertility magic. Consequently, while these figurines may attest to the practice of tattooing in C-Group Nubia, they cannot be used to assess its actual frequency.

In connection with fertility and fecundity, it has been suggested that tattooing served as a rite of passage, signaling the bearer's sexual maturity and enhancing her erotic allure (Renaut 2008, 2014). Others have put forth that tattoos had a protective function during pregnancy and birth, with the geometric designs on the abdomen expanding like a net to "hold things in" (Fletcher 2005). Yet, the evidence from HK27C does not support these interpretations for the elaborate abdominal designs found on the selected women there. The leather headgear and loincloths worn exclusively by the tattooed women at HK27C seems to denote something more than marriageability and childbearing, and instead suggest they had a special standing in their community.[19] Similar leather items have been observed in other Nubian cemeteries, often in association with a limited number of adult females.[20] Much like human skin, leather requires special if unpredictable conditions to survive, and so the frequency of its appearance in tombs may be skewed by accidents of preservation. Nevertheless, the record from the Nubian site of Adindan (see map 1.1), wherein fifty-eight graves contain preserved leather but only two (both female) had perforated leather, strongly suggests that such items were both rare and their use restricted (Williams 1983:table 27).

In Egypt, the cut leather loincloth appears to be an article of male attire (Vogelsang-Eastwood 1993:16–31), but when worn by women, it is in the context of dancing and ritual performance (Decker and Herb 1994:cat. no. R 2.1, 3.26, 3.27). The association of tattoos with dancers and musical performers is also well attested, as previously discussed. All of these characteristics are brought together on a New Kingdom ostracon, a broken pot sherd painted to show an acrobatic dancer clad only in a perforated loincloth with tattoos on her thigh and arm (fig. 1.12).[21] This evidence, combined with previous observations, suggests that the tattooed Nubian women buried at HK27C performed dance (at least in their younger years), and more importantly probably had special knowledge of magic spells and ritual movements linked to fertility and other events that were of importance to their community and their Egyptian patrons. Nubian magic was both feared and prized as being foreign and more potent (Raue 2014). The presence of real Nubian dancers at Deir el Bahari and Hierakonpolis, or figurines marked with obvious and recognizable Nubian traits like the dot-and-dash tattoos, made the rituals they performed in all the more effective.

That such tattoos and the patterns in which they were applied were distinctive markers of cultural affiliation is further supported by another discovery at Hierakonpolis. Using infrared imaging, tattoos were documented on the skin of a young man of the so-called Pan Grave culture, another foreign people resident in Egypt from the later Middle Kingdom. The tattoos on this individual are placed in a highly visible location on his shoulder and chest, and consist of dotted patterns far different from the C-Group examples (Friedman 2016). Thus there can be little doubt that, like the distinctive pottery that defines the various peoples in the Nile Valley, tattoo patterns were also culturally specific and understood as indicative of ethnicity.

Conclusions

In New Kingdom Egypt, tattooing continued to be linked with ritual performance in the artistic record, but seems to have become more discrete and private. Figural tattoos depicting Bes, the god of music, appear on the thighs of nude or semi-nude women on various luxury items of material culture (Bianchi 1988:25–26, figs. 8–11; Keimer 1948:40–42, plates 20–22). These marks would typically have been hidden beneath clothing and only viewable during ritual performances. However, recent examinations have revealed figural and hieroglyphic tattoos situated in more publically visible locations on three women from Deir el Medina (see map 1.1) (Anne Austin, personal communication, January 27, 2016; Watson 2016). One of these women bore more than thirty markings, including designs on her arms and neck. These discoveries serve to show that the artistic record alone (or our interpretation of it) will not suffice to allow us to understand the multivalent and nonstatic use of body ornamentation in ancient Egypt, and the choices made in the formation of an indelible identity over the course of this long civilization.

The tattoos observed on the Gebelein mummies now prove that tattooing was practiced in prehistoric Egypt, as was no doubt also the case in Nubia. Each cultural area developed its own tattoo traditions and techniques: in Egypt it was figural, in Nubia it was pattern-based. New discoveries at Hierakonpolis suggest that tattoos were recognized as identifying markers of specific ethnic affinity between cultures, while within each culture they may have been used in a variety of different ways. The evidence available to date suggests these marks among women in the Middle Kingdom may have signaled initiation into certain cults, access to special knowledge, or were professions of faith, but this was probably not their only purpose. As ethnographic evidence (e.g., Smeaton 1937) indicates, the tattoos could also have been applied for therapeutic or protective reasons, or potentially as beauty aids, among other possibilities. Ultimately, only the individual can help us understand their private motivations, but new imaging techniques such as infrared examinations show that uncovering these motivations is not beyond our reach. There is no doubt a wealth of information in tombs, store rooms, and museums still waiting to be found, and when it comes to the Nile Valley, we have literally just scratched the surface.

Notes

I am grateful to the following people for their assistance, advice, and useful comments on various aspects of this chapter: Ikhlass Abdel Latif, Daniel Antoine, Sean Dougherty, Xavier Droux, Joel Paulson, Anna Pieri, Dietrich Raue, James Rossiter, Alice Stevenson, and Angela Tooley. Excavation and analysis of the C-Group remains at HK27C at Hierakonpolis were facilitated by grants from the National Geographic Committee for Research and Exploration, the Wenner-Gren Foundation, the Michela Schiff Giorgini Foundation, the White-Levy Program for Archaeology Publications, and the support of the Tom and Linda Heagy and the Friends of Nekhen. I also wish to thank the Egyptian Ministry for Antiquities for their kind permission to undertake excavations at Hierakonpolis.

1. Absolute dates follow those in Shaw and Nicholson (2008:350–52).
2. See Bianchi (1988); Gilbert (2000a); Hambly (1925); Keimer (1948); Poon and Quickenden (2006); Tassie (2003).
3. Infrared photographs were taken under flash and ambient light conditions. Earlier observations under infrared imagery were made in 2012–2013 using an IR940 filter (Paulson 2012).
4. The identity and status of these individuals are unknown since details of their burial context are unclear. As reported by Wallis Budge (1920:360), who claims to have been present at the excavation, the woman was without covering and had a single pot containing porridge.

However textile impressions on her shoulder indicate she was covered with a shroud and the veracity of Budge's account has long been questioned. The same questions surround the male, who was said to have been found in a stone-covered grave surrounded by a variety of pots and lithics (Budge 1920:359), none of which can now be identified. All museum reconstructions of his burial have been notional and intended only to provide an example of general Predynastic burial customs.

5   Flexed inhumations are typical for the period.

6   Testing of pretreated hair from the female mummy (UBA-33754) produced a radiocarbon age of 4497+/−32 BP, calibrated to 3349–3093 cal BCE (2 sigma) and with a 41.6 percent probability to 3334–3264 cal BCE (1 sigma). The male mummy (UBA-33753) produced a radiocarbon age of 4461+/−36 BP; calibrated to 3340–3018 cal BCE (2 sigma) and with a 56 percent probability to 3326–3229 cal BCE (1 sigma). These dates were acquired thanks to Daniel Antoine, Marcello Mannino, Paula Reimer, Sahra Talamo, and the Institute for Bioarchaeology at the British Museum.

7   This time frame corresponds to the Naqada II and Naqada IIIA period respectively in the terminology currently used for the relative chronology of early Egypt (see e.g., Patch 2011:212).

8   The correlation between radiocarbon dates and cultural relative dating is not without problems, with radiocarbon dates generally being younger than expected. This is due in part to wiggles in the calibration curve for the 4th millennium BCE. Nevertheless, the recent statistical modeling of radiocarbon dates for the period by Dee et al. (2013) suggests an absolute date for the late and terminal Predynastic period (Naqada IID-IIIA) of 3352–3297 BCE (1 sigma) or 3377–3238 BCE (2 sigma). These ranges fit well with the dates from the Gebelein mummies and the parallels for their tattoos within the datable art of the period.

9   The visual language so dominant in the earlier Predynastic period probably never fell out of use, but was not relevant to the funerary material that makes up the bulk of our information. It has been suggested that drawings on perishable materials like plastered walls or painted linens were responsible for its transmission over time (Hendrickx et al. 2009:211). It is now possible that tattoos may also have served this function.

10 Greywacke is a type of fine-grained, gray-green sandstone that was mined in the desert to the east of the Nile Valley. It is sometimes incorrectly called slate or schist.

11 Copper was present at this time in Egypt, and copper needles were found in the same cemetery, apparently the prized possession of men who kept them in pouches at their hip (Dougherty and Friedman 2008:318). It is possible that cultural norms may have precluded their use in tattooing or perhaps their use by women. In contrast, an intriguing correspondence of copper awls with cosmetic palettes has been observed in a number of graves belonging predominantly to mature women in late and terminal A-Group Nubia (ca. 3100–3000 BCE) (see Nordström 1972:123; 2002:361–72). This co-occurrence of copper awl, palette, and women has been discussed in relation to tattooing practices and practitioners by Hans Ake Nordström (2002:366–67), who suggests tattooing was used as a way to emphasize or define Nubian A-Group ethnic and culture identity at this time of increased contact (not all of it friendly) with Early Dynastic Egypt.

12 A similar function may be proposed for the assemblage from Abydos grave E381, which was also kept in a basket (see Naville 1914:17, plate 3.1; see map 1.1).

13 In the Old Kingdom (Dynasties III–VI) the record is mute regarding the presence of tattooing. This lack of evidence may simply be an accident of preservation, but significant changes in cosmetic practices and presumably body ornamentation are also evident. The palettes so important for preparing cosmetics in the Predynastic period disappear by the end of the Second Dynasty, a process that has been linked to the increased control over the conduits to magical knowledge (or at least its display) by the centralized dynastic state (Baduel 2008).

14 Bianchi (1988:22) erroneously states that the sketch does not represent Amunet but rather a different mummy. This has led to confusion and the mistaken belief that a second tattooed body was found at the same time (Poon and Quickenden 2006:124) or even in the same tomb and that in total there are four tattooed bodies from Deir el Bahari (Graves-Brown 2010:113–15). This is not the case.

15 Renaut (2008:fig. 5) also provides a new drawing of Amunet's tattoos, but assumes that the swelling of the belly in life would have rendered the pattern on the lower abdominal area into a more triangular shape, which he believes served to emphasize the pubic region. This, however, remains to be determined. The drawing provided here is based on what is visible in the photographs only.

16 This identification seems to have discounted the high-quality objects and jewelry found with these women. A review of these is provided by Roehrig (2015).

17 Tooley (2017) has now shown that the cropped hair style on some of the figurines, interpreted as representing the curly hair of Nubians, is in fact only an artifact of preservation. Hair was originally added separately to the figurine in a specific tripartite arrangement, with areas of tonsure creating a hairstyle that was purely Egyptian.

18 See Firth (1927:54, plate 25d), with a different and better picture than Hambly (1925:320–21), where it is misdated.

19 The condition of their teeth also indicates they followed a different diet from the rest of the community.

20 For example, Reisner (1923:304); Säve-Söderbergh (1989:131, 186, 208); Williams (1983:121, 154).

21 Although this woman is not physically different in overall appearance from other depictions of acrobatic dancers, Bianchi (1988) identifies her as a Nubian based on the dotted pattern tattoos.

2

Burik

TATTOOS OF THE IBALOY MUMMIES OF BENGUET, NORTH LUZON, PHILIPPINES

Analyn Salvador-Amores

TATTOOING WAS A PREVALENT PRACTICE DURING THE PRE-HISPANIC (before 1521) and early historic periods (sixteenth to seventeenth century) in the Philippines (Chirino 1969; Salvador-Amores 2013; Scott 1994). *Batek* or *batuk*, meaning "to strike" or "to hit," is the general term for traditional tattoos, although other terms are also used by the various Indigenous ethnolinguistic groups of the country's Cordillera region: *batók* (Kalinga), *fatek* (Bontoc), *bátok* (Ifugao), *bátek* (Ilocano, Ibaloy, Lepanto, Sagada Igorots,[1] and the Itneg of Abra), and *bátak* (Kankanaey). The term *burik* among the Ibaloy-speaking communities in Benguet Province refers to a person that is "tattooed all over the body." Tattoos function as painful rites of passage, bodily decoration, talismans against malevolent forces, marks of bravery, visible markers of religious and political affiliations in the community, and symbols of status or affluence.

Traditional tattoos can still be found today among tribal elders from different Indigenous groups in some villages and urban areas of northern Luzon (Salvador-Amores 2011, 2013). However, the custom of covering the body with traditional tattoos began to decline in the region in the early twentieth century. Remarkably, the most enduring evidence of this practice in the Philippines is the remnants of tattoos found on different body parts of tattooed mummies[2] dating from the thirteenth century CE in Kabayan, one of the oldest Ibaloy tribal settlements in Benguet[3] (Garong et al. 2010; Merino 1989) (map 2.1). Although the practice of full-body Ibaloy tattooing and mummification is now extinct, tattoos found on the skin of the Kabayan mummies serve as a visual and material record of an ancient tattooing tradition.

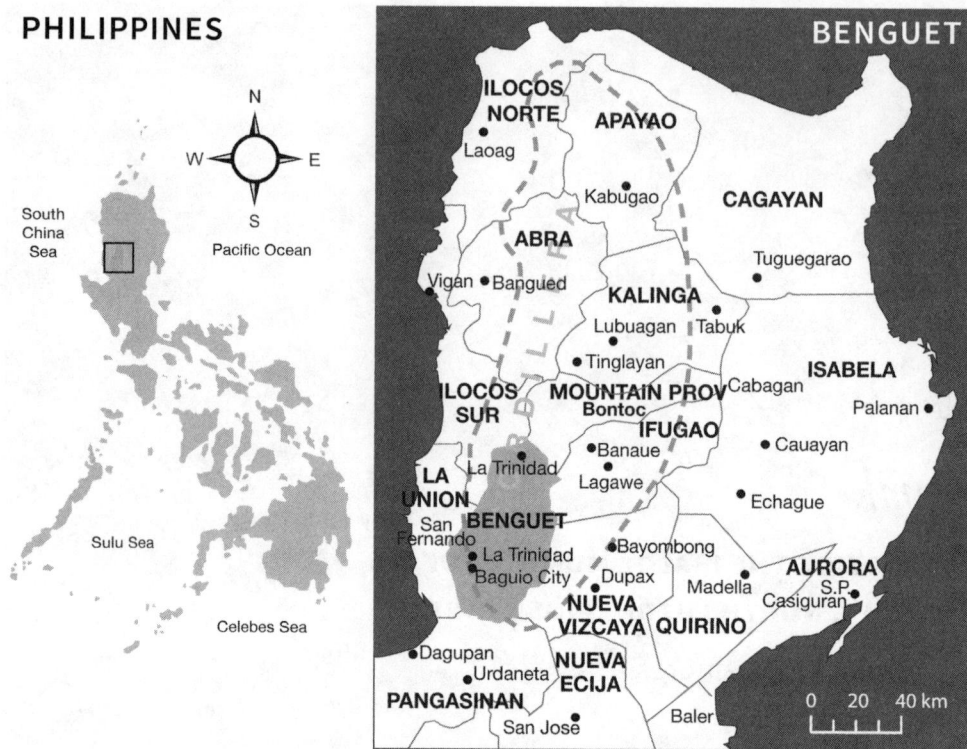

Map 2.1. Cordillera region, north Luzon, Philippines. Kabayan is located in Benguet province, and was once the seat of Ibaloy culture. The Ibaloy reside in the mountain valleys and settlements of the general southeastern area such as Kabayan, Atok, and Kapangan. The predominantly Kankanaey group is found in the northern municipalities of Benguet such as Mankayan, Bakun, and Kibungan. Map modified by Analyn Salvador-Amores and Denes V. Dasco.

Burik in Early Culture and History

Burik refers to the tattoos worn by the Indigenous Ibaloy people, their ancestral predecessors, and other Banao-speaking[4] peoples residing in Mountain Province and adjacent regions of Luzon. The term closely translates to "spotted" (Meyer 1885:512–13; Scott 1975:110). Early historians wrote that the term *burik* "applies to any Igorot [indigene] who is tattooed in a certain manner" (Craig and Benitez 1916:110). This terminology corresponds to the eyewitness account by Filipino writer Eduardo P. Casal, who had seen tattooed Igorots at the Philippine Exposition in Madrid in 1887. The word *burik* contains the root *rik,* which is of Austronesian origin, meaning "speckled," "dappled," and "spotted" (Blust 2011; Blust and Trussel 2012). The Igorot people are consistently referred to as *Iggorot a burikan* ("checkered Igorots") in the Ilocano epic *Biag ni Lam-ang* (*Life of Lam-ang*) (Yabes 1958:296–97, 299–303). In Ilocano, the word is used as an adjective to refer to a person who is "tattooed all over the body" (Rubino 2000:135). In addition, other linguistic evidence may be gleaned from the Indigenous Itneg term *burí,* which means "speckled like iguanas"[5] or "to ornament" (Vanoverbergh 1929:183–84). The same meaning is used in the Kankanaey, Pangasinan, Tagalog, and Bikol languages (Blust and Trussel 2012).

The term *burik* may alternately have been derived from the Banao-speaking people. The Banao region is situated in the western part of the Cordillera Central mountain range of the northeastern Benguet and southwestern Mountain Provinces. Here, two Banao subgroups resided—the Burik and the Busao—both of which practiced tattooing.[6] Early writers confused the term "*Burik*" with the name for Banao-speaking peoples, since *burik* is the local term for the elaborate full-body tattoos of the people.[7]

In 1882, the German scientist Hans Meyer embarked on a three-month journey to the Cordillera Central. There he observed that local men and women were tattooed profusely with elaborate bluish black designs on the wrists, arms, chests, and legs (Meyer 1885:512).[8] Frederic Sawyer, an English engineer who lived in Luzon for fourteen years, also observed:

> You can hardly find a man or woman who has not a figure of the sun tattooed in blue on the back of the hand, for in Central Benguet they worship the sun. Some of them tattoo the breast and arms in patterns of straight and curved lines pricked in with a needle in indigo blue. The Burik Igorrotes tattoo the body in a curious manner, giving them the appearance of wearing a coat of mail. (Sawyer 1900:252)

The Spanish *conquistadores* were captivated by the gold jewelry that bedecked the "scantily clothed" Igorot as well as their "curiously strange body decorations," and in 1887 "four battle scarred Igorots with tattoos" (Scott 1974:12) were sent along with thirty-six other Filipino men and women to participate in the *Exposición General de las Islas Filipinas* in Madrid. The intricate tattoos were an attraction at the exposition.[9] The tattooed participants were chiefs (in Spanish, *gobernadorcillo*) of their respective communities: Oit-tavit and Sumad-en from Bontoc, and Lao-lao and Gumad-ang from Lepanto, Benguet (Anonymous 1887:5, cited in Rovillos 2005:231). They proudly displayed chest and arm tattoos, which had been earned for bravery in warfare, and featured elaborate designs including lines, animal figures, and other geometric patterns. Other details about their tattoos were published in brief descriptions. Gumad-ang possessed curved lines on the back of his arm to signify membership in his tribe in Lepanto, while the heavily marked Lao-lao wore:

> On the back of his right hand a toothed wheel that must represent the sun; another wheel with a cross in the center on his left; a kind of dog figure on the hollow of his chest; the figure of a frog with another of a dog on his left arm, and another two dogs on his right arm; on his chest, abdomen, arms and legs a multitude of scars. (Peréz 1988 [1902]:174–75)

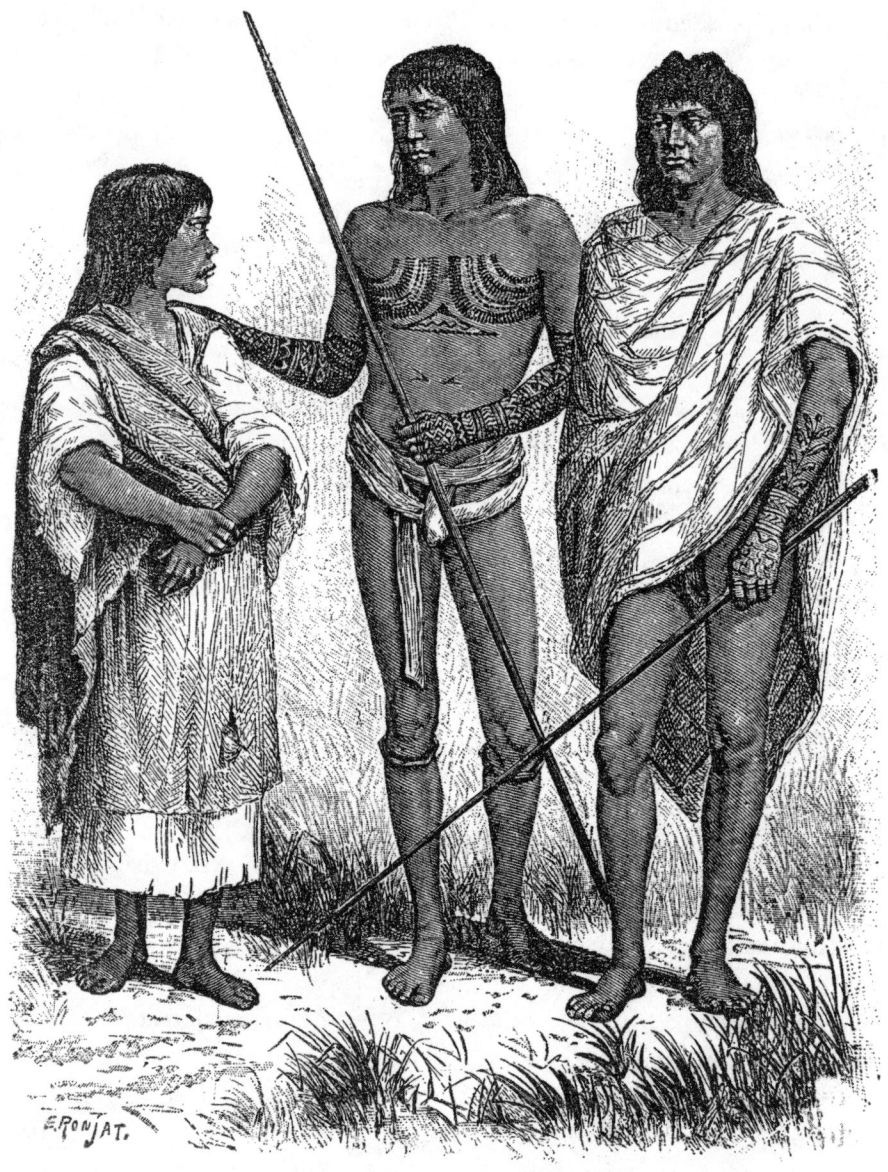

Types d'Igorrotes.

Fig. 2.1. "Types D'Igorrotes" (Types of Igorots) with chest, arm, and hand tattoos. After Marche (1887:153).

These tattoo markings served as both a curiosity and attraction for fairgoers, who recorded them in photographs (Sánchez Gómez 2003:191). Despite reported deaths and other controversies surrounding the display of the tattooed Igorots,[10] the descriptions of their physical appearance have become invaluable for understanding the functions and forms of their traditional tattoos. Moreover, we can discern from this information

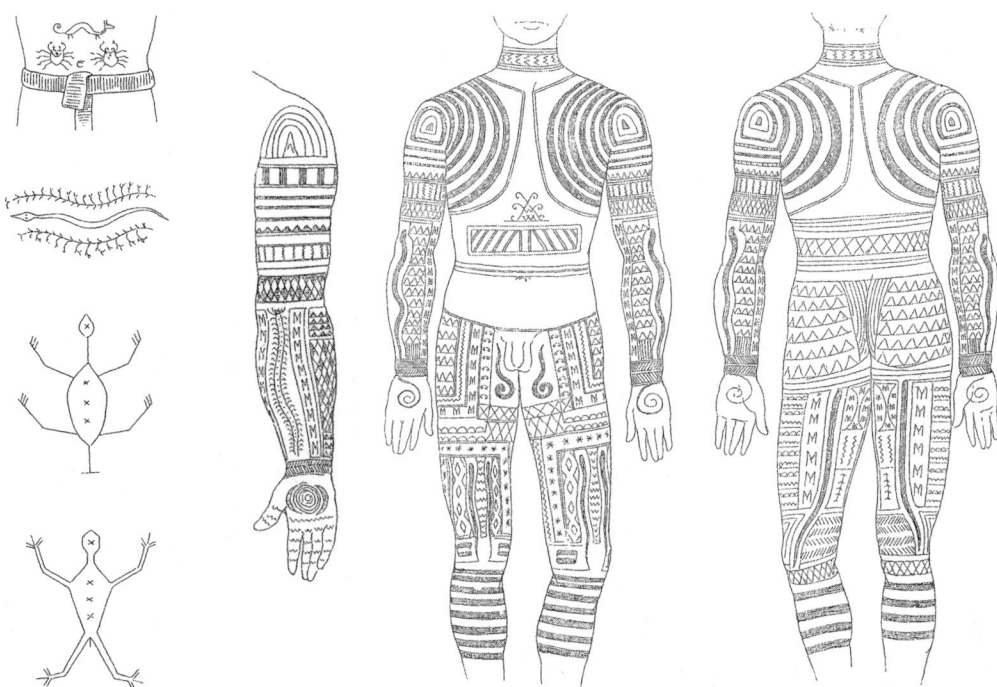

Fig. 2.2. Hans Meyer's detailed illustration of *burik* (tattoos) as seen in the Philippines, 1882. *Burik* is also the name of a tattoo design found on the body and translated as "spotted." The tattoos are comprised of figurative (man, lizard, snake, and scorpion) and geometric designs (lines, circles, stripes, and zigzags). Similar figurative patterns are found on the thighs and buttocks, while the chest, back, and legs display parallel stripes, making the body look like a sailor's striped jacket and the legs like Tyrolean stockings. After Meyer (1885:512–14).

important details regarding the social status of the tattoo bearers as well as the cultural values attributed to tattoos in the past.

Shortly after the Madrid Exposition, several intrepid visitors to the Philippines provided additional accounts of the tattooed Igorot people of Benguet. These European travelers came to the Cordilleras motivated by genuine scientific inquiry and the prospect of "exotic" adventures. For instance, Carl Semper (1975 [1862]:28–99), a German scientist, took interest in Benguet tattoos, which he described as having "designs [with] straight and curved lines, with an exception of a drawing on the back of the hand which could be an outline of the sun." Semper interpreted the sun pattern as a sacred icon, but noted that no special rituals were associated with it. Antoine-Alfred Marche, a French scientist, likened the tattoos to works of art depicted in the illustration by D'Altamonte (fig. 2.1), who accompanied him on his trip to the Cayan and Mancayan areas of Lepanto, Luzon, in the 1880s: "[They were] done with great precision and depicting serpents and flowers sometimes, but most frequently executed with great care and method. As one becomes richer and more powerful, the designs increase" (Marche 1970 [1887]:115).

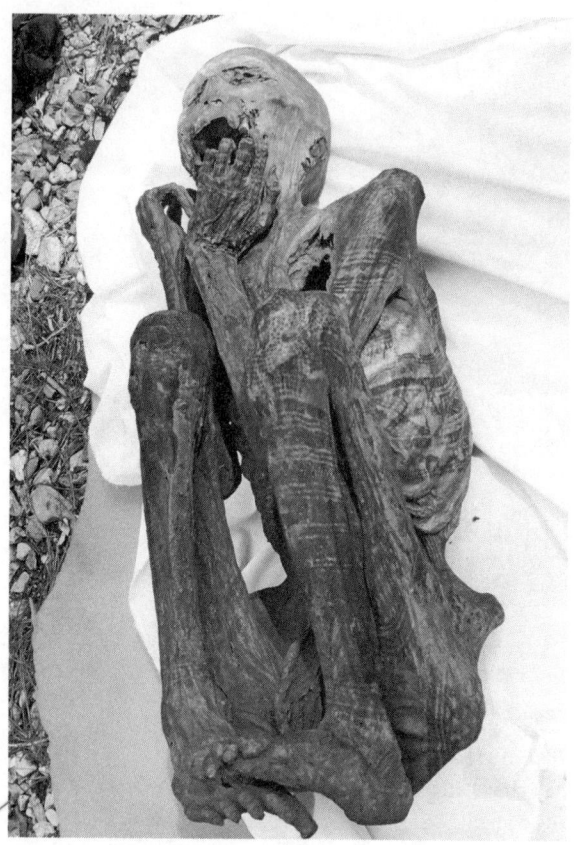
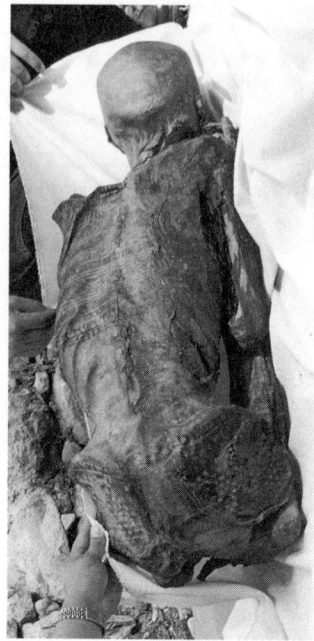

Figs. 2.3 and 2.4. Appo Anno, the seated mummy of Natubleng, Benguet, the Philippines, is clad with elaborate tattoos all over the body (1100–1300 CE). Photographs courtesy of Art Tibaldo.

Hans Meyer traveled to the mountains of the Cordillera in the early 1880s and was perhaps the first individual to draw a detailed depiction of Igorot tattoos (fig. 2.2). His tattoo drawings were accompanied by a description of the tattoos, which he called *burik*. Meyer's drawings show designs that are identical to tattoo patterns dating back to an earlier period (fourteenth century or earlier) and those that appear on the mummy of Appo Anno (figs. 2.3–2.4), which is estimated to be 700 to 900 years old (Merino 1999:99).[11] Beyer (1947:219) observes that mummies "were kept in wooden coffins in a dry niche ... the body was completely tattooed, from the top of the forehead to soles of the feet, with intricate pattern of the type illustrated by Meyer in his monograph on the Igorots in 1885." There are also mummies from other Benguet areas that bear very similar tattoos to those portrayed in Meyer's drawings. Attempts to explain the meanings and symbols of the tattoos found on the mummies were mere speculation, and further in-depth research and investigation are needed to understand their distribution and association.

The custom of tattooing the whole body with decorations resembling a coat of mail with breastplate and backplate (fig. 2.5) was widespread historically in the Philippines and also practiced during the prehistoric period. The early origins of tattooing in

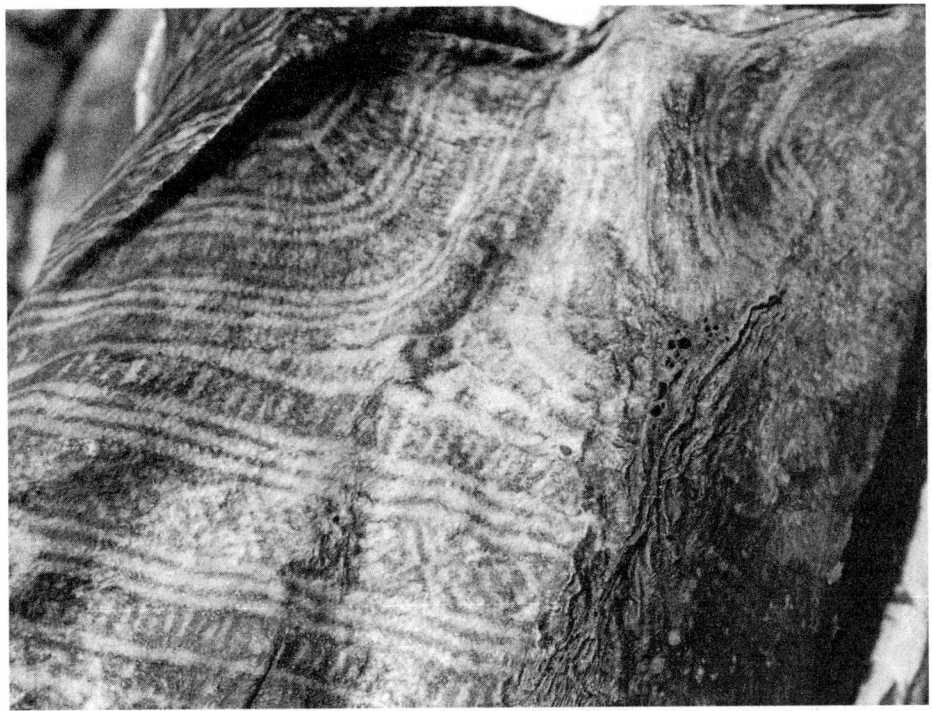

Fig. 2.5. Backplates of Appo Anno, a male mummy of Natubleng, Benguet, the Philippines (1100–1300 CE). One tattoo depicts the anthropomorphic *to-o* (man) tattoo pattern in the center of his back. Photograph courtesy of Art Tibaldo.

Benguet are possibly supported by archaeological finds dating from 370 BCE to 220 CE, including comb-like instruments and two horn chisels that may be tattoo instruments, unearthed in a grave in Arku cave, Cagayan, Benguet (Ambrose 2012:12; Bacus 2002:264; Thiel 1988:248, 262).

Late nineteenth-century documentation of Indigenous tattoos in northern Luzon demonstrates that the human body was fully tattooed with distinct and abstract patterns. Most of the tattoos documented from the pre- and early historic periods were abstract, geometric designs that followed a similar pattern and form covering a man's chest and back, and a large portion of the body. The tattoos of women also appear on both arms and shoulders (Vanoverbergh 1929). There is also a noticeable association between mummy tattoo patterns and designs found on Ibaloy funerary blankets called *pinagpagpagan, dill-i,* and *kuabaw* that wrapped the corpses of affluent individuals. Similar patterns can also be found carved on some of the wooden coffins found in Kabayan (fig. 2.6). At the Timbac rock-shelter site in Benguet Province, a coffin cover of a single broad board decoratively carved with geometric designs closely resembles the tattoo designs found on the skins of the mummified dead (Bagamaspad and Hamada-Pawid 1985:125).

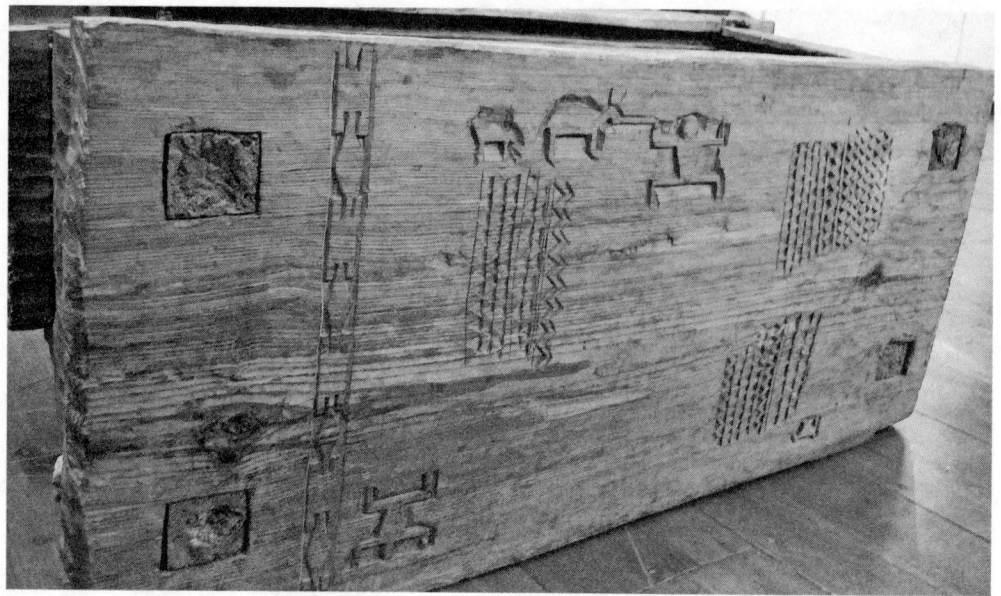

Fig. 2.6. A rectangular wooden coffin possibly used for kinship internment (eighteenth to nineteenth century CE). This coffin is located at the Kabayan Museum in Benguet, Philippines, and has intricate patterns similar to the tattoo designs found on the Kabayan mummies. Photograph © Analyn Salvador-Amores.

By the 1900s observers noted that *burik* was "probably now becoming obsolete, for at least those of the Igorrotes who live near the Christian natives are gradually adopting their dress and customs" (Sawyer 1900:252). The introduction of cotton cloth as a form of clothing had also contributed to the loss of the significance and visibility of full body tattoos. Finally, the cessation of headhunting practices as a result of missionization and threat of imprisonment also contributed to the decline of tattooing practices (Vanoverbergh 1929:189).

Tattooed Mummies and *Burik* Designs

Mummification and tattooing were extensively practiced in Benguet in the past (Merino 1989), but these traditions were prohibited beginning in the late nineteenth century CE during the American colonial period (1898–1946) because they were considered "health hazards" for the local communities. Nevertheless, many of the tattooed Kabayan mummies were maintained in their original burial grounds and rock-shelters over the following generations, while others became relics encased in glass in makeshift museums in Baguio City and Benguet in the mid-1970s. Others were stolen or removed. On August 1, 1973, through Presidential Degree 260, the Kabayan mummies were declared one of the National Cultural Treasures of the Philippines.

The mummies and their tattoos have since become the subject of discussion in television and film documentaries, as well as objects of curiosity to local and foreign tourists visiting Benguet Province. Recent efforts by the local government in Kabayan and the National Museum of the Philippines have proclaimed the need to preserve the mummies and conserve the rock-shelters that house them. In turn, archaeological and conservation research efforts are being undertaken.[12]

In the rock-shelters of Timbac, Benguet, fourteen mummies were found buried in dugout rectangular wooden coffins in the 1970s (Aromin 1985; Salcedo 1980). In a recent report assessing the physical condition of two well-preserved Timbac mummies, archaeologist Ame Garong observed that the majority of mummies found in burial caves are tattooed with distinct patterns and designs that covered the forearms, upper arms (female adults), and the whole body (old and middle-age adult males), including the fingertips (Garong et al. 2012:9–12). Of the fourteen mummies, ten were female and tattooed (ranging from young to middle adult); three male and tattooed (from middle to old age), one of which displayed well-preserved full body tattoos (plate 3).

Generally speaking, the tattoos of Ibaloy men of the historic period were characterized by geometric and figurative designs on the chest, back, sides of the stomach, buttocks, arms, shoulders, hands, fingers, neck, throat, face, and legs. The figurative designs include centipedes (*kamajan*), snakes (*oleg*), lizards (*batingal, karat*), dog (*aso*), and deer (*olsa*). These lifeforms were considered to be omen creatures and also perhaps symbolic representations of gods or their earthly messengers (Moss 1920). The sun (*akew*) and certain plant forms were also employed as tattoo patterns. Geometric iconography included lines, circles, triangles, chevrons, and other shapes. That designs varied from village to village in the past (Moss 1920) provides evidence that tattoos were highly individualized ethnic markers and for some probably marked people of high social status.

My preliminary research on the ethnoarchaeology of tattoos in Kabayan (2012) demonstrated that mummies also possessed "unfinished tattoos" across their bodies. Some of the mummies had tattoos on the forearm, wrists, and elbows, while others had full-body tattoos. It is likely that some of these tattoos were unfinished because the individual died before they could receive a full complement of tattoos. Evidence of full-body tattooing is confirmed in observations made by Augustinian priest Fray Angel Lopez, who wrote:

> The dwellers are most addicted to painting or tattooing their legs, arms, chest and back. The styles they usually adopt are a series of squares formed with alternating dots and lines; one side of the square parallels the vertebrae and the other is perpendicular, leaving the sternum and vertebral column clean. This same combination of lines and dots, but forming circles, serves as the base for the decoration of the legs and arms. (Peréz 1988 [1902]:138)

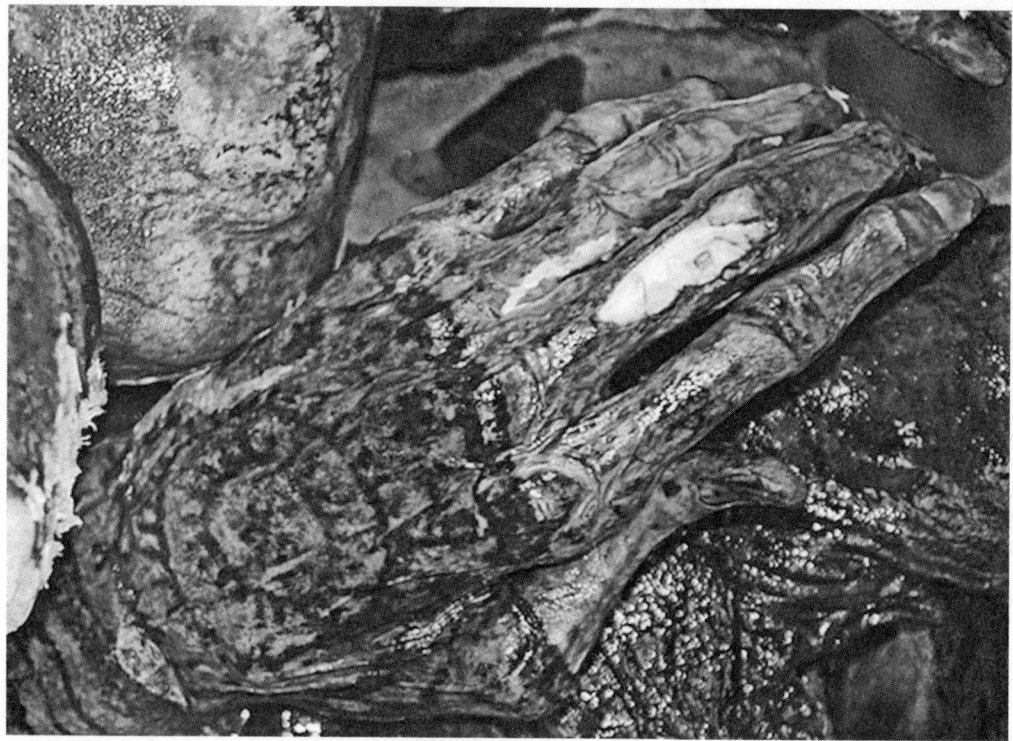

Fig. 2.7. Photographic detail of the "sun tattoo" found on the back of the hand of an undated adult male mummy, Benguet, Philippines. Photograph courtesy of Orlando Abinion.

Aside from the functions of tattoos described previously, the Ibaloy believed that tattoos had the power to prolong life and cure diseases including smallpox (Perez 1979:8).

Other Ibaloy tattoos were believed to embody more magical powers. The ever-present *to-o*, or man motif (see fig. 2.5), represents humankind as a prime element within the context of earthly existence and reality. The *oleg*, or snake, signifies the essence of animism in Ibaloy culture and the belief in spirits, the soul, and life after death.[13] Serpents are said to be the spirits of the ancestors who are believed to know more than humans. Furthermore, *oleg* tattoo designs were thought to possess protective powers for people who wore them (Casal 1998).

Two fully tattooed adult male mummies bear "sun-designs" (*akew*) on the back of their hands (fig. 2.7). These solar motifs were believed to be sacred symbols related to mortuary rituals. Based on oral narratives of Ibaloy elders, the deceased are buried northeast facing the sun. It is at this location that the Ibaloy believe the soul (*kalaching*) awakens and where it will be greeted by the ancestors in the afterlife to become one with the gods beyond the earth-world (*duvong*). This tradition may explain why the Timbac rock-shelters are oriented toward the northeast facing Mount Pulag. *Pulag* is a

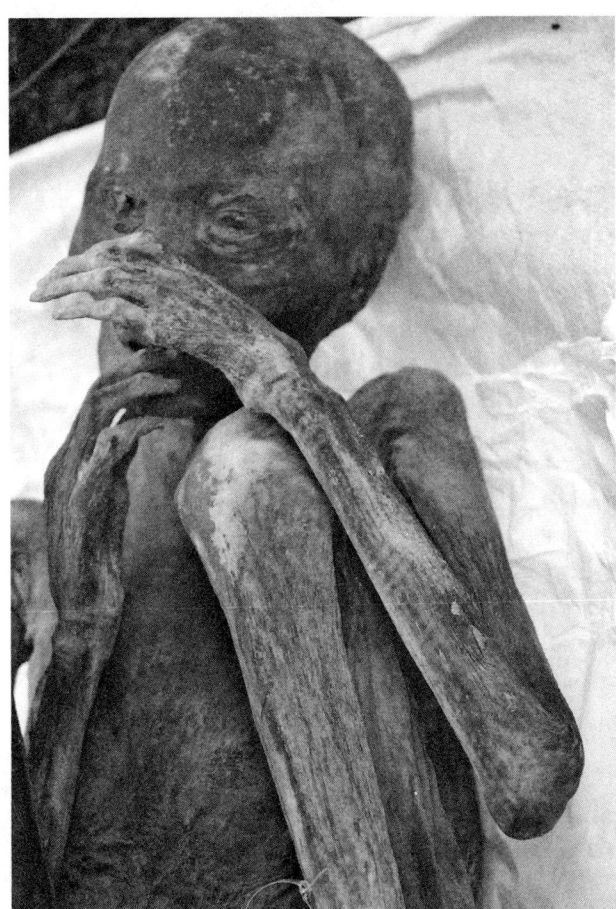

Fig. 2.8. Tattoos on the forearm and upper arm of an undated female mummy, Benguet, Philippines. Photograph © Analyn Salvador-Amores.

term to refer to the place where the spirits of the ancestors (*kaapuan*) converge. Moreover, "the sun was regarded as the most powerful of all deities, and the fact that he was always appealed to in ordeals seems to indicate that he was the god of justice and the supreme ruler" of all (Moss 1920:281).

Female mummies from Timbac are tattooed on the back of the hands, wrist area, forearms, and upper arms (fig. 2.8). Based on archival photographs (see Sinopoli and Fogelin 1998) and illustrations (see Vanoverbergh 1929:222), these tattoos include figurative and geometric designs. Although the functions of these tattoos are not precisely known, it is likely that these bodily adornments marked significant rites of passage and other important life events. These ideas have been corroborated through testimony provided by tattooed elders in Suyoc, Guinzadan, Mankayan, and Banao, who believe that female mummy tattoos were variously a form of adornment, a kind of permanent "clothing," a symbol of affluence or social status, talismans and protective devices from evil spirits, and, more importantly, permanent marks that allowed the ancestors to identify them in the afterlife (Salvador-Amores 2010–2011). The elders also identified

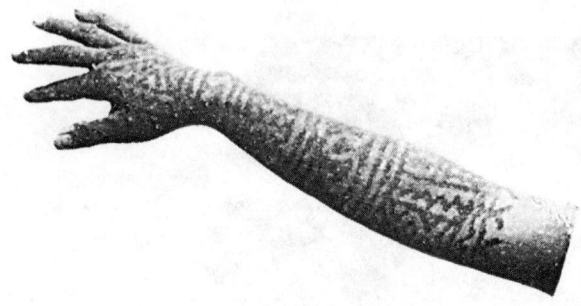

Fig. 2.9. Photograph of an Ibaloy woman's arm and hand showing tattoos resembling those found on undated female mummies of Benguet, Philippines. After Worcester (1906: plate XXV).

the iconography of the ancient tattoo designs as follows: stars (*talaw*), carabao (Filipino water buffalo) jawbone (*pad-padanga*), rice mortar (*pinat-pattu*), basket weave (*inak-akbu*), zigzag lines (*tiniktiku, batikua*), seeds (*pinak-paksey*), and river (*balenay*) represented by curved lines (fig. 2.9).

Early Documentation on the Process of Tattooing

Around 1900, Fray Angel Peréz documented the Ibaloy tattooing process. He observed:

> With three needles joined, the points of which are a millimeter apart like steps, and dipped in a liquid somewhat like ink, made of pig's bile and soot, which mixture, called guisit, they introduce into the skin in the same way as vaccination among us, and it causes inflammation so great that it prevents them from being able to work for some days, which inflammation is always accompanied by a high fever. Among the drawings of animals, the figure of the lizard predominates all of them. (Peréz 1988 [1902]:138)

Some mummies were tattooed with a maguey (*Furcraea foetida*) thorn, a plant that is abundant in Kabayan, Bokod, and other areas of Benguet (Merino 1989:27). The tattooing tool might also be the thorn of a lemon or orange tree (Perez 1979:11), which was dipped into the ink and was used to puncture the skin with the desired designs. The tattooing pigment used to ornament the mummies of Kabayan was comprised of "pounded leaves of a native tomato mixed with soot and water until a consistent and oily ink-like liquid is produced" (Merino 1989:27). In other cases, maguey thorns were dipped into bluish black ink made from the fruit of a plant called luzon viburnum or *atilba* (*Viburnum luzonicum*) (Igualdo 1989:222). According to some tattooed elders in Kabayan, the color of the resulting tattoo is bluish and greenish black.

The nineteenth century description of tattooing in Banao is similar to the tattooing procedures of the neighboring Bontoc region. There, however, the tattooing instrument contained ten needles attached to a piece of bent water buffalo horn. Alexander Schadenberg, a German pharmacist, who made several expeditions to the Cordilleras between 1886 and 1889, collected a similar tattoo instrument.[14] Schadenberg described in detail how the tattooing he saw was executed:

> The instrument for tattooing consists of a thin piece of carabao horn bent at right angles and furnished on the shorter end with sharp pieces of wire. These needles are placed against the skin and driven in by a stroke with a wooden hammer. When about twenty strokes have thus been made, the wounds are rubbed vigorously with soot. The soot is obtained by burning resinous wood, and a pot is held over the flames to collect the soot. (Schadenberg 1975 [1887]:134)

In southern Kalinga Province, Luzon, Whang-Od, a nearly one-hundred-year-old tattoo practitioner among the Butbut Kalinga people, uses a citrus thorn inserted into a perforated stick called the *gisi* ("stick with a thorn") instead of a cactus thorn, and employs a mallet for hand-tapping the designs into the skin (Salvador-Amores 2011:298–300; 2013). Steel sewing needles are also part of her repertoire. Steel needles (*panatak*) were used in tattooing Ibaloy and Kankanaey women in the early twentieth century, but most of them passed away in the 1980s. It is uncertain how sewing needles were introduced in the Cordillera region and how they came to be used for tattooing, though they may have arrived in the 1920s when Catholic missionaries taught sewing and embroidery to young girls (and carpentry to the boys).

In many of the tattooing sessions in southern Kalinga, the tapping frequency was about 90 to 120 taps per minute, with a continuous piercing of the skin (Salvador-Amores 2002). Whang-Od would stop for a few seconds to replenish the ink at the tip of the thorn. It would take an hour or more to tattoo a fairly small design. It takes a day to finish full sleeve tattoos on one arm, and another day for the other arm.

A similar and lengthy process was characteristic of the *burik* tradition in Benguet. According to some of the tattooed elderly women there, the entire tattooing process would take months to finish. Merino noted that the tattoo practitioner would almost become a member of the tattoo client's family. Like other tattoo practitioners working in the Cordillera, the client's family had to provide the tattooist with food and shelter to render the tattoo service (Merino 1989; Salvador-Amores 2011, 2013). Though tattooing of the arms carried a degree of prestige, "not all Ibaloys have their arms tattooed since only those who are *baknang* (affluent) families practice this. However, those who are tattooed may not necessarily be *baknang* but may be descendants of well-known members of the community" (Perez 1979:11).

Tattooing and Wearing *Burik* as a Contemporary Practice

The popularity of tattoos today in urban Manila is manifested in the many national and international tattoo festivals held in Philippine cities and abroad. While in the past *burik* was kin-based and had social and collective meanings among the Ibaloy, in contemporary tattoo practice different sorts of persons seek out these tattoos, and the social linkages are no longer important. The purpose and motivation for using these tattoos have changed (for example, they are often used as an individual form of self-expression).

Dutdutan[15] is an annual tattoo exposition sponsored by the Philippine Tattoo Artists Guild (PHILTAG),[16] an association of 130 licensed professional tattoo artists recognized by the Department of Health as having met the required standards of safety and hygiene.[17] Some attendees at these conventions possess *burik*-inspired tattoo motifs and patterns appropriated from old illustrations and photographs. Knowledge of *burik* tattoos can be gleaned selectively from books, the internet, photographs, and a patchwork of general and second-hand knowledge. Some tattoo artists work in "modernized" *burik* styles, consisting of traditional motifs set in modern arrangements and featuring many graphic figures, such as stylized snakes, dogs, birds, lizards, and other iconography. In the contemporary development of tattooing, traditional motifs persist, while the creativity of tattoo artists emerges through the development of their own style, technique, and interpretation.

Junjun Tabuyog, a tattoo artist who specializes in tribal tattooing with the use of modern tattoo machines, has an album of Cordillera motifs in his catalogue of designs. One of these is the *burik*-inspired tattoo. According to Tabuyog, he found the illustrations from an internet source, and incorporates the designs into his own art. He also noted that many tattoo enthusiasts have taken an interest in the *burik* designs in different tattoo conventions locally and abroad: "A lot of my clients asked me to design a combination of individual designs or even the whole of the *burik* designs tattooed on their chest or on specific parts of their body done with the electric tattoo machine" (Junjun Tabuyog, personal communication, September 27, 2012).

As the experiential nature of tattoos again becomes central in contemporary tattoo practice in the Philippines, there is interplay between the permanence and impermanence of tattoos in the construction of identity inscribed on the skin. In addition, as different actors extract different values from tattoos, they become more individualized rather than part of a collective identity. On the other hand, practitioners and enthusiasts are reappropriating an indigeneity (by referencing Polynesian, Kalinga, or Ibaloy-style tattoos) that is not necessarily regionally or locally rooted, but is an identity built around a specialist activity (i.e., tattooing). This approach is in contrast to the traditional functions of *burik* embodied in the Kabayan mummies and traditional tattoos among the ethnolinguistic groups in the Cordillera who use tattoos as an expression of their ethnic identity.

A handful of modern tattoo artists have adopted the hand-tapped technique of tattooing. Artist Nick Arriesgado used this technique among others to apply *burik*-inspired tattoos on the chest of his client, environmentalist and forester Dada Macusi (figs. 2.10 and 2.11). Macusi collaborated with Arriesgado in the conceptualization of a "Benguet-inspired" tattoo design on his chest. This large tattoo took several months to finish and required three to four hours per session. It was completed with an electric tattooing machine.[18] The chest piece symbolizes the "coat of armor" of Appo Anno,

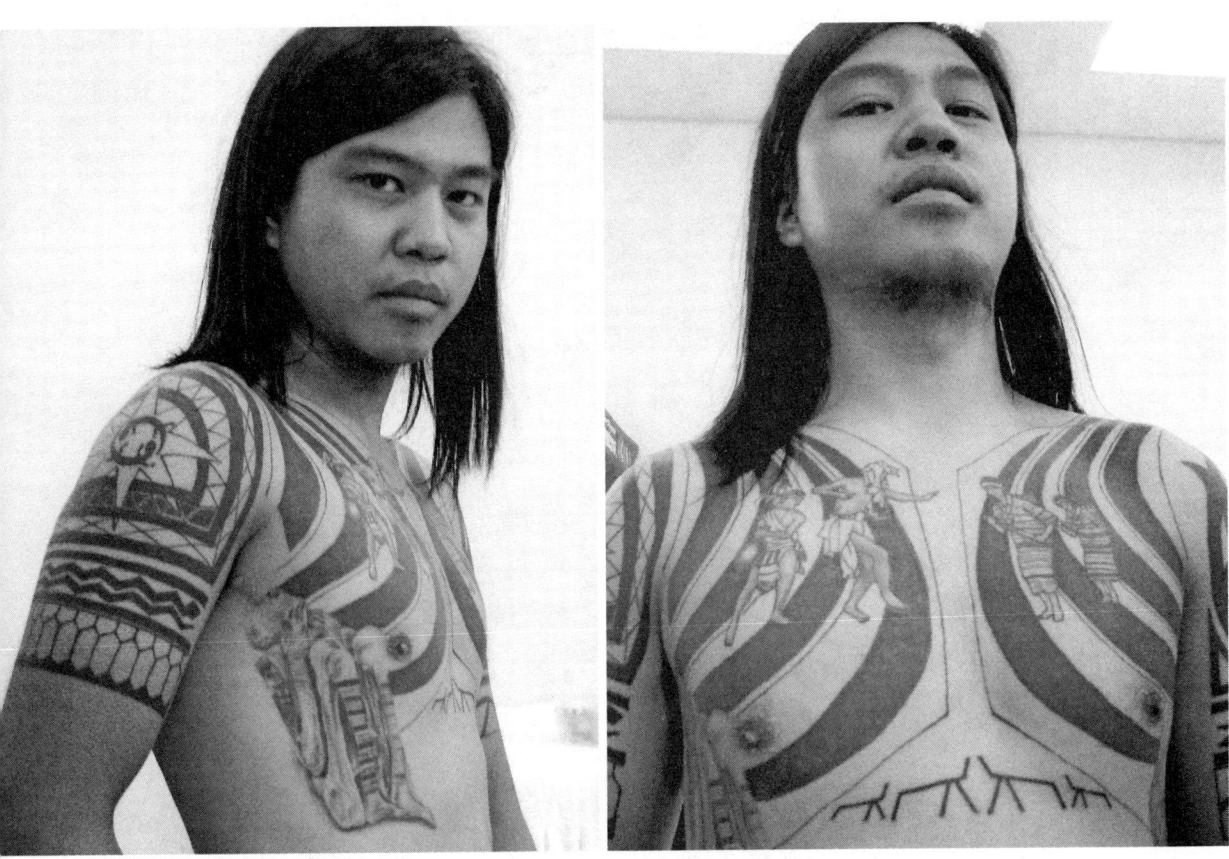

Figs. 2.10 and 2.11. Filipino Dada Macusi's chest tattoos show the "coat of armor" (breastplate) of Appo Anno (1100–1300 CE), a tattooed mummy found in Benguet, Philippines. On his shoulders are Cordillera-inspired motifs produced in a modern technique. Right: Detail of the *tal-lak* with a pair of men and women in a dancing position, over the blackened breastplate. Center: *Aso*, or dog motifs, also found on some tattooed mummies in Kabayan. Photographs © Analyn Salvador-Amores.

the tattooed mummy of Benguet (see fig. 2.3). On the right side of his torso, Macusi displays a tattooed mummy to show the provenance of his tattoo. In the middle of the chest are two pairs of men and women in Benguet native attire performing a traditional dance called *tal-lak* (cf. Bagamaspad and Hamada-Pawid 1985:94).

Other tattoo artists in the Philippines who employ the hand-tapping technique are Daniel Purissima and Agit Sustento. Both are self-taught artists who have fused traditional *burik* designs on their clients and collaborated with other tattoo artists to tattoo *burik* and other tribal-inspired motifs on their skin, like those of the "*Pintados*" of Visayas. The *Pintados* (Spanish, "painted" or "tattooed people") were the heavily tattooed Indigenous inhabitants of the Visayan Islands of the central Philippines. They were first described by Spanish clergy, conquistadors, and colonists in the sixteenth century.

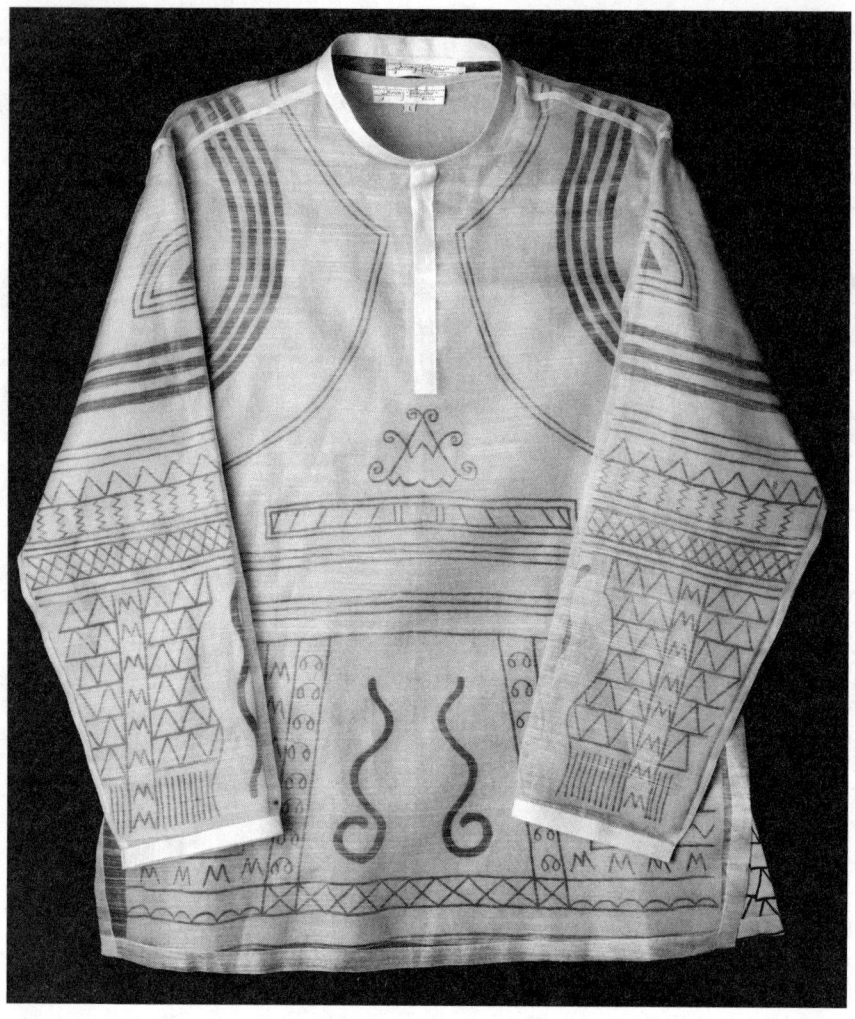

Fig. 2.12. The fusion of *burik* motifs on a contemporary *barong Tagalog* made by En Barong (2012). The *barong* incorporates traditional tattoo motifs inspired by the 1885 drawing of *burik* by Hans Meyer. Photograph courtesy of Neal Oshima and En Barong Inc.

As noted, traditional Ibaloy tattoo designs have been appropriated in contemporary tattoo practice. However, *burik* worn as clothing has also become part of the modern way of (re)expressing identity in the Philippines. In turn, it has become a new fashion statement that is in vogue with urban people in Baguio City and Manila.

Ibaloy tattoos have become recontextualized in clothing designs as expressions of a unique Filipino identity. For example, these ancient tattoo motifs are now visible on everyday garments such as T-shirts and national men's wear (*barong Tagalog*) (see Salvador-Amores 2011). More specifically, the clothing company En Barong recently created a new line of menswear called *Cordillera hinaboe* ("mountain coarse weave") featuring embroidered designs culled from Indigenous tattoo patterns seen in old line drawings and illustrations from the early nineteenth century. There are two versions of the *Cordillera hinaboe*, each of which is manufactured from fibers made from leaves of the *piña*, or pineapple plant. First, the tattoos are embroidered directly on the surface on the *piña* fabric with motifs including mountains, clouds, rice paddies, snakes, and lightning that "represent aspects of their environment and folk beliefs" (Alejo-Hila et al. 2008:258). The second style features the embroidery on the surface of an undershirt made from off-white cotton cloth, which is worn with a plain translucent *piña* over it (fig. 2.12). The designs resemble the *burik* seen in Meyer's 1885 drawing (see fig. 2.2).

The *burik* patterns are inherently similar to the tattoos found on the surface of the *piña* fiber. In turn, they effectively bundle the embodiment of the social character and historical nature of the tattoos within the texture of the fabric in order to transform the status of a once extinct and ancient tattoo to a vibrant and living one. Some *burik* patterns, such as those illustrated by Meyer, were originally borrowed by Roberto Feleo, an artist and fine arts professor at the University of the Philippines in Diliman. Feleo conceptualized the design exclusively for En Barong as early as 1988, although the garment was not manufactured until 2007.

Tattooing was likely one of the earliest types of ornamentation applied to human skin in the Philippines. The designs were ethnic ideograms of the social life of the people. When clothing became part of social life, this form of decoration became part of the embroidery and weaving traditions developed (Alejo-Hila et al. 2008:82). According to Feleo, colonization forced native Filipinos to cover their bodies, which meant covering their tattoos, their original clothing. By putting the tattoo designs on the *barong*, designers have made them visible once again. The use of tattoos and their meanings in fashioning identities through the *barong*, reflects the nation state's respect for and recognition of ethnic groups in the Philippines. This refashioning of tattoos on the *barong*, becomes the connection of the people to the nation, because the *barong*, has achieved status as national attire.

Conclusions

Tattoos (*burik*) found on the mummies of Kabayan, Benguet, are a source of invaluable information regarding the sociocultural beliefs, religious and mortuary practices, and tattooing traditions of the Indigenous Ibaloy people. In the past, *burik* was tattooed on the human body to proclaim ethnic origins, identity, and social status. Today *burik* has been transformed and has acquired new meanings across many different socialcultural contexts as it travels from Indigenous skin to T-shirts, national menswear, and the skins of non-Indigenous contemporary tattoo bearers.

Traditional Ibaloy tattoos have been appropriated in many different ways. Their features have been re-invoked so that the experiential aspect of tattooing (pain and permanence) and the graphic element of the tattoos (pure designs, motifs) are now used by non-Ibaloy to construct contemporary individual and social identities on the skin and through the clothing they wear. The process of disaggregating the traditional tattoo by way of modern tattooing methods and embroidering and printing tattoo patterns on designer and mass-manufactured clothing have created and reinvented new tattoo designs based on timeworn Indigenous motifs. As traditional *burik* now travels across and through different material, technological, and social spaces, its once uncertain future has now been assured through a new generation of bearers.

Notes

I would like to thank Lars Krutak and Aaron Deter-Wolf for the kind invitation to contribute to this volume. A prior version of this chapter addressing the social biography of tattoos was published in *Humanities Diliman* (2012). I would like to express my deepest thanks to Florentino Merino of Kabayan, Benguet, for his time in sharing his knowledge about the mummies in 2003. I extend my gratitude to Lazo and Norma Pucay, who graciously lent me some relevant photographs of the Kabayan mummies, and to the people of Natubleng, Benguet, for their warmth and hospitality during my visit to Appo Anno's burial cave in 2010. B. Lynne Milgram and Thomas Zumbroich provided useful comments and suggestions on the preliminary draft of this paper. I also wish to thank June Prill-Brett for her insightful comments, and Ana Labrador, Assistant Director of the National Museum of the Philippines, who kindly invited me to revisit Kabayan in July 2012. Retired conservation curator engineer Orlando Obinion and Ame Garong of the Archaeology Division of the National Museum of the Philippines shared their preliminary reports on the mummies of Kabayan. I would like to acknowledge the staff of the Kabayan Museum in Benguet, and especially Zosimo Bejar, Virgie Martin, and Clarifel Abellera, for additional information on the mummies. Finally, to the many tattoo artists and enthusiasts I have met at many tattoo conventions, thank you for your interest, time, and attention.

1. Early writers refer to the Indigenous people inhabiting the northern Cordillera region using the collective term Igorot.
2. This is the approximate age of the Kabayan mummies until further radiocarbon dating is conducted for scientific study to ascertain exact age. H. Otley Beyer (1947) writes that the mummies found in Kabayan were believed to be centuries old (150 to 200 years old) and are the ancestors of the present-day Ibaloy. Furthermore, Merino (1999:99) states that: "Mr. Moss, an American who established the elementary school in Kabayan in 1908, recorded that the Kabayan mummies were created about thirty generations ago." Mr. Indo Masao, a Japanese scientist who radiocarbon dated some of the mummies, reported them to be 700 to 800 years old (Merino 1999:99).
3. Otley Beyer (1947:219) also mentions the discovery of mummies not only in Kabayan but also at Mount Santo Tomas near Chuyo and Tunglo. More than twenty mummies were found there in a cave, and at least half were in a fair state of preservation. Mummies have also been found in Sagada, Besao, Bontoc, and Alab, Mountain Province (Keith and Keith 1981:19).
4. The Banao region is situated in the western part of the Cordillera Central mountain range of northeastern Benguet and southwestern Mountain Provinces.
5. The legend of "The Crow and the Lizard" as retold by the elders in Alab, Bontoc, and Tinglayan, Kalinga Province, outlines the origin of tattooing. The pattern found on the lizard's skin is similar to that of iguanas.
6. John Crawfurd (1856:76–77) used these terms to refer to the "wild and independent tribes inhabiting the northern portion of Luzon . . . who tattoo the upper portion of the body and

made the Spanish writers [jump] into a conclusion that they were descendants of the Pacific driven by storms on the coast of Luzon."

7   *Burik* is also an Ilocano term that means "engraving or decoration." The Spanish word *buril* means, "engraving tool." The term *burik-burikan* in Ilocano means "to carve, engrave, sculpture; emboss, design or sketch" (Rubino 2000:136).

8   Remnants of Ibaloy tattooing are seen today on the bodies of elderly women in some areas of Benguet. A separate research project on the tattoos of the Ibaloy women is currently being undertaken.

9   Anales del Museo Nacional Anthropologia (1998); *El Globo* (1887:3); Rovillos (2005); Scott (1974:275); Taviel de Andrade (1887).

10 The *ilustrados* in Europe objected to the Madrid Exposition, believing it to be an assault on human dignity and a misrepresentation of the Philippines (Salman 2001:154; Scott 1974:276–78). Rizal said to Blumentritt "from what I understand, it is not an exposition of the Philippines at all but only of the Igorots" (Salman 2001:154). Byrne (2007:29) argued that the great nineteenth century exposition was an occasion for the metropolitan population to savor the sense of being at the pinnacle to which history has climbed: "It put them, quite simply, in a different class from the rest of the world."

11 A pastor allegedly stole the mummy of Appo Anno around 1918 to get rid of a pagan symbol. It wound up as part of a sideshow in a Manila circus and changed hands a number of times in 1984 before an antiques collector donated it to the National Museum (Dumlao 2013). In 1999, the mummy was retrieved by the National Museum and was returned to its burial site in Nabalicong, Benguet. The Kankanaey celebrated Appo Anno's return with a re-burial ceremony, complete with local rituals. The burial cave where the mummy is now located has iron grills and the local people now maintain the site (*Philippine Daily Inquirer* 2004:A8).

12 Aromin (1985); Baretto (2002); Faylona (2002); Peralta and Legaspi (1968); Picpican (2000, 2003); Salcedo (1980).

13 The cover of a rectangular wooden coffin found in Bangao cave, Kabayan, has two snake figures carved on the lid. Similar snake figures are found on funerary blankets in Benguet and Mountain Provinces.

14 In addition to the photographs he took, Schadenberg collected tattoo instruments used in Bontoc and Abra as part of an ethnographic collection of artifacts for illustration purposes in his lectures at the Amsterdam Colonial Exposition in 1883. Other specimens he collected include instruments for woodcarving, weaving, and blacksmith work. The Schadenberg collections are housed in the Rijksmuseum voor Volkenkunde, Leiden (Brilot 2004:49–51).

15 *Dutdutan* is a Tagalog word derived from *dutdut*, which means "to insert ink with the use of needles."

16 Another tattoo organization in the Philippines is the National Tattoo Artists Association (NTAAS). If a tattoo artist is not a member of either of these two organizations, s/he is considered "underground" and perhaps nonreputable because they lack a legal permit to operate and an official health registration certificate required by the Department of Health.

17 The Department of Health prohibits the use of shared needles in tattooing for fear of HIV-AIDS transmission and requires tattoo artists to wear surgical gloves for the entire process of tattooing.

18 Traditional tattoos also captured the imagination of Filipino-Americans in the United States (Salvador-Amores 2011:312–13; see also Krutak, this volume). Some of these individuals have incorporated *burik* designs in their chest-pieces and other body tattoos (Krutak 2010). These tattoos are created with electric machines and traditional hand-tapping and hand-poking tools.

3

Reviving Tribal Tattoo Traditions of the Philippines

Lars Krutak

WHEN SPANISH CONQUISTADORS LANDED IN THE PHILIPPINES IN 1521, they encountered heavily tattooed local peoples they called "*Pintados*" or the Painted Ones. Five hundred years later, traditional tattooing across the Philippines is nearly extinct. Today, it survives only in remote regions of Mindanao and the Cordillera Region of Luzon (Krutak 2014b).

One of the last remaining tribal tattoo practitioners in the Philippines is ninety-eight-year-old Whang-Od (fig. 3.1), a respected Kalinga elder from the village of Buscalan, who has been tattooing clients for more than eighty years (Krutak 2010). Utilizing the timeworn technique of hand-tapping, she hammers her pomelo thorn tool into the quivering flesh of domestic and international tourists who are in search of a lasting souvenir, as well as local Kalinga villagers who seek to reassert their Indigenous roots in an increasingly globalized world.

Like the tattoos of the Ibaloy (see chapter 2, this volume), Kalinga tattoo motifs were derived from nature: rice bundles, centipedes, python scales, and eagle wings. Generally speaking, women's tattoos were symbols of adulthood, while men's tattoos demonstrated accomplishments on the battlefield (Krutak 2010).

One decade ago, however, the future of Kalinga tattooing was certainly in doubt. Tattoos were no longer being given, and with the passing of successive generations of tattooed elders the custom was rapidly vanishing. But this trend would change around 2006, when Whang-Od began apprenticing her great-niece Grace Palicas to take over

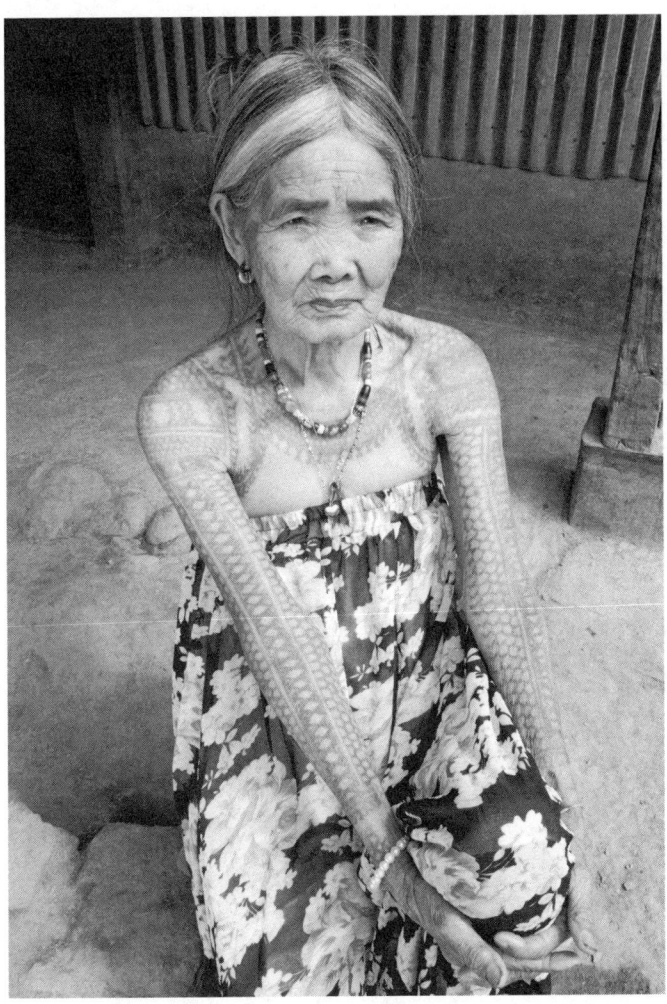

Fig. 3.1. Kalinga elder and tattoo artist Whang-Od, who is ninety-eight years old (2016). Photograph © Lars Krutak.

the practice from her. During the following years, several more young Buscalan women were also trained by the elderly tattoo master to create a vibrant Kalinga tattooing revival that continues to this day.

Mark of the Four Waves

Prior to the contemporary Kalinga tattoo revival, the preservation of Indigenous Filipino tattooing was supported by members of the Mark of the Four Waves Tribe (plate 4). Founded in Orange County, California, in 1998 by Elle Festin and a small group of diasporic Filipinos, the Tribe is a global community[1] of hundreds of men and women of Filipino heritage that seeks to revitalize the tattooing traditions of the many tribal peoples—including the Kalinga and Ibaloy—who call the Philippines

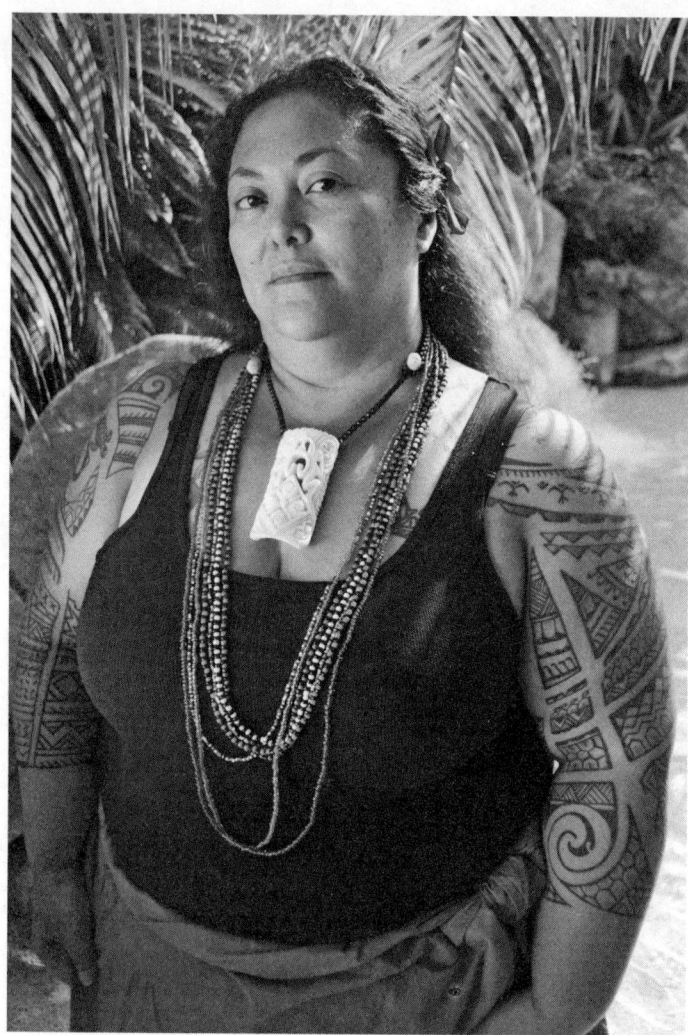

Fig. 3.2. Mark of the Four Waves Tribe member Tina Astudillo-Ash (2012). The Tribe is a worldwide contemporary group dedicated to preserving Indigenous Filipino tattooing. Photograph © Lars Krutak.

home (Krutak 2015). Members of the Tribe work closely with selected tattoo artists, including Festin and his wife Zel, and historians to develop their customized genealogical patterns.

Tribe members come from all walks of life (e.g., professors, doctors, nurses, chefs, police, janitors, musicians, soldiers, firemen, IT professionals) and what they share is a profound sense of brother/sisterhood that is expressed through their boldly patterned tattoos. Tribe member Tina Astudillo-Ash relates: "Having tattoos is essential to who we are. For me, they represent not only who I am but who my people and ancestors were—strong and brave people who have much to be proud of" (Krutak 2010:296) (fig. 3.2).

Mark of the Four Waves member Ryan Mallari has family roots that harken back to the Province of Benguet, home to the Ibaloy mummies. His grandmother was a traditional healer, some even called her a "witch," and when someone was ill in her family

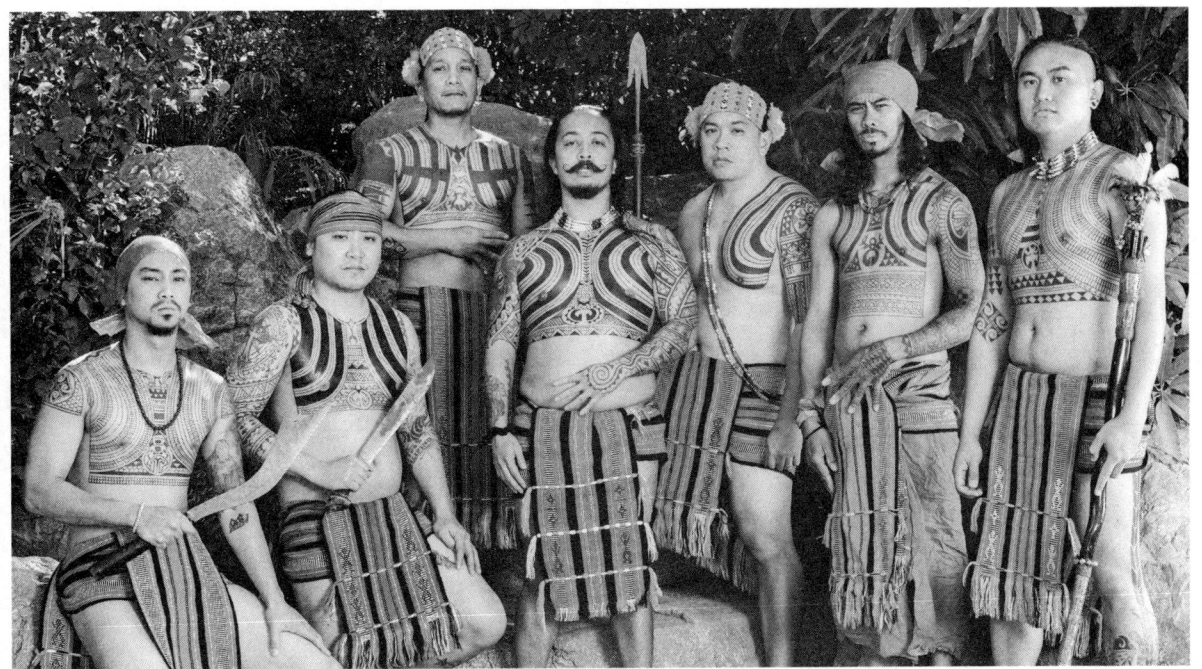

Fig. 3.3. Mark of the Four Waves Tribe members Timothy Cross, Iam Ordaz, Vince Bantilles, Jordan Lumaquin, Ryan Mallari (with spear), Bubu Enay, and Kimo Demingoy, each wearing Ibaloy-inspired tattoo designs (2014). Photograph © Joe Ash / www.ash-photos.com.

she performed certain rituals. "Ginger, salt, and rice were thrown into a bowl of water while she sat in front of an open door calling the sick person's name. She was performing an ancient ritual that was rooted in a Tribal understanding of the soul and the body that I am now only beginning to understand," he says (Ryan Mallari, personal communication, April 7, 2016). "The Ibaloy-inspired tattoos that I wear are an affirmation of that connection and link me to those traditions long lost, lost because of cultural assimilation and the colonization of our traditions and heritage by outsiders. The breaking of skin and imprinting the culture of my ancestors is my own personal revolt against time, forgetfulness, assimilation, and irreverence that would have those traditions disappear. Without a doubt, these tattoos are for my children and those yet to come" (fig. 3.3).

While the tattoos of Tribe members are appreciated for their great beauty, they are not meant to be a fashion statement. Rather they function as bridges that link individuals to their personal and family histories, and for this reason every tattoo is personally sacred. Thus, it is highly taboo and disrespectful for anyone to copy another person's design. In the opinion of the Tribe, tattoos should never be worn lightly, because, after all, they define who you are and remain with you throughout your entire life.

As in many Indigenous cultures around the world, Tribe members believe that tattoos should be earned and not given freely. Consequently, each member participates

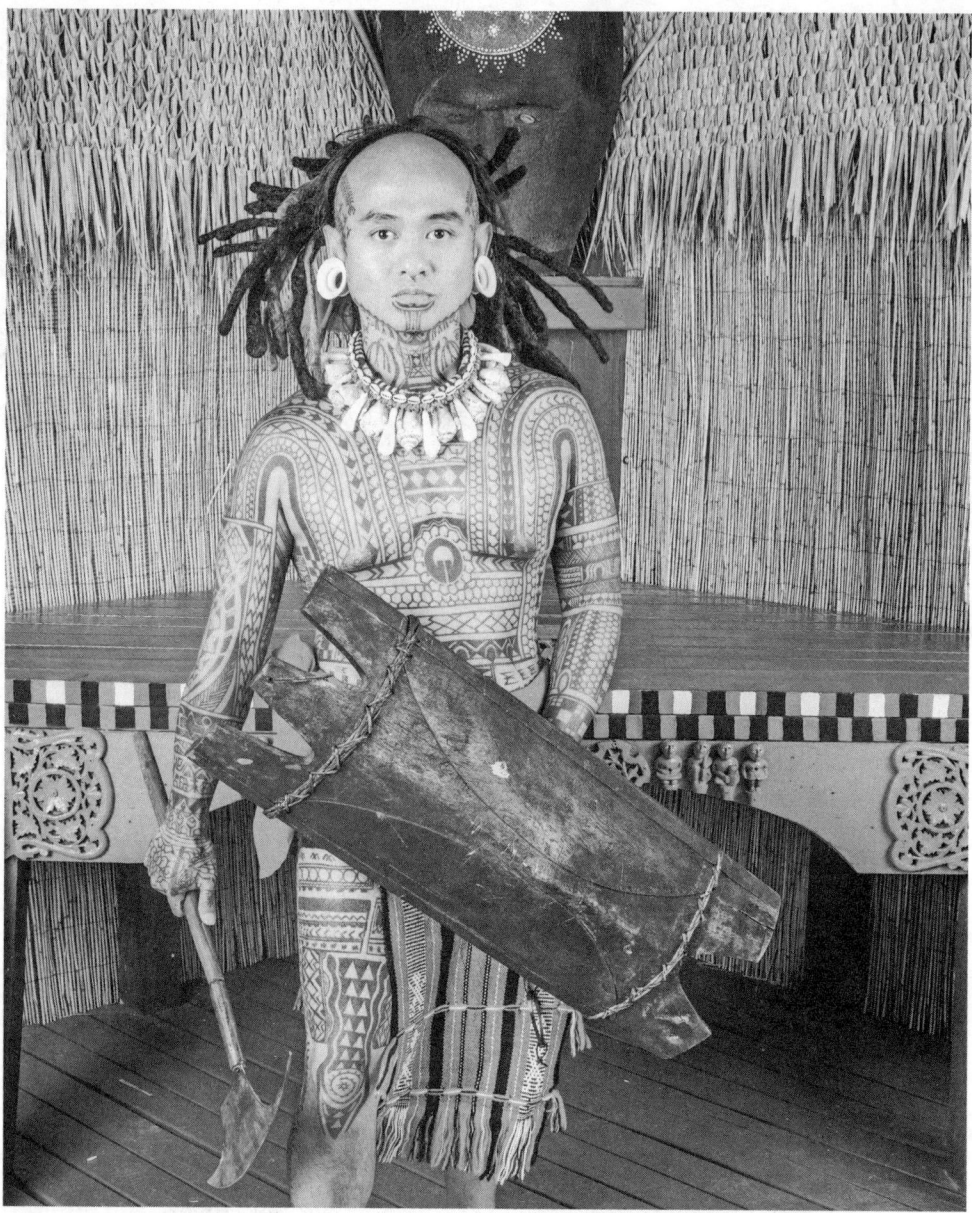

Fig. 3.4. Elle Festin, co-founder of the Mark of the Four Waves Tribe (2014). Photograph © Joe Ash / www.ash-photos.com.

in a lengthy research process whereby s/he uncovers the appropriate tattoo for their body based on several factors, ranging from genealogy to astrology, and to career goals and future aspirations. Tribe members are supported and guided throughout their quest for individual knowledge and consult available reference material in the Mark of the Four Waves library and archives to attain the necessary wisdom from which their tattoos are created. Because much of this reference material is quite old and rare, the Tribe has invested large amounts of money to acquire it. In addition, they have also invested heavily in objects of material culture, such as weaponry, basketry, and textiles, from which they draw inspiration to develop their tattoo designs. Some of these resources are available at Festin's studio *Spiritual Journey Tattoo and Tribal Gallery* in Stanton, California, where he tattoos members of the Tribe (Krutak 2013a).

An accomplished artisan and designer, Festin typically employs traditional tools and techniques (hand-tapping and hand-poking) to produce tattoos. He feels that the handcrafted tattoos he conceives pay homage to the individuals who continue to make Indigenous tattoos, like Whang-Od, and those who came long before her. He says of his work: "Each tap or poke is like a whisper from another time or place. We want to pay our deepest respect to those Tribal artists who came before us, and that is why we give it proper ceremony and ritual when using these kinds of implements. Otherwise, the practice of tattooing will be like an empty vessel, hollow and without meaning" (Krutak 2015:70) (fig. 3.4).

Festin and the other members of the Tribe feel great pride in reawakening the ancient voices of the people to whom these tattooing traditions once belonged. Festin says: "I feel deep down in my heart that I should continue this tattoo revival for those people who are seeking their culture and roots. I want to expose Tribal tattooing's great depth and beauty, because the piece we create together are not flash art you see on other shops' walls. Rather, we create art that has an energy and life of its own and our members are drawn to it because there are so many personal levels of meaning embodied within it" (Krutak 2015:70).

Note

Mark of the Four Waves chapters are located in Canada, Sweden, Germany, Australia, and the Philippines, as well as various US states (e.g., California, Washington, Nevada, Arizona) and metropolitan areas (e.g., Houston, Chicago). Members of unorganized chapters also hail from Italy, France, the United Kingdom, and New Zealand.

4

The Mummification Process among the "Fire Mummies" of Kabayan

A PALEOHISTOLOGICAL NOTE

Dario Piombino-Mascali, Ronald G. Beckett,
Orlando V. Abinion, and Dong Hoon Shin

THE PROVINCE OF BENGUET, SITUATED IN NORTH LUZON, PHILIPPINES, holds a large number of ancient mummified remains, mostly located within the municipality of Kabayan. The mummies are mainly associated with the Ibaloy, one of the several Indigenous groups of Benguet people collectively known as Igorot. The mummies are preserved within wooden coffins carved from hollowed pine tree (*Pinus insularis*) segments in natural shelters or rock caves (Picpican 2003). Many of the mummies of this region are heavily tattooed. Very little information is currently available on the mummification process. Clues regarding the funerary rituals performed in the area have been passed down through oral tradition and suggest that mummification was reserved for the upper social classes and the elderly.

These tattooed mummies are the ancestors of contemporary villagers and have become a regional and national symbol of Ibaloy identity. Today, many tribal members consider the mummies to be sacred beings who actively intervene in the world of the living. In turn, ritual offerings are made to the ancestral dead to appease their spirits and to petition them for blessings in the form of children, wealth, long life, bountiful crops, and domesticated animals (Picpican 2003). Since the tattoos of the dead can be read as biographical statements recounting their deeds in life, the practice of mummification served an important function, because it assured that these achievements would not be forgotten over the ensuing centuries.

Ibaloy Mummification

The information for this study was mainly gathered on site during two surveys conducted by the authors in 2002 and 2012. In addition to ethnographic data, inspections of some of these corpses revealed that desiccation was the principal method of mummification, and that both sexes as well as all age groups were preserved. Evisceration was not evident in these mummies. According to local accounts, a salt solution was introduced into the mouth of the person shortly before or soon after death. The cadaver was then washed. The body was then positioned as though seated on a "death chair" with the head extended backward using a cloth strap. The "death chair" was constructed of local materials, and the seated remains were positioned on a ladder facing toward the front of the traditional stilt house. A scarf or blanket was used to both secure the body and to cover the head. A low fire was lit below the chair to enhance dehydration, hence the name "fire mummies." During the process, bodily fluids were released and collected in a jar. Once the dripping of fluids ceased, the body was exposed to the sun and the epidermis was peeled off by community elders. This action, however, would not compromise the tattoos present on the bodies, because the pigment is deposited in the dermal layer. Juice from the leaves of local plants, including guava (*Psidium guajava*), *diwdiw* (*Ficus septica*), *patani* (*Phaseolus lunatus*), *duming* (*Dolichos lablab*), and *besodak/sopedak* (*Embelia philippinensis*) was applied to the corpse. Also, tobacco smoke was blown into the mouth of the deceased. Once the process was completed, the body was taken into the mountains for entombment.

While some of the information collected may be anecdotal—such as the use of an expensive substance like salt and the possibility of ingesting the solution prior to death—some features reported in these accounts may encourage mummification (Cardin 2014). The seated position may have enhanced desiccation, since the enzyme-laden fluids of the small intestine would have drained out through the perineum. The blanket often used to cover the cadaver may have served a wicking function and increased the rate of water evaporation. Furthermore, the heat created by the fire played a role in the process. The fire would have created a localized environment of decreased humidity and elevated temperature. The wood smoke would have encouraged the process of mummification, especially within an enclosed area such as a traditional house where a preservative microenvironment could be created. The phenolic compounds released from the fire would aid in the preservation of tissues through their antioxidant properties inhibiting the decay of fats, while their antimicrobial action would have prevented bacterial growth. Additionally, as wood smoke often contains formaldehyde and acetic acid, a hostile environment for bacteria would be created, while the ultimate cross-linking of collagen fibers would have expelled water from tissues. In turn, this action decreased the enzymatic action that occurs during decomposition. Finally, the smoke may have created a physical barrier against insect infestation (Beckett et al. 2011).

Nevertheless, some of the reported practices likely played a limited part in the process. The introduction of the salt solution into the mouth seems to have had no impact on organ preservation because the cessation of the peristalsis in a deceased individual would prevent the fluid from traveling beyond the stomach. Similarly, tobacco smoke blown into the mouth would have only limited exposure to the internal tissues.

Paleohistology

To shed further light on the process of mummification practiced by the Ibaloy, the authors examined a soft tissue sample acquired from one of the two mummy burial caves located on Mount Timbac by means of paleohistological techniques (Aufderheide 2003). The sample consisted of soft tissue associated with a rib bone, which had been radiocarbon dated to the eighteenth to nineteenth century CE (Beckett 2013). The surface of the sample was inspected by stereomicroscope before histological study began.

Following initial inspections, the sample was rehydrated with Ruffer's solution, 5 : 3 : 2, for distilled water : absolute ethanol : 5 percent sodium carbonate (Ruffer 1921). After the solution was fixed by 4 percent paraformaldehyde, a gradual series of sucrose (10 percent–30 percent weight/volume) was employed to treat it. The total period for rehydration, fixation, and sucrose treatment was two weeks. Tissues were then embedded in an optimal cutting temperature (OCT) compound and frozen rapidly in 2-methylbutane precooled to its freezing point with liquid nitrogen. Tissue specimens were cut into 12- to 20-micrometer sections on the cryostat, thaw-mounted on gelatin-coated microscopic slides, and stored at 20°C until required. Sections were stained using the hematoxylin-eosin and Masson's trichrome stain, following the methods described by Sheehan and Hrapchak (1980).

The sample was taken from the thoracic cage; it felt very hard and stiff, and exhibited a curved shape. The convex surface appeared like the tendons of various muscles in the thoracic cage, such as the intercostal muscles (ICM) (plate 5a). The effects of tanning, possibly made by fire-induced mummification, could be identified on the convex surface of the sample, therefore confirming historical sources (plate 5b).

On the opposite side (concave surface), the periosteum originally attached to the rib was visible (plate 5c). The rib was not part of the sample as it had been previously separated from the soft tissue. In the cross section of the sample, we clearly found each layer of muscle tendon and rib periosteum underneath it (plate 5d).

Through histological observation, we discovered that the microscopic images were well matched with the gross findings of the sample. In the Masson's trichrome stain, we could see the black tanning on one side and the periosteum on the other. Most of the histological samples belonged to muscle tendon. We believe the tanning process affected the muscle tendon surface. As far as the microscopic features are concerned, muscle tendon of this mummified tissue were mainly composed of collagen fibers and interposing muscle fibers (plates 6a–6c). Although the histological samples were well preserved, we could not see any cell nuclei in the sample examined. This means that karryorhexis had already occurred during tissue degradation in the course of the mummification process (plate 6d).

In our histological investigation on the fire mummy tissue—the first study ever carried out on this type of Southeast Asian mummy—unique findings were expected because the local process of mummification is distinctive when compared to other recorded cases worldwide. However, the current histological appearance suggests that the microscopic findings were not specific in this case. This study was performed on a limited part of a single mummy, consisting of a tendon overlying a rib. Because of cultural norms, additional tissues could not be sampled.

Conclusions

In summary, like for the findings reported from other countries, mummified tissue from this fire mummy was composed mainly of collagen fibers. Although mummy firing and smoking methods were unique from the methodological point of view, the general histological pattern was not so different from that seen in other natural or artificially prepared mummies. In fact, even without any embalming treatment with chemicals, the deceased was mummified and very well preserved for its relative age.

In the current histological investigation, we could also see that the morphological appearance of the cadaver was influenced by special environmental conditions. First, tanning could be identified on the convex surface of the sample. Second, presumptive carbon particles were profusely observed in the collagen fibers. Seemingly, these particles were created by the firing and smoking during the ritual of bodily preservation. Considering that this sample consists of a muscle tendon once overlying the thoracic cage that must have been concealed underneath the skin, tanning of its surface suggests that the fire created this effect. Finally, we noted the co-presence of collagen and muscle fibers in the same part of the investigated sample. Considering the characteristic morphology of muscle tendon, this may be an expected pattern.

5

Identifications of Iron Age Tattoos from the Altai-Sayan Mountains in Russia

Svetlana Pankova

THE ALTAI-SAYAN MOUNTAIN SYSTEM IS A SPECIAL REGION AT THE JUNCture of the vast Siberian taiga (Russia) and the mountainous-steppe expanses of Inner Asia (Mongolia, Kazakhstan, and northwest China). Geographically and culturally the Altai-Sayan mountain region has always been more connected to its southern neighbors, since it was a part of the so-called Great Steppe Belt or Corridor—a habitat and interaction environment for different nomadic groups since at least the first millennium BCE. The various ancient cultures that inhabited this region left behind an extensive archaeological record and are perhaps best known for their burial rites, rich artistic traditions, and the exceptional preservation of perishable materials.

Preserved tattoos have been identified from eight ancient burials in the Altai-Sayan region, and are representative of two cultures spanning the period between approximately 400 BCE and 400 CE (map 5.1). Seven of these burials come from the high valleys of the Altai Mountains and belong to the seminomadic pastoral population of the fourth through third centuries BCE, named Pazyryk after the burial site (Barkova and Pankova 2005; Polosmak 2000; Rudenko 1970:109–14). Burials of these horsemen are famous, containing numerous preserved objects made of felt, leather, wood, and horn that are elaborately decorated with mostly zoomorphic images. The Pazyryks are also known for the custom of deliberate mummification (Barkova and Gokhman 2001; Polosmak 2001:238–55).

An eighth tattooed mummy dating to the third through fourth centuries CE was unearthed at the Oglakhty burial ground in the Minusinsk region, a small mountainous

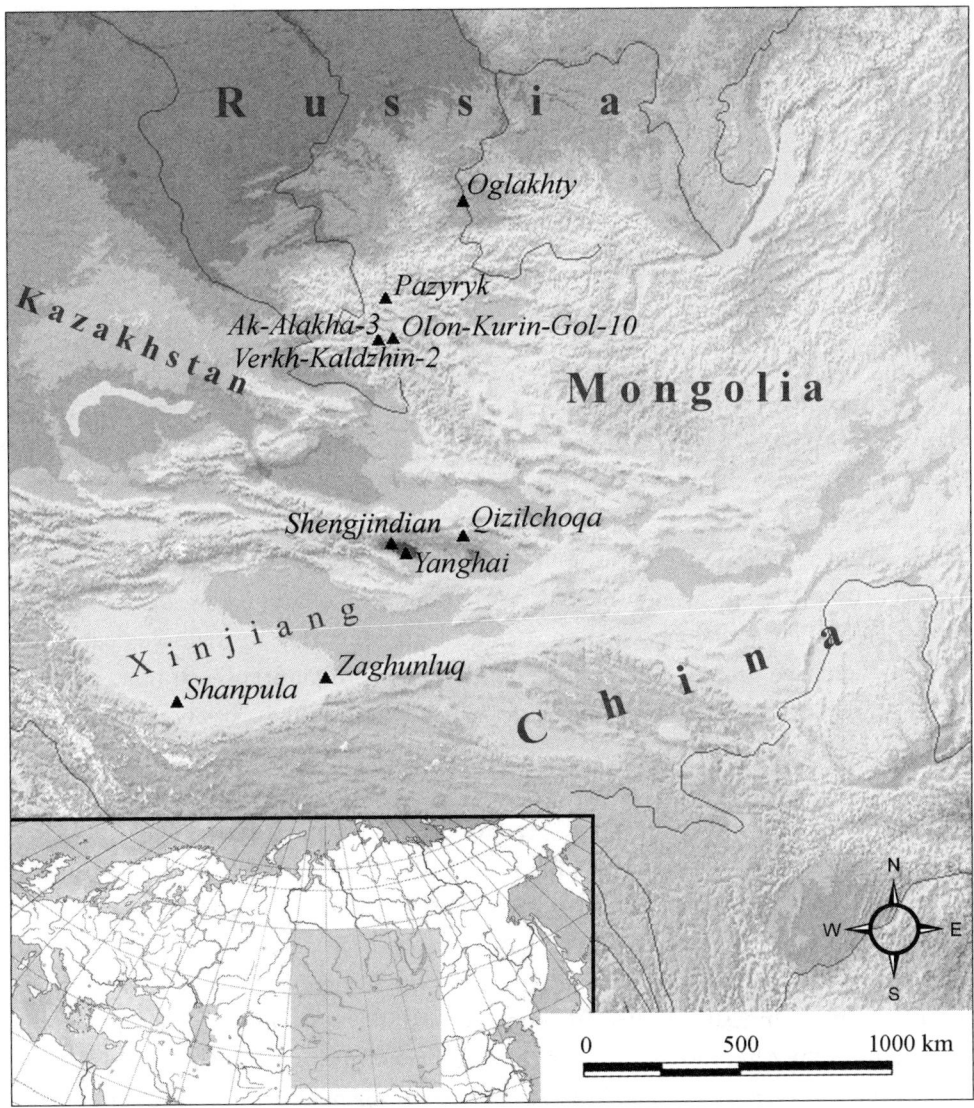

Map 5.1. Ancient tattoo findings in the Altai Mountains (Pazyryk, Ak-Alakha-3, Verkh-Kaldzhin-2, Olon-Kurin-Gol-10), Minisinsk region (Oglakhty), and the Tarim Basin (Yanghai, Shengjindian, Qizilchoqa, Zaghunluq, Shanpula). ▲ = archaeological sites with tattooed mummies.

steppe area encircled by the Sayan ridges at the north of the Altai-Sayan region on the Yenisei River. Little is known about the sociocultural milieu of the people who utilized the Oglakhty cemetery. However, archaeological studies have shown that this ancient population was associated with the early Tashtyk culture (100–400 CE) (Pankova et al. 2010; Vadetskaja 2009:65–75). Recent DNA studies have confirmed that they were Indo-European in origin (Keyser et al. 2009).

Of the eight tattooed Altai-Sayan mummies only three bear visible body markings. The tattoos of the others were, until recently, completely disguised by the darkened color of their skin and the clothing that concealed them. To reveal these ancient skin pictures it was necessary to employ a special photographic procedure that utilized reflected infrared light (Barkova and Pankova 2005). This work was conducted at The State Hermitage Museum in St. Petersburg, Russia.

Mummies of the Pazyryk Burial Mound: A Tattooed Chieftain and Other Marked Nobility

Peculiarities of the Pazyryk culture, including certain types of horse equipment, weaponry, and art objects, testify that the horse-riding population was one of the groups belonging to the so-called "Scythian World," a conventional title given to nomadic steppe peoples who lived across a vast area spanning Northern China to the Carpathian Mountains of Eastern Europe in the first millennium BCE. These tribes were similar in their way of living, economic structure, and social relationships, spoke ancient Iranian languages, and shared a sophisticated worldview rich in mythological traditions. These related peoples also handcrafted elaborate, unique art objects that comprise the so-called Scytho-Siberian animal style, which can usually be easily recognized in archaeological artifacts.

The ancient Greeks called the nomads they first met in Asia Minor and then in the Northern Black Sea region "Scythians" (Herodotus, Book IV; Latyshev 1947a:299, 303; 1947b:250–86; 293; 295–98; 300; 329). In Persian cuneiform sources, similar tribes living on the northeastern frontier of the Achaemenid (Persian) Empire were called "Saka" (Latyshev 1947a:277–79; Struve 1968:25, 30–31, 51–66). Chinese narratives of the time mentioned different horse-riding "barbarians" beyond the northern and western frontiers of the then Chinese states (Reed 2000); some of these groups might have been the inhabitants of the Altai Mountains, but any direct correlations are not available, to date.

The first discovery of ancient Altai-Sayan tattoos was made in 1947 by archaeologist Sergei Rudenko in the Pazyryk Valley, Russian Altai Mountains, approximately 1,600 m above sea level.[1] Rudenko uncovered the tomb of a high-level "chieftain," a man about fifty to sixty years of age with pronounced Central Asian features, who lived in the fourth century BCE. This burial, along with others uncovered several decades later, demonstrated a strikingly original culture that possessed affinities to other nomadic peoples of the Scythian world. The tombs of the Pazyryk people were encapsulated in deep subsurface pits situated beneath large stone burial mounds called kurgans (Rudenko 1970). Because of endemic climatic conditions and the unique construction features of the kurgans, many of these burial chambers were filled with ice over time, effectively preserving their contents from the elements. As a result, human remains and objects made of organic materials, which under normal conditions would have soon been destroyed with the passage of time, have survived to the present day (Rudenko 1953, 1970).

The burial mound that contained the Pazyryk chief, designated Kurgan 2, also contained the body of a woman. Both individuals were intentionally mummified and placed in a wooden coffin (Barkova and Gokhman 2001:80–83). Their skulls were trepanned, and their internal organs were removed and replaced with plant stalks and sedge. The incisions used to open the body were sewn together with horsehair and sinew. Finally, a resinous mixture of shellac, dammar, and wax was applied to the skin to preserve it. The burial chamber of the Pazyryk chieftain and his female counterpart was looted in antiquity and both mummies were undressed, beheaded, and their hands and feet were severed from their bodies.

Tattooed figures of fantastic animals covered the epidermis of the Pazyryk chieftain, including his arms and shoulders, large portions of his lower right leg, and parts of his breast and back. The woman buried in Kurgan 2 had no visible traces of tattoos. The chieftain's body was in a poor state of preservation and was eventually dissected by scientists. However, pieces of his skin, including those that contained tattoos, were conserved (plate 7). Tattoo drawings were later made and brought together in a graphic reconstruction of the chief's heavily tattooed body (Rudenko 1970:figs. 51–54).[2]

In 1949, excavations of Kurgan 5 at the Pazyryk burial ground revealed two more mummified bodies, which were eventually brought to The Hermitage State Museum. This male and female pair remained largely intact, although their clothing was found to have been removed in antiquity. Their desiccated skins are deeply folded, possess a very dark brown color, and show no visible evidence of tattooing.

Pazyryk Tattoos: One Hand-Prick at a Time?

The tattoos found at the Pazyryk barrows were considered unique and believed to be related to the high social status of the individuals buried there. However, a series of more recent excavations on the subalpine Ukok Plateau which borders China, Mongolia, and Kazakhstan have revealed more tattooed mummies from the Pazyryk culture.

In 1993, archaeologist Natalia Polosmak discovered a mummy of a woman (twenty-eight to thirty years old) with tattooed arms in Kurgan 1 at the Ak-Alakha-3 site (Polosmak 1994ab, 2000, 2001:228–37). In 1995, Vjacheslav Molodin excavated a burial in Kurgan 3 at the Verkh-Kaldzhin-2 site that contained a body of a young man (about twenty years old). His shoulder was covered with a fantastic figure combining the twisted body of an ungulate, the head of a bird of prey, and fantastic antlers (Polosmak 2000, 2001:228–37). The skin on his left forearm was not preserved, so it is unclear whether it contained tattoos. At first the bluish black tattoos seen on the Ukok mummies stood out clearly against their light skin, but shortly after being removed from the graves their skin became considerably darker and the tattoos "disappeared." Special techniques were then needed to restore the skin color to its original state (Kozeltsov and Romakov 2000:104). Tattooed mummies from the Ukok Plateau demonstrate that the custom of tattooing in Pazyryk society was not restricted to the high nobility: The young man was an "ordinary warrior," and the woman, buried in full honor but in isolation, may have possessed some special knowledge, being a storyteller, a traditional healer, or a soothsayer (Polosmak 2001:280).[3]

Additional ancient Altai tattoos were discovered in 2003–2004 during the course of a special examination of the mummies at The Hermitage Laboratory for Scientific and Technical Expert Evaluation. This study was initiated because of an unexpected tattoo sighting on a mummy from the non-Pazyryk cemetery at Oglakhty. More specifically, a male mummy from the Minusinsk region, Khakassia, unearthed from the Oglakhty cemetery, was being prepared for study along with other artifacts from this collection. Having disrobed the mummy of its fur clothes, conservators noticed vague blue drawings on the skin. Experts in forensic medicine called in to inspect the mummy suggested using infrared illumination to better reveal the tattoo designs.

The technique of infrared reflectology, in which light in the near-infrared spectrum is captured with special photographic equipment, has been used for decades by art historians and criminologists to detect drawings and inscriptions that have been erased or hidden under layers of dirt, darkened oil, and other pigmented substances. Infrared reflectology is particularly well-suited for detecting carbon-based pigments, such as those used in many ancient tattoos (Pabst et al. 2009, 2010). Carbon-based tattoo pigment invisible to the naked eye absorbs the near-infrared wavelengths, whereas clean skin reflects it intensely. As a result, the dark skin of mummies under infrared light appears quite bright, and the tattoos, if any are present, stand out very darkly. This technique has been used since the 1970s to identify tattoos on mummified human remains from across the globe.[4]

Thanks to photographs taken by means of a Kodak DCS 460 IR camera (infrared diapason ~1 micrometer), the once barely visible tattoos on the Oglakhty mummy became much clearer, as did others invisible to the naked eye (Kyzlasov and Pankova 2004:64). Shortly after the Oglakhty mummy was photographed, the same procedure was applied to the Pazyryk mummies, because it was our hypothesis that additional tattoos would also be found (Barkova and Pankova 2005:48–49). As mentioned previously, the epidermis of most Pazyryk mummies is stained a dark brown color and lines of tattoos are not always readily visible to the naked eye. The skin had probably become so dark because it had been exposed to air during the disturbance activities of ancient looters. The mummies were housed in a museum environment for more than fifty years, and during that time were photographed several times and subjected to X-ray examination. Although the mummies were regularly studied by experts from the biological control, no trace of tattoos had ever emerged. The new investigations using infrared photography revealed that tattoos were located on all four preserved mummies from the Pazyryk burial mounds stored at The Hermitage.

In our attempt to locate new tattoos, it was necessary to prepare the mummies for full body photography. Because the mummies are rigid, we could only take oblique angle

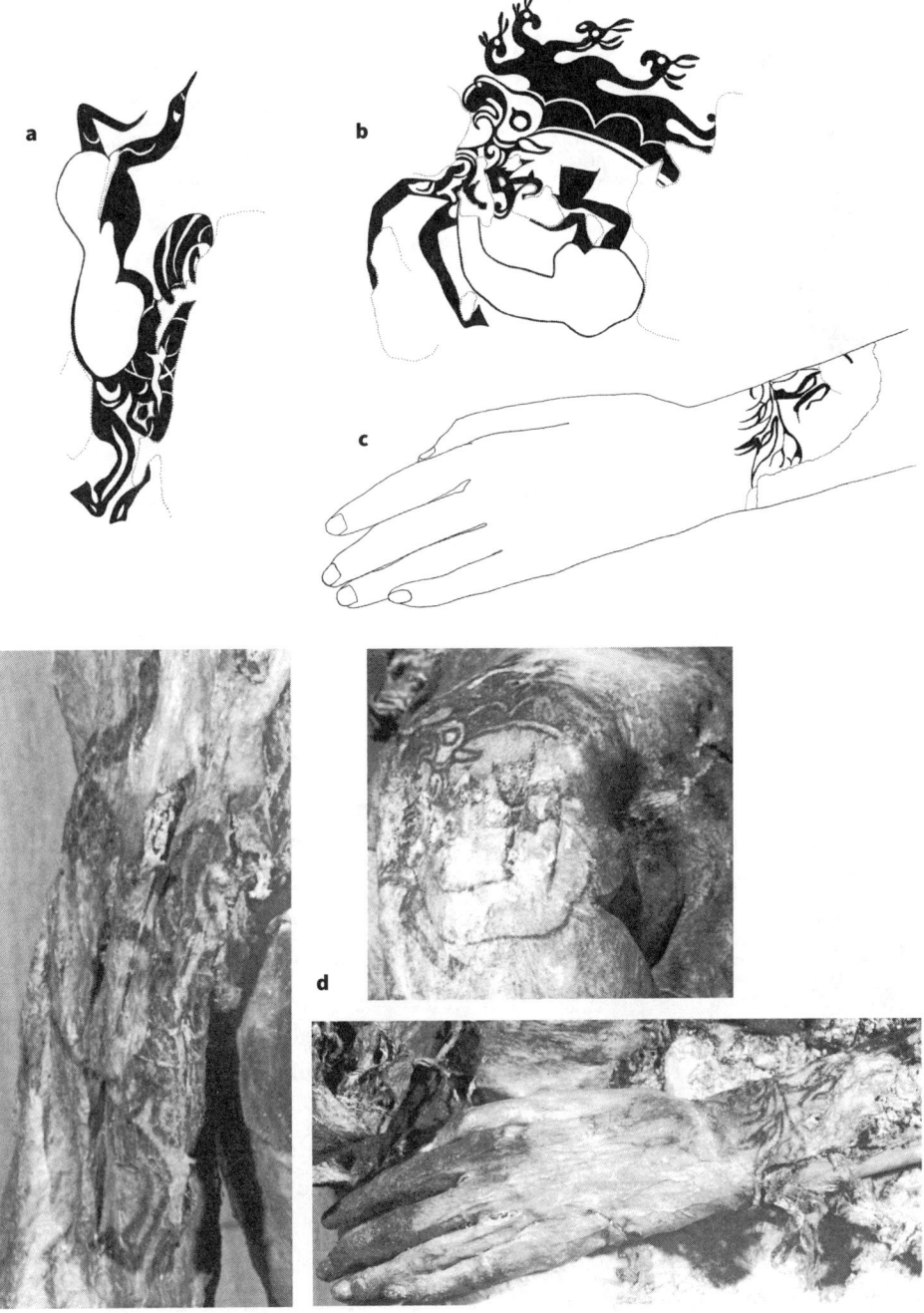

Fig. 5.1. Tattoos on a female body from Kurgan 2 at Pazyryk (fourth century BCE). Infrared photos and drawings: (a) hoofed griffin on the left shoulder; (b) argali, or mountain sheep, on the right upper arm; (c) partial depiction of a deer on the left wrist; (d) and infrared photographs of the same areas. Illustrations by Svetlana Pankova. The State Hermitage Museum, St. Petersburg (Inv. No. 1684/296). After Barkova and Pankova (2005).

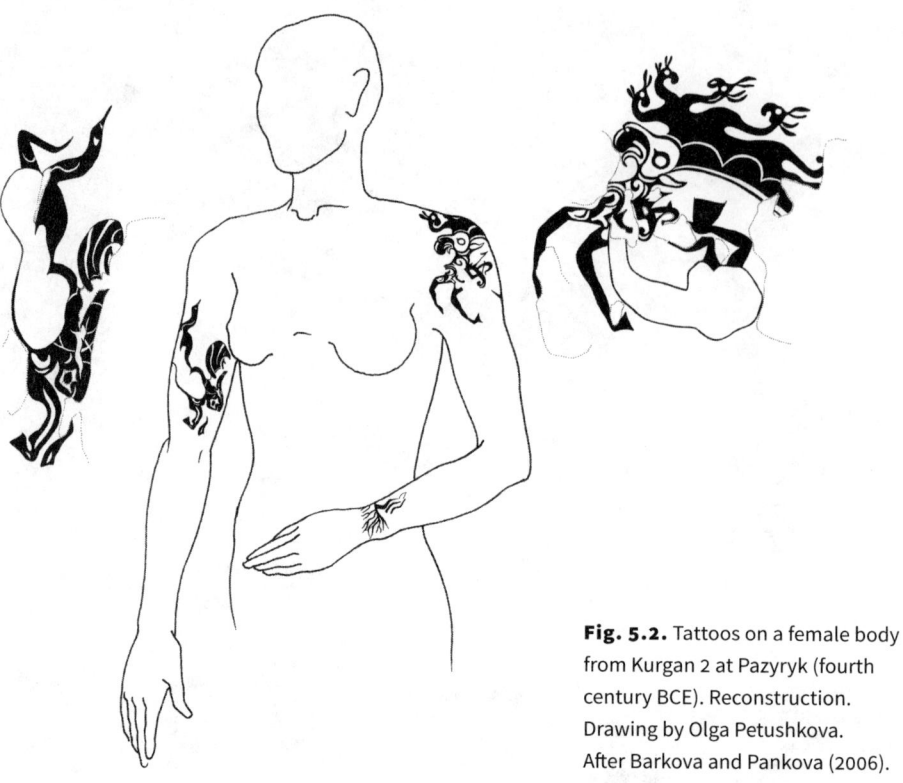

Fig. 5.2. Tattoos on a female body from Kurgan 2 at Pazyryk (fourth century BCE). Reconstruction. Drawing by Olga Petushkova. After Barkova and Pankova (2006).

pictures of the inner sides of the arms and legs. The mummies also possess multiple skin folds that warp their tattoos. Some cuts and seams made during the operation for the long-term conservation of the bodies disturbed the tattoos. These factors hampered the process of making drawings, which were only possible to implement from infrared photos.

The Pazyryk woman from Kurgan 2, whose body was placed in the coffin together with the chief, was in her early forties when she died.[5] Unlike her companion, Indo-European traits prevail in her appearance (Barkova and Gokhman 2001:82). Although her skin was badly preserved in comparison to her male counterpart, her tattoos survived and were easily recognizable under infrared examination because of their similarity to known examples (fig. 5.1). On the woman's left shoulder a fantastic animal is represented. Its body is that of an ungulate and its head resembles a bird of prey. The animal has large antlers, one of which has prongs shaped like the heads of birds. The animal's body is twisted and its entire figure is spherical in form. This same creature also appears on other mummies from Pazyryk and Ukok, and is conventionally called a "horse-griffin" or "hoofed griffin" (Shulga 2010:131–36). On the woman's right upper arm was tattooed an argali (*Ovis ammon*, mountain sheep) with a twisted rump. On the outer part of the left arm, slightly above the wrist, is a tattoo of a deer's antler with

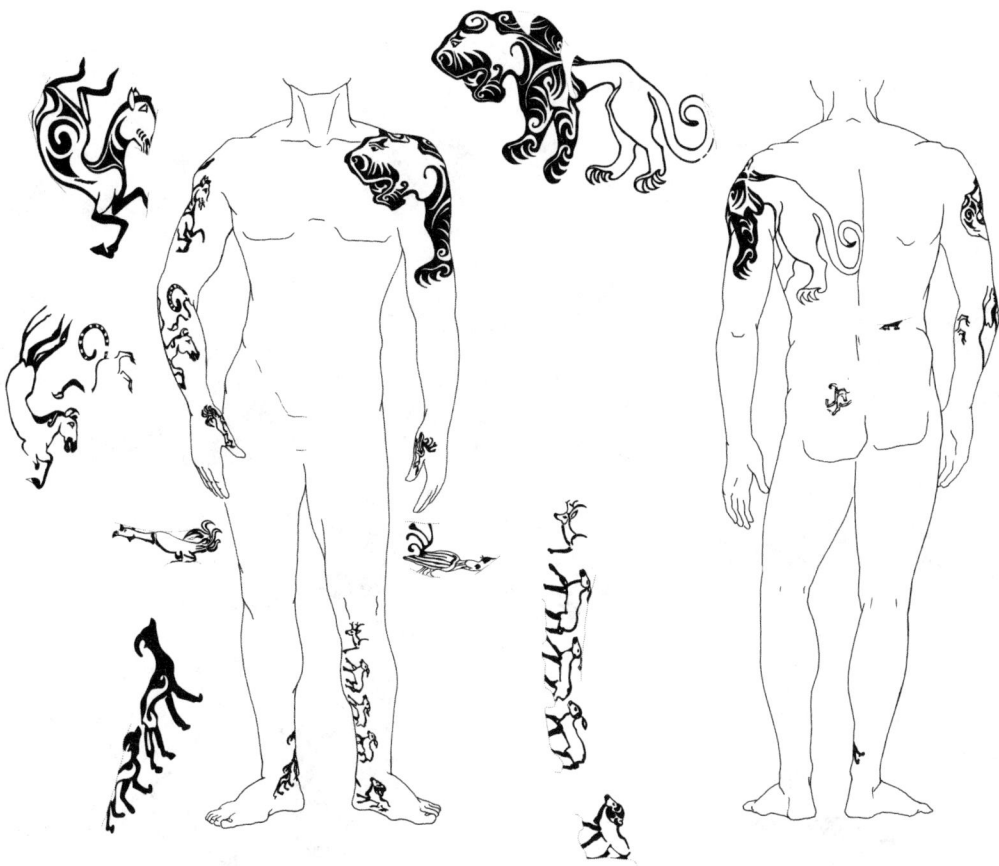

Fig. 5.3. Tattoos on the skin of a man entombed at Pazyryk, Kurgan 5 (fourth century BCE): feline predator (tiger?) on the left shoulder and back; horse on the right upper arm; equine and carnivore figures on right forearm; two zoomorphic figures on the mummy's back and buttock; two birds on each hand; and several ungulates (roe deer, ram, and two goats) mark legs. Reconstruction. Drawing by Olga Petushkova. After Barkova and Pankova (2006).

numerous prongs. It is difficult to say whether this was an independent representation or part of a larger deer figure. The forearm could have been also tattooed, but the skin was not preserved there. Tattoos are absent on both hands (fig. 5.2).

The mummies from Kurgan 5 at Pazyryk are considerably better preserved compared to those from Kurgan 2. They are almost complete and their skin is very dry and dark. The man found in Kurgan 5 died around the age of fifty-five whereas his female counterpart was aged fifty at death. Both were buried together in a large sarcophagus made from the trunk of a single cedar tree (Barkova and Gokhman 2001:85). The man's tattoos are situated on his shoulders, back, arms, and legs (fig. 5.3). Especially impressive is a figure of a feline predator (a tiger?) on the left shoulder, with the rear part of its body, paws, and tail stretching toward the spine (fig. 5.4).

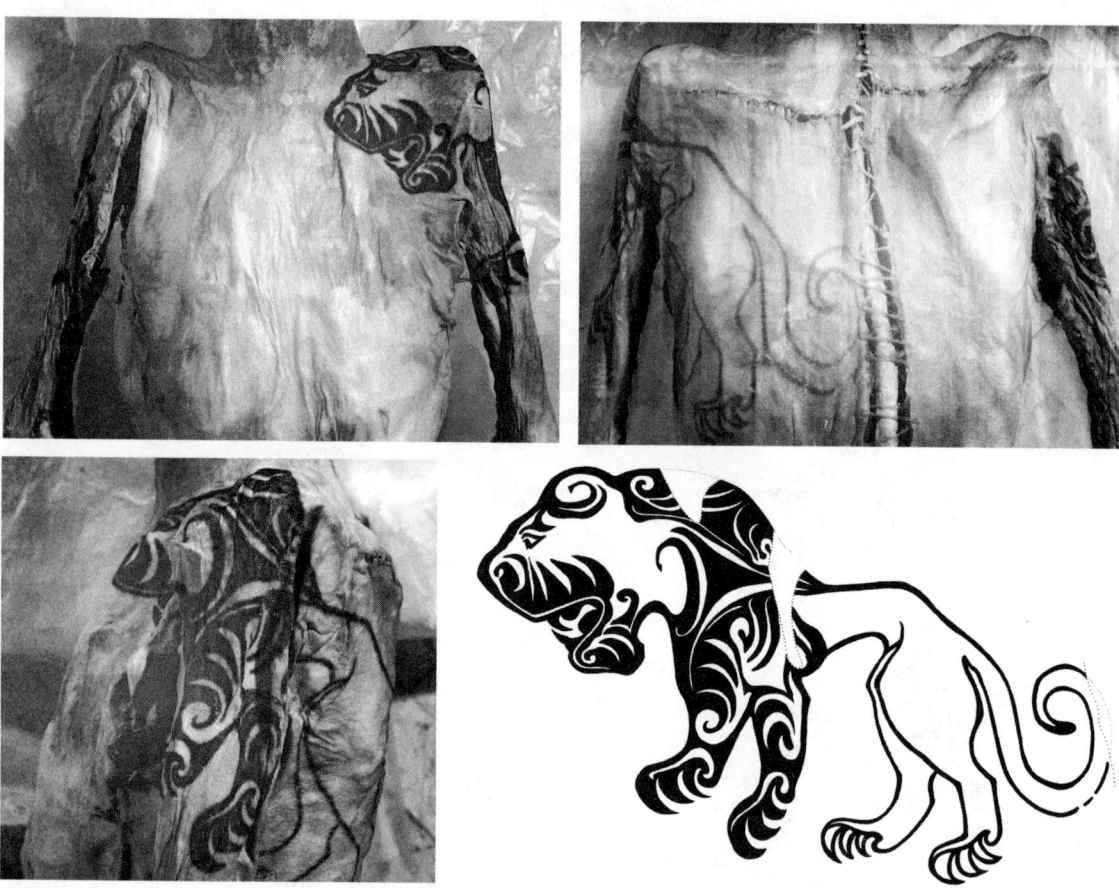

Fig. 5.4. Tattoo of a feline predator (tiger?) on the left shoulder and back of a man buried at Pazyryk, Kurgan 5 (fourth century BCE). Infrared photographs and drawing. Illustration by Svetlana Pankova. After Barkova and Pankova (2005).

A horse was tattooed on the right upper arm of the Kurgan 5 male, its rump twisted and its hind legs thrown upward (fig. 5.5). The right forearm bears a representation of two animals—a horse or koulan (*Equus heminonus*, Asiatic wild ass) and a carnivore with a striped tail twisted in a ring (fig. 5.6). The carnivore is disturbed by a skin seam, but the scene is recognizable thanks to its resemblance to a similar composition with the same animals on the male chieftain from Kurgan 2. Two unclear figures tattooed on the mummy's back and buttock are distorted by a skin fold and seam (fig. 5.7).

Both hands of this second chieftain are tattooed. On the bases of both thumbs there are figures of different walking birds, facing toward the nail. The bird on the right hand is most likely a heath cock or a wood grouse, while the other bird is difficult to determine (fig. 5.8). Both legs are tattooed with figures of ungulate animals: roe deer, a ram, and two goats walking up the leg (figs. 5.9 and 5.10).

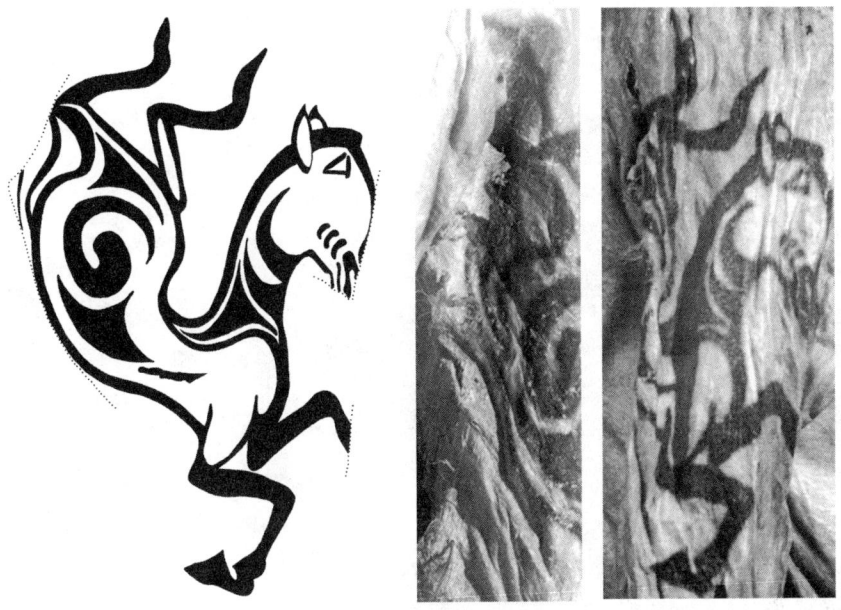

Fig. 5.5. Horse tattoo on the right upper arm of the entombed man at Pazyryk, Kurgan 5 (fourth century BCE). Infrared photographs and drawing. Illustration by Svetlana Pankova. After Barkova and Pankova (2005).

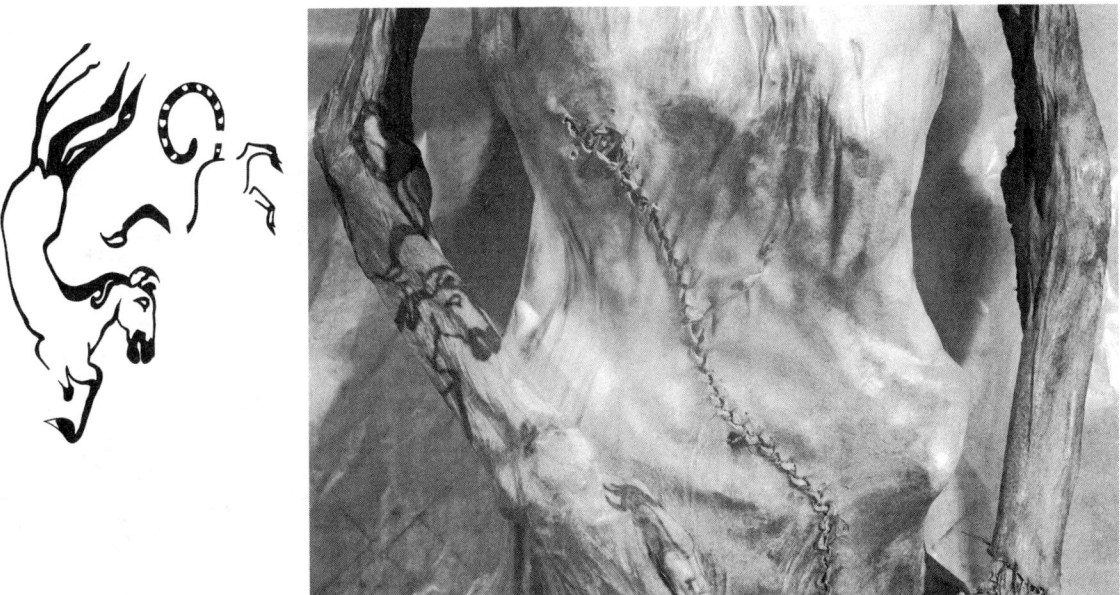

Fig. 5.6. Galloping equid and partial feline tattoo on the right arm of the man buried at Pazyryk, Kurgan 5 (fourth century BCE). Infrared photograph and drawing. Illustrations by Elena Stepanova. After Barkova and Pankova (2005).

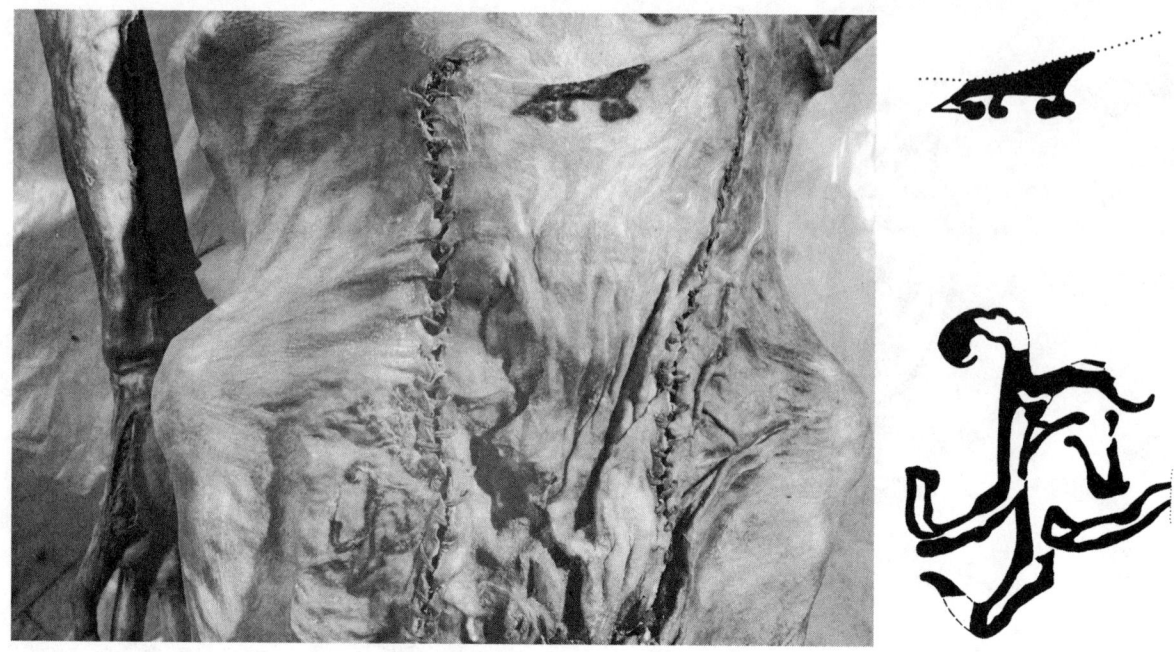

Fig. 5.7. Zoomorphic tattoos on the back and buttock of the man buried at Pazyryk, Kurgan 5 (fourth century BCE). Infrared photograph and drawings. Illustrations by Svetlana Pankova. After Barkova and Pankova (2005).

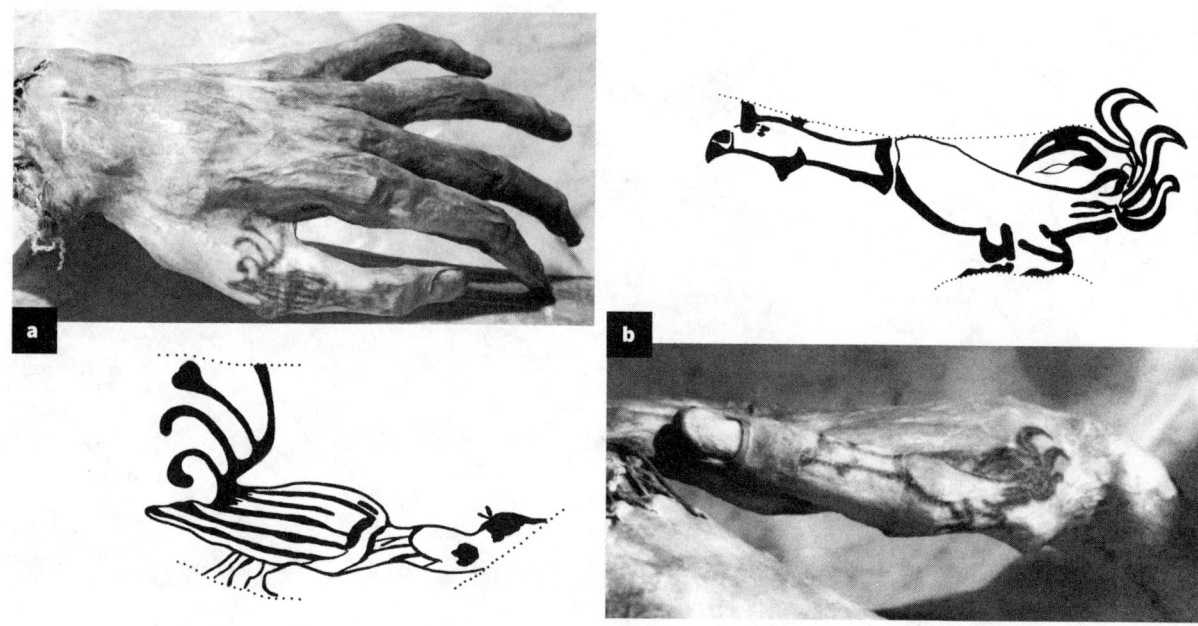

Fig. 5.8. Bird tattoos on the (a) left and (b) right hands of a nobleman buried at Pazyryk, Kurgan 5 (fourth century BCE). Infrared photographs and drawings. Illustrations by Svetlana Pankova. After Barkova and Pankova (2005).

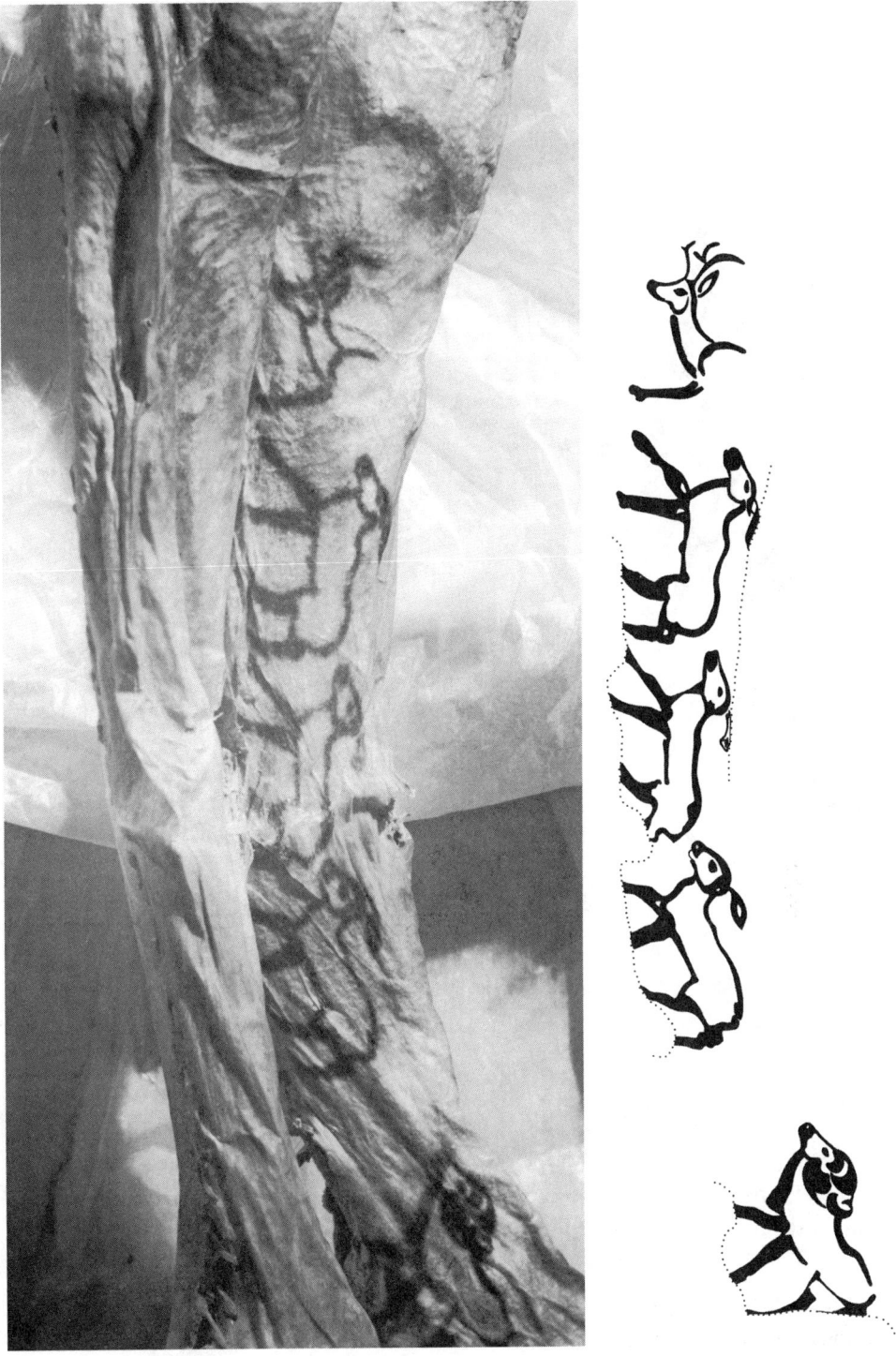

Fig. 5.9. Ungulate tattoos on the left leg of a nobleman buried at Pazyryk, Kurgan 5 (fourth century BCE). Infrared photograph and drawing. Illustrations by Svetlana Pankova. After Barkova and Pankova (2005).

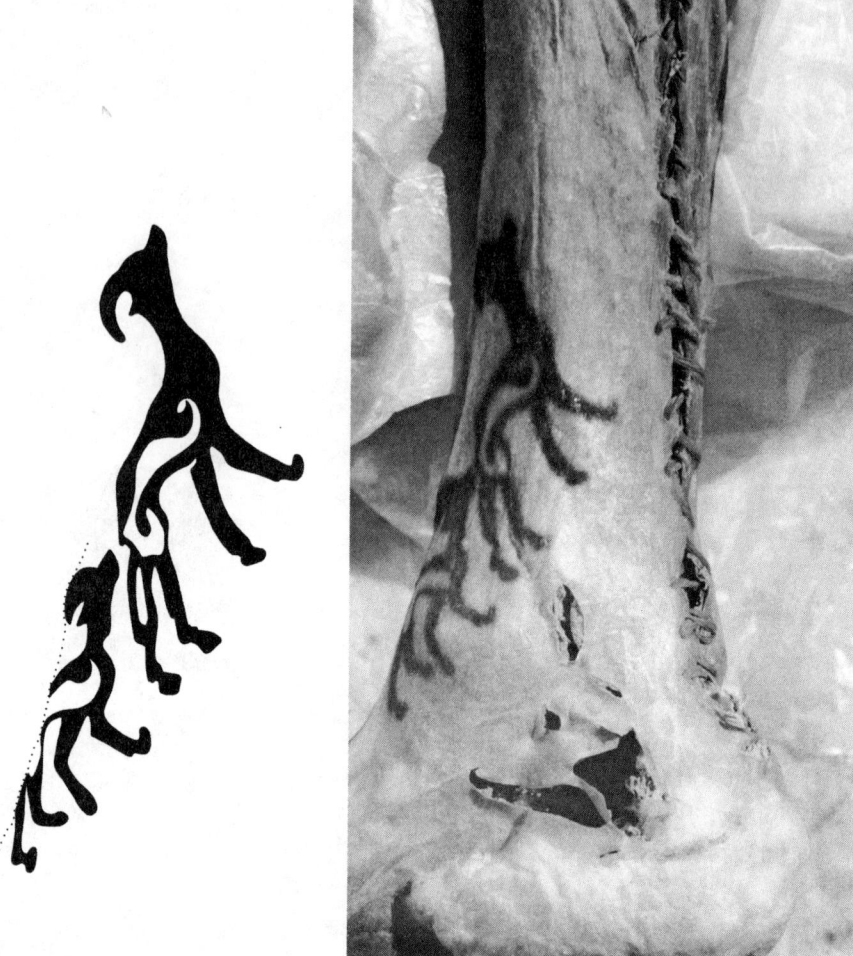

Fig. 5.10. Ungulate tattoos on the right ankle of a nobleman buried at Pazyryk, Kurgan 5 (fourth century BCE). Infrared photograph and a drawing. Illustration by Svetlana Pankova. After Barkova and Pankova (2005).

Tattoos on the female mummy differ from other Pazyryk body marking in terms of their arrangement, in that the shoulders are not tattooed and the forearms are covered by compositions that encircle the extremities (figs. 5.11 and 5.12). The left arm presents a scene in which a large bird of prey claws the neck of a deer or an elk. The tip of the bird's tail or wing is shaped like a bird's head (fig. 5.13). On the woman's right forearm is a complex composition consisting of several figures, including two tigers and a leopard attacking a deer and an elk (fig. 5.14). All elements of the composition are balanced and subjected to the artist's design, suggesting that the tattooing was done according to a draft illustration, stencil, or a predetermined general layout.

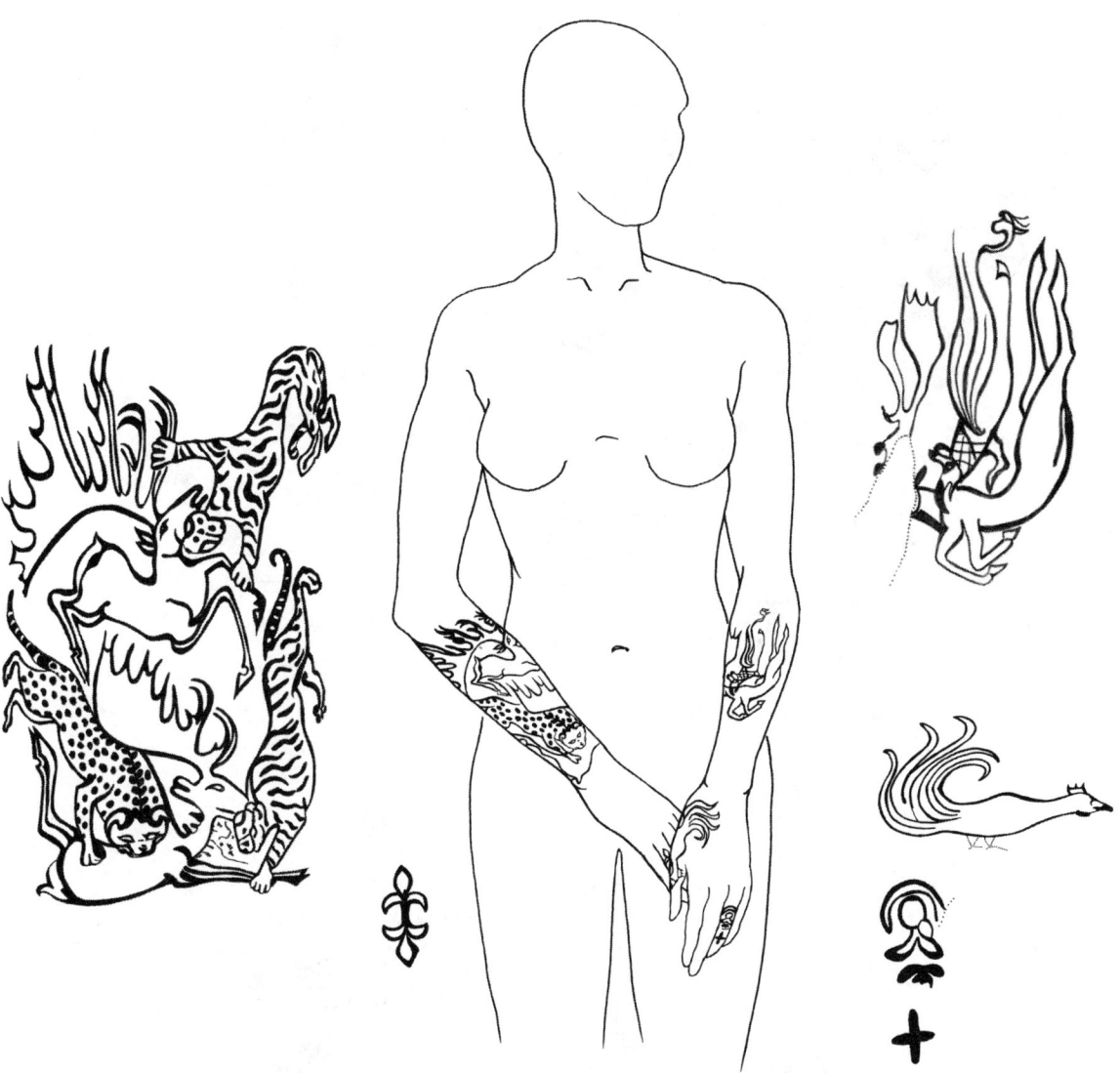

Fig. 5.11. Tattoos on a noblewoman buried at Pazyryk, Kurgan 5 (fourth century BCE): a raptor grasping its prey (left arm); two tigers and a leopard attacking a deer and elk (right forearm); rooster-like tattoo (left thumb); and floraform designs (ring fingers). Reconstruction. Drawing by Olga Petushkova. After Barkova and Pankova (2006).

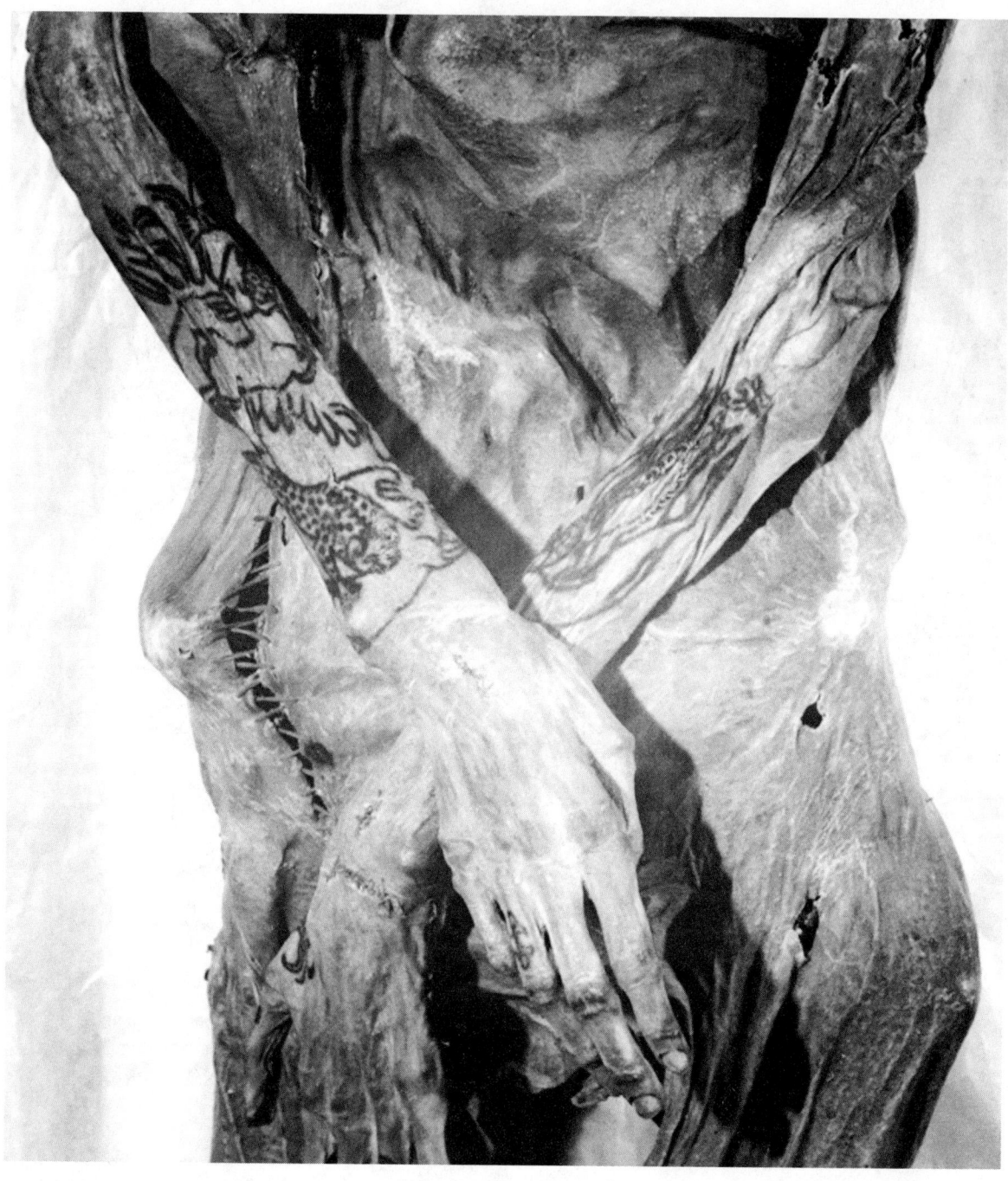

Fig. 5.12. Zoomorphic tattoos on the woman's body, Pazyryk, Kurgan 5 (fourth century BCE). Infrared photograph. The State Hermitage Museum, St. Petersburg (Inv. No. 1687/90). After Barkova and Pankova (2005).

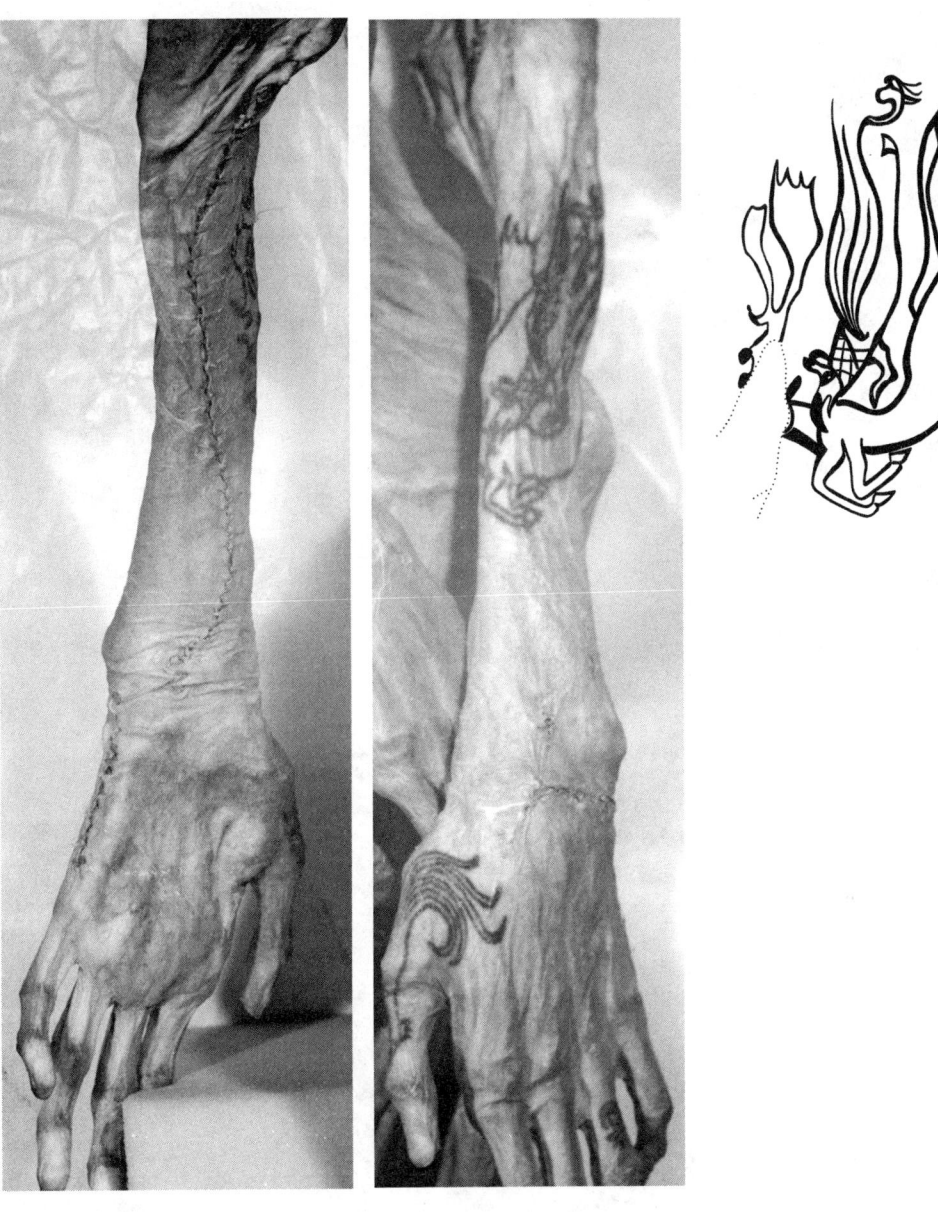

Fig. 5.13. Tattoos of a raptor and its prey on the left arm of the noblewoman buried at Pazyryk, Kurgan 5 (fourth century BCE). Infrared photographs and a drawing. Illustration by Svetlana Pankova. After Barkova and Pankova (2005).

Some tattooed figures are present on the woman's hands. The left thumb carries a representation of a bird, most likely a rooster. On the ring fingers some botanical elements resembling opposing trefoils were depicted, which to date are the only known examples of this tattoo motif among the ancient Pazyryk (fig. 5.15).

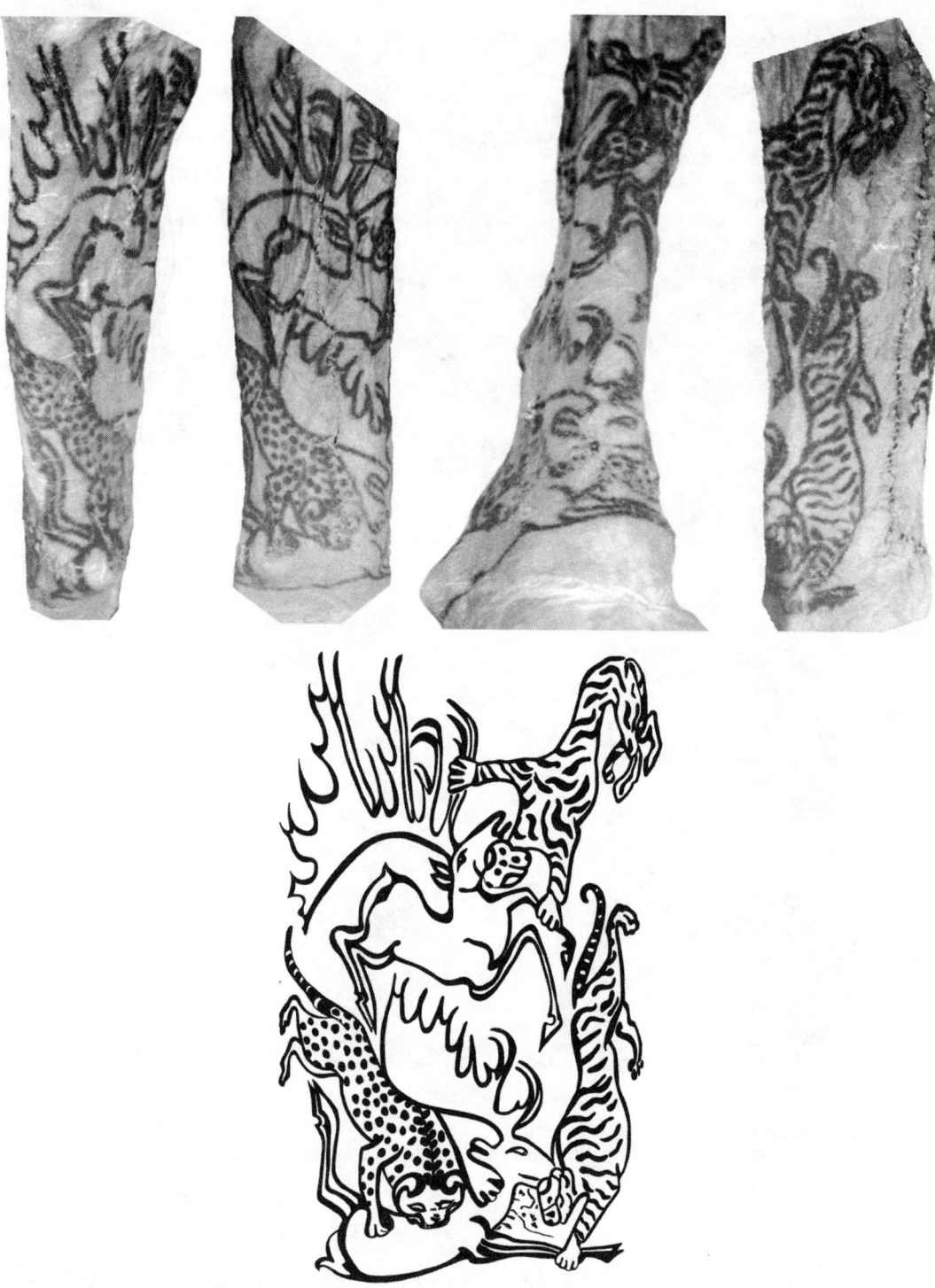

Fig. 5.14. Tattooed composition of three feline carnivores devouring their prey on the right arm of the noblewoman buried at Pazyryk, Kurgan 5. Infrared photographs and drawing. Illustration by Svetlana Pankova. After Barkova and Pankova (2005).

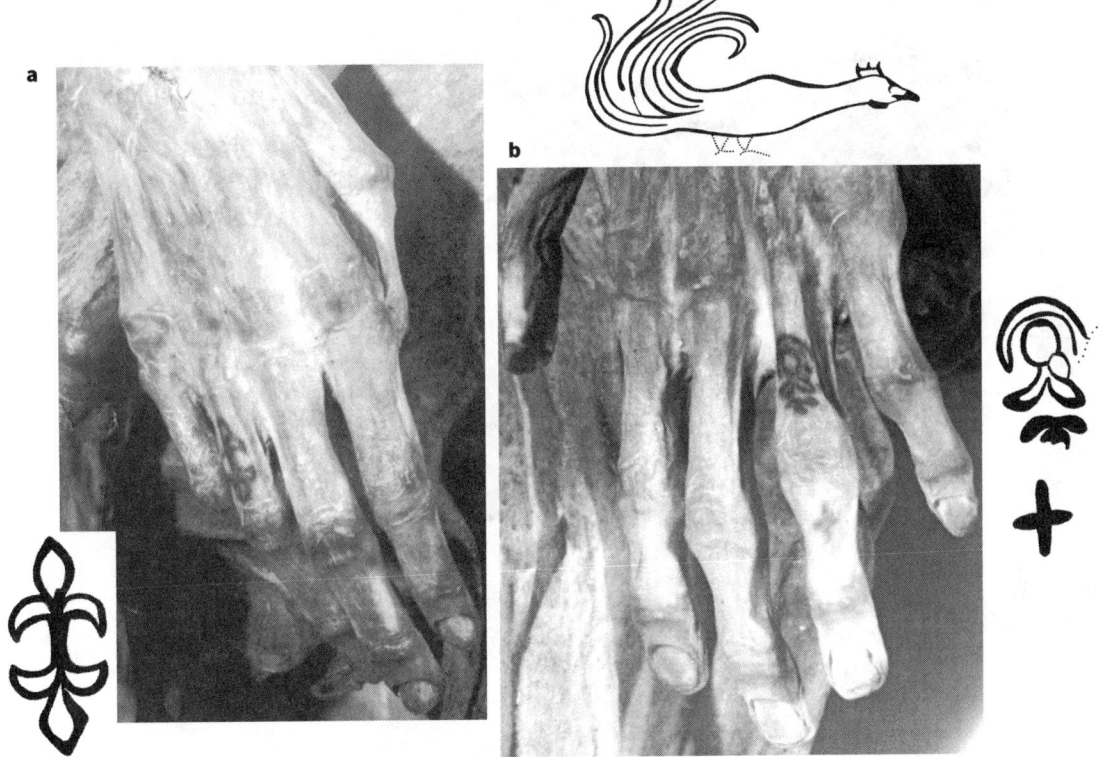

Fig. 5.15. Avian hand tattoo and floraform marks on the (a) right and (b) left fingers of the noblewoman buried at Pazyryk, Kurgan 5 (fourth century BCE). Infrared photographs and drawings. Illustration by Svetlana Pankova. After Barkova and Pankova (2005).

Infrared examinations performed on skin fragments belonging to the Pazyryk chief from Kurgan 2 also revealed two previously unknown tattoos. The first of these appeared on his right thumb, and consists of a representation of a bird with a bushy tail, apparently a rooster (fig. 5.16). The second tattoo appeared on the left foot, beneath the knee. The chieftain's left foot "had been severely hacked by the robbers, and the undamaged parts of the tattooing were insufficient to make sense of the figures" (Rudenko 1970:112, fig. 51). Indeed, this skin piece was torn and crumpled, preventing it from better revealing the scarcely visible tattoo located on the outer part of the foot. In 2013, the skin fragment was restored in The Hermitage conservation workshop and again investigated through infrared photography. As a result, a figure of a fantastic animal measuring 18 by 8 cm came to light (figs. 5.17 and 5.18) (Barkova 2014). The depicted creature is another "hoofed griffin," the sixth figure of its kind on this person's skin. Notwithstanding, this tattooed figure is the first known depiction of a hoofed griffin located on the foot. Previously, creatures of this kind were only known to be depicted on the shoulders and upper arms.

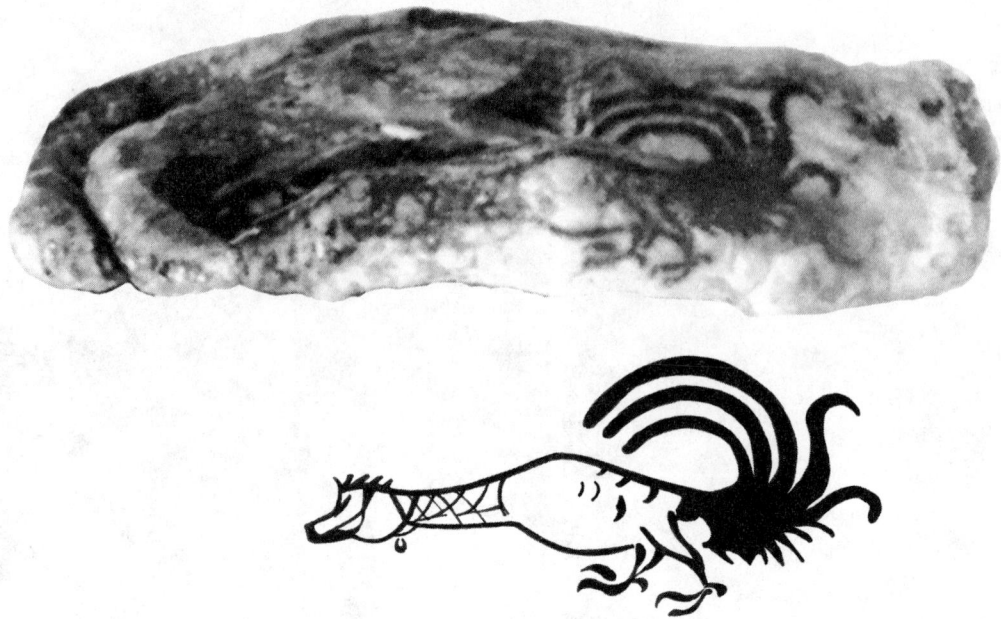

Fig. 5.16. Representation of a bird on the right hand of a man, cut off by ancient looters. From Pazyryk, Kurgan 2 (fourth century BCE). Infrared photograph and drawing. Illustration by Darja Kirilova. The State Hermitage Museum, St. Petersburg (Inv. No. 1684/309). After Barkova and Pankova (2005).

Other skin pieces from the Pazyryk chieftain excavated by Rudenko have not yet been subjected to infrared photography. The drawings of the chief published by Rudenko look quite exact, but it cannot be ruled out that future examinations may reveal new details. None of the Pazyryk mummies display tattoos on their faces, although the face of the woman from Kurgan 5 was partly destroyed and the faces of the Ukok mummies did not survive (Polosmak 2001:233).

There is little information available regarding the techniques and toolkits used by the ancient Pazyryk tattooists. No associated artifacts that could be identified as tattooing implements have been found in the tombs of the Pazyryk population. All the same, it is most likely that tattoos were made by pricking with hand-held needles (see Yablonsky, chapter 15, for Sarmatian tattooing tools).[6] During his preparation of the mummy Rudenko noted considerable depth of the coloring substance in the skin, which made him believe the tattooing was made by pricking. He also postulated that the chieftain had been tattooed long before his death, possibly in his youth, writing: "We are dealing with a stout man with strongly developed subcutaneous fat tissue. The ordinary fat layer, directly under the skin, was not colored, although the muscles under them in the area directly below the tattooing were intensely blackened. At the time he was being tattooed, the chief, if not exactly thin, was not as stout as he became before his death" (Rudenko 1970:112).

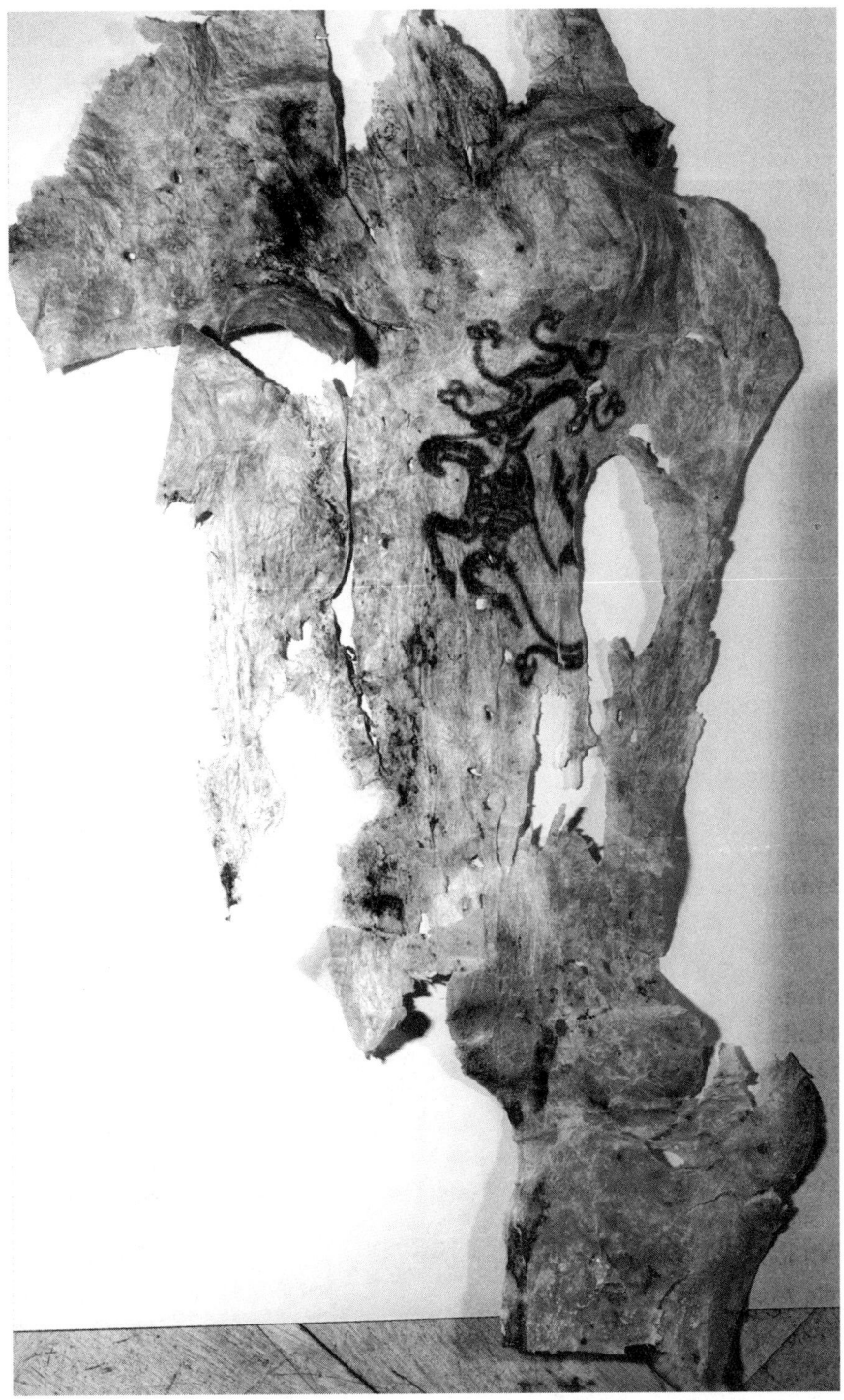

Fig. 5.17. Tattooed figure of a hoofed griffin on the left foot of the chief buried in Kurgan 2, Pazyryk (fourth century BCE). Infrared photograph. The State Hermitage Museum, St. Petersburg (Inv. No. 1684/306). After Svetlana Pankova (2013).

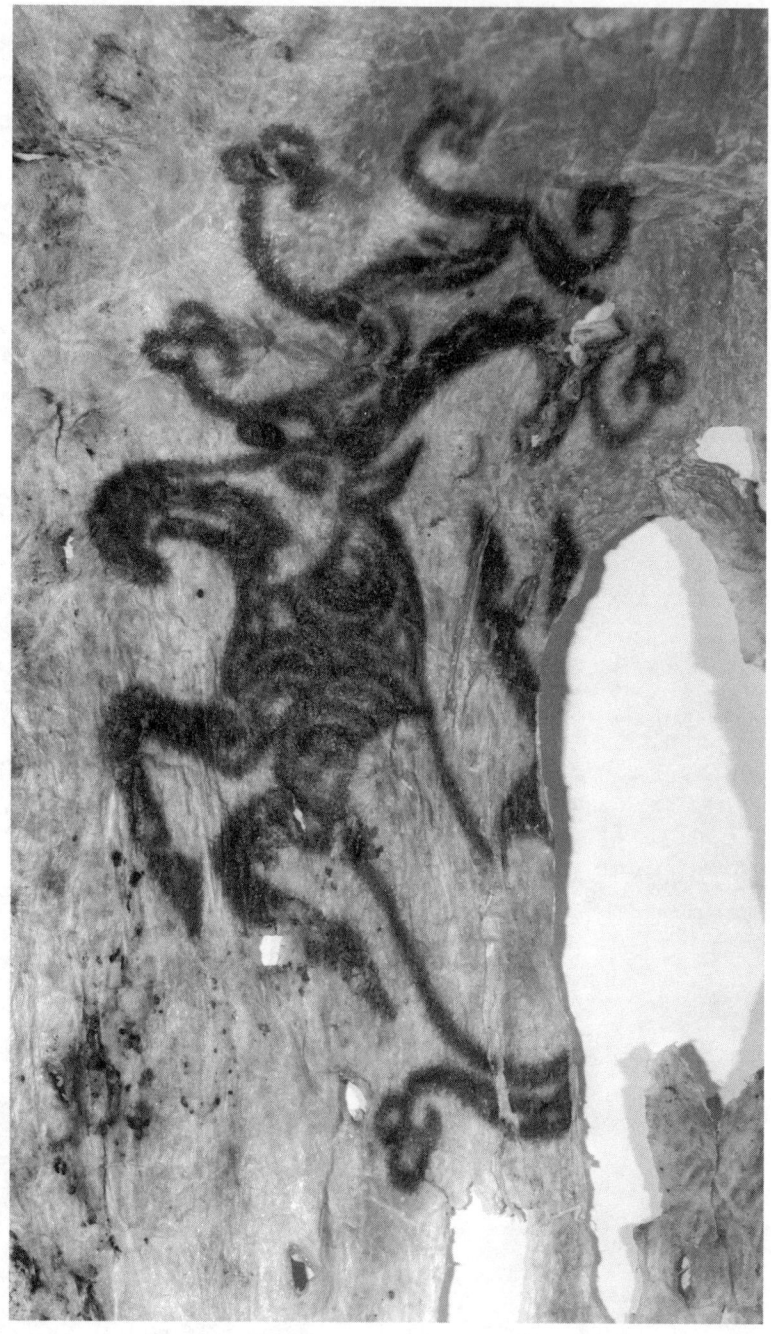

Fig. 5.18. Close-up view of the Pazyryk chief's hoofed griffin tattoo, the sixth found on his body, from Pazyryk, Kurgan 2 (fourth century BCE). Infrared photograph. The State Hermitage Museum, St. Petersburg (Inv. No. 1684/306). After Svetlana Pankova (2013).

A sample of tattooed skin from the Pazyryk Ak-Alakha-3 site was studied by X-ray-spectral microprobe analysis, and resulted in identification of dot areas about 20 micrometers in diameter that contained large amounts of potassium. The presence of potassium suggests that the pigment composition used for tattooing was carbonized vegetable matter or soot (Malakhov et al. 2000:169; Polosmak 2001:231). Relatedly, microchemical and microscopic tests of the tattooed Oglakhty mummy showed that the tattoo pigment also contained soot (Kyzlasov and Pankova 2004:64).

Pazyryk Tattoos and Their Meaning

Most of the images of Pazyryk tattooing represent dynamic animals and creatures of a fantastic appearance. They are depicted in fighting scenes and in processions, but also as single figures. The latter are usually shown in a so-called sacrifice or defeated pose — lying on their backs with hind legs turned up so that the body looks twisted—a position that reflects the result of some confrontation. Pazyryk tattoos demonstrate generally the same characters and iconography as motifs placed on felt, leather, wood, and horn objects, including horse equipment and masks, garments and headdresses, leather, pottery vessels, and coffins preserved in the tombs of the ancient Altai population. Taken together, Pazyryk iconography certainly constitutes a unique artistic oeuvre, although space constraints restrict me from evaluating the possible relationships between tattooed images and similar designs appearing on funerary objects. Notwithstanding, there are tattooed roosters, waterfowl, and blackcocks, horses, rams, deer, and feline predators among the realistically depicted animals. Other creatures look fantastical as they combine features of different animals. These include figures of the so-called hoofed griffins, displaying the body, legs, and hooves of an ungulate along with the head of a predatory bird, antlers with prongs ending in bird heads, and the long tail of a feline. These zoomorphic depictions should not be considered as mere decorations, since their omnipresence on Pazyryk material culture is more likely related to Indigenous mythological and world view ideas, personified in a developed system of intelligible meaningful signs (e.g., Argent 2013; Cheremisin 2008; Hančar 1952). In fighting scenes, predominant among Pazyryk images as well as in other Scythian animal style depictions, the crucial ideas of life, death, and revival through sacrifice were repeatedly embodied (Korolkova 2006:129–34).

The seven mummified human remains preserved in the Pazyryk culture tombs were tattooed. Of three male and three female mummies, four originate from high-level tombs at the Pazyryk type site, and two from less complex burials on the Ukok Plateau, some 200 km distant. One more tattoo representing a fragment of an unclear figure was found on a piece of skin preserved at the Olon-Kuril-Gol-10 site, Kurgan 1, in Mongolia (Molodin et al. 2012: figs. 105–6).

All known Pazyryk tattoos represent a complex that spans a relatively short time period: approximately fifty years, according to dendrochronological and radiocarbon examination of the burial chamber logs. Kurgan 2 at Pazyryk was the earliest, dating to approximately 300 BCE, and Kurgan 5 was constructed about 250 BCE (Alekseev et al. 2005:165–69). The two tombs on the Ukok Plateau were constructed almost simultaneously, about 277 BCE (Sljusarenko 2011:table 2). All of the tattoos found on the mummies exhibit a very similar style, and it has been suggested that some of them could have been made by the same tattooist (Polosmak 2000:100). Of course, this idea can hardly be confirmed, but regarding the short time span between the burials, the question of the artist's hand is quite reasonable.

There is not space in this chapter to compare Pazyryk tattoos on different bodies in detail (see Iwe 2013), but because of the small sample size it is not clear whether the results of such a comparison would reveal new insights or simply raise more questions concerning the possible function(s) of Pazyryk tattoo culture. It is obvious, however, that the tattooing of the young man from the Verkh-Kaldzhin-2 site is much simpler compared to other indelibly marked Pazyryk males. He was the youngest among all of the tattooed Pazyryks, so perhaps it was simply too early in his life to have earned the right to more complex tattooing. As for the differences between female and male tattoos, the only obvious fact is that women had no tattoos on their legs.

Indeed, four mummies feature representations of the fantastic animal figure, the so-called hoofed griffin, placed repeatedly on the shoulders (Kurgan 2 male from Pazyryk site, Kurgan 2 female from Pazyryk site, the female from Ak-Alakha-3 site, and the male from Verkh-Kaldzhin-2 site). Because of its frequent appearance on the skin and its size, the hoofed griffin might be regarded as one of the principal images of Pazyryk tattoo culture. However, this image is missing on the tattooed bodies from Kurgan 5 at the Pazyryk burial ground. On the female body the shoulders are entirely clean, and on the man's shoulder appears a feline predator—likely a tiger. The more recent date of the mummies from Kurgan 5 as compared to the other examples may suggest that importance of the hoofed griffin was replaced by a tiger.

It is at this point mere speculation to suggest that an iconographic shift or a particular life event led to the new tattoo figure on the high status male from Kurgan 5. However, it is generally understood that ancient tattoos were a conservative phenomenon, strictly regulated in traditional societies. This idea is based on ethnographic studies of tattoos whereupon design forms typically remain unchanged for hundreds if not thousands of years (Krutak 2014a; Rudenko 1949:152–53; Schuster and Carpenter 1996). Traditional culture and art are also appreciated as conservative. Indeed, the commitment to ancestral traditions is one of the main differences between Indigenous art works and contemporary art, including the art of tattooing. For example, the frozen mummies of Qilakitsoq, Greenland, dating to the fifteenth century CE, display tattoos that are analogous to those seen on objects of prehistoric Paleo-Eskimo material culture predating the Common Era (Kapel at al. 1991:108–9; see Krutak, chapter 18, this volume).

Furthermore, tattooed persons entombed in Pazyryk kurgans belonged to the nomadic elite. Most likely they were not tattooed with individualistic designs but with those belonging to ruling clans, families, or mythological power and/or totem animals. Thus, observable differences in their tattoos might indeed reflect some important changes in Pazyryk society, including the emergence of a new ruling group or forms of worship. Of course, this idea should be verified on a much wider scale through material culture studies rather than just through tattooing itself. It is worth noting here that apart from Pazyryk tattoos, hoofed griffin images are also found depicted on metal objects from approximately simultaneous burials at the sites of Ordos and Xinjiang in Northern China, as well as on chance finds from Mongolia and the Transbaikal region.[7] Studies of these objects might lead us to a better understanding of Pazyryk tattoo iconography.

Pazyryk tattoos may be considered as a kind of visual language in this nonliterate culture, because they seemingly communicated crucial information to members of local society while also permanently marking the populace's affiliation to it (Polosmak 2001:237). Tattoos are in line with the visible character of the culture, in that they are highly decorative and full of animals and other important imagery. One of the main peculiarities of the Pazyryk skin pictures is that they are almost entirely figurative in nature, with few geometric or abstract signs that prevail in many other ancient tattooing cultures. However, a set of purposefully placed dots tattooed along the spine of the Pazyryk chief from Kurgan 2 and his right ankle was likely related to some therapeutic function (Krutak 1999, 2013b; Rudenko 1970:112).

Tattoos of the Oglakhty Mummy

Unlike the Pazyryk tattoo series, which is relatively well known archaeologically, the tattooing found on a mummy recovered from the Oglakhty cemetery of the early Tashtyk culture is so far unique. Dating to the third through fourth centuries CE, the mummy, as mentioned previously, is almost entirely preserved, and infrared photography revealed the presence of tattoos (Kyzlasov and Pankova 2004; Pankova 2013). The cultural practice of tattooing among the early Tashtyk people had long been assumed by researchers, since burial masks found in tombs decorated with painted designs had been reported for decades (Teploukhov 1929:51). Covering the skulls with clay and adorning the faces of the dead with gypsum masks painted with red, blue, and black ornaments was a peculiar feature of the burial rites practiced by local people from the turn of the Common Era through the sixth and seventh centuries CE (Aufderheide 2009; Vadetskaya 2007, 2009).

In 1969, Leonid Kyzlasov of Moscow State University unearthed a well-preserved male mummy in Tomb 4 at the Oglakhty cemetery. The tomb contained many intact organic objects resulting from the dry microclimate existing in the hermetically sealed wooden burial chamber. Entombed within its walls were the remains of five individuals

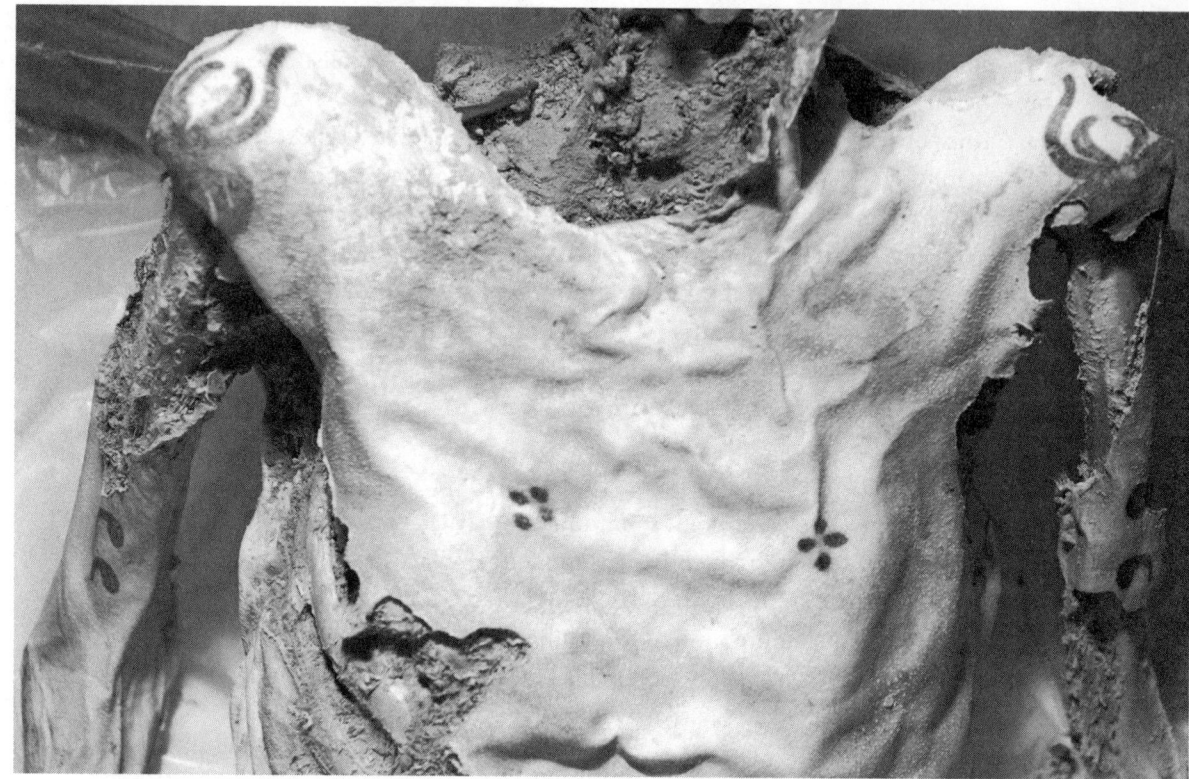

Fig. 5.19. Tattoos of the man from the Oglakhty cemetery, grave 4, front view (third through fourth centuries CE). Infrared photograph. The State Hermitage Museum, St. Petersburg (Inv. No. 2864/71). After Svetlana Pankova (2013).

buried according to different rites. Two of the deceased were dry mummies of a man and a woman. Their skulls were trepanned and their faces were covered with gypsum masks. A third body consisted of the skeleton of a child. Beside them were found two human-size clothed puppets made of leather and filled with grass. Burnt human bones were laid inside their breasts. Among the buried persons' garments were fur coats, trousers, headgear, gloves, a breast cover, and a woolen skirt as well as leather boots. The grave goods also included wooden and ceramic tableware, models of horse bridles, and weapons (Arbore Popescu et al. 2001:81–89, cat. 335–42; Kyzlassow 1971; Piotrovsky et al. 1978:94–96).

The female mummy interred in Tomb 4 was poorly preserved and her skin did not survive. The male mummy was much better preserved and remained clothed until recently. When the man's garments were removed, faded blue figures appeared on his dry wrinkled skin. Although this mummy's skin appeared lighter than that of the Pazyryk mummies, several of its tattoos remained invisible to the naked eye (Pankova

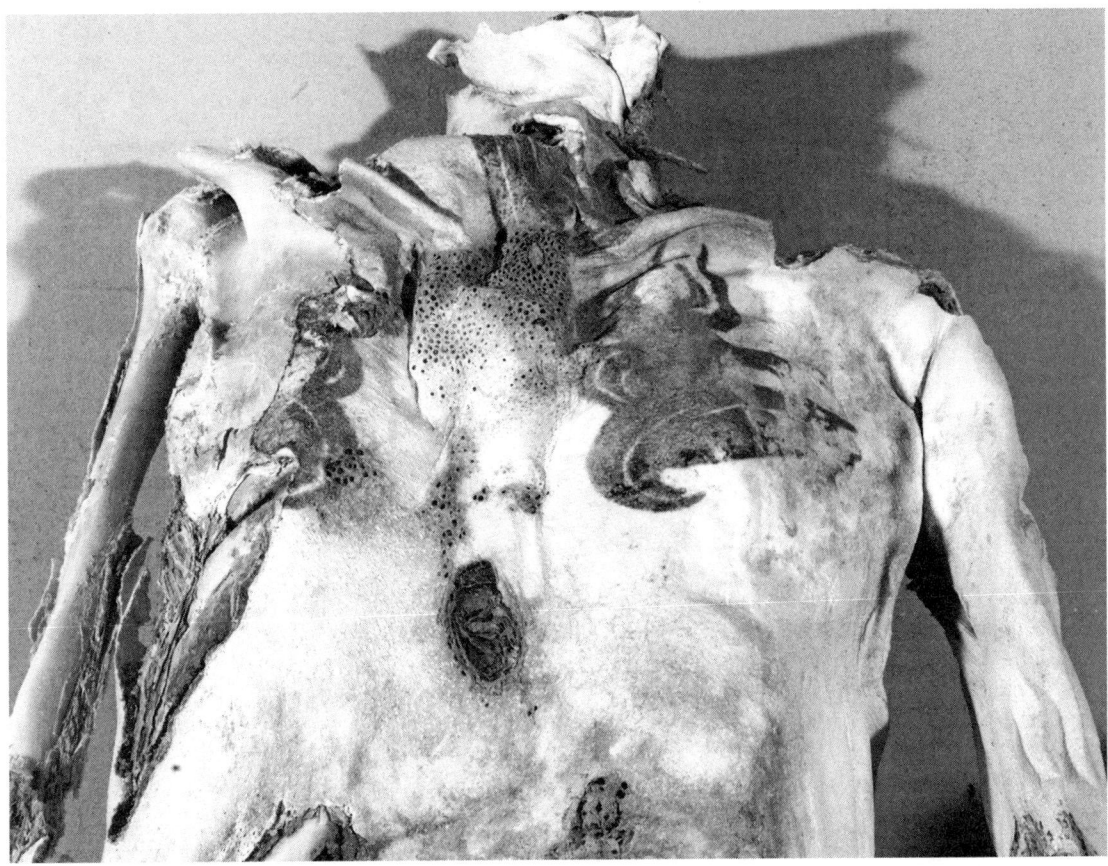

Fig. 5.20. Back tattoos of the male mummy from the Oglakhty cemetery, grave 4 (third through fourth centuries CE). Infrared photograph. The State Hermitage Museum, St. Petersburg (Inv. No. 2864/71). After Svetlana Pankova (2013).

2013: figs. 3–5). Every surface of the mummy's preserved skin was examined at The Hermitage State Museum for the presence of tattoos. In the course of this investigation, thirteen tattoo figures were revealed on the upper back and shoulder blades.

Two identical figures are visible on the shoulders of this individual, although the lower parts of these designs were destroyed because the skin was missing. The upper part of each figure is represented by two pairs of shoots: roundish inner shoots and lyre-shaped outer ones. The preserved dimensions of the figures measure 7.0 by 4.5 cm. Two rosettes, measuring 1.8 by 1.8 cm and consisting of four dots, were symmetrically placed on the breast above the nipples at a distance of 10.5 cm from each other. On each of the upper arms were tattooed two comma-shaped figures measuring 1.5 by 1.5 cm. The skin near these marks is damaged, so it seems possible that initially there were more of these motifs on each of the arms (fig. 5.19).

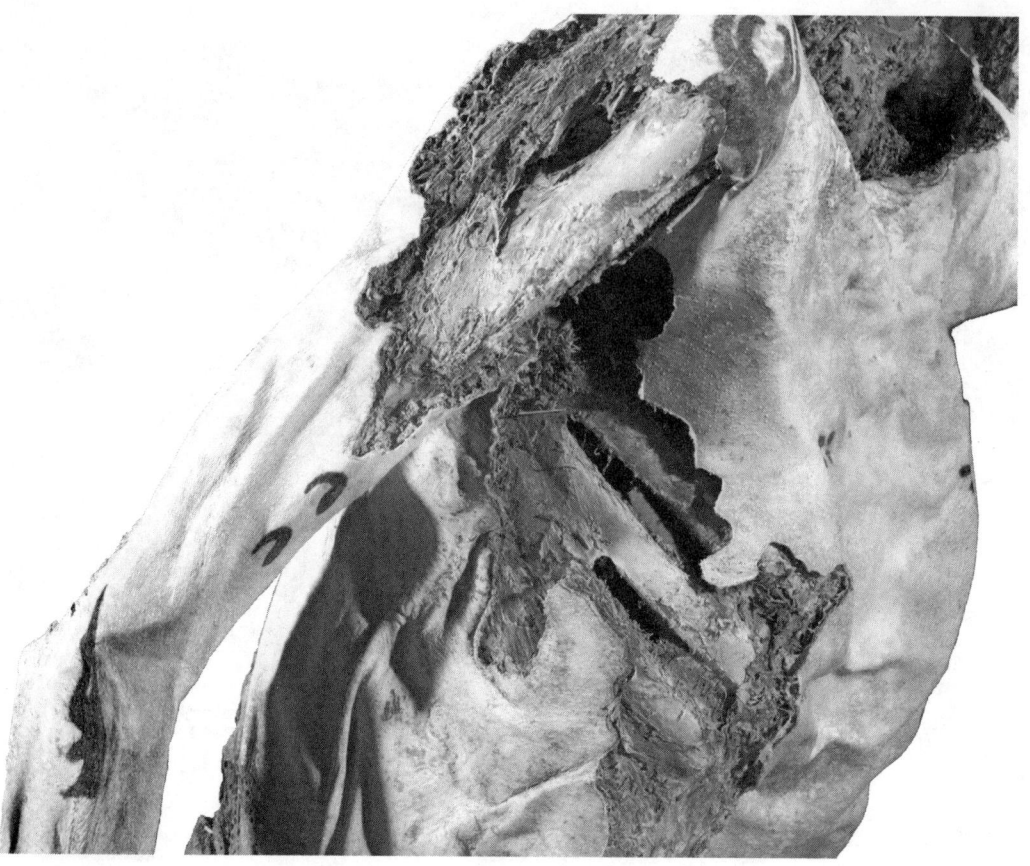

Fig. 5.21. View of the male mummy from the right, Oglakhty cemetery, grave 4 (third through fourth centuries CE). Infrared photograph. The State Hermitage Museum, St. Petersburg (Inv. No. 2864/71). After Svetlana Pankova (2013).

On the back of the mummy, at the shoulder blades, there are two large figures that seem to be identical, though the left figure is severely damaged. The right figure is barely visible to the naked eye, and its outlines are not readily legible. Its size is about 14.0 by 11.5 cm. Both figures are organized in three parts and have tentacle-like shoots. They resemble those on the shoulders and probably represented the same images. The only difference is a spherical detail between the upper shoots. The skin is folded and partly broken, and the figures look slightly distorted (fig. 5.20).

On the upper back of the mummy is a representation consisting of five parallel stripes opened in the center, seemingly enveloping the neck. The skin is distorted by deep folds and completely destroyed at the locations where missing parts of the tattooed depiction would be located, namely at the sides on the neck and on the upper breast.

On the right arm near the elbow a special curvilinear-shaped lancet-like figure with a sharpened end (8 cm in length) is depicted (fig. 5.21). On the inner side of the left

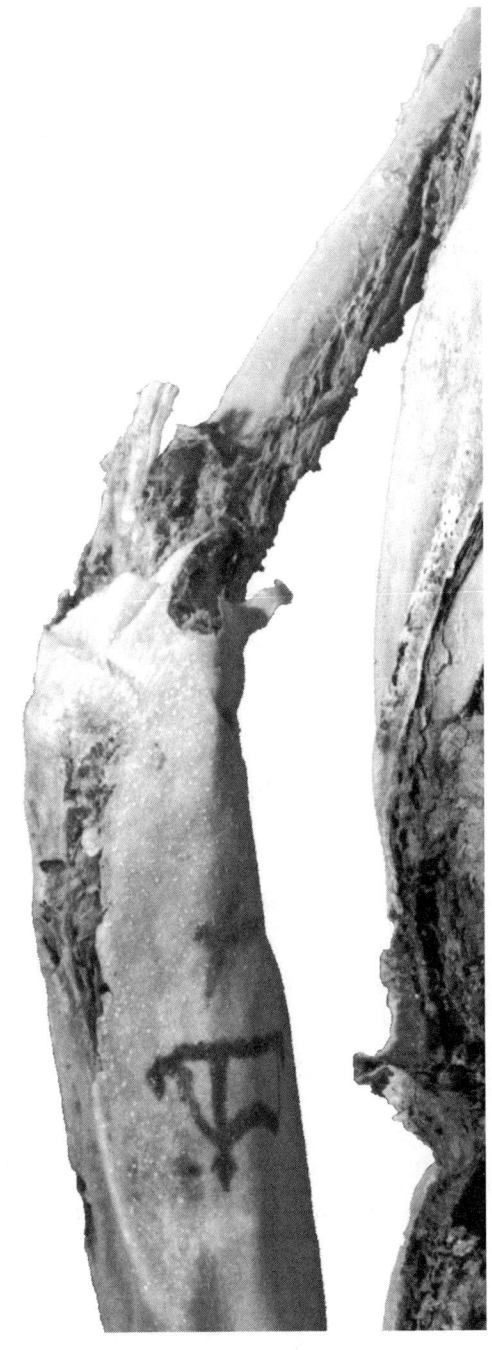

Fig. 5.22. View of the male mummy's left arm from behind, Oglakhty cemetery, grave 4 (third through fourth centuries CE). Infrared photograph. The State Hermitage Museum, St. Petersburg (Inv. No. 2864/71). After Svetlana Pankova (2013).

forearm is a representation of a bow and arrow. The mummy is rigid, and its extremities cannot be easily moved, so this tattoo only could be photographed in oblique projection. Nevertheless, the figure (measuring 6 cm in length) is clearly visible with the assistance of a mirror (fig. 5.22).

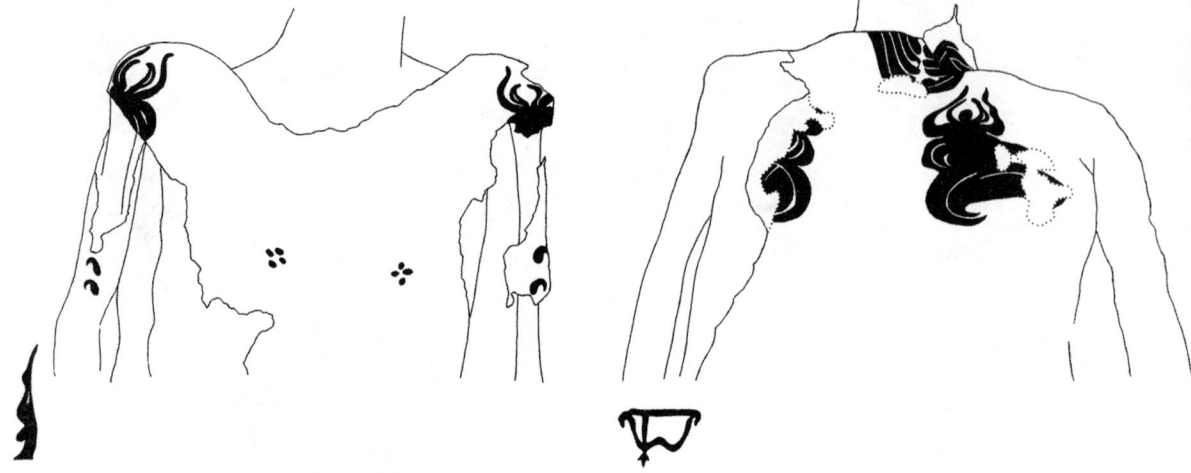

Fig. 5.23. Tattoos of the Oglakhty mummy, grave 4 (third through fourth centuries CE). Reconstruction. Illustrations by Svetlana Pankova.

An important peculiarity of the Oglakhty tattooing is its symmetrical orientation; most of the figures are paired (fig. 5.23). A figure on the upper back is in the center but is symmetrical by itself. Only the tattoos near the elbows have no paired designs, but the skin on the outer side of the left elbow is destroyed, and therefore we cannot formally rule out the presence of a tattoo. The symmetrical arrangement of the tattooing provides the entire composition with a special decorative effect.

The faces of both mummies—male and female—are hidden under the gypsum masks, preventing infrared rays from penetrating them. The masks cannot be removed without destroying them. Thus, the question of facial tattoos among these ancient dead remains unresolved. There is another mummy's head with preserved skin originating from the same cemetery in the collection of the State Historical Museum in Moscow. Infrared photography undertaken in 2014 did not reveal any tattoos on its face. The head belonged to a "halfgrown youth" (Tallgren 1937:76), so the absence of tattoos can perhaps be related to the young age of this individual.[8]

Motifs of the Oglakhty Tattoos

Many of the Oglakhty mummy's tattoos look unusual compared to known examples of early Tashtyk culture art. Surprisingly, an arrow-like figure on the elbow of the Oglakhty mummy resembles a common Pazyryk image—an antler, which is frequently seen on funerary objects but absent as a tattoo placed on the body (Pankova 2013: fig. 9; Rudenko 1970:fig. 96, 101b–c, 102a–c, 160–61). In fact some similarities do exist also in Pazyryk and early Tashtyk material culture, but only further studies can show their significance.

Nevertheless, some tattooed figures have parallels among local materials. For example, elements formed by concentric arcs on the upper back of the Oglakhty mummy can be associated with similar figures on masks painted with blue clay and soot pigment (Pankova 2013:fig. 10). If paintings on masks were really replicas of tattoo designs made on the faces of the dead, these blue and black arcs could express tattoos. Red spirals, usually painted on the same masks, might represent removable depictions. If so, we could imply that local people practiced both rituals. But the question of multicolored tattoos—their specificity and the very ability of applying them in ancient times—is of real interest (see Yablonsky, this volume, chapter 15). References to red and green pigments used for tattoos are present in Chinese sources of the early middle ages. One dating to the sixth century CE tells us that people of southern China "cut their flesh and darken it by rubbing red and green pigment into it" (Reed 2000:7). A ninth century CE document relates that an escaped slave was tattooed "using copperas like ink," explained as a green hydrated ferrous sulfate (Ibid.).

Another image, similar to a tattooed figure, can be recognized on a locally made artifact dating to a later period of the fifth through sixth centuries CE. This item is a wooden slat from collective Tomb 1 at Tepsey III, with carved representations of warriors, one of whom has body markings on his shoulders similar to those preserved on the mummy's skin. Another warrior on the same slat displays a similar motif depicted on his shield (Pankova 2013:fig. 8). This Gorgoneion-like depiction makes me suppose that images of the kind might have a protective, apotropaic function. These representations led us to believe that tattooed images of this kind were actually common and employed for an extended period of time in Minusinsk Hollow.

At the same time, these images display close affinities to others located far beyond the boundaries of the Minusinsk steppe. More specifically, ornaments seen on a locally made woolen skirt from the cemetery of Shanpula in the southern Tarim Basin are very similar (Museum of Xinjiang 2001:fig. 386; Schorta 2001:fig. 92). These woven figures can be traced to imaginary creations related to ancient Chinese *taotie* zoomorphic masks, which were commonly used in ancient times to decorate different objects and rooms because of their protective qualities (Pankova 2013:80–81, fig. 7).

Tattoo Evidence from Neighboring Regions

In the western part of the Scythian World we have uncovered no preserved tattooed mummies, but there are written accounts, iconographic evidence, and tattoo tools that point to the existence of this once widespread tradition. Greek and Latin authors mentioned branding and tattooing among the rites of the Scythians, Thracians (see Zidarov, this volume, chapter 9), Sarmatians, and other Iranian-speaking nomadic tribes of the

Northern Black Sea and adjacent regions (Mayor 2014:104–105; Rudenko 1970:113–14). Greek vase painting recorded some approximate patterns of these tattooing practices, primarily among the Thracians (Mayor 2014:98–109; Zimmermann 1980). Tattoo needles and palettes found in the high-status tombs in the Southern Urals represent tangible evidence of an ancient tattooing tradition there (see Yablonsky, chapter 15, this volume).

In the Asian part of the Scythian World the situation is quite the opposite. There are so far no ancient artifacts that might be identified as tattooing kits. Representations of human figures (on which tattooing could have been recognized) are almost entirely absent in lieu of animal depictions. As described previously, although Chinese accounts from different periods do mention tattooing as a custom of some neighboring groups (Reed 2000), none of these accounts can so far be identified with the nomads of the Altai Mountains or with other nomadic groups to the north and west of mainland China.

The only probable evidence of a Central Asian tattooing tradition besides the tattooed mummies is represented by the so called "deer stones"—late Bronze through early Iron Age vertical pillar-like slabs with relief depictions of animal figures and human weaponry, placed near burials and at commemoration sites.[9] Frequently decorated with belts, necklaces, and earrings, these stones are similar to human figures, and may be personifications of warriors. Stylized figures of deer often encircle these stone stellae and may represent body paintings or tattoos (Gryaznov 1983; Jettmar 1994). These monuments have been found over a vast area, including the Transbaikal region, Mongolia, Altai, Tuva, Jungaria, Kazakhstan, and even farther to the west. Unfortunately, there are almost no surviving mummies from these regions.

It is clear that the ancient tattooing tradition in this part of Asia was not restricted to the Altai-Sayan region. We know this thanks to findings of tattooed mummies in the Tarim Basin burials of China located in the province of Xinjiang. Known tattoos come from different cemetery sites—Qizilchoqa, Zaghunluq, Yanghai, Shengjindian, and Shanpula (see map 5.1)— dating mostly to the first millennium BCE through the early first millennium CE.[10] Most of the documented tattoos from this region consist of curvilinear or angular designs located on hands, though tattooing on the face, upper backs, and arms are also mentioned (Mallory and Mair 2000: plate VII, 142). Certain artifacts found in these cemeteries share features with the Pazyryk materials (Polosmak 1998:341–42; Polosmak and Barkova 2005:99; Shulga 2010:109), including their tattoos. For example, a figure of a burbot (freshwater codfish) from the right foot of the Pazyryk chieftain resembles schematic fish figures tattooed on the hand of a mummy from the Turfan Oasis in northwestern China (Li 2010:10). The piscine tattoo can contribute to the kindred character of these cultures through artistic traditions.

Unfortunately, there is not much available information concerning the tattooed Tarim mummies, even though there are numerous, well-preserved specimens. Therefore, new research should be conducted because it is likely that many new tattoo discoveries will be made.

Conclusions

The tattoo traditions of the nomadic Pazyryk who inhabited the Altai-Sayan mountain region are characterized by a highly decorative style featuring lively animal depictions that are expressive in their design and composition. An early Tashtyk group employed more schematic representations that were both static and symmetrical. However, as the Oglakhty skin pictures are so far the only known examples from the Tashtyk culture, it is too early to make generalizations about their possible functions and meanings. The same is true for the tattoos of other Central Asian groups, like the inhabitants of the Tarim Basin. Nevertheless, there are common features among tattoos from the previously mentioned regions, and this evidence points to a sphere of cultural interaction among these ancient peoples.

Taken together, these findings show that the custom of tattooing was probably quite widespread among the peoples of Central Asia. Therefore, it is necessary to examine every old and newly discovered mummy, even if it consists only of skin fragments, with infrared photography, in an attempt to uncover new insights into the indelible tattoo culture of these ancient peoples. Because tattooing appears to be related to many aspects of ancient Central Asian cultures, the insights will likely enrich our views of these mysterious yet colorful people.

Notes

This work has been done with the support of the Charitable Foundation of Vladimir Potanin.

1. The Altai expedition was conducted by the Institute for the History of Material Culture, Academy of Sciences of the USSR, Leningrad.
2. In 1947, Sergei Rudenko did not have the opportunity to transport the Pazyryk mummies to The Hermitage State Museum, and was forced to leave them in Siberia until 1948, when they were shipped to St. Petersburg (then Leningrad). A piece of tattooed skin from the right shoulder of the chieftain and his severed head has been on display at the museum ever since they arrived there more than sixty years ago.
3. Recent CT scans of this woman's body revealed that she suffered from multiple diseases throughout her lifetime. It has been suggested that she was highly valued by her tribesmen and obtained some treatment from them because she managed to survive numerous debilitating physical ailments. In turn, her special skills and behavior may have contributed to her special position in Pazyryk society as one who "communicate[d] with spirits" (Letyagin et al. 2014:90–91).
4. For example, Alvrus et al. (2001); Armelagos (1969); Kapel et al. (1991:103–104); Smith and Zimmermann (1975).
5. The average age of Pazyryk culture women has been estimated at 33.2 years (Chikisheva 2003:69).
6. It has been suggested that the Pazyryk nomads may also have performed the skin-sewing tattoo technique in antiquity (Rudenko 1970:112).
7. Bunker (1992); Kost (2014: plates 12, 32, 51–53, 57–59, 127); Kovalev (1999); Shulga (2010: fig. 90, 131–36).

8   The exact age of the tattooed person from Oglakhty Tomb 4 has not yet been determined, but he is definitely an adult.
9   Fitzhugh (2009a, 2010); Jacobsen (1993, 2006); Molodin and Polosmak (2005); Savinov (1994); Volkov (2002).
10 Deter-Wolf et al. (2016); Li (2010:10); Mallory and Mair (2000:189, 194, plates VII–VIII); Museum of Xinjiang (2001: fig. 449); Wang (1999:58, 89).

6

Neo-Pazyryk Tattoos

A MODERN REVIVAL

Colin Dale and Lars Krutak

THE SCYTHIANS WERE ONE OF A NUMBER OF TRIBES OF EARLY NOMADIC horsemen (including the Sarmatians, Yuezhi, and Xiongnu) whose realm stretched across the steppes from Greece to Persia to China. The Scythians were primarily an Indo-European people. Through tribal alliances and intermarriage with other groups, they encapsulated several ethnicities, but each tribe shared a common culture bred in the saddle. The flat, barren plains of the East were the shortest link between Europe and Asia, and the horse was the fastest means to traverse these vast distances. Holding reign over all trade, transport, and agriculture in this area contributed to the great wealth of the Scythians, and when a chief died, a large portion of his material fortune was buried with him.

In Book IV of his *Histories*, Herodotus recounted his visit to the Greek trading colony of Olbia in the fifth century BCE, and described the wealth and culture of these tribal horsemen. He took special note of their burial ceremonies, which were lavish events, sometimes lasting a month or more. The bodies of the Scythians were prepared for the afterlife by removing their internal organs. The resulting cavities were filled with grass, sage, and other sweet smelling herbs to hinder decay. The dead were mourned until the spring thaw when a large barrow was excavated into the permafrost and fortified with logs to create a chamber that housed the deceased with their earthly belongings. In some cases a servant, concubine, or several horses were interred in the barrow as well, and a stone burial mound, or kurgan, was built on top (Rudenko 1953, 1970).

The Scythians were equestrians and herders of cattle and sheep. They were hunters of elk, deer, and other game. The life cycle of predator and prey became a focus of their daily lives and their art. This art later became known as the "Animal Style," and the images created by Scythian nomads reflected their lives better than Herodotus could ever have described in words.

A Tsar, Scythian Gold, and Tattooed Mummies

The Russian Tsar Peter the Great (1672–1725) was an avid collector of curios and antiquities, the bulk of which became the foundation for the collections of The Hermitage Museum in St. Petersburg. When his son, Peter Petrovich, was baptized in 1715, a wealthy mining merchant from the Ural Mountains gifted Tsar Peter a king's ransom in Scythian golden objects. The tsar was captivated not so much by the gold items bestowed upon him as by the artistry of their craftsmanship. Within a few months, Peter decreed that all Scythian grave goods would become property of the crown. He furthermore began buying up previously recovered Scythian treasures for his own collection.

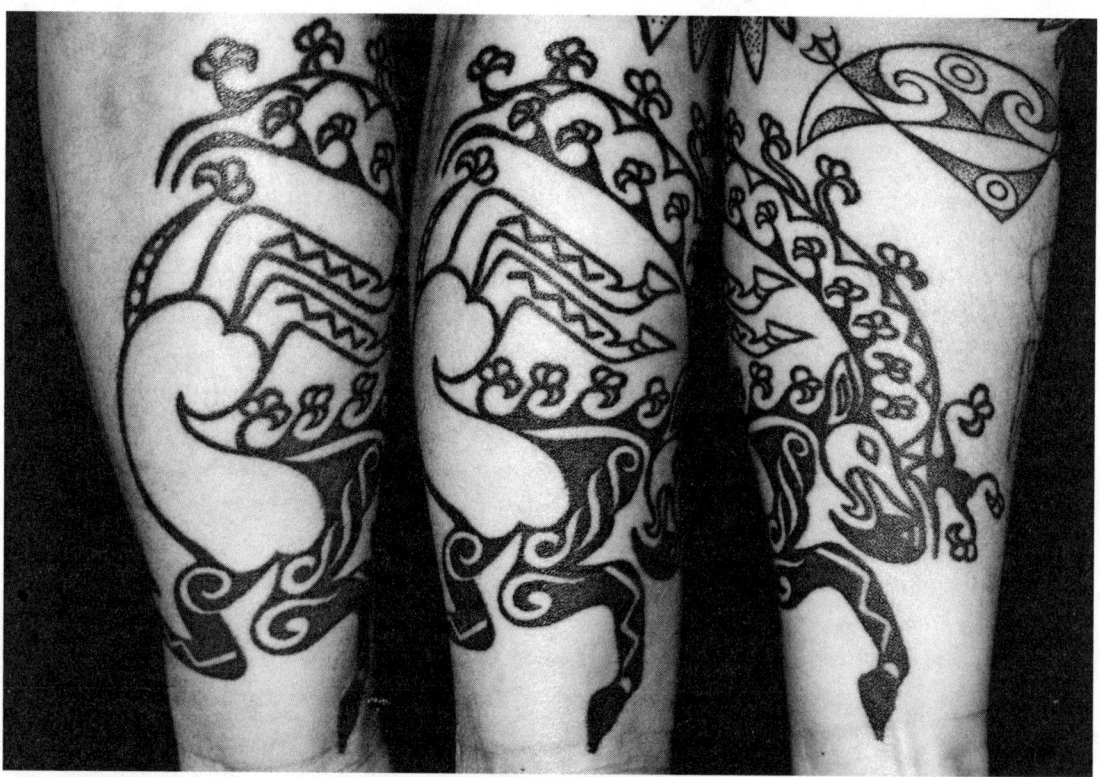

Fig. 6.1. Inge-Mette Petersen's neo-Pazyryk deer tattooed by hand, Copenhagen, Denmark (2014). Tattoos and photograph © Colin Dale / www.skinandbone.dk.

Following the formation of the Imperial Russian Archaeological Commission in 1859, state-sanctioned excavations of Scythian burial mounds and those of related peoples like the Pazyryk began in 1865. The most famous of these expeditions was led by anthropologist Sergei Rudenko, who unearthed five large barrows in the Pazyryk Valley of the Altai Mountains between 1929 and 1949.

The most astounding of the discoveries was the mummified body of a Pazyryk chieftain in Kurgan 2. As described in chapter 5, the mummy's torso and extremities were tattooed with a menagerie of zoomorphic images, including griffins, winged lions, and eagle-headed stags, whose indelible portraits mirrored the more utilitarian art forms of the Scythians (Rudenko 1970:figs. 51–54; see also plate 7). These images are some of

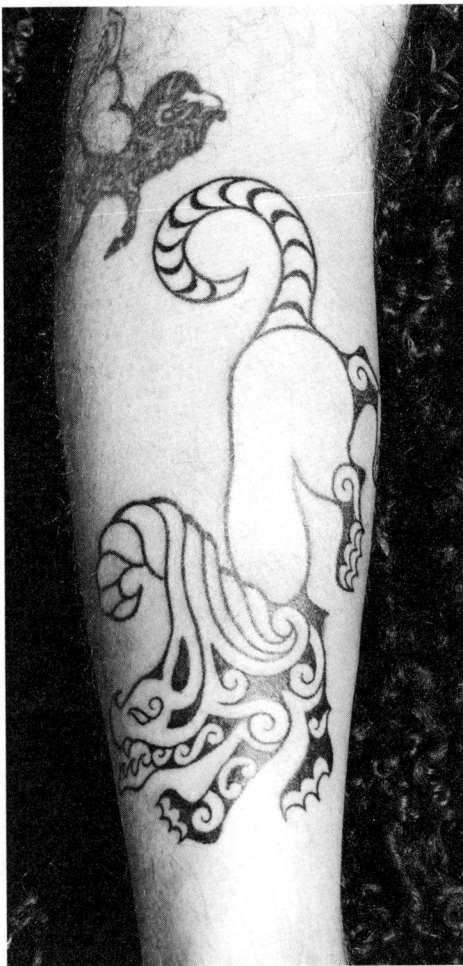
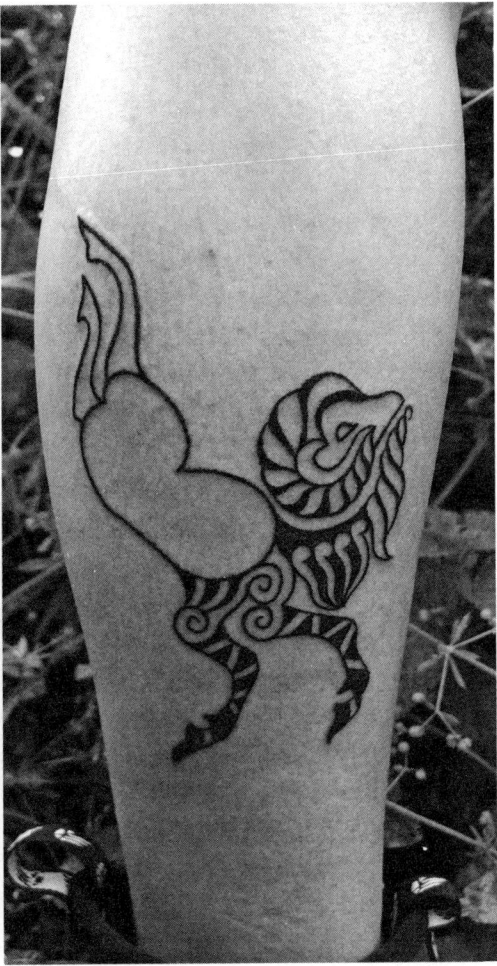

Fig. 6.2. Neo-Pazyryk winged lion tattooed by hand at Lejre Archaeological Research Center, Denmark (2013). Tattoos and photograph © Colin Dale /www.skinandbone.dk.

Figs. 6.3. Neo-Pazyryk ram tattooed by hand at Lejre Archaeological Research Center, Denmark (2002). Tattoos and photograph © Colin Dale / www.skinandbone.dk.

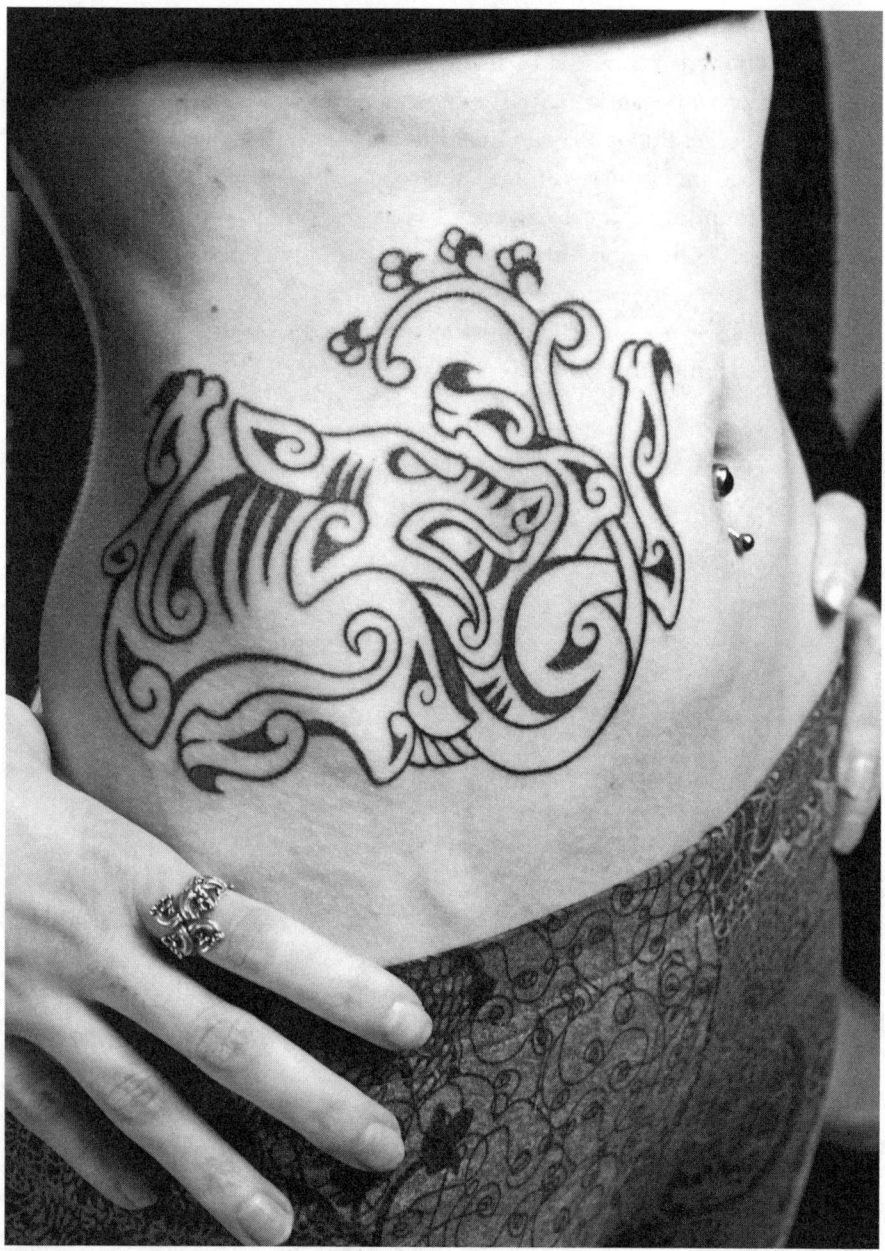

Fig. 6.4. Kiran Shuvalova's neo-Pazyryk wolf tattooed by hand, St. Petersburg, Russia (2013). Tattoos and photograph © Colin Dale / www.skinandbone.dk.

the oldest and most intricate pictorial tattoos known to humankind. Aside from the animal images, there was also a series of dots tattooed along the chieftain's lower back. Although not a copy in form, they were similar in placement (and perhaps function) to some marks discovered on the 5,300-year-old body of the Iceman dubbed "Ötzi" found in the Alps on the Austria-Italy border in 1991 (Krutak 1999, 2013b). Ötzi's tattoos are purported as being part of some form of medicinal therapy (Krutak 2012; Samadelli et al. 2015). Since the Pazyryk chieftain's lower back markings have no relation aesthetically to his other pictorial works, these tattoos may have had a similar purpose.

Rudenko's illustrations of Pazyryk tattoos captured the imagination of a young Danish archaeologist named Søren Nancke-Krogh, who had a complete copy of the chieftain's designs tattooed on his own body. Nancke-Krogh (1969) wrote a short article on the chief's tattoos for the archaeological magazine *Skalk*. It was entitled "Kunsten på Kroppen" (Art on the Body) and featured photos of his recreated tattoos. Although tattooed via electric machine (by Tato Jim in Aarhus, Denmark), Nancke-Krogh nonetheless inspired other individuals to resurrect this ancient art form through receiving their own neo-Pazyryk tattoos. Today, they are collected by lovers of art and history, bonding them through ink and blood to the ancient tattoo traditions of these enigmatic horsemen of the Eurasian steppes (figs. 6.1–6.4).

Pazyryk Tattoos in Canada

Halfway around the world in Toronto, Canada, tattoo artist and medical illustrator extraordinaire Stephen Goltra Gilbert (1931–2014) also brought the Pazyryk chief's tattoos to life. A confessed "tattoo addict," Gilbert encountered tattooing at the age of ten in Portland, Oregon, and by fourteen he bore the number 13 and crossed swords on his legs. Tattooing captivated the young Gilbert because it "seemed at once dangerous and fascinating. The images . . . spoke to me of travel, adventure, danger, and sex. . . . They were forbidden but infinitely desirable" (Gilbert 2000b:8).

As a university student, Gilbert studied art, and after graduation in 1952 he served in the US Army Medical Corps. Following his military discharge, Gilbert studied medical illustration at Massachusetts General Hospital and in San Francisco. In 1973 he became a faculty member in the Art as Applied to Medicine program at the University of Toronto, but tattooing was never far away for him. In the early 1980s, Gilbert studied Japanese *tebori*, the centuries-old method of tattooing by hand, and after retiring as a full professor in 1996, he worked as a tattooist at Abstract Arts Tattoo in Toronto.

Over the course of his artistic career, Gilbert researched and wrote about the cultural history of tattoo. "Tattooing in some form has been practiced in most parts of the world since the Stone Age [and] it never existed in a vacuum. It has always played an important role in the social life of those who practiced it, and throughout history it has appeared in many guises. [I have] a profound and inexplicable fascination with the process of puncturing the skin, letting blood, and consenting to change the body for life. [Tattooing] is something that is sensed intuitively, but behind [its] many uses there lurks a mystery" (Gilbert 2000b:9).

One of Gilbert's tattoo clients was Dave Mazierski, a former student and now associate professor in the Biomedical Communications program at the University of Toronto

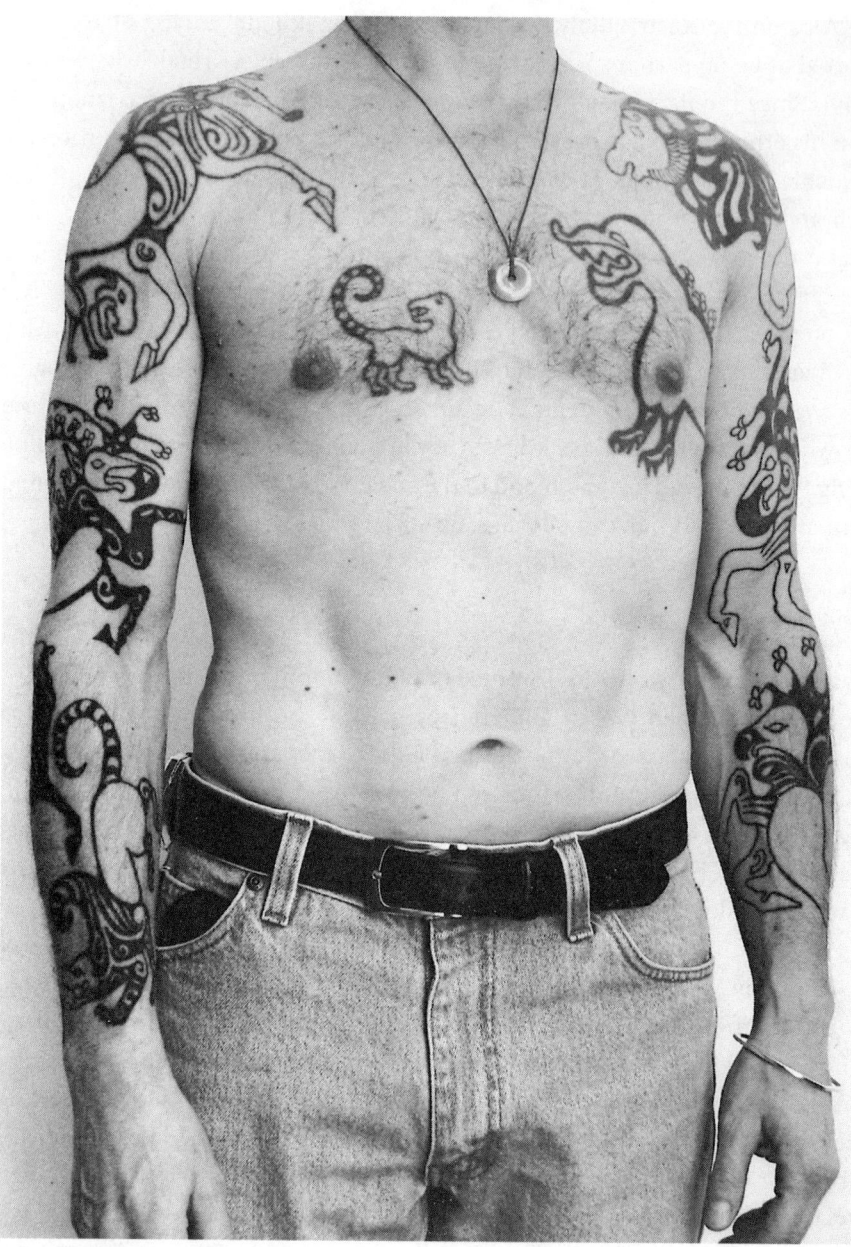

Fig. 6.5. Body tattoos of Dave Mazierski inspired by the ancient Pazyryk chief (2016). Artistry by Steve Gilbert. Photograph © www.calvaria.com.

(fig. 6.5). Mazierski knew nothing of the Pazyryk people or their tattoos until he met Gilbert. "Around 1990, I had a deep interest in Japanese art and culture, and played the *taiko* [drum]. I was familiar with Japanese full-body tattoos, and Steve and I would chat about all of these things, including his interest in *tebori*." Then, Gilbert told Mazierski

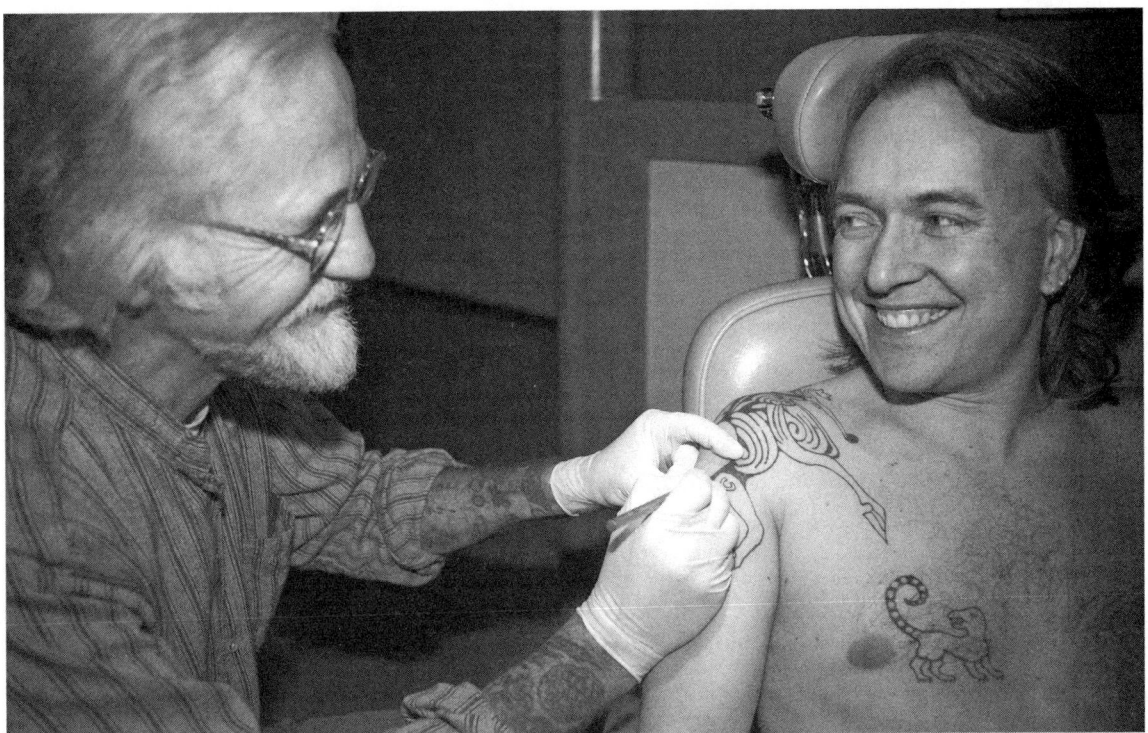

Fig. 6.6. Tattoo artist Steve Gilbert tattooing Dave Mazierski, Toronto, Canada (ca. 1996). Photograph © www.calvaria.com.

about the tattoos of the Pazyryk chief. "They were different from anything else I had seen. Steve offered to give me those tattoos in exchange for letting him 'practice' on me with the *tebori* technique. I was taken by the designs Steve showed me, and I didn't think of anything else—the goal was always to get the 'full set' placed on my body as close as possible to the original."

Gilbert hand-poked the first of many Pazyryk tattoos on Mazierski beginning in 1991, a process that would encompass ten years of collaboration. "By the time we had filled my arms, I think Steve was a bit tired of tattooing in the ancient way. So, he would create outlines of the remaining designs, and after they healed Steve or one of the other artists working at Abstract Arts in those days—Stan Wong and Bill Reid—would fill them in with machine tattooing."

In 2011, Mazierski was invited to travel to St. Petersburg to appear in a television documentary on the American cable *History* channel about The Hermitage, where the remains of the Pazyryk chief are displayed. Prior to the trip, tattoo artist Bill Reid applied the burbot (fish) tattoo on his right shin. While filming in Russia, Mazierski received the tattoo of the four rams running along the left side of the burbot design. At The Hermitage, he met archaeologist Svetlana Pankova (see Pankova, chapter 5, this volume). She informed Mazierski that the mummified right hand of the chief had been found in the museum collections, and infrared photography revealed that a rooster was tattooed on the right thumb. Upon returning to Toronto, Reid added the rooster as well as three additional tattoos that Mazierski was missing: a griffin tattoo above the right foot, a series of dots above the right ankle, and the previously mentioned dots along the lower back.

Mazierski thought his collection of Pazyryk tattoos was now complete, but in 2012 Pankova emailed him noting that another piece of the skin of the chieftain from Kurgan 2 had been found in The Hermitage collections, and infrared photography revealed an elk or stag tattoo on the left foot. Mazierski made a sketch based on the photos Pankova sent him, and Reid completed the tattoo in 2014.

Mazierski remarked that his tattoo journey with Gilbert "was a magical, unique combination of who, what, when, and where" (fig. 6.6). Gilbert passed away in 2014 and in his obituary Mazierski wrote: "Many of his friends, former students and family members carry their own indelible, permanent reminder of Steve's legacy with them. His gentle and caring nature, and his great passion for art, science and truth will always inspire us. . . . There will never be another man like him" (Mazierski 2014).

7

Recovering the Nineteenth-Century European Tattoo

COLLECTIONS, CONTEXTS, AND TECHNIQUES

Gemma Angel

EUROPEAN TATTOOING TRADITIONS ARE PERHAPS THE MOST MISUNDERstood and mythologized of all known cultures that practice the art. Its present-day ubiquity and frequently marginalized status within the nexus of social relations make the European tattoo appear at once familiar and strange. This has been a long-standing state of affairs, which has in turn prejudiced the ways in which European observers have regarded the tattooing practices of foreign and Indigenous cultures. The history of the tattoo in Europe is long but somewhat ambiguous: While early textual and archaeological evidence suggests that tattooing was widely practiced among the Scythians, Celts, Picts, and Germans in prehistoric Europe, the historical picture is far less clear (Caplan 1997:113). The sporadic and discontinuous visibility of the tattoo in European cultural history has thus led historian Jane Caplan to characterize the history of European tattooing by its tendency "to resolve itself into a history of the particular episodes of its emergence into view" (Ibid.:111). These episodes are as diverse as they are sporadic and, despite the limits of the historical record, point to a remarkable tenacity and diversity of practice across national boundaries, historical periods, and cultural milieu.

A number of previously unstudied collections of preserved tattooed human skin specimens are assembled in European medical and anthropological museums.[1] The majority of these collections were gathered during the nineteenth century, when criminological studies of the European tattoo gave collecting practices academic impetus; so it is worth pointing out from the outset that such collections are necessarily limited in their breadth and scope, and the preoccupations of criminologists are clearly reflected in the selection of preserved tattooed images and phrases. Nevertheless, considered alongside other textual and comparative iconographic sources, these collections provide unique material evidence of historical European tattooing techniques, tools, iconography, and contexts.

The Wellcome Collection in London dates from ca. 1830 to 1929 CE and is unique in size and scope, containing 300 examples of dry-prepared tattooed skin. The collection originated in France and historically was part of the Wellcome medical collection now held in storage at the Science Museum archives in London. The tattoos were purchased in Paris on June 15, 1929, on behalf of Victorian entrepreneur Sir Henry Wellcome for his "Historical Medical Museum" (Angel 2012:29–30). Peter Johnston-Saint (1929), the purchasing agent who conducted the sale, wrote that the "skins date from the first quarter of last century down to the present time . . . consisting of skins of sailors, soldiers, murderers and criminals of all nationalities."[2] Aside from Johnston-Saint's brief notes, no other documentary material pertaining to the collection exists within the Wellcome Library archives.

In the absence of archival records, it has therefore been necessary to adopt a more material approach in the study of the Wellcome Collection. Although analytical techniques involving destructive testing may potentially produce information invaluable to both the study of the collection and its future safeguarding, it nevertheless conflicts with one of the primary concerns of the museum: conservation. For these reasons, noninvasive visual material analysis methods have been employed in the study of the Wellcome Collection. This combination of ethnographic object analysis and historical archive research has revealed new insights into the origins and context of the Wellcome Collection tattoos.

With a few notable exceptions, the tattoos preserved in the Wellcome Collection indicate amateur application, most likely by ordinary soldiers, seamen, and semiprofessional tattooists. These individuals, most likely men, either operated an itinerant and opportunistic trade as they moved from place to place, or based themselves at seaports and in barracks. This conclusion is borne out by a combination of close visual analysis of both iconography and the tattooing technique evident in the marks themselves.

Technique Tells a Story: Skin Specimens, Tools, and Pigments

While the specifics of tattooing processes and practices vary widely from culture to culture, the basic principle remains the same the world over: The skin is punctured by a sharp, pointed implement, and pigments are introduced to the wound either on the tip of the tool or by rubbing over the skin after the punctures have been made. The most commonly used method involves applying a series of rapid needle pricks to the skin (hand-poking). Other methods, such as those practiced by the Maori of New Zealand, in which relatively deep grooves are cut into the skin before the pigment is rubbed in, are more akin to carving. More rarely, a skin-stitching method may be used, whereby a needle and pigment-infused thread or a stick dipped in pigment is drawn through the upper layers of the skin (Krutak 2007:146). Many nineteenth-century criminologists interested in the European tattoo read about Indigenous tattoo techniques in anthropological reports and the accounts of explorers, and went on to reproduce general descriptions of these procedures in their own criminological studies (e.g., Lacassagne and Magitot 1881:9–20).[3]

Prior to the development of electric tattooing machines in the 1890s, the techniques and tools used by the European tattooer were simple and often highly unhygienic, a fact that did not escape the attention of medical officers of the navy and other armed services.[4] All necessary equipment would be homemade or improvised from whatever materials were available at hand. The tattoo design would first be outlined freehand onto the skin with a pen—early professional George Burchett is described as using an iodine pencil (Burchett and Leighton 1958:66).[5] Alternately, a pre-drawn design on a sheet of paper or cloth would be laid over the skin and lightly "pricked" out through the template. Since the skin cannot be easily stretched beneath the paper or cloth sheet, this method of design transfer frequently resulted in asymmetric and ill-proportioned tattoos, many examples of which are evident in the Wellcome Collection.

Once the design was outlined on the skin, the tattoo needles were dipped into ink and applied to the skin at an approximate depth of 0.5 to 1 mm. These tools would normally consist of three to five fine points bound together on a long shaft made of wood or some other durable material.

In British tattooist George Burchett's (1872–1953) posthumously compiled *Memoirs of a Tattooist*, the author describes the similarities in the hand-poking methods used by Japanese and European tattooists alike: "The Japanese method is prodding. The ivory needle is held at an angle of between 30 and 45 degrees to the skin and is gently pushed under the epidermis. This, in fact, is the method by which Western tattooists worked before the advent of the electrical tattooing instrument which, itself, employs the same principle" (Burchett and Leighton 1958:65).

A small tattoo such as a name or a date might take less than half an hour to complete, while larger, more complex work requiring detailed shading would take considerably longer, necessitating multiple sessions over weeks or months. In these cases, the outline of the design would usually be completed during the first session, and the shading carried out in subsequent sessions. When analyzing preserved tattoo specimens, the tattooing technique may be identified through close visual observation of the marks themselves. These observations are primarily aimed at visually identifying specific techniques and describing common errors that strongly indicate amateur or unskilled workmanship, as well as outlining the features that constitute a well-executed tattoo.

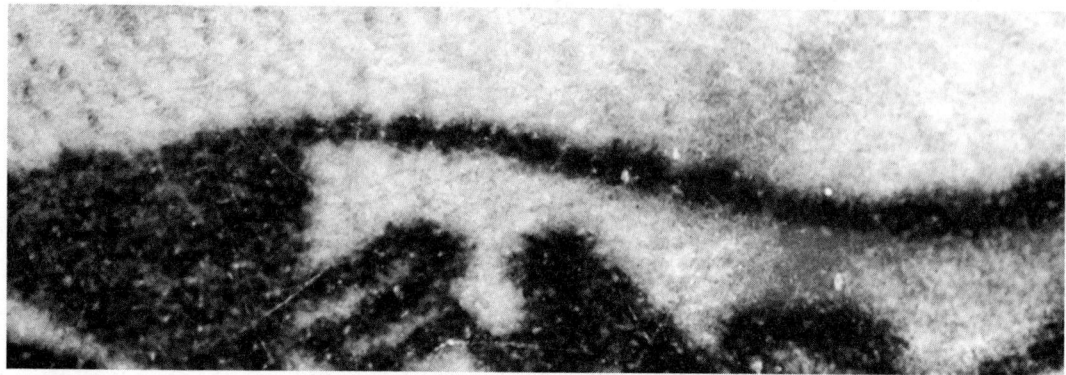

Fig. 7.1. Detail of preserved tattooed human skin (likely from France, ca. 1850–1920 CE), showing beading in the outline. The beading effect is created when tattoo needles penetrate too deeply into the skin and ink spreads into tissue and fat beneath the dermis. Science Museum, London (A733). Photograph by Gemma Angel.

BEADING

Beading occurs when needles penetrate too deeply into the skin and ink spreads into the surrounding tissue and fat beneath the dermis. Visually this appears something like a dot-to-dot drawing, in which a line that should otherwise appear smooth is interrupted by a series of "beads" (fig. 7.1). Beading results from an error in judging the correct application of needle depth (known as the "throw" of the needle, when using an electric tattooing machine), and thus indicates amateur or unskilled work. Awareness of the correct depth at which to apply one's tattoo needles will determine whether the tattoo is well-made, aesthetically pleasing, and will to some extent affect its durability (see "Fading," following).

FEATHERING

Feathering occurs naturally as cells age and pigment particles migrate into neighboring tissues, but it can also develop much earlier when needles are applied to the skin at an angle of less than about 30 degrees, or when too much ink is introduced into the skin too heavily (fig. 7.2). This effect is much more common when hand tools are used in tattooing.[6] Commenting on the handiwork of some of the early professional American tattooists, Samuel Steward describes the way in which poorly applied tattoos degrade over time as a result of excessive feathering:

> Some of the old artists, now dead, did not do work that would be satisfactory by modern standards. They used outline machines that were too thick and heavy, making delicate fine-line work impossible. Their small stuff "closed up"—that is, the slight spreading of the outline that occurs in every tattoo was very marked in their work. A name, for example, in which the letters

were adequately spaced when first put on, might in three years' time become unreadable. The letters "n" and "m" would close together; the loops in the "a" and "e" would come to look like "o." Many of the old boys never really learned to tattoo well during the early years of their experience, and went on to the ends of their lives doing second-rate work, botched, imperfectly shaded and excessively heavy. (Steward 1990:157–58)

APPLICATION OF LINE

Within the Wellcome Collection, the use of hand tools is evident in almost all of the specimens. In this method, hand-manipulated needle bundles of various groupings are used to build up a solid design through a series of individual dots.[7] Unskilled or amateur execution is easier to determine when a hand-poking technique is used, since it is typically far harder to master than machine-operated tattooing. An unskilled tattooer is more likely to produce lines of uneven thickness or lines with a clearly visible string of dots (beading), rather than a smooth, consistent line.

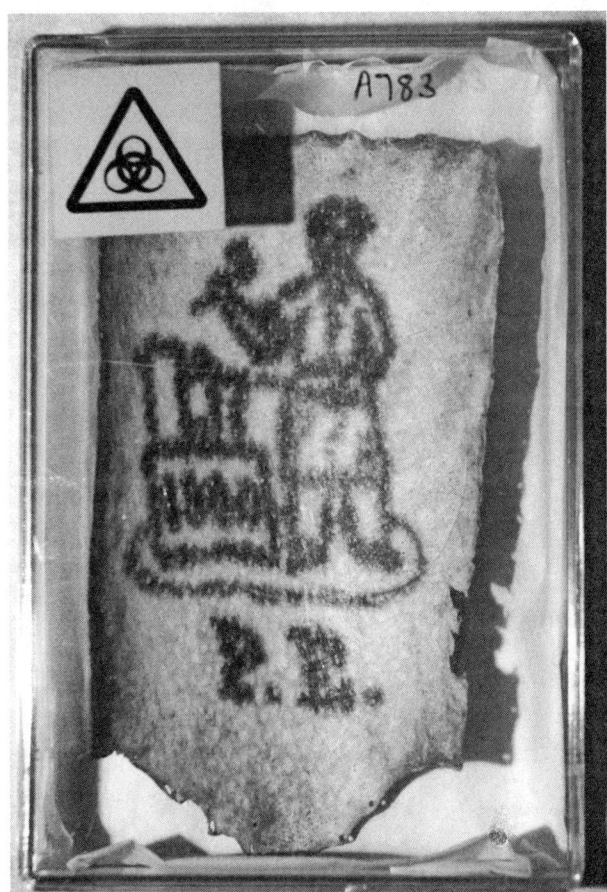

Fig. 7.2. Preserved tattooed human skin from France (ca. 1890 CE), illustrating a figure of a blacksmith with initials. This tattoo shows extreme non-age-related feathering. Science Museum, London (A783). Photograph by Gemma Angel.

PRIOR PREPARATION: STRETCHING OF THE SKIN

Inattentiveness to either of these elements of the tattooing process is usually indicated by the asymmetric appearance of the completed tattoo design. This appearance results from one of two possible causes: lack of artistic skill combined with inadequate design stencils or transfers, or a failure to adequately stretch the skin during tattooing. Many of the tattooed images in the Wellcome Collection are unevenly executed, suggesting minimal or no prior preparation of the design. Tattoos applied in a freehand manner by an amateur practitioner commonly appear asymmetrical once the tattoo has healed (fig. 7.3). When working with preserved tattoos, one must exercise critical judgment to determine whether distortion of a tattoo design has been caused by shrinkage of the skin during the drying process, or poor tattooing technique. In both instances, inadequate stretching of the skin, living or postmortem, will cause distortion of the tattoo.[8]

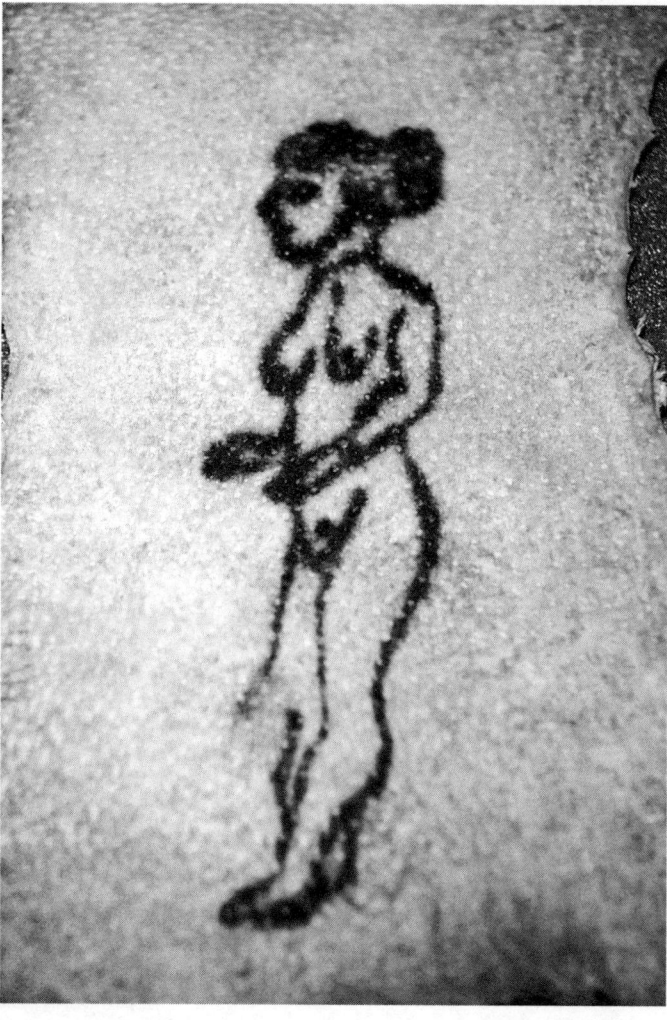

Fig. 7.3. Preserved tattooed human skin from France (nineteenth century CE), depicting a nude female figure exhibiting asymmetric and poorly proportioned design. Science Museum, London (A631).

FADING

Fading occurs naturally to some degree with age, but should never result in a complete absence of ink in whole areas of a design, unless the ink is introduced to the skin at too shallow a depth. This problem is opposite to beading, but results from a similar error of judgment of correct needle depth, and is also common in amateur work (fig. 7.4).

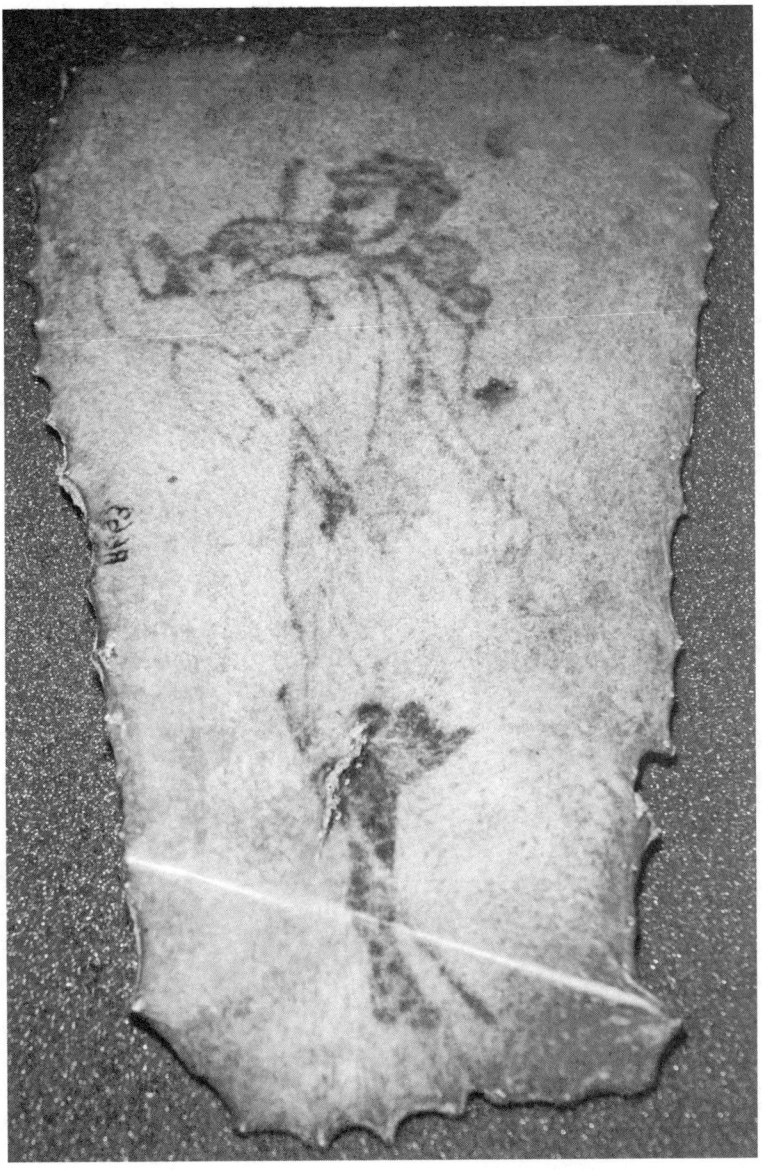

Fig. 7.4. Preserved tattooed human skin (probably from France, nineteenth century CE), showing a figure of a soldier. This tattoo exhibits extreme fading in the central portion of the design because of inadequate depth penetration of ink. Science Museum, London (A663). Photograph by Gemma Angel.

SHADING TECHNIQUE

With respect to the Wellcome Collection, in most cases shading technique does not differ from that used to apply outlines. A "prodding" or "pricking" method using a hand tool is employed to produce individual dots grouped closely together to form colored or shaded areas. Traditional Japanese tattooing and skilled hand-poke artists excepted, this technique tends to produce an undifferentiated block of color with little gradation of light and shade. There are some interesting and varied examples of dotwork shading in the Wellcome Collection, where shading has been used to fill in lettering with solid color, as can be seen in the tattooed phrase "*Enfant du Malheur*" (Child of Misfortune) shown on specimen number A554 (fig. 7.5).

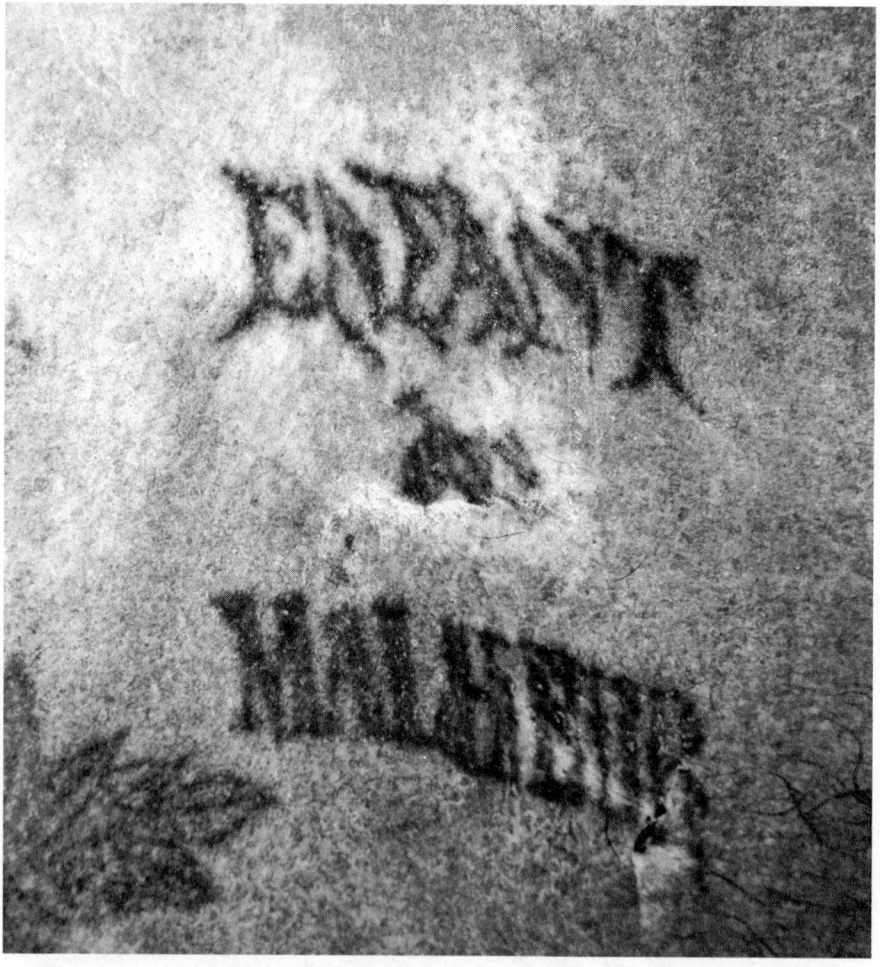

Fig. 7.5. Detail of preserved tattooed human skin from France (ca. 1850–1900), exhibiting dotwork shading within the letters of the phrase "*Enfant du Malheur*" (Child of Misfortune). Science Museum, London (A554). Photograph by Gemma Angel.

Other examples in the collection use evenly spaced dots to give the impression of shaded areas; this technique can be more or less effective according to the skill of the tattooer and the quality of their instruments. Compare, for instance, the crude application of dots to shade the petals of the tattooed flower in specimen A807 (fig. 7.6), with the extraordinarily fine rows of dots depicting hair texture in the female portrait in specimen A629 (fig. 7.7). There is also a handful of tattoos in the Wellcome Collection that show some evidence of machine application. For example, the cross section of a tattoo depicting a female portrait in profile with a checked headscarf (fig. 7.8) shows some very fine line work and patchy coloration using a circular motion, such as is employed when shading with round needle groupings using a machine. This patchy effect occurs when not enough ink is applied to the area, and may in this case be the result of using a needle grouping that is too fine, or possibly using the same fine needle bundle for both lining and shading. This result may indicate the tattoo was created by a relatively skilled amateur with limited resources, or by an apprentice to the profession.

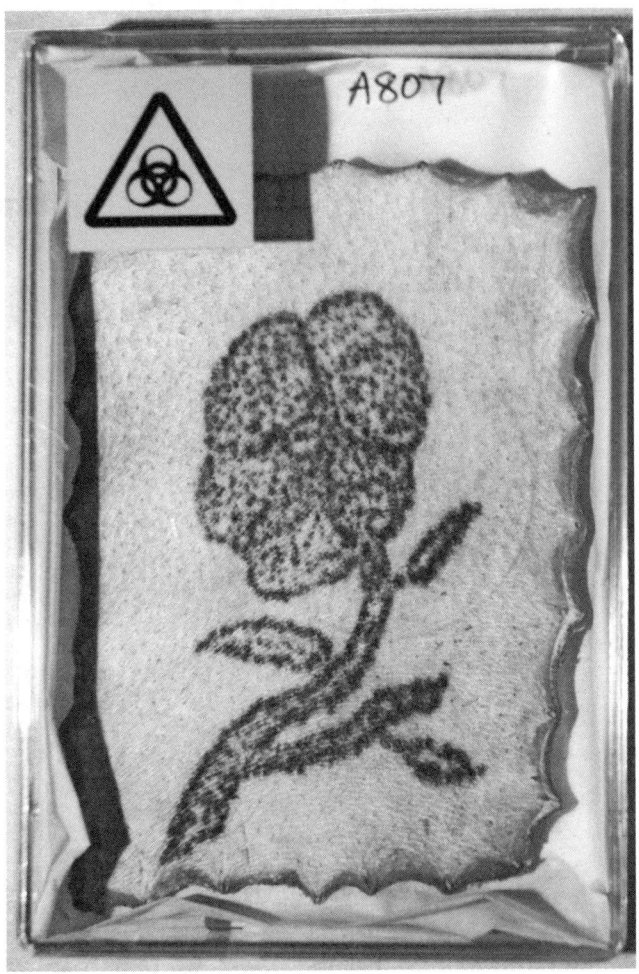

Fig. 7.6. Preserved tattooed human skin from France (ca. 1830–1900 CE), portraying an image of a flower exhibiting crude dotwork shading. Science Museum, London (A807). Photograph by Gemma Angel.

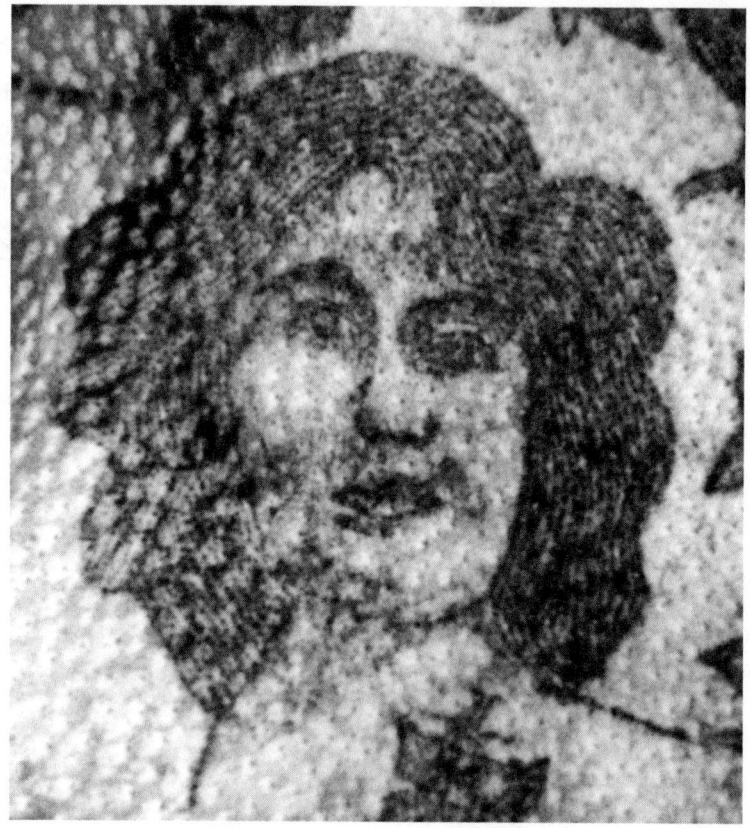

Fig. 7.7. Detail of preserved tattooed human skin from France (ca. 1900–1920 CE), illustrating comparatively skilled hand dotwork shading used to provide texture to a woman's hair. Science Museum, London (A629). Photograph by Gemma Angel.

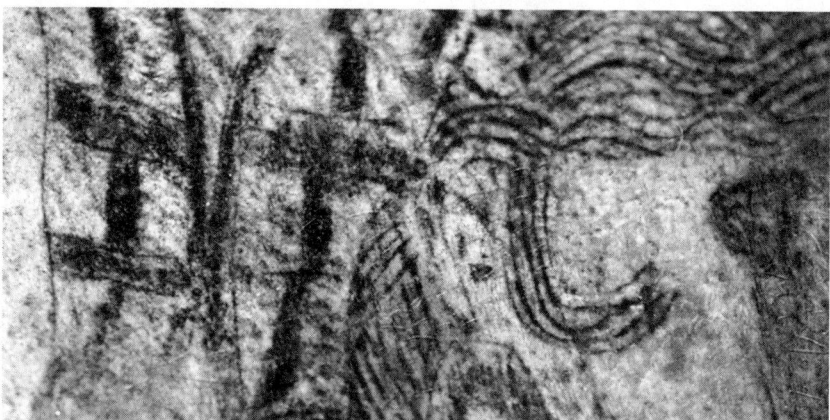

Fig. 7.8. Detail of preserved tattooed human skin (likely French, ca. 1850–1920 CE), showing the smooth, fine outlining indicative of an electric tattoo machine. Examples of machine application are fairly rare in the Wellcome Collection. Science Museum, London (A584). Photograph by Gemma Angel.

PIGMENTS

As well as considering the traces of tattooing technique, some interesting observations may be made regarding the pigments used in the collection. Tattoo ink was limited to black for most tattoos during the nineteenth century. India ink produced the best results and was favored by professionals who could afford to invest in quality pigments. However, the majority of tattooists would have mixed their own pigments using carbon-based materials such as soot (lampblack) and charcoal, which could be mixed into a solution with water, saliva,[9] or urine. Other colorants could include writing ink, bleachers blue, or indigo, which produced a blue-black result.

Red tattoos were far less common because the ores involved in the manufacture of red pigments are highly toxic.[10] Red mercuric sulphide occurs naturally, and has been manufactured for use as a pigment since the Early Middle Ages. The pigment was referred to interchangeably as vermilion or cinnabar, although vermilion became the more commonly used term by the seventeenth century (Harley 1982:125). Red pigments were not commonly used in European tattooing prior to the twentieth century, before which time red inks tended to be used sparingly for small areas of embellishment.

The Wellcome Collection includes only a handful of tattoos containing red dye; out of 300 tattoos only thirty-one contain red pigments. There is marked variability among these pigments, which may be described as fitting into one of three categories: intense, almost iridescent red; dull purple-brown red; and pale rose. The majority of red tattoos fall into the third group, in which the pigment tends to be exceptionally degraded compared to the black ink used in the same designs. There are, however, a few specimens that exhibit exceptionally bright red ink that has lost none of its vivid color (plate 8). Viewed under a light microscope, initial analysis of skins containing these reds suggests that these pigments likely exhibit a high cinnabar content, which would be consistent with nineteenth-century wet-process vermilion production.[11]

Most cinnabar was mined in China during the nineteenth century, and Chinese vermilion was considered a superior hue to European red pigments. Because of the high cost of Chinese cinnabar, European vermilion often contained adulterants that reduced color saturation and made the pigment more susceptible to light-degradation over time. These adulterants might include materials such as brick, orpiment, iron oxide, Persian red, iodine scarlet, and minium (red lead) (Eastaugh et al. 2004). The inclusion of these other substances may explain why there is marked variability among tattoos in the Wellcome Collection containing red inks, in terms of both permanence and vibrancy of color. A visual comparison of red pigments from the collection suggests that a small number of the Wellcome tattoos were created using true Chinese vermilion, and therefore may have been obtained by their bearers while in Asia, where purer forms of cinnabar-based pigment were more widely available.

Amateurs, Opportunists, and Itinerants:
The Late Nineteenth-Century Tattoo Trade

When considered in conjunction with historical literature on the nineteenth-century European tattooing milieu, the technical elements of tattooing previously described can provide a valuable insight into the provenance of preserved tattoo collections for which limited archival documentation survives. While a number of professional tattooists were practicing during this period (predominantly in the United Kingdom and the United States), only a handful of tattoos in the Wellcome Collection bear the signs of professional workmanship. A professionalized trade had not yet emerged in France in the 1890s, and most tattooists were occupied in other trades.

An interesting glimpse of the tattooists' trade can be found in Dr. Daguillon's 1891 study of the tattoos of the insane (1895:175–99), in which he lists the primary professions of the tattooers, as well as those of the asylum inmates. Of the sixty-five tattooed men observed at Ville-Evrard Asylum near Paris, fourteen cases were tattooed by soldiers, eleven by sailors, ten by ordinary workmen, six by vagrants, six by professional tattooists, five who tattooed themselves, two tattooed by children, one by an inmate of a military prison, and one by a prostitute, the only mention of a female tattooist. Nine cases lacked any data on the tattooists's profession (Ibid.).

Daguillon's figures, though limited, reinforce the assumption that tattooing was predominantly carried out socially among comrades in specific military and manual labor occupations. This is also reflected in his data on the "salaries" of the tattooist: in forty-three cases the tattoo was executed for free; on five occasions they were paid for "in kind" (for example, with a cup of black coffee, a glass of wine, or dinner). Only in eight instances were tattoos paid for in cash, with prices ranging from twenty centimes up to two francs. The tattoos executed by professionals were included within this category.

While studies such as Daguillon's can provide interesting data on the nineteenth-century tattoo milieu, such material is inherently limited by its sample and scope. Specifically, the ways in which the tattoos of working and lower class Europeans were characterized by the middle class medico-legal professionals of the period raises the issue of class-bias. Numerous late nineteenth-century nobility and royalty were famously tattooed by the early "tattoo art stars" such as Burchett and Sutherland Macdonald, and received a great deal of high profile commentary by the contemporary press. Therefore it is evident that the contemporary fascination with the practice was not limited to the soldier, seaman, or "recidivist," as assumed by many nineteenth-century criminologists writing on tattooing. Indeed, a far more complex and nuanced class picture emerges from the historical material. British royal military figureheads in particular appear to have played a part, for example, in reinvigorating long-standing traditions of pilgrimage tattooing on journeys to the Middle East and Asia, reinforcing the practice of "souvenir" tattooing already popular among the lower ranks. The frequency of souvenir tattoos within the Wellcome Collection may in fact attest to this popularity.

European Tattoo Iconography: Contexts and Collections

The iconography of tattoos preserved in museum collections can reveal further insights into nineteenth-century European tattooing contexts and communities. Before describing the range of images and text found within the Wellcome Collection, it is however, worth considering the taxonomies of tattoo motifs formulated by late-nineteenth century scholars—not least because these taxonomies frequently correlated tattooed image(s) with the moral character of the tattooed. These characterizations would persist well into the twentieth century. It is also important to note that while these categorizations are inherently limited and even potentially misleading, the Wellcome Collection was assembled during a period when the development of such taxonomies held strong interpretative currency. Indeed, the range of iconographic examples held in this collection strongly reflects the collecting priorities and interests of these scholars.

One of the earliest attempts at classification by genre of tattoo images was produced in 1855 by French medico-legal expert Auguste Ambroise Tardieu (1818–1879).[12] Tardieu studied the tattoos of fifty-one inmates at civilian prisons and hospitals, assigning the images he observed to seven different categories, listed in order of frequency: (I) miscellaneous figures; (II) military emblems; (III) love tokens; (IV) initials, names, and dates; (V) religious emblems; (VI) professional or trade emblems; and (VII) obscene images. All of these categories can be identified within the Wellcome Collection, and Table 7.1 notes the frequency with which particular motifs appear according to an updated classification scheme. Some motifs also cross categories; for instance, a regimental insignia may also fall into the naval (anchors) category.

Other broad image categories represented in the Wellcome Collection include: slogans and declarations; names, dates, initials, and love tokens; memorial tattoos; female figures and busts; male figures and busts (which may be divided between those in regimental costume and historical characters); animals; plants and flowers (frequently represented either in pots or as single stems, and often accompanied by a phrase and/or initials);[13] inanimate objects (such as bicycles); and trade insignia. There is also a handful of miscellaneous designs so idiosyncratic that they confound categorization entirely—a pig riding a bicycle, for instance.

Based on the range of iconographic images and phrases, it seems reasonable to conclude that the majority of tattoos in the Wellcome collection belonged to members of the Foreign Legion[14] and other soldiers, as well as marines and ordinary working men. Whether many of these individuals also served time in military or civilian prisons is far more difficult to determine. Johnston-Saint's (1929) journal record claims that at least some of the preserved tattoos had come from "murderers and criminals of all nationalities."[15] However, this is difficult to determine based on an analysis of tattoo iconography and nineteenth-century criminological sources.

One example of this difficulty can be found in the tattooed skin fragment from a left forearm (fig. 7.9). This specimen bears two tattoos that match descriptions of typical

Table 7.1. Commonly occurring categories of tattoo motifs within the Wellcome Collection, London (ca. 1830–1929)

Category	Description	Frequency*
Military	Regimental insignia	20
	Regimental names	12
	Military costume and weaponry	18
	Medals	3
	Other (name, date and number)	2
Naval	Anchors	9
	Nautical stars	9
	Other (ships, fish, mermaids)	3
Souvenirs (geographic)	Sahara	2
	Africa	1
	Tonkin	1
	Tunisia	1
	Algeria	1
	China	1
	Morocco	1
Patriotic	Coats of arms/flags	5
	Slogans**	3
Religious	Islamic (crescent moon and star)	7
	Christian (crucifixes***)	3
Circus performers	Clowns (male)	3
	Tight-rope walker (female)	1
	Juggler (male)	1
	Strongman	1
	Dancers/acrobats (female)	3

* This column notes the number of tattoos, rather than individual specimens of preserved skin, each of which may carry several tattoos.
** "Honour au Armes"; "Republique Française" x 2
*** In the case of specimen number A617, the tattooed crucifix represents a gravestone, and therefore also falls into the category of memorial tattoos.

"criminal tattoos" found in the criminological literature. Perhaps the most interesting of these tattoos is the phrase "*Mort aux Vaches*," which is faintly visible running vertically down the left edge of the specimen. This phrase literally translates as "Death to Cows," and was a slur directed at the French police.[16] The particular phrase apparently originated during the Franco-Prussian War (1870–1871), when French soldiers used it as a term of abuse for the German *Wache* (guard, or sentinel). The similarity to the French *vaches* may explain the evolution of the expression, which was extended as an insult specifically to the police and gendarmes, and finally to anyone in uniform. The insult was considered so provocative that some offenders appeared in court charged with verbally abusing officers of the law. Writing in 1901, author Anatole France gives some insight into the use and meaning of this expression in his satirical *L'Affaire Crainquebille* (*The Crainquebille Affair*), in which the hapless Jerôme Crainquebille is accused of insulting a police officer. During his trial, his defense clarifies the terms of the insult for the court: "My client is accused of having said: 'Death to cows!' The meaning of this phrase is in no doubt. If you flip through the dictionary of slang, you will read: 'Vachard, lazy, idle; stretching lazily like a cow, instead of working.'—Cow, who sells out to the police; snitch. 'Death to cows!' is said in certain circles" (France 1901:46–47).

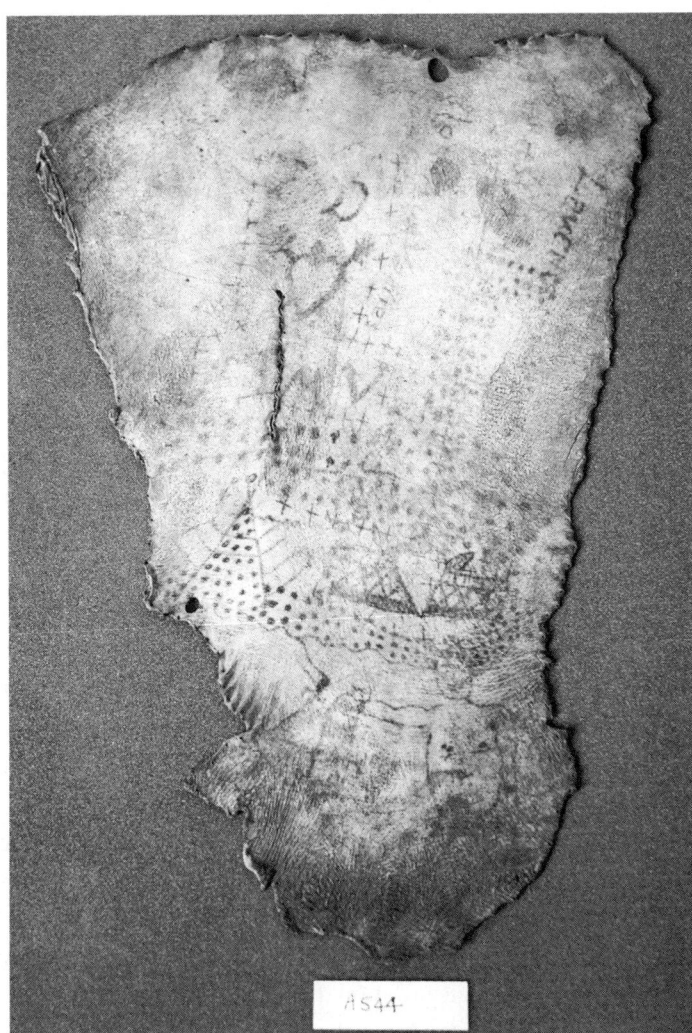

Fig. 7.9. Preserved tattooed human skin from left forearm and hand (likely French, ca. 1850–1920 CE) including the phrase "*Mort aux Vaches*" (Death to Cows) and geometric designs, a tattooed heart pierced with arrows, and a male figure. Science Museum, London (A544). Photograph by Gemma Angel.

According to some writers, a shorthand version of this expression consists of three dots arranged in a triangle, tattooed between the forefinger and thumb. This anti-police slogan has been strongly associated with criminality, and the shorthand version in particular has been read as a form of obscure and cunning criminal argot. Twentieth-century French criminologist Jean Graven (1960:91) writes that, "A variety of dots . . . speaks its own more discrete and mysterious language, which initiates find easy to decipher." However, the signification of the three-dot tattoo varies greatly depending on national and historical context. For example, it has also been associated with sailors, who traditionally received three dots to mark their first voyage. In his lengthy (and frequently contradictory) account of the iconography and meaning of "criminal tattoos," Graven (1960:90) also reports that, "A ring or bracelet with a diamond designates penal servitude." French police superintendent Jacques Delarue confirms this interpretation in his 1950 book *Les Tatouages du "Milieu,"* in which he reproduces drawings of these motifs (Delarue 1990:50, 64).

The interpretation of tattoos comprised of diamonds, and geometric patterns of dots is problematic when one considers the complex cultural exchanges that were often involved in tattoo acquisition among Europeans. In this respect, the modern European tattoo contrasts with the traditional tattooing of many Indigenous societies in a variety of ways. For example, modern European tattoos are not intrinsically connected to one's place in the community, the motifs are not prescribed, and the tattooing process is not culturally embedded in ritual practice. In addition, historic European tattooing was seldom performed therapeutically, and the multiple designs worn by one individual were not generally conceived as a single, interconnected form. This very mutability is a defining feature of the European tattoo: It is frequently marked by heterogeneity, assimilation of foreign tattoo styles, and idiosyncrasy, which arises from an individualism that links specific marks with personal experience.

The tattooed forearm skin (see fig. 7.9), for instance, presents a highly complex array of tattooed symbols that may have multiple cultural reference points. The numerous dots, arranged in vertical and horizontal rows, are interspersed with a series of small crosses, and bear striking resemblance to the traditional geometric tattoo patterns found among the Berber in North Africa.[17] On the other hand, the image of a tattooed heart pierced with arrows and a male figure, Latin lettering, and, of course, the confrontational phrase *Mort aux Vaches,* are distinctly European, as is the French surname "Lavene," which is tattooed vertically down the forearm and possibly presents the name of the individual to whom the tattoo belonged. Therefore, these tattoos may represent broad transcultural influences, rather than a life of criminality and penal servitude, as some criminologists assumed.

The only specimens in the collection that have been categorically connected to a criminal context are a pair of large skin pieces, A555 and A542. These remarkable tattoos occupied the abdomen and right- and left-hand side of the chest of a man identified only as "Fromain" (Angel 2015:211–14). These tattoos are also among the few examples of professional handiwork in the Wellcome Collection (fig. 7.10).

In 1901, French police officials photographed Fromain for the purposes of documenting his tattoos. The original photographic plate is retained in the collection of the Archives de la Préfecture de Police in Paris (Ibid.:211). Ironically, there is nothing in the iconography of his tattoos that would suggest a link to a criminal milieu.[18] Given the frequency of traditional military designs, and taking into account observations of tattooing technique, as well as the historical diffusion of tattooing among military populations, it seems more than likely that the majority of tattoos in the Wellcome Collection were produced in barracks, at sea, or in ports, workshops, and pubs using limited resources by nonprofessionals—a few striking examples of more skilled work notwithstanding.

Fig. 7.10. Preserved tattooed human skin, taken from the anterior torso of a Frenchman identified as "Fromain" (ca. 1901–1929). These tattoos are among the few in the Wellcome Collection that appear to have been applied by a professional tattooist. Science Museum, London (A555, left; A542, right). Photograph by Gemma Angel.

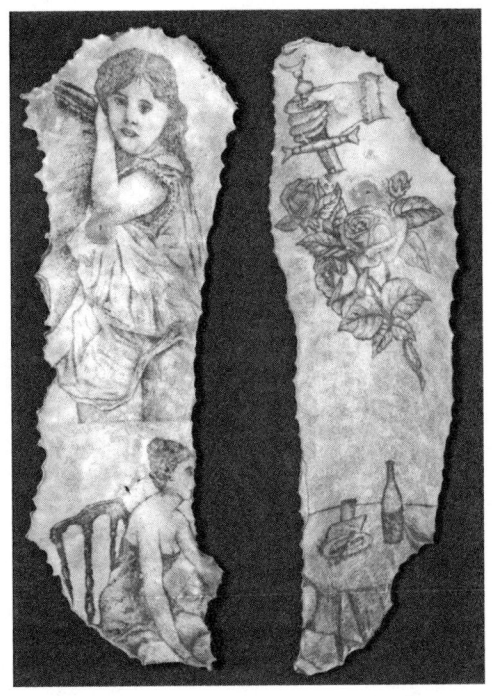

From Iconography to Archive

In addition to iconographic parallels with examples of nineteenth-century tattoos recorded in photographs, the Wellcome Collection tattoos share similarities with many of the hand-traced tattoo drawings collected by scholars such as Alexandre Lacassagne (1843–1924) and published in their works on criminology and the tattoo. That many of these tracings have comparative equivalents among the preserved specimens further suggests that the Wellcome Collection was originally assembled in accordance with the research interests of nineteenth-century criminologists. Examples of similar iconography, such as tradesmen's tattoos depicting various tools, and often presented within a wreath alongside a name, initials, or date, are commonplace. Compare, for example, Lacassagne's tracing of a tinsmith's insignia, with compass, hammer, and shears (fig. 7.11), with the tattooed anvil, hammer, compass, and set square in specimen number A669 (fig. 7.12). Other examples of insignia incorporating tools may not represent tradesmen's tattoos but refer to membership of specific military corps. Specimen number A696, for example, includes the tattooed name "H HEYNAUT" and the year "1856" beneath a crossed shovel and pickaxe—the traditional trade tools of miners, as well as the insignia of engineer battalions.[19]

Perhaps the most striking example of iconographic similitude between Lacassagne's collection of tattoo design tracings and the Wellcome preserved skins is the tattoo of a circus strongman, or wrestler. In Lacassagne's text, this motif is described as the professional emblem of a *lutteur*—a fighter, or wrestler—and may take several forms,

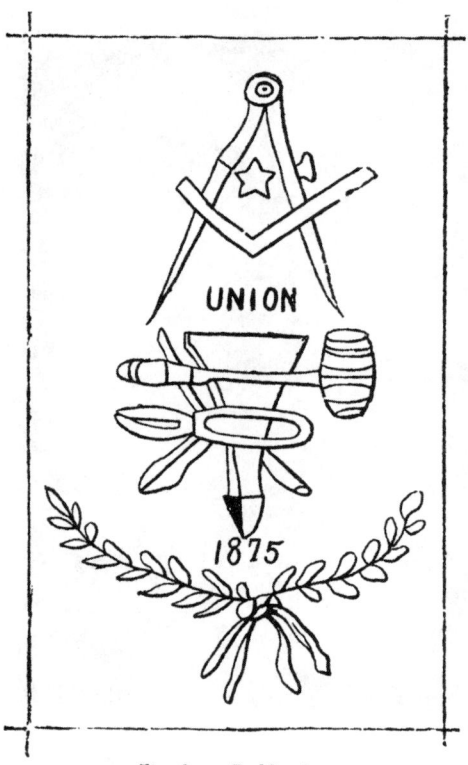

Fig. 8 — Ferblantier.

Fig. 7.11. Tinsmith's insignia, including compass, hammer, and shears, traced from the skin of a tattooed subject (dated to 1875). After Lacassagne and Magitot (1881:32).

Fig. 7.12. Detail of preserved tattooed human skin (likely from France, ca. 1850–1920 CE), showing a tradesman's emblem including an anvil, hammer, and compass. Science Museum, London (A669). Photograph by Gemma Angel.

including a wrestler with weights or dumbbells; two wrestlers in combat; or weights, dumbbells, or cannonballs (Lacassagne 1881b:42). The figure accompanying Lacassagne's text shows a man in a close-fitting long-sleeved shirt, through which his pectoral muscles have been crudely defined, shorts, and what may be stockings (fig. 7.13). He stands with his left hand on his hip and the right arm is raised, a block weight gripped in the hand. The attire of this figure is reminiscent of the classic stage costume of French strongmen performing in carnivals and circuses during the late nineteenth century. A very similar tattooed figure is preserved in specimen number A593 (fig. 7.14). In this example, the strongman is wearing a distinctive costume with the addition of stars decorating his shorts. The tattooist, though unskilled in shading techniques, nevertheless attempted to define the musculature of the figure, marking the pectorals, biceps, and thighs with crudely dotted lines and heavy areas of solid shading. The figure's pose is identical to the tracing reproduced in Lacassange's text. Tattoos depicting circus and other performers make up a small proportion of the Wellcome Collection—a mere nine individual

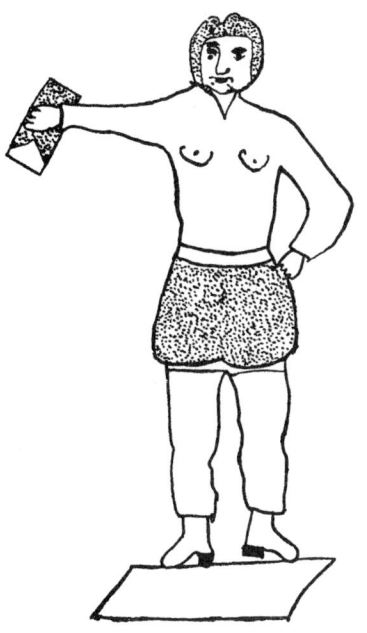

Fig. 7.13. Late nineteenth century tattoo showing a fighter, or strongman's insignia, traced from the skin of a tattooed subject. After Lacassagne (1881b:28).

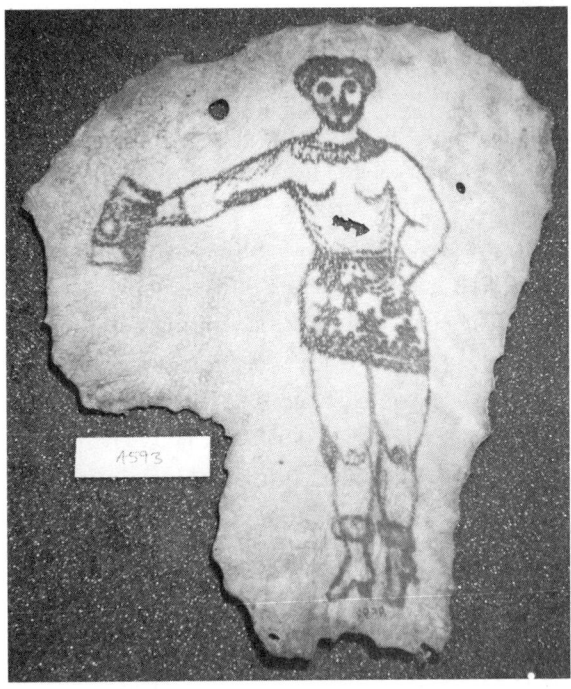

Fig. 7.14. Preserved tattooed human skin (likely from France, nineteenth century CE), depicting a circus strongman. Science Museum, London (A593). Photograph by Gemma Angel.

motifs, or 3 percent of the whole collection. Nevertheless, if Lacassagne's interpretation of these kinds of motifs as "professional emblems" is correct, it is intriguing that this rather marginal professional group is represented in tattoo collections at all.[20]

Lacassagne assembled his first collection of tattoo tracings during 1879–1880 in Médéa Province of Algeria, where he gathered tattoo imagery from the bodies of men enlisted in the 2nd African Battalion (known as the *Bats d'Af*), as well as men serving time in military prisons. During the late nineteenth century, there were four single penal battalions of Infanterie Lègére d'Afrique (Africa Light Infantry), which was composed of French civilian or military criminals, as well as the all-volunteer Légion Étrangère (Foreign Legion). Lacassagne collected his data on the tattoos of 360 soldiers from the 2nd *Bats d'Af*, who had been enlisted in the penal battalions for offenses such as desertion, selling their military-issue effects, or stealing from their comrades (Lacassagne 1881a:290). The remainder he gathered from the military prisons. Lacassagne (Ibid.:289) writes that he "gathered about sixteen hundred tattoos. This collection, which I believe to be unique, is of great importance, since it represents absolutely accurate drawings, inscriptions or emblematic statements on the skin of four hundred people."

In his first published study, Lacassagne did not reproduce any illustrations of regimental motifs, focusing instead on trade emblems and inscriptions. He considered the influence of military life to be a weak factor in the acquisition of tattoos (not at all comparable with the naval milieu, where tattooing was—he believed—a way of life). Rather, Lacassagne identified time spent in prison to be the major factor in the acquisition of tattoos among the battalions he studied: "The large number of tattoos almost always gives the measure of the criminality of the tattooed or at least an appreciation of the number of his convictions; and his stay in prison" (Ibid.:291).

The correspondence is striking between Lacassagne's study of French colonial regiments in North Africa and the range of military tattoos from this region represented in the Wellcome Collection. There is a considerable number of tattoos in the collection that refer to specific African Infantry regiments. Specimen number A775, for example, bears the shorthand regimental inscription of the 2nd *Zouaves*: "2.Z" (fig. 7.15).[21] Other regiments appearing in emblems and inscriptions include the 1st and 3rd *Zouaves*, the 12th *Hussards*, 6th *Chass d'Af* (*Chasseurs d'Afrique*—a light cavalry corps of the French Armée d'Afrique), as well as numerous *ligne* regiments. Although the geographical parallels with Lacassagne's collection of images are certainly significant, none of the regiments represented in the Wellcome Collection previously mentioned were penal battalions. Historically, it was overwhelmingly those groups of men enlisted in penal battalions whose tattoos were the subject of criminological interest.

Significant collections of photographs of tattooed soldiers from the North African penal battalions were also gathered during the late nineteenth century. The majority of these photographs are held in private collections and little is known of their provenance. Jérôme Pierrat and Éric Guillon's 2004 book *Le Tatouage à Biribi*, for example, contains seventy-five black and white photographs of tattooed men from the disciplinary battalions in Algeria, known colloquially as "Biribi."[22] The photographs in this collection of portraits are typically taken against a black background, and are cropped to frame the naked bodies of the tattooed men from the waist up. There are a great many motifs in common between the tattoos depicted in this collection and those preserved in the Wellcome Collection, including phrases such as *Enfant du Malheur* (Child of Misfortune), *Pas de Chance* (No Chance), *Robinet d'Amour* (Love Tap), and *Sans Pitie* (Without/No Pity). Mementos and references to places such as *Souvenir D'Afrique, Maroc,* and *Tunisie* also appear, as do numerous female portraits, military busts, wreaths, lions, leopards, flowers, daggers, and more. Despite the close similarities between the repertoires of motifs, it has proven impossible to make any unequivocal connections between collections of photographs such as those in Pierrat and Guillon's book and collections of preserved tattoos. So while these photographs provide an important resource for the purposes of comparison of iconography and milieu, it has not been possible to conclusively establish whether the Wellcome Collection tattoos were collected from the bodies of North African military soldiers in these locales.

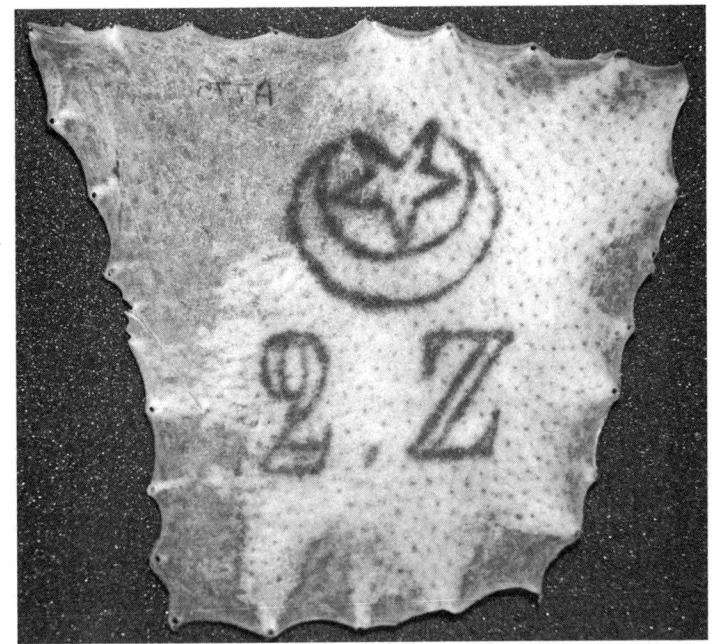

Fig. 7.15. Preserved tattooed human skin from France (ca. 1850–1900 CE), showing the shorthand regimental insignia of the 2nd *Zouaves*, African Infantry regiment. Science Museum, London (A775). Photograph by Gemma Angel.

Conclusions

Material-ethnographic analysis of the tattooed skins in the Wellcome Collection reveals a complex assemblage of multiple biographies, elusive associations with geographies and social groups, and collecting practices suggesting close connections with nineteenth-century criminological studies of the tattoo in particular. An analysis of the type and range of tattoo iconography within the collection demonstrates close affinities with tattoo imagery amassed by criminologists such as Lacassagne as a part of their studies of the tattoo, suggesting that this collection was assembled according to similar principles and preoccupations. The geographical specificity of some of this iconography suggests a military context for many of the tattoos, though not necessarily a penal context. The connection between the tattoos of Fromain (see fig. 7.10) and the photograph held in the police archives in Paris, however, demonstrates that in at least one instance, the context of the prison is relevant. Moreover, the disparity between the geographic locale of the military tattoos and the Parisian police records relating to Fromain further suggests that this collection was assembled over an extended period of time and drawn from a diverse range of sources and unknown individual doctors, criminologists, and collectors.

Although only a fraction of the range of examples of nineteenth-century European tattoo iconography held in storage at the Science Museum in London is represented here, what emerges from these analyses is consistent across the collection as a whole. The Wellcome Collection reveals an episode in the history of the European tattoo during which scholars sought to pathologize a practice that was widespread among working-class men employed in physical labor, including soldiers, sailors, manual tradesman, and circus athletes. Based on the range of images and text in this and other comparative European collections, it is possible to conclude that tattooing in Europe during the nineteenth century was a largely folk art practice performed by nonprofessionals, which combined local traditions with imagery assimilated from encounters with non-European tattooing practices. Tattooing in these contexts may in itself be regarded as a form of collecting, frequently associated with travel, cultural exchange/appropriation, and group allegiance—whether as part of a trade or a regiment—whose roots may be traced to long-standing traditions of Christian pilgrimage tattooing.

Notes

1   In Paris, the anthropology department of the Muséum National d'Histoire Naturelle holds fifty-six pieces of dry-preserved tattooed human skin within their collection. Similarly, the Department of Forensic Medicine at Jagiellonian University in Krakow, Poland, has sixty wet-prepared tattoos; the Instituto Nacional de Medicina Legale e Ciências Forenses collections in Lisbon, Portugal, contains seventy wet-preserved tattoos; anatomist Ludwig Stieda also reported a collection of 200 dried pieces in Königsberg, Germany, in 1911; and there are many more examples of smaller collections in London, Berlin, and Austria (Angel 2013:135).
2   Journal entry dated Saturday, June 15, 1929.
3   French physician and criminologist Alexandre Lacassange sets out six different categories of tattooing technique; the fifth of these, which he terms "*tatouage sous-épidermique,*" describes skin-stitching methods.
4   French naval surgeon Ernst Berchon condemned tattooing as a major health risk. Berchon (1869) claimed that tattooing among seamen could result in serious infection, which in extreme cases could lead to amputation. He managed to convince the French naval ministry to ban the practice in 1861; however, the order was not enforced in practice.
5   Since its publication, tattooist George Burchett's *Memoirs* has been generally accepted as a rare example of a first-hand twentieth-century account of the life and trade of one of the first professional British tattooists. However, as Jon Reiter's recent scholarship reveals, "It is written in the first person, though it is actually a posthumous compilation of Burchett's own archives of newspaper and magazine interviews, tattoo and other memorabilia, plus some additional information provided by the Burchett family" (Reiter 2012:212). Regardless of its veracity as a first-hand account, the description of tattooing methods is nevertheless accurate.
6   I draw on both personal experience working in UK tattoo studios and with tattooing clients here; similar observations can be found in a range of historical practical tattooing guides and tattooists' memoirs (e.g., Burchett and Leighton 1958; Morgan 1912; Purdy 1896; Steward 1990).
7   Typically a grouping of three or five needles would be used for line work, or seven for very large, bold designs that would be later filled in with solid shading.
8   Although some distortion of the tattoos will occasionally occur in dry-preserved specimens as a result of shrinkage during the drying process, it is relatively straightforward to establish whether this is the primary cause of the uneven appearance of a tattoo. Close observation of skin grain patterning across the whole specimen will often determine whether poor preservation technique is the culprit.

9   Saliva was commonly used to mix pigments, moisten needles, or even clean the skin before, during, and after tattooing. These unsanitary practices were reported in a number of medical journals, and were implicated in the spread of infectious diseases such as syphilis and tuberculosis. For an overview of cases, see Angel (2013:165–79).

10 Cinnabar, the common ore of mercury, was highly valued for its bold red pigment despite its toxicity.

11 Further work involving material sampling will be undertaken to establish whether the pigment structure bears these observations out under higher magnification. I thank Dr. Ruth Siddall at University College London Earth Sciences for her collaboration and expertise in identifying these pigments.

12 Tardieu's taxonomy was reworked and refined by a number of other criminologists, of whom Alexandre Lacassagne was the most significant.

13 The most common flower is the pansy, the French flower of remembrance, which appears thirty-six times.

14 Specimen number A532, for example, is tattooed with a "grenade" insignia and regiment number, a popular regimental motif of the Foreign Legion. The addition of a wreath framing the grenade is very similar to the 2nd infantry regiment insignia, which usually depicts the grenade within a horseshoe.

15 Journal entry dated Saturday, June 15, 1929.

16 "Death to Pigs" would be the equivalent insult in English.

17 It is important to point out that these tattoo motifs among the Berber are usually applied to women as protection and fertility symbols. On balance, the French phrases present on specimen number A544 are suggestive of a soldier of one of the French colonial regiments who was stationed in North Africa. It was not uncommon for soldiers to acquire tattoos in the regional style while stationed abroad. As outsiders to the region, the issue of gender-appropriate tattoos in that culture may have been considered unimportant. Numerous tattoos in the Wellcome Collection make explicit reference to a North African military context, for example specimen numbers A626 and A532.

18 Images and discussion of Fromain's tattoos appeared in several criminological texts throughout the mid-twentieth century. See Angel (2015) for discussion of the various erroneous interpretations of these particular tattoos.

19 The 317th Engineer Combat Battalion officially used this insignia from 1943. It usually appeared with the Lorraine Cross and oak tree representing the Argonne Forest, with the motto "By Industry and Honor." Although this example is specific to US troops during the Second World War, many regimental symbols and insignia were used informally by servicemen, and went through many stylistic changes over a long period of time prior to their official adoption by military authorities. Although this particular example has its origins in US-French Allied operations in France during World War I, the crossed pickaxe and shovel predates this period, possibly deriving from nineteenth-century penal battalions.

20 Dr. Daguillon (1895:177–78) also records a "fairground athlete," a "dramatic artist," and a "body builder" among the tattooed patients he studied at Ville-Evrard asylum.

21 The *Zouaves* were largely raised by short-service conscription from the French settler population.

22 Biribi was a French game of chance that was made illegal in 1837; it was known as a "cheat's game." In the French Army, "to be sent to Biribi" was a slang expression for being sent to the disciplinary battalions in the North African colonies.

8

After You Die

PRESERVING TATTOOED SKIN

Aaron Deter-Wolf and Lars Krutak

HISTORIC COLLECTIONS OF TATTOOED HUMAN SKIN, SUCH AS THE pieces from the Wellcome Collection described in chapter 7 of this book, are found in institutions and private collections throughout the world, including Paris, Lisbon, Krakow, Berlin, Bucharest, and Tokyo. These assemblages generally date to the nineteenth and early twentieth centuries, and while the specific impetus for the collections is sometimes murky, most appear to have been gathered from members of lower social classes as part of anatomical and medical studies. With the exception of examples from the Fukushi Collection (Hardy 1987) in Tokyo, many were likely obtained from bodies of the deceased without the prior consent of their bearers.

The rapid proliferation of tattooing in Western culture over the past two decades has accompanied widespread acknowledgment of the personal significance that tattoos hold for their bearers, as well as recognition of the artistic value of the tattoos themselves (Bezu 2013; Davidson 2017; Davis 2015). As a result of these shifting views, the collection and preservation of tattooed skin from deceased individuals has emerged from the shadows of morbid curiosity and is poised to become part of the global consumer economy. Toward this end, two organizations have recently been launched that will work with tattooed individuals who want to have their tattoos preserved after their death.

In 2014, Dutch tattoo artist and illustrator Peter van der Helm launched the Foundation for the Art and Science of Tattooing,[1] an organization based in Amsterdam that may be the first commercial tattoo preservation business in the world (fig. 8.1). "We as

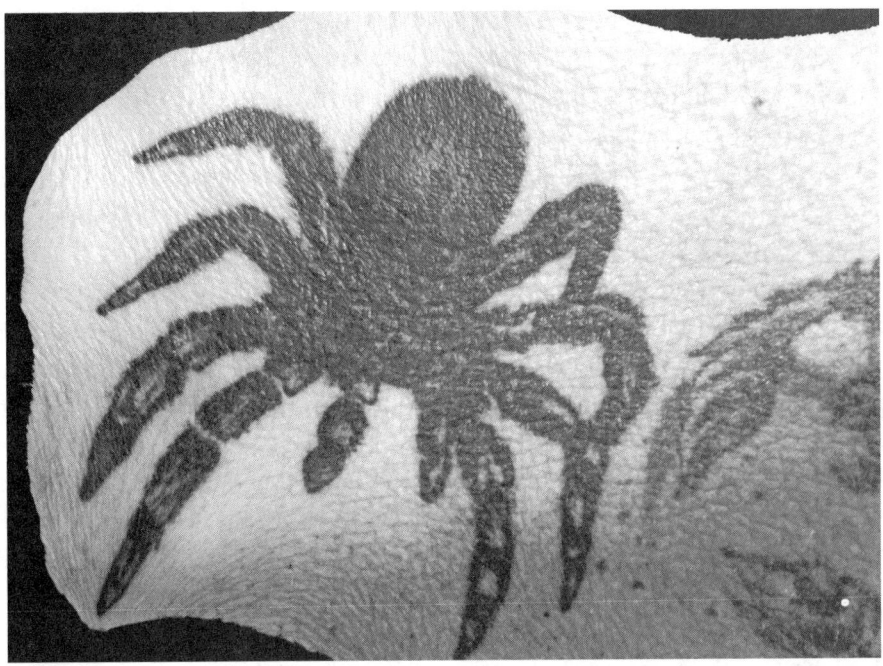

Fig. 8.1. Modern tattoo preserved by the Foundation for the Art and Science of Tattooing (Amsterdam), at the request of the deceased (n.d.). Photograph courtesy Peter van der Helm.

tattoo artists, enthusiasts, and lovers all have our tattoos done with special meaning and purpose," van der Helm told *Inked Magazine* in 2013 (Connell 2013). "Not all of them might be good to use in our service and some of them you might definitely want to take to your grave but others can be an inspiration for people in the tattoo world and around you like friends and family who couldn't understand the tattoos while you were around."

"Everyone spends their lives in search of immortality and this is a simple way to get a piece of it," van der Helm was quoted as saying to Reuters news agency in a separate interview (Deutsch 2013). "Everybody with tattoos has that idea. It's not a new idea, we just found a way to actually do it."

Van der Helm's process begins after an individual dies. Their tattooed skin is removed by a pathologist and either frozen or packaged in formaldehyde, ideally within forty-eight hours of death. The specimen is then sent to a processing center where water and fat are gradually extracted and replaced with silicone or another liquid polymer in a process known as plastination. This technique was developed in 1977 by the German Anatomist Gunther von Hagens at the University of Heidelberg's Institute of Anatomy. Von Hagens patented the process in 1977 and 1982, and used the technique in the mid-1990s for his exhibition *BODY WORLDS*, which displayed preserved human bodies and body parts.

Those interested in donating their tattoos to the Foundation for the Art and Science of Tattooing for preservation must complete a donation form available on the foundation website. Although the form indicates intent, it does not constitute a binding contract. Enrolled participants may withdraw from the program at any time without providing a reason. Participants must also pay a cost to fund preservation, with about €300 covering preservation of a single four-inch tattoo (plate 9).

According to the donation form, preserved tattoos will be managed as "anatomical works of art," to be used "exclusively for research, educational, therapeutic and artistic purposes." Donors may request that their tattoos not be displayed, and may also specify that they can be displayed anonymously. In addition, the specimens may be loaned out to the family of the deceased in perpetuity, with the option of return to the foundation for curation and storage at any time.

While the first clients were American, van der Helm's foundation is steadily gaining a predominantly European clientele. To date the foundation has preserved five tattoos, all of which are on loan to relatives of the deceased. Most of the donors enrolled in

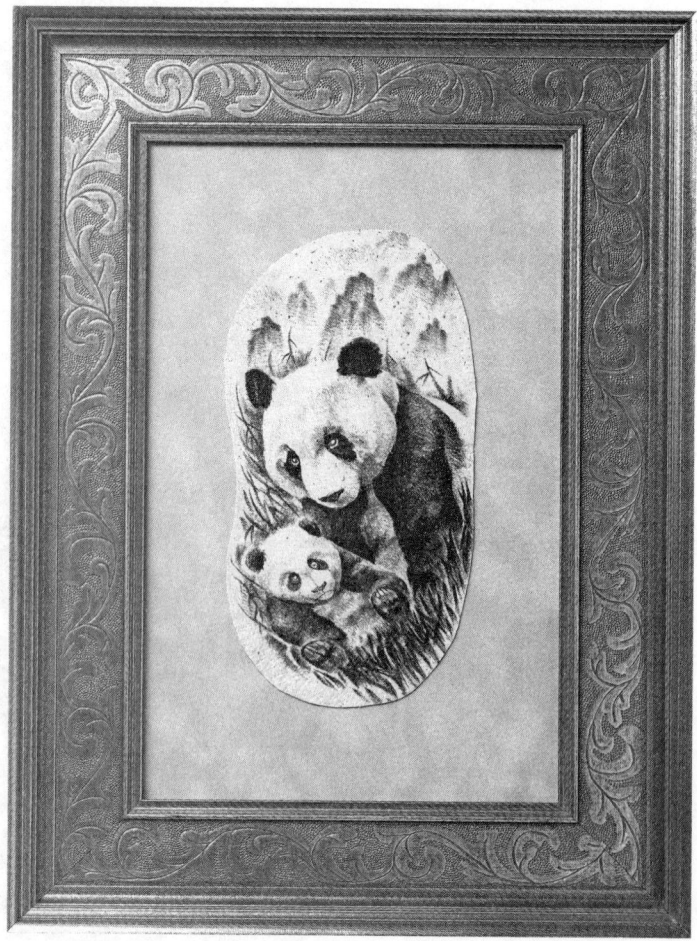

Fig. 8.2. "Pandas." Tattoo preserved by the National Association for the Preservation of Skin Art (NAPSA), 2015. Tattoo art by Bryan Krause. Photograph courtesy of Charles Hamm/NAPSA.

the foundation are still alive, van der Helm told us: "Not everyone deceases in a rapid manner, and I wish my clients long and happy lives" (personal communication, March 13, 2016).

On the other side of the Atlantic, another organization of tattoo enthusiasts and artists based in the suburbs of Cleveland, Ohio, invented a process to help people preserve their tattoos for posterity. The National Association for the Preservation of Skin Art (NAPSA)[2] was launched in 2015. Its founder is Charles Hamm, a heavily tattooed former Klynveld Peat Marwick Goerdeler (KPMG) partner and entrepreneur. Hamm has hundreds of hours of tattooing on his body, including several tattoos designed by family members. Each one of his body marks carries personal and family meanings, and Hamm wanted to preserve them physically after death for those people he loves most. This inspired him to create NAPSA.

Lars Krutak visited NAPSA headquarters in January 2016 and spoke with Hamm and his staff. Hamm told Krutak: "I will be cremated eventually, but I want to leave my wife, children, and family a part of me. An urn of ashes on the mantelpiece is one

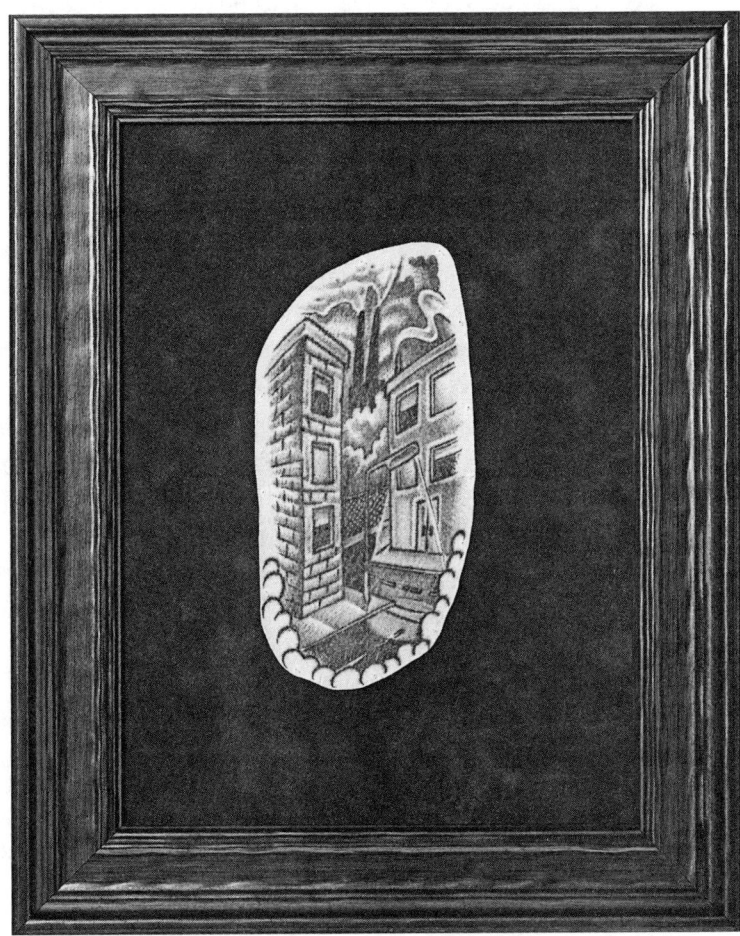

Fig. 8.3. "Cleveland Street." Tattoo preserved by NAPSA (2015). Tattoo art by Al Garcia. Photograph courtesy of Charles Hamm/NAPSA.

PRESERVING TATTOOED SKIN

thing, but a beautifully framed tattoo is another and certainly more appealing to look at. You can also remove the frame and touch the tattoo, touch the person that you want to remember for eternity."

Reflecting on the project, Hamm noted it took a lot of planning and research to develop the proprietary process to preserve the tattoos. "We had nothing to test it on. Luckily, I had a dramatic weight loss of 100 pounds, so I went to a plastic surgeon and asked if he could cut that skin off [pointing to his sides]. I asked him, 'Could you draw a line around the areas you'll be cutting?' He said 'Yes!' and then I replied, 'I am coming back next week with two tattoos in those spots, and I want that skin back after you're done!' So that's how we tested the process and it worked to perfection."

Upon its launch, NAPSA required a one-time registration fee of $115 and an annual payment of $60. Once enrolled, you could opt to register one tattoo about the size of a chest piece for postmortem preservation. Members could also pay additional fees to preserve other tattoos or to double the size of the ink to be commemorated. Membership also required that a beneficiary be designated, and they would be responsible for notifying NAPSA about the death of a client within eighteen hours. Beneficiaries would receive a $2,000 stipend from the to-be deceased to defray the costs of preserving the tattoo.

NAPSA's tattoo preservation efforts were dissolved in February 2016.[3] A new company, Save My Ink Forever (SMIF)[4], emerged, and now tattoo preservation is managed directly through funeral homes and crematoria that are preferred providers in the SMIF network. Before NAPSA's preservation efforts ceased, two dozen tattoos were conserved there (examples are shown in figs. 8.2 and 8.3). As of April 2016, three tattoos have been preserved by SMIF, and their list of clients continues to grow as more preferred providers are added.

SMIF encourages interested clients to sit down with their families and discuss their desires before reaching out to a funeral home director. After these conversations take place, the funeral home will then contact SMIF for a kit to temporarily preserve the tattooed skin. Once SMIF receives the skin, it takes two months to process it before it is returned framed to the beneficiary. Like every great painting, every tattoo has a story, and SMIF wants to preserve as many tattoos as possible.

Notes

1. www.wallsandskin.com/preserveyourtattoos/.
2. www.savemyink.com.
3. Today, NAPSA has focused its efforts on becoming one of the largest online tattoo communities through its dedicated website. To date, it features the largest directory of worldwide tattoo events, maintains a massive virtual gallery of tattoo art, and has developed a tattoo artist-specific live streaming app for video coverage of tattoo and art sessions, among other things.
4. www.savemyink.tattoo.

Part 2

Tools

9

The Antiquity of Tattooing in Southeastern Europe

Petar N. Zidarov

About 460 BCE, Herodotus (Book V, 6) wrote that among the Thracians, "to be tattooed is a sign of noble birth, while to bear no such marks is for the baser sort." This curious testimony is among the first written evidence of the practice of voluntary tattooing in the written history of mankind. Contrasting accounts explain that Thracian women began to tattoo in an attempt to reclaim their bodies after being forcibly marked by Scythians while in captivity[1] or were tattooed by their husbands as a punishment for killing Orpheus.[2] The credibility of these early literary accounts may be questioned as heavily biased, considering the use of *otherness* as a literary technique (Dimova 2014:36; Hartog 1988). While a critical assessment of Herodotus's narrative on Scythian customs suggests that the Father of History relied heavily on informants who were mixing observations and ideology (Ivantchik 2011), the reliability of literary evidence on early historic tattooing in southern Europe is to a certain extent indirectly confirmed by extant mummified tattooed bodies buried roughly during Herodotus's time in Siberia and the Altai Mountains of Central Asia (see Pankova, chapter 5, this volume), and by images of tattooed Thracian women and goddesses illustrated on Athenian and Apulian red-figure pottery made throughout the fifth and fourth centuries BCE (fig. 9.1).

Contrary to Herodotus's account, the tattoos depicted on Apulian red-figure pottery are located exclusively on the hands and feet of goddesses and Thracian women, but not on depicted Thracian nobles (Tsiafakis 2015; Zimmermann 1980:166). These marks usually consist of relatively simple geometric patterns and compositions including straight

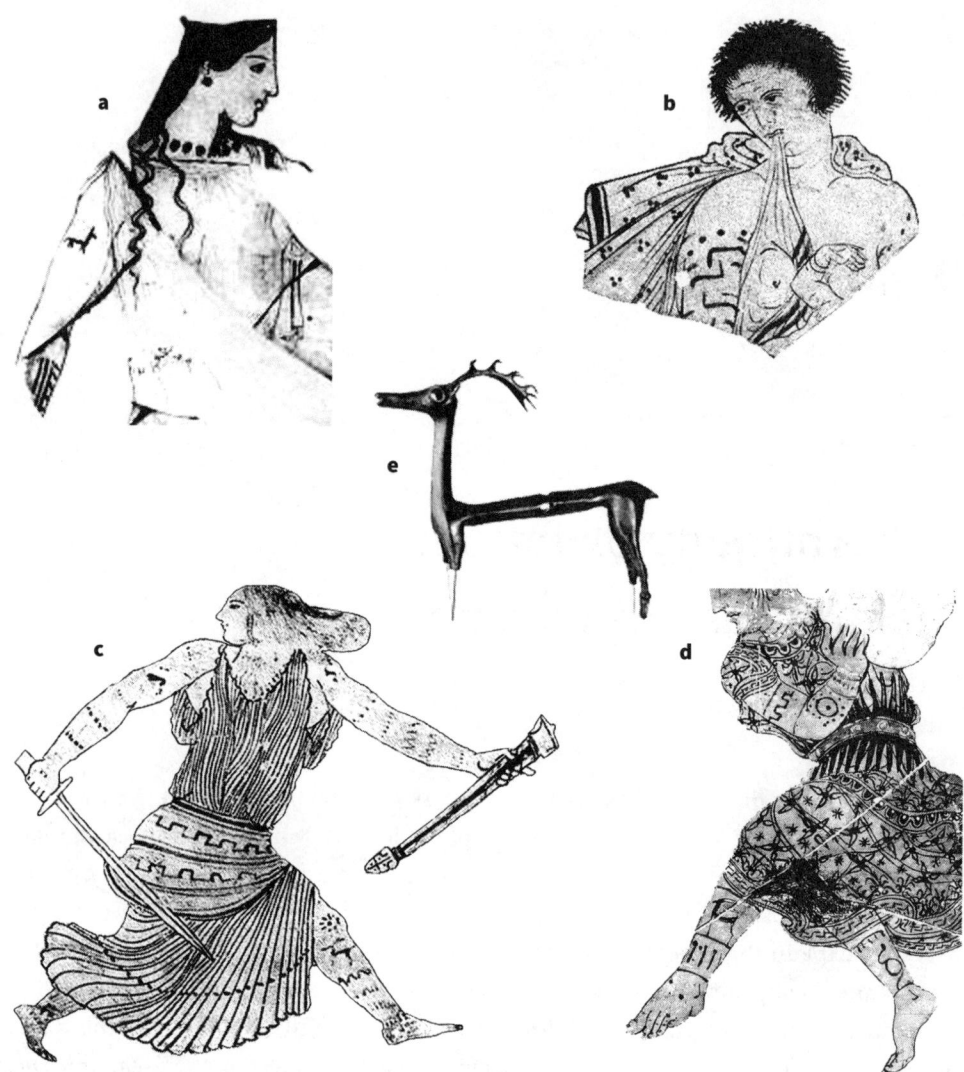

Fig. 9.1. Examples of ancient artwork depicting possible Thracian tattoo designs: (a-d) Illustrations of women on Athenian and Apulian red-figure pottery (fifth and fourth centuries BCE). (e) Bronze stag from Sevlievo, Bulgaria, kept at National Archaeological Museum Sofia (Photograph courtesy of Krassimir Georgiev). Drawings modified after artifacts from: (a) National Museum of Athens, (b) British Museum, (c) Munich Antikensammlungen, (d) Allard Pierson Museum Amsterdam.

lines, chevrons, meanders, and crosses (Tsiafakis 2015; Vasileva 2016:30; Zimmermann 1980:184), all of which are reminiscent of Thracian clothing and textiles depicted both on red-figure vessels and on ceramics from southwestern Bulgaria referred to as *Tsepina* (or *Tsruncha*) (Domaradzki 1990, 1994; Georgieva 2003; Hänsel 1976). The few recurring Thracian figural tattoo patterns that appear in pictorial sources include the sun, the snake, and the deer, the latter in seemingly canonical postures reminiscent both of an extant object from the area of Sevlievo in Bulgaria (Aruz et al. 2000:1; Casson and Venedikov 1977:16; Karadzhinov 2013) (fig. 9.1e), as well as of imagery seen on the tattooed mummies from Pazyryk (see Pankova, chapter 5, this volume).

Interestingly, images of tattooed bodies are almost absent in the native Thracian context. They do not appear in either regional metalwork, on the portraits of nobility known from monumental tombs, or on decorated ceramics used in the Greek colonies along the Thracian coast and distributed farther inland. The only exceptions are two massive parade greaves (leg armor) of Thracian rulers dating to the fourth century BCE. These artifacts depict female faces bearing possible tattoo designs, and were found among the rich sepulchral deposits in the Vratsa tumulus (known also as Mogilanska mogila) in northwest Bulgaria and in a burial mound near Agighiol in southeast Romania.[3] The ornamentation on the Vratsa greave consists of medium-wide equidistant horizontal bands covering only the right half of the face (fig. 9.2a). The bands on the greave from Agighiol cover the entire face and run horizontally between the eyes and mouth. Additional marks are arranged in a radial pattern at the chin and follow the curvature of the nose and superciliary arch, eventually crossing at the forehead.

Both these decorated—likely tattooed—faces, as well as unadorned female faces depicted on other parade greaves from Thrace, are usually identified as divine characters.[4] Similarly, depictions of tattooed bodies that appear during the Archaic period of Greek art (ca. 800–479 BCE) are likewise considered indicative of the superhuman nature of the portrayed characters (Fellmann 1978:29). It therefore remains uncertain to what extent this iconography could be taken as literal pictorial evidence supporting Herodotus's claims for voluntary tattooing of humans.

Taken together it seems likely that if Herodotus's information regarding Thracian tattooing was based on observation, it was already rather outdated in his time, and had been superseded by later influences derived from different sources of origin. Instead, a glimpse of what the actual early tribal tattoos of the Thracians could have looked like may perhaps be gained by examination of the skillful artistic renderings of wild animals and fantastic creatures featured on locally produced silver horse trappings, like those from Letnitsa, Vratsa, and Zlatinitsa-Malomirovo in Bulgaria (fig 9.2b–g). The compositions of these pieces are based on principles of bilateral and rotational symmetry and appear so aesthetically modern that some have been adopted as corporate logos (e.g., that of the *Bulgarian e-Journal of Archaeology*).[5]

Ornamented Prehistoric Terra-Cotta Figurines

Artistic depictions of possibly tattooed bodies have also been recovered during excavations at sites across the Near East and southeastern Europe dating to the sixth and fifth millennia BCE. These artifacts consist of a significant series of terra-cotta figurines in the shape of humans, animals, and fantastic zoomorphic creatures, some of which are decorated with incised or painted ornamentation closely following anatomic details

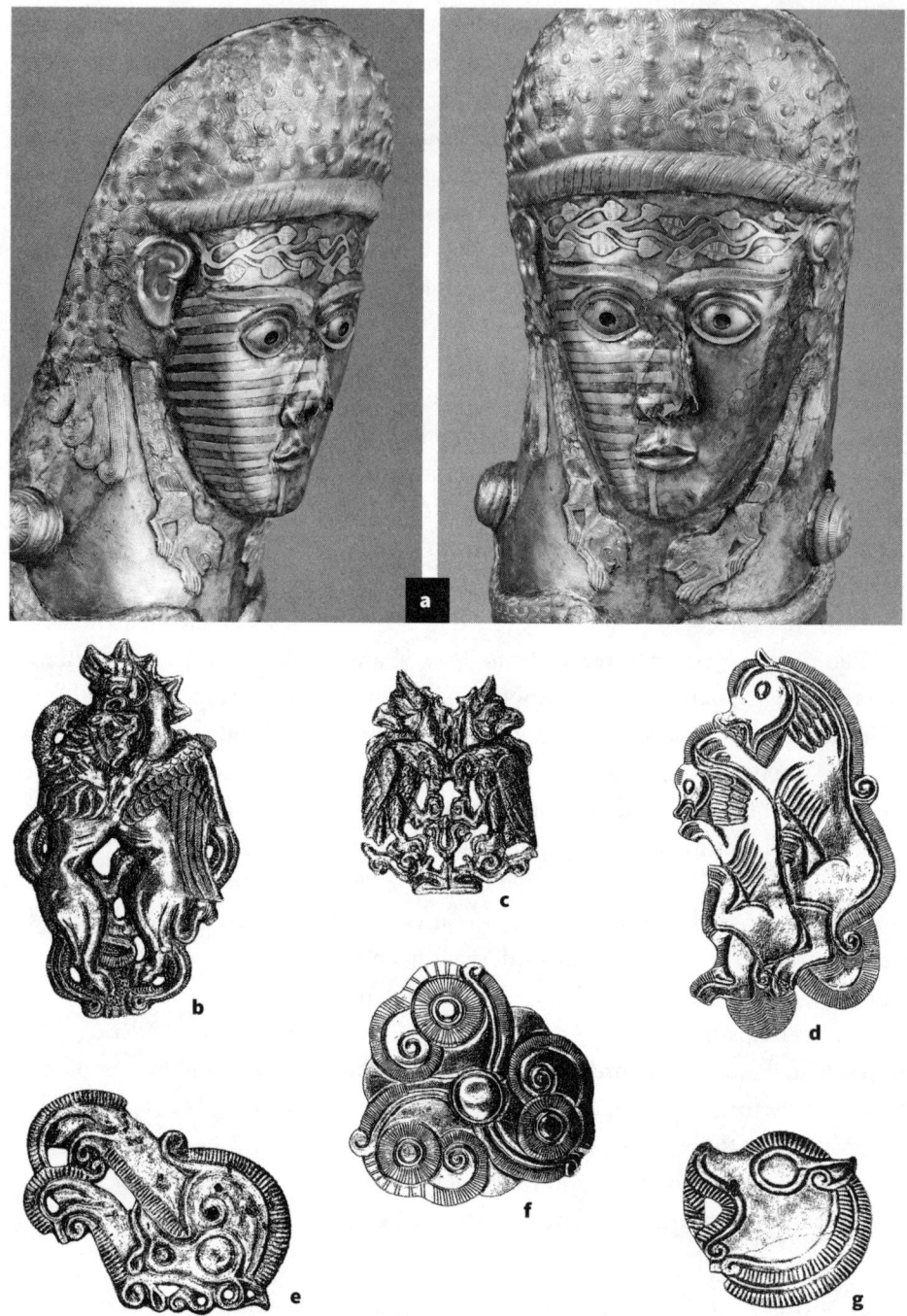

Fig 9.2. Thracian metalwork exhibiting possible tattoo motifs (Bulgaria, fourth century BCE). (a) Detail of upper portion of a parade greave from the Mogilanska tumulus, Vratsa (photograph courtesy of Krassimir Georgiev). (b through g) heraldic imagery on silver horse trappings from the Letnitsa treasure (b, c) (modified after Rabadzhiev 2015), (d, e) Mogilanska tumulus (modified after Teodossiev 2015), and (f, g) Malomirovo tomb (modified after Agre 2015).

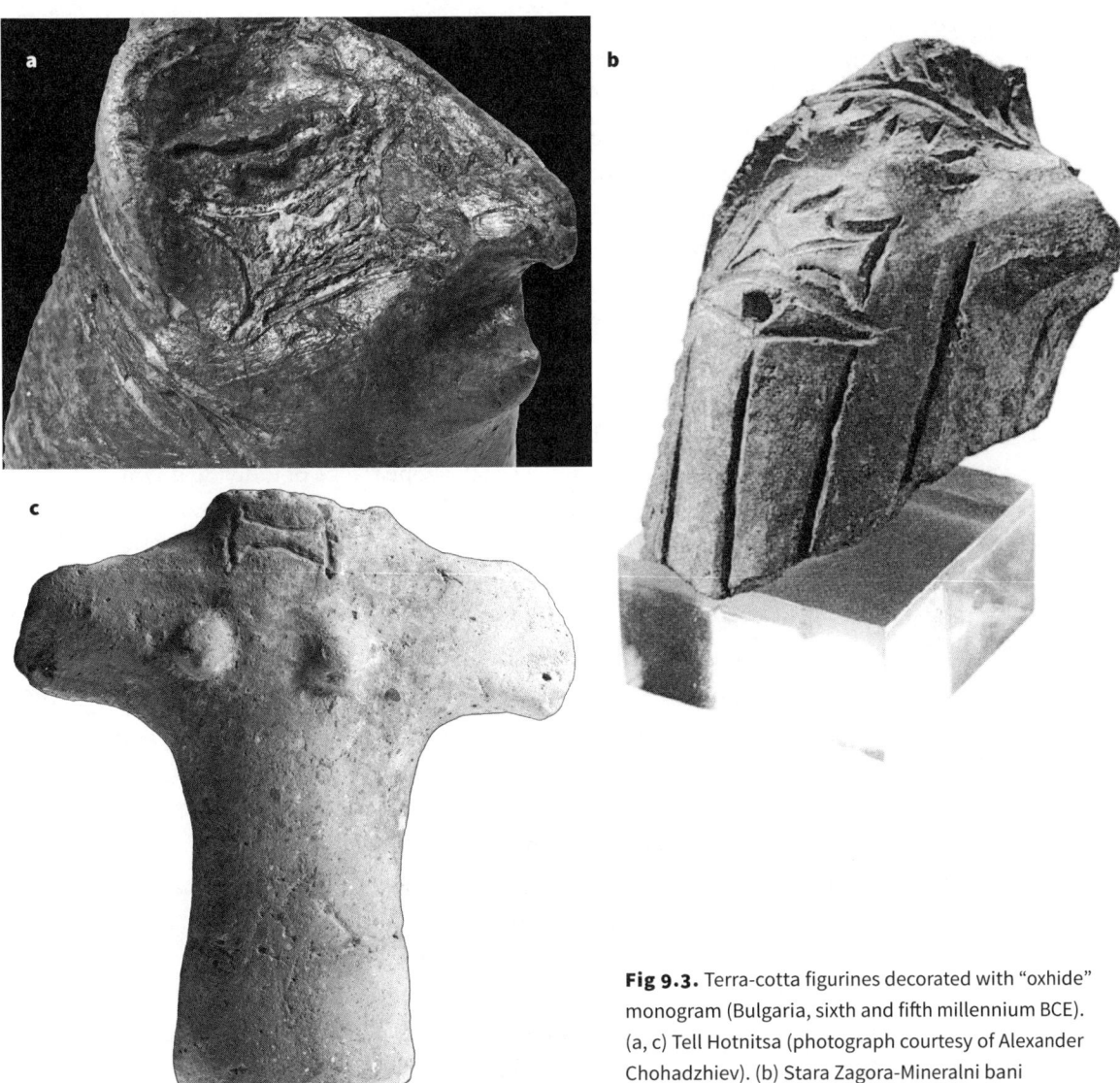

Fig 9.3. Terra-cotta figurines decorated with "oxhide" monogram (Bulgaria, sixth and fifth millennium BCE). (a, c) Tell Hotnitsa (photograph courtesy of Alexander Chohadzhiev). (b) Stara Zagora-Mineralni bani (photograph courtesy of Tsvetan Chetashki).

(figs. 9.3 and 9.4) (Hansen 2007, 2011). As with figurines from elsewhere in the world, their ornamental design likely provides a glimpse into the repertoire of possible motifs and compositions that could have been rendered as temporary or permanent body art.[6] One unresolved issue is whether these figurines represent humans, gods, imaginary ancestors, or supernatural beings employed in some form of ritualized activities or acting as vehicles for sympathetic magic.[7]

While some of these figurines were dumped with rubbish in the streets and in pits and around settlements (Gaydarska et al. 2005; Müller 2012), others are buried in graves and cenotaphs alongside high-value artifacts (Slavchev et al. 2015; Ţerna 2013; Vajsov

2002). These varying attitudes toward the production, consumption, and deposition of figurines hint at their differential use and the likely function of some as effigies of real persons or ancestors (Todorova 1986:196–203). Therefore, it seems justified to analyze the decoration of these figurines as a proxy for human body treatment.

The transferability of ornamental motifs and compositions between material culture and tattoo designs is known from ethnographic documents and is considered a potential correlate for temporary and permanent prehistoric body art (Streit 1935:681). Nevertheless, this transferability of patterns and designs also makes it difficult to determine whether ornamentation depicted on figurines represents textile patterns or body art forms, since costume design may also be decorated with linear ornamentation (e.g., Lüning 2005). Some of the useful working criteria for assessing possible body art depicted on (apparently) human figurines include the positive/negative correlation between ornament and anatomical shapes, as well as the appearance of individual symbols and designs on places like the face, which are unlikely to have been covered by cloth (see figs. 9.3a and 9.4e). However, even when the depicted ornamentation clearly follows the body contours, it is difficult to discern representations of tattooing from temporary application of paint or even scarification (see Renaut, chapter 17, this volume).

Throughout the sixth millennium BCE, figurines from southeastern Europe are rendered in a schematic manner with triangular heads and exaggerated noses, and most artistic attention is paid to variations in shapes, proportions, and posture. Less common examples, including figurines from Ovcharovo-Gorata (see fig. 9.4a) and the later Bulgarian Neolithic assemblages from Samovodene, Usoe (see fig. 9.4b), and Durankulak, display linear and punctated ornamental designs.[8]

The early fifth millennium BCE witnesses a trend in which the shapes and proportions of human figurines become more naturalistic, while at the same time faces retain a schematic modeling. It is during this same period that some full-bodied female figurines become covered with culture-specific incised ornamentation. Some of these are covered with geometric motifs and compositions executed with incision or painting, in frequencies that vary depending on the local chronology and cultural sequence (see figs. 9.3 and 9.4). Simple dots and incisions are most often used to mark anatomical features, such as eyes, mouth, hair, and elements of the costume including belts, straps across the chest, shirts, pants, hats, and even masks.

Corresponding figurines with male attributes are rather rare among the southeastern European examples, and those that exist are usually devoid of linear designs. Therefore, if one considers the "population" of figurines representative of the associated human population, it would seem that body decoration was far more frequent among women than men, a trend mirrored in many Indigenous societies (e.g., Krutak 2007). A similar female-focused tradition of body decoration is perhaps presented in the find of six couples of female and male (androgyne) figurines dating to the Cucuteni A period (ca. 4600–4100 BCE) at Dumești, Romania. In that assemblage the female figurines are completely covered with incised decoration, while the male characters seem to wear only

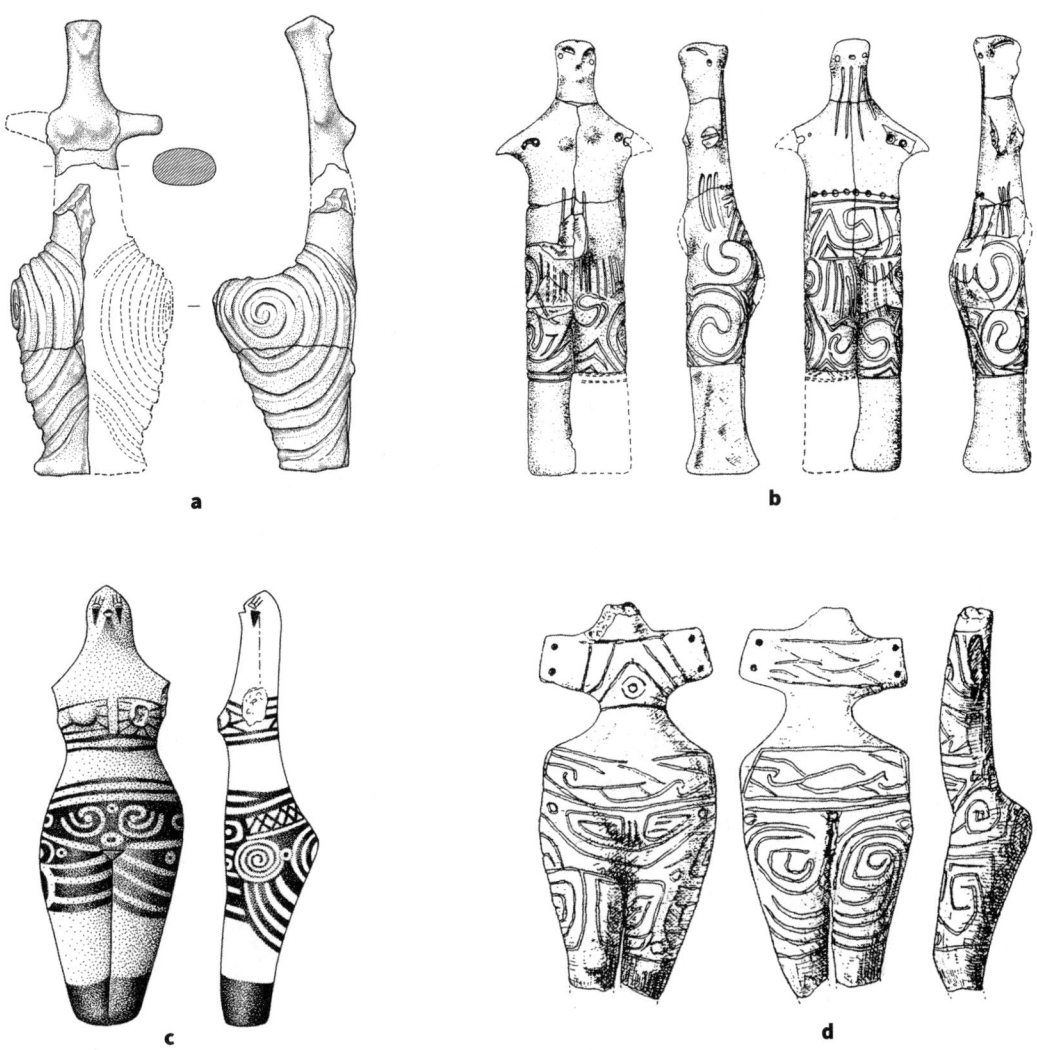

Fig 9.4. Decorated terra-cotta figurines (Bulgaria, sixth and fifth millennium BCE). (a) Ovcharovo-Gorata (drawing reproduced courtesy of Ivan Vajsov). (b) Usoe (drawing reproduced courtesy of Ivan Vajsov). (c) Polyanitsa (redrawn after Todorova and Vajsov 2001: plate 54.609). (d) Golyamo Delchevo (redrawn after Hansen 2007: fig. 123).

waist and shoulder straps (see fig. 17.11 and accompanying discussion by Renaut, chapter 17, this volume) (Draşovean and Popovici 2008: figs. 74–76; Maxim-Alaiba 1987).

Other archaeological examples of decorated figurines from southeastern Europe exhibit linear patterns at key locations on the face, including examples from the Bulgarian sites of Gradeshnitsa, Polyanitsa, and Golyamo Delchevo (see figs. 9.4c and 9.4d). Other samples from Pietrele in Romania display motifs limited to the torso, pelvis, and upper leg.

The specific motifs depicted on figurines from the region vary widely, and may consist of individual symbols or signs, friezes, and complex compositions. In some instances, intricate compositions covering the torso, breasts, and/or the legs of these artifacts have been interpreted as elements of clothing, although that interpretation is far from conclusive. There does appear to be a positive correlation between certain patterns and where they appear on the bodies of figurines. For example, spiral patterns most often decorate the buttocks or the belly, while the latter may be also marked by rhomboids.

Isolated patterns (monograms) are among the most suggestive examples of decoration on figurines that may represent tattooing (see fig. 9.3). The so-called oxhide pattern appearing on either side of the Danube River and Balkan mountain range is among the best recognizable single motif. These monograms are located across the body, although almost never on the arms.[9] Specific examples include marks depicted on the neck (Hansen 2007:238, fig. 137; Todorova and Vajsov 2001: fig. 54.608), the chest (Hansen 2007:335 fig. 189.10; Kalchev 2005:43), on the belly (Mitkova 2005; Todorova and Vajsov 2001: fig. 54.607), over the loin (Draşovean and Popovici 2008:153), on the back (Atanasova 2011: fig. 5; Todorova and Vajsov 2001: fig. 51.599), and on the thighs (Vajsov 1998: fig. 2.3).

Some of the same iconographic elements depicted on these figurines also appear as isolated patterns on stamp seals (*pintaderas*), which may have been used for application of temporary designs to human skin and/or leather.[10] The most popular patterns found on stamp seals from the early sixth millennium BCE include wavy lines, concentric circles, spirals, meanders, triangles, crosses, swastikas, and intertwined horizontal S-shaped patterns.[11]

Copper Age Tattoo Masters from Pietrele

Beyond possible depictions of tattooing in the figural art of southeastern Europe, another category of considerably less known and rarely studied archaeological data also has the potential to contribute considerably to our knowledge of the earliest stages of tattooing: the tools for applying tattoos. The conventional technology for the execution of tattoos facilitates the insertion of a pigment (most often from crushed or pulverized carbon) beneath the epidermis using a fine, sharp needle. In some places around the world individual needles were bound tightly together in a bundle (e.g., Deter-Wolf et al., chapter 13, this volume; Krutak 2014a; Robitaille 2007). These multipoint tools were especially useful for creating wide lines or filled areas, the application of which using a single needle would pose a major test to the patience of both the tattooist and the tattooed. Although no such instruments have been securely identified to date from ancient Thrace, this may well reflect the poor state of research in settlement studies from this region and period (Popov 2015) or the use of perishable materials such as thorns of wild plants.

The spatial association of sharp needles and ochre pigments in caves in southern France has long been discussed as possible evidence that tattooing could have been practiced in Europe since the late Paleolithic (e.g., Péquart and Péquart 1962). However, the 1991 discovery of the mummified Iceman in the melting glaciers of the Ötztal Alps on the Austrian-Italian border confirmed unequivocally the use of tattooing, likely for medicinal or therapeutic purposes, by at least 3300 BCE (Kutschera et al. 2000). Recently Deter-Wolf and colleagues suggested that the sixty-one tattoos on the Iceman's body seem to reflect a mature stage of development of a tattooing tradition (Deter-Wolf et al. 2016).

It is possible that bone needles were used for tattooing in the Balkans a millennium before the Iceman's death, among the Late Copper Age (4500–4200 BCE) inhabitants of the tell, or artificial mound, settlement near Pietrele, Romania, on the shore of the Danube River (Zidarov 2009). While fieldwork at the site is still in progress and contextual data is not yet solidified, the continuing study of the Pietrele collection has revealed further evidence for the possible use not only of individual needles as tattoo implements, but also of needles bundled in combs, which may indicate the presence of relatively specialized tattoo "masters" even at this early age.

Tell-like sites similar to Pietrele appeared in the Lower Danube area during the early fifth millennium BCE (Reingruber 2014), probably as a result of colonization processes from Upper Thrace in southern Bulgaria where this settlement pattern evolved over a millennium earlier (Todorova 1978, 1982). However, the sudden appearance of weaponry (Boyadzhiev 2011; Ivanova 2008) and a number of local adaptations, such as specialized cattle and sheep herding and dairying strategies, likely indicate processes of delayed acculturation and cultural hybridization of several communities.[12]

Excavations at Pietrele revealed parallel habitation on and off the limits of the tell itself, as well as maintenance of far-reaching contacts for procuring copper and Mediterranean shells used for exotic ornamentation. The inhabitants of Pietrele also achieved a certain degree of monumentality in their architecture, with alternating episodes of house burning and rebuilding, using considerable amounts of clay-plaster daub (Hansen 2015; Reingruber 2011; Reingruber et al. 2010).

Although tell communities rarely exceeded twenty households, the excavations at Pietrele revealed a considerable degree of differentiation among the house inventories. For example, the data indicate varying degrees of knowledge and specialization in hunting, fishing, and the use of medicinal plants as compared to textile production and animal husbandry in neighboring households (Benecke et al. 2013; Hansen et al. 2008; Reingruber 2012). Tell sites are sometimes considered to be social arenas used predominantly for ritual performance rather than regular habitation (Bailey 1999; Raczky et al. 2011). However, the accumulation of household waste and other signs of habitation at the tell site suggests no significant spatial differentiation between domestic and ritual activities.

The bone and antler artifacts from Pietrele form a large and diverse collection of various tools, weapons, ornaments, and figurines numbering over 2,000 objects (Benecke et al. 2013; Hansen 2011; Zidarov 2008). Various types of animal bone awls and pins are among the most ubiquitous finds, and vary greatly in terms of size, shape, and species (Nørgaard 2011; Zidarov 2007). Most of these tools are sized to comfortably fit in a human hand and would not have been hafted, or set into in a handle, with minor exceptions. Two exceptions consist of very thin pointed implements fashioned from split and ground hare or sheep/goat metapodials and finely carved rib slivers of larger mammals. These items are far more fragile, and likely would have required binding or hafting (fig. 9.5 and plate 10). These tools typically measure 50 to 70 mm (rarely exceeding 100 mm) in length, 4 to 7 mm wide, and no more than 1.2 mm thick. The diameter of the point, measured at 50 mm from the tip, usually does not exceed 0.3 to 0.5 mm.

The first type of needle is produced by axial division of metapodials of small mammals about the size of a hare. Once halved, the two parts were extensively ground to achieve the desired outline and dimensions. The distal epiphyses are often partially retained and although all of their sides and surfaces are ground flat, sometimes a hollow cavity remains on the ventral side, where occasionally residues of red or white mineral pigments could be observed. The second type of needle is made from the compact tissue on the diaphyseal wall of similarly sized long bones. These tools typically lack remains from epiphyseal articulations, and are made either from splintered bones or prepared blanks that have been ground flat but exhibit occasionally shallow furrows filled with residues of red or white pigments.

The observation of over 2,000 bone and antler artifacts from Pietrele reveals that similar pigments are generally absent on other types of bone tools. So, the chance that pigments randomly accumulated on the surfaces of the needles found at Pietrele as a result of post-depositional taphonomic processes is considered unlikely.

One group of bone needles from Pietrele was recovered from a burned-out structure identified within Trench F (see fig. 9.5c and 9.5d) (Hansen et al. 2007). As a result of the high temperatures generated during the conflagration of that house, the organic component of the bone was pyrolized, and the mineral components were bound together in a monolithic calcinated block, wherein the needles were stuck sidewise together as if hafted in a comb. Unfortunately the preservation of this find is too poor for reconstructing details.

Another set of better preserved bone needles from Trench B at Pietrele excavated in 2011 (Hansen et al. 2012) exhibits remains of linearly arranged traces of red ochre on their edges, indicating they may have been bound together into a single multipoint tool (see plate 10). The needles are rectangular to triangular in cross section, and are considerably curved along their length. The longest (broken at the base) is 125 mm long, and measures 1 mm across at 5 mm from the tip. All of the needles display curved cross sections at their bases. The differential degree of curving allowed a reconstruction of the order in which they could have been tightly arranged while in use. This reconstruction matches closely the linear arrangements of ochre residues with imprints of fiber strings, indicating that the needles were likely bundled into a multipoint comb. It is

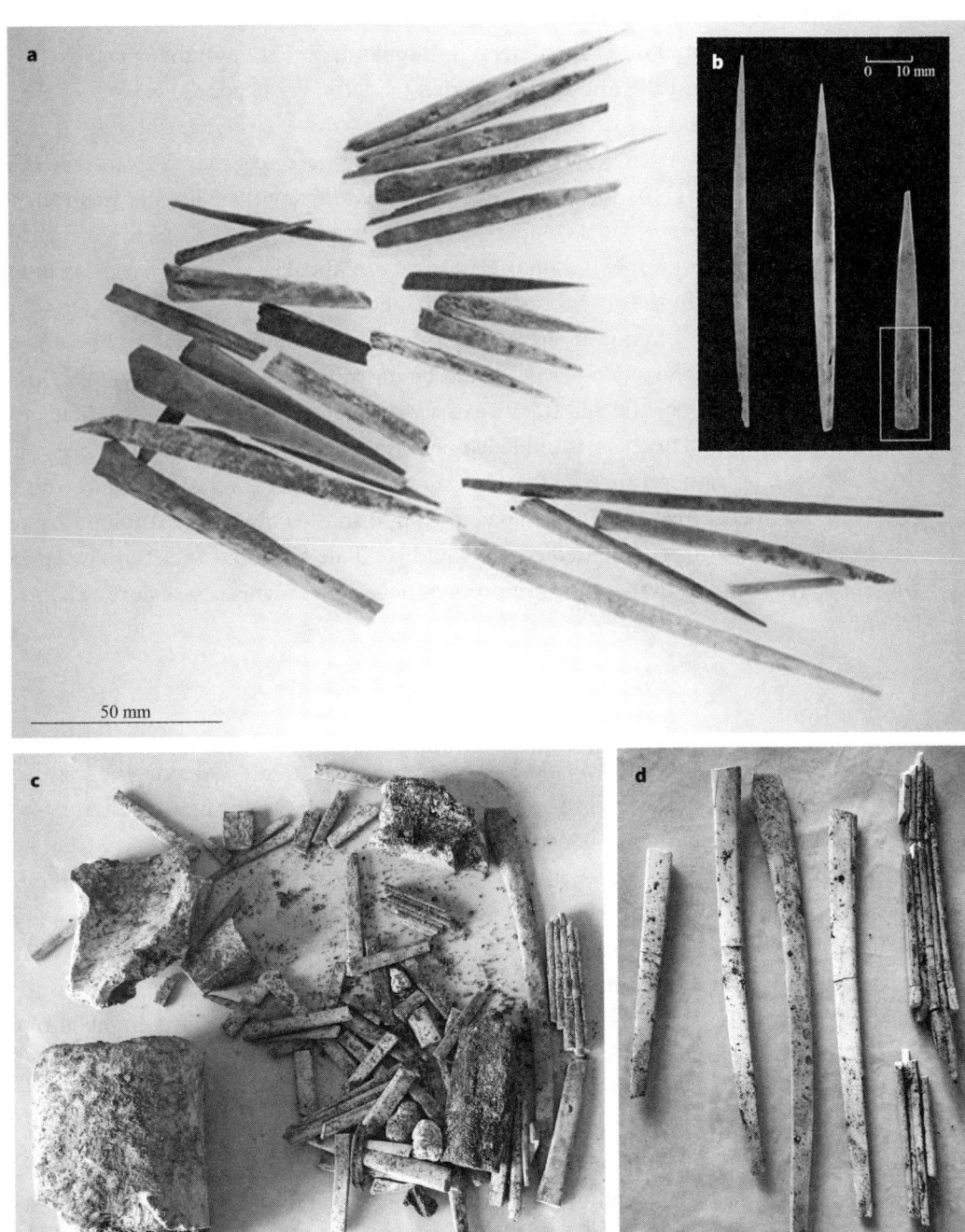

Fig 9.5. Bone needles and a fragmented comb from Pietrele, Romania (ca. 4500–4200 BCE).
(a, b) Collection of individual needles from various levels and features across the settlement. (c, d) Collective find (Inv. No. P06-F370) from burned house in Trench F (c) before and (d) after conservation. Photographs courtesy of (a) Svend Hansen, (b) Petar Zidarov, and (c and d) Cristina Georgescu.

possible that such tools could have been used for scratching skin (see Deter-Wolf et al., chapter 13, this volume) or to apply ochre to human hair, although the appearance of ochre residues only on the finest bone needles (Zidarov 2008, 2009) also allows for a different interpretation.

Systematic use-wear analysis on all objects of this category may help to quantify the specific function(s) the tools from Pietrele served during their use life (see Deter-Wolf and Clark, chapter 16, this volume). The identification of various residues such as pigments, binders, or even blood on their surfaces might also indicate that these tools were used to tattoo. In the absence of such data, however, the preliminary criteria for assigning a tattooing function to these bone needles are mainly intuitive and based on comparative studies and analogies. It should be noted that: (a) the bone needles from Pietrele are extremely brittle and fracture easily throughout their length; (b) their tips are so thin, sharp, and brittle, it is unlikely they would penetrate more resilient material than soft skin or leather; (c) very often the gap between teeth is very small, and would allow for no thicker fiber than hair to pass through; and (d) the combination of five to seven needles in a sharply pointed comb would facilitate tattooing wide lines or infilling solid areas, similar to the wide, multiprong tools from Polynesia (see Furey, chapter 11, this volume).[13]

Conclusions

A considerable body of archaeological, iconographic, and written sources suggest that tattooing was likely practiced in southeastern Europe at least during two archaeologically well-documented episodes: first, during the sixth and fifth millennia BCE, and later, during the fifth through fourth centuries BCE. Unfortunately, beyond the contestable pictorial and written account, the only secure evidence documenting the practice of tattooing in the distant past remains in the survival of tattooed human skin. While many more case studies examining possible tattooing in ancient southeastern Europe may be expected in the future, with the absence of new discoveries of preserved human mummies such as the Tyrolean Iceman, our picture of ancient tattoo traditions will likely remain devoid of "hard proof."

We can understand that tattooing meets basic human social or psychological needs, as evidenced by its repeated invention and transmission throughout history (and prehistory) in very different communities and under different cultural conditions. Yet without the personal accounts of those who made and wore tattoos in antiquity, the meanings of these marks will remain largely elusive, except when we are able to draw parallels from other cultures and glean insights from the archaeological record.

Thankfully, there exists considerable interpretive potential in combining literary, pictorial, and archaeological sources for developing a multidimensional understanding of tattooing in ancient and prehistoric societies in southeastern Europe. But this argument depends largely on the social context of their creation and use. Future research would benefit from focusing attention on the agendas of ancient authors, the technological development of various tattooing implements, and the use and deposition of decorated figurines. In addition, new information might be gleaned from further examining the use and exclusion of certain symbols in ancient art, and the additional nonverbal messages of figural compositions. Finally, systematic comparative studies of tattooing practices among contemporary and ethnographically documented societies would help to refine our understanding of the social functions tattoos might once have had.

Notes

I am grateful to Aaron Deter-Wolf and Lars Krutak for the stimulus and patience during the preparation of this paper. I would also like to extend my gratitude to a number of colleagues who shared thoughts, references, and granted rights for using their photos and drawings: Tsvetan Chetashki, Alexander Chohadzhiev, Juliy Emilov, Georgi Ganetsovski, Cristina Georgescu, Krassimir Georgiev, Svend Hansen, Stoyan Ivanov, Petar Kalchev, Małgorzata Grębska-Kulow, Emil Nankov, Volodya Popov, Meda Toderaș, Ivan Suvandzhiev, and Ivan Vajsov.

1. "But their (Scythian) wives used to tattoo the wives of the Thracians (of those Thracians, that is, who lived on the northern and western frontiers of Scythia) all over their bodies, drawing figures on them with the tongues of their buckles; on which account, many years afterward, the wives of the Thracians who had been treated in this manner effaced this disgrace in a peculiar manner of their own, tattooing also all the rest of their skin all over, in order that by this means the brand of disgrace and insult which was imprinted on their bodies, being multiplied in so various a manner, might efface the reproach by being called an ornament" (Athenaeus, Book XII, 27).
2. Phanokles, in Joannis Stobaeus, *Florilegium* 64, 14; Plutarch, *Moralia* 557d.
3. Berciu (1971); Marazov (1980:80–82, 2010); Teleaga (2010); Torbov (2005).
4. For example, the Great Goddess on the greaves from Vratsa and Agighiol; Bendis on the silver greaves from Zlatinitsa; and Pallas Athena on a bronze greave from Golyama Kosmatka (Agre 2011:45–72; Dimitrova 2015:173–78; Marazov 2011:174).
5. http://be-ja.org.
6. Boghian (2010); Comșa (1994); Kunter (1971); see also discussions in Friedman, chapter 1, and Renaut, chapter 17, this volume.
7. Bailey (1994); Hansen (2007); Marangou (1992); Ucko (1962).
8. Hansen (2007:363, fig. 202); Krauß et al. (2014); Todorova (1980); Todorova and Vajsov (2001); Vajsov (1998).
9. A cruciform design placed on the left shoulder of a figurine from Tell Arpachiah in Syria (Hansen 2007:fig. 43.14) is representative of a different cultural tradition.
10. Atakuman (2015); Dzhanfezova (2003); Lichter (2011); Makkay (1984); Skeates (2007).
11. Atakuman (2015); Lichter (2011); Makkay (1984).
12. Benecke (2001); Benecke et al. (2013); Bréhard and Bălășescu (2012); Bréhard et al. (2014); Gillis et al. (2013); Radu et al. (2016).
13. Future studies on this topic should ideally compare ethnographic tools with the numerous prehistoric objects from Pietrele at various magnifications and employ for use-wear and residue analysis to identify the most reliable criteria for their most plausible identification as tattooing tools.

10

Balkan Ink

EUROPE'S OLDEST LIVING TATTOO TRADITION

Lars Krutak

Since 2009, Bosnian researcher Tea Mihaljevic (née Turalija, 2011) has conducted more than two dozen interviews with traditionally tattooed Catholic women and men from Bosnia and Herzegovina. The oldest tattooed woman she has met, Marta Kuna of Osmanlije (Kupres Municipality), was born in 1917, but her story and those of the many other Bosnian and Croatian Catholics who wear these ancient symbols are waiting to be told (fig. 10.1).

It is not known when or where the practice of tattooing originated among the Catholics of this part of the Balkan Peninsula. However, it has been demonstrated (see Renaut, chapter 17, this volume) that it was an autochthonous tradition of Thraco-Illyrian cultures that inhabited the Balkans prior to 300 BCE. Moreover, Croatian anthropologists Ćiro Truhelka (1896) and Mario Petrić (1973, 1976) wrote that the combinations of cruciforms, celestial bodies, and other natural symbols that comprise this graphic tradition predated Christianity. British travel writer Mary E. Durham (1929:121–22), who traveled extensively across the region in the early twentieth century, was told by a local priest, "They have a number of curious pagan beliefs, which they will not tell me. I have found that they believe in two powers—Light and Darkness—which are in conflict—Good and Evil. These tattoos are in some way connected with this belief. So is the Serpent, which they sometimes tattoo and also draw on the walls."

Bosnian Catholics called the tattooing process *bocati* or *sicati* (Bosnian, "to sting," "to prick," or "to cut") whereas Durham's Catholic informants in northern Albania

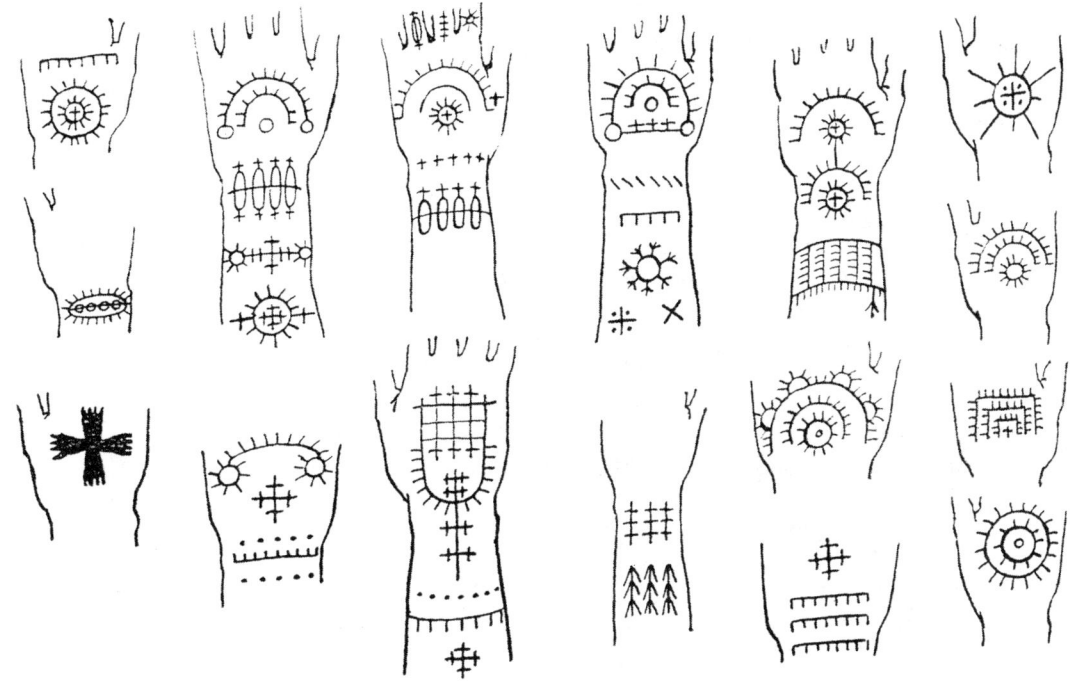

Fig. 10.1. Bosnian Catholic tattoos (ca. 1908). Redrawn after Durham (1929:105).

called it *sharati* ("to color"). Croats who fled Bosnia during Turkish rule to settle as refugees in Dalmatia and Slavonia termed it *bocanje* or *sicanje* (Croatian, "stinging," "pricking," "tattooing"). In Bosnia, some of the traditional patterns were as follows: *kolo* ("the circle"), named after a customary dance, *klas* ("ear of corn"), *ograda* ("fence ring"), *narukvitza* ("bracelet"), *grancitza* ("small pine twig"), *eliza* ("fir tree"), *krizh* or *krizhevi* ("cross," "crosses"), and Sun, Moon, and Morning Star (Krutak 2007:46) (plate 11).

The tattoo patterns were traditionally applied by old women, who first stenciled the design onto the skin with the blunt end of their tattooing needle or a chicken feather. Sometimes the design was carved into a piece of willow or ash bark and stamped onto the epidermis. Generally speaking, tattoo pigment consisted of the soot of resinous pinesap collected on a plate and then combined with honey and water, saliva, and mother's milk from women who had a male child with blue eyes.[1] However, many other substances could also be combined with soot[2] to produce tattoo ink, including milk from a black sheep, horse milk, egg yolk, juniper berry juice, holy water, or sugar (Tea Mihaljevic, personal communication, March 27, 2016). Mihaljevic's informants stated that after the design was pricked into the skin with one or more "hot" needles, a piece of blue indigo paper was applied to the wound for one day to enhance the color. This type of paper was once common as a tobacco wrapper.

Certain significant Christian days of the year were preferred for tattooing: Annunciation Day (March 25), Good Friday, Palm Sunday, and St. John's Day (June 24) were tattooing days, but March 19 (St. Joseph's Day) was the most common.[3] Truhelka's informants stated that tattooing was performed in spring because the wounds healed more easily during this time. However, he argued that there was a deeper religious meaning associated with the timing of the tattooing rite that "had disappeared from popular consciousness" (Truhelka 1896:497). More specifically, he believed that tattooing was connected to the position of the Sun, fertility, and the spring equinox, because St. Joseph's Day fell on the eve of the spring solstice.

As noted, tattooing was especially connected to religion. One of Durham's (1929:104) female informants explained: "All the family comes to see it done," because "Christ suffered for us, [and] it is right we should suffer for Him." Similarly, Marta Kuna told Mihaljevic, "It was Good Friday and Jesus suffered on the cross, [so] we put [the tattoo] in His name."

However, tattoos had other religious functions. During the Turkish occupation of Bosnia and Herzegovina (1463–1878), Catholics were forced to convert to Islam. "Our oral traditions handed down from our grandmothers recorded that Turkish chiefs (*Begs* or *begovi*) ravished our beautiful girls by force," Mihaljevic says. "These women would rather die, so they committed suicide, sometimes by jumping from cliffs, to escape the clutches of the Begs. If they refused their advances, the Turks would murder them. Begs had the right to sleep with Christian women on their first wedding night. So our people tattooed their hands, fingers, chests, foreheads with crosses and other ancient ornaments in order to protect themselves from Turks." Tattooed elder Ljuba Šimić of Rastičevo village remembered: "Turks despised the cross so cross tattoos were a form of protection." Mihaljevic also added: "Our children, male and female, were also taken to Turkey as slaves, so they too were marked. This was done so that they would always know that they were Catholic once, even if converted to Islam."

The Turkish occupation of Bosnia and Herzegovina lasted until the nineteenth century. Afterward, there was a succession of governments, including those headed by Austria-Hungary (1878–1918), the Kingdom of Yugoslavia (1918–1941), and later Socialist Yugoslavia (1945–1992). With the integration of the country into a communist state, tattoo practices were largely discouraged because they were considered "primitive" in contrast to the modernist and nationalist ideology of the evolving nation.

"The state did not persecute, imprison or openly repress those people clinging to their national identity and traditions like Bosnian-Croat tattooing," says Zagreb-based tattoo artist Zele (personal communication, February 28, 2016). "But there was a lot of prejudice toward them, because the intellectual elite looked down on these people as backward, primitive, narrow minded, and inferior. They were mainly rural farmers with little education, and it was believed that such people would not be able to advance into higher positions in the state-run economy or administration so they were discriminated against. Throughout the 1950s the state enforced mandatory education programs to help modernize its rural communities. And even in the most traditional regions, people stopped tattooing around this time because they were made to feel ashamed of their tattoos."

Many of Mihaljevic's informants offered similar testimony (see Turalija 2011) (plate 12). "It was not desirable to express our faith during the communist times," says Šimić. "After the war, tattooing died out."

"Even the church was persecuted during those times after WWII," explains tattooed elder Marica Džeko (b. 1933) of Botun village. "I was tattooed when I was five or six years old. And many people who had crosses on their hands had problems with the communist authorities back then. I remember one woman who had many crosses on her hands and chest and they wanted to fire her from her job."

Mihaljevic's grandmother Bosiljka of Begovo Selo village (b. 1931) remembered that tattooed people were "despised" when the Communists arrived, and they were no longer welcome to express their Catholic faith in this way. "The Communists banned it . . . and our tattoo custom disappeared suddenly after they came, because they thought it was primitive."

Anica Radoš of Mlakva village (b. 1923) exclaimed: "We stopped doing it and I didn't tattoo my children. We were hiding it from the Communists. They didn't like to see it!" (Turalija 2011).

Traditional Balkan Tattoo Revival

Bosnian-Croat tattooing is Europe's most ancient and enduring tradition of permanent body marking. It survived the centuries as a largely uninterrupted traditional practice that reaffirmed religious faith, cultural identity, and timeworn customs and beliefs that were never completely eradicated. Zele affirms that traditional Balkan tattooing should be revered as part of their national heritage, "because it is a precious and fragile part of our cultural legacy to the world."

Zele, born on the Dalmatian coast in Sibenik, vividly remembers the first time he created a Bosnian-Croat–inspired tattoo. In 1994, a soldier from Bosnia and Herzegovina came to me for a little *jelitza* (cross) tattoo on his trigger finger (fig. 10.2). "He explained that this tattoo would represent his Croatian roots and defiance to his enemies. To be honest with you, I had little knowledge of these ancient tattoo traditions before meeting this man and he actually introduced them to me."

With his interest piqued, Zele visited several Bosnian and Croatian villages with his friend German journalist Michael Laukien (Laukien 2000). He managed to meet many tattooed women but their knowledge of the tattoo designs and associated meanings was limited. "The motivation for getting the tattoos was purely religious, for cultural identification and aesthetics. There was no mention of medicinal, magical, or ritual

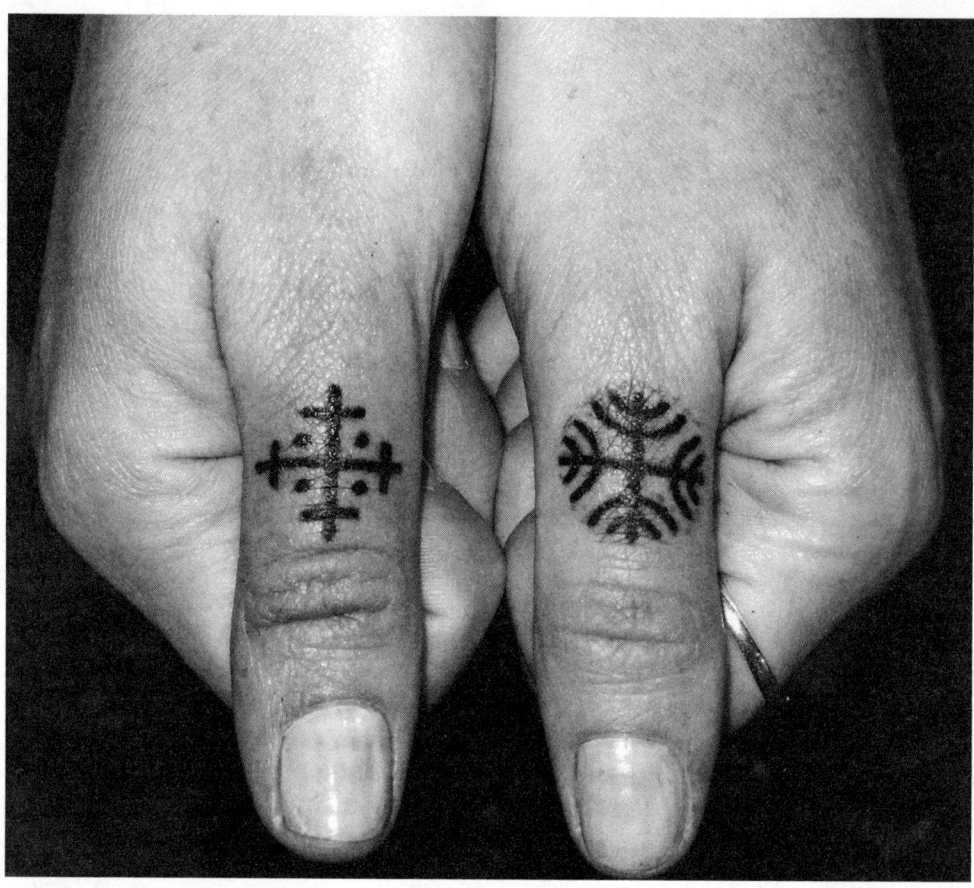

Fig. 10.2. Thumb tattoos displaying traditional Bosnian-Croat iconography (2015). Tattoos and photograph © Zele, Zagreb Tattoo / www.tetoviranje.com.

associations," he says. "But these aspects most probably existed in pre-Christian periods but were forgotten later on. It's a shame that Truhelka didn't do more because I think he had the opportunity to do so. Thus, I believe we missed our chance to delve deeper into the matter, and we are too late to do anything more than to document what is known, preserve the old photographic materials, and bring these materials together in a book that can be shared with the world" (figs. 10.3 and 10.4).

Another Croatian tattooist, Sasha Aleksandar, hails from Slavonia but works from his studio in the seaside town of Rovinj. He inked his first traditional tattoo around 2000 on a woman who was inspired by her grandmother's tattoos. Since that time he has created dozens of tattoos derived from customary Bosnian-Croatian designs, including large backpieces comprised of patterns illustrated in the published works of Truhelka[4] (figs. 10.5 and 10.6).

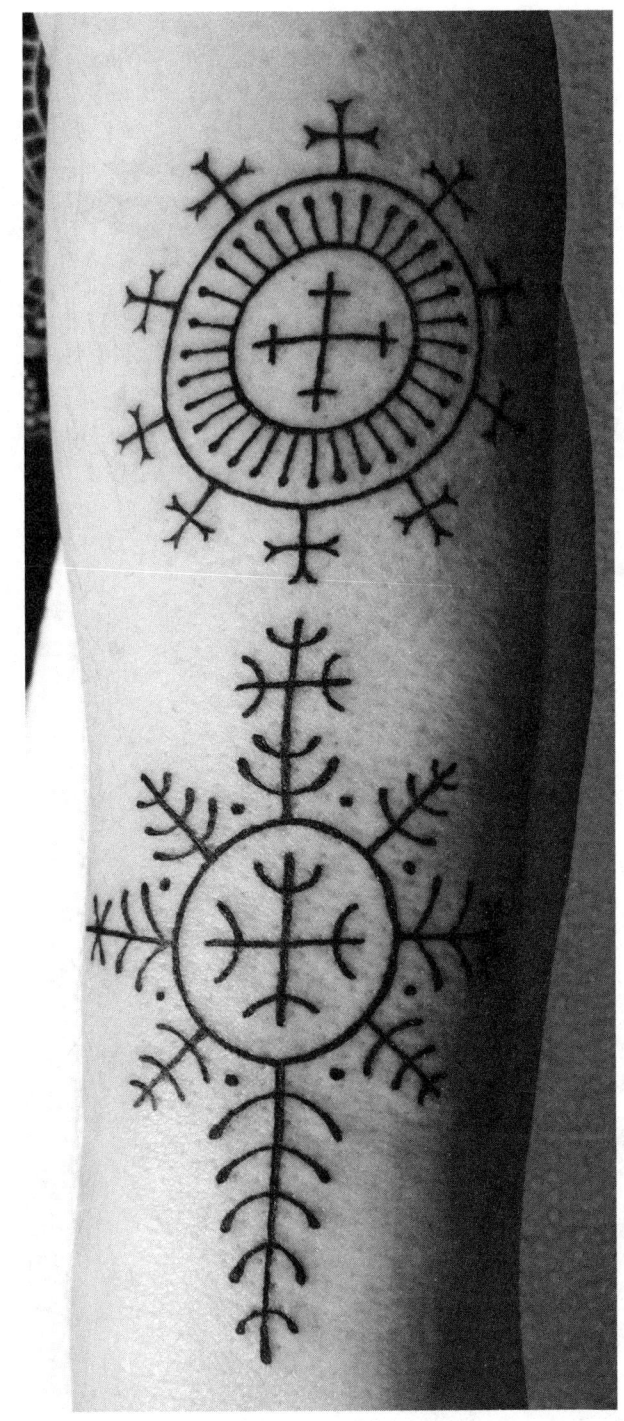

Fig. 10.3. Bicep tattoos utilizing ancient design work from the Balkans (2015). Tattoos and photograph © Zele, Zagreb Tattoo / www.tetoviranje.com.

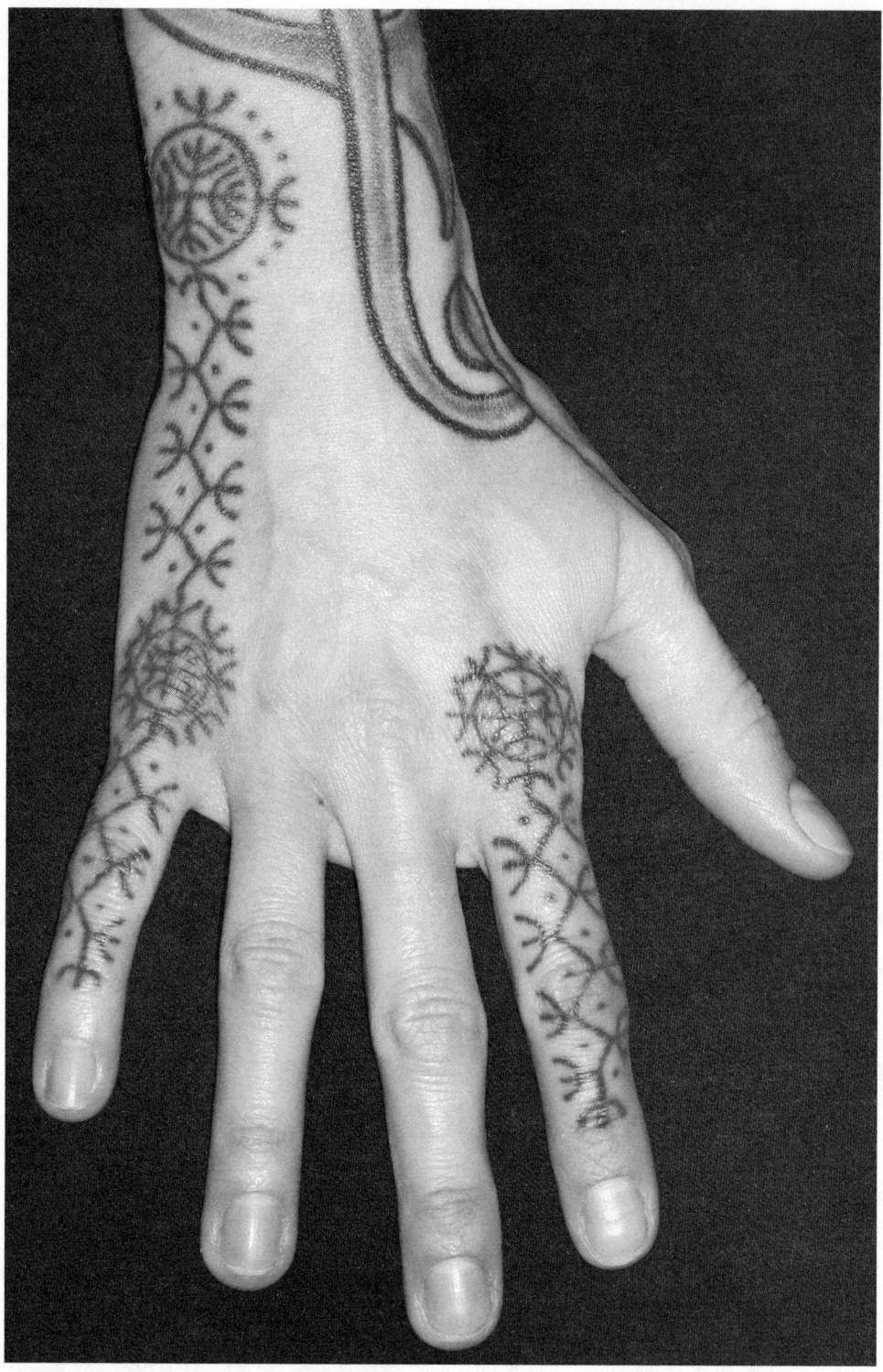

Fig. 10.4. Hand tattoos inspired by traditional Croatian designs (2015). Tattoos and photograph © Zele, Zagreb Tattoo / www.tetoviranje.com.

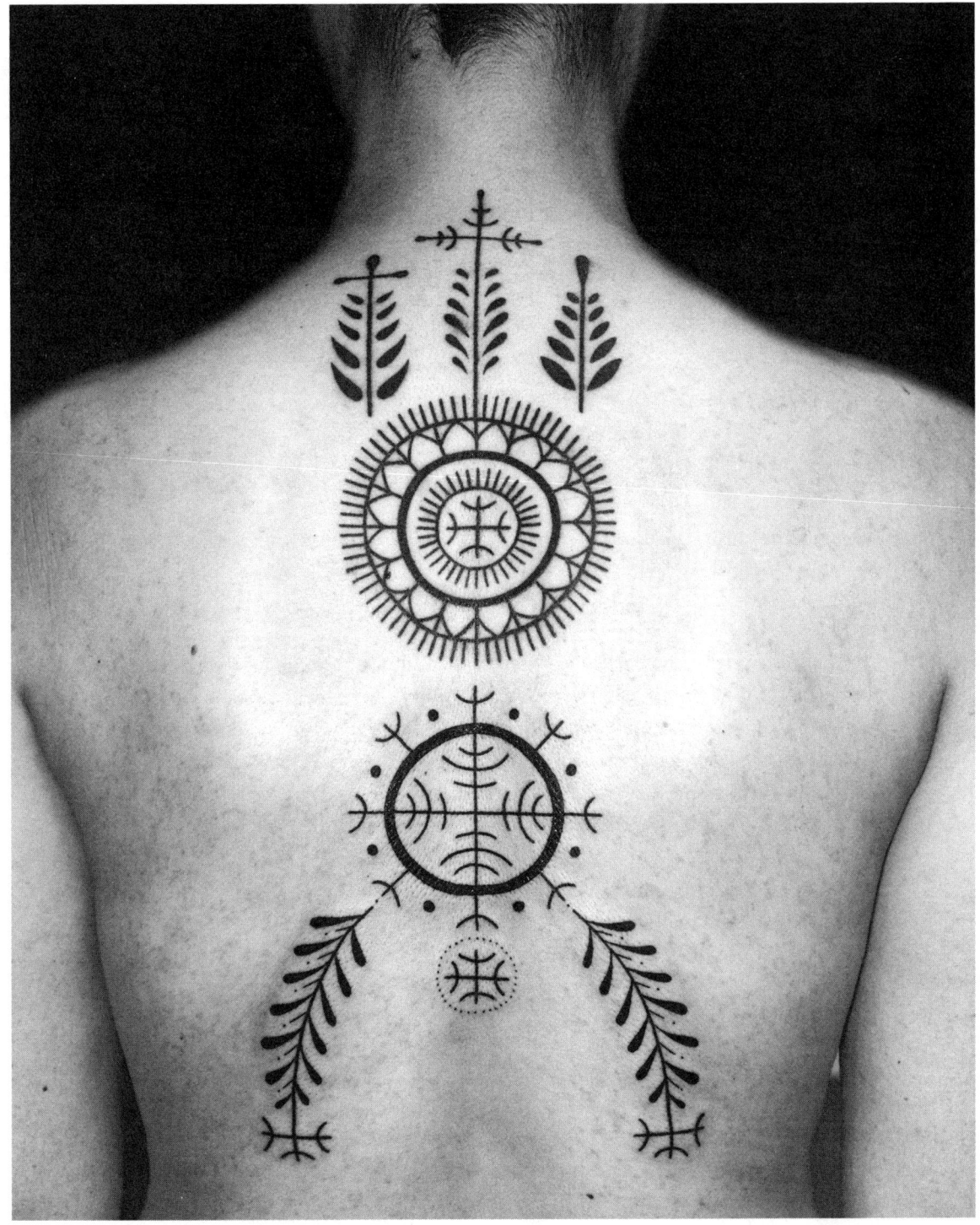

Fig. 10.5. Bosnian-Croat inspired backplate with sun wheel, wheat stalks, fir branches, and cruciform elements based on traditional designs (2015). Tattoos and photograph © Sasha Aleksandar, Orca Sun Tattoo / www.orcasuntattoo.com.

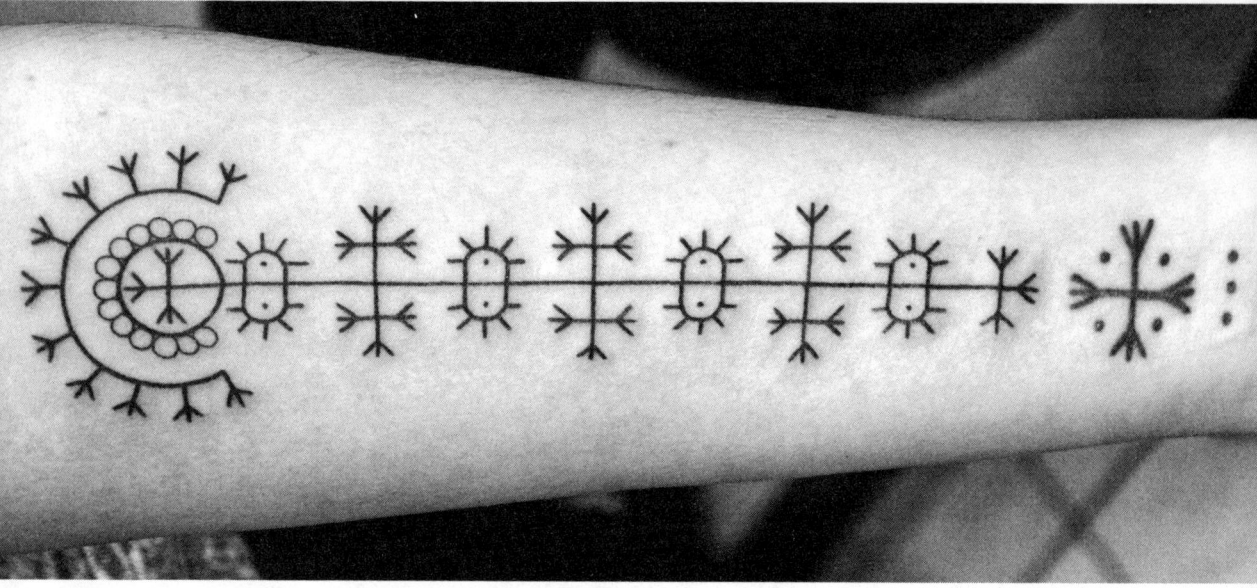

Fig. 10.6. Forearm tattoos in the Bosnian-Croat style (2015). Tattoos and photograph © Sasha Aleksandar, Orca Sun Tattoo / www.orcasuntattoo.com.

"I think today where everything is becoming culturally homogenized people are now returning to the past in their search for identity," Aleksandar says. "I know a few women living abroad who want something as a reminder of their Balkan ancestry. So I created this beautiful backpiece for a woman from Slavonia. Her family moved to Croatia from Bosnia and her grandmother had tattoos on her hands. Even as a child she always liked her grandmother's tattoos but she wanted something larger placed on her back."

Aleksandar also tattoos men with traditional Balkan patterns, but he says his male clients usually prefer smaller designs than women do. These tattoos typically take the form of cross tattoos placed on the right shoulder or a cross inked on the index finger.

Notes

1. In some areas of Bosnia (e.g., Kraljeva Sutjeska), mother's milk was procured from a woman with blue eyes. Her male child also bore the same eye color (Tea Mihaljevic, personal communication, March 27, 2016).
2. Tattoo soot was also produced from charred pumpkin stems.
3. Tattooing could also be applied during Lent.
4. Backpieces such as these are not traditional in the sense of their placement on the body. Customarily, Bosnian-Croat women were tattooed on both hands, forearms, sternum, or forehead.

11

Archaeological Evidence for Tattooing in Polynesia and Micronesia

Louise Furey

During the European exploration voyages of the late eighteenth century, Captain James Cook wrote about the practice of "*tattow*" or "*tatau*" in Tahiti. Phonetically the word *tatau* resembled "tattoo," an existing English word for a drumbeat, and the association was possibly reinforced by the sound made by tapping a mallet against the comb haft. Cook and his compatriots were fascinated by the practice and by the varied designs encountered on each island group of the South Pacific, many of which were illustrated by artists accompanying the voyages. Tattooing in that part of the world shares a common ancestry, although the purpose and meaning of tattooing differs from place to place, as does the form of the implement used.

Traditional tattooing implements in Polynesia are hafted at an angle to the handle, which is struck with a light mallet causing the teeth of the comb to pierce the skin of the subject. Elsewhere in the world, tattooing implements are either hafted in line with a handle or are handheld, and applied to the skin directly or through the technique of skin-stitching (Robitaille 2007). The perpendicularly hafted tattoo implement and use of a mallet is associated with speakers of the Austronesian family of languages, originally prevalent throughout southern mainland China, Island Southeast Asia, and the islands of the Pacific.[1] Recent research on distinctive handheld obsidian tools described from archaeological sites in Papua New Guinea, Solomon Islands, and Vanuatu suggests their use as skin piercers, possibly in association with charcoal and ochre pigments (Kononenko 2012; Kononenko and Torrence 2009; Kononenko et al. 2016). While some sites are associated with the Austronesian speakers, others in Papua

New Guinea date from mid-Holocene (ca. 1650–2000 BCE) sites, suggesting that the history of skin marking in this region is complex.

Tattoo implements in Oceania vary through time and space in terms of material, size, and shape. The history of tattooing using hafted implements in this part of the world mirrors closely the story of the settlement of the Pacific by Austronesian speakers, and may have had its origins in Neolithic Southern China prior to 1500 BCE (Robitaille 2007:159), but by the time it reached the geographic margins of Polynesia it was unique in terms of the associated rituals, meanings, and elaborate designs.

Research continues into the story of the settlement of Oceania, traced not through tattoo practices but primarily by ceramic designs. Briefly, ceramics bearing distinctive decorations define the Lapita Cultural Complex that appeared about 1300 BCE in the previously aceramic archaeological record of the Bismarck Islands to the northeast of Papua New Guinea (map 11.1). The decorative designs are in some cases elaborate, with stylistic faces possibly representing ancestor figures, presented on ornately shaped vessels such as pedestaled bowls, cylinder stands, and wide dishes intended for display and presentation (Kirch 1997:143; Sand 2015). No exact correlates of this decorative style have been found farther west, although a similar dentate stamp technique for applying the decoration was being used (Bedford 2015). The Lapita Cultural Complex (named after the place in New Caledonia where the ceramics were first found) included domesticated plants and animals of Southeast Asian origin, shell ornaments, and styles of ground adzes that were not known to the existing non-Austronesian speaking populations who had entered Near Oceania from the northwest (Kirch 2000).

Although there are general similarities in material culture of the founding Austronesian-speaking population with that in the broad homeland area of Island Southeast Asia, there is no one traceable origin of the Lapita people because of adaptation and cultural borrowing that occurred before entering the Bismarck Archipelago in Near Oceania.[2] In that region, borrowing from existing populations took place as well as technological innovation. The Lapita period only lasted about 500 years (Sand and Bedford 2010), and during that time the Lapita people settled the islands of Near Oceania, then extended across the first of the larger water gaps (300 to 350 km) to the uninhabited islands of Santa Cruz in the Southeast Solomons, Vanuatu, and New Caledonia, and finally across 800 km of water from Vanuatu to Fiji and Tonga by about 850 BCE. This continually unfolding and complex story is one involving multiple cultural interactions with existing people throughout Near Oceania who were biologically and linguistically diverse.

People bearing Lapita ceramic pottery arrived as far east as Tonga and Samoa by 850 BCE. Over the next millennium Lapita settlers of Tonga and Samoa developed through an Ancestral Polynesian culture to become Polynesian linguistically, socially, and culturally (Kirch 2000). Innovation in watercraft and sails provided the means to cross water gaps exceeding 1,500 km. The onset of cyclical El Niño conditions, which brought long periods of westerly winds in contrast to the usual prevailing easterly winds,

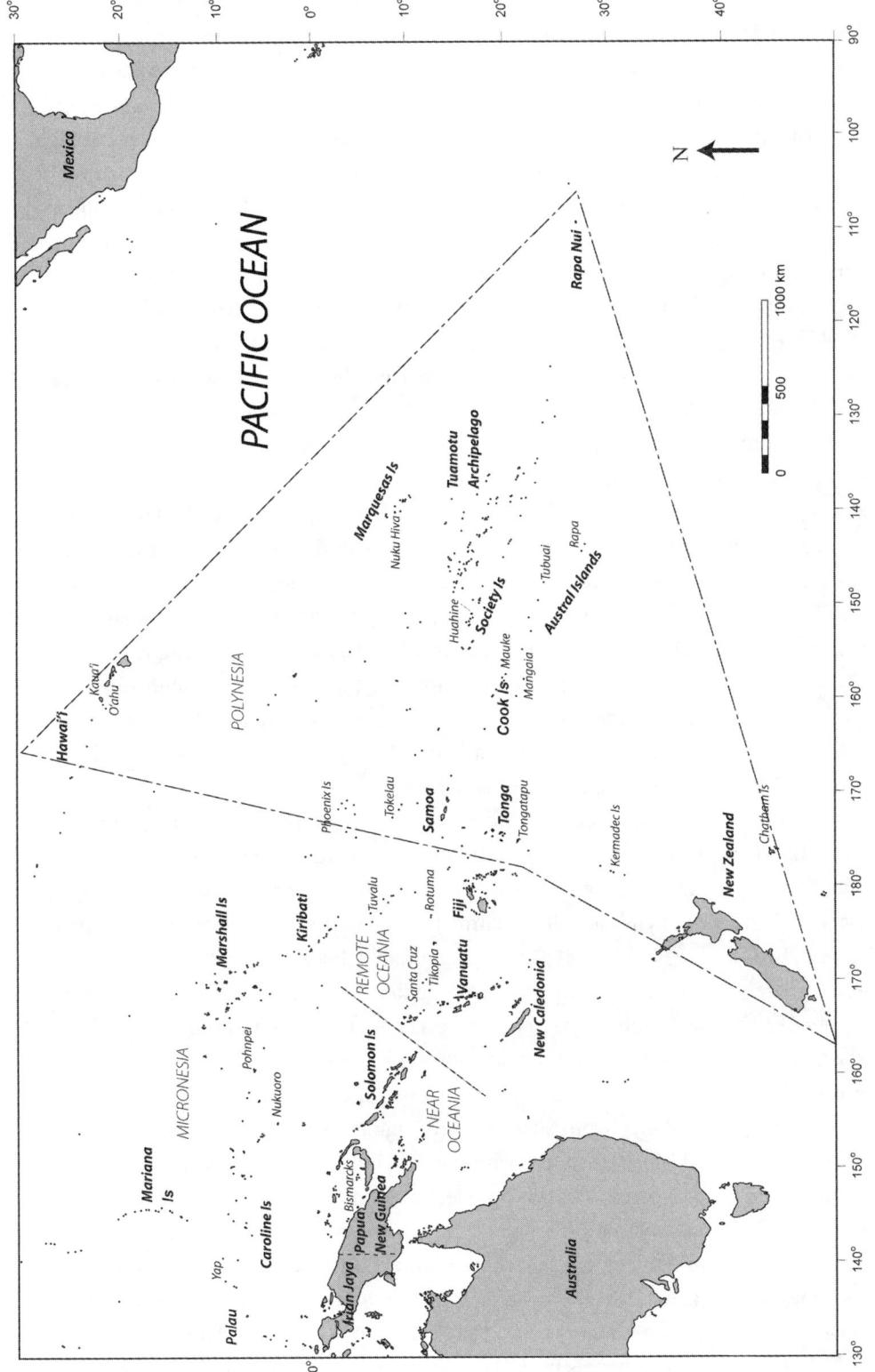

Map 11.1. The Pacific Ocean, focusing on Near and Remote Oceania, and the Polynesian triangle defined by Hawai'i, Rapa Nui (Easter Island), and New Zealand.

may also have facilitated long-distance voyaging (Anderson et al. 2006). Settlement of the Cook Islands, Society Islands, and Marquesas Islands took place by 1100 CE, with the margins of Polynesia shortly following thereafter: north to Hawai'i, east to Rapa Nui (Easter Island), and lastly south to New Zealand approximately 1300 CE (Anderson 2014).

The settlement story for Micronesia is also complicated, with several source areas providing founding populations for different island groups. Linguistic studies reveal that languages in Palau and the Mariana Islands, in far western Micronesia, are most closely related to those of Island Southeast Asia, particularly the Philippines and the northern Indonesia region (Kirch 2000:167), whereas farther east in Micronesia, the languages belong to the Oceanic subgroup of Austronesian languages, which encompasses all languages of Near Oceania, Central and East Micronesia, and Polynesia. Yap was most likely settled from the Bismarck Archipelago about 1250–1350 BCE, with the Marshall Islands and Kiribati (Gilbert Islands) settled from the Solomon-Vanuatu area slightly later in time (Clark 2014).

The distinctive Lapita ceramic surface decoration motifs have been interpreted as being modeled on tattoo designs (Kirch 1997:142). The blunt-toothed dentate combs used to dent the clay and create the ceramic patterns (Ambrose 2007) further reinforce this inferred relationship. However there is no lineal relationship between Lapita designs of 3,300 to 2,900 years ago and Polynesian designs on various organic materials over 1,000 years later. Over time and with eastward expansion, Lapita designs became simplified (Sand 2015), and in some cases disappeared altogether, although undecorated pots continued to be made on some islands. Alternately, Ambrose (2012) has proposed that woven fiber work (mats and baskets) with decorative patterns may have been the inspiration for the ceramic designs.

Despite tattooing being associated with Austronesian speakers in Island Southeast Asia, investigations at over 200 sites containing Lapita ceramics in Near and Remote Oceania have yielded no tangible archaeological evidence of the form of tattoo combs later prevalent in East Polynesia. Initial claims for bone tattoo combs from the Lapita site To.1 on Tongatapu (Poulsen 1987) are questionable, because reanalysis of the site stratigraphy suggests that these artifacts were in a later intrusive feature and probably date to about 1450 CE (Smith 2002:213). There is general agreement among archaeologists working in Remote Oceania that tattooing using a hafted skin puncturing technique was brought into the region with the Austronesian-speaking migrants, and therefore the lack of evidence from sites of Lapita age is probably related to materials used (Kirch 1997:131). While bone preservation is variable in Lapita sites, absence being solely due to bone degradation cannot be used as an all-encompassing explanation. One simple and logical explanation for the lack of bone tattoo combs in Lapita sites is that use of bone instead represents a post-Lapita, and possibly a Polynesian, innovation.

Austronesian speakers have employed a range of materials for puncturing the skin. To the west, in island and mainland Southeast Asia, thorns of citrus (family Rutaceae) are used to pierce the skin, whereas in Polynesia, shaped implements of bone and pearl shell (of the pearl oyster, *Pinctada* sp.) appear in the archaeological and ethnographic records. On Micronesian island groups a variety of materials are used including thorns, fish spines, and bone. Shell of black-lipped pearl oyster (*Pinctada margaritifera*) was used archaeologically in Central and East Polynesia (Kirch et al. 1995; Molle and Conte 2013), but not apparently in West Polynesia. Bone tattoo tools may have been adopted out of necessity in Polynesia and Micronesia since citrus is not endemic to those areas (Robitaille 2007). Sour orange (*Citrus macroptera*) and pomelo (*Citrus maxima*) were introduced into Fiji, Tonga, and Samoa as part of the Lapita suite of cultivated plants, and in Fiji in particular, thorns of pomelo continued to be used for tattooing in historic times (Whistler 1991, 2009:57–60).

In Polynesia there exists a general similarity in tattoo comb styles that mirrors other aspects of material culture. Within Eastern Polynesia voyaging and interaction between the Cook Islands, Society Islands, and Marquesas Islands continued after initial settlement and ensured similarity in cultural practices for a time (Walter 1996). Settlers from this area to the farthest land masses of Hawai'i, Rapa Nui, and New Zealand carried with them the same East Polynesian culture. However on reaching these geographic boundaries, isolation from the homeland area encouraged rapid culture change and development of distinctive societies.

The following island-by-island summary of tattooing technology draws both from the archaeological record and from accounts that document the form of tattooing instruments at and after European contact. Archaeological evidence for tattooing is variable, even in those island groups (with the exception of New Zealand) where tattooing remained culturally important until the time of European missionary influence (D'Alleva 2005; Roth 1905:292). Drawing on other sources of information is therefore important to review the overall distribution of tattooing and the materials used for tattoo implements.

Western Polynesia

Ethnohistoric and ethnographic sources document that tattooing took place throughout Western Polynesia, and many examples of tattoo combs have survived in museum collections. However, archaeological evidence of tattooing in the region is rare and relatively recent in origin. The elusive connection between the well-developed East Polynesian tattooing technology and its inferred presence in the earlier Lapita, and post-Lapita ancestral Polynesian cultural complexes has not yet been discovered.

TONGA

Four tattoo combs from a (reinterpreted) post-Lapita context at site To.1 on Tongatapu probably date to about 1450 CE. Three of the toothed combs have lengths between 27 and 31 mm and are 6 to 7 mm wide, with between six to nine teeth (plate 13). The remaining example has four extremely long teeth and may have had more. Whether the combs are of Lapita age or later is relevant, but significantly they are confirmation that bone material will survive in archaeological sites in Tonga by this date, and there is an expectation that more will be found in the future given the right circumstances.

An example collected from an unknown Tongan location in the 1770s by Captain James Cook is very similar to the described Samoan implements of the same period, and quite unlike the archaeological examples from Tongatapu. The implement has a total of twenty-nine fine teeth from five bone combs joined to a turtle shell backing plate by fiber (Kaeppler 1978a:212). Combs of varying width, with between six and sixty teeth, were in use in the early eighteenth century (Roth 1906:7). It is likely that combs at the upper end of the reported range of teeth would have been composite implements not unlike the example collected by Captain Cook.

Regular voyaging and social interaction between Tonga and both Samoa and Fiji took place before and after European contact (Kaeppler 1978b). Samoans fulfilled an important role in the very structured hierarchical Tongan social system, and tattooing of high ranked Tongans was carried out by Samoan tattooists. Although it cannot be implied that all historically collected tools may have been Samoan in origin, the close relationship undoubtedly led to similarities in styles.

SAMOA

Tattoo implements are elusive in the 2,500-year-old archaeological record of Samoa despite investigations at a range of sites over several decades. Bone and shell have not preserved well, partly as a result of soil conditions affecting long-term artifact survival, and evidence for use of shell and bone tools is generally scarce (Davidson 2012:4).

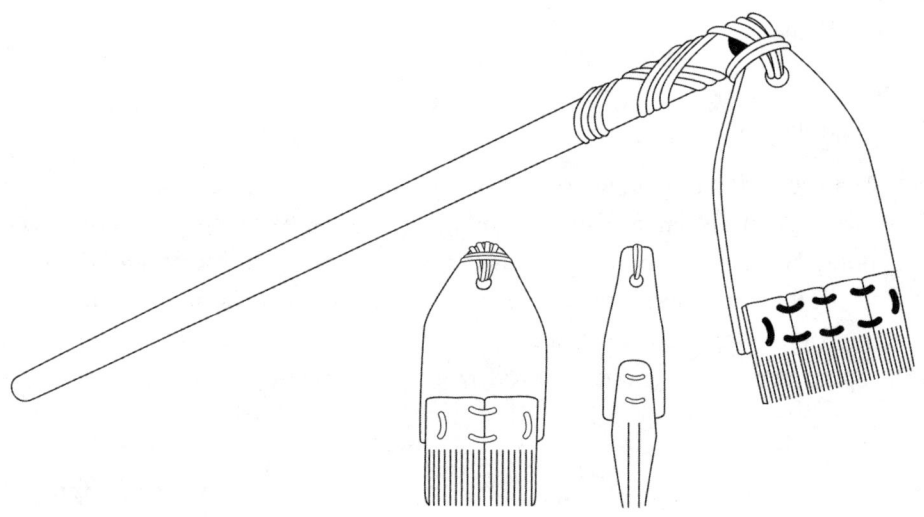

Fig. 11.1. Bone composite tattoo comb form with turtle shell backing plate, Samoa (late nineteenth to early twentieth century CE) (after Hiroa 1930:636). Drawings by Louise Furey.

Late nineteenth and early twentieth century Samoan tattooing implements were of composite form, with short-length combs made from ground tabs of pig teeth or human bone attached to flat backing plates of turtle shell (fig. 11.1). Implements range from those with only a few teeth to broad examples involving multiple combs lashed together (Handy and Handy 1924:22). The turtle shell plate was about 2 mm thick and had a beveled lower edge, overlapped by the upper end of the bone comb (Hiroa 1930:636–41). Comb types had specific tattooing uses, including creating dots, fine lines, and thicker lines. Composite tools with between forty-one to forty-six teeth and measuring 49 to 52 mm wide were made by lashing up to four combs together and used for infilling areas between lines. Handles were made from wood or bamboo, and lashed to the turtle shell plate using coconut fiber. A coconut leaf midrib was used for the mallet, coconut shell for the mortar for grinding the pigment, and wood for the pestle. None of these materials survive long term, although it is expected that the bone would have better preservation.

FIJI

Fiji was first settled by Austronesian speakers bearing the Lapita Cultural Complex, and later by migrants from the west who introduced new material culture and cultural practices, as well as linguistic and genetic influences. The island group had regular ongoing contact with Tonga and Samoa to the east, but is different culturally.

No tattoo combs have been found in archaeological sites on Fiji, although there are several historical accounts documenting the practice.[3] Combs in museum collections are made from thorns bound together, as well as from turtle shell, fish bone, shark tooth, and bone (for example: Pitt Rivers Museum 1899.62.432; Auckland War Memorial Museum 31506, 31507). Two-pronged tools are well documented (see previously cited examples), but composite toothed instruments like those found in Tonga and Samoa are not recorded from Fiji. Fijian tattooing differs in many ways from the practice elsewhere in Polynesia, including that only women are tattooed, and tattooists are exclusively women. In this sense Fiji is more closely aligned with the Polynesian Outliers, where tattooing doesn't strictly follow the norms of Polynesia proper.

POLYNESIAN OUTLIERS

Northwest of Fiji and to the north of the Solomon Islands, there are small isolated islands known collectively as the Polynesian Outliers. Inhabitants speak Polynesian languages and their cultures are predominantly Polynesian. Some of the islands were populated by Lapita people around the same time as West Polynesia, with later settlers bearing fully developed Polynesian culture arriving from the east 700 to 1,000 years ago. Each of the islands may have been settled from Western Polynesia directly, or more likely by way of eastern outliers including Tuvalu, which had Fijian influences (Clark 2014; Kirch 2000).

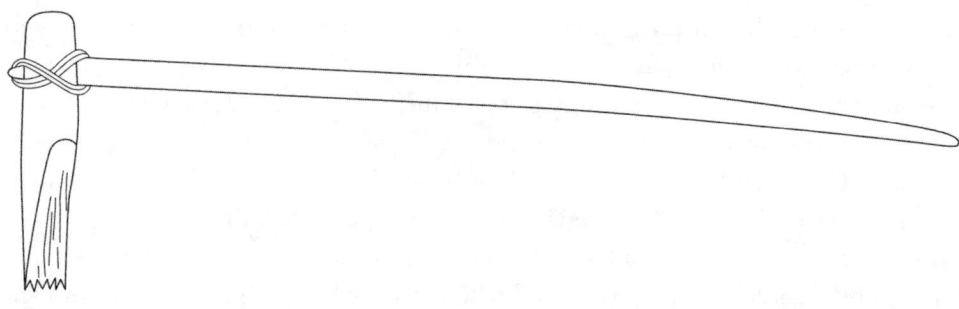

Fig. 11.2. Tattoo comb from Tikopia (twentieth century CE) (after Pendergrast 2000:20). Drawing by Louise Furey.

Knowledge of past occupation of these remote islands is in most cases limited, and none have archaeological evidence of tattooing, although on some islands the practice existed up until recent times. A full exploration of the historical record of tattooing for the Polynesian Outliers is outside the scope of the present effort. Taken as a whole, however, the corpus of tattooing here is remarkably coherent and homogenous. Like in the larger island groups, missionary influence may have been responsible for the abandonment of tattooing.

TIKOPIA

There are good accounts of tattooing in Tikopia in the twentieth century (Firth 1936; Pendergrast 2000), but no tattoo combs have been found in the archaeological record (Kirch and Yen 1982). Although changes in material culture and diet in the early thirteenth century suggest a new, probably Polynesian cultural influence, Tikopians believed tattooing was introduced more recently from Rotuma, approximately 800 km to the east (Firth 1936).

Modern Tikopian tattoo implements are made from the humerus of the brown booby (*Sula leucogaster*), a large seabird. One side of the shaft is cut away at the end and teeth similar to long serrations formed on the projecting tip (fig. 11.2). A hole is drilled through the bone at the opposite end for inserting the tapered end of the handle. Associated tools consist of a mallet made of coconut midrib, a pigment dish of coconut shell, a pestle made of wood, and a bamboo storage container (Pendergrast 2000).

Central and Eastern Polynesia

In contrast to Western Polynesia a relatively large number of tattoo combs are known from archaeological contexts in Central and Eastern Polynesia, which include islands of the Cooks, Society, Marquesas, Tuamotu, Australs, Rapa Nui, Hawai'i, and New

Zealand. There is variation in shape of the combs at the haft end, in material and in width, suggesting that tattooing was well developed by 1200–1400 CE. There is no archaeological evidence for the composite tool forms that developed later in some of these places.

The Southern Cook Islands, situated centrally between West and East Polynesia, are separated from Western Polynesia by a water gap of about 1,500 km. Regular contact between West and East Polynesia was not sustained after the eastern island groups were settled. However within Central Polynesia there was regular voyaging between the Cook Islands, Marquesas, and Society Islands for some centuries after settlement, with movement of finished adzes and other tools (Allen 2014:10).

COOK ISLANDS

Archaeological evidence of tattooing in the Cook Islands comes from only a few places, although historically the practice was carried out on all islands (Hiroa 1927). The styles of comb used bear similarities to forms present in other East Polynesian island groups.

Eight tattoo combs dating from the fourteenth century were recovered at Tangatatau Rockshelter on Mangaia (Kirch et al. 1995). Four tools of the assemblage are illustrated in fig. 11.3a–d. One comb is made of a flat tab of bone and the other three are fashioned from bird bone. Lengths range from 25 to 34 mm. Teeth number between six and eleven, and there are perforations for binding the comb to the handle. The upper ends of the comb include both straight and concave forms. Individual teeth have been formed by filing away the spaces between, leaving, in most cases, parallel grooves on one side of the body.

Combs at Anai'o on the island of Mauke also date to the fourteenth century (Walter 1998). Like the Tangatatau examples, the three combs are perforated for haft attachment (figs. 11.3e–g). Two of the Anai'o combs are made from mammal bone and the other from pearl shell. The pearl shell comb (see fig. 11.3f) is curved on one edge, straight on the other, and square across the top. Two of the combs are toothed, while one of the mammal bone examples is plain, possibly representing a tool blank awaiting teeth. Two of the Anai'o combs were found within the outline of a house (Richard Walter, personal communication, October 2, 2015).

Combs are also reported from Vairoronga on Mangaia, and from Nikaupara on Aitutaki (see illustrations in Mangos and Utanga 2011:44).

In the early twentieth century, tattoo combs on Aitutaki, the northernmost of the Southern Cook Islands, were described as toothed and fashioned from the bone of a bird (Hiroa 1927). The absence of accounts of tattooing from other islands in the Cooks in the nineteenth and early twentieth centuries is possibly a direct result of a ban imposed by Christian missionaries. Tattooed individuals were seen during the late eighteenth century voyage of Captain James Cook, but no surviving examples of tattoo combs are known in museum collections.

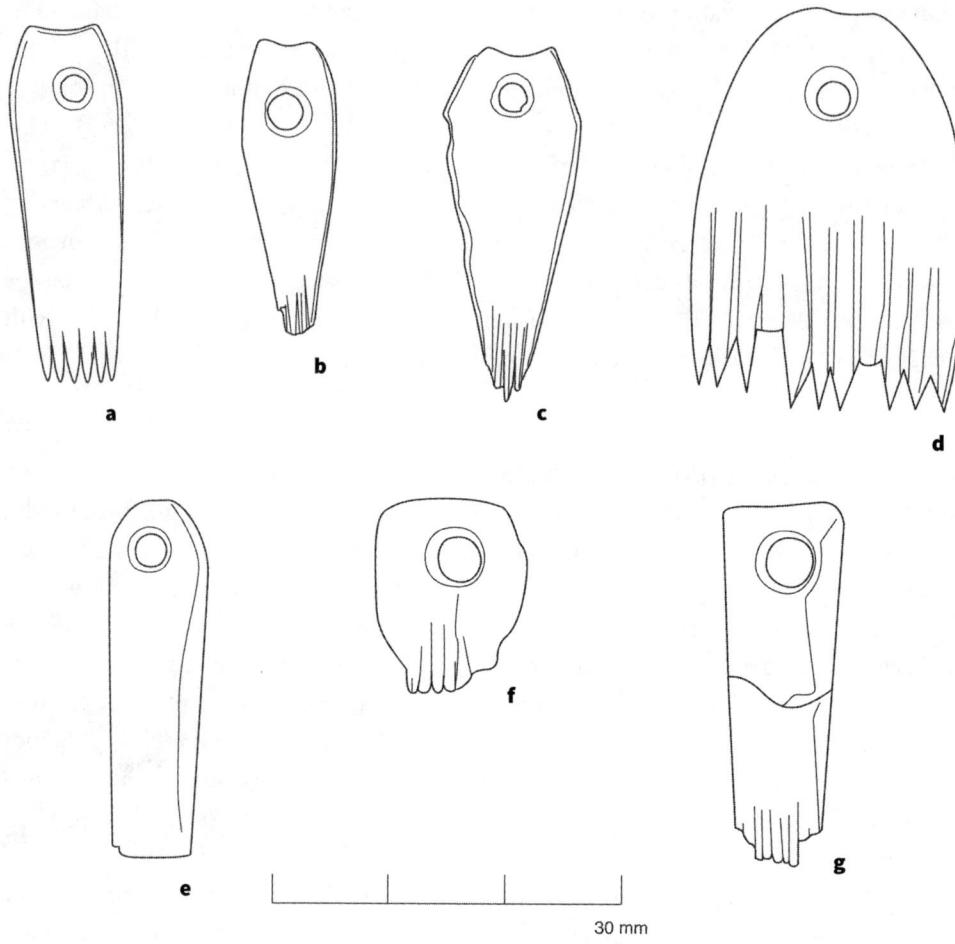

Fig. 11.3. Tattoo combs from the Cook Islands (fourteenth century CE): upper, Tangatatau Rockshelter, Mangaia; lower, Anai'o, Mauke: (a through e, g) bone; (f) pearl shell. Drawing by Louise Furey.

AUSTRAL ISLANDS

The Southern Cook Islands and Austral Islands form a continuous chain of volcanic islands, with the Austral Group (Rimatara, Rurutu, Tubuai, Ra'ivavae, and Rapa) at the eastern end. The full settlement history of the islands is not well known, although dates for settlement are similar to those for the Society Islands.

A material culture collection from Atiahara on the island of Tubuai is East Polynesian, the undifferentiated material culture present directly after settlement, which is similar across a wide area of the Cook, Society, Marquesas, Mangareva, Hawai'i, and New Zealand Islands (Walter 1996). Four near-complete combs are toothed bone, while two are pearl shell, four are plain bone (fig. 11.4), and two fragments are also bone. The plain examples (fig. 11.4b and f) are most likely blank tabs ready for the addition of

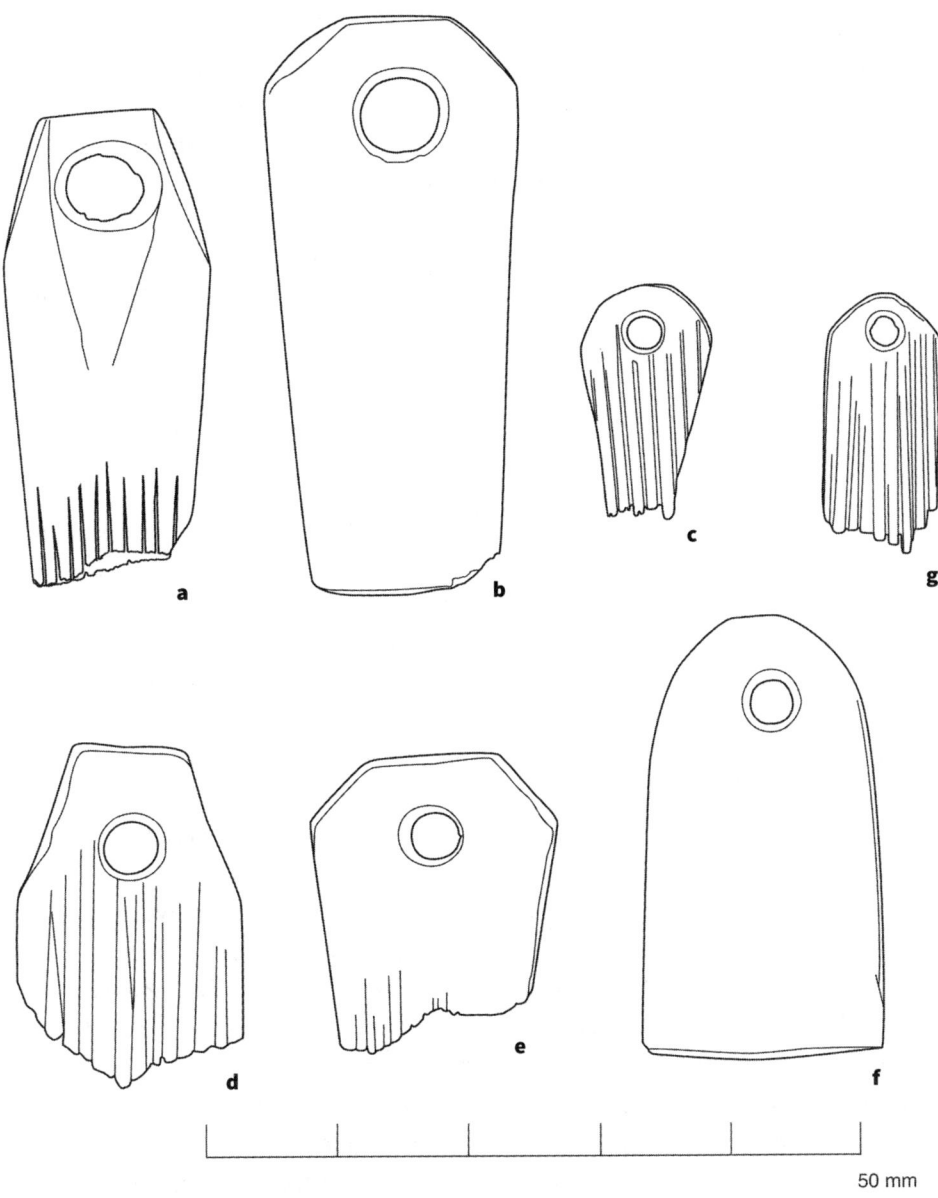

Fig. 11.4. Tattoo combs from Atiahara, Tubuai, Austral Islands (thirteenth to fourteenth centuries CE): (a through f) bone; (g) pearl shell. Drawings by Louise Furey.

teeth, rather than intended to be used in this form, as the squared lower ends would not cut the skin unless beveled and sharpened. The two pearl shell examples (see fig. 11.4g) are incomplete but the presence of parallel striations on both sides of the body suggests that teeth would have been present, and five of the six bone combs have striations on both sides. Eleven are perforated for hafting, and the other example is missing that

ARCHAEOLOGICAL EVIDENCE IN POLYNESIA AND MICRONESIA

part of the comb but was probably also modified for hafting. None have the scalloped upper end for fitting around the handle which is present at Tangatatau Rockshelter, Mangaia, but five have the rounded upper edges like one of the combs from Tangatatau. The remaining five have an angled reduction on each side at the haft end, a form also present at Tangatatau as well as Houhora in New Zealand and Hanatekua in the Marquesas Islands.

Radiocarbon dating indicates that Atiahara was occupied several times between the late thirteenth and late fourteenth centuries CE (Hermann et al. 2015:7). While it is not known which of the three occupation layers the tattoo combs can be assigned to, the dates are in general agreement with the age of combs from both Tangatatau and Anai'o in the Cook Islands.

SOCIETY ISLANDS

One tattoo comb and one unfinished blank fashioned from pearl shell have been found at Vaito'otia, and one at Îles-du-Vent on Huahine (figs. 11.5a–b). The finished objects, like the pearl shell examples from the Marquesas, differ from other pearl shell combs in the hafting modification. Each has a semicircular central groove similar to a broken out perforation, and also notches on the outside edge for holding the lashing firm (Molle and Conte 2013:223–24). Dating results from Vaito'otia are unreliable but occupation was probably between 1100 and 1200 CE (Anderson and Sinoto 2002).

No bone tattoo combs have been found in archaeological contexts in the Society Islands, despite the widespread use of bone implements at European contact. Complete combs, with handle, were observed during voyages by Captain Cook in the late eighteenth century (fig. 11.5c–e). They include narrow toothed combs and wider composite combs. Cook described tattoo implements as pieces of flat bone or shell, with three to twenty teeth (Roth 1905). The selection of narrow or wide combs depended on the design to be tattooed. Artist Sydney Parkinson, who accompanied Cook on that voyage, wrote that implements were one or two flat pieces of bone, five inches in length (Ibid.:287). An unusual example from Cook's voyage (see Kaeppler 1978a:152) appears to have three teeth that would form a circular impression. No archaeological examples of this type are known from East Polynesia, although a circular example from Hawai'i is discussed by Allen (2006).

MARQUESAS ISLANDS

Ten pearl shell tools and one bone comb were found in the dune site of Hane, on Nuku Hiva in the Marquesas Islands. The dating of Hane is problematic, with multiple dates giving conflicting results. However, the lower levels of the site, from which the combs were recovered, were deposited between the late tenth and early twelfth centuries CE (Allen 2014:7). None of the pearl shell combs are complete lengthwise but range from 16 to 40 mm for near complete examples. They are broader than bone examples at between 11 and 25 mm, and the narrowest example is of similar shape to the bone

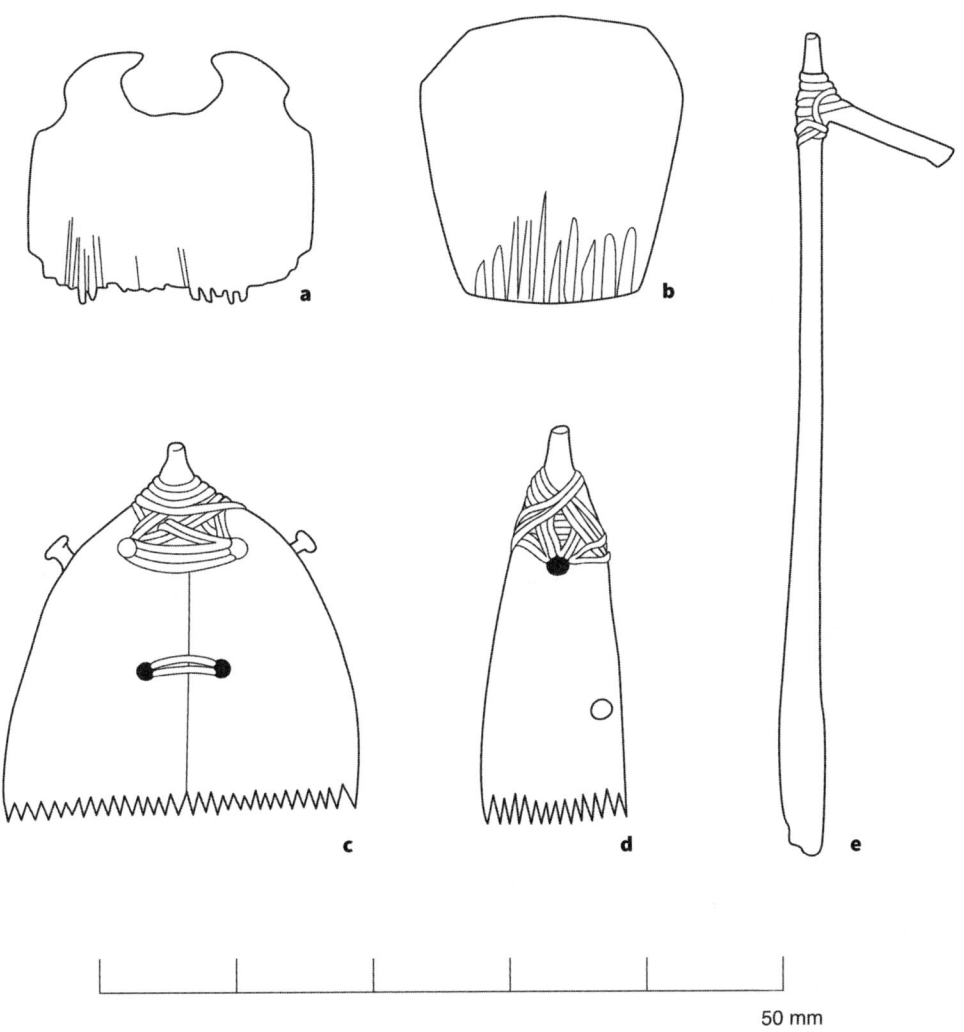

Fig. 11.5. Tattoo combs from the Society Islands, ca. 1100–1200 CE: upper (archaeological specimens): (a) Vaito'otia, pearl shell; (b) Îles-du-Vent, pearl shell; lower: combs from Tahiti illustrated during Cook's voyage (c, d) bone composite combs; (e) hafted comb (after Kaeppler 1978a:212, fig. 429). Drawings by Louise Furey.

comb, which is 33 mm in length with twelve teeth (fig. 11.6a–c). Pearl shell combs have between fifteen and twenty teeth. The haft modifications of pearl shell combs are not unlike the examples from the Society Islands but are quite unlike those from Atiahara and Anai'o. The narrow comb is replicated in bone and pearl shell, but the wide comb is only made in pearl shell. The shape of the narrow combs is similar to examples recorded by Langsdorff, who was a member of the Russian expedition to Nuku Hiva in 1804 (Thomas 2005:16), suggesting this style continued to be used for hundreds of years.

ARCHAEOLOGICAL EVIDENCE IN POLYNESIA AND MICRONESIA 171

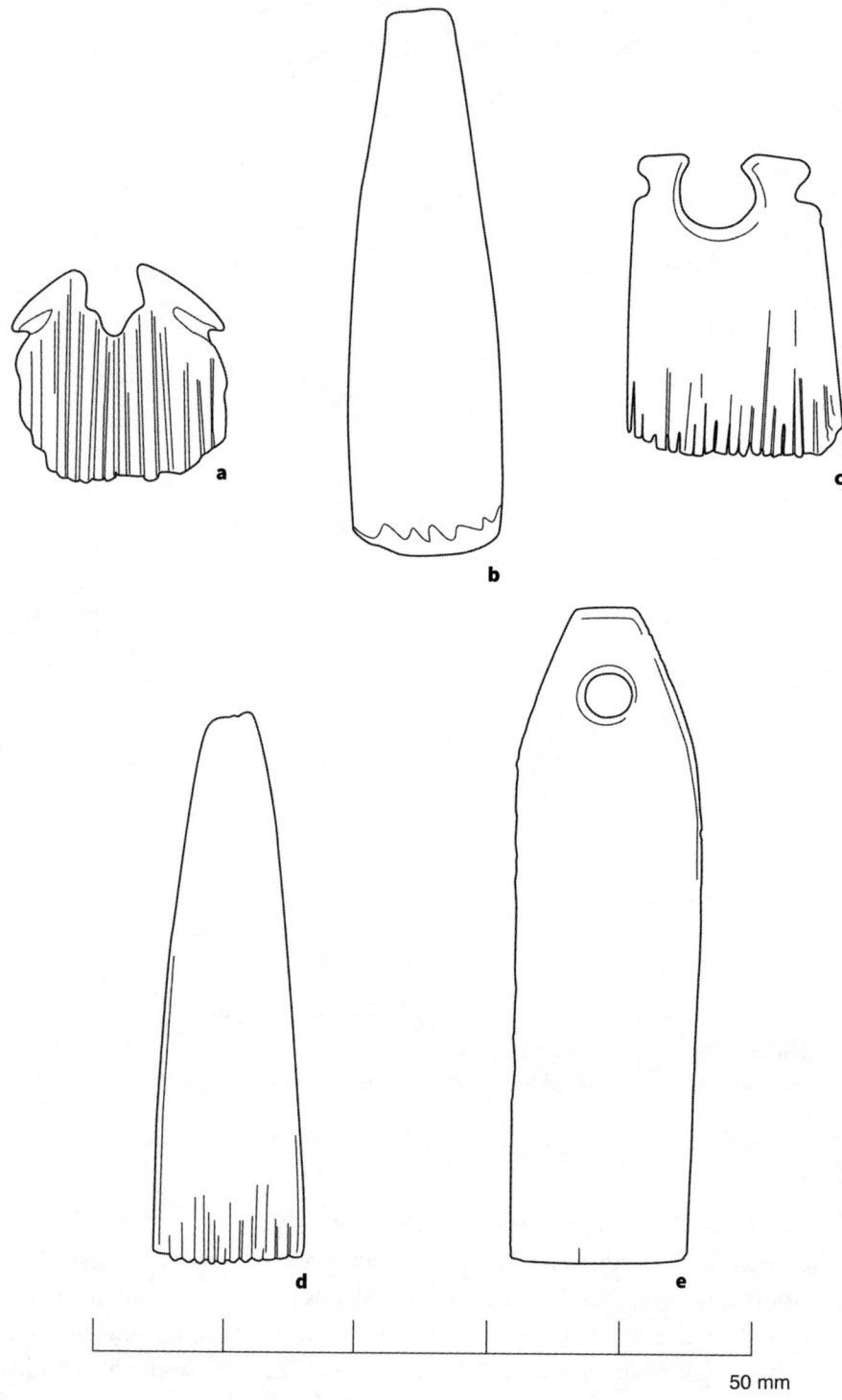

Fig. 11.6. Tattoo combs from the Marquesas Islands (late tenth through twelfth centuries CE): (a, b) Hane, pearl shell; (c) Ha'atuatua, pearl shell; (d) Hane, bone; (e) Hanatekua, bone. Drawings by Louise Furey.

A bone comb from Hanatekua, on Nuku Hiva, has no reliable age estimate (fig. 11.6e) but, on the basis of material culture at the same level, can be assigned to a slightly later age than the lower levels of Hane (Sinoto 1970:110). There is a perforation for hafting, and the upper sides angle inward. The object is possibly a blank as there are no teeth.

The site of Ha'atuatua, also on the same island, has yielded a complete specimen of pearl shell, dated to between 1275 and 1475 CE (Rolett and Conte 1995:223)(fig. 11.6c). This tool measures 23 mm in length and 16 mm wide; it has twenty-one teeth and associated parallel grooves on the body. The haft lashing modifications are very similar to those from the Society Islands and unique to the use of pearl shell, possibly because the width of the shell combs required modifications to hold them secure against the handle.

In the early twentieth century on Nuku Hiva, combs of different lengths were used to make straight lines and small curves. Those for straight lines tapered to the haft end, were unusually long at about 75 mm long, toothed, and made of bone. Combs ranging in size from 78 by 14 mm, to 38 by 2 mm, with between two and twelve teeth, were collected in the early twentieth century by German physician Karl von den Steinen (1925:83). He described use of a range of materials including bird bone, human bone, fish bone, stingray barb, and turtle shell. Unusually, the narrow tapered ends were inserted into a slit in the handle (Handy 1922), a form of hafting not reported elsewhere in Polynesia.

RAPA NUI

Four bone combs have been found in archaeological excavations on Rapa Nui (Beardsley 1996; Ferdon 1961:247–48). Examples in museum collections in Vienna and Berlin are made of bird bone, measure between 75 and 90 mm in length, between 7 and 8 mm maximum in width, and have five to seven teeth (Métraux 1971:237–38). One example (fig. 11.7) tapers to a rounded butt, or to a slight knob on the end, although this might also be interpreted as a lashing notch on each side. A complete example with handle attached (Métraux 1971:241, fig. 32.1) is noticeably different from Marquesan and Society Island examples in the positioning of the comb on the shaft of the handle. Implements from other islands, with the exception of Hawai'i, have the comb hafted near the end of the handle. The described lengths of the tattoo combs from Rapa Nui place them at the upper end of length range for all tattoo combs in Polynesia.

HAWAI'I

Tattoo implements have been excavated from several islands in Hawai'i. Single narrow bone combs were used but, with modification, they could be joined to make wide composite combs. Several composite examples are reported from Makani'olu Shelter (site 02) on O'ahu (Allen 2006; Emory 1946). One consists of four combs that collectively have a length of 44 mm, width 42 mm, and thirty-five teeth (fig. 11.8). This composite comb has a broad, plain frame on each of the outer units, and is grooved.

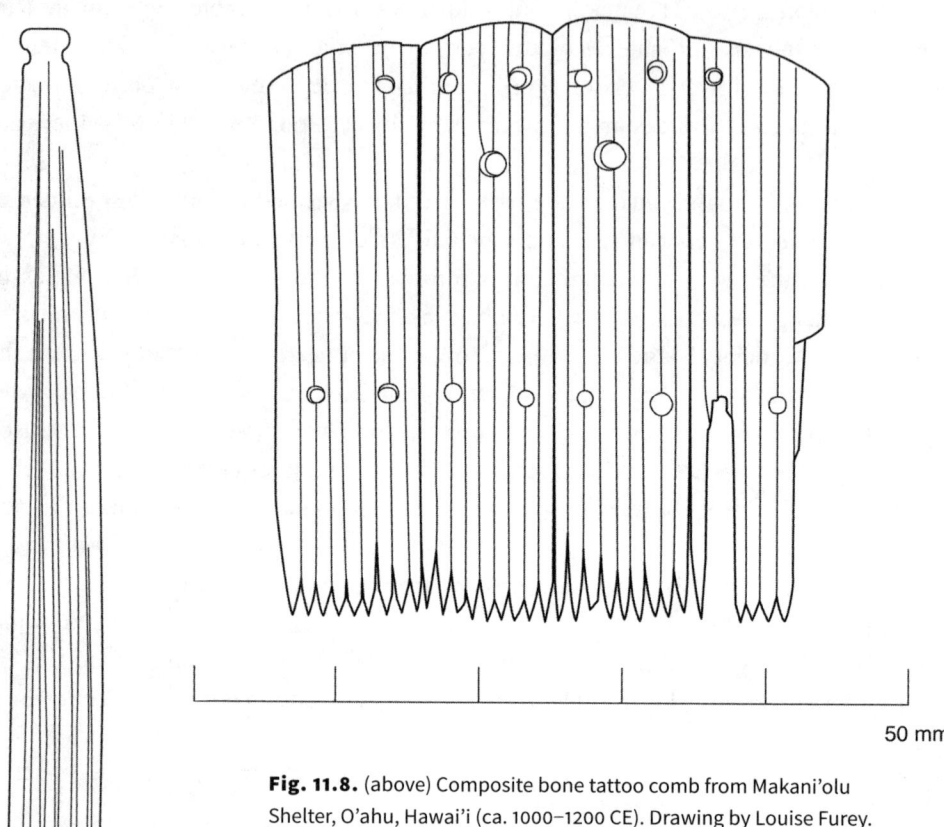

Fig. 11.8. (above) Composite bone tattoo comb from Makani'olu Shelter, O'ahu, Hawai'i (ca. 1000–1200 CE). Drawing by Louise Furey.

Fig. 11.7. (left) Bone tattoo comb from Rapa Nui (Easter Island) (early twentieth century CE) (after Ambrose 2012: fig. 2). Drawings by Louise Furey.

Small aligned perforations on each individual comb are for binding to the narrow bone backing strip or brace, and the central two units have a larger hole placed centrally in width for hafting attachment. The upper ends are straight or slightly angled so that when placed together there is a slight curve overall.

Another composite comb from Makani'olu consists of two combs, each with three small holes and one large hole and an upper end angling to an apex. The comb length is 40 mm, composite width 22 mm, and it has thirty-four teeth. Deeply incised parallel grooves extend the length of the comb, a feature unique to Hawaiian combs. Interestingly, the outer margin on both combs is plain, forming a frame to the completed comb.

From the same site another composite implement was made from the humerus of a seabird cut diagonally through the shaft at one end, with no haft modification, and was possibly handheld (Allen 2006).

The Makani'olu Shelter is one of the oldest sites in this part of O'ahu (Kirch 1985). A recent synthesis of Hawaiian radiocarbon dates suggests settlement of O'ahu sometime between 1000 and 1200 CE (Kirch 2011), although reassessment of settlement dates on the main island of Hawai'i favors the first decades of the thirteenth century CE (Reith et al. 2011). If this is the case, early settlement of O'ahu, and therefore the Makani'olu Shelter, might also be younger than Kirch (2011) proposes.

Five combs have been reported from the Nu'alolo Kai site on the island of Kaua'i, (Ingalls 2011). The two largest combs resemble those from Makani'olu, and are made from a large bird bone shaft and unidentified mammal bone. The bird bone example is a blank and lacks finished teeth. The three remaining combs are fashioned from the humeri of Newell's shearwater (*Puffinus newelli*) and exhibit between three and six teeth.

An historically collected toothed comb in the collection of the Peabody Essex Museum (illustrated in Allen 2006:109) tapers toward the haft end, like the Rapa Nui and Marquesan examples, and is also attached to the handle some distance from the end. None of the reported archaeological examples have the same tapered shape, so it is unclear how representative this sole surviving example is of tattoo instruments from Hawai'i.

NEW ZEALAND

The large number of combs from archaeological contexts on New Zealand is in marked contrast to elsewhere in Polynesia. These artifacts have been recovered from various contexts and time periods over a wide geographical area from the top of the North Island to the lower South Island. Combs from the first decades after Polynesians arrived in New Zealand in the late thirteenth to early fourteenth centuries CE are both narrow and wide. By the sixteenth century, combs in New Zealand are uniformly narrow, suggesting a related change in tattoo designs over time. However, the wider combs are made from tabs of moa bone (large flightless extinct bird) or tabs ground from sea mammal tooth. Moa were extinct by the mid to late fifteenth century CE and sea mammal teeth were rarely available after that time, which limited the available materials for wide combs. Pearl shell does not grow in the temperate waters of New Zealand, and no composite combs have been recovered.

At Wairau Bar, one of the earliest dated settlement sites on the east coast of the South Island, nine combs were uncovered from undated contexts (Duff 1956), but radiocarbon dates place overall site occupation in the early to mid-fourteenth century CE (Jacomb et al. 2014). The combs range from between 24 to 34 mm in length and 7 to 20 mm in width (fig. 11.9a–h). Five are made of thin ground tabs derived from a split sea mammal tooth, two of tabs of moa bone, one is a split segment of bird bone, and the other a split section of mammal bone. All but one has remnant teeth, varying from five to seventeen in number. In all examples parallel longitudinal incised lines are present on one side, extending from the distal end to near the haft area while the reverse side is plain. Sides of the combs are parallel, or taper slightly toward the teeth. Haft forms are very similar, with a central perforation near the haft end and a concave upper edge, with sides above the teeth grooves reduced in width.

Over 1100 km to the north, there is a site at Houhora, North Island, which is of similar age to Wairau Bar (Anderson and Wallace 1993; Furey 2002). Eight combs are less well preserved than those at Wairau Bar, and several are missing the teeth. Lengths range from 25 to 51 mm and widths from 8 to 25 mm (fig. 11.9i-l). The number of teeth range from six to eleven. Materials include a ground tab from a sea mammal tooth, a ground tab of moa bone, and bird bone. All have perforations for hafting, although the shape of the upper end varies from straight to having sharply angled upper ends. None is the same shape as the Wairau Bar combs. The largest shaped tab of moa bone has been noticeably reduced in thickness at the lower end but has no evidence of teeth.

Tattoo combs from other, slightly later, sites date to the late fourteenth or early fifteenth centuries CE. All are consistent in width (8 mm) and in length (27 to 28 mm) despite being from geographically separate areas. The combs are made from split bird bone and are significantly smaller than those from Wairau Bar and Houhora.[4] All have teeth or short parallel lines at the blade end on one side to indicate presence of teeth. Hafting modification is a perforation or a broad notch on each side at the proximal end. Four slightly longer combs from Shag River, South Island (McGovern-Wilson et al. 1996), are 5 to 10 mm wide and 25 to 38 mm long. Three have teeth and one is plain. The haft forms differ from other examples of a similar age: two are plain without notching or perforations, and two have very reduced sides formed by notching and a scallop at the end.

The largest single assemblage of tattoo combs from New Zealand were looted in the 1930s from a *pa* (fortified site) named Oruarangi, which dates from between approximately 1500 CE and the 1830s (Furey 1996). A total of 152 intact combs eventually found their way into museum collections, plus broken pieces. The combs range from well-finished items to rough slivers of bone (plate 14). Most are made from the longitudinally split leg bones of seabirds, while a small number are fashioned from dog or human bone.

The Oruarangi combs are 18 to 127 mm long, but 81 percent are less than 59 mm long (Furey 1996:54–57), and 85 percent are 3 to 8 mm wide. There are three types: Of the first type, 43 percent have teeth that can be extremely fine. While having a similar width to other types of combs, the majority are between 4 to 7 mm wide and the narrowest are only 2 mm wide. The second type, accounting for 29 percent, have shallow longitudinal parallel lines extending from the cutting edge for up to 10 mm, forming serrations at the cutting edge but no separate teeth. These implements are possibly spent, worn combs which previously had teeth, or acted in a similar way to the plain-edged

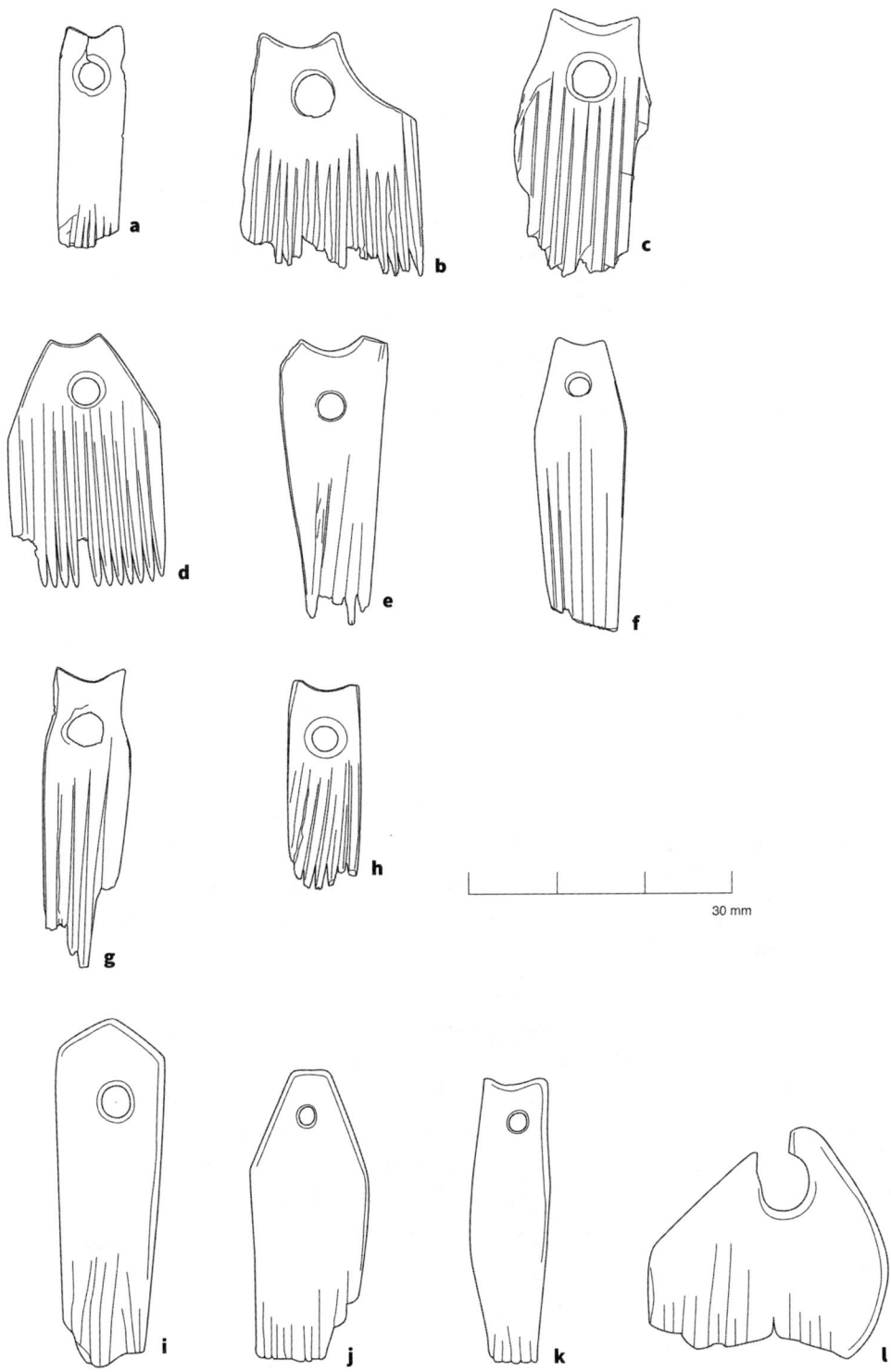

Fig. 11.9. Bone tattoo combs from New Zealand (late thirteenth through early fourteenth century CE): (a through h) Wairau Bar; (i through l) Houhora. Drawings by Louise Furey.

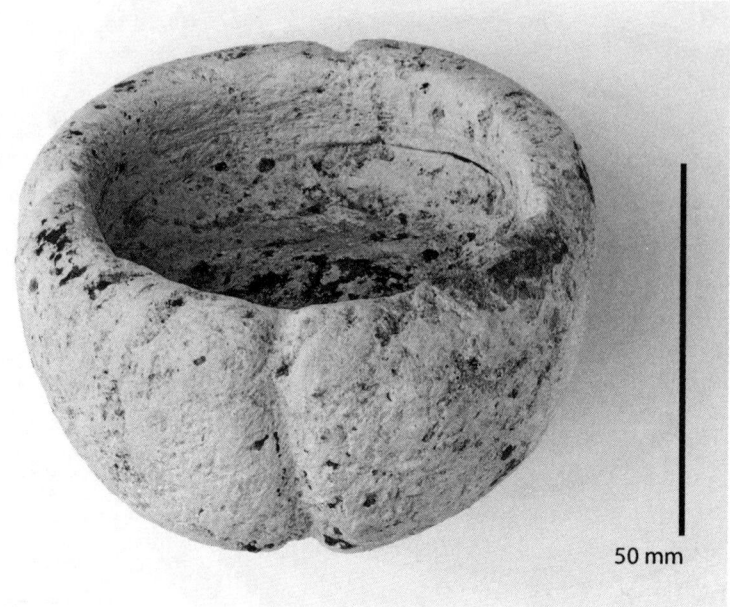

Fig. 11.10. Pumice pigment container for mixing tattoo ink, Oruarangi, New Zealand (ca. 1500 CE). Photograph © Auckland Museum.

combs but allowed pigment to be introduced into the skin via the longitudinal grooves. The grooves can be on one or both sides, contrasting with the combs from the earlier 1300–1400 CE period that only have lines on one side. The cutting edge is always straight. The third type is unique to New Zealand and has a cutting edge that is plain, either straight or rounded, and between 2 to 9 mm wide. This type makes up 28 percent of the assemblage, and fits the description of the implement used to make the cut and create grooves (Best 1904).[5]

Haft modifications of Oruarangi combs are of several types: plain-ended implements (65 percent), which often have an unground proximal edge suggesting they were unfinished tabs; with notches on either side at the haft end (22 percent); or have a perforation for lashing attachment (12 percent). In a few examples there are multiple notches on each side, and two examples with both a hole and notches.

In tropical Polynesia accounts of tattooing describe mallets of light wood, coconut leaf-rib or bamboo, and split coconut shell containers for mixing the black pigment. In New Zealand's temperate climate, alternatives had to be found to the tropical coconut, resulting in the creation of a more durable container made, rarely, from wood (Wardwell 1994:214) and more commonly pumice, which is readily obtained from the inland volcanic zone of the North Island, or as sea-rafted pumice from coastal locations. These containers are shaped by grinding, with small hollowed-out cavities in the interior that often exhibit residual pigment staining (fig. 11.10).

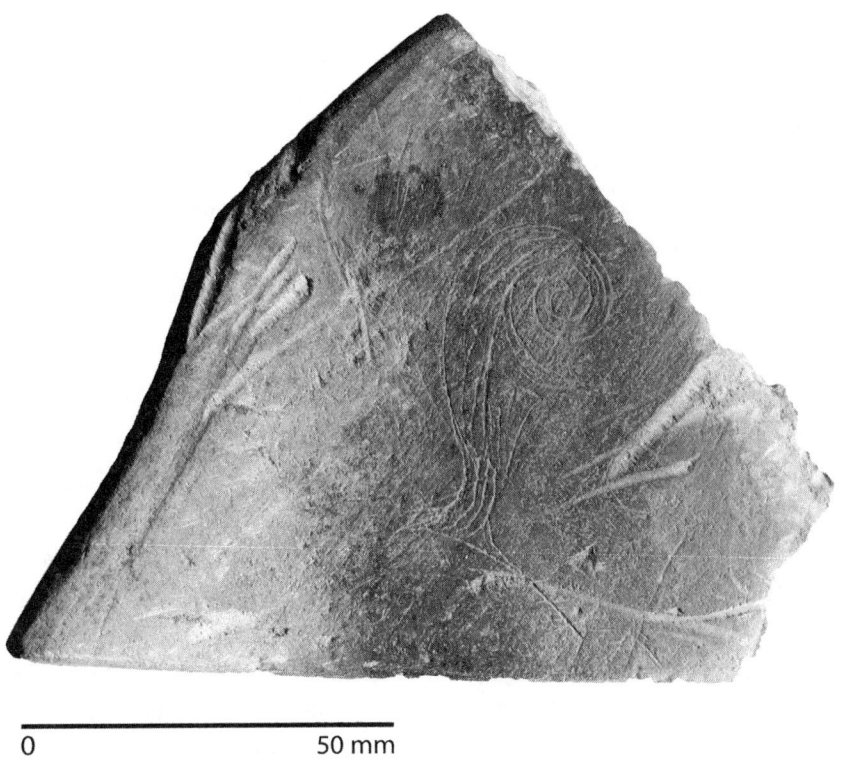

Fig. 11.11. Sharpening stone (*hoanga*) with incised tattoo design. Raupa, New Zealand (seventeenth through eighteenth centuries). Photograph © Auckland Museum.

Although the method of manufacturing combs has not been described, tools involved would have included sharp stone flakes such as obsidian or sharpened shell fragments used for scoring cut lines in the bone, and sandstone abraders for smoothing and sharpening edges. An abrader from Raupa, near Oruarangi, uniquely has a tattoo design scratched into it (fig. 11.11), perhaps the preliminary sketch created by the tattooist before transferring the design onto the skin (Prickett 1990).

The size and type of combs achieved different results, with some implement types used exclusively for particular designs on the face (Best 1904; Robley 1987; Te Awekotuku 2007). The range of tools produced two main effects: plain-edged implements to cut the skin (to outline), and serrated-edged, or toothed, implements to introduce the ink (to shade). While the historic accounts all refer to the use of split seabird bones, there is a single later nineteenth-century reference describing the use of a thorn to prick, and a shark tooth to cut the skin (Robley 1987). No evidence of shark teeth used for this purpose has been found archaeologically.

European contact introduced new materials that were readily adopted into Maori material culture. A unique New Zealand tattooing kit in a leather pouch contains combs made from iron and bone and is believed to have been used prior to the 1840s (Palmer 1958). The iron tools are indistinguishable from bone tools in size but differences are apparent in the haft: the bone examples are plain, and the iron combs have small lugs on each side near the upper end. Traditional tattooing of Maori men was last commonly practiced in the second half of the nineteenth century, but facial tattooing (*moko*) using bone implements continued to be practiced on some women into the 1920s, with a shift toward using darning needles into the 1940s (Te Awekotuku 2007).

Micronesia

Micronesia is made up of over 2,000 small islands grouped into archipelagos of low atolls and high islands. Reflecting the origins of the founding populations, there is cultural diversity in the different groups of islands. Geographically the islands are north of the equator, situated above Melanesia. No tattoo combs have been found archaeologically in Micronesia. This is understandable in the island groups where thorns were used exclusively, but less easy to explain where bone combs were used historically.

The multi-origin settlement of Micronesia is reflected in the practice of tattooing across the island groups. On settlement, tattooing would have followed the custom of the homeland. Over time changes would have occurred resulting from contact between island groups and the influence of immigrant populations. Missionary influence during the historic period caused tattooing to disappear on many islands. Early accounts from the eighteenth and early nineteenth centuries illustrate the designs, and later ethnographies add detail on individual tattoo patterns still surviving but do not report on the practice itself. A comprehensive account of historic observations relating to tattoo in Micronesia is given in Ambrose (2012).

In the far west, tattooists in Palau used thorns, as well as bone tools that were perforated for attachment to the handle and featured two to three teeth. Practitioners in the Caroline Islands used bone combs, while those on Pohnpei and Nukuoro employed citrus thorns or bone implements. Further east, tattooists on the Marshall Islands used bone combs, fish spines, or thorns bound together and hafted at an angle to the handle. Blades from the Marshalls were narrow with three to five teeth, but some wider examples had up to twelve teeth. On Kiribati (previously known as the Gilbert Islands) tattooists used citrus thorns as well as bone combs.

The distribution of use of different materials does not display a clear pattern. Use of bone follows the Polynesian practice, and there may have been influence from the Polynesian Outliers in the region, but use of thorns and fish spines is more suggestive of older traditions linked to Island Southeast Asia.

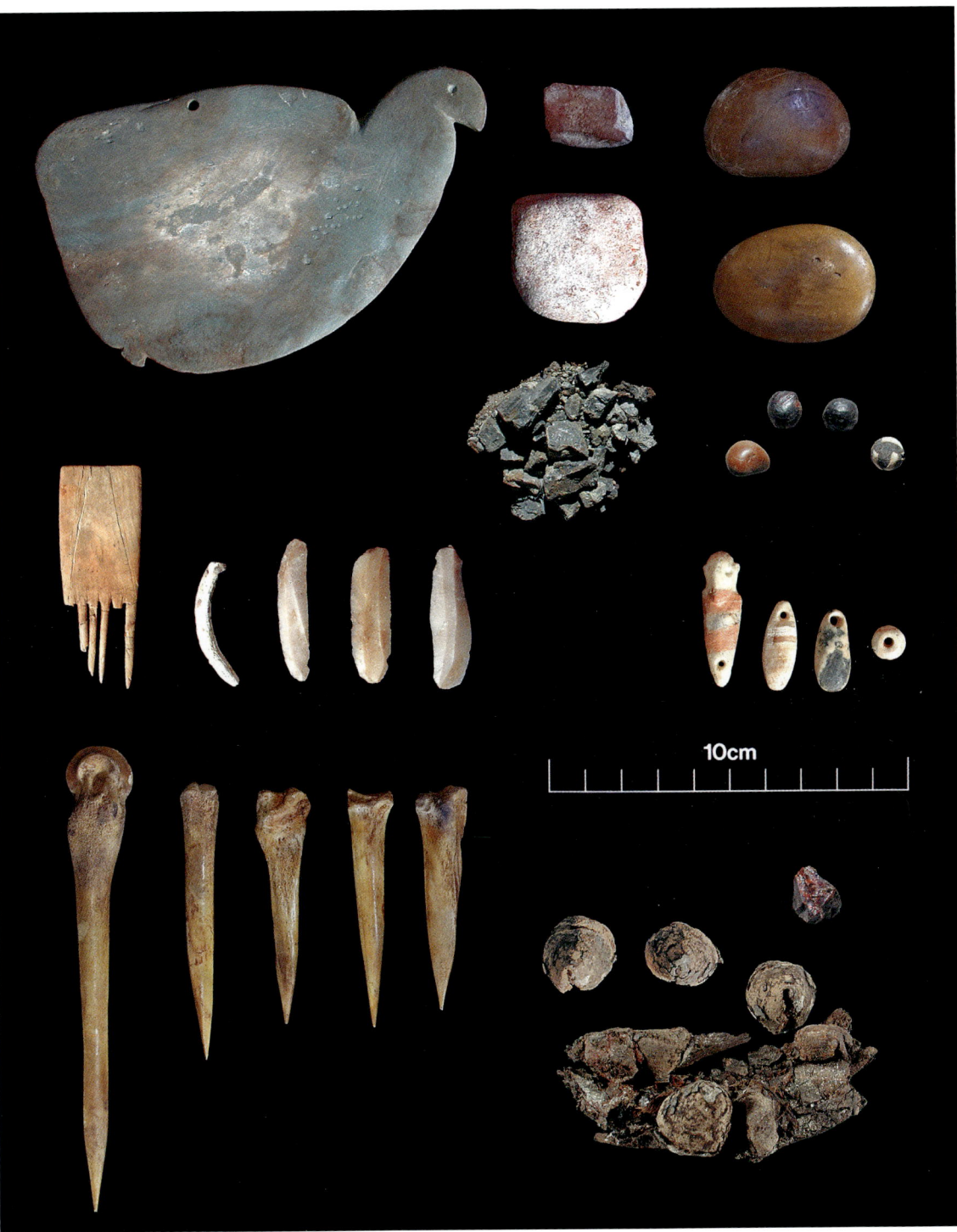

Plate 1. Assemblage of materials found in the burial of a Predynastic woman at Hierakonpolis, Egypt (HK32 Burial 333), which may include implements for tattooing (ca. 3600 BCE). Photograph by Renée Friedman, courtesy of the Hierakonpolis Expedition.

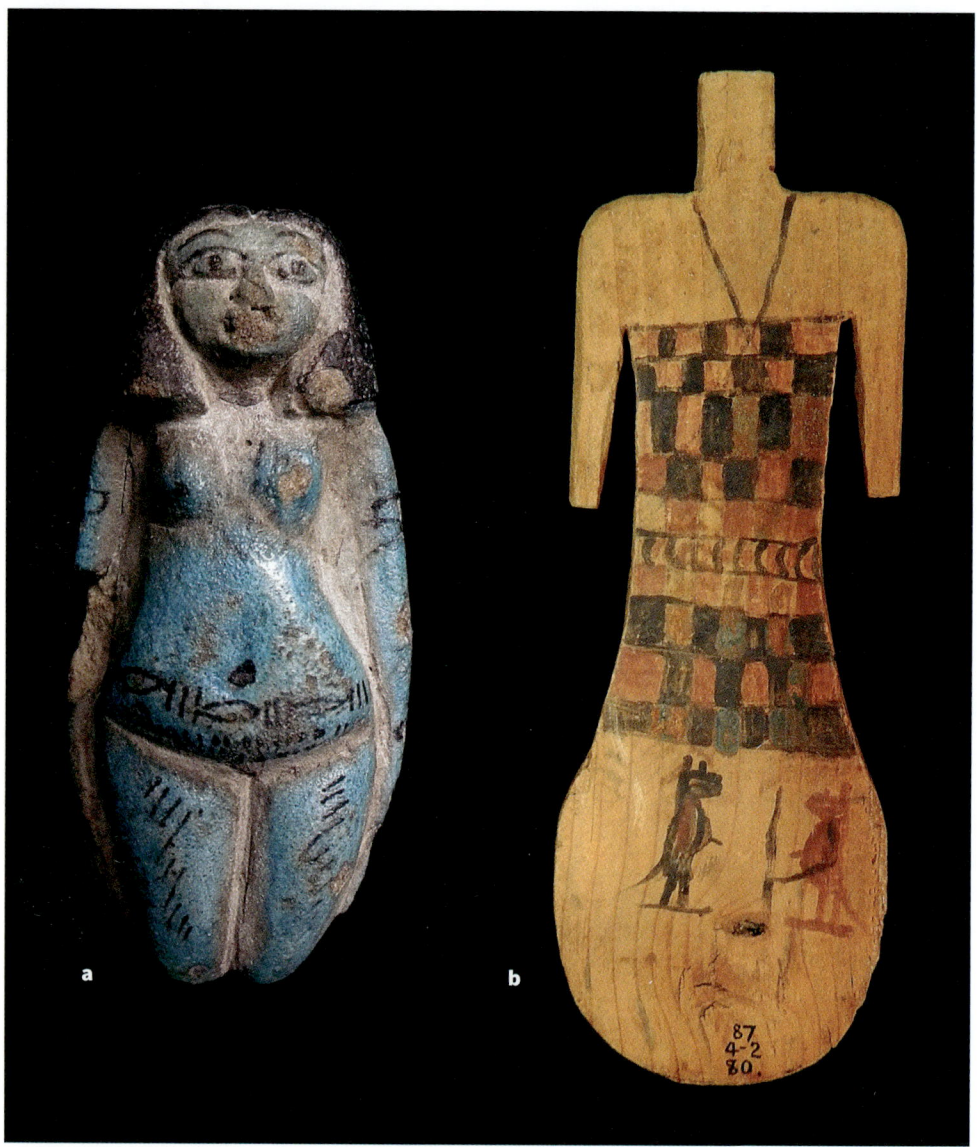

Plate 2. Egyptian figurines with decoration possibly representing tattoos from the Middle Kingdom: (a) faience figurine with tattoos on truncated legs (ca. 1980–1800 BCE); (b) wooden paddle doll, back view, with tattoos of the goddess Tawaret (ca. 2050–1800 BCE); not to scale. Photographs by Renée Friedman. British Museum, London (EA52863, EA33627).

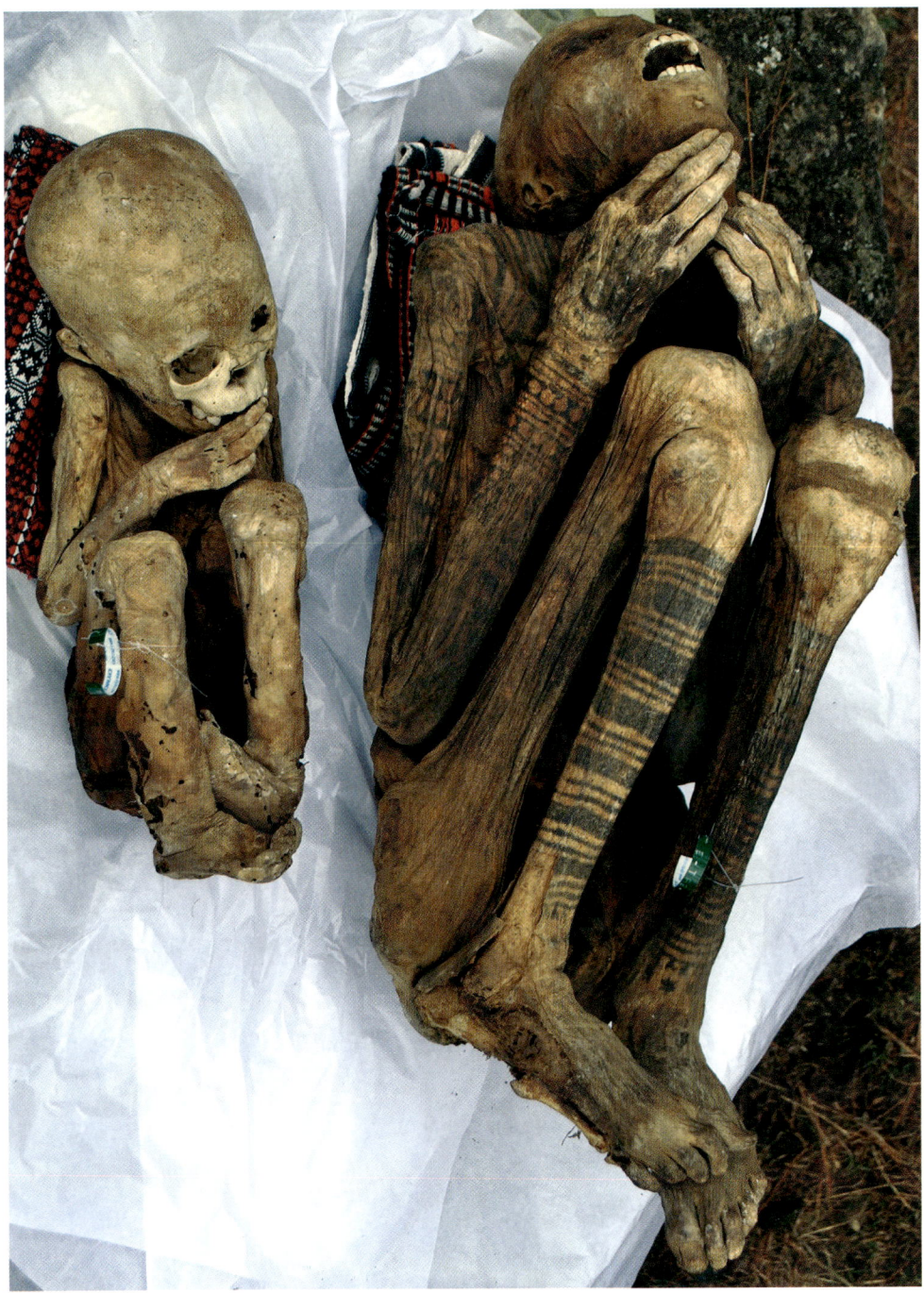

Plate 3. Male mummies from the Timbac rock-shelters, Benguet Province, Philippines. The adult mummy on the right has full-body tattoos, while the one on the left (child) has no traces of tattooing, indicating it has not participated in rite of passage ceremonies. Photograph © Analyn Salvador-Amores, 2012.

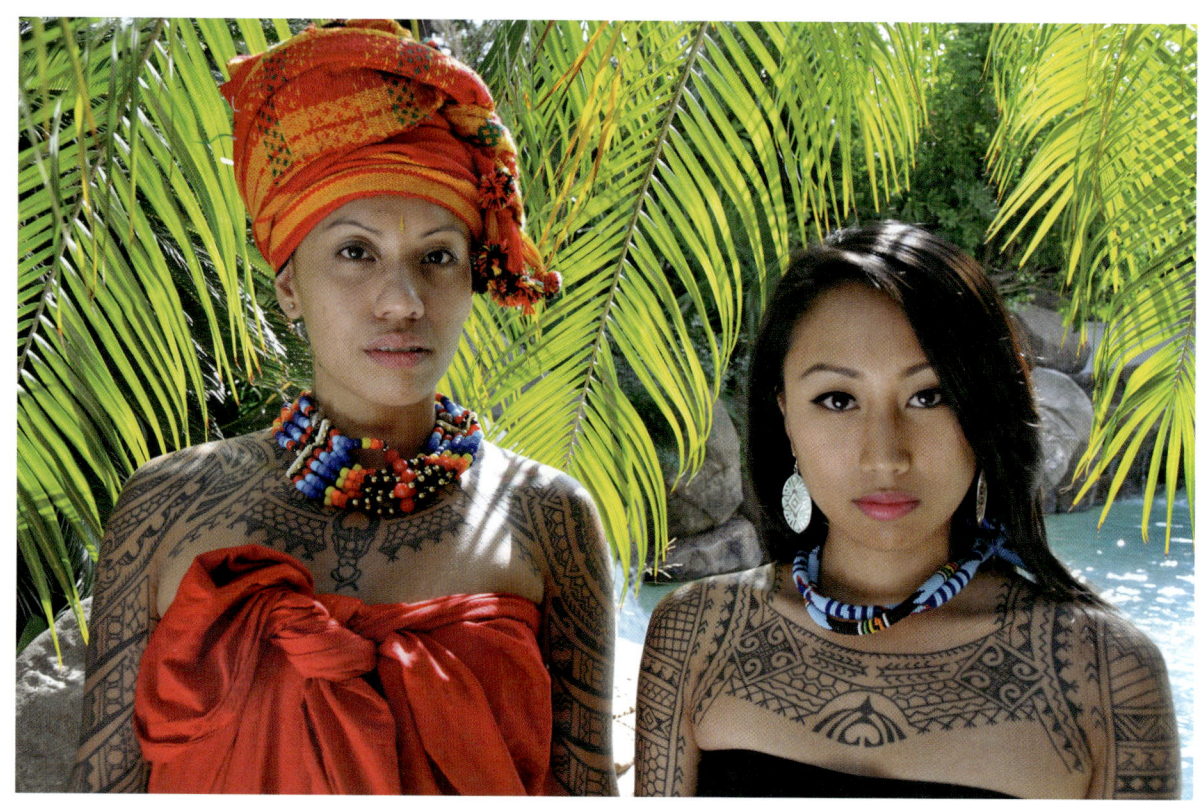

Plate 4. Bianca Gutierrez and Irene Mangon of the Mark of the Four Waves Tribe, an international organization of men and women formed in 1998 and dedicated to the preservation of Indigenous Filipino traditional tattooing. Photograph © Lars Krutak, 2012.

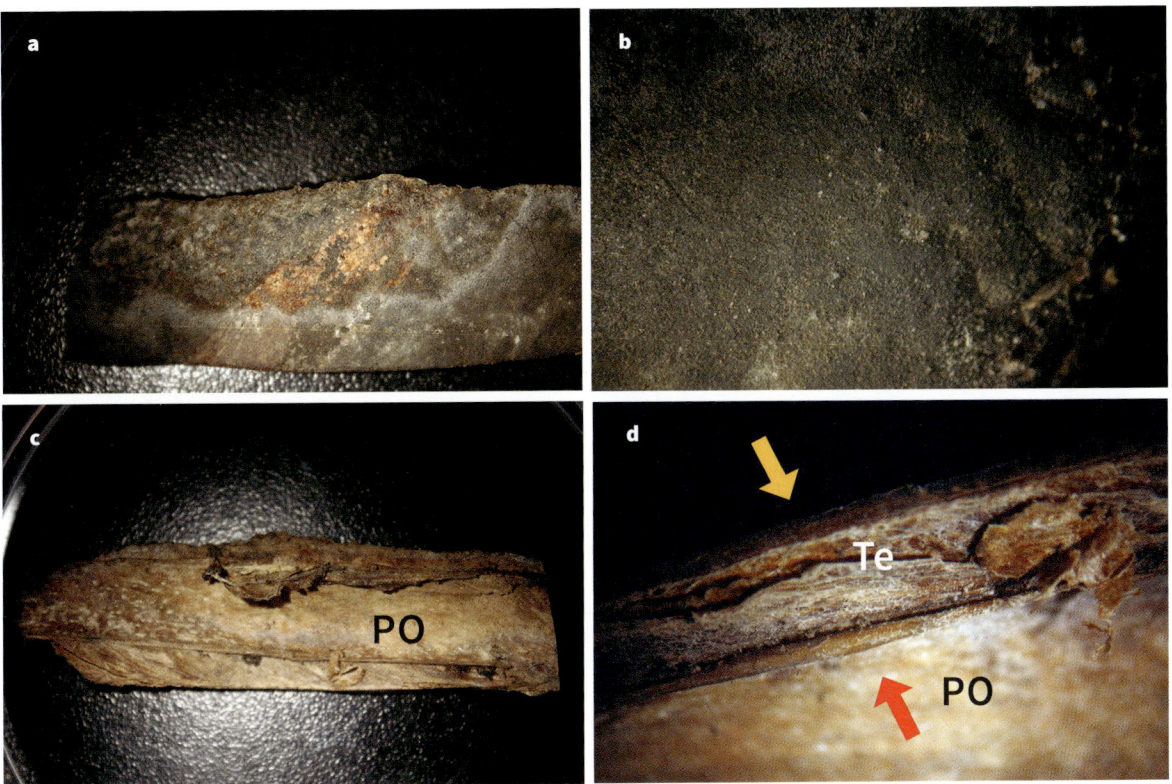

Plate 5. A soft tissue sample taken from the thoracic cage of a Timbac rock-shelter mummy, Benguet Province, Philippines. The sample dates to the eighteenth to nineteenth century CE and (a) illustrates the convex surface, while (b) represents the magnified image of (a). The effects of tanning, possibly the result of fire-induced mummification, can be observed. On the opposite side of the sample, (c), the periosteum (PO), originally attached to the rib, is visible. In the sample cross section (d), each layer of muscle tendon (TE) and rib periosteum were clearly visible. Yellow and red arrows indicate convex and concave surfaces of the sample, respectively.

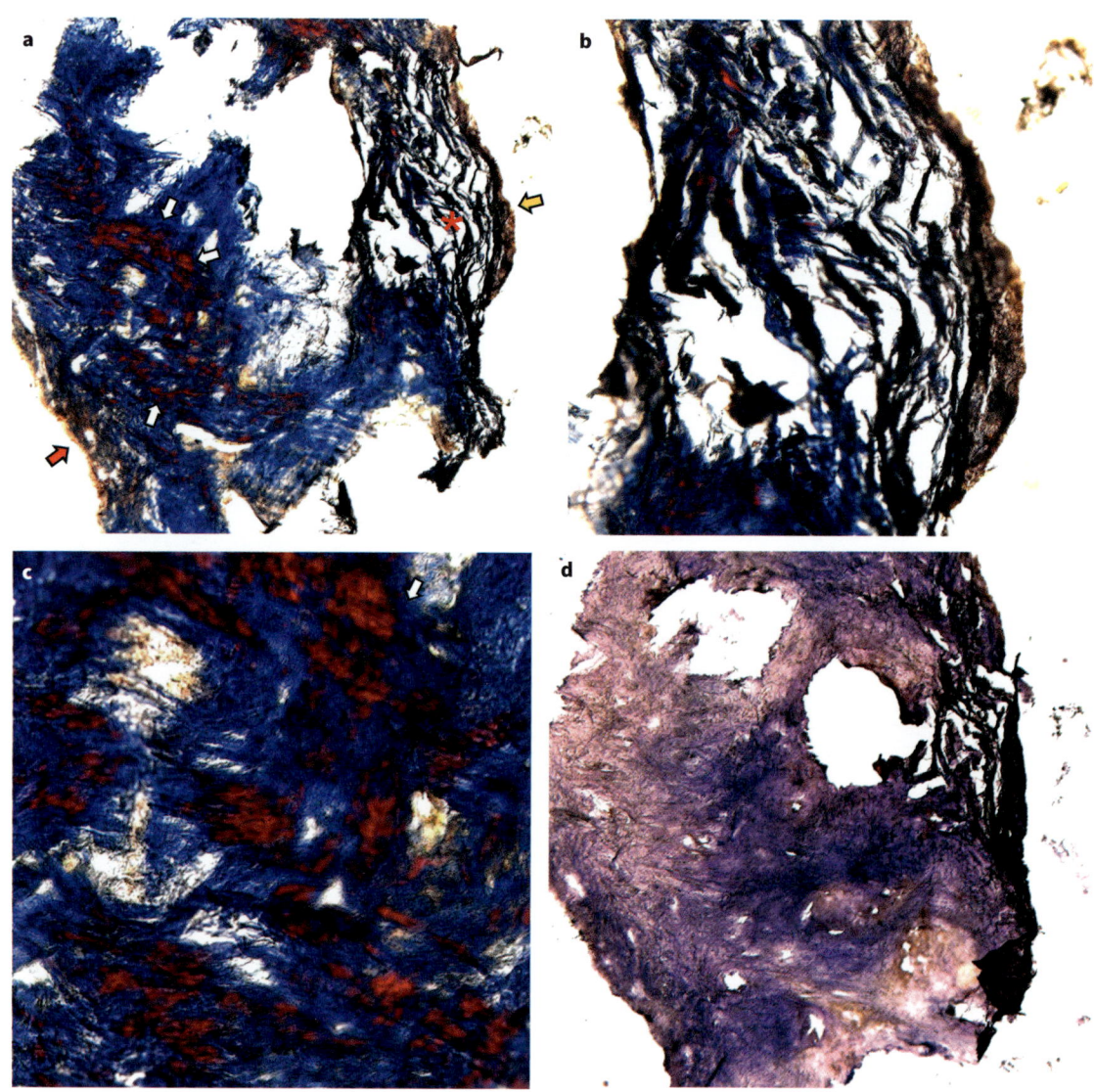

Plate 6. The histological study of the Timbac mummy's soft tissue sample was the first ever carried out on a "fire mummy" from Kabayan, in the Philippines. In the cross section slide (a), yellow and red arrows indicate convex and concave surfaces of the sample, respectively, and the red asterisk demarcates the tanning. Most of the tissue is mainly composed of collagen fibers (stained in blue), while the muscle fibers (red structures indicated by white arrows) are interposed between them. Slide (b) represents the tanning in magnification. Collagen fibers are blackened by presumptive carbon particles, and slide (c) shows the collagen and muscle fibers in magnification. After staining sample sections with hematoxylin and eosin (d), we could not see any remaining cell nuclei.

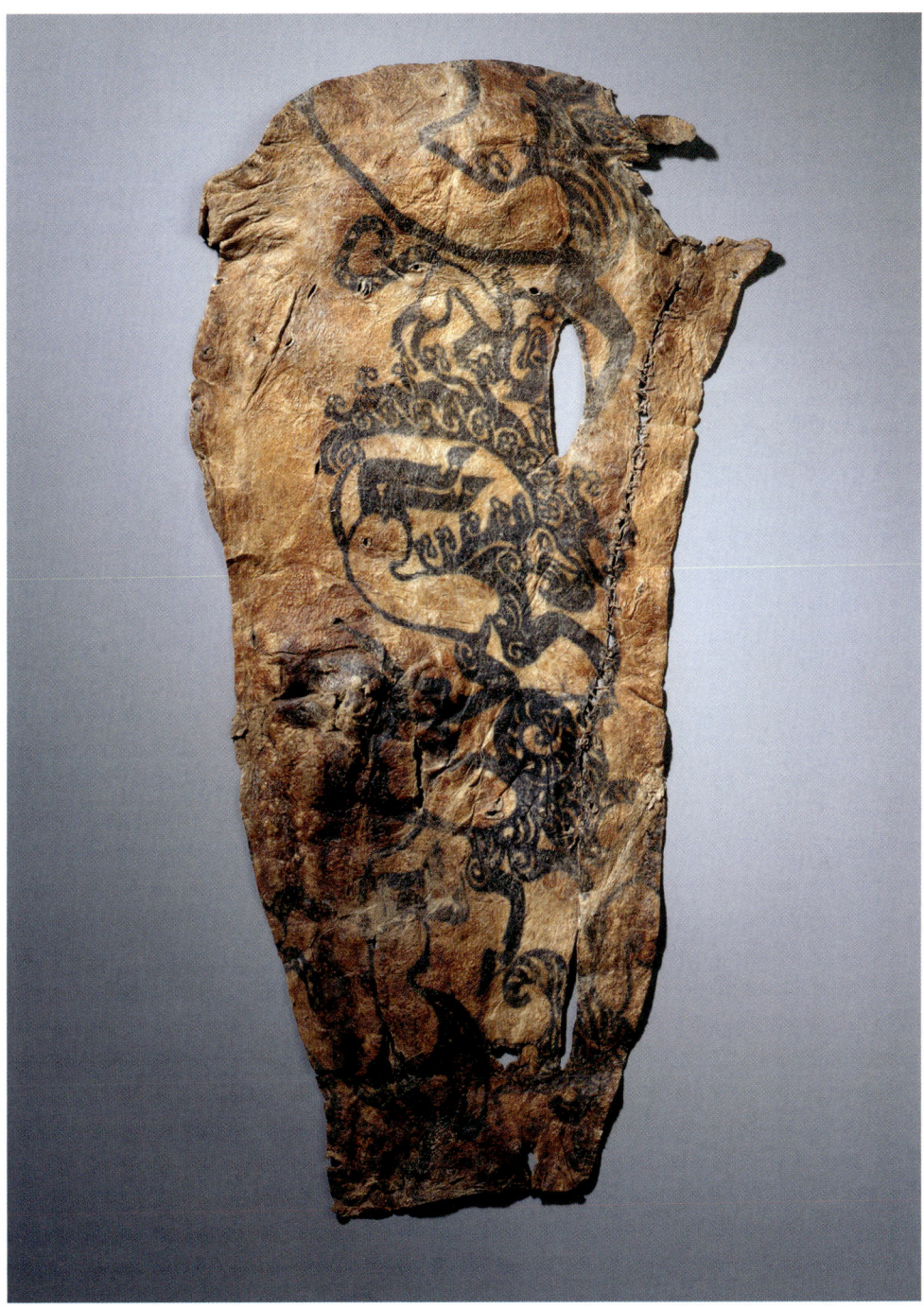

Plate 7. Tattooed skin from the right shoulder of a Pazyryk chieftain, from Kurgan 2 at Pazyryk, Russia (fourth century BCE). The scene depicts a feline predator (tiger) with striped tail, a mythological hoofed griffin, and a wild ram with spiraling horns. The State Hermitage Museum, St. Petersburg (Inv. No. 1684/298), Russia. Photograph © The State Hermitage Museum. Photograph by Vladimir Terebenin.

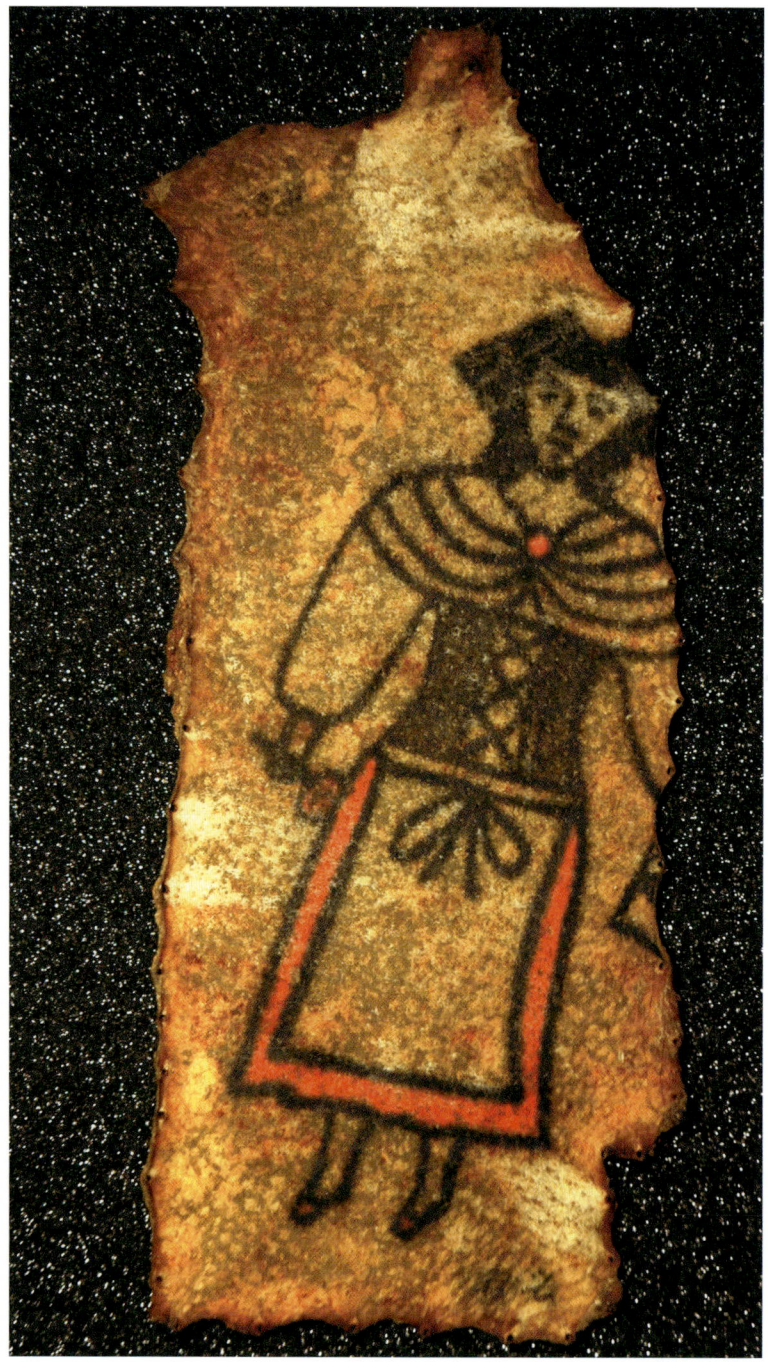

Plate 8. Preserved tattooed human skin from the Wellcome Collection (ca.1830–1929), collected from France and depicting a female figure holding a rose in her right hand. This tattoo shows a rare example of preserved bold red pigment. The persistence of the red in this tattoo suggests the ink used here contained a high ratio or quality of vermilion (mercury sulphide). Science Museum, London (A687), photograph by Gemma Angel.

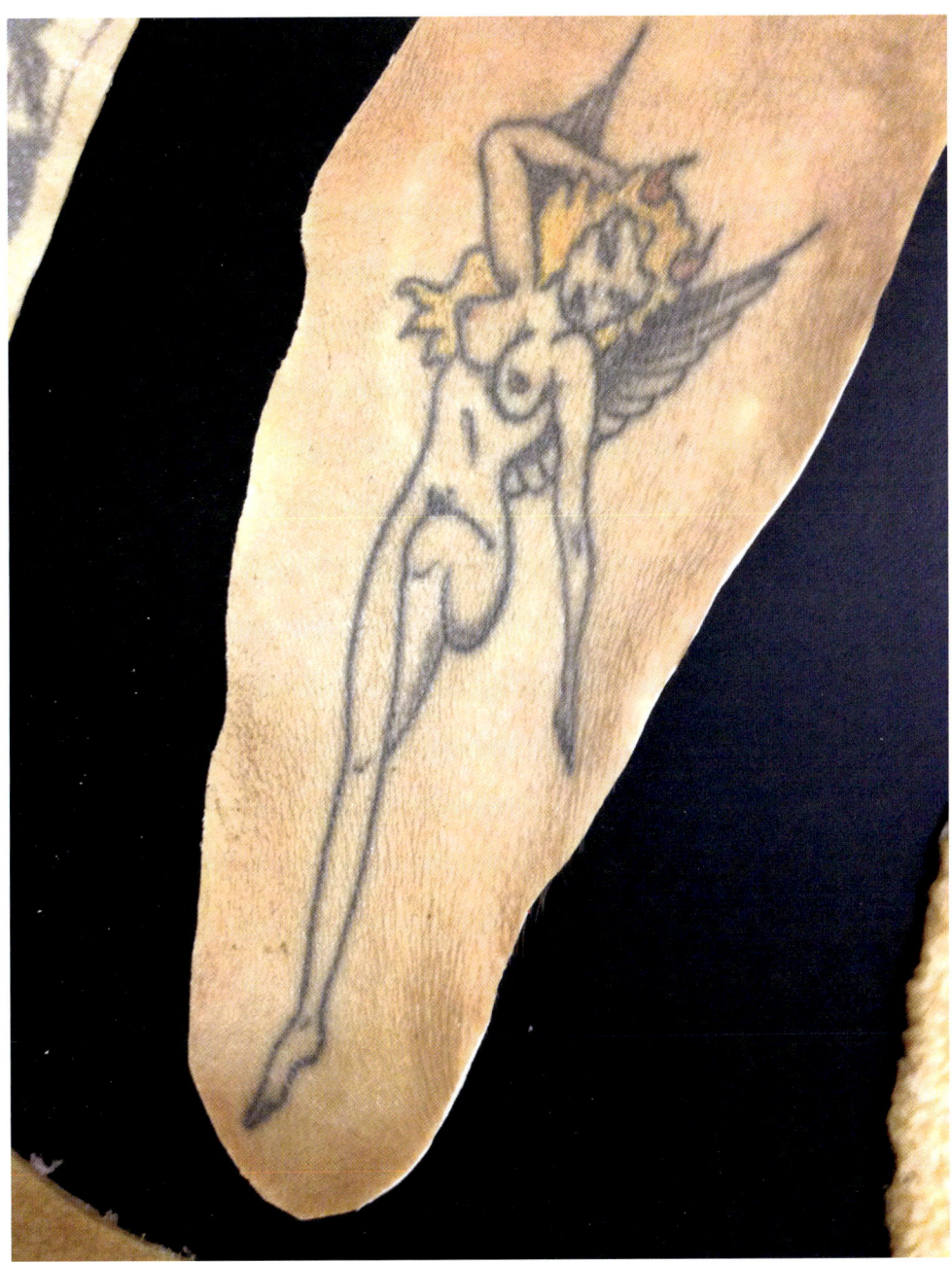

Plate 9. A modern tattoo preserved at the deceased's request by the Foundation for the Art and Science of Tattooing, Amsterdam (www.wallsandskin.com). Tattoos donated to the Museum collection are curated as anatomical works of art for research, educational, therapeutic, and artistic purposes. Photograph courtesy Peter van der Helm.

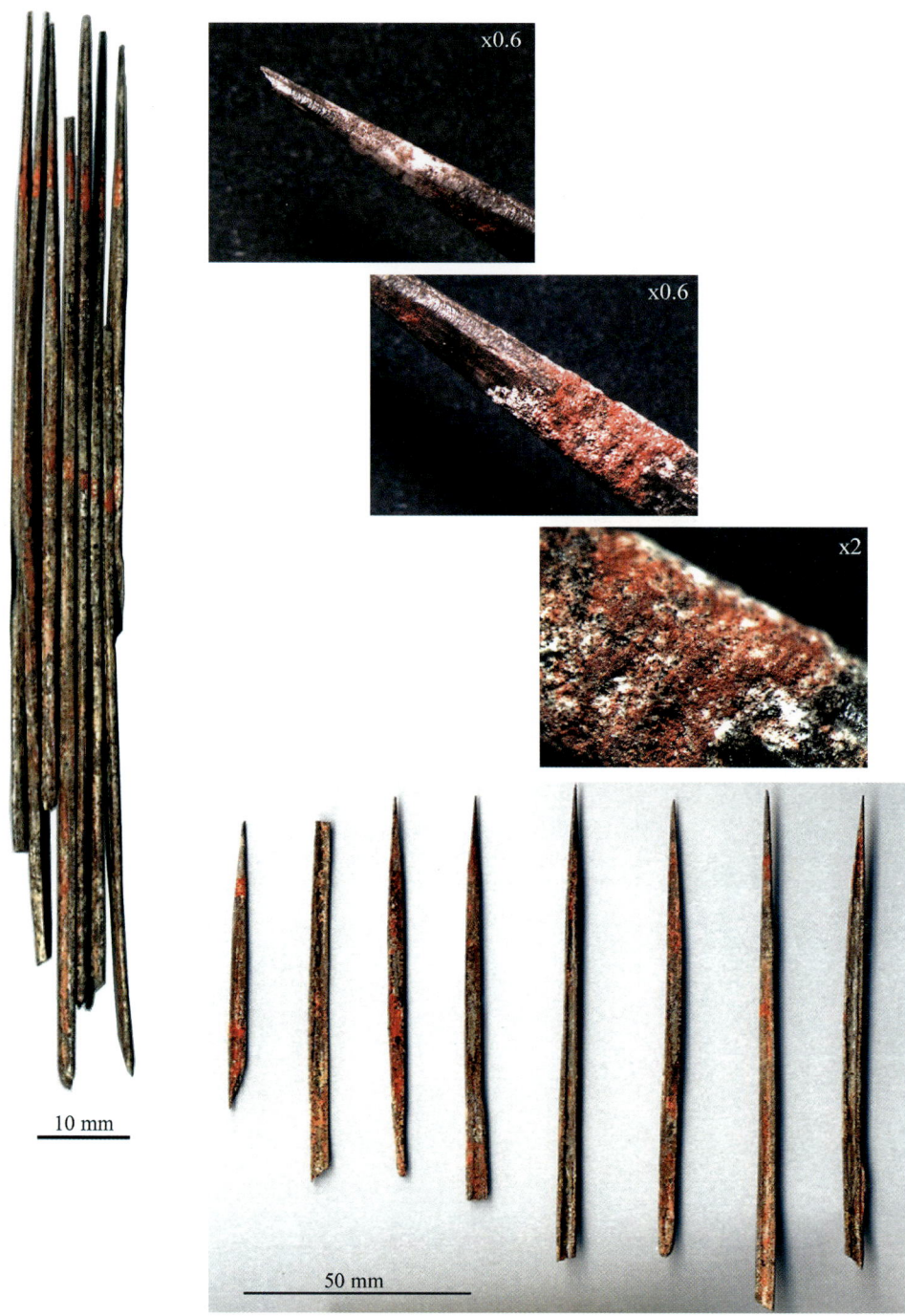

Plate 10. Bundle of eight bone needles excavated in 2011 from Trench B at the Late Copper Age site of Pietrele, Romania (4500–4200 BCE) (Inv. No. P11-B51-1003). The needles are shown bundled together (left) and separated from one another (bottom). Red ochre pigment is visible toward the tips of these tools under magnification (x0.6 and x2). Red linear banding across the grouped needles suggests they were bound together into a single, multipoint implement. Photographs by Petar N. Zidarov.

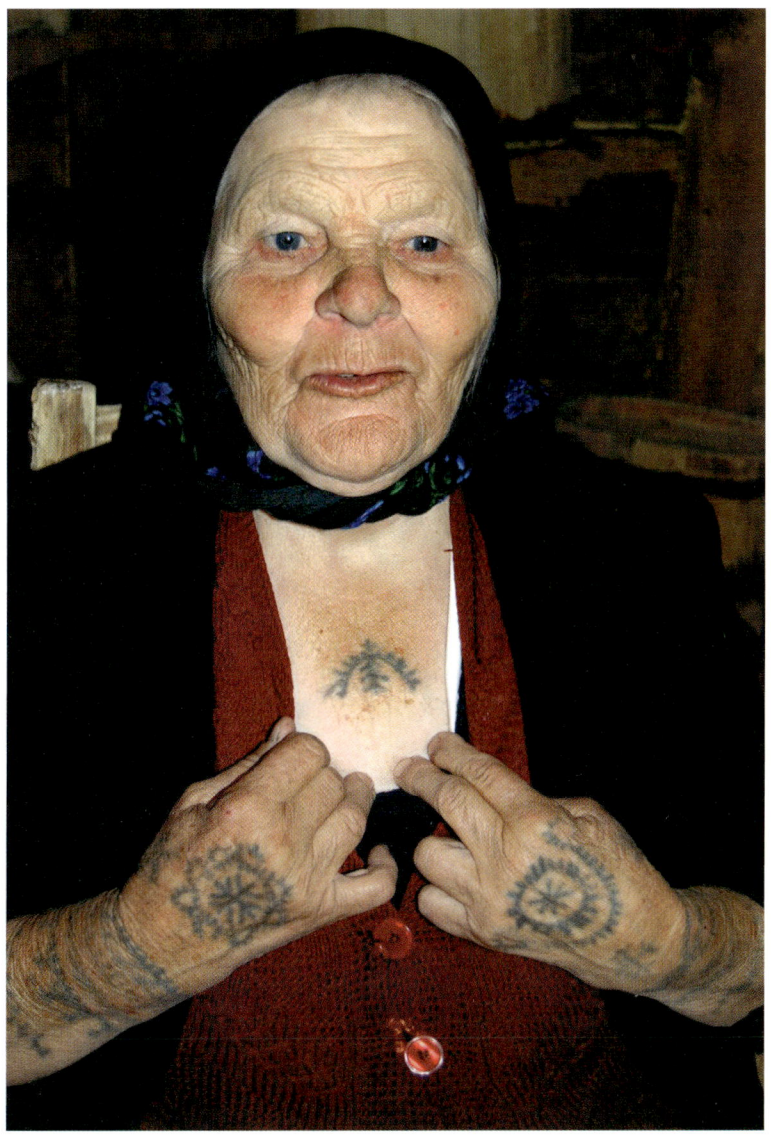

Plate 11. Jela Sivonjíc, a tattooed Bosnian Catholic woman from Zubovići village (2012). Bosnian-Croat tattooing is Europe's most ancient and enduring tradition of permanent body marking. It survived the centuries as a largely uninterrupted traditional practice that reaffirmed religious faith, cultural identity, and timeworn customs and beliefs. Photograph courtesy of Tanya Kanceljak.

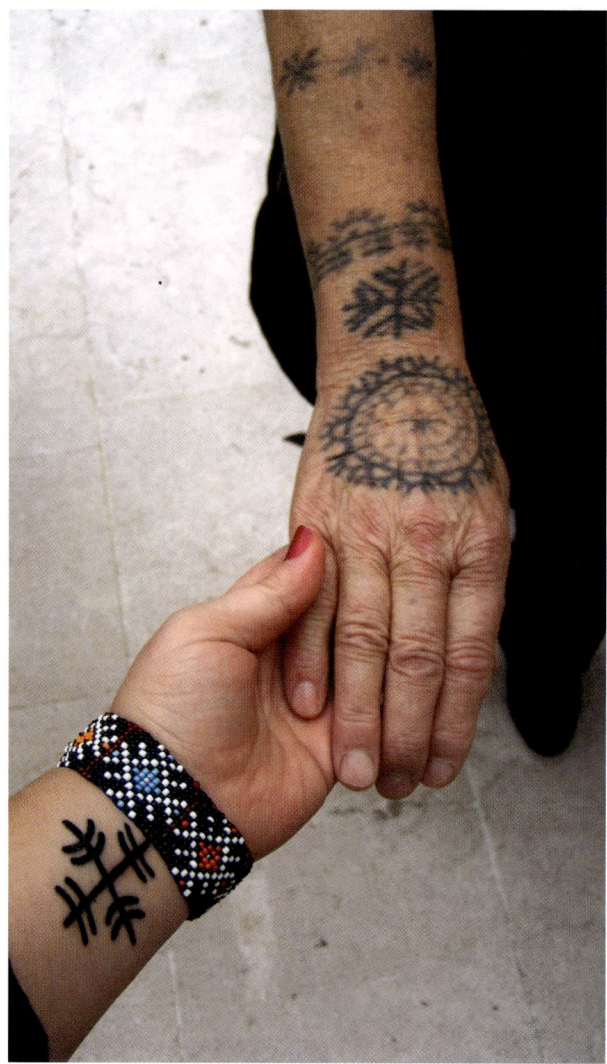

Plate 12. Traditional Croatian tattoos with contemporary revival tattoo worn by Tea Mihaljevic. During the Turkish occupation of Bosnia and Herzegovina (1463–1878), Bosnian women were tattooed with Christian symbols, especially crosses, to repel the amorous intentions of Turkish men. Photograph courtesy of Tea Turalija Mihaljevic.

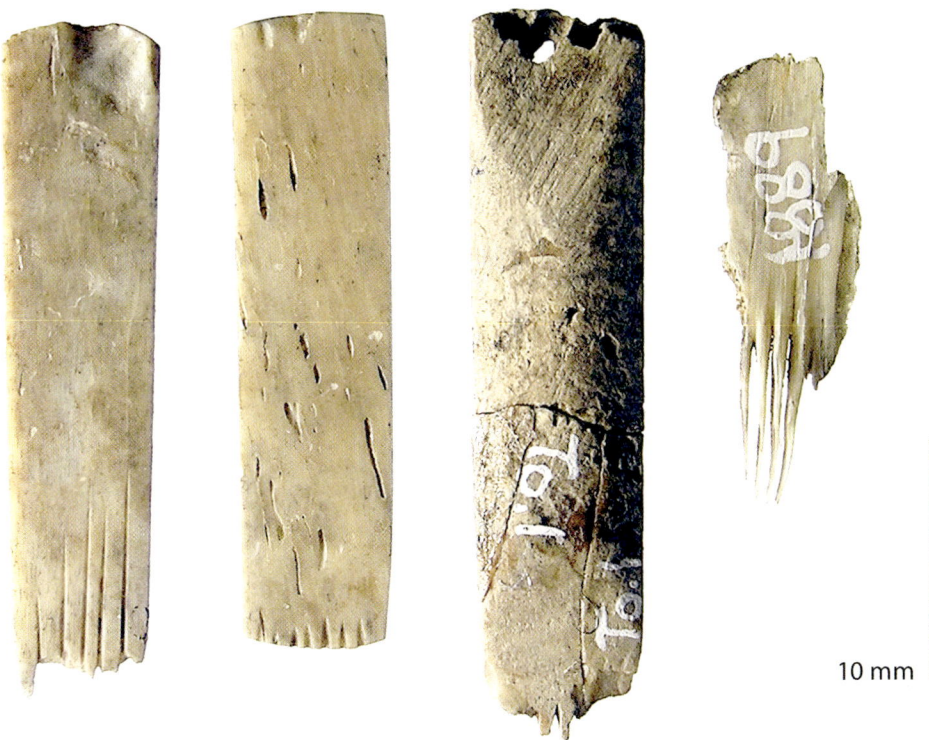

Plate 13. Bone tattoo combs from site Tongatapu To.1, Tonga. These tools were originally interpreted as originating from Lapita occupations, but subsequent reanalysis suggests they are from a later intrusive feature dated ca.1450 CE. Photograph by Wal Ambrose.

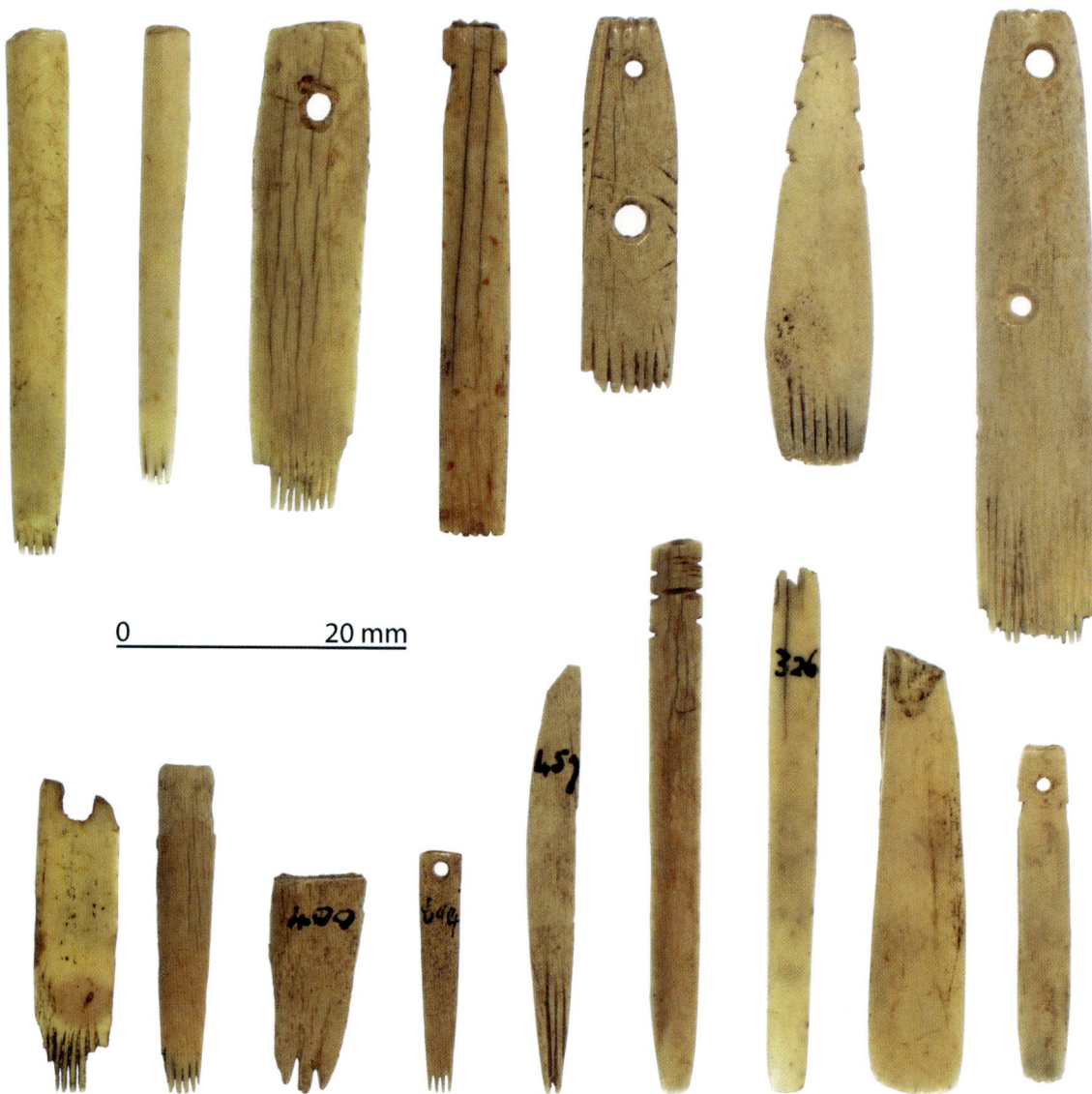

Plate 14. Selected bone tattoo combs from the site of Oruarangi, New Zealand (ca.1500–1830 CE) showing the variations on the cutting edge, including finely pointed, serrated, and plain ended. Many tattoo combs from this site are made from the split leg bones of sea birds, although a small number are also fashioned from dog or human bone. Photograph © Auckland Museum.

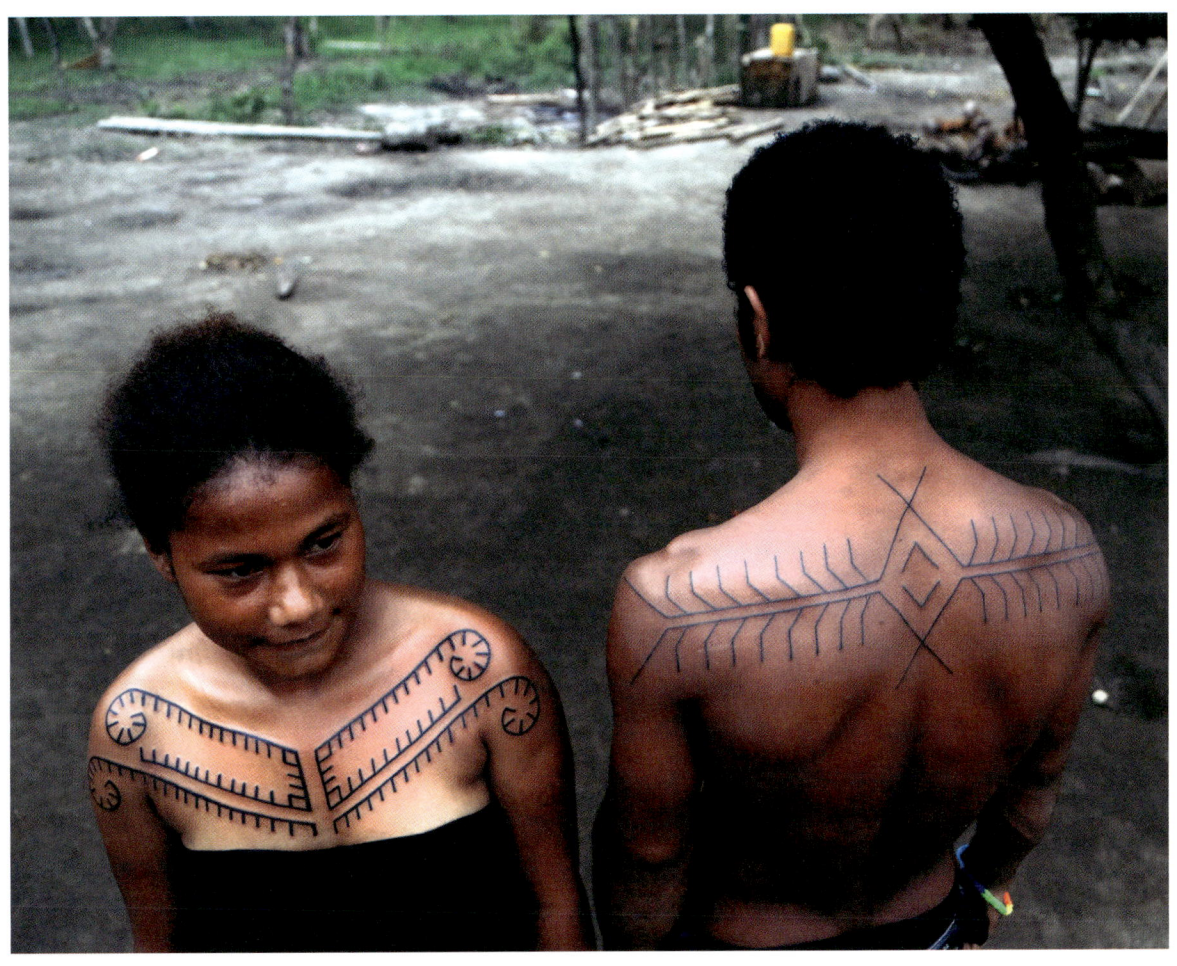

Plate 15. Magaiva Oini Opu and Ofoi Isoaimo Auki from Inawi Village, Mekeo, Papua New Guinea (2013). These bold markings relate to familial patterns and represent the first traditional tattoos given in Mekeo territory in some eighty years. Tattoos and photograph © Julia Mage'au Gray / www.teptok.com.

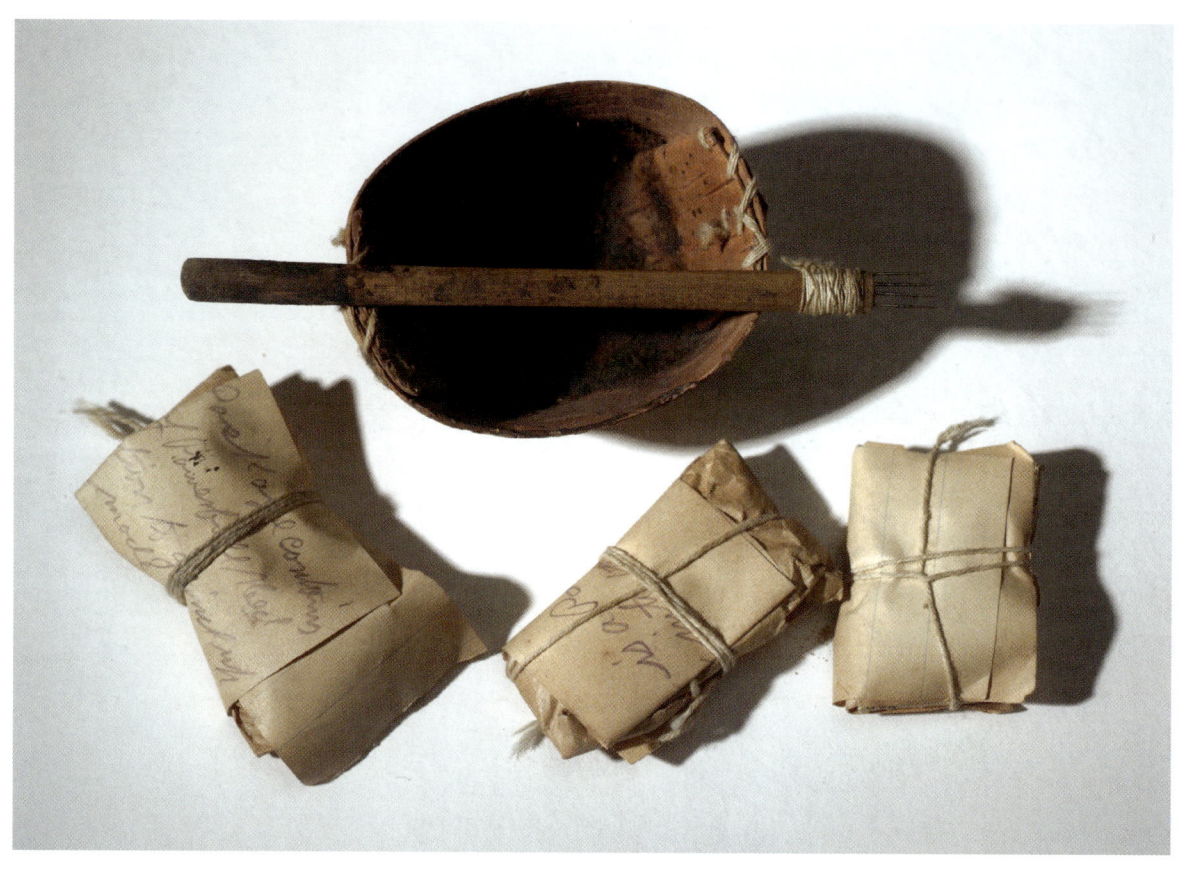

Plate 16. Early twentieth-century Menominee tattoo toolkit collected by Alanson Skinner in 1912 in Wisconsin for the American Museum of Natural History. The kit contains paper bundles of wood charcoal, a bent birch-bark pigment container, and a four-point tattooing tool comprised of steel needles tied to the end of a wooden handle. Image courtesy of the Division of Anthropology, American Museum of Natural History (Catalog No. 50.1/6643 A-E).

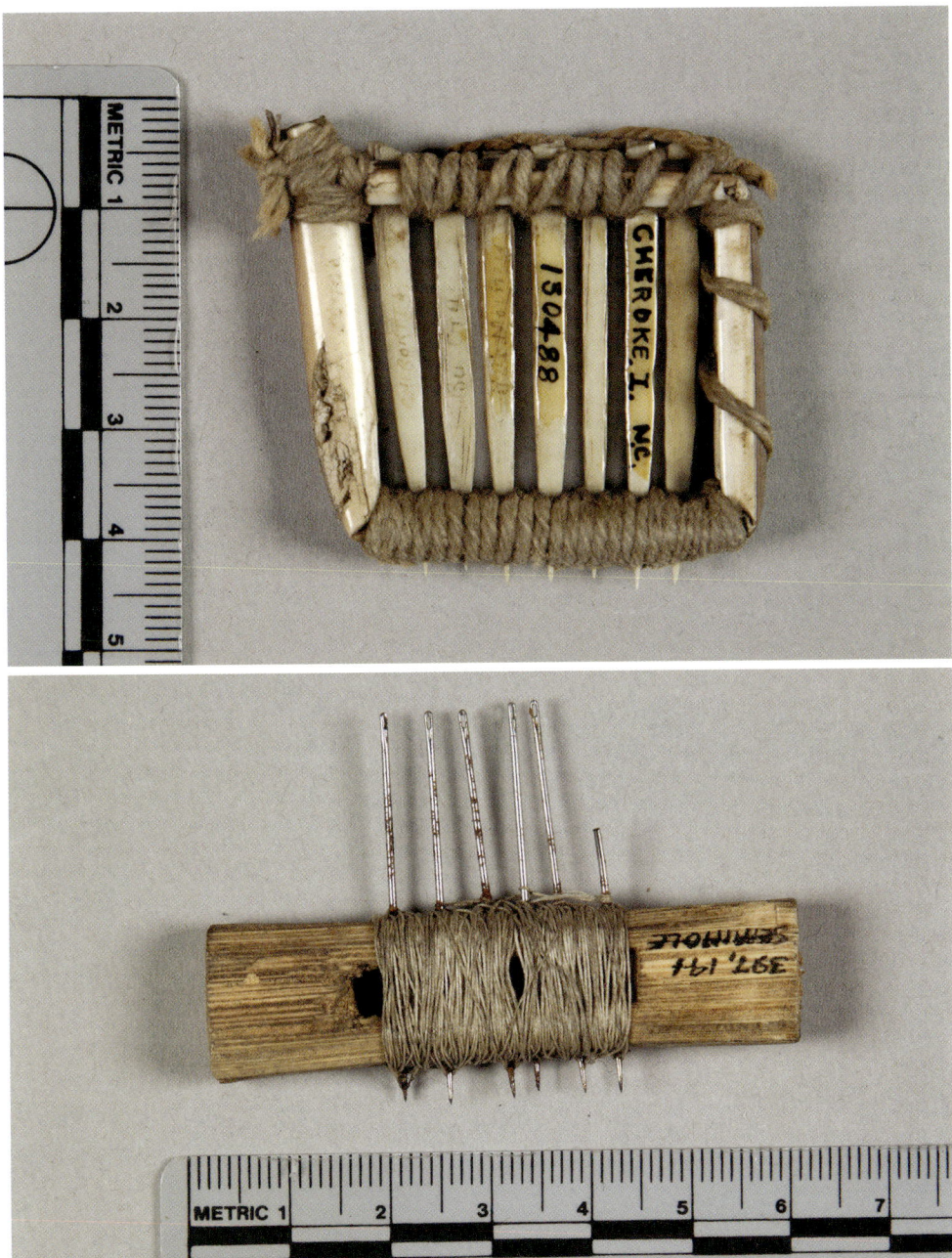

Plate 17. Examples of historic Native American scratchers: (top) turkey bone tines with bent turkey quill frame, collected from the Eastern Band of the Cherokee Indians in 1888 (National Museum of Natural History catalog #E130488-0); (bottom) steel sewing needles set within a hollowed palmetto stem, acquired from the Seminole in 1956 (National Museum of Natural History catalog #E397141-0).

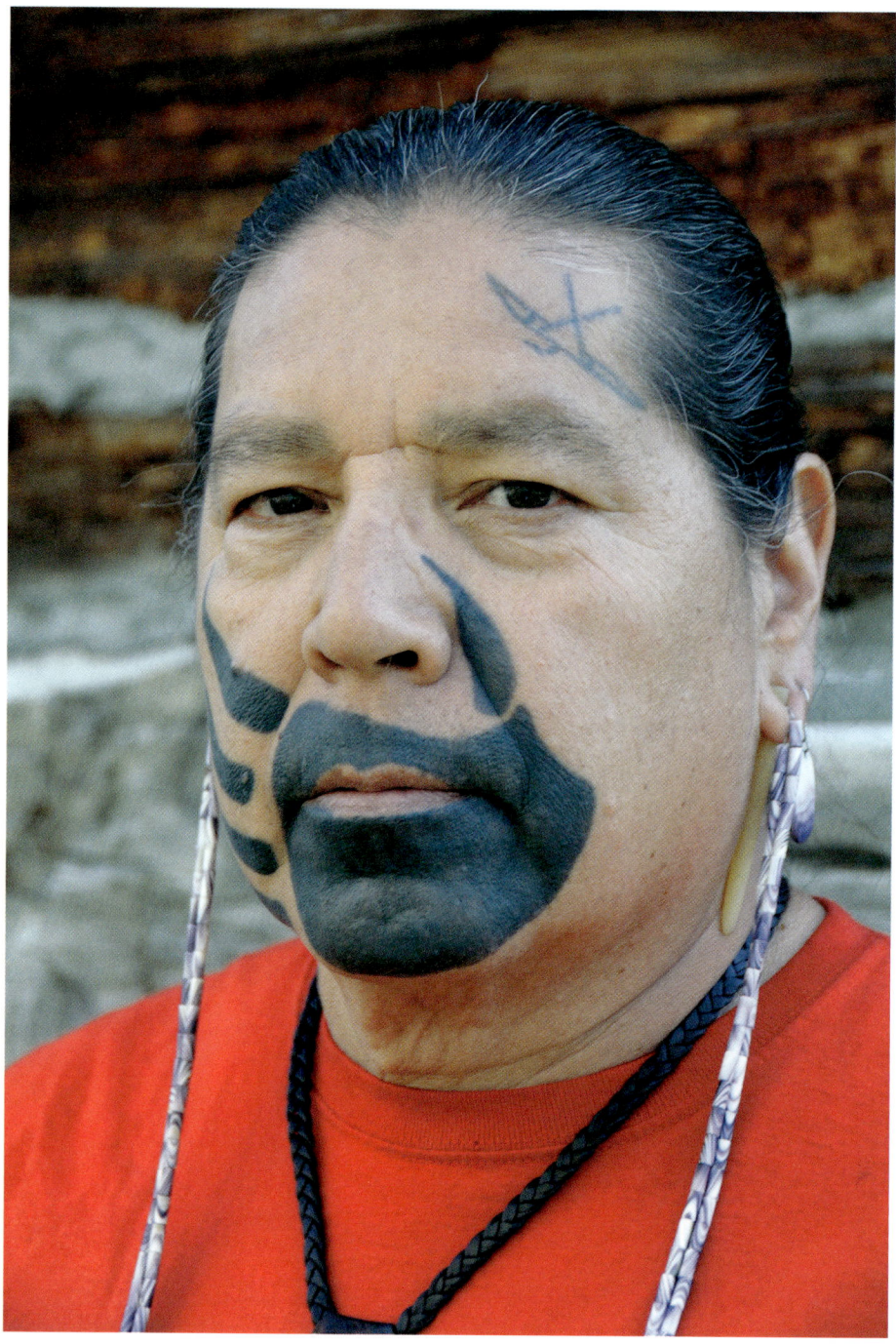

Plate 18. Alan White (Cayuga) bears a medicinal Thunderbird tattoo on his forehead and a bear claw on his face. He is a member of the Bear clan, a medicine clan, and descended from a long line of healers in New York State. White finds his healing medicine in dreams and visions sent to him by the Bear Spirit which he honors with the facial tattoo. Photograph © Lars Krutak.

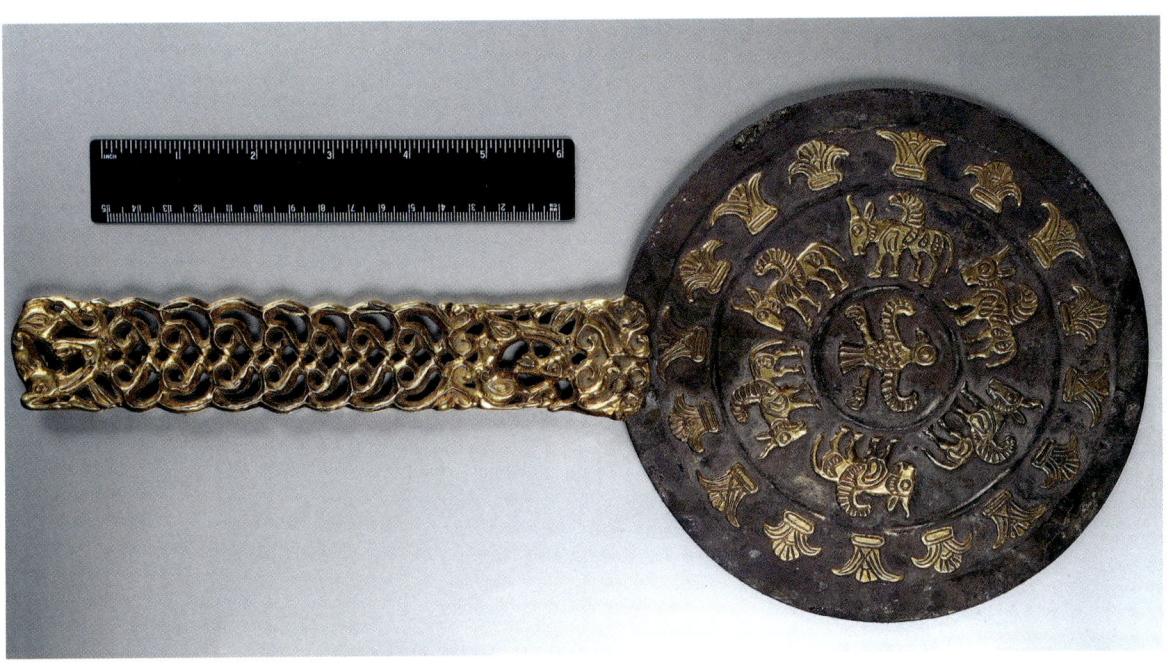

Plate 19. Rear of a silver and gold mirror from Kurgan 1, Burial 2, from the Filippovka 1 burial ground, Russia (PP 19971/10, DR-2295). The length of the handle measures 20 cm, while the diameter of the mirror measures 17.75 cm. Photography by Olga Anikeeva. Courtesy of the Orenburg Governor's Museum of Local Lore and History.

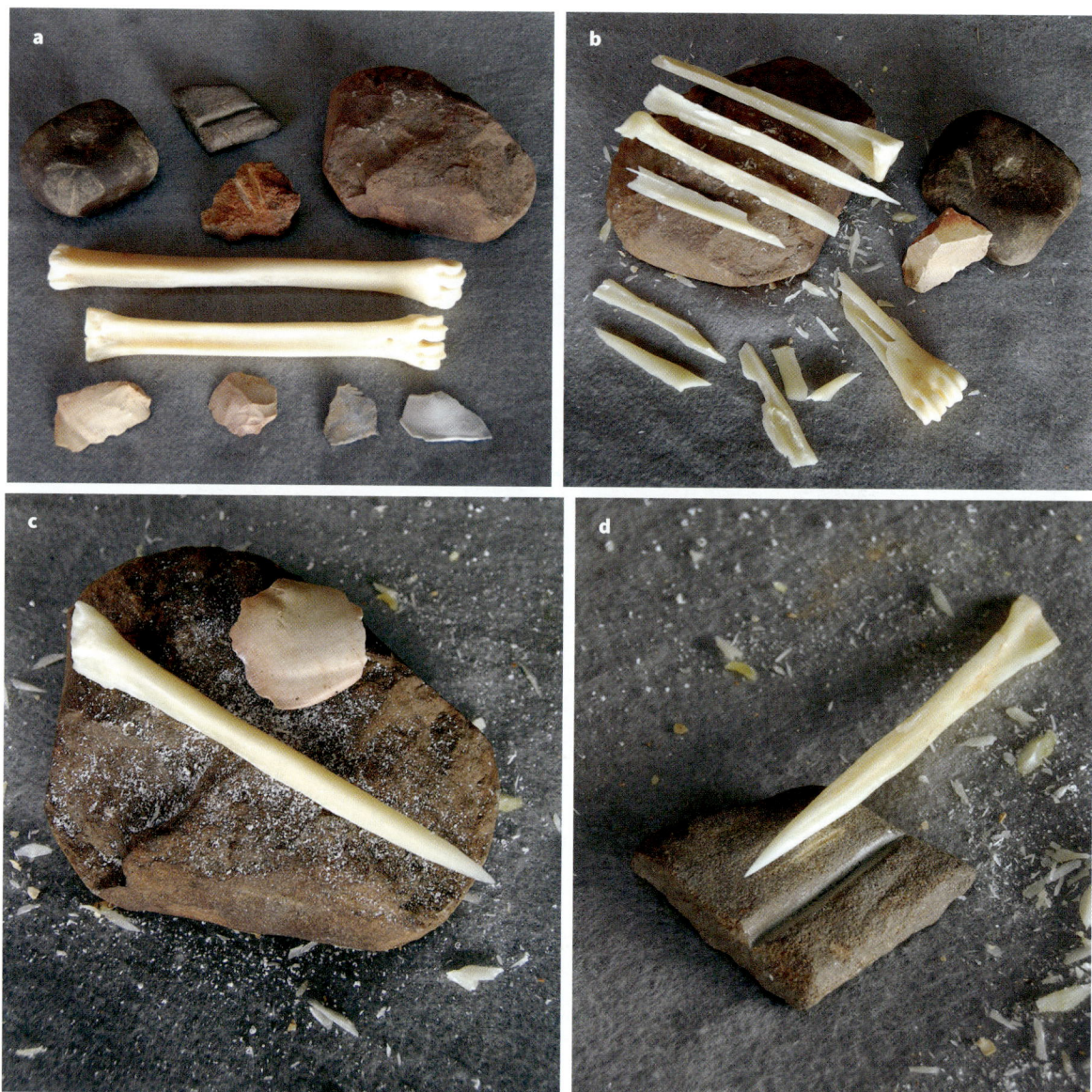

Plate 20. Manufacture of deer bone tools for experimental tattooing: (a) unworked bone shown alongside stone tools used in manufacture; (b) deer bone is scored with chert tools and split using flake wedges and bipolar percussion; (c) removal of bone splinters and initial shaping with chert flakes; and (d) final sharpening by longitudinal grinding on abrasive stone.

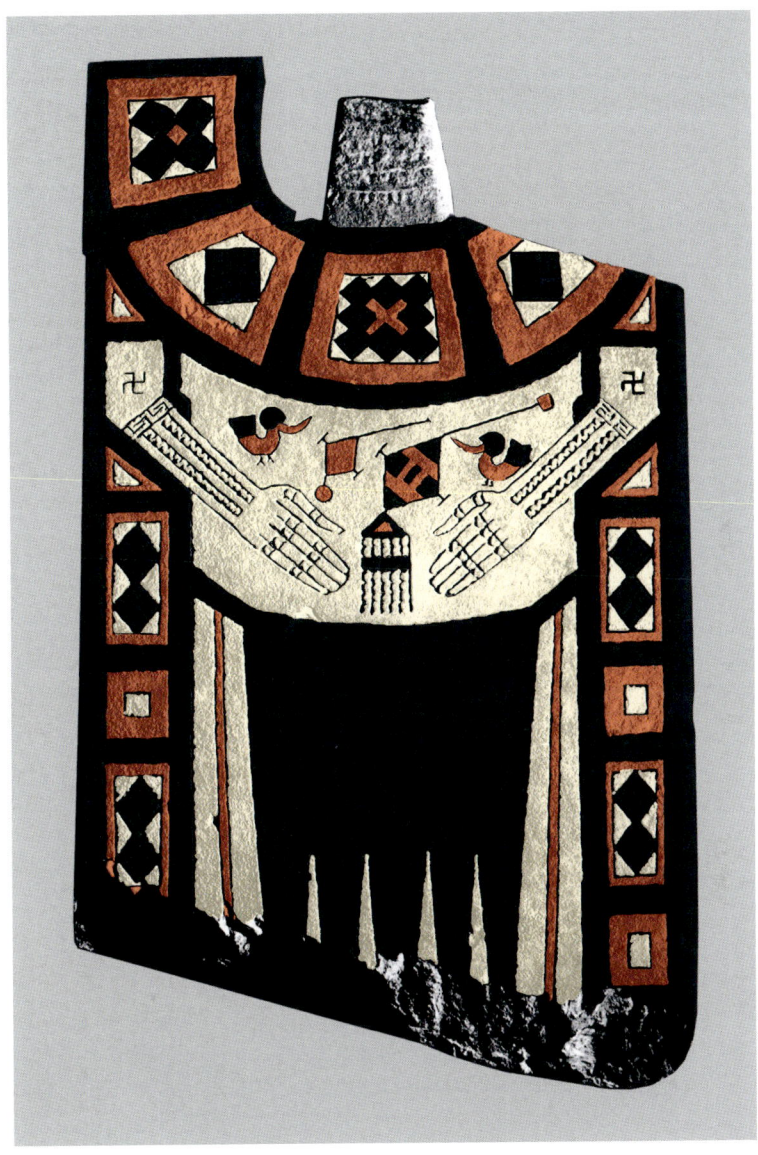

Plate 21. Female Daunian stela (circa 600–500 BCE), Museo archeologico nazionale di Manfredonia, Italy, photography with original colors reconstructed by Norman (2011b:43, fig. 3.10 and plate 1, after Nava 1980: no. 622, plate 198). Writers of antiquity documented tattooing traditions among several Iapygian peoples of which the Daunians were one. Although the precise function of Daunian tattoo remains unknown, ancient ceramics and monumental stelae affirm that women favoured intricate hand tattooing.

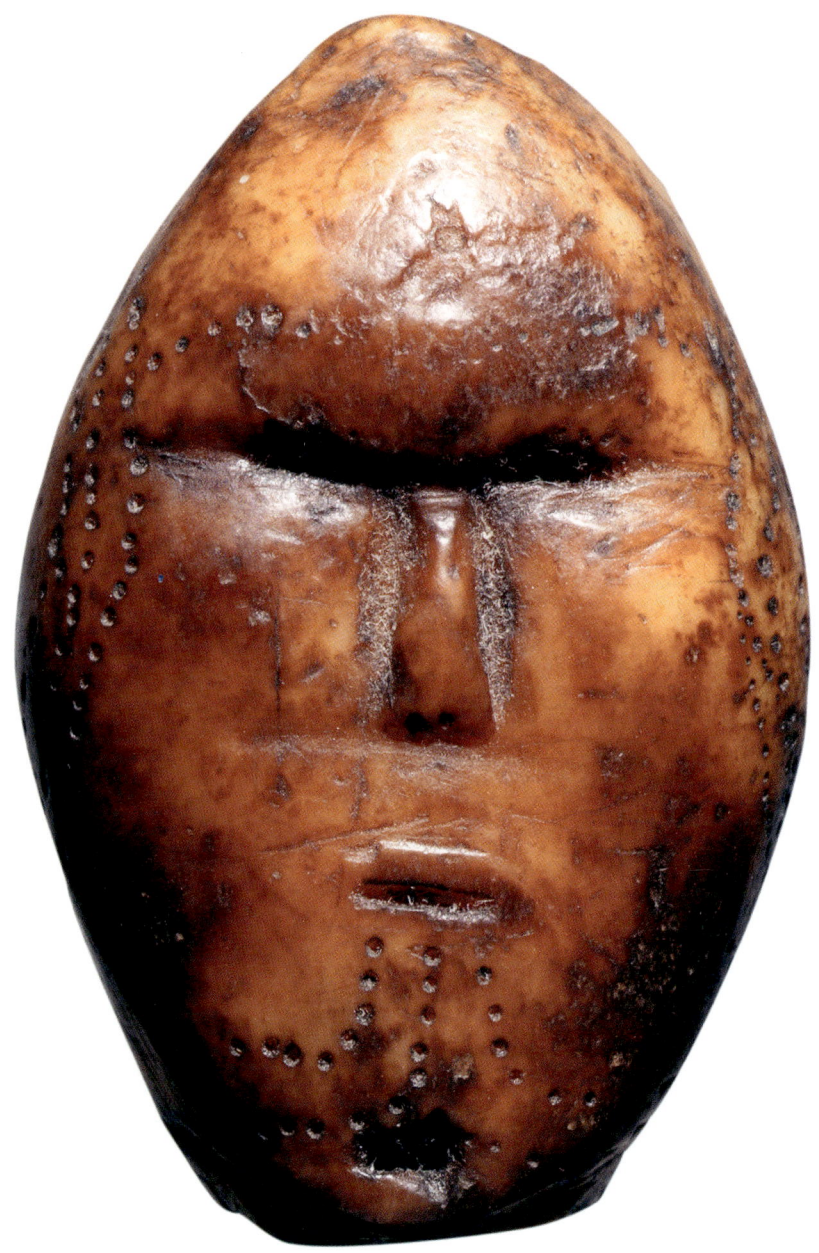

Plate 22. Punuk figure head. Walrus ivory, height 13 cm, St. Lawrence Island, Alaska. In the Punuk period, new styles of tattooing emerged on St. Lawrence Island, including bands of tattooing on the cheeks that sometimes circled the face, and various forms of chin and body designs. The cheek bands on this female figure likely represent charms against infertility. Collection of Bill and Carol Wolf, New Jersey.

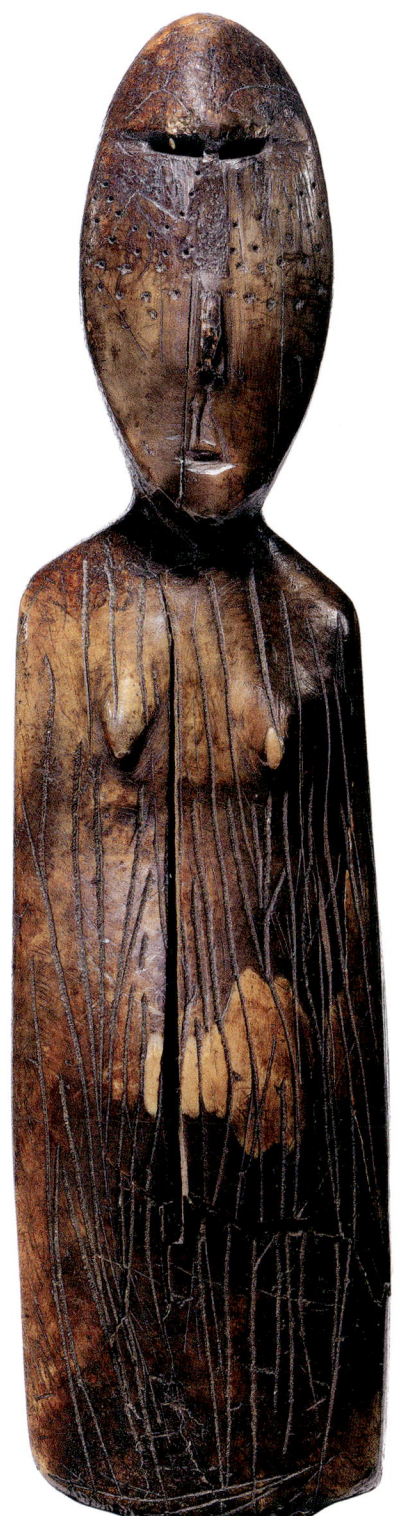

Plate 23. Okvik female figure, walrus ivory, height 15.25 cm, Bering Sea region, Alaska. Heavily marked with body striations and drilled facial perforations possibly representing tattoos, this early Okvik sculpture might have been used in hunting or fertility ceremonies. The deeply cut eyes and small mouth may have been "fed" with offerings, although other objects of this form possess eyes inset with jadeite (Carpenter 2011:112, fig. 25). The flowing curvilinear forehead markings and dot-like facial motifs closely resemble aspects of historic female tattoo traditions of West Greenland and the Inuit region. Donald Ellis Gallery, Dundas (Ontario) and New York City.

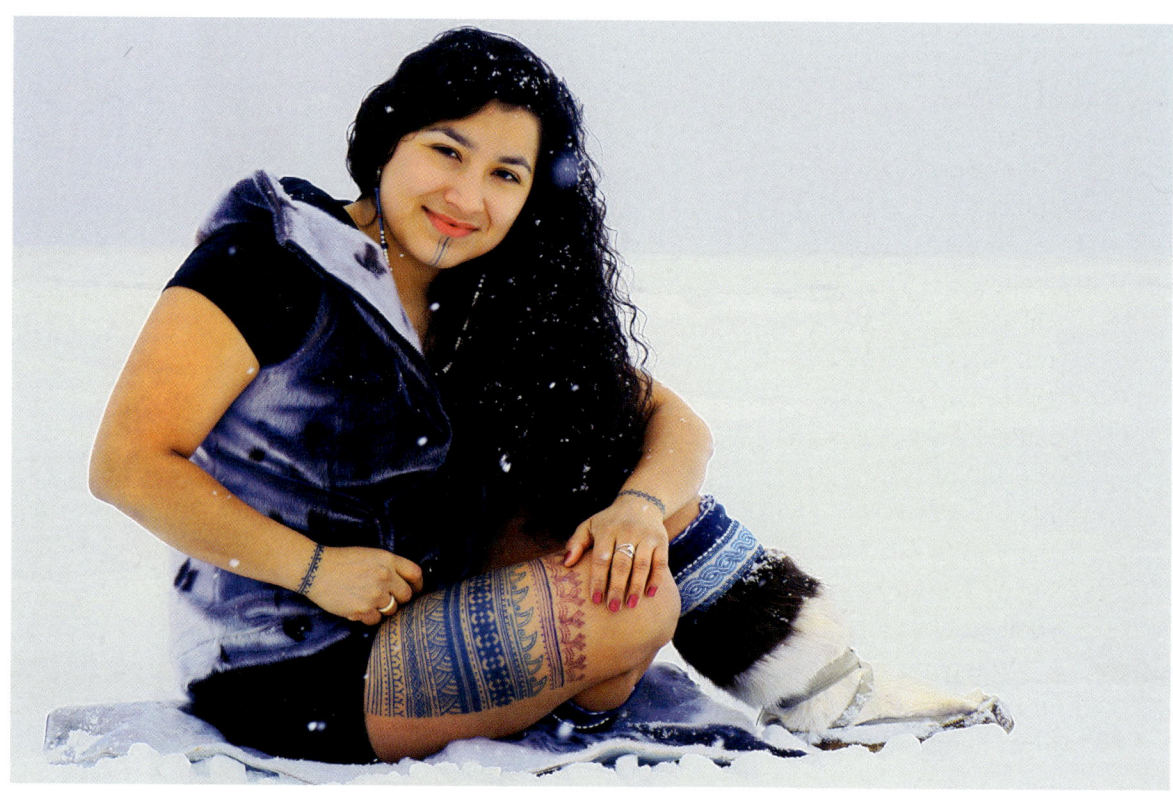

Plate 24. "Birthing Tattoos" of Iñupiaq/Kiowa artist Marjorie Tahbone, of Nome, Alaska. Thigh tattoos such as these ensured that the first vision a newborn baby witnessed was a thing of beauty. Tattoos by Elle and Zel Festin, Spiritual Journey Tattoo / www.spiritualjourneytattoo.com. Photograph © Kalynna Ashley.

Discussion

The role of tattooing in Polynesian societies is complex and multidimensional. Prior to European contact there was diminishing use of tattoo on some islands, or apparent complete absence. British anthropologist Alfred Gell (1993) identified a correlation between tattooing and hierarchical social systems but cautioned that multiple factors should be taken into account including cosmology, group identity, identity of self, rank, and concepts of rite of passage. These concepts would have been incomprehensible to the casual observer not steeped in the culture. In particular, the practice of tattooing by New Zealand Maori was bound by very strict social rules to protect the individual from spiritual harm and was accompanied by *karakia* (prayers).

At the time of European contact, tattooing was documented from some island groups, but was sparse or absent on other islands. Tattooed individuals were not encountered on the islands in the Tuamotu Group; Niue; Rapa and Tubuai in the Austral Islands; Tongareva, Pukapuka, Rakahanga, and Manihiki in the northern Cook Islands; or on Rekohu Chatham Island to the east of New Zealand (Ibid.). In contrast, individuals in Samoa, Society Islands, and New Zealand were highly tattooed at first contact with Europeans. There are historically collected examples of tattoo combs from islands such as Samoa yet no archaeological examples, contrasting with Tubuai where there are known archaeological examples (Atiahara) but no historic records of tattooing. Where tattoo survived, missionaries attempted to ban the ongoing practice, but in some cases with limited success.

Without ethnographic or historic accounts, tattooing would have a very low visibility in parts of Polynesia and Micronesia since there is very little tangible evidence in the archaeological record. Leaving aside Gell's postulated correlation between the level of sociopolitical organization and the continuation of the practice over time, if tattooing was introduced to each island at the time of initial settlement, then a greater archaeological footprint might be expected. Poor preservation of organic material has already been canvassed in relation to Samoa and Tonga, but does not apply universally throughout Polynesia. Limited archaeological investigations and sampling on some island groups, particularly in the Cook Islands and East Polynesia, is another likely explanation for this absence, and therefore might be remedied over time with further investigations.

Another possible explanation for the sparse archaeological evidence of tattooing relates to the procedure itself. Ethnographic accounts from various islands describe tattooing tools stored in a case containing combs, handles, mallet, and maintenance tools for sharpening the blunted combs (Firth 1936:174; Handy and Handy 1924:22–23; Hiroa 1927:363,1930:636, 639). The kit would belong to the tattooist and therefore be removed from the location where the tattooing was carried out, possibly a house or shelter built specifically for the tattooing event (Handy and Handy 1924:22). Where the kit was stored between uses is not described in any account. Tattooists are described as craftspeople or specialists (Firth 1936:174; Hiroa 1930:636, 639; Métraux 1971:237), and not every village would have had such an expert. This could account for the lack of evidence even at sites where large excavations have been conducted. The excavated context in which tattoo combs are found is rarely reported: only at Anio'o in the Cook Islands can it be said that two of the combs were found within a house (Richard Walter, personal communication, October 2, 2015), and apart from an account that some combs were found together in Oruarangi, New Zealand, the *pa* was looted in such a way that no features would be detected.

Within Polynesia there does appear to have been change in the style of combs over time, although the only reference points are the earliest settlement sites and the historic period with up to a 700-year gap in between (New Zealand and Hawai'i are the exceptions). The earliest dated evidence for bone and pearl shell combs is from East Polynesia (1000 to 1100 CE, Hane and Vaito'otia), with a number of places in wider East Polynesia (Mangaia and Anai'o in the Cook Islands, New Zealand, Hawai'i, Austral Islands), demonstrating tattoo was widespread by the fourteenth century. Distinguishing the earliest occurrence of combs is made more difficult by problems with dating and refinement of settlement chronologies, in addition to absences and sampling issues described above.

Narrow and wide combs were initially used in the Society Islands and the Marquesas, although the pearl shell combs tend to be wide and the bone examples narrow. Cook Islands and New Zealand have both wide and narrow combs. The Austral Islands also had wide and narrow combs, and in Hawai'i the narrow combs were intended to be bound together as a wide composite, making the Makani'olu Shelter combs the oldest examples of the composite form. However Hawai'i also has combs formed on the cut end of the shaft of a bird bone, an unusual departure from the recognizable standard formal shape of comb. This style of comb was possibly unhafted.

At European contact both wide and narrow combs were in use, although the wide combs were of greater width than those in the settlement period as a result of the joining together of multiple single combs. This is evident in Hawai'i and the Society Islands, and inferred for Samoa, since although ethnographically collected combs are composite, there are no earlier forms known. New Zealand is the exception, since there is no evidence of wide combs at contact, nor are there perforations on the combs to allow joining together, and in fact combs in New Zealand became narrower over time. The development of composite combs and flat plates in Western Polynesia occurred after the Polynesian Outliers were settled, since this form is not recorded anywhere in Micronesia or on the small outlier islands.

The haft lashing forms from the Society and Marquesas Islands in the early period are unique. Although confined to wide pearl shell combs, these styles are not evident in Atiahara or the Cook Islands sites that also have pearl shell examples. Perforations for hafting to the handle are most common in sites in New Zealand (Wairau Bar, Houhora,

Whitipirorua, Harataonga, and Hot Water Beach), Hawai'i, Atiahara, Anai'o, and Tangatatau, although there is variation in the shape of the upper edge. Rounded, squared, scalloped, and angled upper edges are evident. Notches and lashing protuberances are only present in sites in the Marquesas and Society Islands, related specifically to wide pearl shell combs, but notching is also present on narrow combs in two New Zealand sites (Shag River, Washpool). By the late eighteenth century in New Zealand, notching on narrow combs or a plain haft is most common with a low incidence of perforated hafting technique.

The piercing edge is either toothed or serrated, and in late New Zealand there is also the development of a plain chisel-like form. Parallel grooves on one or both sides of the body for an irregular distance from the teeth are generally present. In Hawaiian examples the grooves extend along the length of the comb and are possibly intended to also be decorative. From all locations there are also examples with teeth but without grooves. Although the intended purpose of grooves was to deliver ink to the teeth it may not have been necessary, and it is instead possible that the grooves were a result of the filing or cutting of the teeth.

While all of the described examples are flat or slightly curved following the shape of the bone, an unusual example from the Society Islands drawn by the artist accompanying Cook (see Kaeppler 1978a:152) has a multi-toothed bone implement that would leave a circular dotted impression. A similar mark would be left by the toothed bone shaft from Hawai'i, illustrated in Allen (2006:119).

Conclusions

Perpendicularly hafted tattooing tools are widely associated with Austronesian language speakers, who transported them into Oceania during the Lapita period. However, the absence of bone tattoo implements from Lapita sites suggests use of bone was a later development. Bone combs therefore developed in Polynesia at an unknown time but certainly prior to 1100 CE. Because bone combs are also present in the Polynesian Outliers which were settled from Western Polynesia, it is most likely that bone combs were carried into Eastern Polynesia from Western Polynesia. However, it remains possible that bone combs were an East Polynesian innovation spurred by an absence of suitable thorns, and the idea transmitted to the homeland area as a result of ongoing contact. The distribution of bone combs in the geographic area called Micronesia is mixed, with bone being used on the Caroline Islands and Polynesian Outliers, and a dual use of thorn and bone implements in Pohnpei in the Marshall Islands. It is possible, given the place of origin of each island group in Micronesia, that bone combs entered Micronesia from the Samoan-Tongan area, with transfer of the technology farther west. Farther west again, in insular Southeast Asia, New Guinea, and Timor-Leste, only thorn implements were used.

Use of bone combs and pearl shell would have allowed tattoo designs to develop further, with more extensive skin coverage, particularly where wide combs were used for producing large areas of black and infilling. In New Zealand the late narrow chisels allowed deep gouging of the flesh, and there is no evidence of the designs having large blocks of pigment.

In summary, tattooing with perpendicularly hafted implements was a technological development that originated in Island Southeast Asia or southeastern mainland China and spread eastward to Polynesia and Micronesia. Despite changes in use of material, and in comb shape and size, the use of the distinctive perpendicularly hafted comb remains relatively unchanged over several thousand years. Differences in comb size and shape reflect development within each island group, which is also evident in the designs recorded in historic times. Archaeological evidence for tattooing is lacking from Near Oceania and West Polynesia generally, but in East Polynesia the presence of tattoo combs in multiple places suggests tattooing was an important part of ancient life.

Notes

I am indebted to Wal Ambrose for advice, references, and for use of figure 2 in this essay. Thanks also to Patrick Kirch, who provided images of Mangaian combs not yet published, and Mara Mulrooney, Curator, and Charmaine Wong, Archaeology Collection Manager of the Bishop Museum, who generously supplied images and measurements of Hawaiian and Marquesan combs. Richard Walter gave additional information about Anaiʻo. Thanks also to Rangitane o Wairau, Kaitiaki (guardians) of Wairau Bar, for permission to reproduce images of the combs. Briar Sefton, Anthropology, University of Auckland, provided help with figure 1 in this essay, and Milvia Goldstein drew the illustrations.

1. Some tribes among the non-Austronesian speaking Naga (India and Myanmar), Chin (Myanmar), and Drung (China) also tattooed or hand-tapped with perpendicularly hafted implements (Gros 2012; Parkitny 2010; Saul 2006).
2. Near Oceania is defined as the islands in the western part of the Pacific closest to New Guinea, including the Solomon Islands and Bismarck Archipelago. Here, islands, if not visible from one to the other, have short water distances of approximately 100 km between them. Remote Oceania is to the east of the Solomon Islands, where distances between islands or island groups are greater.
3. For example, Brewster (1922); Kleinschmidt (1984); Ratzel (1896); Thompson (1940); Wilkes (1845); Williams and Calvert (1859).
4. Furey (1990); Law (1972); Leach (1979); and Leahy (1974).
5. Plain tattoo implements, called chisels, were used on the face and created a relief similar to wood carving. Deep grooves with raised edges enhanced the tattoo effect.

12

Reading Between Our Lines

TATTOOING IN PAPUA NEW GUINEA

Lars Krutak

PAPUA NEW GUINEA IS THE SECOND LARGEST ISLAND IN THE WORLD. Roughly the size of California, it is one of the most rural countries on the globe, with only 18 percent of its six million inhabitants living in urban areas. Incredibly, over eight hundred Indigenous languages are spoken in PNG, accounting for 20 percent of the world's total.

Just as Papua New Guinea (PNG) is linguistically diverse, it possesses numerous tribal tattooing cultures. And as far back as elders can remember, tattooing has been a local tradition of nearly every coastal people. Here, among the Motu, Waima, Aroma, Hula, Mekeo, and others, women were heavily tattooed from head to toe,[1] resulting in some of the most complete body coverage in the Indigenous world.

In the early to mid-nineteenth century, however, tattooing largely disappeared in PNG for a variety of reasons: tribal warfare ceased, missionaries discouraged initiation ceremonies, and tattoos associated with highly ritualized Motu trading voyages (*hiri*) became obsolete as these seafaring traditions were gradually abandoned (Ryan 1970).

The *Hiri*

Motu tattoo sessions for women were usually performed in relation to lengthy and dangerous trading expeditions called *hiri*. These voyages were undertaken in large double-hulled sea-going canoes (*lakatoi, lagatoi*). *Hiri* expeditions, which were symbolically complex, typically lasted six to eight months, and in rare instances one or more years. During the *hiri*, the first-born daughters of *lakatoi* owners were secluded in a village house, along with ten to fifteen daughters of other expedition members, until the voyage had been completed (Krutak 2014c).

During the girls' seclusion, many ritual restrictions were placed on them, and female "guardians" watched their every move, because breach of taboo could spell disaster for the *hiri*. For example, girls were compelled to sleep on their back (faces up) every evening, because if they slept on their sides or on their stomach it was believed that these movements would capsize the *lakatoi* on the open sea (Ibid.). Girls were also forbidden from consuming large meals, because this action might sink the boat or make it heavy, resulting in its inability to move quickly on its journey. Moreover, girls could not sit cross-legged upon the floor of the seclusion house, and whenever they prepared to sit or stand they first walked in a circle, so as to help propel the *lakatoi* on its journey. In the Motu village of Gaba Gaba I was told that men in the sea canoes would know that rules had been broken in the seclusion house if they encountered frequent big waves and violent storms during their voyage (Ibid.).

Girls that were the third, fourth, or fifth-born daughters could also be tattooed after a *hiri* returned to their home village, but more ceremonial emphasis was placed on the tattooing of an expedition leader's eldest daughter (*hudiha hahine*) and her cohorts (fig. 12.1). This custom is linked to an ancient myth where the first *lakatoi* builder mandated that the eldest girls in seclusion should be tattooed by female relatives while the expedition was at sea. The mythic creator of the *hiri* also instated the religious taboos that were to be obeyed while the girls were in seclusion.

Once the *lakatoi* returned, the newly tattooed *hudiha hahine* and a few pairs of other girls were washed, oiled with coconut oil, and dressed in new grass skirts. Then they boarded a small canoe to meet the *lakatois* anchored offshore. Because of the lengthy period of seclusion, the girls' skin had become pale and this enhanced the boldness of their newly acquired tattoos. The girls then sang songs of welcome, the verses being repeated several times over. The lyrics to one of these tunes, recorded in the village of Gaba Gaba, are:

> At low tide, we will hold hands and we will swing our grass skirts;
> To welcome our lakatois coming in.
> Two or three pairs of us will always welcome our lakatois home;
> That brings us wealth from the Gulf. (Ibid.:22)

Girls who were not first-born could also be tattooed during minor village events, especially while turtle hunters were out at sea. For example, certain clans were specialists in turtle hunting and these animals were captured in large nets. Turtle hunting expeditions typically lasted two weeks and while men were out hunting, girls that were not firstborn would be secluded in a village house and tattooed. Here, they observed similar ritual restrictions as the first-born daughters during the *hiri* seclusions.

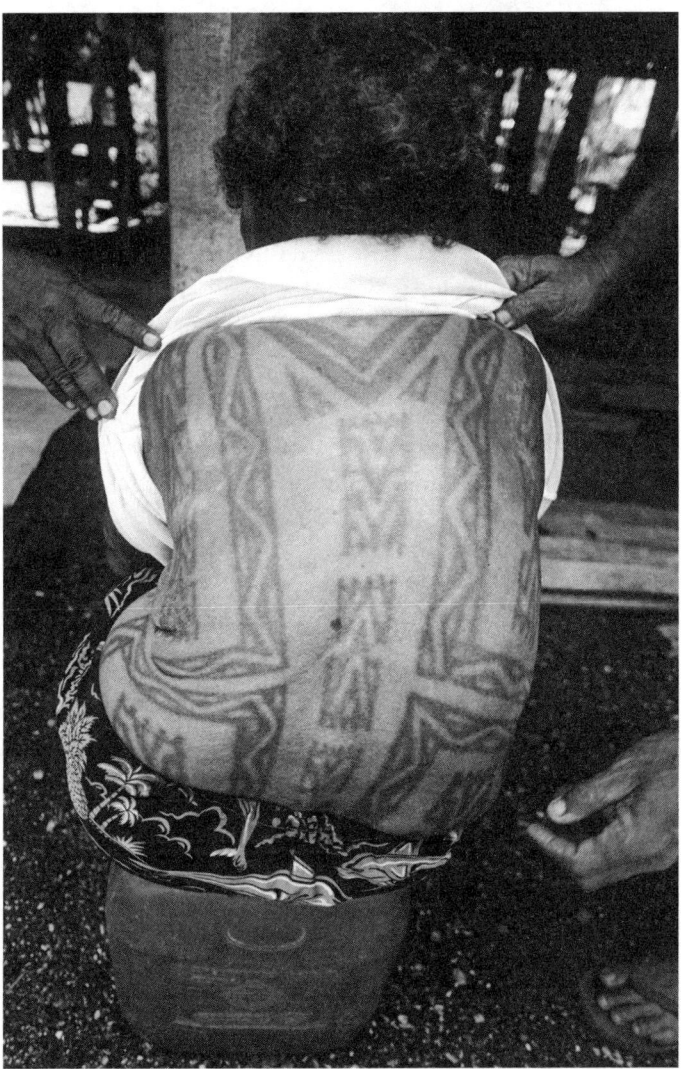

Fig. 12.1. Back tattoos of Motu elder Ade Baroa from Gaba Gaba village, Papua New Guinea (2012). She was the last Motu elder in her village with full body tattooing. Photograph © Lars Krutak.

First-born daughters were entitled to special facial and leg designs. These motifs proclaimed to all villagers that their fathers had successfully participated in the *hiri*. Younger daughters of *hiri* leaders, or those that were not first-born, were not allowed to wear these designs.

Tep Tok (2015): The Papuan Tattoo Revival

In 2015, a groundbreaking documentary film, *Tep Tok: Reading Between Our Lines*, was released.[2] *Tep Tok* is the story of four women of PNG and Australian descent who explore their village tattooing traditions and journey across Pasifika cultures (Samoa, Tahiti, the Cook Islands, and New Zealand) to resurrect them.

Tep Tok co-producer Nata Richards (Hula) explains that tattooing practices were discarded quickly in her home village of Vula'a. She and Frank Kolou, of neighboring Kamali village, attribute these dramatic shifts to the arrival of the church and missionaries long ago. "The fact that our grandmothers are tattooed and our mothers are not is a clear indication of how fast and final the stop[page] . . . took place." Kolou, whose mother is the last fully tattooed Hula woman in his village, recounted his childhood memories: "All these kids are going to church. The pastor [was] saying these patterns [will] become like ghosts. . . . And this is when [and where] the [tattooing] culture [was] being phased out" (fig. 12.2).

Filmmaker Julia Mage'au Gray (Mekeo) also attributed the demise of tattooing among her people to missionaries: "My mother and aunties were not traditionally tattooed either. . . . [And] when we ask the old women why [they stopped], they always repeat with the same answer: 'It was because of the missionaries.' "

Today, only a few fully tattooed elderly women remain in coastal Papua. When these individuals are gone, the tattoo knowledge they embody and in their collective memory will be lost, making the task of resurrecting traditional tattooing even more difficult. Ranu James (Motu), whose ancestral roots are tied to Gaba Gaba village, explains that time is the worst enemy: "Our old ladies are dying and the knowledge or our *revareva* [tattooing] is dying with them . . . and we don't have time to catch it. We've only got as long as they have and they are old women now. Losing [this] would be like being totally displaced in your own culture. Being unable to identify yourself and connect you with *who* you came from and *who* you are."

Tattoos in coastal PNG were closely linked to one's tribal identity. Each tribe had unique patterns that revealed where an individual came from and what group you belonged to. For women, they also signified rites of passage into adulthood. For example, Hula women who had completed the final phase of their tattooing were celebrated at an initiation feast called *kapa* that was held annually at the ceremonial house (*dubu*) in the village center (Guise 1899:216). At the climax of this two-day ceremony, known as *kuiriga*, the freshly tattooed women ascended the *dubu* platform to prepare themselves for the forthcoming public display of their newly transformed bodies.

A similar ceremony occurred in Waima villages. For girls who had been fully tattooed, a feast was prepared to celebrate their transition into adulthood. The girls formed a procession and were led through the village to publicly display their tattooed bodies (Krutak 2014c). Unmarried young men would show their admiration by throwing betel nut skins at the girls (fig. 12.3). Then a special song was sung and repeated several times by the girls, who were later joined by the young men:

> Shell ornaments hang down;
> From our backs . . .
> [The men then countered:]
> Let me dance, you are ready to be married! (Ibid.:23)

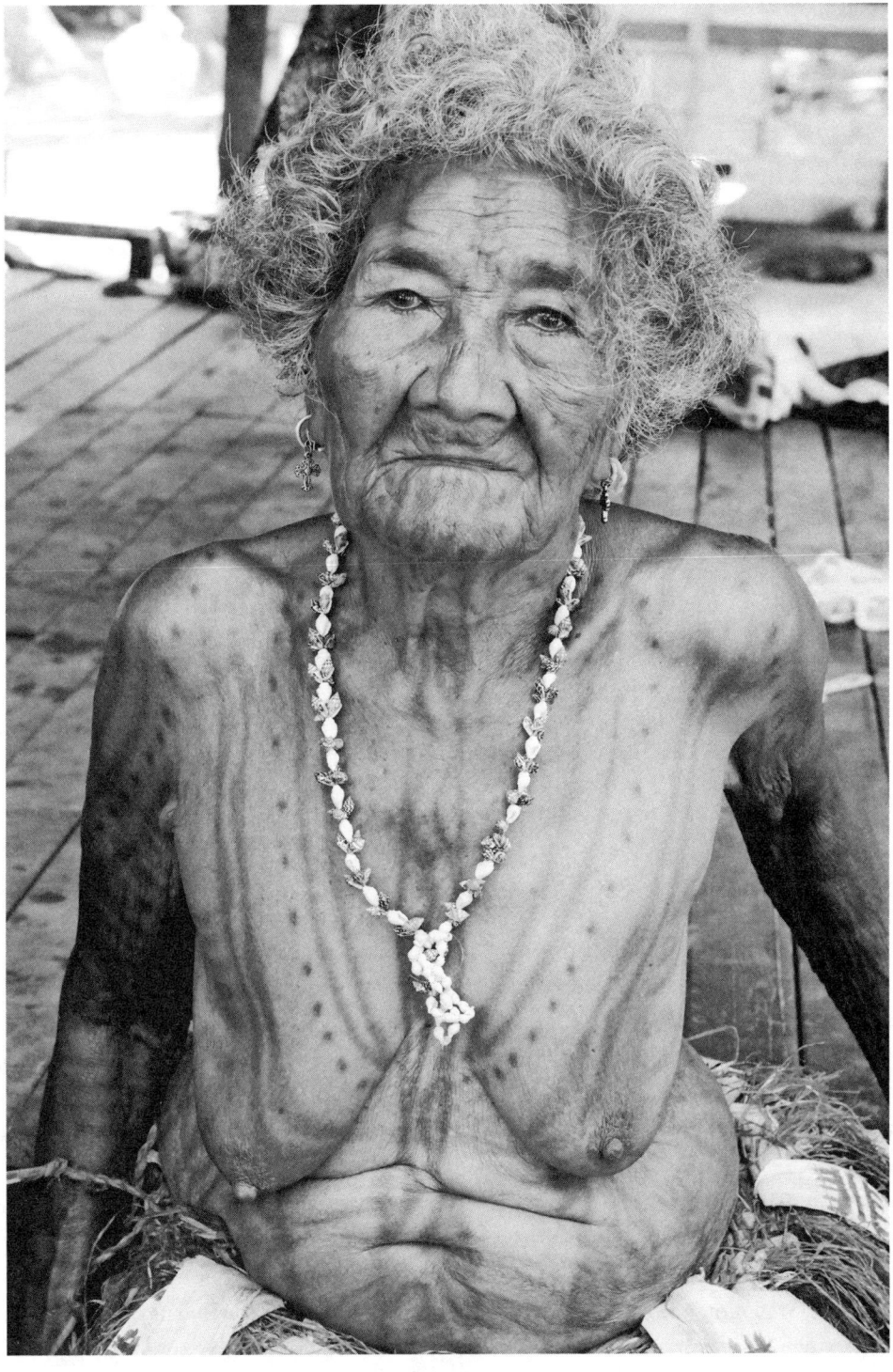

Fig. 12.2. Hula elder Vali Kolou of Kamali village, Papua New Guinea (2012). She was the last Hula elder in her village with full body tattooing. Photograph © Lars Krutak.

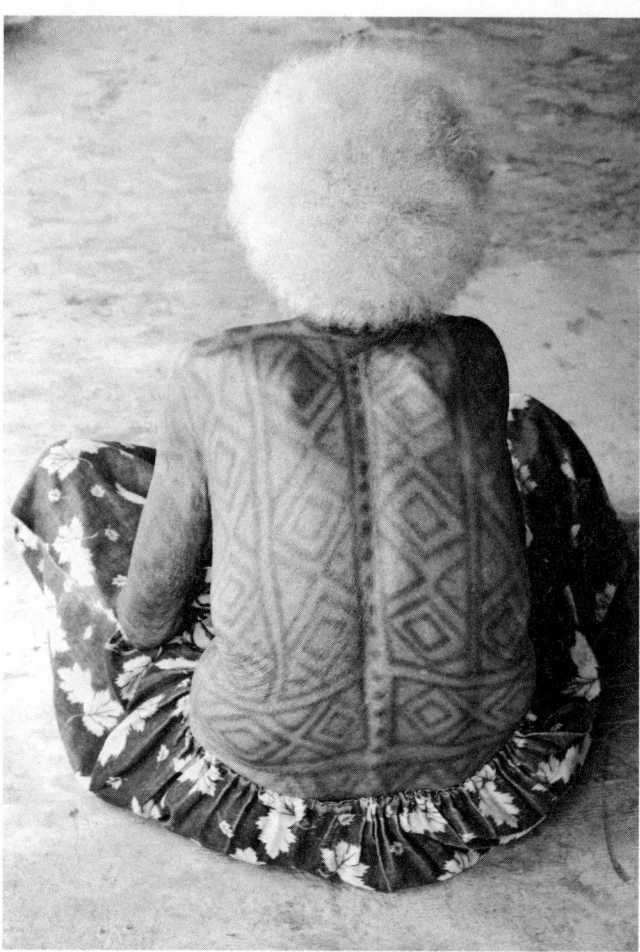

Fig. 12.3. Back tattoos of Waima elder Taitá Koroka of Hisiu village, Papua New Guinea (2012). After she received her tattoos as a young girl, she joined a procession of other newly tattooed women to publicly display their newly transformed bodies in the village. Photograph © Lars Krutak.

"Losing the tattoo meant that we were losing [our] culture and identity," notes Gray. "We lose our elders' knowledge and vision. We lose who we are as women. We lose that connection to the past, and that would be horrible. We no longer have the tattooists; [they are] gone. She was the one who told the story, worked out what was appropriate for you, and she put that on you. Her role has gone. So what we are trying to do is to bring her back. It's our job to make tattoos fit now."

A pivotal moment in the journey to reclaim Papuan tattooing occurred in 2012 in Samoa. During filming of *Tep Tok*, master tattooist Sulu'ape Sa'a Alaiv'a Petelo suggested that someone needed to pick up the traditional tools in order to make the revival possible. Gray remembers that moment: "We started this *Tep Tok* journey with this sort of pilgrimage to Samoa to see traditional *tatau* [tattoo] in practice, and to be tattooed. For us, at that point [we wanted] to raise awareness . . . and to carry our *bubu's* [grandmothers'] tattoos on us. That is how far we had thought. And then what we learned is

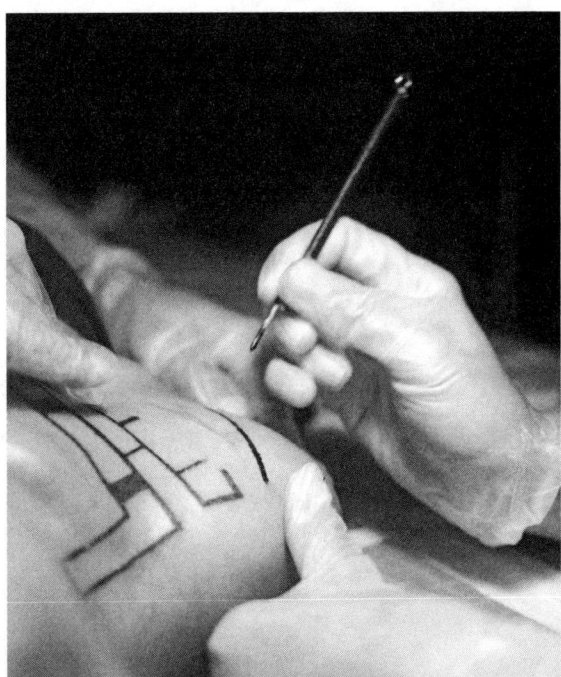

Fig. 12.4. Tattooist Julia Mage'au Gray at work, Papua New Guinea (2013). Tattoos and photograph © Julia Mage'au Gray / www.teptok.com.

that if you are really serious about bringing back this tattooing practice, then you need to pick up the tools. And so we did."

Since that fateful encounter in Samoa, Gray lived for six months in New Zealand, apprenticing with a host of traditional tattooists (plate 15). There she learned how to hand-tap and hand-poke tattoos. Afterward, she began tattooing family members back in the Mekeo heartland of PNG; those were the first traditional tattoos given there in some eighty years. Gray also tattooed her *Tep Tok* collaborators, including James. She said, "Ranu told me, 'I cannot pick up the tools, but I will give you my skin until you perfect it. And then you will tattoo my children.'"

Gray and her *Tep Tok* collaborators hope that their project will instill pride in Papuan tattooing again by showcasing it to the world. These signs on skin are not just pictures; they are stories about their lives and journeys through it (fig. 12.4).

Gray explains: "Polynesian cultures are tattooing [again]. They have had their renaissance. They have brought it back, and we are not . . . [We] need to remember what we have is incredible. We can keep it alive and it is up to us. And if we don't do it, then we're being negligent and lazy. We are not being at our full potential [and] it would be a waste."

Coastal women continue to draw tattoos on their faces and bodies at large public festivals, like the Motu *Hiri Moale* festival held annually in the capital of Port Moresby. Participants express pride in their tattooing traditions, but the challenge is to translate that into something more permanent (fig. 12.5).

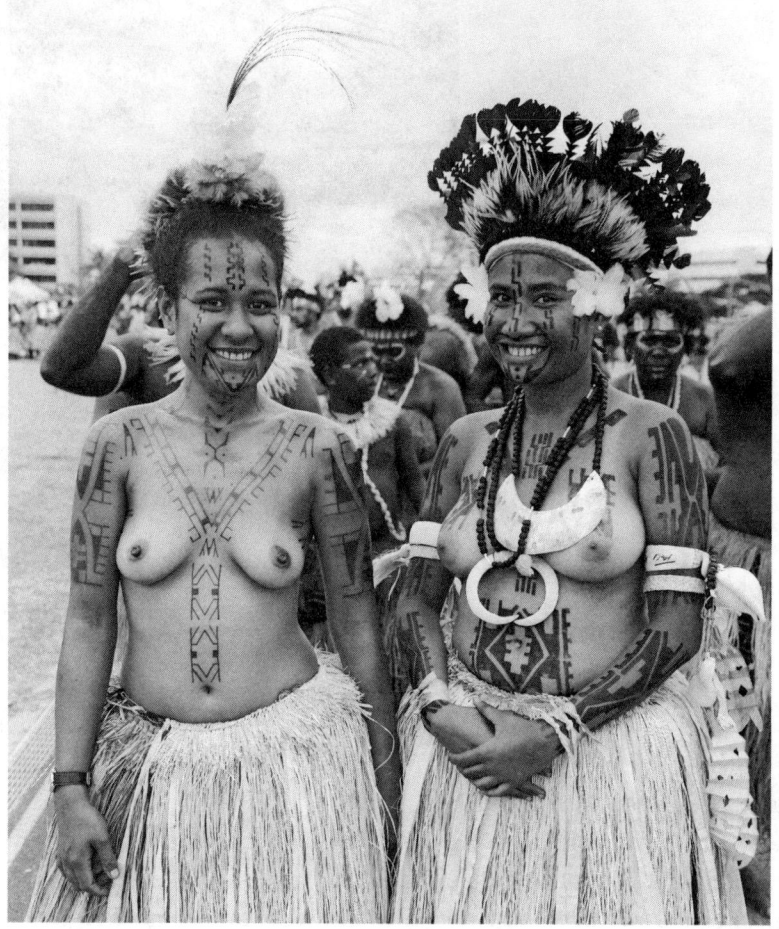

Fig. 12.5. Motu women at the annual *Hiri Moale* festival with painted-on tattoos, Papua New Guinea (2013). Terita Gamoga Toea (left) also wears tattoos (*revareva*) on her chest. Tattoos and photograph © Julia Mage'au Gray / www.teptok.com.

"Why are they drawing instead of not tattooing? Because there are no tattooists and no one to teach the practice," Gray says. "The designs are alive. It is there, it is in our minds, we appreciate it. [But we need] to stop the drawing and make it real. . . . It is possible, it [is] doable, [and] this is only the beginning."

Notes

1. Coastal Papuan men typically displayed chest, arm, or back tattooing related to their exploits in combat (see Krutak 2007). Men among the inland Managalase were tattooed all over their bodies with patterns associated with complex initiation rituals (Krutak 2013c).
2. Material quoted from the *Tep Tok* documentary appears throughout this essay. It is reproduced courtesy of Sunameke productions, www.teptok.com.

13

Scratching the Surface

MISTAKEN IDENTIFICATIONS OF TATTOO TOOLS FROM EASTERN NORTH AMERICA

Aaron Deter-Wolf, Benoît Robitaille, and Isaac Walters

PRIOR TO ACCULTURATION NATIVE AMERICAN GROUPS THROUGHOUT the Eastern Woodlands of North America engaged in numerous forms of permanent and semipermanent body modification. Specific traditions, their underlying significance, and associated technologies varied widely, but included piercing, ear stretching, dental and cranial remodeling, suspension, scratching, and tattooing. While some of these practices were imposed on individuals as punishment, many were aspired to as marks of social or spiritual achievement and bestowed as part of elaborate public rituals.

Although more than a millennium of Native American body modification is documented in the iconographic, ethnohistorical, and ethnographic record of North America, our understanding of the archaeological footprint of these traditions remains incomplete. Thankfully this pattern has begun to change over the past decade, as objective and informed research has allowed us to reevaluate conventional wisdom and misunderstandings regarding the archaeological record of Indigenous and ancient body modification. Toward that end, archaeological evidence, ethnohistorical and historical data, and use-wear analysis can be combined to reassess archaeological identifications of tattoo tools from North America's Eastern Woodlands. Of specific interest here is the perceived intersection of scratching and tattooing technologies, and a typological dilemma that results from historic misunderstanding of these practices.

Issues in Identifying Tattoo Tools

Successful identification of tattoo tools in archaeological collections from North America or elsewhere requires overcoming issues related to artifact preservation and recovery, culture change, traditional artifact classification systems, and the biases and misunderstandings of previous researchers. Ancient tattoo tools were likely made from a wide variety of resources, including bone, ivory, shell, metal, stone, and botanical materials (Deter-Wolf 2013b). However, many of these materials will not preserve well in the archaeological record. Depending on the site setting and soil chemistry, items including thorns, small bones, and biodegradable elements such as wooden handles, leather wrappings, fiber bindings, and feathers are unlikely to be preserved.

For those tattoo tools and tool elements that do survive, successful archaeological identification may be hindered by recovery and processing techniques. The ¼-inch mesh screens that are standard for North American archaeology may not catch small tools and tool fragments. In addition, overly enthusiastic artifact cleaning and the application of preservatives or chemicals intended to stabilize an artifact can obliterate or mask suggestive use-wear patterns and residues.

Traditional tattoo technology from North America and throughout the Indigenous world changed dramatically beginning in the fifteenth century following the introduction of European trade goods. Steel sewing needles were rapidly and widely adopted following first contact, and in many places they quickly replaced Indigenous tattoo tools (Ibid.:43). This initial culture change was followed by centuries of forced missionization and acculturation, which included the suppression of Indigenous tattoo traditions, resulting in the knowledge of traditional tattoo tools being largely lost. As a result, archaeologists investigating precontact sites in North America do not have reliable documentation of Indigenous tattoo tools to compare with their collections.

Because of this lack of comparative data, many possible tattoo tools have been subsumed into traditional artifact classification schemes (Deter-Wolf 2013a:21; Tassie 2003:86). For example, pointed bone tools will typically be assigned to a functional category such as awls or needles, while stone implements could be catalogued and reported as gravers, points, or blades. Archaeologists may also assume that minimally reworked faunal materials constitute food remains rather than tools, and as a result, specific elements such as fish teeth or spines that could have been used to tattoo may never be individually examined beyond initial species identification.

Finally, archaeological identification of tattoo tools can be hindered by antitattoo bias and scholarly misunderstandings of the practice. Until recently, academic treatment of tattooing and other forms of body modification was filtered through the lens of Western and Judeo-Christian history, in which these traditions were regarded as curiosities or marks of barbarism rather than integral parts of Indigenous cultural expression. These biases were inadvertently reinforced in the 1980s and 1990s by well-intentioned but misinformed studies fixated on body modification as a facet of the

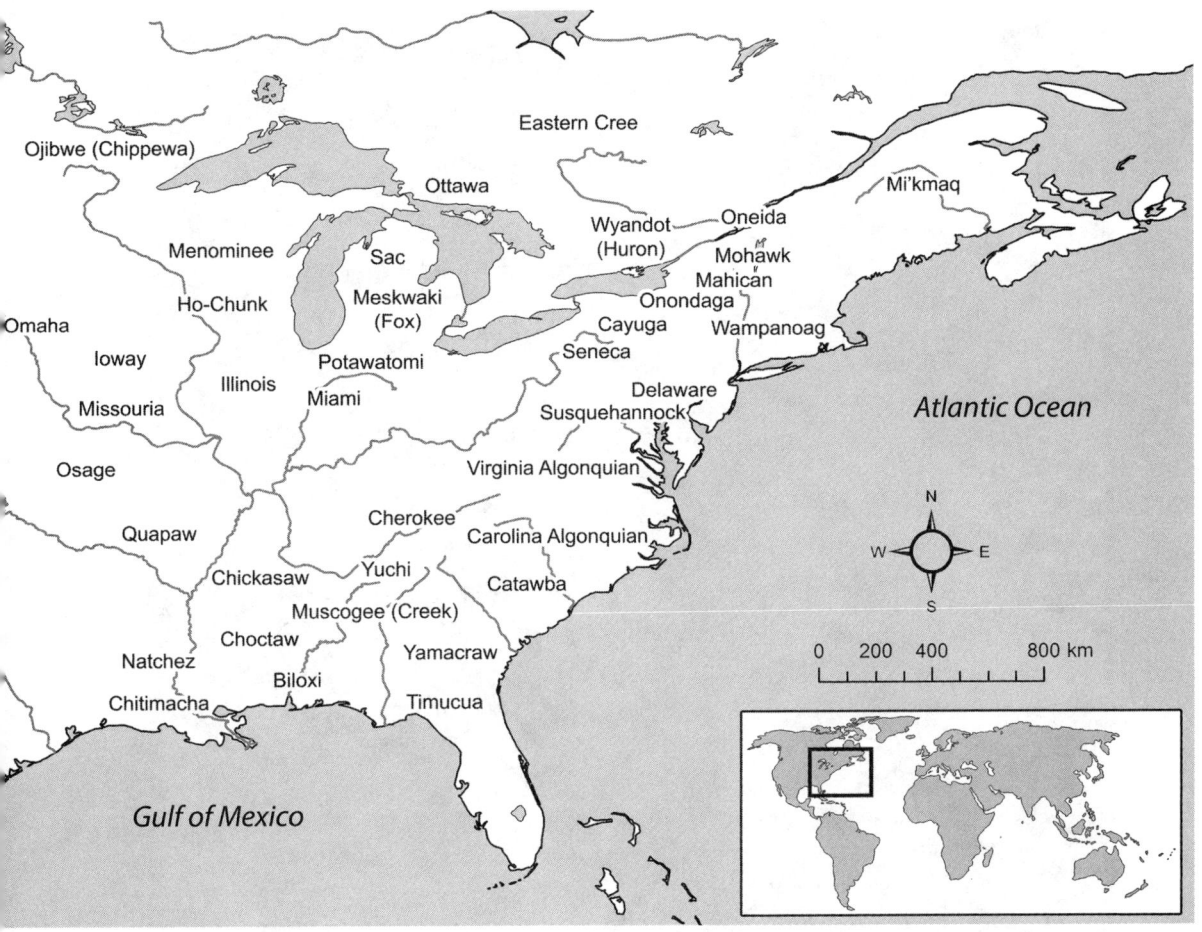

Map 13.1. North America's Eastern Woodlands, identifying historically documented Native American tattoo traditions.

"Modern Primitive" movement (Lodder 2011). The net result of this process has been an academic discourse largely disconnected from any methodological and/or technological understanding of Indigenous tattooing and body modification.

Tattooing in the Eastern Woodlands

The Eastern Woodlands of North America comprise a regional culture area beginning along the coastal margins of the Atlantic seaboard and Gulf of Mexico, spreading north to the subarctic regions of Canada and generally bounded to the west by the Mississippi River (map 13.1). This vast region is home to Indigenous Native American peoples, who over some thirteen millennia prior to European contact left behind an archaeological record indicative of their complex and varied cultures.

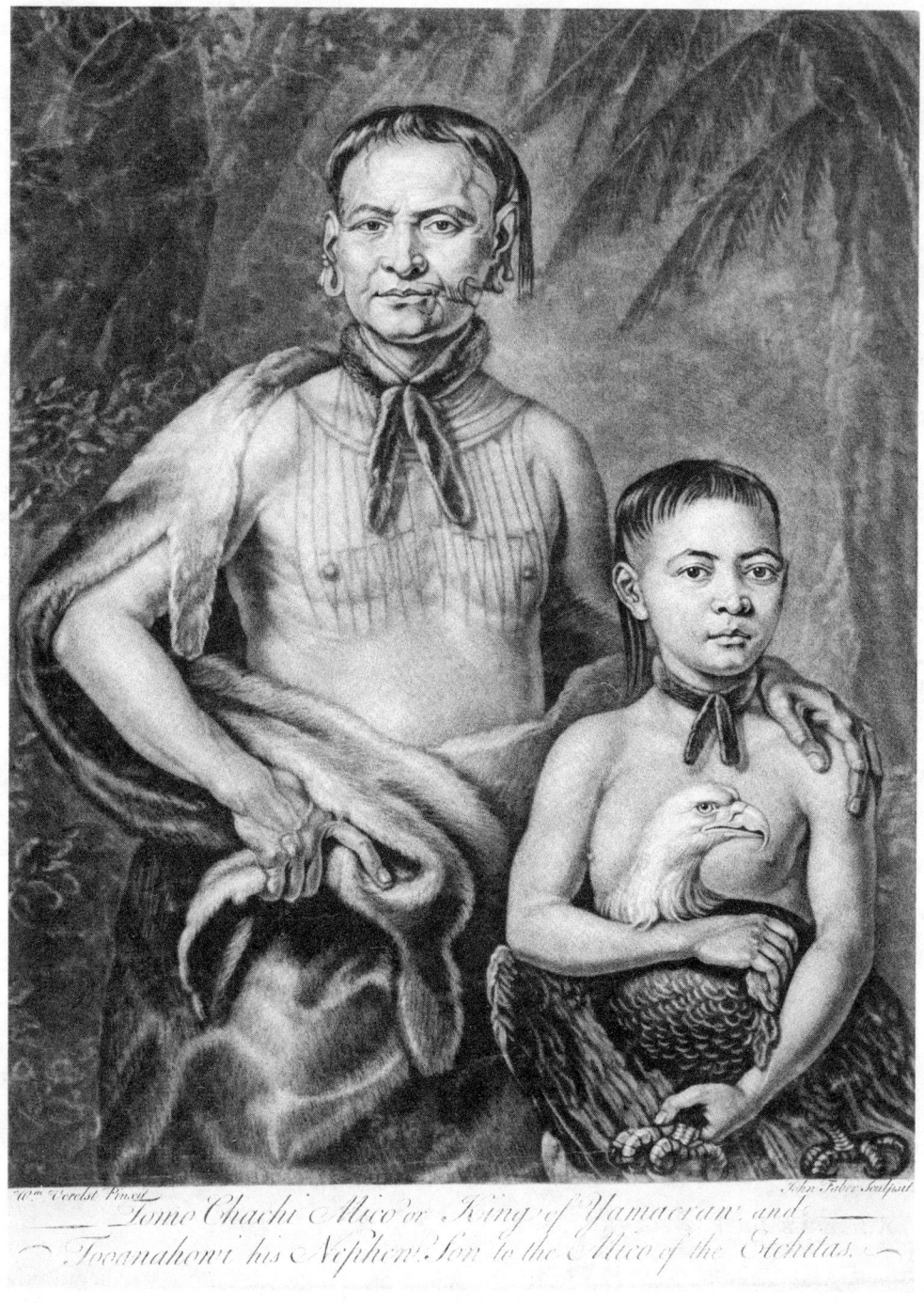

Fig. 13.1. Tattoo marks on the Yamacraw leader Tomochichi. Mezzotint by John Faber the Younger (1739) based on a 1735 painting by William Verelst.

Although the exact antiquity of tattooing in the Eastern Woodlands is unknown, ancient art from the region as well as from the neighboring Great Plains suggests that traditions of permanent body marking may have existed as early as the first centuries CE, during the Woodland period of regional prehistory (ca. 1000 BCE to 900 CE) (e.g., Steere 2013). A rich body of figural art suggests these traditions flourished during the ensuing Mississippian period (ca. 900 to 1600 CE). The ubiquity of pre-contact Native American tattoo traditions is perhaps also reflected in accounts of Europeans and Euro-Americans who traveled through the region beginning in the sixteenth century. Historic accounts from that time document that many, or perhaps most, Native American societies of the Eastern Woodlands practiced tattooing prior to acculturation (see map 13.1), including the Timucua, Chickasaw, Choctaw, Chitimacha, Natchez, Muscogee, Yuchi, Cherokee, Virginia Algonquian, Quapaw, Mohawk, Delaware, Seneca, Illinois, Menominee, and Ojibwe (Deter-Wolf and Diaz-Granados 2013; Krutak 2014a) (fig. 13.1).

The Indigenous tattoo traditions of the Eastern Woodlands were broadly extinct by the mid-nineteenth century as a result of prolonged acculturation and cultural fracturing caused by epidemics, forced removal, and relocation. This process took place prior to any formal study or documentation of tattooing practices, and consequently specifics of tattooing in the region remain poorly understood. To the west on the Great Plains, groups including the Osage, Ioway, Omaha, and Cree did not suffer the impacts of disease and forced relocation to the same extent as groups east of the Mississippi. Consequently the tattoo traditions among these peoples, including their associated rituals and material culture, endured for at least another half century and were documented through ethnographic study.[1] These accounts contain much more specific information about Native American tattooing than exists for the Eastern Woodlands, and so serve as an invaluable comparative data set.

Although limited in scope and specificity, historical accounts and the art historical record have nevertheless allowed us to gain some understanding of Native American tattooing in the Eastern Woodlands during the sixteenth through eighteenth centuries CE, and thereby hypothesize regarding pre-contact traditions. The motivations for tattooing varied somewhat by tribal affiliation and gender (Krutak 2013d, 2014a; Wallace 2013). Tattooing among Native American men in the Eastern Woodlands broadly served to invoke guardian spirits, document war honors, and signal group affiliation. These marks were applied incrementally during an individual's life to commemorate rites of passage and feats of bravery. While documentation of tattooing among Native American women in the Eastern Woodlands is far more meager, the marks likely indicated adulthood, and identified family and/or group membership. Tattoos on both men and women demonstrated elevated social status, and in the Great Lakes region medicinal tattoos were also used to treat specific pains and ailments (Krutak 2014a).

Native American tattoo technology in the Eastern Woodlands varied widely prior to European contact, and included single-point and multipoint tools made from animal bone, fish teeth, stone, and possibly thorns and other botanical material (Deter-Wolf 2013b). These tools were applied directly to the skin through the technique known today as hand-poking. Tattooing mainly employed carbon-based pigments inserted into the skin at the tip of the tattoo implement or introduced by rubbing onto the punctured skin surface.

To date there are three extant, documented examples of historic Native American tattoo toolkits from the Eastern Woodlands. Two kits collected in the early twentieth century among the Menominee in Wisconsin now reside in the collections of the American Museum of Natural History (plate 16) and the Oshkosh Public Museum (fig. 13.2). A third kit collected by American anthropologist and ethnographer Frances Densmore among the Ojibwe (Chippewa) is now in the collection of the State Historical Society of North Dakota (fig. 13.3). Both Menominee kits contain wood or plant charcoal used as a base for tattoo pigment, and all three toolkits include surfaces for mixing and holding ink. The Ojibwe example and that from the American Museum of Natural History both include bark or bentwood containers, while the Menominee kit from the Oshkosh Public Museum includes a pigment-stained ceramic sherd that apparently functioned as a palette. Most importantly, all three kits contain tattoo implements consisting of wooden handles between 120 and 160 mm long with either four (Menominee) or five (Ojibwe) metal needles hafted longitudinally to the end of the handle using thread or cordage. The tines on these tools are set slightly apart from one another at 1- to 2-mm intervals, with the total width of the tips measuring less than 9 mm.

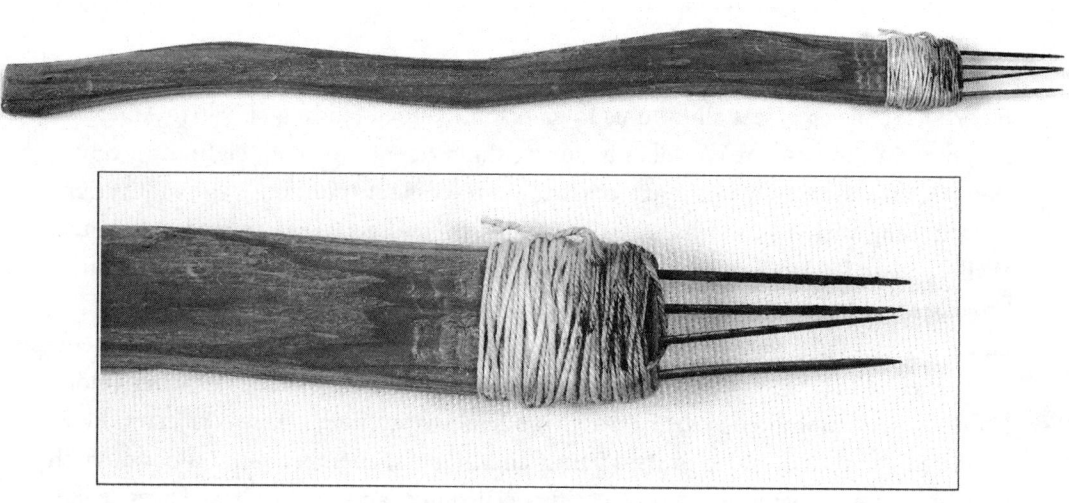

Fig. 13.2. Early twentieth century Menominee tattoo tool, made from metal needles tied to the end of a wooden handle. Image courtesy the Oshkosh Public Museum (Object ID I92.5.14.10).

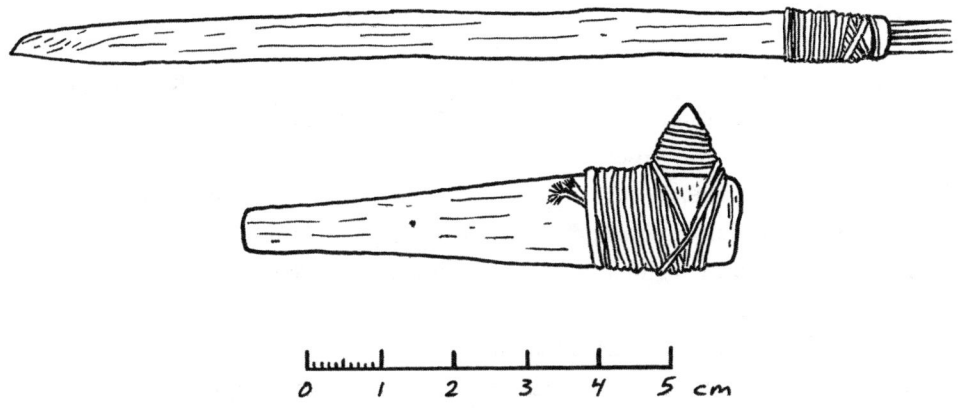

Fig. 13.3. Tattooing (top) and bloodletting (bottom) implements from an early twentieth century Ojibwe tattoo kit. The tattoo tool has metal needles at the tip, while the "lance" has a triangular flint blade. Both feature wooden handles (North Dakota State Historical Society, Catalogue SHSND 694). Drawing by Aaron Deter-Wolf.

In her 1928 report to the Bureau of American Ethnology, Densmore (1928:333, plate 46) references the Ojibwe tattoo tool as a "surgical appliance," and describes its use in inserting medicinal pigment comprised of carbonized plant remains, bear gall, and water beneath the skin. This process was undertaken as a means of treating headaches, rheumatism, and goiters rather than being part of a decorative tattoo tradition. Indeed, by the time Densmore collected this tool, tattooing among the Woodland peoples had been reduced to a strictly curative/therapeutic practice that survived alongside medicinal bloodletting.[2]

The Ojibwe kit also includes an implement consisting of a small (~10 mm) triangular flint blade set at 90-degrees into the end of a 70-mm-long tapered wooden handle (see fig. 13.3), along with a replacement blade and leather tool cover. Densmore (1928:333, plate 46) identifies this tool as a "lance," and in accompanying text describes that it was "tapped with the thumb and finger of the right hand" to create a gash for letting blood.[3] In some cases, an accompanying funnel made from a hollowed-out horn was placed over the incision and the other end sucked on by the practitioner to encourage blood flow.

The coexistence of bloodletting tools and tattooing tools within the same toolkits among both the Ojibwe and Menominee led to some historical misunderstandings about which implements were actually used to tattoo. Ethnographer Huron Smith (1923:350) records that, among the Menominee, "Some of the men have 'tattooing outfits,' which are not really tattooing outfits as we understand the term, but rather blood-letting instruments." Similar cases of misidentification are also well documented in the Oceanian context, where bloodletting instruments have repeatedly been confused with tattooing tools (Robitaille 2007:161).

Scratching

Confusion regarding identification and function of bloodletting and tattooing tools is also present in examinations of ancient Native American culture. Excavations at prehistoric sites throughout the American Southeast and Midcontinent have recovered sets of small, split bone implements which, when found in situ, were often arranged parallel to one another and recovered from burials (fig. 13.4). Most of these tools date to the Mississippian period of regional prehistory, although some examples have also been recovered from the preceding Woodland period.[4]

The Woodland period is marked archaeologically by increased population sedentism corresponding to the spread of horticulture, ceramic production, construction of earthen mounds, increased social stratification, and the appearance of regional ceremonial complexes such as the Adena and Hopewell. The Mississippian period is the final prehistoric stage in the region, and is identified by widespread adoption of maize agriculture, settlement of permanent, sometimes fortified villages, a proliferation of mound sites overseen by complex chiefdoms, and the presence of distinctive art and ritual practices linked to influence from the paramount site of Cahokia along the Mississippi River near St. Louis, Missouri. While some Mississippian chiefdoms began to decline by the late fourteenth century CE because of factors including regional drought and political turmoil, in some areas Mississippian societies persisted until after European contact. Although the introduction of European diseases and armed conflicts caused dramatic upheaval and ultimately brought about the collapse of Mississippian chiefdoms, many precontact cultural elements and ritual practices persevered among subsequent Native American groups.

There is a clear and well-recognized connection between the sets of archaeologically recovered multipoint bone implements and compound tools used historically for scratching rites among various Native American groups including the Cherokee, Muscogee, Yuchi, Catawba, and Seminole (plate 17). During scratching rites, these tools were dragged across a recipient's limbs and torso deeply enough to draw blood. Scratching was performed in conjunction with stickball games and annual community-wide ritual events, where it served to purify and fortify participants.[5] Variations of the practice were also used for therapeutic and punitive purposes (e.g., Buswell 1972:182–87; Mooney 1902:476). In 1902, ethnographer James Mooney described a scratching rite among the Cherokee that was performed as part of instruction in tribal lore: "They sat up all night talking, with only the light of a small fire burning in the middle of the floor. At daybreak the whole party went down to the running stream, where the pupils or hearers of the myths stripped themselves, and were scratched upon their naked skin with a bone-tooth comb in the hands of the priest, after which they waded out, facing the rising sun, and dipped seven times under the water, while the priest recited prayers upon the bank" (Mooney 1902:230).

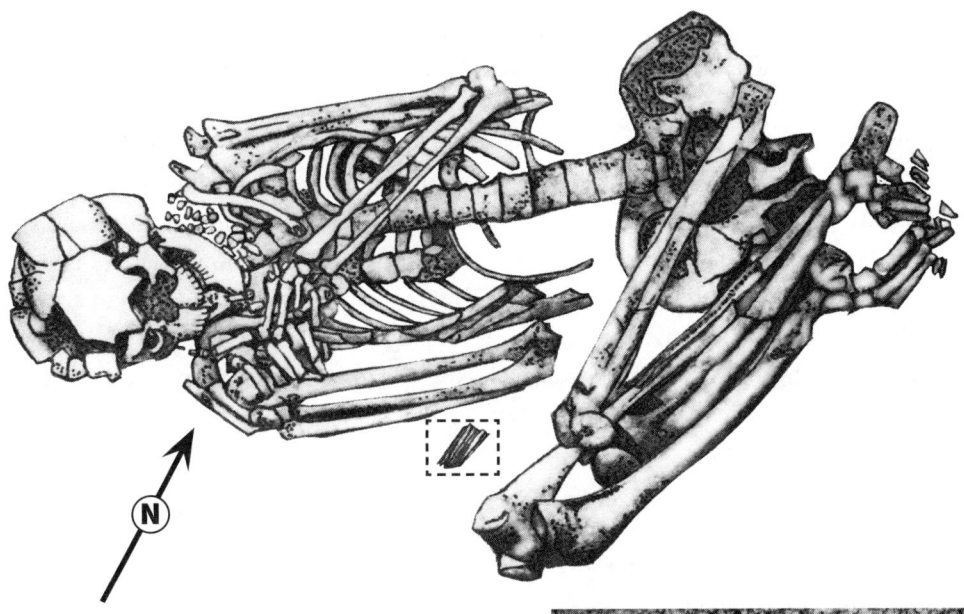
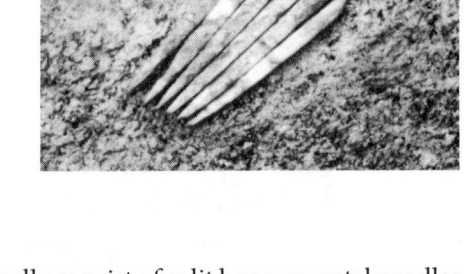

Fig. 13.4. Drawing of Burial 6 from the Town Creek site (31Mg2), Montgomery County, North Carolina, (ca. 1150–1250 CE), and in situ view of the associated turkey bone scratcher. Photograph courtesy of the Research Laboratories of Archaeology, University of North Carolina at Chapel Hill (RLA Neg. No. 141, taken by J. L. Coe, 1937).

Historic examples of scratching tools generally consist of split bone or metal needles set separate from one another within a frame made from a bent feather shaft or wood block. Some Native American groups used other tool types for scratching, including snake teeth, thorns, and garfish jaws.[6] However, this discussion focuses only on the multipoint bone implements, which have been mistaken by some researchers as being tattoo tools.

SCARIFYING AND SCARIFIERS

Modern ethnographic discussions now refer to the ritual activity described previously as "scratching." However, for five centuries many European and Euro-American sources identified the practice as "scarification." This terminology dates back to a 1768 account from among the Muscogee by French captain and explorer Jean Bernard Bossu (Bossu 1768:24–25, as cited by Swanton 1928:365),[7] which may also be the first European documentation of Native American scratching. The use of the term *scarification* in this context is technically correct from a historical European language perspective, since the English word *scarify* is ultimately rooted in the Greek *skariphasthai* (σκαρῐ́φᾰσθαι, "scratch an outline"), from *skariphos* (σκάρῐφος, "stylus") (Oxford English Dictionary 2016). By the fifteenth century the verb *scarify* was used in both French and English to reference shallow incisions made in the skin, particularly for medical purposes.

Over the past half century the term *scarify* has undergone considerable semantic drift, and is now used primarily to reference the deliberate creation of culturally significant scar tissue (e.g., Demello 2007:235). Traditional scarification practices take on a variety of forms, including the insertion of inert material within a wound to create a raised keloid, cutting or chiseling flesh to create patterns of scar tissue, and the removal of strips of flesh (e.g., Pales 1946). Regardless of the geographic, temporal, or cultural setting of the various forms of scarification, they all share intent: the voluntary intentional creation of visible scar tissue.

A form of scarification was practiced historically on North America's Great Plains, where Native Americans including the Arapaho, Crow, Lakota, Blackfoot, and Hidatsa used metal or flint knives to remove flesh offerings during mourning rituals, rites of passage, and ritual events such as the Sun Dance.[8] In 1896 James Mooney recorded a particularly vivid description of this process and its intent as performed by the Arapaho Chief Black Coyote, or Watonga (fig. 13.5):

> In his portrait . . . a number of scars will be noticed on his chest and arms. The full number of these scars is seventy, arranged in various patterns of lines, circles, crosses, etc., with a long figure of the sacred pipe on one arm. According to his own statement they were made in obedience to a dream as a sacrifice to save the lives of his children. Several of his children had died in rapid succession, and in accordance with Indian custom he undertook a fast of four days as an expiation to the overruling spirit. During this time, while lying on his bed, he heard a voice, somewhat resembling the cry of an owl or the subdued bark of a dog. The voice told him that if he wished to save his other children he must cut out seventy pieces of skin and offer them to the sun. He at once cut out seven pieces, held them out to the sun and prayed, and then buried them. But the sun was not satisfied, and soon after he was warned in a vision that the full number of seventy must be sacrificed if he would save his children. He then did as directed, cutting out the pieces of skin in the various patterns indicated, offering each in turn to the sun with a prayer for the health of his family, and then burying them. Since then there has been no death in his family. In cutting out the larger pieces, some of which were several inches long and nearly half an inch wide, the skin was first lifted up with an awl and then sliced away with a knife. This had to be done by an assistant, and Black Coyote was particular to show me by signs, sitting very erect and bracing himself firmly, that he had not flinched during the process. (Mooney 1896:898)

In addition to the scars from his flesh offerings, Black Coyote also owned chest tattoos (Krutak 2014a:162). These marks are visible as nested circles in the portrait that accompanies Mooney's account (see fig. 13.5), and functioned as tribal identifiers. Unlike the flesh offerings described previously, Black Coyote's tattoos were applied to his skin using bundled yucca spines.

Native American scratching did indeed leave behind faint scars. In 1953, author and ethnographer Louis Capron wrote: "You can always tell, for several months thereafter, when a Seminole has been to the Green Corn Dance. The scratch marks will show below his sleeve" (Capron 1953:192). However, unlike the Arapaho flesh offerings, the creation of visible scar tissue was not the principal, intended outcome of scratching rites. Rather, the importance of these rituals lies in the release of blood. Consequently it has been suggested that scholars abandon the term *scarification* when discussing Native American scratching: "For though scarring produces blood and blood-letting may produce scars, ambiguity will be reduced if the intended function of the rite is permitted to dictate the terminology" (Buswell 1972:193–94). Nevertheless, use of the terms *scarification* and *scarifiers* to reference Native American scratching rituals and tools has persevered among some archaeologists and museums.

Within the archaeological literature, individual components of the multipoint bone scratching tools described previously and illustrated in fig. 13.4 have been identified variously as pins, needles, and awls. However, when recognized as the elements of a compound tool, they are typically addressed as *scarifiers* both in typological classifications and in functional descriptions.[9] Because these tools are indeed used to make shallow incisions in the skin, use of the term *scarifier* is—once again—technically correct from a European linguistic perspective. However, employing this terminology ignores modern understandings of both body modification and Native American scratching, and contributes to ongoing confusion regarding Native American body art.

Discussion

Confusion regarding the functional use of the multipoint bone tools is additionally complicated by analyses suggesting the artifacts were used both for scratching and tattooing.[10] Contrary to these interpretations, there are no ethnographic studies documenting Native American use of these distinctive tools for any purpose other than scratching. The proposed dual function of scratchers as tattoo tools is also entirely unsupported in the ethnohistorical and archaeological data. Moreover, in the world sample of tattooing cultures, there are no examples of needle-based tattoo implements also being used for other forms of body art. Even the Maori of New Zealand, whose combination of tattooing and scarification led many observers to believe their facial markings were the result of a dual-function operation, actually employed separate, specific tools for the chiseling and tattooing aspects of *moko* (Te Awekotuku 2007).

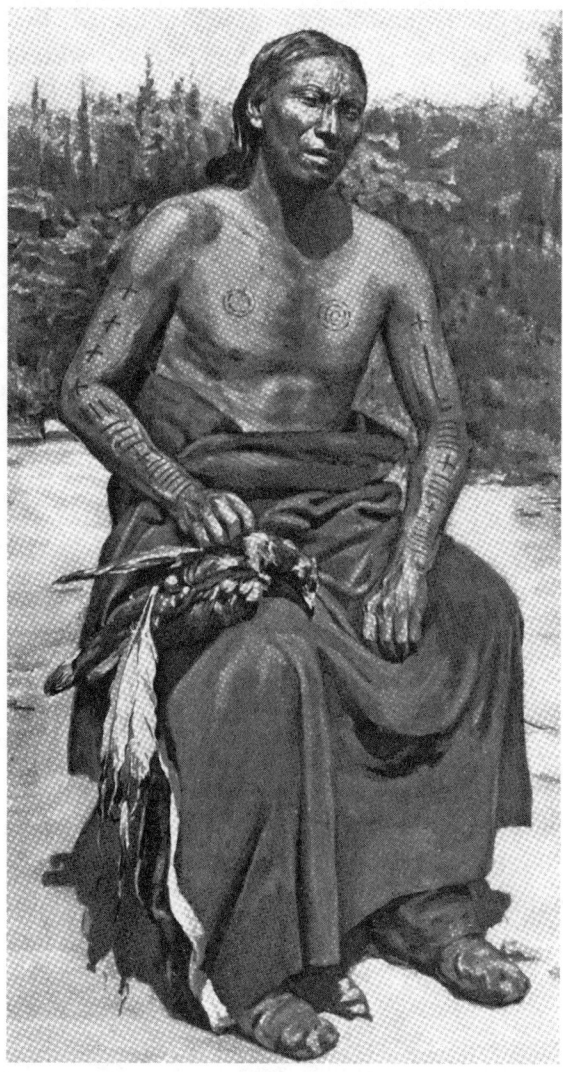

Fig. 13.5. Scars on the arms and tattoos on the chest of the Arapaho man Black Coyote (Watonga) (1896 CE). After Mooney 1896: plate CV.

Instead, the traditional assignment of a joint bloodletting/tattooing function to Native American scratchers appears to be based entirely on secondhand conventional wisdom.

There are only a few European ethnohistorical accounts describing multipoint, compound tattoo implements from the Eastern Woodlands, including five from the eighteenth century CE, and two from the twentieth century.[11] These accounts record tattoo tools consisting of between two and twelve metal needles arranged beside one another on the tip of a handle. In Louisiana, French historian and naturalist Antoine-Simon Le Page du Pratz (1947 [1758]:346) describes "six needles in a piece of wood in two rows, in such a manner that they only stick out about the tenth part of an inch," while in eastern Canada tattoos were given using "two or three well-sharpened fish or animal bones, which they bind separate from each other to the end of a piece of wood" (Raudot 1904 [1709]:64–65). Among the twentieth-century Menominee in Wisconsin, ethnologist Alanson Skinner (1921:134) records a tattoo tool "composed of several [bone] needles set in a handle made of the thick, strong quill of some large bird, from which the covering had been stripped. The upper end had been folded over and thrust into a longitudinal slit made in its own shaft. The needles were fastened in a row in the distal end."

In his seminal work *The Southeastern Indians*, anthropologist and historian Charles Hudson (1976:30) wrote that after European contact, "in some places tattooing was done with five or six needles tied to a small piece of wood in such a way that all the points were aligned like the teeth of a comb." This statement is presumably based on the same ethnohistorical data outlined previously, although no source is provided. Hudson then goes on to note that Southeastern groups used "an instrument like this *not to tattoo*, but to administer ritual scratching" (emphasis ours). As exemplified by the initial passage from Hudson, it is possible to confuse historic Native American tattoo implements with multipoint scratchers based only on ethnohistorical descriptions, since both tool types consist of needles or sharpened bones hafted parallel to one another on a piece of wood or bent feather shaft. This similarity may also explain initial misconceptions of the joint scratching/tattooing function of scratching tools. However, through recent research we can now link ethnohistorical descriptions of tattoo implements from the Eastern Woodlands to actual ethnographic examples of Native American tattoo tools (see plate 16, figs. 13.2–13.3).

While both multipoint scratchers and tattoo implements exhibit sets of parallel tines, there are important technological differences between the tool types with regard to the arrangement of needles and the hafting style. The individual points on scratchers are spaced 5 to 7 mm apart in most historic examples, resulting in a total tool width that typically exceeds 30 mm. This arrangement reflects the intended purpose of the tool, which is to create shallow, parallel cuts.

The 1- to 2-mm tine separation and total tip width of >9 mm exhibited for the Eastern Woodlands tattoo toolkits described previously appear somewhat wider than the needle spacing on comparative historic tattoo tools from the adjacent Great Plains. Multipoint implements from that region, including examples collected from among the Osage, Plains Cree, Ioway, and Missouria (fig. 13.6) exhibit needles typically set more closely adjacent, though with similar total tip widths. Regardless, the needle spacing and tip width of historic tattoo tools from both the Eastern Woodlands and Great Plains present a clear technological benefit over widely spaced scratcher tines, in that they allow a tattooist to more easily create both individual solid lines and solid color infill within discrete areas. The wide tool widths and widely spaced tines found on scratchers would be impractical for tattooing any design other than equally spaced parallel lines and/or dots, and even in this regard would be largely limited to flat areas of the body. There are no credible depictions of historic Native American tattoos that show such patterns.

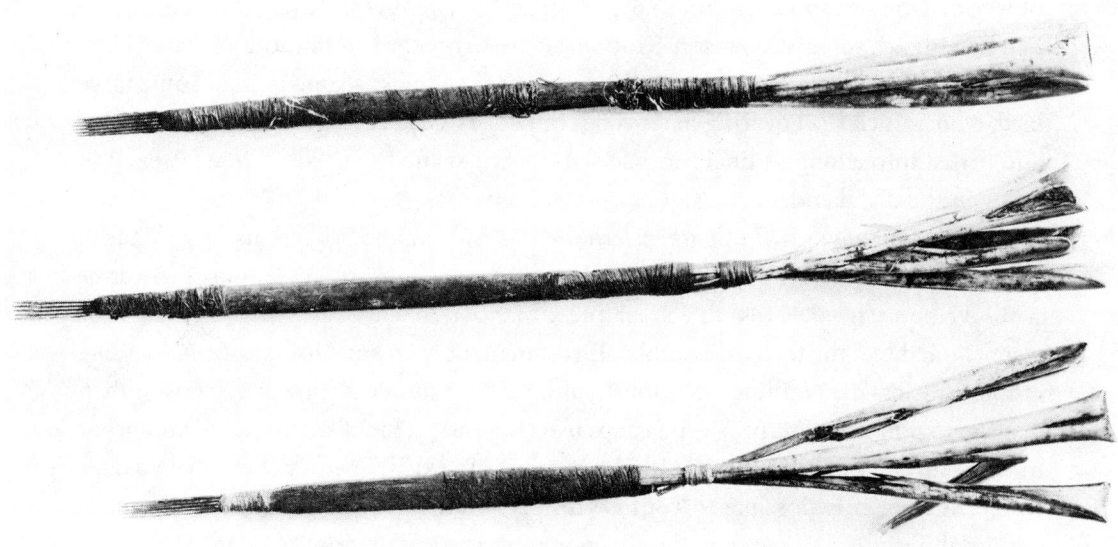

Fig. 13.6. Osage tattoo tools consisting of metal needles tied to the ends of wooden handles (late nineteenth or early twentieth century). The opposite ends feature folded quill rattles (Manuscript 4558, Box 33, National Anthropological Archives, Smithsonian Institution, Suitland, Maryland).

Finally, the long, narrow handles of historic tattoo tools allow them to be held and manipulated between the thumb and first two fingers like a brush or pencil, providing control over the depth and angle of puncture. These handles also facilitate the attachment of significant ritual paraphernalia such as feathers, bells, and rattles. This hafting technique stands in contrast to the square or rectangular wood and feather-shaft frames of historic scratching implements, which are designed to be held firmly between the thumb and three to four fingers as they are pulled downward or laterally across the flesh of the recipient.

Broadening the comparative scope, Native American scratchers are substantially wider, and most important, their points are much more widely spaced in relation to one another than almost all tools from the worldwide sample of Indigenous tattoo implements. Other examples of wide multipoint tattoo tools do appear historically in far eastern India, Myanmar, and Oceania. However, like the Native American tattoo tools and unlike scratchers, those comparative implements all exhibit closely spaced teeth. In addition, as described and illustrated by Furey (in chapter 11, this volume), the wide tools from these other areas tend to be specialized parts of multi-implement tattoo kits.[12] They were used for creating wide lines and broad fills, and are accompanied by additional significantly narrower implements. No such additional tools are associated ethnographically or archaeologically with Native American scratchers.

Finally, the microscopic use-wear patterns created on bone scratchers clearly indicate these tools were not used to tattoo. Experimental use-wear analysis has demonstrated that tattooing with sharpened bone implements results in overall rounding of the apical tip, flattening of bone fibers, and smoothing of manufacturing patterns along the longitudinal axis within the final 3 mm of the tool tip (Gates St-Pierre 2017; see also Deter-Wolf and Clark, chapter 16, this volume). Overall, these wear patterns are consistent with repeated linear piercing of soft or wet hide to a very shallow depth.

In 2013 the senior author of this essay examined use-wear patterns on two sets of Mississippian multipoint bone artifacts identified as *scarifiers* and housed in the collections of the Illinois State Museums (ISM) at Dickson Mounds Museum in Lewistown, Illinois. These included ten bird bone points from the site of Dickson Mounds and seven split bone implements from the Vandeventer site, both in Illinois. The tools from Dickson Mounds were recovered from Burial 475, the grave of an adult male, where they were arranged parallel to one another above the right shoulder, forming a multipoint implement approximately 70 mm wide (Harn 2013). The individual tines measured between 7.3 and 7.6 cm in length and lay touching or slightly separated from one another, all with their tips oriented toward the feet of the buried individual. No specific provenience or positioning is known for the examples from Vandeventer.

Microscopic use-wear examinations revealed that the tips of the individual bone points varied from slightly rounded to beveled, and in some cases bi-beveled. All seventeen tools exhibited longitudinal striations consistent with manufacture and

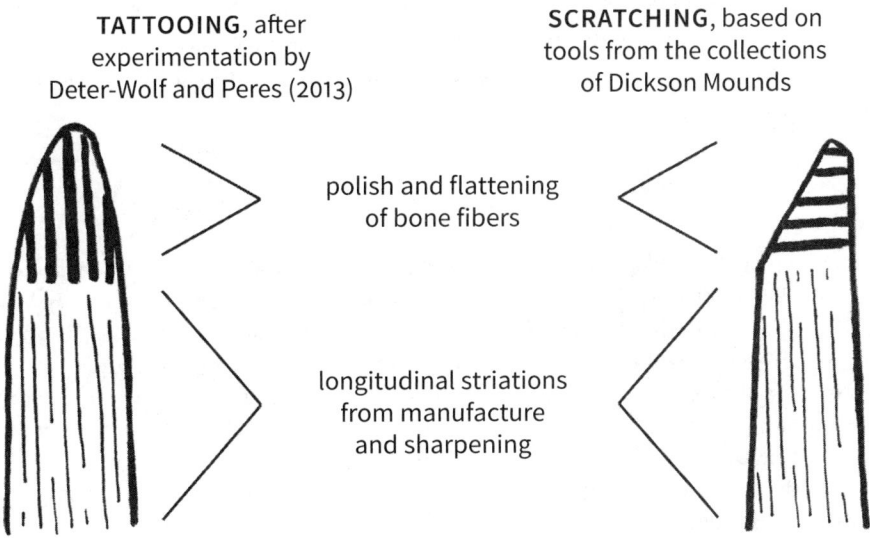

Fig. 13.7. Schematic representation of use-wear analysis on bone tools, comparing the results of experimental tattooing (left) with wear patterns on Mississippian period scratchers (ca. 900 to 1600 CE) from the collections of the Illinois State Museum, Dickson Mounds (right). Drawing by Aaron Deter-Wolf.

sharpening on an abrasive stone surface. However, none exhibited flattening of bone fibers or smoothing of manufacturing patterns at the tips consistent with directly piercing skin or soft hides. Instead, these tools exhibit transverse polish running perpendicular to the tool shaft (fig. 13.7), wear patterns that are consistent with being dragged in a linear fashion through soft hide or skin at a shallow depth, rather than being used in a piercing motion.

Conclusions

Scarification, scratching, and tattooing are not the same. They are fundamentally different forms of body modification, and for their Native American practitioners were associated with distinct rituals, imbued with different meanings and symbolism, and performed with separate tools. While to non-Native observers the tools used for these different activities may share certain general characteristics, they were not the same implements and are not functionally or ritually interchangeable. Although scholars have generally abandoned the term *scarification* to describe Native American scratching rites, the word has persevered as a typological category and descriptor for the unique multipoint compound tools with which the activity was historically performed. Moreover, these tools are often erroneously identified as having been dual function—being used for both scratching and tattooing. These misunderstandings have led archaeologists to misidentify the actual role of these tools, and in doing so, to misinterpret Native American ritual practices and traditions of body alteration. Based on the data presented here, scholars can perhaps now abandon both the scarifier typology and misidentification of a tattooing function for these tools once and for all, and instead discuss the distinctive artifacts of Native American body modification in terms meaningful to their actual use.

Notes

The authors would like to thank Alan Harn, Mike Wiant, and the staff of Dickson Mounds Museum for their hospitality and for facilitating access to their collections. Anna Cannizzo of the Oshkosh Public Museum, Mark Halvorson of the State Historical Society of North Dakota, and Adam Watson of the American Museum of Natural History provided assistance identifying and documenting the tattoo tools in their collections. The senior author wishes to thank Tennessee State Archaeologist Mike Moore for his continued research support. This chapter is based on the conference paper "Kanukaski (I am Scratching it): Examining the Artifacts of Native American Body Art in the Eastern Woodlands," presented at the 79th Annual (2013) Meeting of the Society of American Archaeology in Austin, Texas.

1   See Harrington (1913); La Flesche (1921, 1930); and Skinner (1926).
2   Hilger (1992 [1951]:93–95); Landes (1937:138); Skinner (1921:133).
3   The resemblance between this instrument and European bloodletting fleams is so striking as to suggest that the form of the Ojibwe tool may have resulted from post-contact Euro-American influence.

4   The examples of these tools recovered from Mississippian contexts are too numerous to exhaustively summarize here; see, however, Coe (1952:309, 1995:238–40); Conrad (1991:147, 149); Goodman (1984:14); Harn (1980:16, 26); Jolley (1978:58); Kimball et al. (2010:46); Morse (1960:346); Morse and Morse (1990:58); Morse et al. (1961:126, fig. 75); Perino (1968:61); Santure and Esarey (1990:88, 91, 104); Williams (1954:247); and Winters (1974:38). For a Woodland period example, see Mills (1904:47).

5   Gilbert (1943:195); Mooney (1902:230, 476); Speck (1909:115, 121); Sturtevant (1955:177–79).

6   See, for example, Howard (1990:137), Lawson (1709:43), and Peres and Deter-Wolf (2016:109, table 10.2).

7   "Le harangue finie, le Chef leur fait des scarifications aux cuisses . . ." (Bossu 1768:24–25).

8   For example, MacLeod (1938); Voget (1998:43–44); Weitzner (1979:254–55).

9   For example, Conrad (1991:147, 149); Goodman (1984:14); Harn (1980:16, 26); Jolley (1978:58); Morse (1960:346); Morse and Morse (1990:58); Morse et al. (1961:126, fig, 75); Perino (1968:61); Polhemus (1998:225); Santure and Esarey (1990:88, 91, 104); and Wilson (2010:574).

10 Boudreaux (2005:335); Kimball et al. (2010:46); Santure and Esarey (1990: 89–91); Strezewski (2003:240); Tubbs (2013:195, 197).

11 Bonin (1887:218); Dumont de Montigny (1753:140); Hilger (1992 [1951]:94); Le Page du Pratz (1947 [1758]:346); Long (1791:48); Raudot (1904 [1709]:64–65); Skinner (1921:134).

12 Although less widespread than the better known Oceanic examples, multi-instrument tool sets featuring wide needle arrays along with narrower combs and suited to a variety of functions are also known to have been used among some Naga groups of far eastern India and northwestern Myanmar. One such set was notably collected by the early twentieth century ethnographer Henry Balfour among the Konyak Naga at Tamlu. These tools are now part of the collection of the Pitt-Rivers Museum at Oxford University, England (Accession numbers: PRM1936.4.11, PRM1936.4.12, PRM1936.4.13, PRM1936.4.14, PRM1936.4.15, PRM1936.4.16, and PRM1936.4.17).

14

Native North American Tattoo Revival

Lars Krutak

Even though their lands, cultures, and identities have been fractured, diminished, and transformed by centuries of colonialism and forced acculturation, today tattoos are helping to heal those wounds inflicted upon Native North American communities.

"Tattooing was practiced by almost every Indigenous nation across Canada and the United States," says Nlaka'pamux tattoo artist Dion Kaszas. "And the revival of cultural tattooing has become a medium of reclaiming our Indigenous identities and even our bodies from the colonial machinery which sought to divide us, control us, and wipe us out."

Historically, Native North American tattoos functioned to initiate individuals into adulthood, cure bodily complaints, reflect social status, document martial achievement, and to channel and direct supernatural forces (Krutak 2014a). But tattoos also communicated lineage and group affiliation as well as cultural pride and ancestral heritage.

Michael Galban (Washoe/Mono Lake Paiute), a Public Historian and Curator at the Ganondagan Seneca Art and Culture Center near Rochester, New York, says it is important to reconstruct this cultural practice. "I certainly think it is a recapturing of a tradition, a way to tie yourself to the past. It also reminds yourself of your place in [Indigenous] culture and is a vehicle to outwardly project that sense to the world. Decolonization is a very complicated process—and tattooing [can] be a part of that process if it is informed with the truth."

Galban, whose wife, Tonia, is Akwesasne Mohawk, wears many hats. Apart from his duties at Ganondagan he is a skilled artisan handcrafting quillwork (bags, moccasins, mitts, headdresses), elm bark containers, effigy bowls and ladles, and snowshoes, as well as traditional tattooing implements. But only recently has he begun to tattoo with the implements. "I have a list of folks who want to get tattooed. But I originally just designed tattoos for people, and it takes a long time. I really spend a lot of time thinking of them, what they do, what their role is in the local Haudenosaunee community, and how they see themselves. If I am going to tattoo someone I want it to feel right."

For Kaszas, a personal tragedy inspired him to start tattooing in the old way. In 2010 he was working as a kickboxing instructor in British Columbia and was mentoring a promising young man. "I suspected he had Indigenous heritage and asked him about it. To which he replied, 'No.' But I knew he had Cree roots. A short time after this conversation he tragically took his own life. This weighed heavily on my heart and as I sat at his funeral I decided I needed to find a way to help Indigenous people become proud of who they are . . . an anchor to reconnect them to their ancestors and cultural heritage. And this is when my tattoo revival movement was born."

At first, Kaszas looked toward the tattoo cultures of Polynesia for guidance. "Inspiration and courage came from the voices, practices, and journeys of the many Pacific Island tattoo artists and cultural practitioners. Even though I had not met many of the people I considered my mentors and teachers in person, it was their work and their courage that led me to my revival efforts. And I was particularly drawn to something one Maori tattoo bearer said: 'Moko [tattoo] inscribes your soul, it uplifts your senses, and it changes you forever. It is the ultimate engagement of oneself with one's body, because it cannot be removed.' "

Kaszas has relearned the traditional tattooing techniques of his Nlaka'pamux ancestors—hand-poking and skin-stitching. One of his recent clients is Nêhiyawahk (Cree) educator Carla Wells-Listener of Maskwacis, Alberta (fig. 14.1). For twenty years she was drawn to a historical portrait of a Cree woman with traditional facial tattoos, and when she found Kaszas she wanted to bring these tattoos to life. "I wanted an Indigenous person from Canada to make this tattoo. It has strengthened my tie to the ancestors and brought groundedness in my thoughts and energy. I send him many blessings for helping me to revive this ancient symbol of womanhood. And I'd love to see other Cree women sport the *iskwew-asasow* (chin tattoo)."

Kaszas's tattoo revival project is making great headway, and he says most of the response and interest has been from people of his generation (figs. 14.2 and 14.3). Recently, he developed a residency-style training program at the University of British Columbia–Okanagan to help fulfill the need for trained cultural tattoo artists who can serve their communities and nations. The training program included coursework in traditional tattoo techniques and tool manufacture, cultural and spiritual safety, and a certificate program in blood-borne pathogens. It also provided a platform from which to inform participants of the meanings and functions of Indigenous tattoos.[1]

Back in New York, I asked Galban why he thought it was important to educate all generations of Indigenous people about the meaning and history of Haudenosaunee

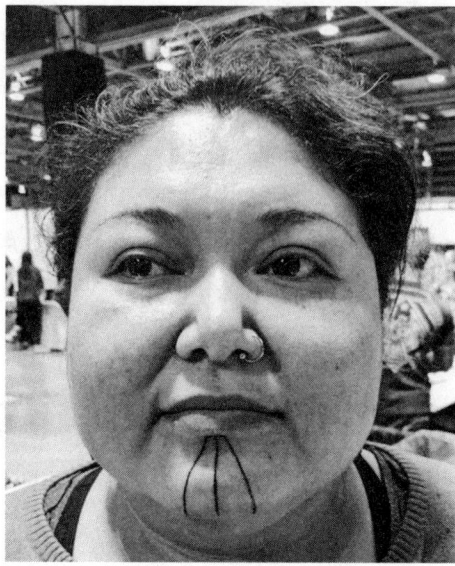

Fig. 14.1. Carla Wells-Listener (Cree) from Alberta, Canada, proudly bears the facial tattoos of her ancestors (2016). Tattoos and photograph © Dion Kaszas / www.indigenoustattooing.com.

tattoos through the programs at Ganondagan. He says, "I want to responsibly inform folks about what I have come to understand as the functions of these practices. Not to drive the path of the practice, but to expose people to what we know about it so that the future of the revival has a strong base to work from. For many, it's simply about what looks cool, but the old designs aren't simply about aesthetics. They are evocative of culture and worldview. In fact, the old tattoos were taboo for a long, long time."

Indeed, many elder tribal members cautioned those who sought traditional symbols, because the patterns conveyed an ancestral tie or were highly personal or supernatural in nature (plate 18). Peter Jemison, Director of Ganondagan and Faithkeeper to the Cattaragus Seneca Nation, explains: "To reuse that, if you are not part that tradition, raises questions," if not spiritual risks.[2]

But gradually over time the reluctance to embrace these time-honored traditions faded. "It started with the very inquisitive internet generation; questions about worldviews and the past were being asked and answered," Galban explains. "Back in the 1990s I began to ask some of the old folks about tattoos, and the answers I received were very conservative. I asked esteemed Onondaga elder Huron Miller about it, he was one of the most informed Haudenosaunee I knew, and he flatly denied the tradition. For him, and his lifetime and even the lifetimes of his grandfathers, he was right. I had to reconcile this long absence of tradition with what I was discovering in the writings of the past."

Then Galban began to collect his own Woodlands-style tattoos. And they raised awareness almost immediately.

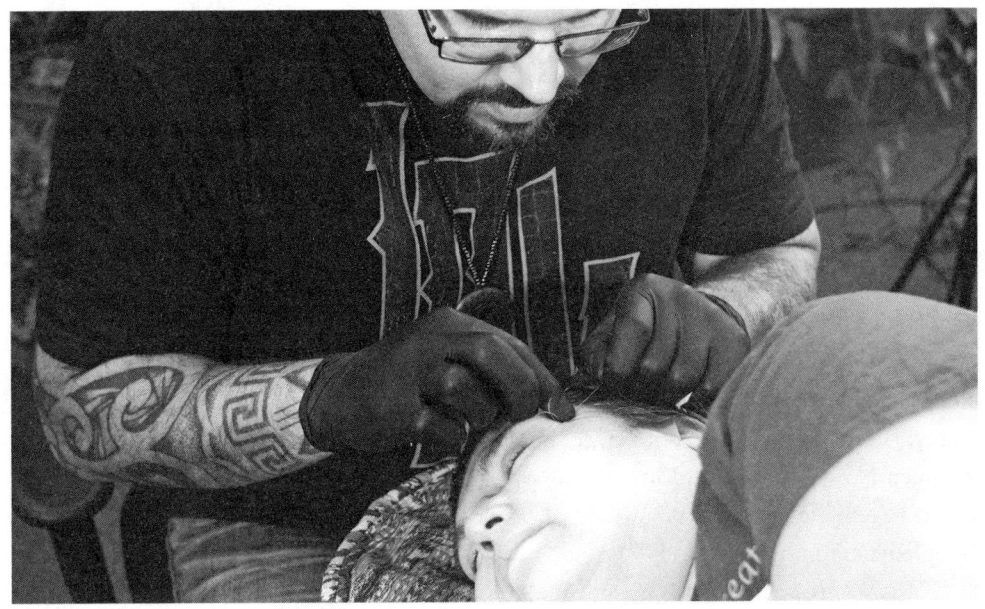

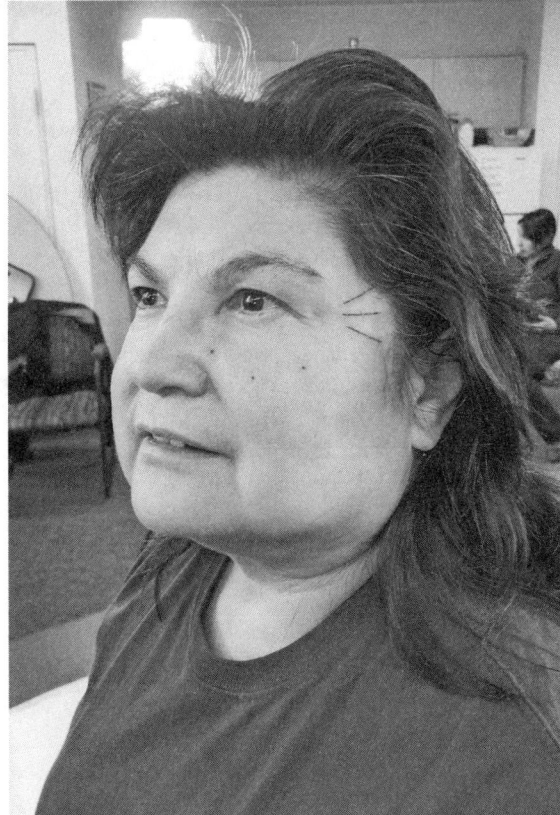

Figs. 14.2 (top) and 14.3 (bottom). Tattoo artist Dion Kaszas ('Nlaka'pamux) skin-stitching fellow tribal member Molly Toodlican, 2016. The tattoo is significant because it is the first traditional facial tattoo executed in 'Nlaka'pamux country in more than seventy years. Photographs © Kiano Zamani.

"I remember getting stopped in my wife's longhouse during midwinter ceremonies, mid-dance (!), to talk about tattoo customs. People wanted to know. I began to have formal and informal discussions all around Haudenosaunee territory and even back in the late 1990s organized our Dance & Music festival around body modification! Some of our board members quit because they were opposed to the concept."

Although Galban certainly did not discourage the tattoo revival, he refuses to take credit for jumpstarting it. But he is very interested in what will happen to it in the near and distant future.

"I think the more informed people are about the old practices, the better and more structured perhaps the practice will become. My hope is that the tattoo tradition returns to the rite of passage ceremonies which exist in many Indigenous communities around the world today. If we can shift over the 'warrior' emblems of the past to our reality as modern Native people and return the power of distinction to them, I think it would extend the life of the revival and only bolster the already strong cultural identities that people have today."

Kaszas agrees. "Tattoos are permanent symbols of who we are, where we come from, and they connect us to our ancestors," he says. "They testify to the resilience of our Indigenous cultures and peoples. They proudly declare that we're still here and that we will *always* be here!"

Notes

This chapter is based on several interviews with the following individuals: Dion Kaszas (personal communications, August 26, 2012, and March 4, 2016); Michael Galban (personal communications, October 18, 2016; June 28, 2013; and August 5, 2013); and Carla Wells-Listener (personal communication, March 3, 2016).

1. Kaszas posts regular updates about his various tattoo projects, research findings, and personal journey to help encourage other Indigenous peoples to reclaim their traditional tattooing practices via his website (www.indigenoustattooing.com).
2. Exhibition text panel from "Indian Ink: Iroquois and the Art of Tattoos," Iroquois Museum, May 1–November 30, 2013 (see also Krutak 2014a:214).

15

The Discovery of a Sarmatian Tattoo Toolkit in Russia

Leonid T. Yablonsky

SOME OF THE WORLD'S MOST ANCIENT TATTOOS WERE DISCOVERED ON the Russian (former USSR) frontier in the early 1950s. Burial mounds, or kurgans, excavated in the Altai Mountains of Central Asia revealed the mummified remains of heavily tattooed individuals belonging to the Pazyryk archaeological culture of the fifth through third centuries BCE (see Pankova, chapter 5, this volume) (map 15.1). These mummies were found in two kurgans and were preserved because of cryosolic- or permafrost-affected soils (Rudenko 1953:136–40).

More recently in 1993, tattooed mummified remains of a woman were also uncovered after excavations at the Ak-Alakha-3 burial ground on the Ukok Plateau located in the Altai Mountains (Polosmak 2000:fig. 3) (see map 15.1). In 1995, another tattooed mummy was unearthed in the Altai at the Verkh-Kaldzhin-2 site. This male individual bore spectacular figures of an ungulate on his shoulders (Molodin 2000:fig. 143). These and other tattooed Altai mummies were the focus of a special study by The State Hermitage Museum, St. Petersburg, Russia, in which all of the Pazyryk tattoo designs were published for the first time (Barkova and Pankova 2005).

Although other ancient nomadic peoples inhabiting the Eurasian steppes of the southern Ural Mountains to the west of the Altai also practiced tattooing, these cultural traditions have received little attention in scholarly circles. The indelible custom of tattooing among one of these groups of Eurasian nomads, the Sarmatians, is evident in recent archaeological discoveries of their material culture, including implements that may be tattooing tools. These cultural materials, which have never been described in

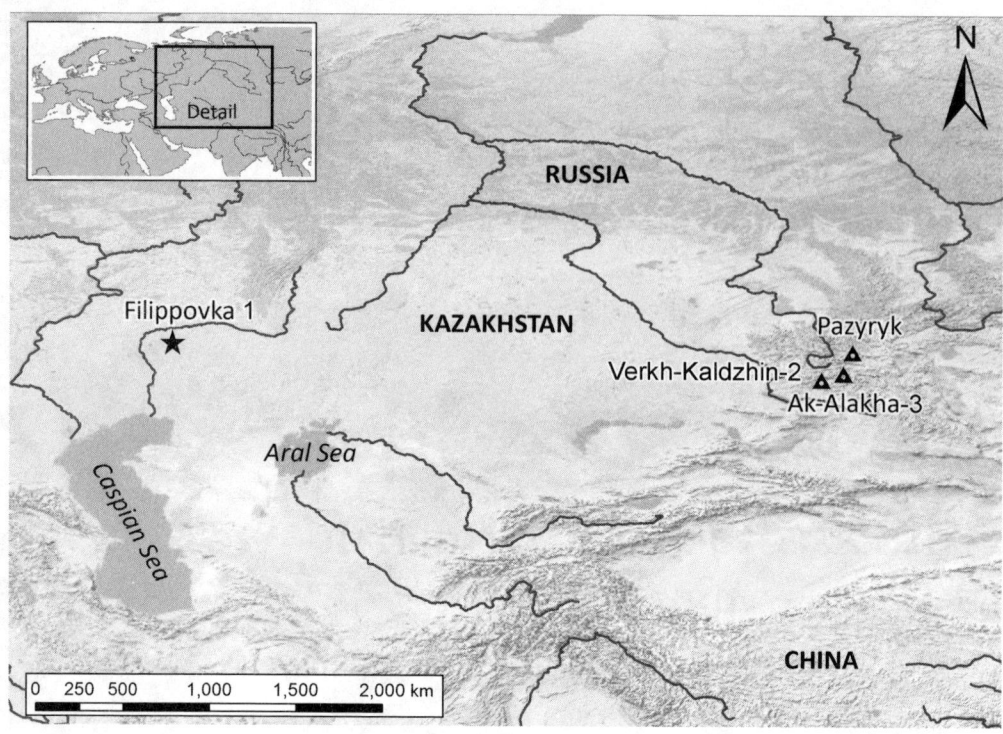

Map 15.1. Eurasian steppe country with archaeological sites discussed in this chapter.

detail before, may represent the earliest archaeological evidence of tattooing technology from the region, and therefore have an important role to play in reconstructing the tattoo history of the ancient nomadic horsemen of Eurasia.

Brief Historical Review: Scythian and Sarmatian Nomads of the Steppes

Thousands of burials and kurgans created by early nomadic peoples have been excavated in the Eurasian steppes, but until recently little was known about the custom of tattooing among these ancient populations. Although crystolic conditions preserved tattooed human remains of several Pazyryk individuals in the Siberian Altai, the warmer climates and loess soils characteristic of the Pontic-Caspian steppe farther west have not preserved organic human remains and thus mummies are absent here. Nevertheless, tools possibly employed for tattooing have been found repeatedly at some sites, especially the Sarmatian burial ground of Filippovka 1 dating to the fourth century BCE.

The Sarmatians were not the only local people to practice tattooing during this time. The Scythians, a mighty warlike people who inhabited the Pontic-Caspian steppe of the northern Black Sea and Fore-Caucasus region, set up a powerful state that existed from the second half of the seventh century BCE until the third century BCE. These Eurasian nomads did not leave any traces of written language. However, some kings' names are known from ancient Greek and Persian texts, which also play a significant role in describing aspects of their nomadic culture. For example, the Greek historian Herodotus (ca. 484–425 BCE) visited Greek colonies and collected data about the nomads who inhabited the borderlands of the Northern Black Sea region. In particular, his research concerned the Scythians, who were the Greek colonists' closest neighbors. Herodotus also wrote about their burial ceremonies, and one of their most peculiar features: the construction of kurgans—artificial earthen burial mounds above the tombs.

The Scythians' eastern neighbors were the nomadic tribes of Sauromatians, and later Sarmatians. While Herodotus knew almost nothing about these nomads who lived across the Volga River and in the Transurals region, the first-century Greek historian Diodorus Siculus tells us that the Sarmatians were contemporaries of the Scythian kingdom to the west, and contributed to its downfall in the third century BCE (Yablonsky 2014a:17). For nearly 1,000 years, from the fifth century BCE until approximately 400 CE, the Sarmatians controlled the steppes of eastern Europe and central Asia via horseback, moving constantly across the landscape searching for new pasture for their herds of cattle, sheep, and horses. As a transient people who left behind no permanent settlements, archaeological data plays a crucial role in reconstructing their cultural history. The remarkable burial ground of Filippovka 1 is therefore important, because it yields extensive evidence of the Sarmatian's rich cultural heritage, including material objects likely related to their tattooing practices (Pshenichnyuk 201; Yablonsky 2010, 2013, 2014b).

Filippovka 1

The Filippovka 1 site is located between the Ural and Ilek Rivers in the Orenburg region of Russia's Urals, and was excavated between 2004 and 2007 (see map 15.1). Several archaeological complexes excavated at the site have produced possible tattoo tools and revealed new information on the burial rituals of the Sarmatian nomads. These findings are fully described here for the first time in English.

COMPLEX 1

Complex 1 was found in Burial 4 of Kurgan 15. The skeleton belonged to an elderly woman, approximately fifty to sixty years of age, positioned on the floor of one of the *podboy* niches, or a side niche in one of the burial pit walls. She was accompanied by a diverse array of equipment indicative of her high status (fig. 15.1a–e). Within the grave, two iron needles, a small bronze wheel, and a piece of chalk were found near a large clay vessel. A decorated bronze mirror (fig. 15.1e) was also entombed with the woman, and the remains of a leather case adhered to the mirror's surface. Additional burial objects were set under the discoidal mirror and are described in the following discussion.

Burial 4 also contained a bone stenciling tool or marker (fig. 15.1a, fig. 15.2). This tool is blunt at the distal end, circular in cross-section, and features seven ring-shaped

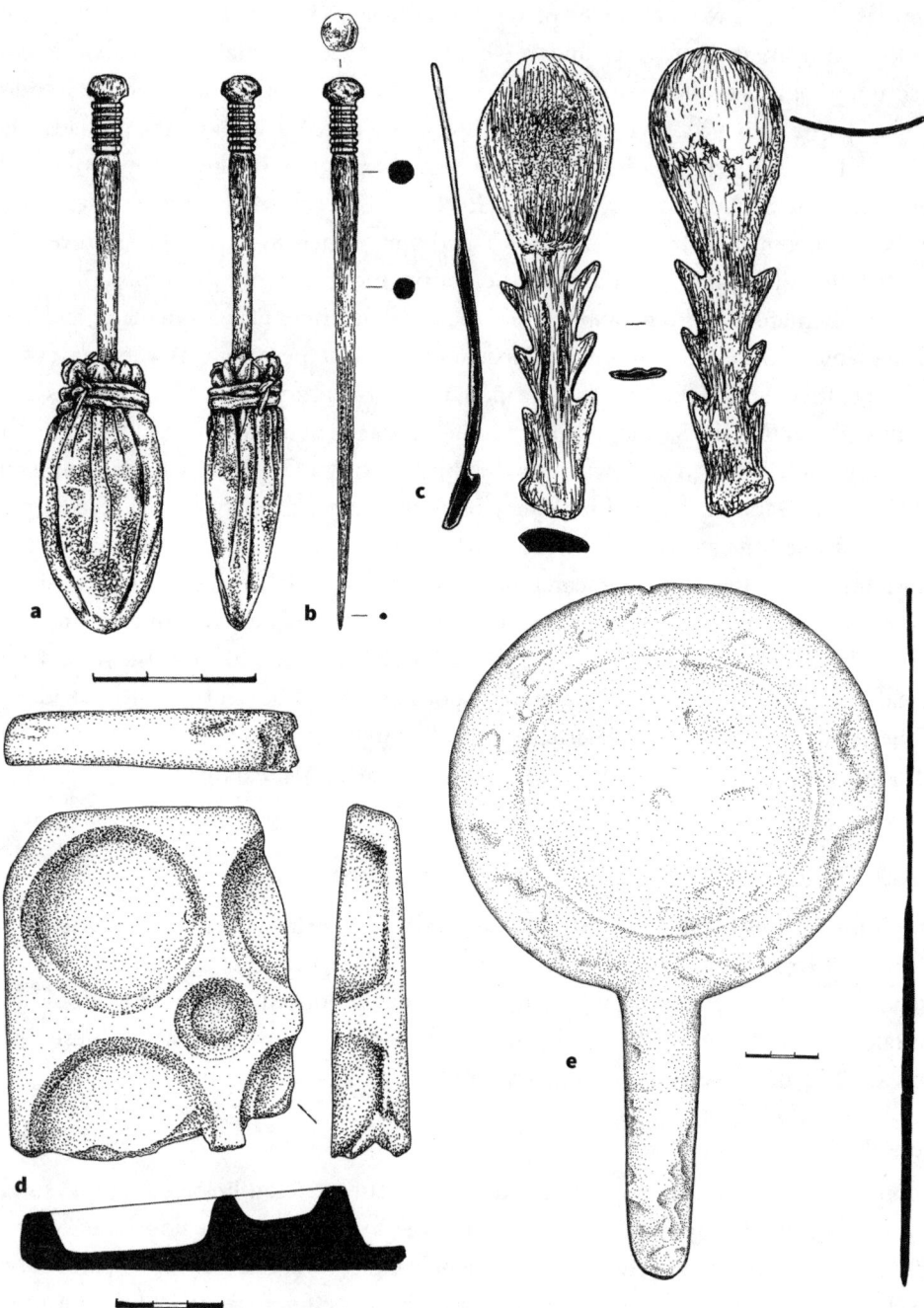

Fig. 15.1. Tattoo tools and related artifacts from Complex 1 recovered from Kurgan 15, Burial 4, Filippovka 1 burial ground, Russia (fourth century BCE): (a) leather pigment bag (KP 18980/21), H. 5.1 cm, W. 2.3 cm; (b) bone stencil or marker (KP 18980/20), L. 10.3 cm; (c) bone spoon (KP18980/23), L. 8.7 cm; (d) stone palette (KP18980/22), H. 12.5 cm, W. 12 cm; (e) bronze mirror (KP18980/19), H. (of handle) 9.1 cm, D. (of disk) 13.7 cm by 13 cm. Illustrations by Olga Frizen. Collections of the Orenburg Governor's Museum of Local Lore and History.

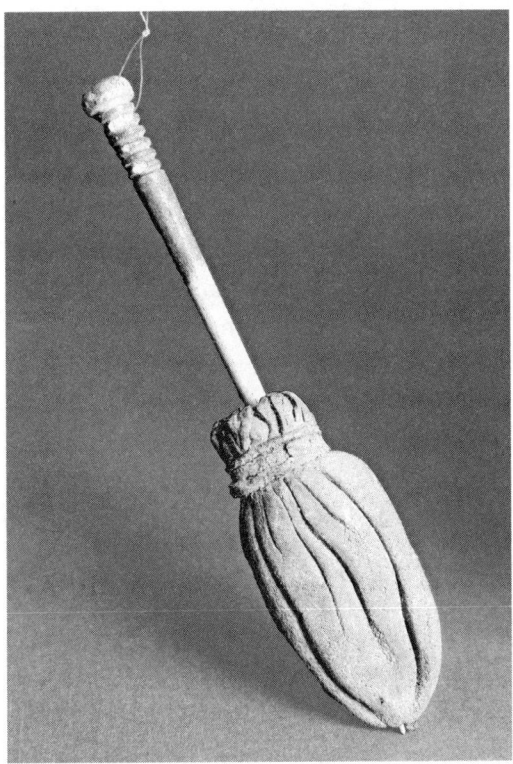

Fig. 15.2. Leather pigment bag holding a bone tattoo stenciling tool, recovered from Kurgan 15, Burial 4, Filippovka 1 burial ground, Russia (fourth century BCE) (KP 18980/20-21). Photography by Alexander Mirzokhanov. Courtesy of the Orenburg Governor's Museum of Local Lore and History.

notches. The distal end of the tool was held within a well-preserved leather pigment pouch, fitted with a leather cord at the neck to seal its contents.

Burial 4 in Kurgan 15 also included a small bone spoon made from an animal rib (fig. 15.1c), a fragment of belemnite, and an iron knife. Belemnites, or fossilized marine cephalopods, are often found in women's graves and are believed to have been used in Sarmatian magico-religious rituals. The spoon handle displays three flat triangular ridges on each side, which are swept toward the bowl and resemble stylized animal horns. The iron knife (not illustrated) had a flat handle and curved saber-edged blade turned upward at the tip.

A stone palette, presumably used for grinding and mixing paints or pigments, also was present in the Kurgan 15 grave (fig. 15.1d). This square-shaped object, which is incomplete, was manufactured from gray-brown sandstone and featured four circular flat-bottomed recesses surrounding a smaller central cup.

COMPLEX 2

Complex 2 was found in Burial 4 of Kurgan 29. The skeleton was placed in a *podboy* niche. It was a woman who died between the ages of eighteen and twenty years. She was positioned on her back, with her head directed south, face up, with arms extended along the body.

A circular stone palette with nine slanted circular recesses (fig. 15.3) was uncovered in the southwest corner of the niche, with a stone pestle resting in its central cup. This polished argillite mixing pestle was convex on one face and concave on the opposite surface, suggesting that one face was used for grinding and the other for pounding pigment. Both the palette and pestle are highly polished and show heavy wear.

Other associated funerary objects from Burial 4 in Kurgan 29 included an assemblage of beads found near the cervical vertebrae, two beaded bracelets on the wrists, and stone pebbles placed at the left shoulder. These later objects may have functioned as pounders to grind pigments.

Yet another assemblage of items was deposited at the foot of the burial. These included a bronze mirror (fig. 15.4a), a piece of clay with traces of finger streaks on its surface, and a 10- cm-long iron needle resting on the surface of the mirror. Beside the mirror a bone spoon (fig. 15.4b) was recovered, along with two fossil *Gryphaea* shells (fig. 15.4c), fragments of clay pots, and an iron knife.

COMPLEX 3

Complex 3 was discovered in Burial 2, Kurgan 1. This rich cultural deposit consisted of a burial pit covered with a wooden panel, below which was buried a woman aged 30 to 35 years. Two red sandstone mixing palettes (hereafter called Palette 1 and Palette 2), were found below her feet. Palette 1 displays five cup-shaped depressions for mixing. The four larger outer depressions are approximately 3.4 cm in diameter, while the central cup measured 1.2 cm in diameter. The pestle is pear-shaped and flattened in cross-section.

Palette 2 was discovered lying upside-down and beneath Palette 1. It is rectangular in form with no traces of ornamentation (fig. 15.5). Seven rounded depressions were carved into its surface. Four of these are located at the corners of the object and three more appear on the transverse axis between the corners. A rectangular pestle was found deposited above Palette 2.

A hollowed-out horse canine tooth located near the palettes held ground red ochre. In close proximity to the tooth were several egg-shaped pebbles of a dark gray metamorphic rock. These pebbles exhibit abrasions on their surface, suggesting they were used as whetstones for sharpening thin items such as needles.

Many other prestige objects accompanied the woman in Burial 2 of Kurgan 1, including a large, elaborate, beautiful silver mirror that was placed beside the body (plate 19). The mirror's handle is decorated with gilded stylized animals, with embossed ornamentation on the back depicting an eagle surrounded by a procession of six winged bulls and sixteen floraform designs. Each hoofed bull is shown with four legs, one ear, and a long, straight horn protruding from the crown of the head. An annular yoke is depicted on each bull's neck underneath the ear. Teardrop-shaped motifs are situated on the thighs and sometimes on the trunk, and are characteristic of the so-called Scythian-Siberian "animal-style" artistic tradition. The bulls' wings are located in the middle of the back and curve forward.

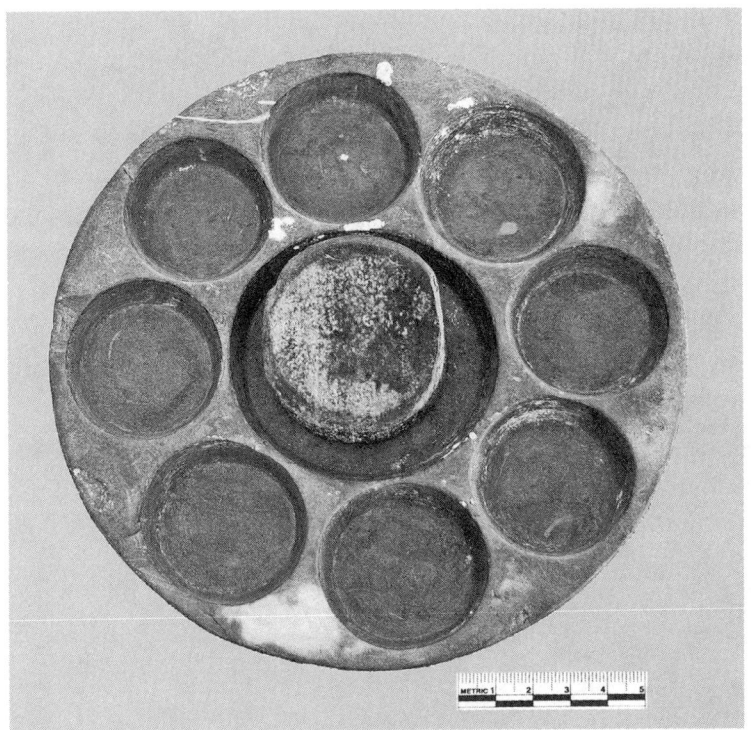

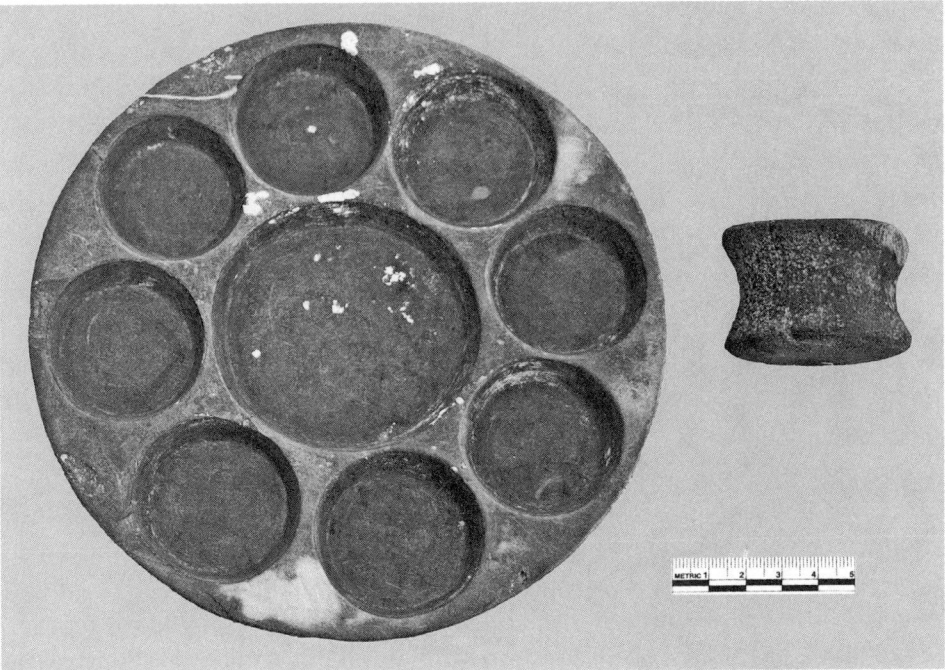

Fig. 15.3. Discoidal stone mixing palette and argillite pestle recovered from Complex 2, Kurgan 29, Burial 4, Filippovka 1 burial ground, Russia (fourth century BCE) (KP 19353/52-53). Palette, Diam. 14.3 cm; Pestle, H. 4 cm, D. 5.5 cm. Photography by Olga Anikeeva. Courtesy of the Orenburg Governor's Museum of Local Lore and History.

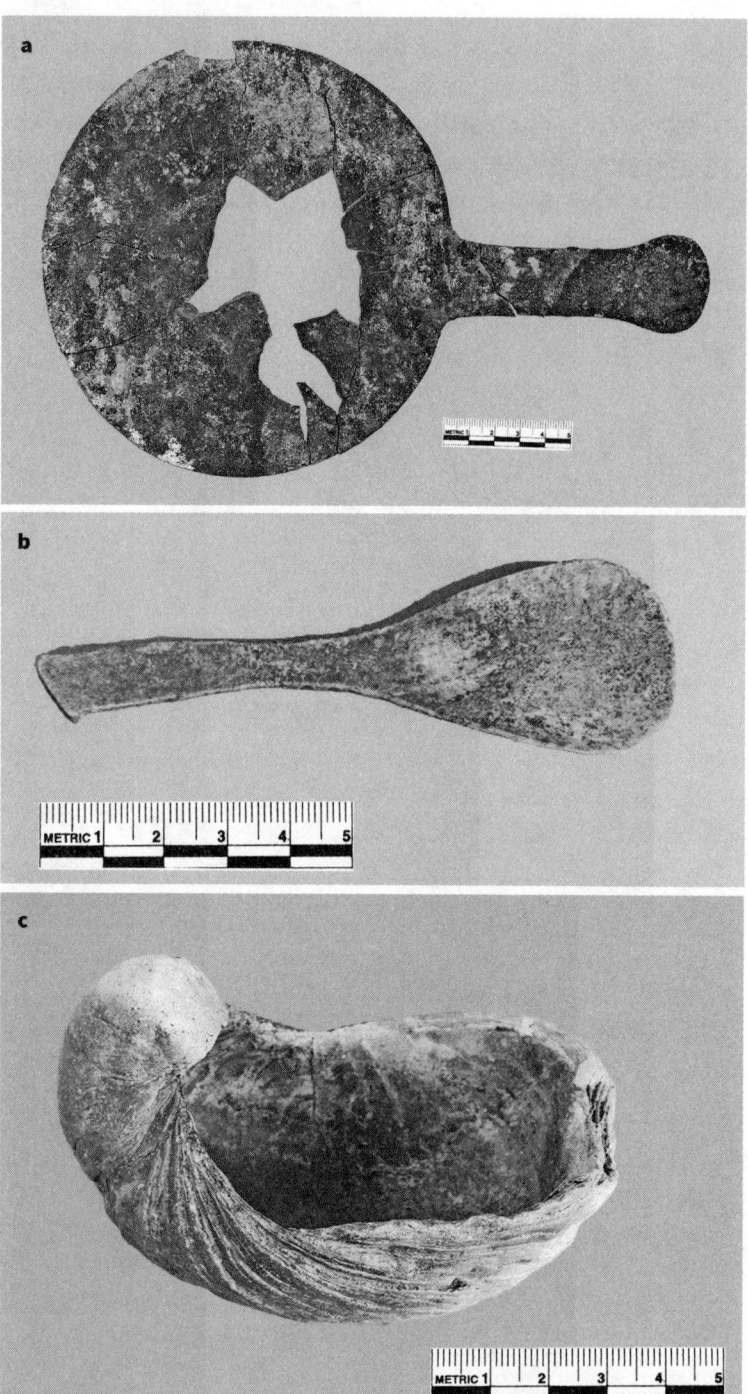

Fig. 15.4. Additional artifacts recovered from Complex 2 in Kurgan 29, Burial 4, Filippovka 1 burial ground, Russia (fourth century BCE): (a) bronze mirror (KP 19353/55a); (b) bone spoon (KP 19353/78b); (c) fossil *Gryphaea* shell (KP 19353/56). Photography by Olga Anikeeva. Courtesy of the Orenburg Governor's Museum of Local Lore and History.

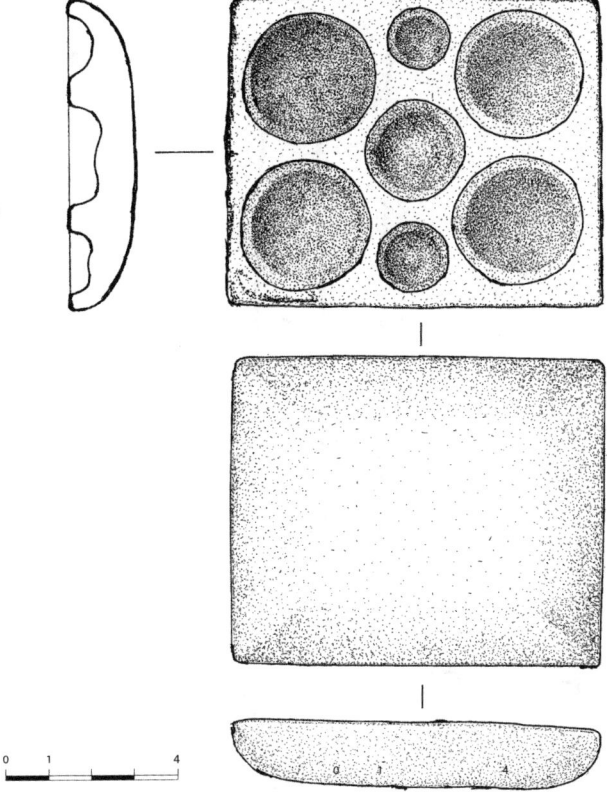

Fig. 15.5. Red sandstone mixing palette (Palette 2), recovered from Kurgan 1, Burial 2, Filippovka 1 burial ground (KP18957/56), Russia (fourth century BCE): H. 9.2 cm, W. 8.8 cm. Illustrations by Konstantin Okorokov. Collections of the Orenburg Governor's Museum of Local Lore and History.

A total of fifty-two additional artifacts were found under the mirror in Burial 2, including a rectangular whetstone made of red sandstone (fig. 15.6a), and a bone spoon with a carved handle depicting a stylized figure of a ram (fig. 15.6b). Also beneath the mirror, six gold needles and three iron knives were found. The six gold needles can be divided into two types: Type 1, having twisted handles, and Type 2, displaying a looped end for threading (figs. 15.6d–i; figs. 15.7 and 15.8).

The three iron knives were situated beneath the gold needles. Knife 1 has a single-edged blade measuring 2 cm wide and a handle inlaid with gold. Knife 2 is narrower, with a blade width of ~1.2 cm. Knife 3 measured ~1.4 cm in width, and exhibited a handle lined with gold leaf. The end of the blade is bent upward, and a sliding iron loop is present at the distal end of the knife handle.

Nearby, excavations recovered a leather pouch containing black pigment and a composite object consisting of three elements: a turquoise rod, a gold knob of truncated conical shape, and a glass bead mounted through the top opening of the golden knob by a wooden pin. The purpose of this object remains unknown. Beside the composite object lay a miniature bronze spoon with a handle made of wire wound around a rod and forming a loop at its distal end. Bronze and flint arrow points were also uncovered in close proximity.

A SARMATIAN TATTOO TOOLKIT IN RUSSIA

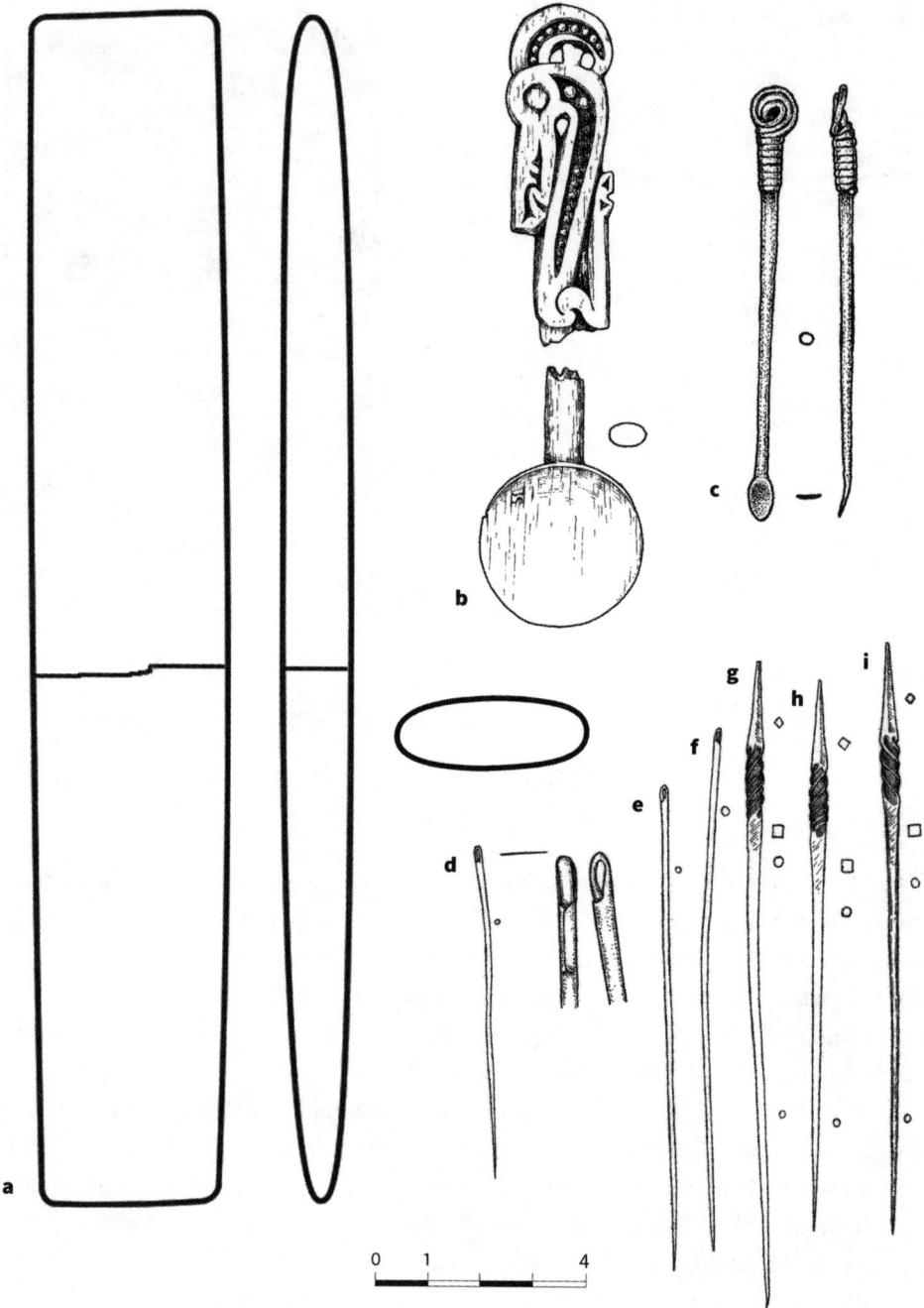

Fig. 15.6. Artifacts from Complex 3 –found underneath the mirror at Kurgan 1, Burial 2, Filippovka 1 burial ground, Russia (fourth century BCE): (a) red sandstone whetstone (KP19971/48), L. 23.5 cm, W. 3.8 cm; (b) bone spoon with carved handle (fragment) (KP19971/27), L. ~11.5 cm; (c) bronze spoon (KP19971/16), L. 8.8 cm; (d through i) gold needles: Type 1 (twisted handles, KP 19971/50-52, DR-2274-76), L. 10.5 to 12 cm; Type 2 (looped end, KP 19971/54, DR-2278, KP 19971/49, DR-2273, KP 19971/53, DR-2277), L. 6.4 to 10 cm. Illustrations by Konstantin Okorokov. Collections of the Orenburg Governor's Museum of Local Lore and History.

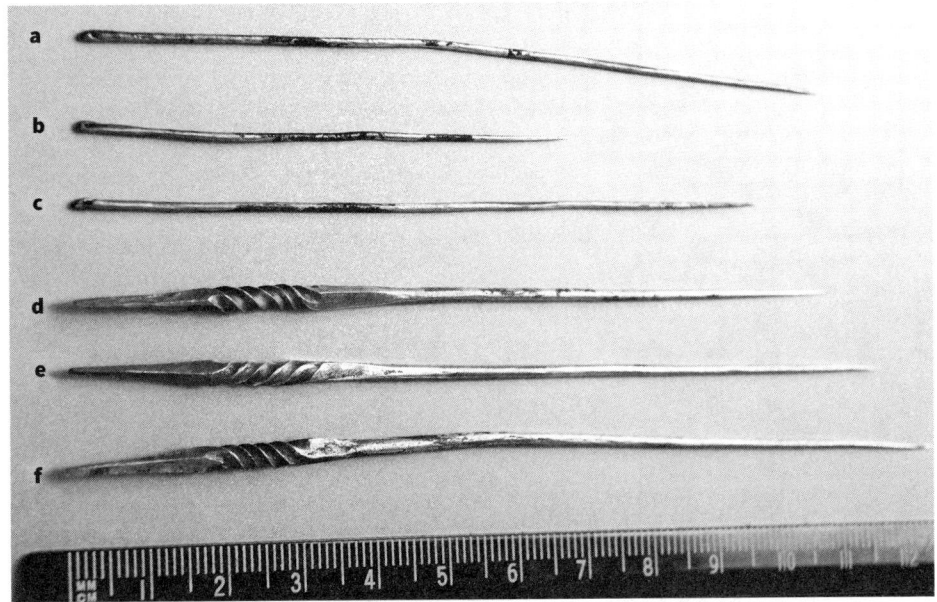

Fig. 15.7. Gold tattooing instruments from Kurgan 1, Burial 2, Filippovka 1 burial ground (KP 19971/49-54, DR 2273-2278), Russia (fourth century BCE). (a through c) Type 1, twisted handles; (d through f) Type 2, looped end. Photography by Olga Anikeeva. Courtesy of the Orenburg Governor's Museum of Local Lore and History.

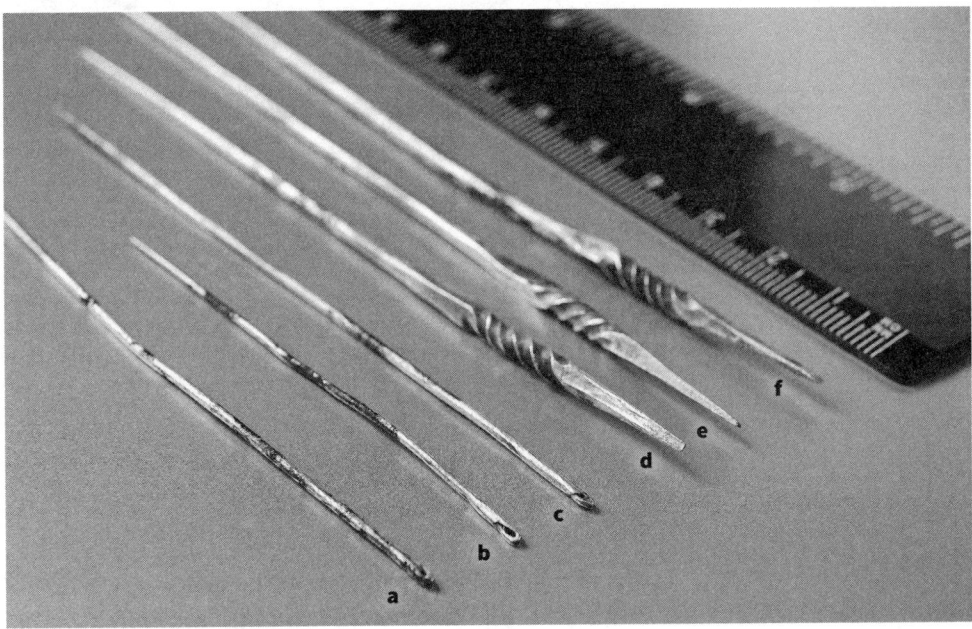

Fig. 15.8. Detail of the tops of gold tattooing instruments from Kurgan 1, Burial 2, Filippovka 1 burial ground (KP 19971/49-54, DR 2273-2278), Russia (fourth century BCE). (a through c) Type 1, twisted handles; (d through f) Type 2, looped end. Photography by Alexander Mirzokhanov. Courtesy of the Orenburg Governor's Museum of Local Lore and History.

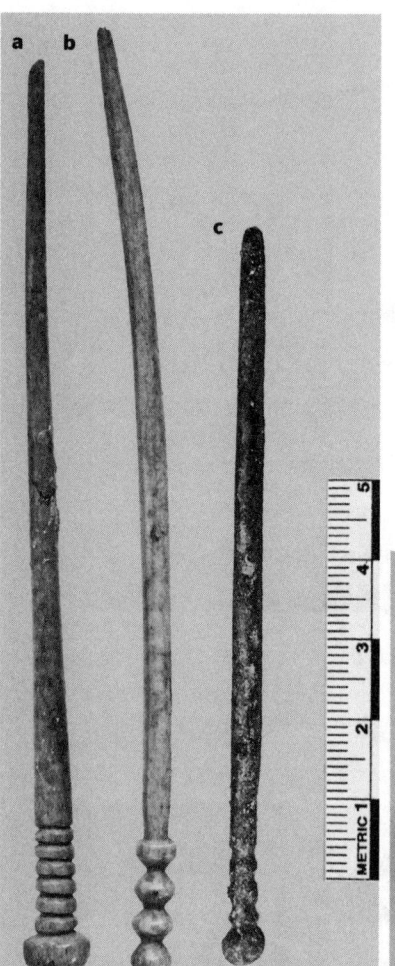
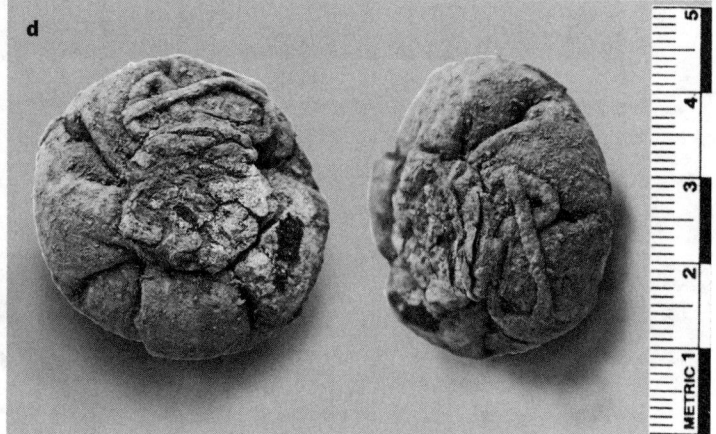

Fig. 15.9. Tattoo stencils or markers and pigment bag from Complex 3, recovered from Kurgan 1, Burial 2, Filippovka 1 burial ground, Russia (fourth century BCE): (a) bone marker (KP 19957/62), L. 11.2 cm; (b) bone marker (KP 19957/61), L. 11.7 cm; (c) bronze marker (KP 19957/69), L. 13.8 cm; (d) leather bag containing black pigment (KP 19957/73), L. 3.5 cm, W. 3.5 cm. Photography by Olga Anikeeva. Courtesy of the Orenburg Governor's Museum of Local Lore and History.

Three stenciling tools or markers were located under the pigment pouch (figs. 15.9a–b)—two made of bone and one made of bronze. Marker 1 is slightly arched, circular in cross-section, with a pointed proximal end and a knob on the opposite tip (fig. 15.9a). A succession of circular grooves is carved below the knob to facilitate handling and manipulation. Marker 2 has the same form but possesses fewer carved grooves (fig. 15.9b). The third marker, made of bronze, was situated in the same area (fig. 15.9c). This object was manufactured with three circular rolls for handling and is slightly flattened at its base.

Beneath the bronze marker were found fragments of twigs and another leather pouch filled with black pigment (fig. 15.9d). The pouch was originally spherical, but had become flattened under the weight of the sediment covering it. The neck of the pouch was tied with a leather strap. The remnants of a Persian walnut shell were situated beside this pouch. This shell could have been used as an organic pigment storage container or as raw material from which to produce tattooing pigment itself.

Tattooing Tools Categories

Several categories of artifacts possibly associated with ancient Sarmatian tattooing were recovered during excavations of the Filippovka 1 burial ground. A summary of these cultural deposits follows.

STONE PALETTES

These sandstone palettes are up to 2 cm thick. They can be divided by shape into square (see fig. 15.1d), rectangular (see fig. 15.5), and discoidal forms (see fig. 15.3). The surfaces of these stone objects were well polished. Circular cups, from five to nine in number, were present in the thicker palettes. Within these cups organic pigments were graded and separated. The central cup on these palettes was likely intended for mixing the actual tattooing pigment.

SPOONS

Small spoons can be classified into different types based on shape, with each form having had a different function:

Type 1. These implements were made from bone. They had an oval scoop and a long handle (see figs. 15.1c, fig. 15.4b, fig. 15.6b) and were often decorated in the tradition of the so-called Scythian-Siberian animal style (see fig 15.1c, fig. 15.6b). Spoons of this type were used to transfer pigments from storage containers to the palette cups.

Type 2. These tools were made of bronze. They are small, oval-tipped spoons with rod-shaped handles topped with twisted elements to facilitate handling (see fig. 15.6c). They probably were used to stir the tattoo pigment in the center cup of each palette.

MIRRORS

Mirrors are typically bronze and disc-shaped with a long handle. Most often, the end of the handle has an extension, which is a stylistic chronological marker that allows us to date them to the end of fifth through fourth centuries BCE.

Mirrors had a special, symbolic meaning in the early nomadic funeral rite of the north Pontic steppe region (Khazanov 1963). During the funeral ceremony they were usually broken as a symbol of their master's death, and only fragments of mirrors have been found in graves. However, when mirrors are found with possible tattooing implements, they are always intact, and in these cases we can assume that they were placed there for tattooing use in the afterlife. Sarmatian mirrors of silver and gold have also been found, including the exquisite silver and gold gilt mirror from Burial 2, Kurgan 1 (see plate 19).

KNIVES

Three iron knives were found in association with the possible tattooing equipment from Burial 2, Kurgan 1. While it is not known how or if these tools were used in Sarmatian tattooing, these artifacts differ from utilitarian examples by virtue of their curved upper blade tip. Their possible ritual purpose is further emphasized by the presence of gold inlay on the handles.

STORAGE CONTAINERS FOR TATTOO PIGMENTS

These storage containers were found in large numbers at the Filippovka 1 cemetery. Most of these objects took the form of small leather pouches cinched with a drawstring about their necks (see figs. 15.1a and 15.2). However, a horse tooth container was found stuffed with red ochre. It is possible walnuts found near the mixing palettes in Burial 2, Kurgan 1, were also used as pigment receptacles or were organic sources for tattooing pigment.

PIGMENTS

Excavators identified evidence of organic coloring materials that were perhaps used as tattooing pigments, but these were not well preserved. Inorganic pigments were found in three complexes: with or near the palettes, under the elaborate mirror, and also in a large basket, which stood at the head of the individual in Burial 2, Kurgan 1.

Of the pigments found in association with the palettes, one inorganic sample displayed a pinkish yellow color and was composed of a mixture of sedimentary iron minerals. Another inorganic sample was found in the horse tooth receptacle found near Palette 2 in Burial 2, which contained red ochre manufactured from a mineral of the hematite (iron ore) family. In addition, a small piece of yellow ochre was found in association with one of the palettes. The pigment was manufactured from a mineral of the limonite (iron ore) family.

Two leather pouches stained with a powdery black charcoal pigment were found beneath the mirror in Burial 2, Kurgan 1. A piece of bright red ochre was also collected at this location. A basket was placed at the head of the woman in Burial 2, Kurgan 1. This basket contained two leather pouches stained with charcoal. A piece of yellow ochre was also found in association with the basket.

Taken together, the composition of the pigments and their association with mixing palettes suggests that Sarmatian tattoos were multicolored.

MARKERS

These markers were presumably used to draw stencils on the human skin or to add pigment into an open piercing. These objects were manufactured of bone (see figs. 15.9a and b) and bronze (see fig. 15.9c). One marker was found placed within its associated leather pigment bag (see fig. 15.2).

TATTOO NEEDLES

The needles for tattooing were made of iron and gold. The iron needles excavated at Filippovka 1 were not well preserved and had become badly corroded. However, the basic features of the iron needles can be seen in their well-preserved gold counterparts.

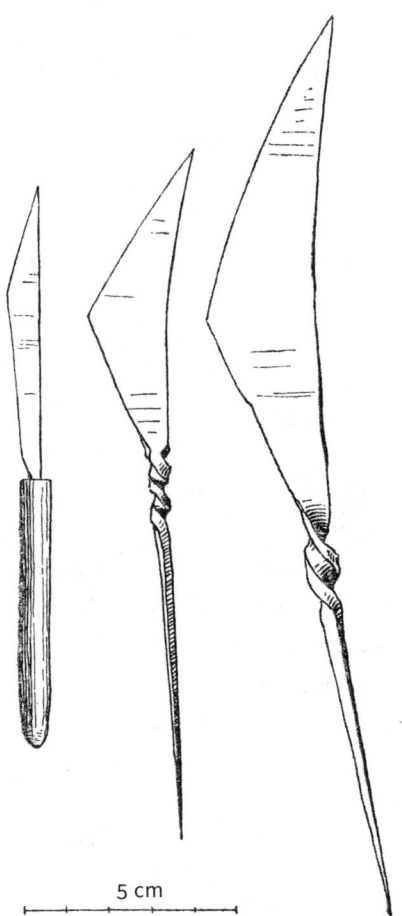
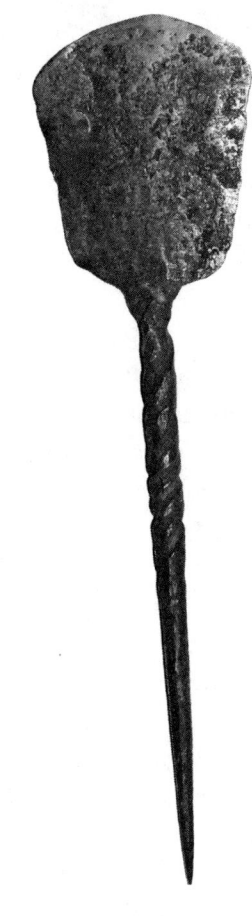

Fig. 15.10. Makonde metal scarification tattooing tool (*chipopo*) (ca. 1950), Mozambique. Redrawn after Dias and Dias (1964: fig. 20).

Fig. 15.11. Hamar scarification tool, Ethiopia, 13.5 cm long. Manufactured by a tribal blacksmith in 2007. Collection of Lars Krutak.

These gold needles, six in number, were collected from Burial 2, Kurgan 1, and can be divided into two types: The first type of tattooing needles possessed sharp proximal points with twisted handles and tapered flat edges at their distal ends (see figs. 15.7d–f and figs. 15.8.d–f). Presumably these were used to hand-poke or prick-in tattoos, a common technique employed across the Indigenous world. The tapered flat edges would have been effective in scraping away flowing blood from the tattoo incisions, so the tattoo artist could effectively monitor the process. Similarly crafted tools are used today among scarification tribes in Africa for this purpose (figs. 15.10 and 15.11) (Dias and Dias 1964:58).

The second needle type is cylindrical, displaying a sharp end and an eye for the threading of sinew or other thread (see figs. 15.8a–c and figs. 15.9a–c). These types of implements may have been used to "stitch-in" tattoos, a technique of tattooing widely employed by Eskimo-Inuit peoples across the Arctic (Krutak 2014a), the Yupiit and Chukchi of northeastern Siberia (Bogoras 1904–1909), and the Evenki (Hiekisch 1879:72; Middendorf 1875:1428) and Selkup (Middendorf 1875:1461) of Siberia. It has been suggested that the Pazyryk nomads may also have performed this tattoo technique in antiquity, since eyed needles have been found in association with high-status burials (Rudenko 1970:112).

Conclusions

Tattoos of the ancient Altaic nomads of the early Iron Age have long been known because of the extraordinary and accidental preservation of their mummified human remains. Farther west on the north Pontic steppes of the southern Urals, however, local climatic conditions were not favorable for artificial mummification, and tattooing has not been preserved on human skin.

Recent archaeological research at the Filippovka 1 burial ground has produced an assortment of artifacts suggesting that the ancient Sarmatian people practiced tattooing during the fourth century BCE. This mortuary complex, located today between the Ural and Ilek Rivers near the northern border of Kazakhstan, has revealed a plethora of material culture related to tattooing praxis, including colored pigments, beautifully crafted bronze mirrors, stone mixing palettes, iron and gold needles, bone and bronze stenciling tools, and whetstones for sharpening tattooing implements.

While mirrors, needles, pigments, and whetstones could have been used to perform several functions, at Filippovka 1 they were always found in association with stone mixing palettes and stenciling tools, suggesting a special purpose. This assemblage of materials is consistent with the essential elements of ancient and Indigenous tattoo toolkits identified elsewhere around the globe (Deter-Wolf 2013a). Moreover, these cultural materials were found repeatedly in several funerary complexes and not in other contexts across the site. Unfortunately, similar toolkits have not been found in other Sarmatian cemeteries dating back to the early Iron Age, and so the specific function of these materials from Filippova 1 remains elusive. However, given ethnographic and archaeological parallels, it is possible that these unique artifact assemblages from Filippovka 1 constitute a Sarmatian tattoo toolkit, and therefore represent the earliest archaeological evidence of tattooing technology from this region.

These tools have only been found in association with women's burials at Filippovka 1, perhaps indicating that tattooing was a female prerogative and a female-centered profession. This suggestion is bolstered by evidence that Sarmatian women carried out ritual activities at the family, clan, and tribal level (Yablonsky 2009). Because the hypothesized tattoo complexes at Filippovka 1 were found to be associated with objects of worship, we can assume that if tattooing was indeed practiced, it was likely a ritualized aspect of the Sarmatian funerary cult. In turn, Sarmatian cultural values were transmitted through tattooed human skin during one's lifetime and after death.

16

Further Evaluation of Tattooing Use-Wear on Bone Tools

Aaron Deter-Wolf and Tara Nicole Clark

TATTOOED, MUMMIFIED REMAINS DEMONSTRATE THAT THE PRACTICE of permanently marking the human skin spans five continents and at least 6,000 years of human history (Deter-Wolf et al. 2016). However, the quest to comprehend the antiquity, scope, and role of tattooing among past cultures cannot be limited to those exceptional instances where tattooed human flesh survives in the archaeological record. Rather, scholars must pursue other lines of evidence in the study of tattooing if we are to understand this ancient and global phenomenon in a holistic manner.

Tattooing comprises a socially and ritually significant activity spanning hundreds of cultures and thousands of years, but at present the practice appears to have left very little evidence in the way of material culture remains. Some ancient tattoo tools were undoubtedly made from small, fragile, and biodegradable materials that have not been preserved in the archaeological record. However, implements manufactured from durable materials such as stone and bone should have been able—depending on local preservation conditions—to better survive the ravages of time. Although many of these tools have likely been excavated or collected, relatively few have been formally recognized as tattoo implements. The successful identification of these materials must overcome a host of issues, which, as discussed by Deter-Wolf and colleagues in chapter 13 of this volume, include inadequate artifact preservation and recovery methods, cultural changes, conflicting traditional artifact classification systems, and the biases and misunderstandings of previous researchers.

Experimental research in tattooing pig skin with bone and stone tools suggests that use-wear analysis—the examination of microscopic patterns created by friction when a tool is used—might provide a means for identifying tattoo implements in archaeological collections.[1] Further examination on this topic remains to be done, including testing the replicability of previously documented microwear and evaluating the suitability of pig skin as a proxy for living human flesh in tattooing use-wear studies.

Typological Classification

One of the major issues hindering successful identification of tattoo implements in archaeological and museum collections relates to artifact typologies and modern assumptions of tool function. In the absence of distinctive tools that can be directly linked to historic practices (such as the perpendicular-hafted implements from Polynesia and Micronesia described in Furey, chapter 11, of this volume), archaeologists must instead build a convincing case for tattooing function on an artifact-by-artifact basis. Supporting evidence for these assertions may include but is not limited to archaeological provenience, association with other artifacts, and comparative ethnographic, historical, and art historical data (Deter-Wolf 2013a; Tassie 2003).

The classification of bone tools presents a special dilemma for modern scholars, who are left with a legacy of research that relied on the formal attributes of artifacts to assign typological categories and perceived functions (see Gates St-Pierre and Walker 2007). Pointed bone tools from the archaeological record, for example, have been typically assigned to categories such as "awls" or "pins," based mainly on morphological attributes including their pointed tips and long, narrow shafts. Unfortunately the tool typologies imposed by modern scholars and the implicit functions connected to those categories may have little, if any, relationship to the emic viewpoint—that is, how the tools were manufactured, used, and understood by the cultures of origin.

Some pointed bone artifacts were indeed used by people in the past to pierce holes in various materials, thereby meeting the basic definition of "awl" (Gates St-Pierre 2010:72). However, other bone tools exhibiting the same narrow, pointed form might have been used for creating basketry, woven matting, and incised pottery, for piercing wood, processing nuts and plant foods, fastening clothing or pinning hair, as gaming pieces and cooking or dining utensils, as personal ornamentation, and, as most relevant for our purposes here, as tattoo implements (Gates St-Pierre 2007; 2010).

Both single-point and multipoint bone implements were used for tattooing by Indigenous cultures throughout the world, including in eastern North America (Deter-Wolf 2013b) and throughout the Pacific (Robitaille 2007; see also Furey, chapter 11, this volume). However, it is important to acknowledge that not all ancient and Indigenous tattoo implements were made from bone. Ethnographic and historical accounts reveal that prior to adopting metal tools, tattooists across the globe used implements fashioned from a wide variety of lithic, faunal, and botanical materials that varied according to region and culture (Krutak 2007). The present focus on bone tools is based instead on prior research and the availability of comparative bone tool use-wear studies from the Old and New Worlds.[2]

As demonstrated in chapter 13 of this volume, not all pointed bone implements from the archaeological record were used for tattooing. To correctly interpret and understand the role of tattooing in past cultures, scholars must therefore be able to differentiate between those artifacts used for tattooing and those that were not. While archaeological data including provenience and association can be vastly informative in this regard, that information may be absent for historic, private, and museum collections.

Other avenues of analysis and identification must be developed through which to identify possible tattoo tools in the absence of contextual data and for cultures and regions where comparative ethnographic and historical data are unavailable. Toward this end, studies of microwear on bone tool assemblages (e.g., Buc 2011; d'Errico and Backwell 2009; Gates St-Pierre 2007) have demonstrated that wear patterns created during the use life of a tool can provide a direct, objective means of assessing function. Therefore, successful identification of the wear signature associated with tattooing may provide an alternative approach for identifying ancient tattoo implements.

Previous Research

Previous experimental analysis by the senior author (Deter-Wolf 2009, presented in Deter-Wolf and Peres 2013) sought to examine the efficacy of tattooing with single-point bone implements as well as other tool types drawn from the ethnographic and archaeological record of eastern North America.[3] The results of that study demonstrated that single-point bone tools were—by modern standards—better suited for applying tattoos than other implements, including tools made of thorns, fish teeth and spines, and implements fashioned from chert or flint. During tattooing of pig skin, sharpened bone implements were able to insert pigment beneath the epidermis in an even manner and without breakage (Ibid.). However, specific ethnohistoric and ethnographic identifications of non-bone tattoo implements among Native Americans (see Deter-Wolf 2013b; Krutak 2014a) reveal that the perceived effectiveness of one tool type over another in a modern setting does not, by itself, allow for conclusions regarding the function of implements from the archaeological record.

The initial study was followed in 2011 by examinations focused on assessing the evidence for tattooing with bone needles from a microwear perspective (Deter-Wolf and Peres 2013). That work sought to identify the microscopic wear patterns left behind during tattooing in the hopes that those marks might be sufficiently distinctive to use as baseline data in interpreting the function of bone tools from the archaeological record and/or museum collections.

To study the use-wear signature created by tattooing, pointed bone tools made from the antlers of white-tailed deer (*Odocoileus virginianus*) were used to mark lines of 200 punctures onto a segment of fleshed rib cage from an adult male pig (Ibid.). The tools' tips were examined both before and after tattooing, using a scanning electron microscope. Comparison of the tool tips in pre- and post-tattoo microscopy revealed morphological changes on the terminal 0.5 mm of the tips, including rounding of the tips, flattening of bone fibers, and smoothing of longitudinal manufacturing striations. While these were originally characterized as general morphological changes instead of distinctive wear patterns (Ibid.), they can now be understood to represent a light use-wear signature resulting from a combination of the tools' relatively short use life (i.e., how many punctures were made) and application to wet (as opposed to dry or tanned) skin.

The 2011 investigations provided interesting data regarding the applicability of microwear studies in identifying ancient tattoo implements. Specifically, the study suggested that the appearance of a use-wear signature on bone tools consistent with repeatedly piercing soft or wet hide to a very shallow depth (~0.5 mm) might be presented as evidence in support of a tattooing function. However, the 2011 investigations based characterizations of microwear on three tools used to administer only 200 punctures each. Broadening the sample size and extending the duration of testing might therefore help refine understanding of the resulting use-wear patterns. In addition, the previous examination relied on microwear created by tattooing pig skin. Although forensic studies routinely use porcine skin as a proxy for human skin (see following discussion), there have been no prior assessments as to whether tattooing the skin of a dead pig will create the same microwear patterns as tattooing the skin of a live human.

Methods and Results

As with prior experimental analysis (Deter-Wolf and Peres 2013) the current examination employed bone tools fashioned from the metatarsals and metacarpals of adult male and female white-tailed deer (plate 20a). All bones had been largely defleshed through natural processes prior to collection, and were subjected to final hot water maceration prior to tool manufacture. Following maceration, the bones were degreased using a hot water and dish soap mixture, and sanitized in a 3 percent solution of hydrogen peroxide and water.

The cleaned bones were repeatedly scored along their longitudinal axis using a chert graver spur and flake corners before being split between a limestone anvil and hammerstone using a large flake as a wedge (plate 20b). Removal of remaining marrow residue and bone splinters along the lateral margins of the split pieces was accomplished with chert flakes and scrapers. The tool tips were initially shaped by shaving using chert flakes (plate 20c), followed by longitudinal grinding using increasingly fine-grained stone surfaces (plate 20d), resulting in tips that appeared pointed in profile and rounded in cross section.

The porcine test subject consisted of the fleshed belly of an adult male pig, purchased from a butcher and stored under refrigerated conditions. The meat was allowed to rest at room temperature for 30 minutes prior to tattooing. The authors and three other volunteers acted as the human subjects for the study. While petroleum jelly is sometimes applied to the skin during modern professional tattooing to reduce needle drag and eliminate incidental ink staining on the surface of the epidermis, none was used during the current analysis to eliminate possible effects on the resulting microwear patterns.

Each bone tool was treated in 91 percent isopropyl alcohol for five minutes and allowed to air dry. The tools were dipped in commercial black tattoo ink prior to tattooing, and re-dipped as necessary during testing. A total of four tools were used to tattoo human skin during the experiment. Subject 1 was tattooed above the left lower tibialis posterior muscle with lines measuring a total of 80 mm, consisting of approximately 350 punctures. Subject 2 was tattooed on the left teres major muscle with three solid dots consisting of approximately 250 punctures. Subject 3 was tattooed on the lower

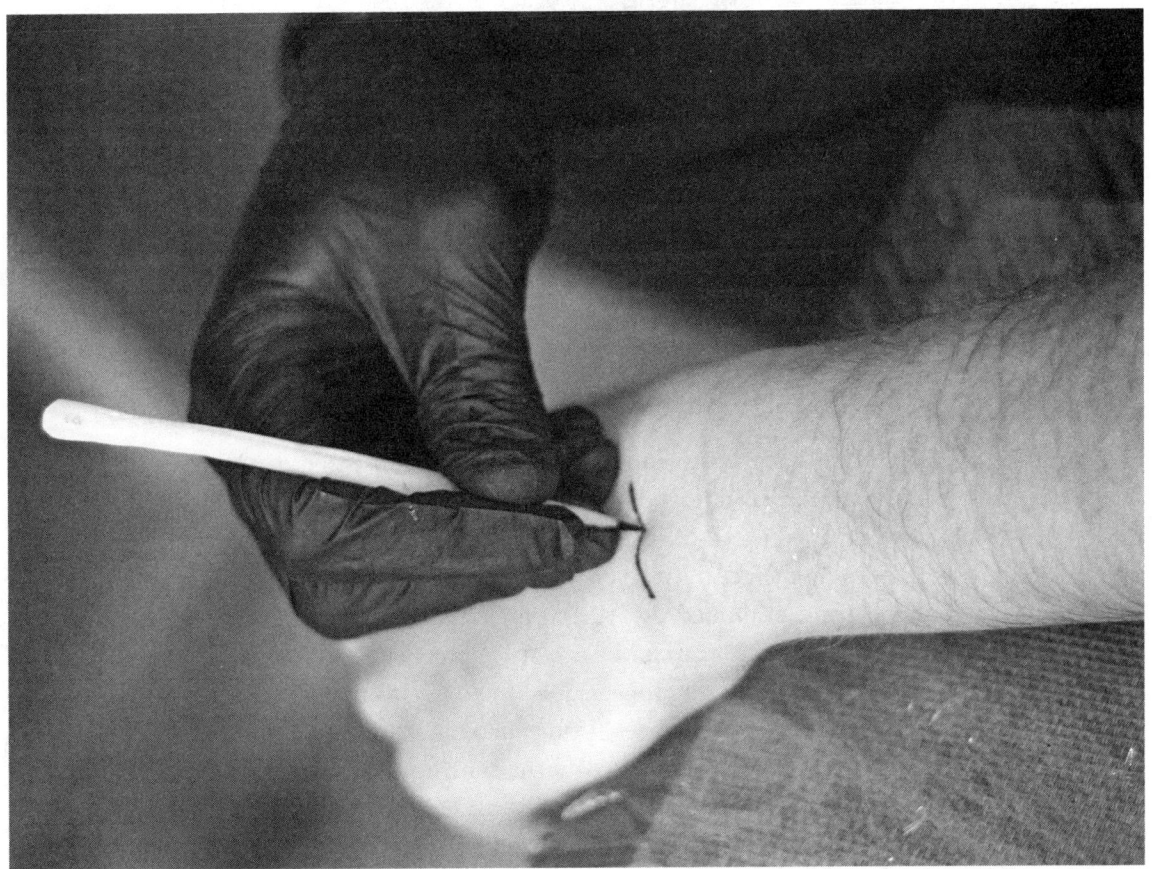

Fig. 16.1. The senior author, Aaron Deter-Wolf, tattoos his left wrist using a deer bone tool (2016). Photograph by Ethan Freeman.

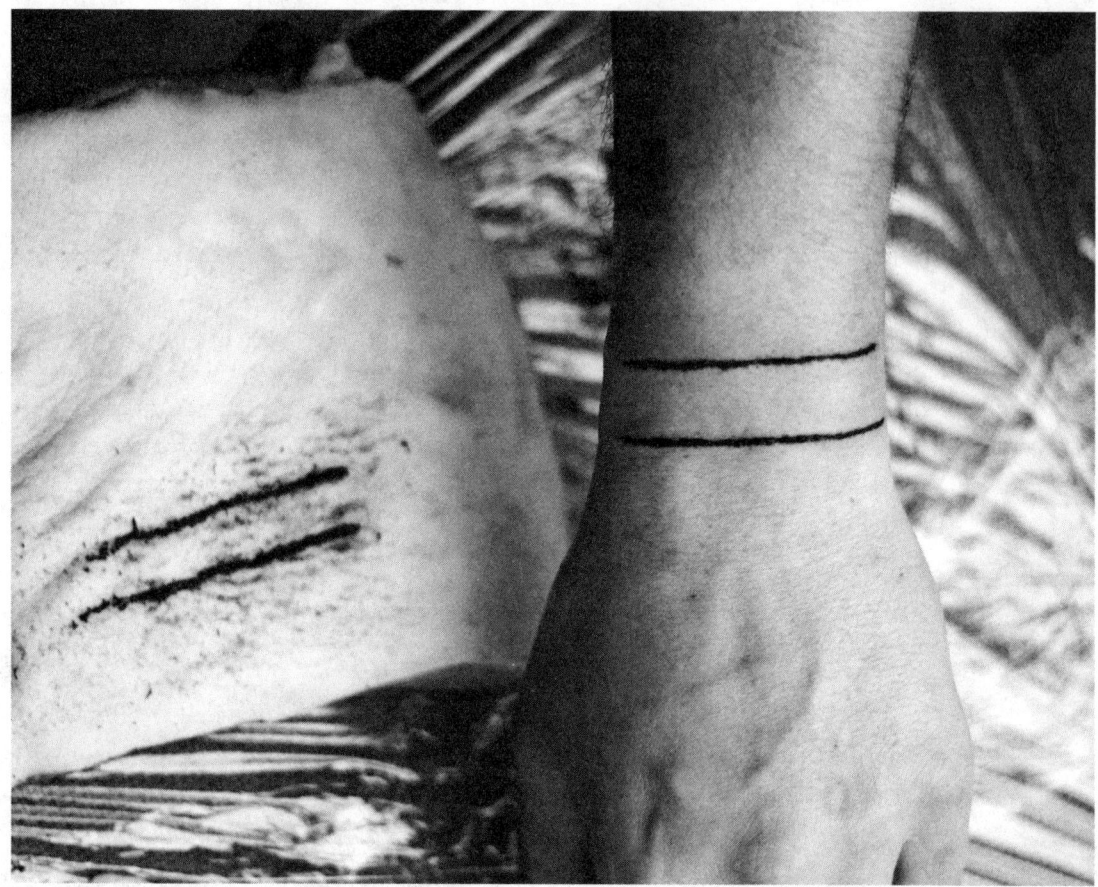

Fig. 16.2. Comparison of lines tattooed on human skin and pig skin (2016). Photograph by Ethan Freeman.

right triceps with lines measuring a total of 90 mm and consisting of approximately 400 punctures. Subject 4 was tattooed on the dorsal surface of the left wrist with lines measuring a total of 127 mm and consisting of approximately 1,500 punctures (fig. 16.1). All of these marks were then duplicated on pig skin with separate tools (fig. 16.2).

All bone tools were examined before and after tattooing using both a Reichert 570 stereo star zoom (0.7x to 4.2x) and Graf Apsco Steri-ette 412 microscope at 40x magnification. Prior to testing, all tools exhibited tips that to the naked eye appeared pointed and displayed smooth surfaces. Under magnification the tips exhibited flat to beveled profiles. Trace manufacturing patterns consisting of sporadic transverse to oblique "chattermarks," and longitudinal gouges created during lithic scraping were present (fig. 16.3a and c). These marks were overlaid and in some cases partially to fully obscured by the buildup of narrow light to medium longitudinal striations over 100 percent of the original tip surface as a result of grinding. Some silica crystals and small particles from the stone surfaces were embedded within these striations.

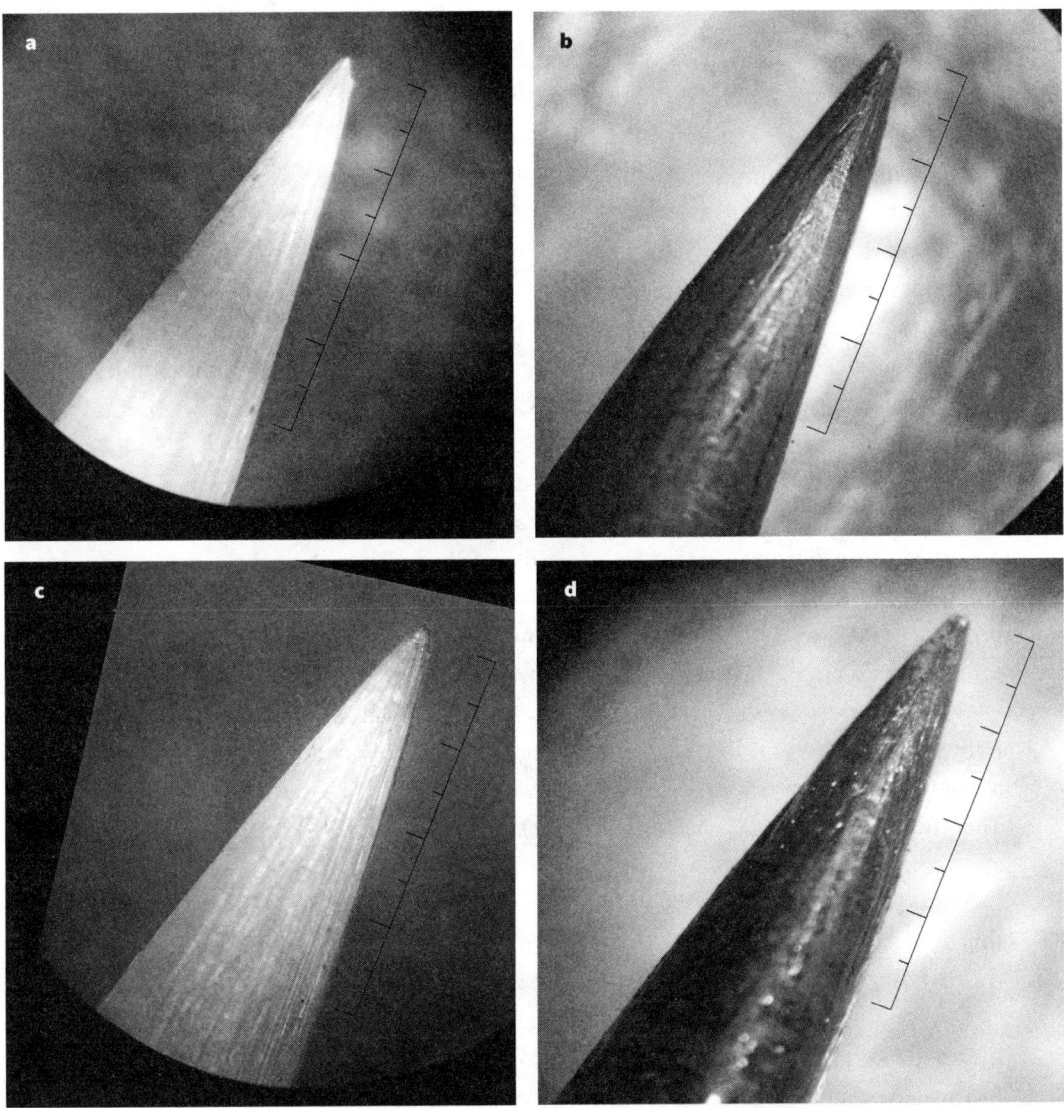

Fig. 16.3. Microscopic images (2016) showing bone tool tips before and after tattooing 127-mm-long lines on human skin (a, b) and pig skin (c, d). Scale bar = 4 mm.

Following tattooing, the tools used on human skin exhibited microwear consisting of rounding of the tip, flattening of raised bone fibers and smoothing of longitudinal manufacturing marks, and the development of low-level polish along the highest points of topography (fig. 16.3b). These morphological changes were present in the final 2 mm of the tool tip. At 40x magnification, microwear on tools used to mark pig skin was similar enough to that created by tattooing human flesh as to be indistinguishable to the authors (fig. 16.3d).

Discussion

This examination sought to replicate and further assess use-wear patterns created by tattooing with bone needles, and to evaluate possible differences in microwear created by tattooing pig skin and human skin. The patterns observed during these tests were consistent with previous investigations, and may be best characterized as demonstrating the repeated piercing of soft or wet hide to a very shallow depth. At the same time, the investigation demonstrated that there was no observable difference in microwear signatures resulting from tattooing skin of deceased pig and live human skin.

Previous use-wear experiments have demonstrated that awls and bone implements used for piercing dry and wet hides will exhibit wear patterns extending some 10 to 50 mm from the tip (Buc 2011:553; Byrd 2011:86; Legrand and Sidéra 2007:73–74). In some instances, these tools will also develop transverse wear created by twisting as they are applied (Byrd 2011:77; d'Errico et al. 2003:264–65). As described above, wear patterns observed following tattooing were limited to the final 2 mm of the tool tip and oriented along the longitudinal axis. No transverse wear was created during the tattooing process. The patterns resulting from tattooing therefore stand in distinct contrast to microwear created by using bone tools as true awls.

Earlier experimental tattooing studies by Deter-Wolf and Peres (2013) conducted only limited testing on the skin of dead pig. It was therefore anticipated that tattooing a live test subject over a greater duration would necessitate regular tool resharpening. This did not prove to be the case, since a single tool was used to tattoo Subject 4 for approximately 1,500 punctures without any drop-off in the quality of ink deposition or increased discomfort on the part of the subject. Therefore, while one may speculate that this activity would obscure or obliterate microwear traces (in the case of bone tools, through linear abrasion), the actual extent of that impact has not been assessed.

Although the structure of human skin is morphologically similar to that of other higher order primates (Lavker et al. 1991), use of these other species for scientific or medical experimentation raises numerous ethical considerations. However, the skins of other common laboratory animals exhibit morphological differences from human skin in terms of thickness, tightness, and structure, making them unsuitable surrogates (Lavker and Sun 1982; Liu et al. 2010). Various anatomical and dermatologic examinations have demonstrated that pig skin exhibits close correspondence to human skin in terms of morphology, cellular composition, and immunoreactivity (Avon and Wood 2005; Meyer et al. 1978). As a result, pig skin is often used in place of human flesh for forensic studies investigating topics such as wound healing, pressure and bite marking, and exposure to heat, electricity, and radiation (see discussion in Summerfield et al. 2015).

Most important for the current study, pig skin and human skin exhibit a marked correspondence in terms of epidermal thickness, elasticity, and texture. Pig epidermis measures 0.03 to 0.14 mm thick, which encompasses a range similar to that of the average human.[4] In addition, the surfaces of pig skin and human skin are comprised of fine intersecting lines and exhibit an elaborate understructure of ridges (Montagna and Yun 1964). It is therefore not surprising that tattooing both dead pig and live human skin with bone tools results in comparable use-wear patterns.

The main difference between tattooing deceased porcine and live human skin observed during the current test related to the manner in which the surfaces held pigment. Excess ink could be easily wiped from human skin using distilled water and a paper towel, but excess ink on the surface of the pig skin was difficult to remove without forceful rubbing and repeated application of isopropyl alcohol (see fig. 16.3). The specific reason(s) for this difference are unclear, though it may perhaps relate to the absence of oils on the surface of the dead skin.

Conclusions

While this study reiterates that tattooing with bone tools creates an identifiable microwear signature, it is by no means the last word in attempting to identify ancient tattoo implements through use-wear analysis. Further work remains to be done in assessing the microwear signature of tattooing, including comparative studies of other tool types, and attempting to address the issue of tool resharpening. In addition, examinations by scholars more versed in use-wear analysis and with the aid of higher magnification are likely to further refine our understanding of the microwear patterns created on bone tools used to tattoo.

Use-wear analysis is not well-suited to every situation, because microwear examinations are time consuming, require specific expertise, and in many cases would be impractical to perform on every tool in a collection. Issues that can impact the survival of microwear include possible reuse for nontattooing activity, when and how artifacts are deposited in the archaeological record (e.g., immediately after use, following breakage, or after resharpening), soil conditions, postdepositional processes such as heating and weathering, and archaeological recovery, cleaning, and preservation strategies. Nevertheless, the growing body of use-wear data presents one possible means of separating potential tattoo tools from other bone implements in archaeological and museum collections, and when combined with other lines of evidence can help inform a well-reasoned identification of ancient tattoo tools.

Notes

We extend our gratitude to Tanya Peres for her ongoing advice and guidance on all zooarchaeological matters, and to Christopher Pliny for his encouragement to undertake this research. Sunny Fleming and Roger McCoy of the Tennessee Division of Natural Areas facilitated microscope time, while Ethan Freeman provided photo and video documentation for the project. Christian Gates

St-Pierre, Benoît Robitaille, and Sarah Levithol Eckhardt all provided reviews of the draft manuscript. Finally, we thank Colin Dale, who provided essential guidance on bone tool tattooing and sterilization.

1. Deter-Wolf and Peres (2013); Gates St-Pierre (2017); Kononenko (2012); Kononenko and Torrence (2009); and Kononenko et al. (2016).
2. For example, Buc (2011); Byrd (2011); d'Errico and Backwell (2009); Gates St-Pierre (2007); Gates St-Pierre (2017); Legrand and Sidéra (2007); and LeMoine (1997).
3. Gates St-Pierre (2017) recently presented a significant new study on use-wear created from tattooing pig skin with bone tools, which due to its late addition cannot be fully summarized here. That effort documented the formation of polish, smoothing of surfaces, and rounding of edges in the final 3 mm of tool tips.
4. The thickness of the human epidermis varies between approximately 0.06 and 0.1 mm, reaching up to 0.6 mm on the palms and soles of the feet (Wang and Sanders 2005:263).

Part 3

Art

17

What to Make of the Prehistory of Tattooing in Europe?

Luc Renaut

ALTHOUGH ÖTZI (CA. 3370–3100 BCE) STILL REPRESENTS THE OLDEST direct evidence for the practice of tattooing in Europe (Deter-Wolf et al. 2016), the specific antiquity of the tradition is unknown. In the absence of tattoos preserved on human skin other than Ötzi, and given the shortcomings in reliably identifying ancient tattoo tools from the region, the anthropomorphic representations of possibly tattooed figures recovered from the Upper Paleolithic period (ca. 50,000 to 10,000 years ago) through the Bronze Age (ca. 2300 to 1200 BCE) are a promising resource through which to interpret possible ancient European tattoo traditions. However, while many of these artifacts have been invoked as evidence of tattooing practices, few survive close scrutiny.

Paleolithic

It has been suggested that various sharp or pointed bone or stone tools recovered from Paleolithic archaeological contexts may have been used to introduce coloring substances under the epidermis. In the past this hypothesis was notably defended by several scholars.[1] French archaeologists Marthe and Saint-Just Péquart (1962) suggested that the direct association of these tools with red ochre[2] at the site of Mas d'Azil, France, and an absence of parietal art from the site, suggested the ochre was used for body decoration and specifically for tattooing (Péquart and Péquart 1962).

This identification was recently revisited by Aaron Deter-Wolf (2013a), who suggests that finds of possible tattoo implements in association with pigments and a suite of other tool types may be archaeological indicators of a "tattoo toolkit." However, any identification of ochre use for tattooing in the Upper Paleolithic runs up against a major obstacle: ochre-based tattooing has never been conclusively identified in either ancient or Indigenous practices. Moreover, the histological analysis of ancient tattooed human remains and the ethnographic record both reveal that pre-industrial tattooing inks were largely derived from soot or ground charcoal (Krutak 2013b; Pabst et al. 2009, 2010; see also Pankova, chapter 5, this volume). Although Paleolithic cultures may very well have used ochre and other pigments to color their skin in a temporary manner, the evidence for assigning these pigments and associated tools a tattooing function remains at best uncertain.[3]

Human Effigies, Hatching, and Stippling (38,000–8,000 BCE)

Partial or complete three-dimensional human effigies constitute another line of evidence for possible tattooing in the Upper Paleolithic period. For example, in the late nineteenth century it was suggested that a series of engraved reindeer antlers from La Madeleine, France, represented human forearms bearing chevron-shaped tattooed marks "such as are still in our own times made on this part of the forearm among some savages" (Lartet et al. 1875:137)[4] (figs. 17.1a and b). However, an alternative interpretation of these marks was offered by archaeologist Henri Breuil (1907:23), who, after examining similar designs, concluded "that these hands are the deformed representation of a fish's tail while the tattooed arm is merely its body."[5]

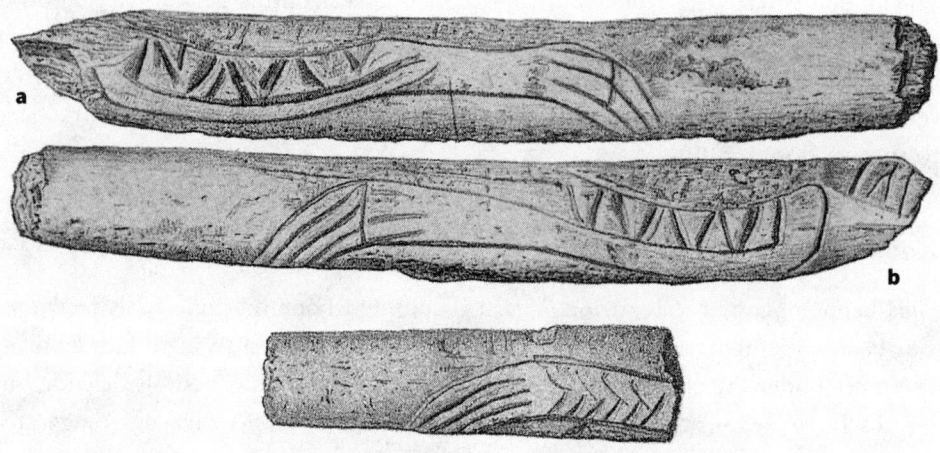

Fig. 17.1. Engraved reindeer antlers found between 1863 and 1865 at the La Madeleine rock-shelter (Tursac, Dordogne, France). 100 by 14 by 13 mm (19.1a). British Museum inv. Palart. 355 (19.1a). Magdalenian (15,000–10,000 BCE). Lithographs published by Lartet et al. (1875: B. plate IX, 1a and b; B. plate XVII, 6).

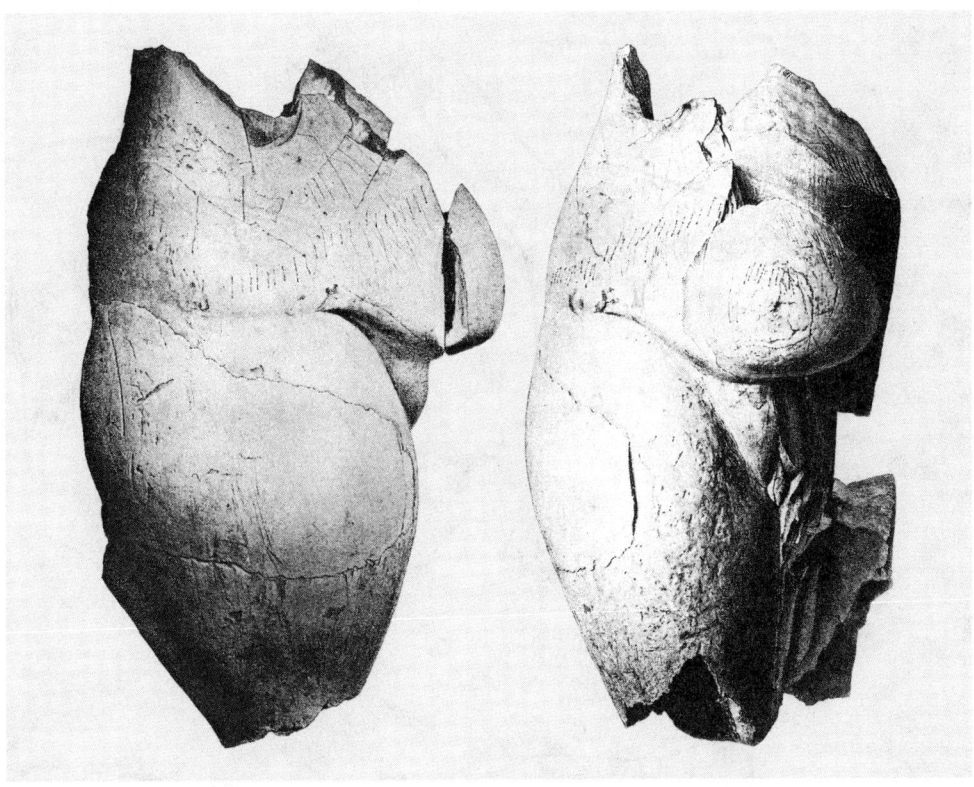

Fig. 17.2. *La Poire* ("The Pear"). Ivory statuette found in 1892 at the Grotte du Pape (Brassempouy, Landes). 79 by 55 by 41 mm. MAN 47333. Gravettian (26,000–20,000 BCE). Photographed by Piette (1895: plates II and III).

Already in the nineteenth century, the hatching and stippling patterns that figured on some anthropomorphic effigies were believed to be representations of abundant body hair, a feature regarded as a mark of "primitiveness" by evolutionist scholars of the time. French archaeologist Édouard Piette (1895:144) therefore thought he recognized "rows of hairs arranged in bands [that] cover the stomach above the navel" on the figurine known as *La Poire* (The Pear) of Brassempouy, France (fig. 17.2). The engraved bone known as *La Femme au Renne* (Woman under the Reindeer) from the Laugerie-Basse rock-shelter in France (fig. 17.3) also struck him as possessing "abundant body hair. The hairs represented by hatching appear very long on the thighs and short on the mound of Venus. They are arranged in thin bands along the stomach and chest. These bands appear to indicate darker areas and form actual stripes. Hirsute races certainly existed in the past" (Piette 1895:145–46). However, other scholars have recognized that the depictions of human body hair are extremely rare or even nonexistent in Paleolithic art. One recent interpretation has suggested that instead of marks indicating hair, *La Femme au renne* of Laugerie-Basse bears "stretchmarks associated with pregnancy," while *La Poire* of Brassempouy presents "tattoos or scarifications" (Duhard 1996:142).

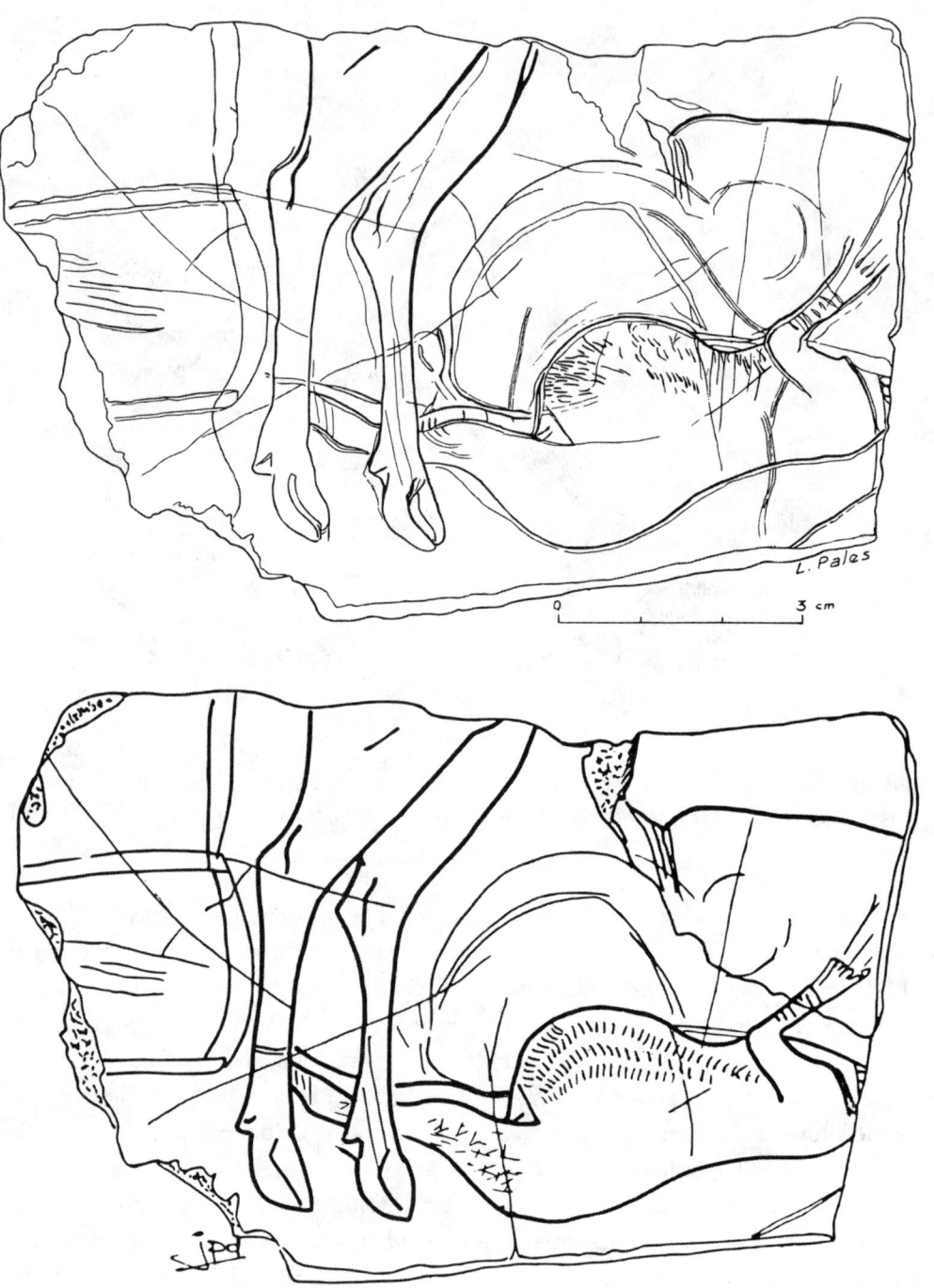

Fig. 17.3. *La Femme au Renne* ("Woman with Reindeer"). Engraved bone found in the 1860s at the Laugerie-Basse rock-shelter (Les Eyzies-de-Tayac-Sireuil, Dordogne). 65 by 100 mm. MAN inv. 47001. Upper Magdalenian (11,500–10,000 BCE). Line drawings by Pales and Tassin de Saint Péreuse (1976:122, fig. 38) and Duhard (1996:163, fig. 93).

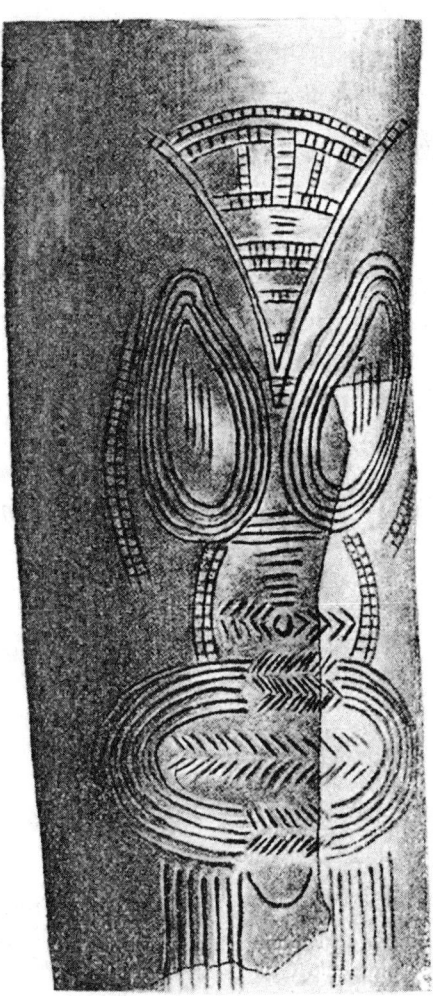

Fig. 17.4. Engraved mammoth ivory, found in 1895 or 1896 at the Předmostí site near the town of Přerov (Moravia, Czech Republic). National Museum, Prague. Gravettian (?) (26,000–20,000 BCE). Engraving published by Obermaier (1912:300, fig. 192a).

This last hypothesis was also brought forth in the case of the Venus of Predmost (Czech Republic), an engraved mammoth tusk depicting a female body composed of geometric designs (fig. 17.4).[6] Prehistorian Hugo Obermaier (1912:301) believed that actual tattoos were represented on her triangular face as well as on her stomach and pelvis. Notwithstanding, this same object was presented in other early publications as being one of the main pieces of evidence for the practice of scarification during the European Paleolithic. More specifically, the chevrons along with the vertical and horizontal lines that fill out the Venus of Predmost's anatomical structures were argued to play no role whatsoever in the analytical or stylized treatment of the human form. Consequently, "these lines can be interpreted as scarification marks" (Wernert 1939:220). This same interpretation has also been offered for *La Poire* of Brassempouy (see fig. 17.2) and for *l'Archer* (the Archer) of Laussel (Dordogne), whose torso features a series of actually very faint parallel striations.

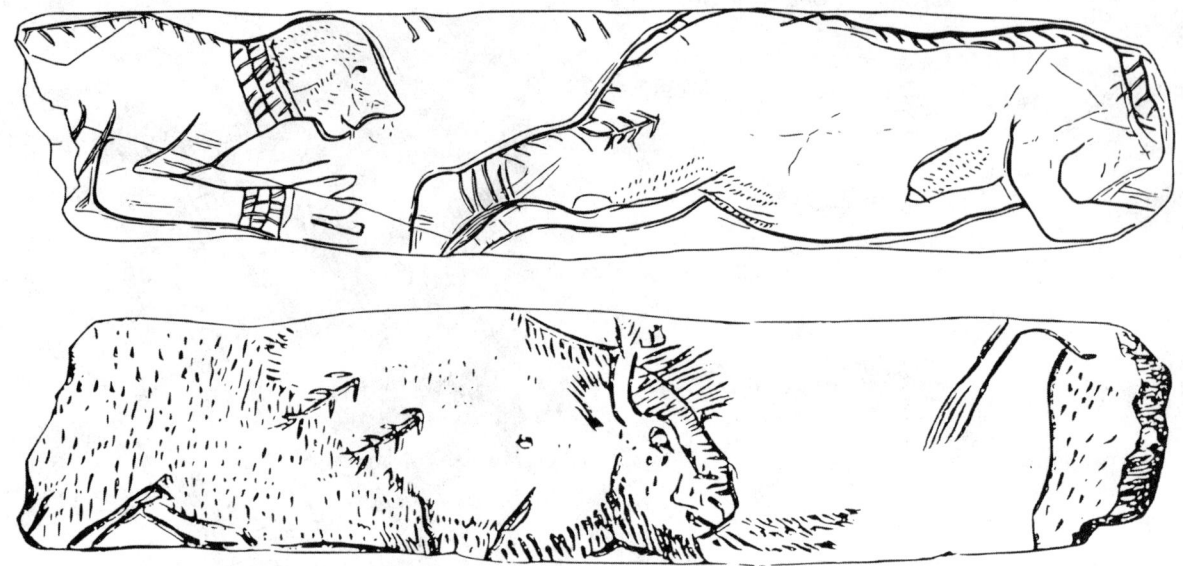

Fig. 17.5. Engraved bone plate found in 1931 at the Isturitz Cave (Saint-Martin-d'Arberoue, Pyrénées-Atlantiques, France). 121 by 23 by 2 mm. MAN inv. 84772. Early Magdalenian (15,000–13,000 BCE). Line drawing of the back: Pales and Tassin de Saint Péreuse (1976:81, fig. 28). Line drawing of the front by Saint-Périer (1932:43, fig. 1).

Many areas on the body of the two women engraved on the front of a bone plate recovered from the cave of Isturitz, France (fig. 17.5), feature stippled parallel lines (nape of the neck and occiput, cheeks, breasts, pubis, and anterior face of the thighs). While some scholars have again interpreted these markings as body hair (Saint-Périer 1932:41–44), others suggest the marks on this image and other female representations (*La Poire* of Brassempouy, *Femme au Renne* of Laugerie-Basse), "could represent body hair, a piece of clothing, body painting or scarifications" (Walter 1995:267). In addition, the neck, wrists, and ankles of these figures are marked with parallel lines and transversal strokes suggestive of necklaces and bracelets. The posterior outline of the legs and back is defined by oblique parallel dashes, an outlining technique that is also found on other Magdalenian anthropomorphs such as the *Chasseur à l'Aurochs* (the Auroch Hunter) from Laugerie-Basse and *l'Homme à l'Ours* (Man with Bear) from Mas d'Azil cave in France. This technique may simply be "a graphic technique to give an impression of depth" (Duhard 1996:107). A similar technique is also known to have been frequently applied to zoomorphic representations. The branched or barbed design engraved on one of the women's outer thighs (see fig. 17.5) also appears twice on the bison engraved on the reverse of the Isturitz blade. The meaning of this secondary design, recurrent in Paleolithic art (especially on portable artifacts), remains unknown (Pozzi 2004:173), though based on the shape I believe it may represent a harpoon head.

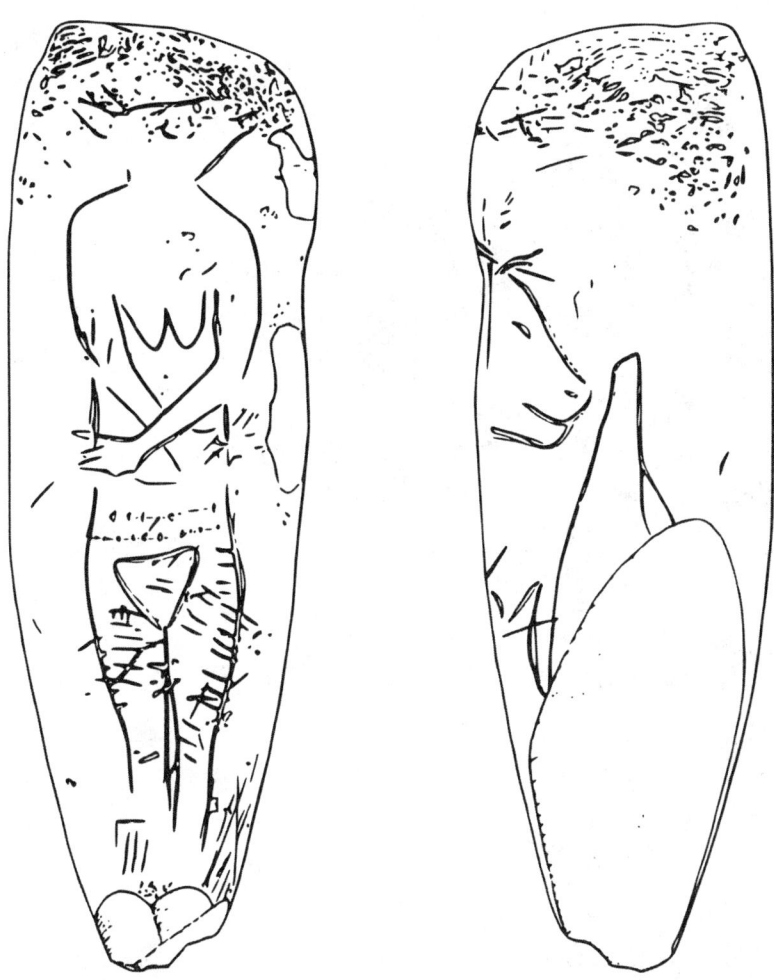

Fig. 17.6. Engraved pebble found in 1883 at Tolentino (Marche, Central Italy). 127 by 41 by 21 mm. Ancona, Museo Archeologico Nazionale delle Marche inv. 8803. End of the Upper Paleolithic (10,000–8,000 BCE). Drawing by d'Errico in Massi et al. (1997:33, fig. 6).

The Isturitz bone plate invites comparison with an image engraved on a piece of chert from Tolentino, Italy (fig. 17.6), which also combines images of a human on the front side and of an animal on the back side. The female figure on its front side is an animal-headed hybrid, wearing what could be identified as a double belt of beads around her waist. The parallel incisions that cover her legs do not lend themselves as easily to interpretation. It has been suggested that they may depict body hair (Massi et al. 1997:39). However, these long, bold dashes seem ill chosen to represent female leg hair, especially when considering the engraver's obvious understanding of controlled line work, as demonstrated by his use of fine lines and delicate stippling to render the figure's belt.

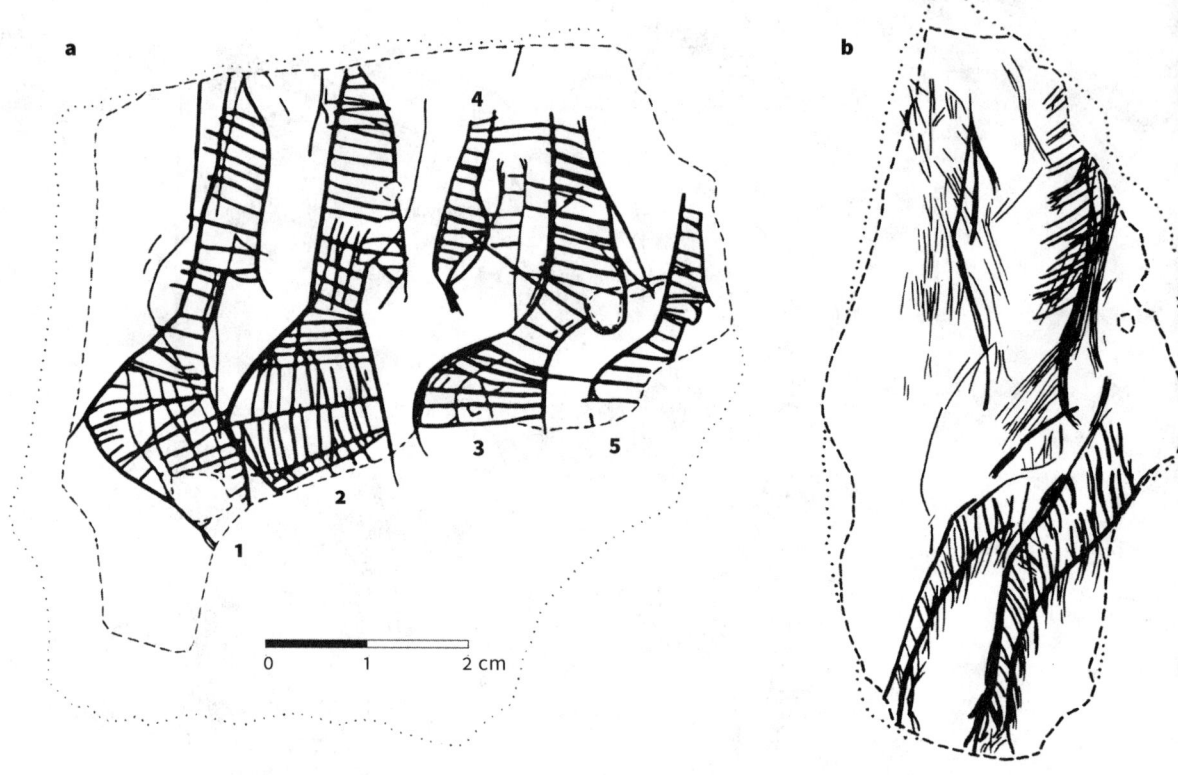

Fig. 17.7. Engraved slates n. 87 and n. 316 from Gönnersdorf (Rhineland-Palatinate, Germany), found in 1968. Upper Magdalenian (13,500–11,500 BCE). Schloss Monrepos Museum (Neuwied). Drawings courtesy of G. Bosinski (Bosinski et al. 2001).

The use of dashes and hatching also appears on a small proportion (forty-two = 10 percent) of approximately 400 engraved female depictions from Gönnersdorf, Germany. These designs, conventionally designated as "clothing" (Bosinski et al. 2001:197), were not necessarily meant to represent decorations or actual bodily accessories. Indeed, the Gönnersdorf engravers either chose to superimpose contour lines (i.e., 15 percent of sample), or to fill the interior surface with patterns (10 percent, but almost never applied both treatments to the same piece (Ibid.). In my sample of forty-two groups of figures, thirty-five (83 percent) display hatching on the lower limbs, while the outlines of seven others are completely filled in (e.g., fig. 17.7a). On a second (fig. 17.7b), the strokes flow over the outline, forming an image that might suggest fur clothing. But one must keep in mind that such engravings are exceptional within the overall corpus. The considerable graphic investment that they display may not have served any kind of figurative objective. Consequently, in this case it would appear excessive to suggest that we are dealing with representations of clothing or body markings.

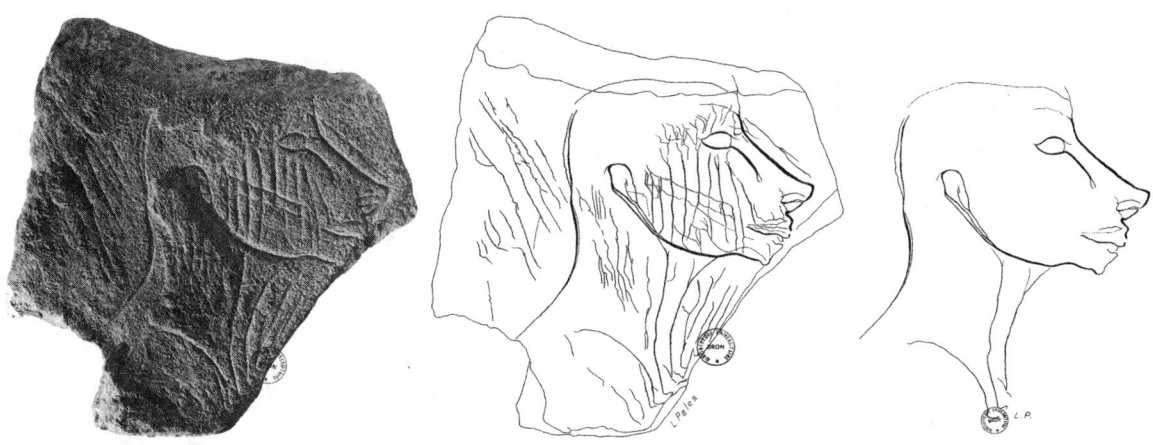

Fig. 17.8. Engraved profile on a limestone plate found in 1938 at La Marche Cave (Lussac-les-Châteaux, Vienne, France). 125 by 120 by 15 mm. MAN inv. 82791. Early Magdalenian (15,000–13,000 BCE, stratigraphic layer dated to 12,300 BCE). Photographed and drawn by Pales and Tassin de Saint Péreuse (1976: plates I–III).

A famous limestone plate from the cave of La Marche, France, one of the hundreds of such pieces discovered at this site, is engraved with the profile of a man whose cheek bears what appear to be several long gashes (fig. 17.8). While it has often been suggested that these gashes represent body painting or scarification (e.g., Airvaux 2001:97), others have questioned this interpretation: "The vertical strokes are reminiscent of the linear, raised or depressed and sometimes keloidal scarifications found among certain tropical African populations. A case could be made in favor of this hypothesis, but these strokes also appear on the front and back of the character's neck. This leads one to wonder if they may not be present for other reasons, including the very basic possibility that they were simply applied to fill up space" (Pales and Tassin de Saint Péreuse 1976: observation n°1).

Most of the engravings from La Marche present a very busy graphic style. Countless linear and curvilinear strokes are layered onto figurative designs that are themselves superimposed onto one another (Pales and Tassin de Saint Péreuse 1976). To view these plates as mere prehistoric sketchpads does not satisfactorily account for such a deliberate oversaturation and obscuring of the surface. This peculiar treatment may instead be the result of repeated performative acts of ritual or magical marking.

Another Venus, discovered in 2008 at Hohle Fels in Germany (fig. 17.9) and dated to ca. 38,000 BCE, is the most ancient example of human figurative art known to date (Conard 2009). What may be a suspension ring sits in place of its head, and following the roughing out of the form, the surface was repeatedly marked with deep horizontal grooves across the abdomen, pubic triangle, and lower back. Semicircles adorn the upper part of the breasts, and oblique dashes appear on the back and arms. In 2015, the site of Hohle Fels yielded a second fragmentary female figure, whose surface also

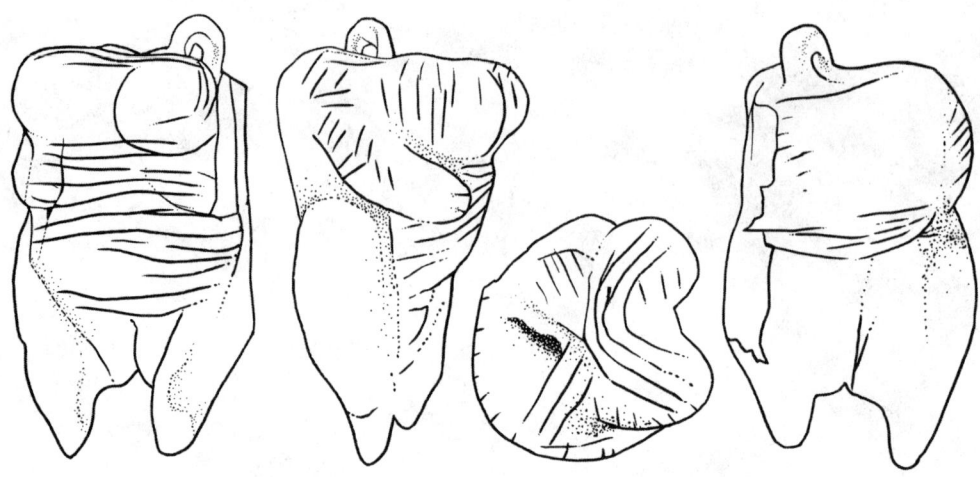

Fig. 17.9. Ivory statuette discovered in 2008 at Hohle Fels cave (Schelklingen, Swabian Jura, southwestern Germany), 65 by 35 by 31 mm. Blaubeuren, Urgeschichtliches Museum. Early Aurignacian (ca. 38,000 BCE). Drawing by the author.

features numerous parallel incisions (Universitaet Tübingen 2015). Parallel strokes (numbering six or seven) are again incised on the upper left arm of the "Lion Man" of Hehlenstein-Stadel (Kind et al. 2014). However, the left and right "arms" of this figurine have more the appearance of feline front legs and paws than of human arms (Kind et al. 2014:138).

Although the incisions on the Venus of Hohle Fels are suggestive of tattooing, body paint (Salomon 2009:90), or "clothing or wrap of some kind" (Conard 2009:250), this type of decoration also frequently appears on tools and on most of the nonhuman figurative carvings from the Swabian Jura mountain range of Germany. Examples include a horse's head from Hohle Fels (reticulated lines) (Conard and Floss 2001); a bear, a mammoth, and a bison from Geißenklösterle cave (parallel incised lines on the legs, flanks, and back); the "Adorant" (Worshipper) of Geißenklösterle (parallel incisions across the arms); a mammoth from Vogelherd (repeated bands of cross-shaped incisions); a lion from Vogelherd (reticulated incisions on the flanks, stippling); and a lion's head from Vogelherd (reticulated incisions behind the jaw), etc. The fact that incisions appear on both humans and animals (and tools) suggests that they do not represent clothing, tattoos, or scars.

From the Neolithic to the Iron Age

The expansion of Neolithic cultures between the Levant, Anatolia, and southwestern Europe was accompanied by a marked increase in the production of zoomorphic and anthropomorphic (predominantly female) figurines (Rollefson 2008). Painted and

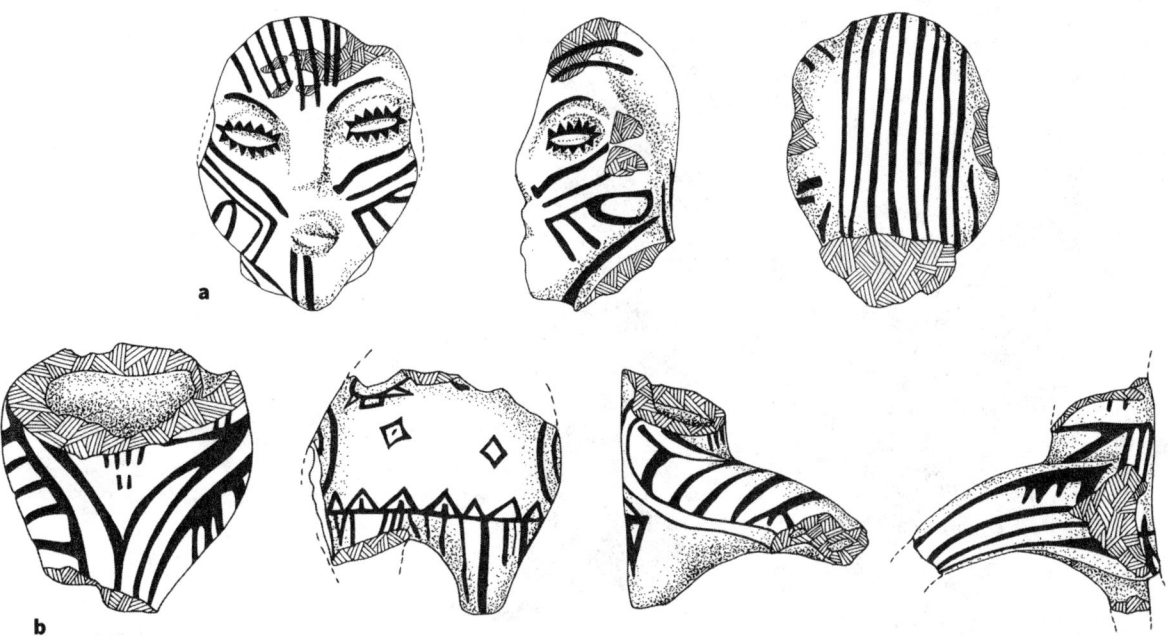

Fig. 17.10. Head of a figurine from Sitagroi (Macedonia, Greece). Burnished red fired clay, black paint, 52 by 37 by 26 mm. Pelvis and thighs of a sitting figurine from Sitagroi (Macedonia, Greece). Burnished orange fired clay, black paint, 70 by 85 by 83 mm. Sitagroi phase III (ca. 4400–3500 BCE). Renfrew et al. (1986: figs. 9.27 and 9.14, and catalog 168 and 169). Published with the permission of the Cotsen Institute of Archaeology Press, UCLA.

incised decoration remains rare on figurines produced during early phases of Neolithic expansion (ca. 10,000–7000 BCE). In Europe, graphic treatment of the surface begins to appear with increased frequency around 5300 BCE (Nanoglou 2015). Paleolithic hatching and stippling give way to more organized compositions: parallel lines, lattice patterns, spirals, triangles, and lozenges are repeated, alternated, and symmetrically arranged to cover important portions of the figurine's surfaces. The old hypothesis according to which this repertoire of designs represented cosmic or religious symbols (e.g., Kruta 1992:97; Nikolov 1989) has been abandoned, and today archaeologists tend to view such decorations as depictions of body ornamentation (clothing, bands of fabric, accessories, body painting, or tattooing) (e.g., Bailey 2005:101,156,162), once again leading us to question if the decorative features applied to these figurines were actually intended to reflect the appearance of living people.

The head of a figurine from Sitgaroi, Greece (Renfrew et al. 1986:239), also appears to be adorned with body painting or tattooing (fig. 17.10a). Other similarly adorned objects have been described as wearing clothing (Renfrew et al. 1986:233) (fig. 17.10b). But any suggestion that this kind of line-work might constitute true to life depictions of actual bodily ornamentation can be viewed with legitimate skepticism, given that it

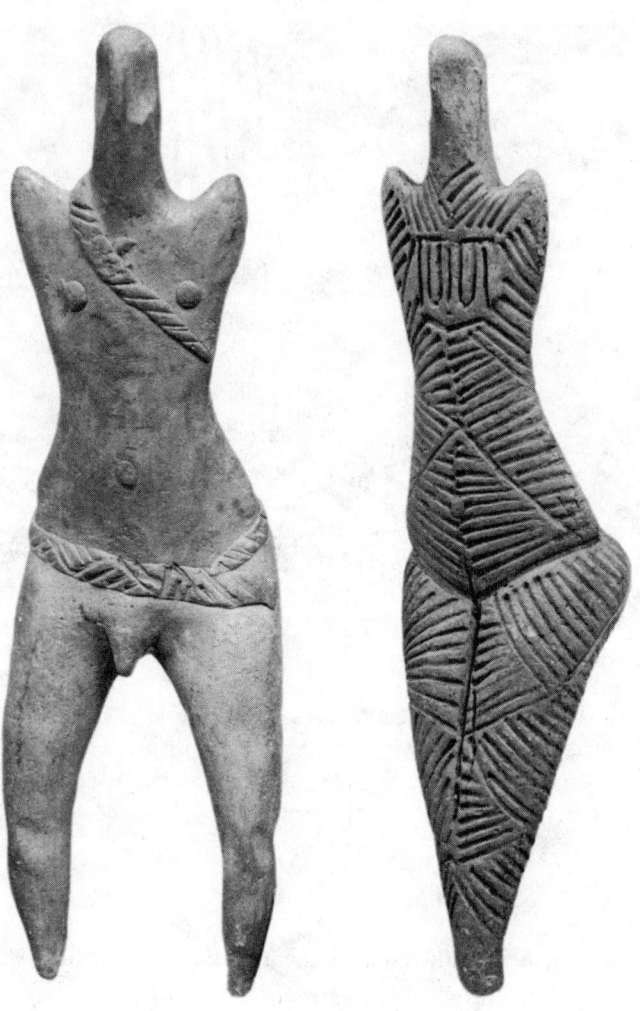

Fig. 17.11. Dumeşti-Între pâraie (Vaslui County, Northeastern Romania). Fired clay, detail: male figurine and female figurine. Cucuteni A3 (ca. 4200–4050 BCE). Vaslui Museum (Romania). Photograph courtesy of Mantu et al. (1997:124, fig. 191 and catalog 52a, 52b).

is also a decorative feature of vases and of terra-cotta miniatures such as tripods and zoomorphic modeled containers (Renfrew et al. 1986:421–23).

The very distinctive ornamental vocabulary that appears on figurines from the Cucuteni culture of Romania and Ukraine (fifth and fourth millennia BCE) features parallel incisions arranged either in conjoined triangular compartments, in lozenges (on the torso, the stomach, and the back), or in spirals (on the buttocks) (see Boghian et al. 2014). These incisions are often filled in with white or red paint, a surface treatment that does not readily conform to the tattooing hypothesis. Instead, the women in these depictions seem to have been bound in ropework or perhaps wrapped in long interwoven bands of fabric. This latter impression is reinforced by a set of figurines from Dumeşti, Romania (Bailey 2005:88–90, 2010:118–19). Six female representations are almost entirely covered with the same distinctive pattern of zoned incisions, while six male figures (with modeled penises) are only "clad" in two clay bands. These latter objects are also decorated with incisions: the first set runs up the back, drapes over the shoulder, and falls across the chest, while the second encircles the hips (Mantu et al. 1997:52a-b) (fig. 17.11).

Male figurines from Tăcuta, Romania, wear the same kind of accessories (Boghian et al. 2014:fig. 4, nos. 3–4). The bands of clay applied to the top of the body are suggestive of costume elements rather than of tattooing or body painting. Proceeding by analogy, one may be tempted to interpret the decorative elements present on the female figurines as depictions of pleated and/or ornate wrapped garments. But here again, there is an absence of solid evidence to confidently state that the decoration of these figurines was intended as a realistic depiction of the appearance of living people.

Earlier statuary produced by the Vinča culture (Serbia and Kosovo, 5250–4500 BCE) also gives the same impression: these anthropomorphic figurines are incised with straight and curved lines that appear to depict anatomical elements (fig. 17.12) (eyes, eyelashes, pubic triangle, fingers), clothing (collar notches and shirt cuffs, skirts, aprons, pendants), and decorative or symbolic patterns (angular or sinuous spirals on

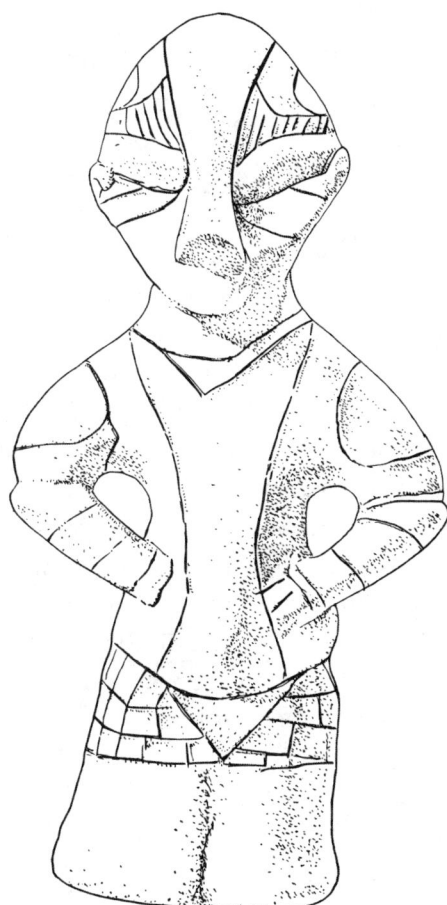

Fig. 17.12. Terra-cotta figurine found in 2002 at Bardhosh (Kosovo, North of Pristina). Vinča Culture (5250–4500 BCE). Orange clay, traces of brown slip, 29.7 by 15 cm. Kosovo National Museum (Pristina), BA 1/02. Drawing by the author.

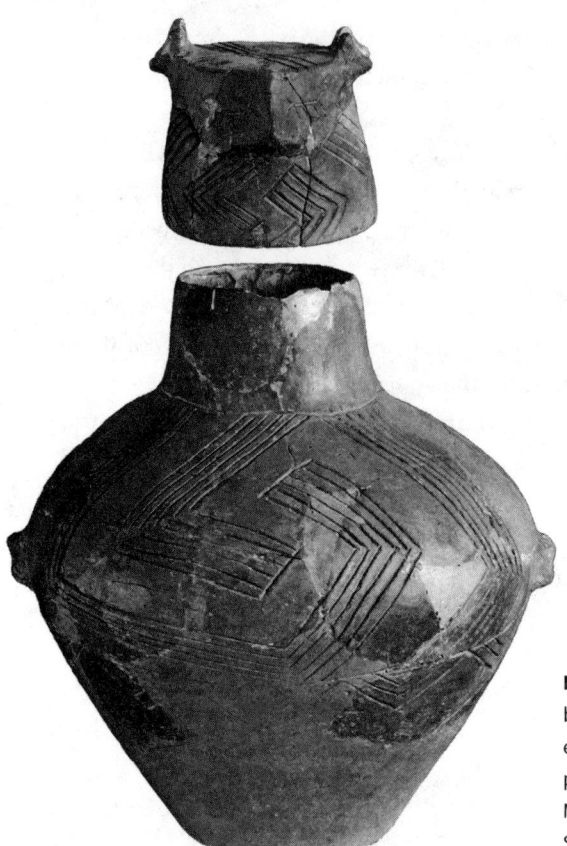

Fig. 17.13. Storage jar (29.8 by 9 cm) with lid (10.7 by 11.8 cm) from Parța (Romania, Timiș county, excavations Gheorghe Lazarovici). Banat Culture phase IIA (= Vinča Culture, phase B1) (ca. 5000 BCE). Muzeul Banatului Timișoara, 747. Photographed in Schier (2005:73, nos. 31 and 32).

the stomach, hips, or skull). Once again, it should be noted that this type of decoration is also found on common ceramics and other anthropomorphic or zoomorphic terracotta miniatures, such as the lid of a feline head–shaped vase from Parța, Romania (fig. 17.13), which bears zigzag designs that are merely extensions of the decorations applied to the container's body. In this case the craftsperson clearly did not intend to produce a realistic depiction of the animal's features. The same can be said about the anthropomorphic Vinča terra-cotta pieces.

One must be equally cautious when interpreting the traces of decoration that remain on many of the Cycladic marble figurines deposited in Aegean tombs during the third millennium BCE (fig. 17.14). Most of these bodily adornments were originally applied in red pigment. In a commentary accompanying her survey of Cycladic figurines, archaeologist Elizabeth Hendrix (2003) hints that these decorative elements (dots, dashes, zigzags), while not representing tangible features (eyes, jewelry, hair), could represent body markings applied to actual living people (painting, scarification, or tattooing). Again, no compelling evidence is brought forth in support of what is, in any case, offered as a mere suggestion. The presence of additional sets of eyes, in particular, leads us to think that the decoration of Cycladic figurines might instead be ritual markings executed exclusively on figurines to reinforce their efficacy.

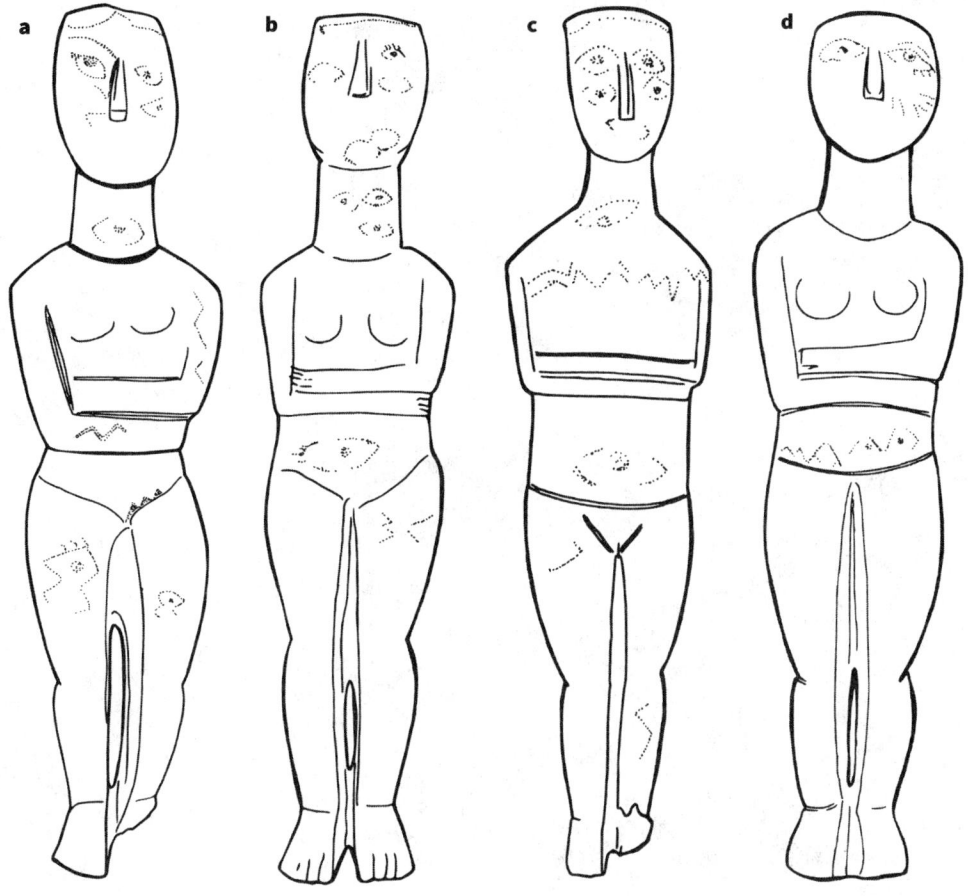

Fig. 17.14. Cycladic carved marble figurines, ca. 2500 BCE; line drawings by Hendrix (2003: figs. 1 (right), 4 (right), 8 (right), 10). Courtesy of the Trustees of the American School of Classical Studies at Athens. The dotted lines indicate traces of paint that are currently almost erased: (a) From Keros Island (Kavos), 54.5 cm. Naxos, Archaeological Museum, Chora, 4691; (b) From Keros Island (Kavos), 58 cm. Naxos, Archaeological Museum, Chora, 4181; (c) Unknown provenance, 39 cm. Naxos, Archaeological Museum, Chora, 4675; (d) Naxos Island, Spedos Necropolis, tomb 14, 33.5 cm. Athens, National Archaeological Museum 6140.20.

Tattooed Women on Both Sides of the Adriatic (by 650 BCE)

Marshaling several lines of concordant evidence, archaeologist Camilla Norman (2011a) has recently drawn attention to figured stelae on which representations of tattooing can be confidently identified. These rectangular limestone slabs were produced in Daunia (Apulia, Italy) and form a fairly coherent ensemble dating back to the seventh and sixth centuries BCE (Nava 1980). Combining deep rectilinear incisions with the occasional use of low relief, Daunian sculptors produced orthogonal depictions of men and women wearing ceremonial garments:[7] clothing decorated with geometric borders and a variety of scenes (weaving, hunting, fishing, cooking, banquets, meetings, processions, martial games, battles, etc.); and fibulae, necklaces, pendants, collars (for

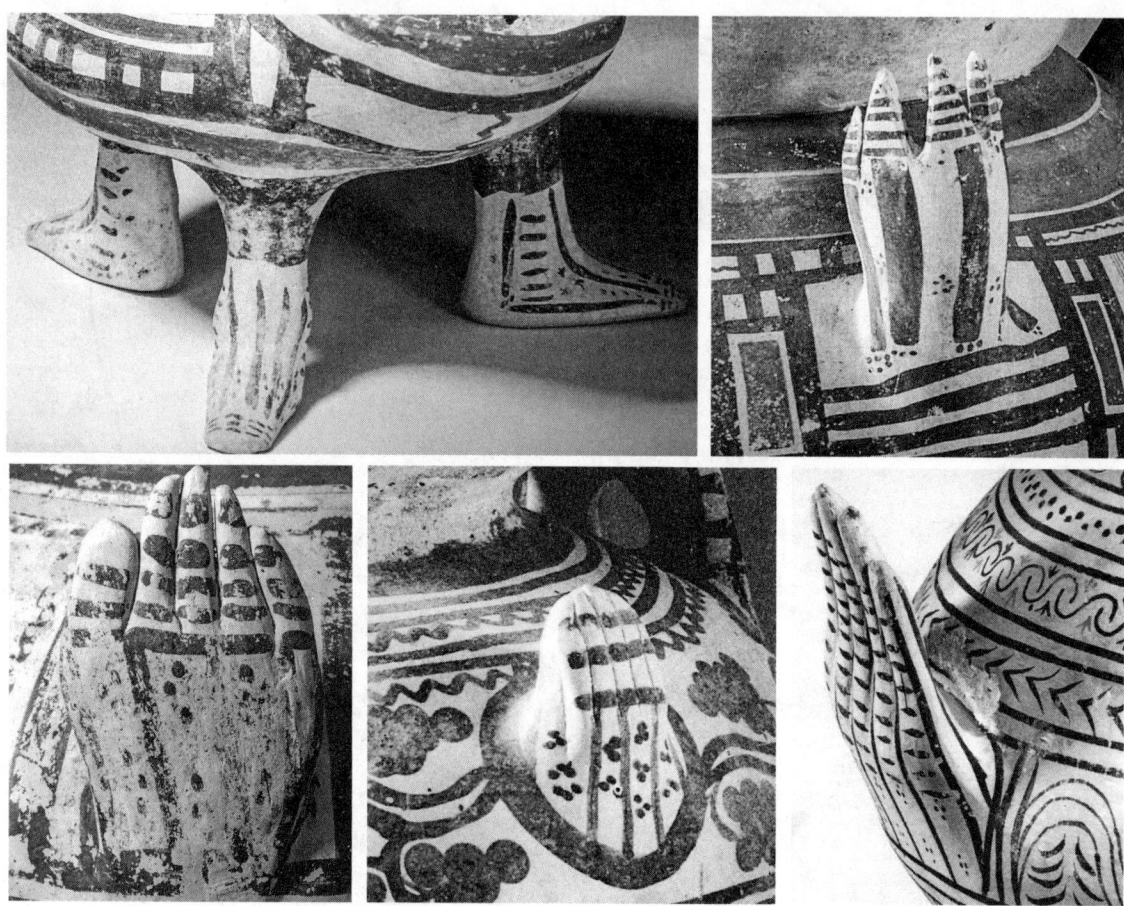

Fig. 17.15. Decorative modeled hands and feet on indigenous Daunian ceramics (Swiss collection) (ca. 500–300 BCE). After Chamay (1993: nos. 198, 210, 211, 212, 227). Courtesy of Association Hellas et Roma, Genève.

women), weapons (for men). Hands and forearms are generally shown emerging from the clothing. The depictions of apron-clad women (probably a marker of nubility) are decorated with an isolated, often diamond-shaped and occasionally cruciform design placed above the elbow; with lines, rectangles, or parallel meanders on the forearms; and with lines and dots on the back of the hand and with transversal dashes across the outer surface of the fingers (plate 21). Norman points out that the decoration of the forearms, in contrast to the costume elements, is never enhanced with color (reds, ochres, white, traces of which subsist elsewhere on the stelae). This, along with the fact that the use of gloves as fashion accessories was unknown during Mediterranean antiquity, reinforces the notion that these artworks depict tattooing and not pieces of clothing.

Similar decorations appear as decorative elements on a number of examples of Daunian pottery from the fifth and fourth centuries BCE (Chamay 1993:198, 210–12,

227; Chamay and Courtois 2002:37, 40) (fig. 17.15). They are rendered in black paint on modeled hands and feet. While the ornamentation of the belly, collar, and handles of these pots varies from one piece to another, the designs applied to the hands remain fairly constant: dashes across the outer surface of the fingers; vertical lines (or bands), between which groups of three or four dots form triangular- or diamond-shaped patterns, run along the back of the hands.[8] A late fourth century BCE funerary painting from Arpi, Italy, provides yet another example of a woman whose forearms are marked with parallel lines (Norman 2011a:150, fig.14).

This iconographic evidence should be considered in light of the testimony provided by the writers of antiquity, according to whom the Daunians were one of three Iapygian groups whose origins could be traced back to Illyria. This fact neatly coincides with archaeological recognition of the close cultural kinship between the Iapygians of Apulia and the Thraco-Illyrian cultures established on the eastern shores of the Adriatic. Moreover, additional ancient written (e.g., Herodotus and Strabo) and iconographic sources (Renaut 2011; Zimmermann 1980) make a very strong case for the existence of a vigorous tradition of female tattooing in the Balkans in antiquity. This tradition is evidenced by many Greek vases dating to the fifth and fourth centuries BCE, on which Thracian women are depicted with tattooed dots, dashes, and concatenated chevrons on their legs, arms, neck, chin, and on the bridge of their feet. In all likelihood this tradition of female tattooing is the same one that has carried on into the twentieth and twenty-first centuries in Bosnia-Herzegovina and Croatia (Truhelka 1896; see Krutak, chapter 10, this volume), Albania (Durham 1929), and northern Greece (Krutak 2007).

Conclusions

Upper Paleolithic representations of human bodies featuring cross-hatching and stippling constitute, all things considered, a relatively minor group within an ensemble that does not generally reserve a particular decorative treatment to the surface of the body. I am surprised at the degree to which the depiction of clothing and adornment, despite their use being well attested in the archaeological record (Taborin 2004; Vanhaeren and D'Errico 2011), tends to be absent from anthropomorphic representations (Duhard 1996:142–43). Regarding tattooing or other forms of body marking, one must keep in mind that absence of evidence is not evidence of absence. But, strictly speaking, the most ancient evidence of human cultural practices at our disposal remains mute on this subject, despite what has often been said and written.

In this art form dominated by outlining, the graphic treatment of the surface of the human body remains anecdotal. Infilling with lines and dots may represent early attempts at strengthening the visibility of representations and/or to bestow upon them certain aesthetic qualities, much in the same way as done for utilitarian objects. This overwrought graphic approach draws on an often limited vocabulary, sometimes to the point of incoherence as exemplified by the La Marche engravings. In some rare instances, at Isturitz and Tolentino for example, depictions of clothing and adornment can be identified,[9] but in no way can these be confidently interpreted as body painting and even less as tattooing.

WAS LUCIEN BERTHOLON RIGHT AFTER ALL?

The interpretation of artifacts from southeastern European Neolithic sites calls for a more cautious approach. Ötzi is there to remind us that tattooing (therapeutic and non-ornamental in his case) was undoubtedly practiced in Europe by the fourth millennium (Deter-Wolf et al. 2016; Renaut 2004b). Several lines of evidence converge to establish the presence of a vibrant tradition of female tattooing some 2,500 years later in the same southeastern quarter of Europe (Thrace, Illyria, Daunia). One could be tempted to trace this later tradition back to the Neolithic by establishing a connection with the refinements in the decoration of female figurines observed over the intervening period. This would in a way give reason to North African scholar Lucien Bertholon, who saw the markings on Danubian and Aegean effigies, Thracian tattooing, the Egyptian depictions of tattooed Libyans, and the female tattooing practices observed during his lifetime, as expressions of a single "archaic" tradition embracing the whole eastern half of the Mediterranean Basin (Bertholon 1904).

One should, however, hesitate to draw meaningful comparisons between the female figurines of southeastern Europe and those found elsewhere that feature markings that can be securely interpreted as tattooing, such as those from the C-Group archaeological culture (ca. 2300 to 1500 BCE) which have been found in northern Nubian archaeological contexts starting at the end of the third millennium BCE (see Friedman, chapter 1, in this volume, fig. 1.8). The lozenge-shaped punctate markings that sometimes appear on these figurines have also been found tattooed on actual skin remains from the same archaeological culture as well as on three mummified women (quite probably of Nubian origin) buried around 2000 BCE in the royal necropolis at Deir el Bahari (Upper Egypt) (see Friedman, chapter 1, this volume). On the other hand, the decoration of European Neolithic figurines does not lend itself to the same kind of unequivocal interpretation, in that it is not necessarily figurative and that the same patterns also appear on zoomorphic statuettes, vases, and terra-cotta miniatures. Clearly, in this region more than elsewhere, people were particularly inclined to apply a similar decorative repertoire to a variety of artifacts that included female figurines. Should one consequently infer that women of that place and time were tattooed? I should think not. Presume, perhaps, but not without risking heading down the wrong track.

BELOW AND BEYOND THE ALPS

One last point is worthy of our attention: Heavily decorated Neolithic figurines and general evidence of tattooing have not been found north of the Alps. Ancient texts have been cited for many decades to argue in favor of the existence of tattooing traditions among the Celts (e.g., among those populations inhabiting the British Isles and in Germany, before and after the Roman invasions), but those accounts do not hold up to intense scrutiny (Renaut 2004a:5—32). Moreover, human remains and convincing anthropomorphic representations with permanent body markings have not been located.[10] This leads us to imagine that female tattooing, well attested as an ancient and durable Near Eastern practice, may well have spread to Europe through cultural transfer from the east. Ötzi's tattoos suggest that this process is likely to have unfolded during the Neolithic. Although he was admittedly only tattooed with short linear therapeutic marks, there is no reason to believe that the women of his tribe did not wear and monopolize a form of decorative tattooing from which men would have been exempt. Gendered ornamental tattooing of women does, after all, coexist elsewhere with non-gendered therapeutic tattooing practices (see Krutak 2013b, 2014a).

All things considered, there is no secure evidence for ornamental tattooing in Europe before the Iron Age. This practice could have reached the southeast quarter of Europe as early as the Neolithic period, but this remains a mere supposition. As for the men and women of the Paleolithic era, the material legacy they left behind suggests that tattooing had not yet entered the repertoire of practices they used to mark and decorate their bodies.

Notes

The author would like to thank Benoît Robitaille for translating this chapter into English.

1. Cheynier (1931); Déchelette (1907:41, 48; 1908:206–7, 510); Péquart and Péquart (1962:211–14, 241–44).
2. Paleolithic ochres were clay earth pigments that were most commonly a red color caused by hematite and were also yellow or brown caused by goethite and/or limonite.
3. Based on ethnographic data summarized by Audoin and Plisson (1982) and Salomon (2009), coloring substances such as red ochre may have served diverse functions in the prehistoric and ancient cultures. These include decorative and symbolic applications, as well as technical and practical uses including: finishing abrasive (hematite); degreasing agent used for the drying of glues, resins, and hides; cosmetic pastes (grease + iron oxides); and to repel insects and vermin from the skin of both the living and the dead.
4. In all cases, translations of original French sources were provided by Robitaille.
5. See also Deffarge et al. (1975:4).
6. For a possible second female figure from this site, engraved with similar designs, see D'Errico et al. (2011).
7. On the subject of female dress in particular, see Norman (2011b) and Verger (2008).
8. The hypothesis favoring tattooing over henna is the most plausible of the two, since henna only appears in the Mediterranean world by the middle of the first millennium BCE, at which time it is still was only known as a perfume (Renaut 2009).
9. For further discussion of questionable cases, see Pales and Tassin de Saint Péreuse (1976).
10. On the subject of Alfred Dieck's complete falsification of the evidence for tattooed "bog people," see Van der Sanden and Eisenbeiss (2006).

18

Sacrificing the Sacred

TATTOOED PREHISTORIC IVORY FIGURES OF ST. LAWRENCE ISLAND, ALASKA

Lars Krutak

Beginning in the late nineteenth century around the Bering Strait, ornate pieces of carved fossil ivory bearing decorations unlike anything previously known from the Eskimo region began appearing in museum collections. These small, deeply patinated artifacts, which originated from ancient village sites across the region and passed from the pockets of Indigenous collectors to American whalers, teachers, traders, and museum curators, were evidence of a distinctive and scarcely known prehistoric maritime culture of northwestern Alaska and neighboring Siberia. Beautifully incised harpoon heads and socket pieces, animated zoomorphic drum and box handles, anthropomorphic figures inscribed with tattoos and body ornaments, and other objects of "unknown use" largely comprised the "high fossil ivory culture" of a society that appeared to have been centered on St. Lawrence Island, parts of the adjacent Asiatic coast, the Diomede Islands, and portions of the Seward Peninsula of Alaska (Hrdlička 1930:174).

By the mid-1920s anthropological interest in the origins of these Paleo-Eskimo peoples peaked (Collins 1937:iii), resulting in a series of archaeological expeditions to the Bering Strait that continues to the present day. On St. Lawrence Island and the neighboring Chukotka Peninsula of Russia, excavations revealed a succession of closely related and partially overlapping cultures—Okvik/Old Bering Sea (~50 to 800 CE) and Punuk (800 to 1200 CE)—whose settlements and cemeteries exhibited some of the finest art ever produced by a hunting society.[1] Lured to the Bering Strait by vast herds of ivory-bearing sea mammals like walruses and large whales, these maritime peoples

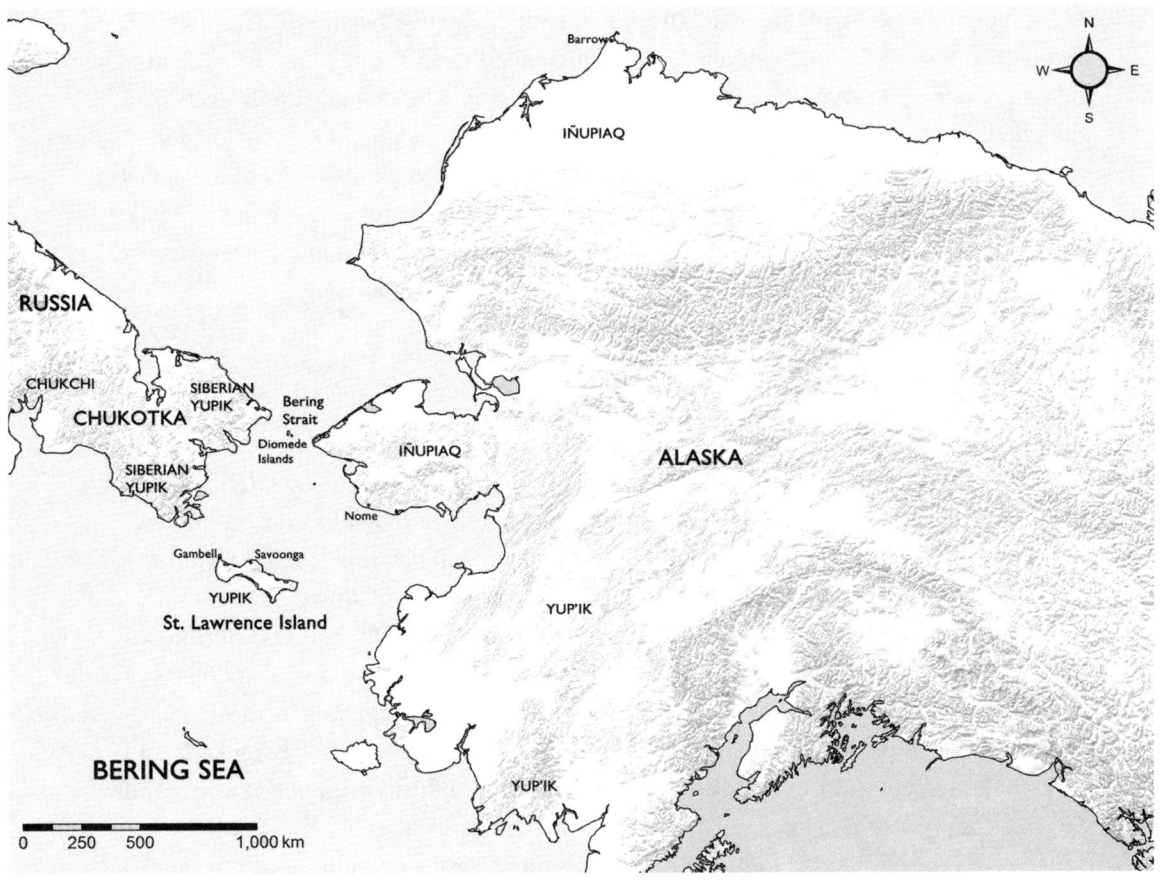

Map 18.1. The Bering Strait region, with locations of sites and historic cultures discussed in this chapter.

from Asia were led by shamans, whaling captains, and notable warriors. Both men and women of these peoples tattooed their bodies and crafted human figurines, or "dolls," that often displayed ornate and naturalistic personal adornments, including amulet straps, beaded headbands, and permanent body markings that have counterparts in recent history and practice.

Although the visual language of Okvik/Old Bering Sea and Punuk hunting iconography and ornamentation can no longer be read precisely, fundamental themes in this material culture have been identified based on the ethnographic record, thereby connecting the worldview and spiritual practices of these ancient peoples to their contemporary descendants (Crowell 2009; Fitzhugh and Crowell 1988). In art historical circles, however, the functions of prehistoric anthropomorphic sculpture are relatively less well understood. Our knowledge of these enigmatic objects is unfortunately limited because of their relative rarity, the uneven degree of their preservation, and the paucity of published information describing their use(s) in the historic era.

Ethnographic data recorded in the nineteenth and early twentieth centuries CE among the Yupiget (Yupik, singular) of St. Lawrence Island and the Chukotka Peninsula of Siberia, the Yupiit (Yup'ik, singular) of mainland Alaska, and the Chukchi and Koryak of far northeastern Siberia, as well as related archaeological and other evidence, challenge longstanding beliefs about the functions of prehistoric Paleo-Eskimo figures from the Bering Strait (map 18.1). Examination of these agentive religious objects, which were used in ritual sacrifice, ceremony, and performance, allows us to suggest new interpretations of their roles in ancient arctic society.

Cultural Chronology, Cosmology, and Ceremony

The earliest prehistoric culture associated with St. Lawrence Island, Alaska, and the neighboring coasts of the Chukotka Peninsula (Siberia) is known as Okvik/Old Bering Sea (Gerlach and Mason 1992; Mason 1998). Excavations initiated in 1928 on St. Lawrence Island and in the nearby Punuk Islands by Henry B. Collins (1929, 1937) of the Smithsonian Institution revealed a sequence of three stages of this culture—Okvik/Old Bering Sea I (~50–400 CE), Old Bering Sea II (400–800 CE), and Old Bering Sea III (400–800 CE)[2]—derived from studies of stratigraphy, artistic styles, and objects of material culture (Collins 1961). Okvik/Old Bering Sea (OBS) appears in the archaeological record as a fully developed maritime Eskimo culture on St. Lawrence Island and Chukotka, but with unclear antecedents and geographical origins (Fitzhugh and Crowell 2009:34).

The OBS people resided in permanent villages and perfected hunting technology to capture the largest sea mammals—walrus and whale—as well as smaller game. The rich ecological landscape that surrounded them, combined with the apparently complex social and political life of their communities, is marked by the development of a major sculptural tradition in ivory and wood (Carpenter 2011). Most Okvik/Old Bering Sea artifacts, and especially hunting paraphernalia (e.g., harpoon heads, harpoon counterweights), are highly contoured and adorned with spirit and animal forms that seem to emerge from the ivory. Works portraying human beings, especially those of women, are usually carved in high relief, displaying anatomical features, such as breasts, distended abdomens, and pronounced genitalia. Other anthropomorphic "ivories" are seemingly androgynous in form with appendages and bodily features (i.e., arms and legs) reduced to formless nubs that barely protrude from elongated torsos (Krutak 2009).[3] These characteristics may have been functional, as recent history and practice demonstrate that dolls lacked limbs to facilitate the changing of outer garments (Linn and Lee 1999).

Many of the prehistoric dolls from St. Lawrence Island display deeply incised lines on their faces and bodies that likely represent tattoos, sacred hunting visors (for men), charm headbands or headdresses, ceremonial parkas, and *uyaghqutat* (amulet straps in the St. Lawrence Island Yupik language) (figs. 18.1 and 18.2), all of which have modern

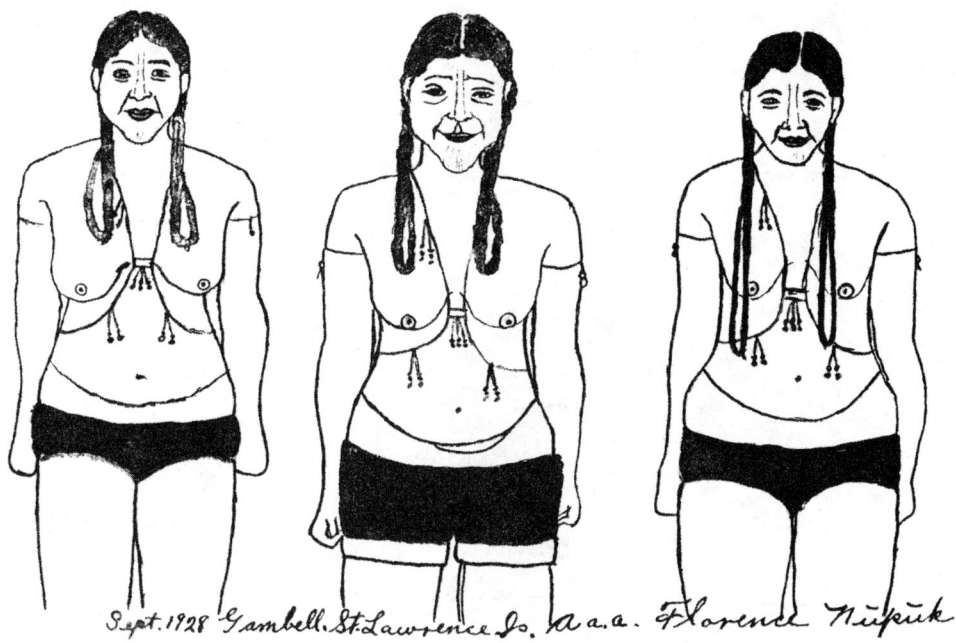

Fig. 18.1. Drawing of tattooed women wearing amulet straps (ca. 1928), by St. Lawrence Island Yupik artist Florence Nupok (Napaaq). Redrawn after Appasingok et al. (1985:70, fig. 33).

analogues in the twentieth century. Such indelible realism suggests that tattooing and other forms of ceremonial adornment were not only traditional ancient customs, but they also worked as vehicles for transforming the body through ritual means (Krutak 2009). While these ancient rituals remain poorly understood, the ethnographic record provides clues to their meanings and functions.

Before the arrival of Presbyterian missionaries at St. Lawrence Island in 1894, the religious practices of the local Yupiget can be best described as animistic (Hughes 1984:273). Deities and various spirits (e.g., ancestral, animal, and environmental) were beseeched and propitiated to ensure good hunting and to assuage the advances of malevolent supernatural entities believed to be the harbingers of sickness, disease, and misfortune (Krutak 1999, 2007, 2009). Shamans, who could be male or female, and Indigenous whaling captains were the primary practitioners of ceremonial culture. Women of the household also participated in specific ritual activities and fulfilled a central position through the performance of magical incantations, by feeding sacred household hunting and apotropaic amulets and charms with tallow and by creating beautifully designed clothing that attracted game animals (Chaussonnet 1989). An old Siberian Yupik man told the Russian ethnographer Waldemar Bogoras: "[I]t is a mistake to think that women are weaker than men in hunting-pursuits," because while a man wanders in vain about the sea and wilderness, searching for game, women who "sit by

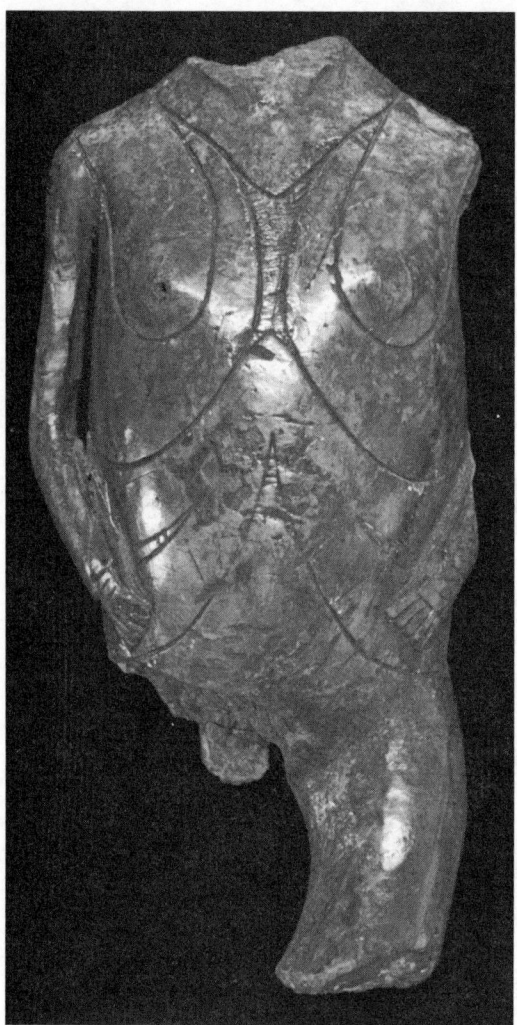

Fig. 18.2. Old Bering Sea II (400–800 CE) figurine. Carved walrus ivory, H. 11.4 cm. This full-figured female figurine was uncovered in a 1934 excavation at the ancient village of Kukulik, St. Lawrence Island. A series of amulet straps drape the torso. University of Alaska Museum of the North, Fairbanks, Alaska (1-1934-1542).

the lamp are really strong, for they know how to call the game [animals] to the shore" (Bogoras 1904–1909:359).

The supernatural was present everywhere in the landscape on St. Lawrence Island. Places along hunting or travel routes became sacred because they were inhabited by deceased ancestors and local spirits that were often animal (Krutak 2007:155). Daily life revolved around increasing one's awareness of the balance between humanity, nature, and the metaphysical. Maintaining this harmonic relationship was critical because the perpetuation of life was dependent upon the interconnections between these worlds. Indeed, humans, animals, spirits, ancestors, and everything in the multilayered and carefully ordered universe were believed to share the same fundamental essence or "vital principle" (Bogoras 1901:32). The concept of transformation—humans into humans, humans into animals, animals into humans, animals into animals, spirits into animals, spirits into humans, spirits into spirits—permeated mythological traditions and daily life and was expressed in many forms of material culture. "Persons" were constituted of multiple attributes extending beyond the human domain. Moreover, the souls of humans and animals were conceived to be very similar, and were both "subject to the same range of emotions and thoughts, of resentments and desires" (Hughes 1984:274).

Around the Bering Strait, and especially on St. Lawrence Island, annual rituals focusing on the procurement of game were a significant part of religious life. Yupik hunters paid their respects to the spirits of slain sea mammals—and the deities and ancestral spirits who assisted them in the hunt—through prayer, song, and offerings of food, water, and blood sacrifice.[4] Siberian and St. Lawrence Island Yupik deities with influence over the sea animals, such as the Grandfather (*Apa*) of game called Kiyaghneq, who resided in the heavens, and the "mistress of sea animals," who lived in the sea with her husband, were honored in ceremonies that continued until recent times (Bogoras 1904–1909:318, 401; Crowell 2009:206; Hughes 1959:73).

Families and clans each had their respective ceremonies, and through giving thanks to the sea mammals that sustained them it was believed they would return to be hunted anew the following year. If the proper acts of consideration were not carried out, the animal spirits and their masters would be offended and withdraw, no longer offering themselves to humans. Moreover, as St. Lawrence Island elder Estelle Oozevaseuk noted: "If you don't hunt them, they will just go down, dying, but if we can hunt them, they'll multiply. That's what we Eskimos believe" (Crowell 2009:206). For the Indigenous people of Bering Strait, death was seen as an integral and necessary part of the cycle of life and renewal.

Many of these traditional hunting or "thanksgiving" rituals featured the use of material culture seen adorning the bodies of ancient Okvik/Old Bering Sea dolls. Writing about 1930, archaeologist Otto Geist described the use of visors during clan whaling ceremonies held in spring during a new moon (fig. 18.3). The visors, along with other ceremonial paraphernalia, were contained in a pouch that held all of the valuable and sacred charms of the family. These sacred bundles were passed down to the oldest son from generation to generation (Geist 1927–1934a:n.p). St. Lawrence Island Yupik historian Paul Silook, who provided volumes of ethnographic material for visiting scientists, added that such visors or "beaks" were also used during ceremonies after a polar bear hunt:

> The [whaling charm] bag [has] two beaks attached to it [that] are used by the boat captain and the boat striker whenever a whale or polar bear is killed. The boat captain always carries it [the bag] back and forth every hunting day and the proper place in the boat is at the bow of the boat. When a whale is killed before the beaks are put on, the captain touches the whale, as dipping it to the whale so the bag touches the whale, and then beaks can be worn. At the time of moon worship[5] it can be carried by the boat captain. (Silook n.d.:n.p.)

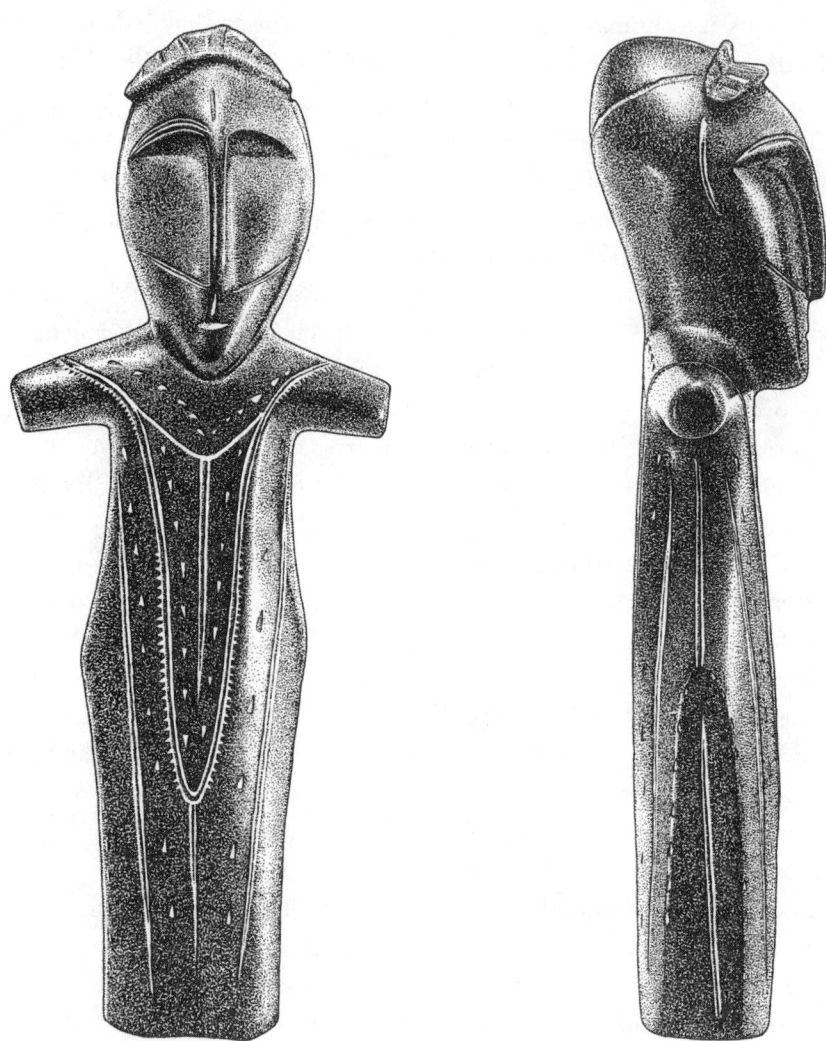

Fig. 18.3. Okvik figure with hunting visor. Carved walrus ivory, H. 13 cm. St. Lawrence Island, Alaska (ca. 250–100 BCE). He is dressed in a ceremonial garment. Drawing by Kathleen Borowick. Rock Foundation, New York (A7958).

Ethnographer Waldemar Bogoras (1904–1909:260) provided two early depictions of these visors, stating they "represent masks at the same time. One has on it the images of killer-whale and two walruses; another, the face of a walrus without tusks; a third has two eyes, which are said to represent whale's eyes." In unpublished field notes, Bogoras (1901:2, 31) added that these designs "represent animal forms or human faces regarded as belonging to the genius [or resident spirit/spiritual counterpart termed *yua*] of the same . . . In their mythology, animals change into men [and vice versa] by simply pushing up the beak or muzzle, like a mask, and change back by pulling it down again."

Another important Yupik hunting ceremony was *Ateghaq*. This rite marked the annual launching of hunting boats (*angyaq*) on St. Lawrence Island and Siberian shores. In Siberia, the ceremony featured facial painting with designs honoring those sea mammals that would "bring good fortune" to the family holding the ceremony. Participants donned white ceremonial rain parkas of walrus and seal intestine that were never worn at any other time, except when a whale was taken (Apangalook 1985:204–9; Hughes 1959:72–73). The best foodstuffs (walrus oil mixed with greens and boiled reindeer meat and fat) were prepared by the wives of the boat captains/owners, some of these morsels were broadcast into the air to feed the spirit of Kiyaghneq, the Supreme Being or Creator, and into the sea to feed the "mistress of the sea animals" and her husband Ka'cak (Bogoras 1901:32; Hughes 1959:73). While the boat owner (*angyalek*) fed the gods and sang songs of pleading (*ivaghulluk*), his wife kindled a ceremonial fire near the *angyaq*. The *angyalek* then threw more bits of the sacrificial meat mixture into the flames to "feed the god" (Hughes 1959:73).[6]

Bogoras (1901:32) stated that the ceremonial parkas worn during *Ateghaq* were of the same form worn by the deities Ka'cak and his wife, and that the *angyalek* and his wife wore a peculiar headdress simulating that worn by the sea deities themselves (Ibid. 1901:32, 34; Bogoras 1904–1909:393). Bogoras also observed that two seal oil lamps were used in the ritual. Upon one lamp was placed a small wooden image of Ka'cak. The other lamp served as the location where Ka'cak accepted his sacrifices.

On St. Lawrence Island, the archaeologist Otto W. Geist witnessed *Ateghaq* ceremonies in the 1920s performed by members of the Aymaramket clan, who were originally from Siberia. In these rites, sacrificial offerings to the ancestors were of paramount concern:

> Now [he] took some of the sacrificial mixture of Siberian reindeer fat chopped finely and sacrificed this three times towards the water. Turning around, he sacrificed towards the boat rack and to the house, then to the mountains—the burial place of their fathers and ancestors. During this sacrificing he mumbled some words which I could not understand. It seemed to me that he was calling names; most likely of the departed ones[7] while he was facing the mountain and throwing the bits of sacrifice towards it. (Geist, 1927–1934b:2–3)

The roles and functions of these and other Bering Strait Yupik hunting ceremonies were embedded in family and clan contexts, just as they probably were in ancient times. Cultural mores, such as ritual beliefs and practices, taboos, hunting rules, modes of conduct, and tattoo styles,[8] were inherited from previous generations of family members and essentially constituted a "law of the ancestors" (Tein 1994:124). Although the Yupiget offered sacrifices to different deities who controlled the spirits of the game, those made to honor the ancestral dead probably constituted the main feature of ceremonial life. These ancestors controlled the cycling of human souls and hovered near their gravesites, waiting to reenter the community through newborn children with their namesakes (Jolles 2002:117; Silook 1940:108). Therefore, keeping the favor of the deceased close to the living was of paramount concern.

A World Turned Inside Out and Upside Down

According to Bering Strait Yupik concepts of the afterlife, the land of the dead was seen as similar to that of the living, but in many ways turned inside out and upside down. In a myth recorded by Siberian Yupik elder Tassan Tein (1994:121), the deceased lived in villages with their dogs. Their cemeteries contained dwellings instead of graves, and when a human died the ancestors held a "festival" to celebrate. Presumably they were eager to receive the name-soul of their deceased relative, which would eventually be recycled back into the world of the living. Similar descriptions of the land of the dead were recorded for the Yup'ik region of mainland Alaska. In a well-known tale of a Yup'ik girl who visited the afterlife, schoolteacher Edward W. Hawkes reported:

> Even the animal shades [spirits] were not forgotten, but inhabited separate communities in human shape. She found the [human] inmates of this region leading a pleasant but somewhat monotonous life, free from the hardships and from the sleet and cold of their earthly existence. They returned to the upper world during the feast to the dead, when they receive the spiritual essence of the food and clothing offered to their namesakes by relatives. According to the generosity or stinginess of the feast givers there was a feast or famine in spirit land, and those who were so unfortunate as to have no namesake, either through their own carelessness [i.e., childless couples] or the neglect of the community [because the deceased was odious], went hungry and naked. This was the worst calamity that could befall an Eskimo, hence the necessity of providing a namesake and of regularly feeding and clothing the same, in the interest of the beloved dead. (Hawkes 1914:29–30)

On St. Lawrence Island and neighboring Chukotka, the feast of the dead (*Aghqe-saghtuq*) was a complex ritual. It was performed in the summer and marked the end of the ceremonial year (Blassi 1985:245). After a successful whaling season, boat captains invited their relatives and clan elders to meet at their individual worshipping places, usually at the village cemetery.[9] Among the Siberian Yupiget the place of sacrifice was located at the gravesite of a beloved ancestor (Hughes 1959:77). Here, the gravestone, which was a large rock, was removed and replaced with a fire pit. Small pieces of meat and fish were placed on the head stone and cut into even smaller pieces. These were thrown into the ceremonial fire by the master of ceremonies, who chanted: "Gather here all [ancestral spirits], here take of food." It was implied by this action that the food then appeared anew in the afterlife (McIntyre 2005:40). Reindeer bones were tossed into the flames and the oldest relative of the deceased then stood at one side of the fire with the remaining attendants at the other. The elder removed a few dead coals from the fire and daubed each attendant while stating: "Now all sickness will leave here." Eventually the gravestone was replaced and the attendants returned home.

In 1912, Smithsonian ethnologist Riley Moore described a similar memorial feast at Gambell, St. Lawrence Island:

> The place of worship is a shallow depression in the earth, circular in form and about a foot across. Sometimes it is on top of a small mound a few inches in height. More often than not they are located in cemeteries. When the ceremony is completed small stones are laid in the hollow, much like eggs in a nest, to prevent the grass from growing there and these are not disturbed until the next time the boat captain has a successful season at whaling. All worshippers sit in a circle around the "altar" and the stones are removed from the fireplace. The boat captain who is master of ceremonies places a little bunch of dry [moss] in the hollow and prepares to strike a fire. Before lighting it, however he calls out . . . "Our grandfathers who are dead, bring us fire" [or "Come so-and-so and gather beneath our fire so we can feed you" (Blassi 1985:243)]. He then lights the fire and a few minute fragments of meat from the whale's flukes and the walrus cub's flippers are burned in the flame, the flippers being fed to the fire by the captains who brought them. The captains do this one at a time and as each bit of meat is torn off he calls the name of one of his male ancestors and follows this by going over the list of diseases which commonly afflict the Eskimo. Then each worshipper eats a small amount of food which he has brought with him for the occasion, after which all stand up together facing the fire and each brushes down the front of his body with his hands as if he were brushing something away from it. Then turning their backs to the fire, each man brushes down his own back, much as he did the front of his body. This is done to brush away any disease which may at the present or at any future day afflict them. (Moore 1912:1–2)

The act of brushing off disease also figured prominently during actual St. Lawrence Island funeral rites. After the deceased had been ritually prepared in their home for burial, the funeral procession traveled to the "Destroying Place." At Gambell village there were two such locations, where the eldest living relative of the deceased used the wooden vessel for bathing the corpse to "sweep away" any residual sickness from the bodies of the other funeral attendees (Hughes and Hughes 1960:96). St. Lawrence Island elder James Aningayou stated this action was a way to "sweep off sickness on that dead person from the whole family and let it all be buried with him" (Jolles 2002:189). Most of the personal property of the deceased was subsequently broken, and the clothing cut from the deceased's body, after which the deceased was eventually interred within a rock pile upon the frozen tundra. Before the funeral party returned home, a series of expiatory ceremonies were performed to purify them from having made contact with the deceased.

Not all spirits of the dead rested quietly, and individuals who brought harm against others in their lifetimes often became evil spirits after death (Tein 1994:121). The deceased could also become a malevolent entity if a living relative was to blame for the death of the deceased through a breach of a taboo (Murphy 1964:68). In such cases, several measures were employed to defend humankind from the "shade" of the dead or the spirits that caused the shade's death. On St. Lawrence Island one of these measures was tattooing. Pallbearers who came into direct contact with the dead were ritualistically tattooed at their primary joints. These locations were the locus of tattoo because they were the seats of a person's limb-souls, and it was therefore at these points that the evil spirit would attempt to enter the body.[10] Tattoo pigment comprised of human urine, soot, and other apotropaic substances like graphite, warded off the evil spirit.[11]

The action of destroying the personal property of the dead was fairly widespread across the Yupik region. These traditions have led art historians, anthropologists, and others to suggest that the dismemberment or decapitation of ancient Okvik/Old Bering Sea and later Punuk human figures may have been performed during a similar type of funerary ritual, whereby the figure was "killed," presumably to release any malignant powers manifested in them (Krutak 2009:203), to forestall their reanimation by evil spirits after the death of the owner (Hollowell 2009:281), or to release the spirit of the object so that it could accompany the owner to the afterlife (Linn and Lee 1999:15). All, some, or none of these hypotheses might be correct. Because in the land of the dead everything is reversed, when an object of a dead person is broken "it was thought to become whole in the Other World" (Tein 1994:119). But there are other possibilities.

Bogoras's (1904–1909:349–50) work with the Siberian Chukchi people revealed that "sacred" anthropomorphic fireboards were perhaps a family's most sacred item. These items were carved of wood or ivory, and some were inherited from preceding generations. Not only were they employed to ignite life-giving fires; they were also used in sacred rites associated with securing and protecting game animals through various sacrifices, and were believed to embody apotropaic powers (Bogoras 1904–1909:356). Fireboards were also believed to be animate and sentient; they were fed at their mouths with tallow or marrow at each sacrifice. Drill holes became the eyes of the fireboard, and the squeaking noise produced by the drilling was conceived of as its voice. When it came time to destroy an antiquated fireboard it was sacrificed in a ceremonial fire, and its human-like head might be cut off and joined to the family's string of charms used to repel evil spirits (Bogoras 1904–1909:350). Prehistoric ivory doll heads separated from their bodies may have served a similar function, since several have been found with suspension or mounting holes indicating continued ritual significance after dismemberment (Wardwell 1986:47, fig. 26; 1992:plate 1).[12]

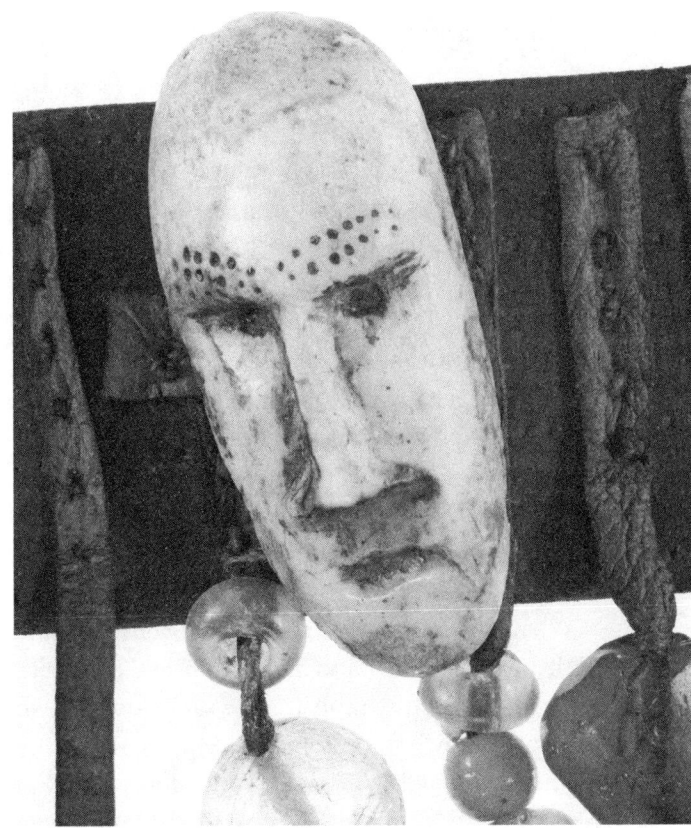

Fig. 18.4. Charm belt. Archaeologist Otto Geist collected this object from St. Lawrence Island whalers about 1928. The small ivory face hanging from the belt has dot-patterning, probably representing a hunting visor, that closely resembles ancient Okvik/Old Bering Sea tattooing forms. University of Alaska Museum of the North, Fairbanks, Alaska (64-021-0134).

Okvik/Old Bering Sea peoples also employed anthropomorphic ivory fireboards. Most of these ancient objects date to the earliest period of Old Bering Sea culture—Okvik—and are missing their heads (Feng 2013:337). However, one example excavated at an Old Bering Sea II site near Gambell, St. Lawrence Island, maintains its head but seems to have been discarded once its usable surface was exhausted (Wardwell 1992:plate 7). These ancient objects were probably used in connection with sea mammal hunting rituals, as they were among the historic Maritime Koryak of Siberia, who fed them with sacrifices of food and regarded them as the "deity of the household fire . . . the helper in the hunt of sea mammals [and] the guardian of the family hearth." (Jochelson 1908:34).

In the historic period, small anthropomorphic ivory heads were worn on the body, either attached to amulet straps under one's clothing or hung on amulet belts that secured the outer parka. One such charm belt from St. Lawrence Island in the collections of the University of Alaska Museum of the North, Fairbanks, displays numerous amuletic attachments, including one prehistoric harpoon head and a carved ivory human head resembling more ancient Okvik/Old Bering Sea–style sculpture (fig. 18.4). Otto Geist, the collector of the object, reported that no man would be successful in a whale hunt without such a charm belt.

Guardian Figures

Anthropomorphic "guardian" figures were widely used by the Siberian Chukchi and Koryak as well as by Yupik peoples inhabiting St. Lawrence Island and neighboring Chukotka. Household guardians protected the living from wandering evil spirits or were used by their owners as spiritual helpers to capture prey, among other things. In the Siberian Yupik region, such family fetishes (*tunghialkutat*) were said to be permanent fixtures and thought to be inherited from generation to generation in the male line (Tein 1994:119).

Guardians displayed enlarged heads and mouths but lacked arms or legs. To keep their favor, the head of the household fed them small pieces of meat from freshly killed game and uttered incantations to them. It was taboo to destroy the figures because such an act was "equivalent to murder of one of the members of the patriclan or of a family member where the fetish was found" (Ibid.). On St. Lawrence Island, similar figures comprised of a simple head and torso were hung from the center pole of the winter house (*mangteghapik*) or tied to the outer flap at the back of the house to "keep watch" and protect its inhabitants from disease-bearing spirits (Collins 1930:130).

Whaling captains kept similar figurines with their religious paraphernalia.[13] They fed them with blubber and meat before and after whale hunts and later destroyed them by fire at the Destroying Place, the same location where elderly and other individuals were voluntarily put to death by means of assisted suicide (Geist and Rainey 1936:123; Leighton and Hughes 1955:331). Paul Silook told Henry Collins that these figures were thought to be the "owners" of the ceremonies where they were employed, but not always representations of dead ancestors (Collins 1930:131). As spiritual helpers they communicated with their human counterparts in dreams, and advised them of specific ceremonial activities necessary to bring success. If their commands were not obeyed, the human owner would "die in a moment" (Silook 1940:49).

Human figurines or "idols" were also employed to assist individuals in weather forecasting and fertility ceremonies on St. Lawrence Island. Geist witnessed numerous small wooden figures discarded just outside of Gambell, probably at the Destroying Place, and noted that "[n]early all were at least partly charred, while some were almost completely burned.... Most of these, my host explained, were weather idols" (Geist and Rainey 1936:30). Geist also collected realistic wooden carvings representing women, sometimes holding their children. According to VanStone (1959:20), "Shamans carved such figures and prescribed them for use as charms by barren women who wished to have children." Presumably, the infertility treatment was effected by releasing the spiritual malady from the woman's body and transferring it into a doll surrogate.[14] The doll was then either left at the place of worship intact or destroyed by breaking ("killing") the surrogate disease-carrier. Collins (1930:55) recorded several sites of fertility rituals around Gambell, each of which was composed of a kind of shrine made of rocks. He wrote: "Women who had no children used to go with [their] husbands to pray for a child. [They] would make small offerings at the place. Name is . . . 'Calling Place.'"

Smithsonian ethnologist E. W. Nelson (1899:435) also recorded the use of fertility figures in the Central Yup'ik region of mainland Alaska. Apparently, these types of dolls could bring about the preferred sex of a newborn: "As a rule, married women are very anxious to have a son, and in case of long continued barrenness they consult a shaman, who commonly makes, or has the husband make, a small, doll-like image over which he performs certain secret rites, and the woman is directed to sleep with it under her pillow."

Tattooed Guardians and Tally Marks

Other guardians or assistants resembling stick-like figures were tattooed on the body (fig. 18.5). Among the Yupiget of St. Lawrence Island and Siberia, the figures were called *yugaaq* ("powerful" or "important person"), and presumably represented an ancestor or other sentient being who protected individuals from evil spirits associated with the land and sea, the spirits of the evil dead, and evil spirits associated with unknown areas where one had not previously traveled (Krutak 2014a:35–36). The *yugaaq* of a new mother was also believed to protect infants from evil influences.

When I interviewed St. Lawrence Islanders about these kinds of tattoos in 1997, I was given the following information. Alice Yaavgaghsiq, the last living tattooist of the island,[15] said: "Sometimes when a mother loses her child, a baby, they do that [tattooing]

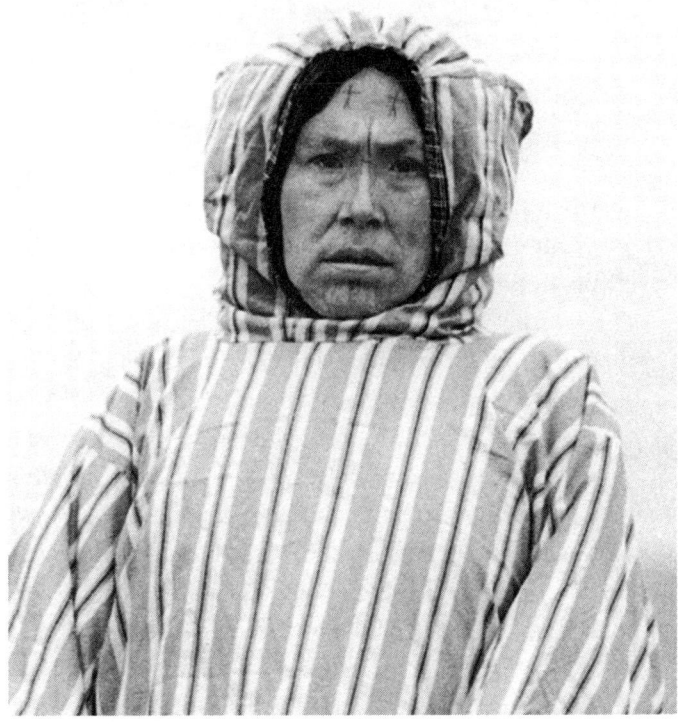

Fig.18.5. Guardian tattoos, or *yugaaq*. Polly Apeyeka of St. Lawrence Island displays tattooed anthropomorphic guardians on her forehead. Photograph by Leuman Waugh, 1930. National Museum of the American Indian (N42762).

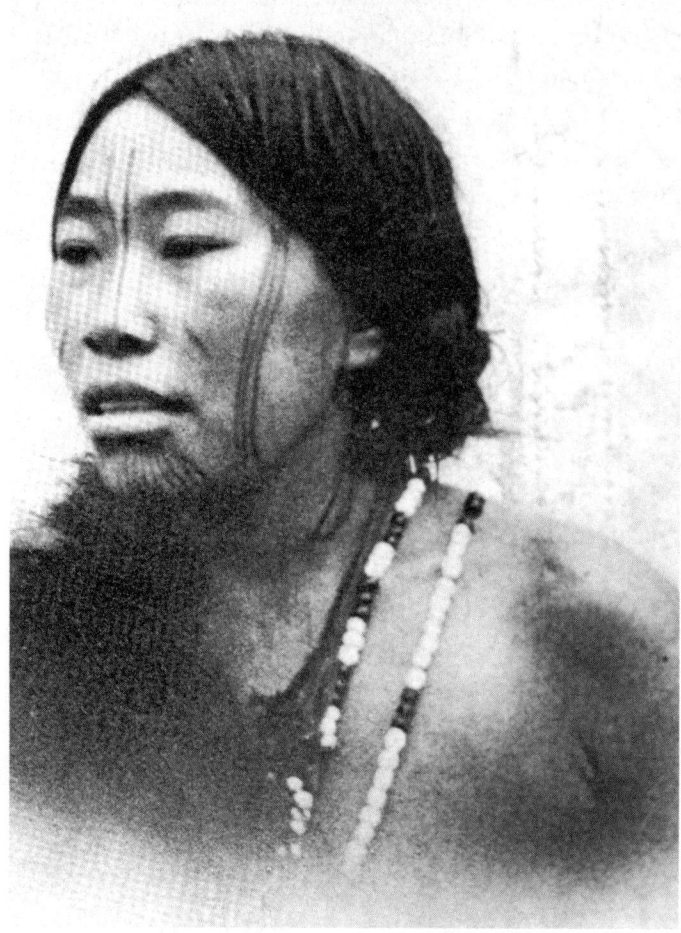

Fig. 18.6. Chukchi women of Siberia were sometimes tattooed with three lines on their cheeks as a fertility charm. This woman (photographed ca. 1900) wears these tattoos. After Cantwell (1902).

when they keep dying." Another aged island resident Mabel Toolie said her aunt had a "little man" tattoo "to scare the spirits away while she was sleeping. These are for protection." (Krutak 2014a:36)

Other historically documented tattoos, such as three tightly grouped lines tattooed on the outer cheeks of Chukchi, Siberian and St. Lawrence Island Yupik women, were believed to cure infertility problems (fig. 18.6). Sometimes similar groupings of lines appear on the cheeks of prehistoric Punuk figures (fig. 18.7; plate 22). In 2001 Estelle Oozevaseuk, a female elder living in Gambell, told me a story about Ayngaangaawen, a girl from the extinct village of Kukulik (*Kookoolok*). Ayngaangaawen always refused to get her tattoo marks because of the accompanying pain, and so she never received them. Consequently she could not bear healthy children, and they all died as infants. Distraught over the loss of her offspring, she finally agreed to become tattooed, and "when she got some marks she had children" and they lived into adulthood (Krutak 2014a:36).

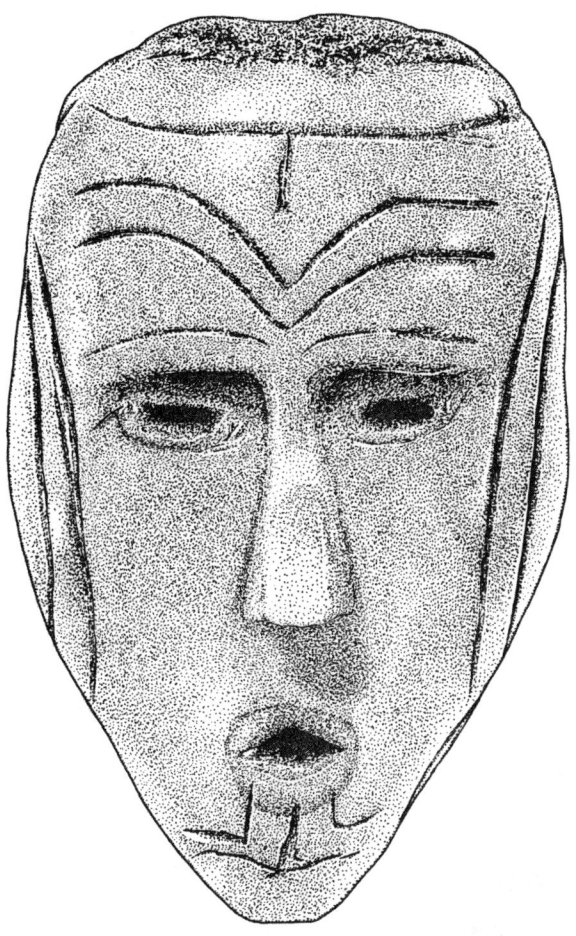

Fig. 18.7. Punuk doll head, St. Lawrence Island, Alaska (ca. 500–1000 CE). Carved walrus ivory, H. 5.1 cm. The bands of tattooing on the cheeks, V-shaped forehead design, and chin markings likely indicate this is a portrait of a woman. Similar cheek and chin tattooing patterns have been recorded on St. Lawrence Island within the historic period. A charm band circles the crown of the head. Drawing by Kathleen Borowick. Rock Foundation, New York (A8035).

Tattoo "foils," like guardian tattoos, have also been employed by both ancient and more contemporary peoples in the Bering Strait region. Boys and girls were marked by tattoo artists underneath the lip with circles or lunettes, or at both corners of the mouth with angled cruciform elements to disguise the wearer from disease-bearing spirits. Paul Silook explained in the 1940s: "You know some families have the same kind of sickness that continues, and people believed that these marks should be put on a child so the spirits might think he is a different person, a person that is not from that family. In this way, people tried to cut off trouble" (Krutak 2014a:37). Sometimes female shamans, who were also tattooists, applied these kinds of tattoos on the body or affixed other marks that were considered to have medicinal value. Some examples from St. Lawrence Island are as follows: a mark over the sternum, which is the shaman's cure for heart trouble; "a small straight mark over each eye, the cure for eye trouble; various other small marks on the body used as remedies from time to time by the shaman (Anderson and Eells 1935:175); [i]f his head aches always he should have a tattoo in [front] of his ears" (Silook 1917:86).

Two lines placed near the eye of a man from St. Lawrence Island observed by E. W. Nelson in the 1880s represented one of these types of medicinal marking. Such markings also appear on ancient Okvik/Old Bering Sea and Punuk culture ivory carvings depicting men and women from St. Lawrence Island.[16] In the Diomede Islands of the Bering Strait, the ethnologist George B. Gordon (1906:81) observed a man with tattooed marks on both cheeks close to the mouth, others on the temple, and two more on the forehead. These three sets of marks on his face were explained as "medicine" and their presence was said to have directly benefited the wearer.

Other tattoos for men and women, some of which resembled those previously mentioned, marked significant individual or family achievements. In the Diomede Islands and at Point Barrow on Alaska's northernmost land, successful whaleboat captains and harpooners wore facial tattoos comprised of many indistinct lines or dots. These markings either resembled a broad band across each cheek from the corner of the mouth toward the ear or one or two tattooed lines formed by dots that began below the nostrils

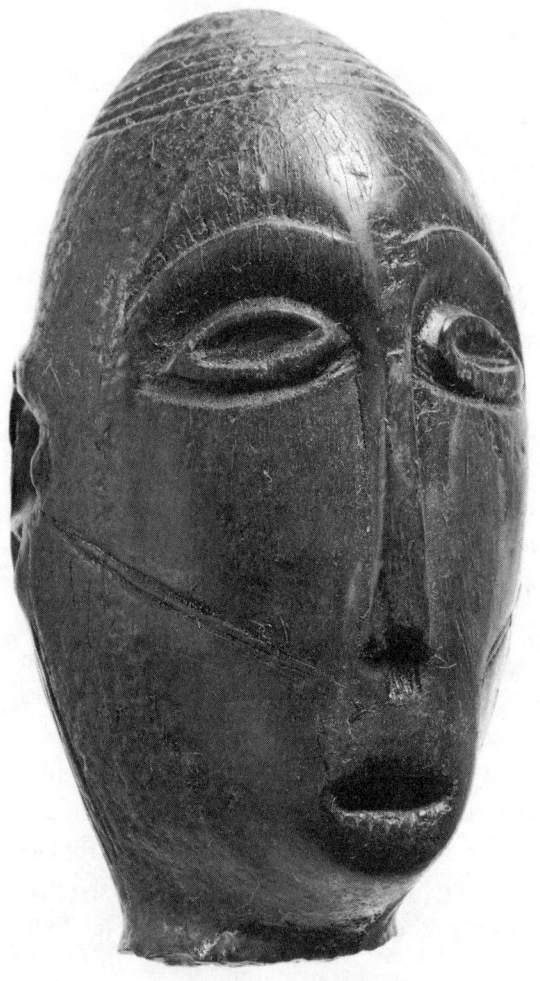

Fig. 18.8. Okvik head with facial tattoos, said to be from one of the Punuk Islands, Bering Sea, Alaska (ca. 100–400 CE). Walrus ivory, H. 7.2 cm. The doll's head with tonsured hair probably represents a great hunter with tattoo tally marks running across the cheeks and under the nose. On the forehead, a series of lines marks the location of his hunting visor. Collection of Perry J. Lewis and Basha Lewis.

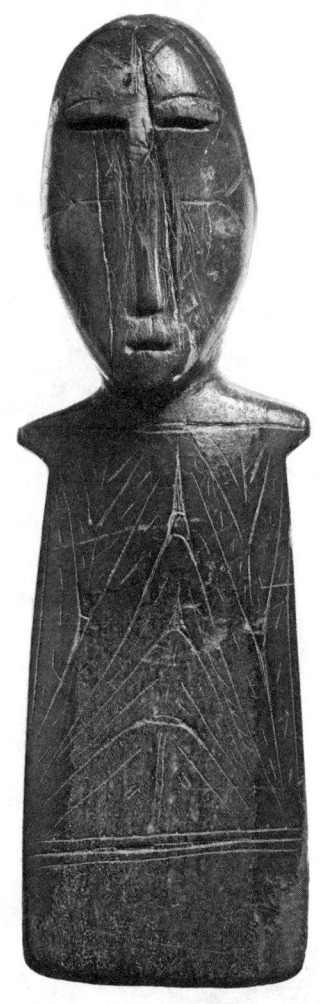

Fig. 18.9. Okvik figure with tattooed fluke tails on cheeks, said to be from one of the Punuk Islands, Bering Sea, Alaska (ca. 100–400 CE). Carved walrus ivory, H. 15.1 cm. Although the spurred lines radiating across the torso may represent an elaborately styled ceremonial outer garment, it is more likely that they signify amulet straps, the waistband of an undergarment, and perhaps tattoos. Princeton University Art Museum, the Lloyd E. Cotsen, Class of 1950, Eskimo Bone and Ivory Carving Collection (1997-106).

and moved upward across each cheek (Bogoras 1904–1909:408; Murdoch 1892:139) (fig. 18.8; see fig. 18.3). In such cases, a new dot or line was added for every whale struck with the harpoon. Barrow whalemen further denoted their hunting prowess with body tattoos in the form of flukes: "[The hunter] Amaiyuna had the 'flukes' of seven whales in a line across his chest, and Mû'ñialu had a couple of small marks on one forearm" (Murdoch 1892:139). Around Bering Strait, both whalemen and the wives or daughters of great whalers were entitled to whale marks or fluke tails near the corners of their mouths (Bogoras 1901:22; Gordon 1906:plate IX),[17] whereas among St. Lawrence Island and Siberian Yupik women facial (cheek) tattoos of whale flukes called *veghaq* reinforced this symbolism (figs. 18.9, 18.10).

Naturalist John Murdoch (1892:139) recorded that at the village of Nuwuk on the end of a point just north of Barrow, Alaska, one man "had a narrow line across the face, over the bridge of the nose . . . [and] he had killed a man." The male tradition of

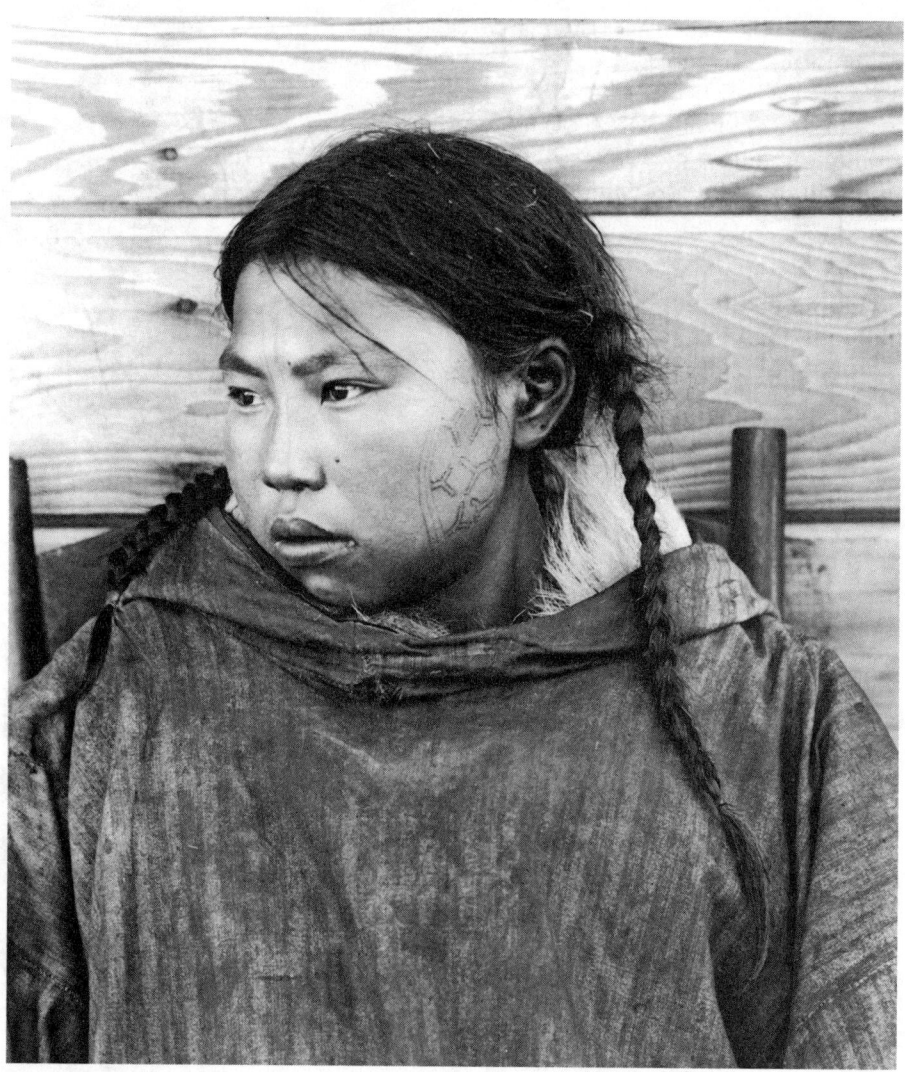

Fig. 18.10. Siberian Yupik girl with fluke-tail tattoos. Bering Strait Eskimo myths tell that the spirit and life force of the whale is a young woman, and facial tattoos of whale flukes, called *veghaq* in Siberian Yupik, reinforced this symbolism; they also commemorated the hunting exploits of male family members. Photograph by Waldemar Bogoras, 1901. Special Collections, American Museum of Natural History, New York (2533).

tattooing over one's nose was common across the Canadian and Alaskan Arctic. In all locations the markings either denoted a successful warrior who had taken human life or an individual who had killed a whale (Krutak 2014a:48–49). Interestingly, each of these types of linear tattooing has been seen adorning the faces of ancient prehistoric doll heads from St. Lawrence Island and Little Diomede Island,[18] demonstrating 2,000 or more years of continuity in tattooing praxis (Krutak 2009:197, 199).

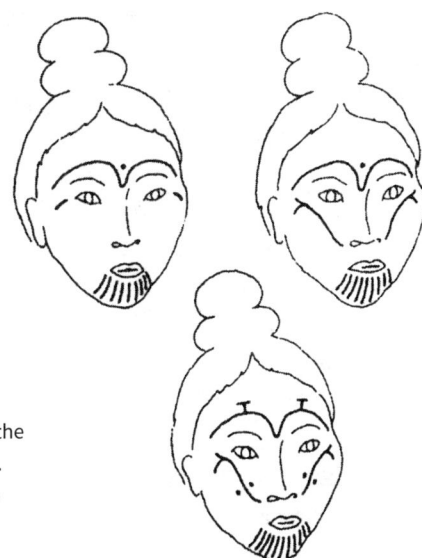

Fig. 18.11. Greenland mummy tattoos. Reconstructions of the Qilakitsoq mummies, West Greenland (fifteenth century CE). A similarly tattooed woman from the Godthaab Fjord region was painted in 1654 and now hangs in the National Museum of Denmark. Drawing by the author.

Many of the heavily tattooed Okvik/Old Bering Sea and Punuk dolls appear to depict women, with their facial markings combining to represent a whale tail. The V-shaped motif appearing on the forehead combined with arching lines moving from the nose upward across the cheek resembles one large whale fluke rising upward from its base on the chin. This iconography also appears in the facial tattoos of Greenlandic and Inuit women of the historic period (fig. 18.11, plate 23). In the Inuit and Greenland regions, mythological tales connect a woman's tattooing to the Sea Goddess or "mistress of marine animals," who controlled the movements of all sea mammals (Krutak 2014a:23). After death it was believed that a woman's soul must pass the house of this deity, and if she were not handsomely tattooed she would be refused passage to the land of "blessed" located in the sky and filled with bounty.[19] Inuk filmmaker Alethea Arnaquq-Baril observed: "If a woman killed an animal, sewed her first pair of boots or a sealskin parka, she was tattooed to commemorate those accomplishments. If you're handsomely tattooed, then obviously you have done many good things in your life and you have a high tolerance to pain, and also an inner strength. [Because] if you quivered or couldn't sit still while being tattooed, then the tattoos would look bad. So having beautiful tattoos represents [many things and] it means you are a mature, strong, good, and ideal woman" (Krutak 2014a:28).

Shaman's Helpers

A final category of human figurine in use around Bering Strait and the Yup'ik region of mainland Alaska in the historic period was the shaman's doll or "helper." On St. Lawrence Island, Geist met several practicing shamans in the 1920s who were freelance spiritualists and the carvers "of the many dolls, idols, [and] fetishes... found in many of the island homes" (Geist and Rainey 1936:34). A shaman usually had one or more helper or "tutelary" spirits "who are men, bird, fish or animals of any kind [but] most are people" carved into human form (Collins n.d.:n.p). St. Lawrence Island shamans "claimed that the [primary] helper was the spirit of some dead person" (Keim 1969:143–44). These powerful objects were regularly fed with tallow, tobacco, and other substances to keep their favor. Across the Yup'ik area of mainland Alaska, helpers were believed to have the ability to speak, walk, cry, and even wear out their clothes as they carried out errands for the shaman (Fienup-Riordan 1995:315; 1996:131–32). They were employed to forecast the future, cure barrenness, retrieve the lost souls of human patients, and fight evil spirits. Helpers were believed to be sentient and human-like, and because they were animated by the spirit of the deceased they were also embodied by a soul or *yua*, "its human being" or "its person." This animated, resident ancestral spirit was envisaged as a little person and was represented as such in ivory or wooden figures from prehistoric to modern times.

The special powers of a shaman's doll helper were derived from the spirit residing within the object, not from the actual item itself. Therefore, it was very important to render these powerful objects realistically through exquisite craftsmanship, and their finely carved nature suggests an extraordinary function. Facial features, personal tattoos, and ceremonial outer garments were carved with precision because ancestral spirits were attracted to and pleased by beautiful things. And if ancient dolls were individual representations of powerful ancestors, then it would have been extremely important to capture their unique portraits. But is there more here than meets the eye?

As previously mentioned, anthropomorphic guardians were attached to the human body via amulet straps, belts, and tattoos. Similarly, many Okvik/Old Bering Sea and Punuk ivory dolls were perforated with suspension holes and probably served similar functions (see perforation beside upper left breast in fig. 18.12). Because of the placement of the holes, some of these objects must have been worn upside down on the neck or body (Wardwell 1986, plate 62, 1992: plate 5; Wolf 2015:35). Inverted figures such as these have been found worldwide and presumably signify a deceased ancestor (Carpenter 2011; Schuster 1970). That is because, as mentioned, death is an inversion of life and the afterworld was turned upside down and inside out.

In addition to the various ways St. Lawrence Island and Siberian Yupik peoples attempted to confuse the spirits of disease through employing tattoo foils that changed their physical appearance, there were, of course, many other traditional practices aimed at disguising one's identity from malevolent forces (Krutak 2009:194, 202), and it is likely that some anthropomorphic charms worn or carried about the body might also have provided this function. From an ideological standpoint they provided their human owner with the appearance, body, or perhaps the soul of a powerful ancestor or helping spirit to confound or help battle disease-bearing and other evil spirits. In this way, an individual who carried a helper figure, or had anthropomorphic *yugaaq*

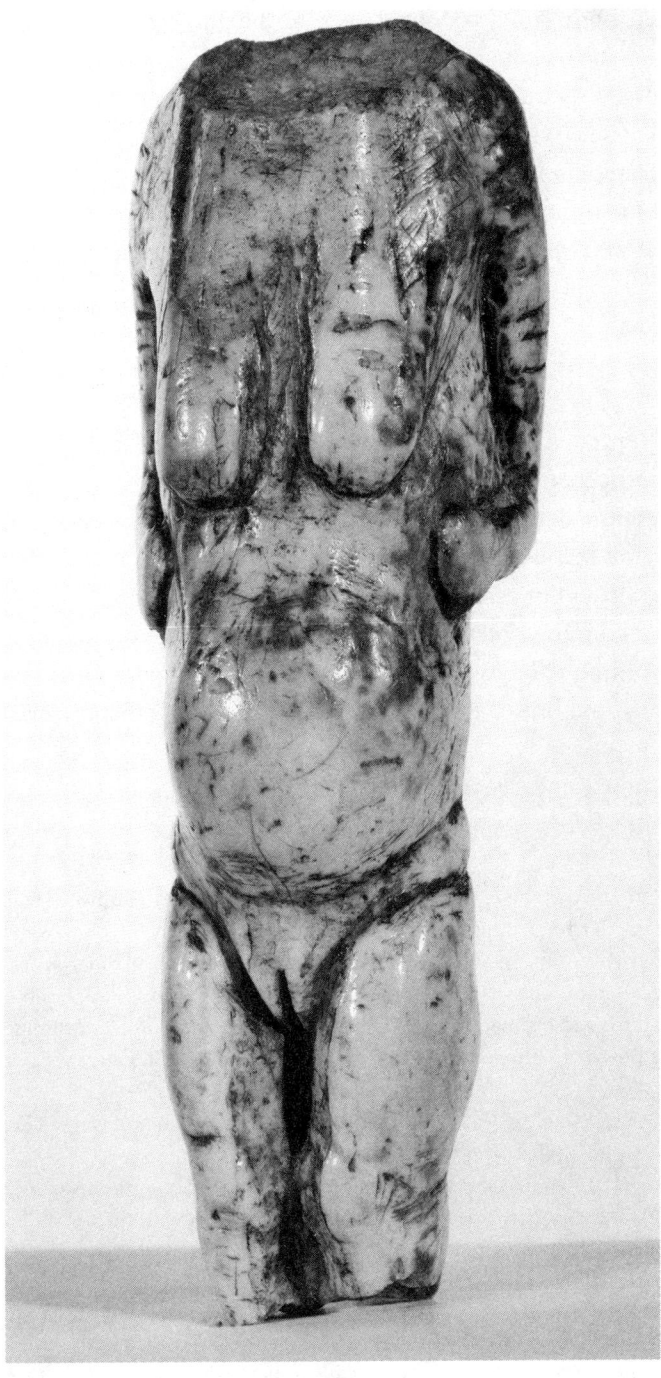

Fig. 18.12. Punuk tattooed figurine, walrus ivory, H. 11.7 cm. Naturalistically carved, this apparently pregnant female object displays arm, shoulder, and breast tattoos. It was excavated off the eastern end of St. Lawrence Island on one of the Punuk Islands in 1928. A perforation above the left breast had been made as if for suspending, perhaps on an amulet strap. Department of Anthropology, National Museum of Natural History, Smithsonian Institution, Washington, D.C. (A244107-0).

tattoos, on their body could become one with the ancestral and other helping spirits though mimicry.

Once the owner of a helper died or the power of the helper was exhausted, it was either discarded on the landscape or otherwise destroyed through ritual dismemberment.[20] Decapitation or breakage was necessary so that the helper could become "whole" again in the afterlife (Tein 1994:119). There it would find renewed use in the world of ancestral spirits who were believed to employ their own family guardian figures to repel evil (Ibid.:121).

Conclusions

Paleo-Eskimo figurative carving and tattooing practices reflect deeply embedded religious beliefs associated with the protection and recycling of life around the Bering Strait. Ethnographic data combined with archaeological and iconographic studies of Okvik/Old Bering Sea and Punuk ivory figures document a rich body of information concerning the ancient interplay of spiritual and ancestral forces from which all life was created, proceeded, and upon which it depended. The functions of tattooed Okvik/Old Bering Sea and Punuk dolls appear to represent a critical component in the process of drawing supernatural power toward the living as well as transporting it for use in the afterlife.

Notes

1. Carpenter (2011); Fitzhugh et al. (2009); Meldgaard (1960); and Wardwell (1986, 1992).
2. These dates are derived from Fitzhugh (2009b:90).
3. "One-without-Arms" or "Armless" was a supernatural character in Siberian Yupik mythology born of a sea goddess and man. Despite his deformities, he manifested the ability to transform people into birds and ordinary objects into sailing vessels, among other things. He also used his amazing powers to kill powerful men in Chukotka and on St. Lawrence Island (Bogoras 1913:421–22).
4. In former times, dogs were also sacrificed and their meat and blood were offered to the spirits. of the air and sea (Hughes 1959:73, 78).
5. St. Lawrence Island whalers did not worship the moon. Rather, "moon worship" refers here to rites in preparation for the whale hunting season that began with the first full moon of winter, usually in late January or early February (Jolles 2002).
6. "Not having fed all the spirits, to go out onto the sea is impossible—the gods are offended and do not wish for good luck. The spirits would drive away all the sea animals from the 'evil' hunter who departs from the established rule" (Hughes 1959:73).
7. St. Lawrence Islander Paul Silook (1940:35) noted that such sacrifices were for "feeding their ancestors' spirits."
8. Paul Silook (1917:n.p.) wrote of clan tattoo designs: "All of the tribes have their [tattooing], except it may be the Siberian woman had different from here. It is said that Kukulik [an extinct village], East Cape, South East Cape and some other part [of St. Lawrence Island] have different tattooing."

9. In Siberia, the feeding of ancestors also took place at old abandoned underground houses or whale jawbone poles that symbolized the spirits of ancient leading clan members (Krupnik and Chlenov 2013:133–34).
10. Inuit (or, Eskimos generally) and St. Lawrence Island Yupiget, in particular, like many other circumpolar peoples, regarded living bodies as inhabited by multiple souls, each soul residing in a particular joint. The ethnologist Edward Weyer (1932:321) observed: "All disease is nothing but the loss of the soul; in every part of the human body there resides a little soul, and if part of the man's body is sick, it is because the little soul had abandoned that part, [namely, the joints]." And if one of these souls is taken away by evil spirits, the member or limb to which it belongs sickens and possibly dies (Bogoras 1904–1909:333).
11. Similarly, all of the houses in the community were circled with human urine or lamp soot to close them down after a funeral, and children were marked upon their faces with apotropaic graphite as a preventative measure.
12. Old Bering Sea artisans also carved ivory human heads in the round. Often a cylindrical hole drilled into the neck of these objects may indicate they were affixed to a staff, charm belt, or other ritual object (Wardwell 1986:68–69, figs. 65, 67).
13. Geist collected one house idol shaped like a mask for the University of Alaska (VanStone 1959:plate 1, fig. 2). This finely carved wooden face hung on the interior wall of a St. Lawrence Island house and was fed whale, walrus, and seal blubber to insure a successful hunt (VanStone 1959:20).
14. This activity can be likened to the "sweeping" or "brushing" away of sickness from the deceased during mortuary rituals.
15. Across the Arctic, women worked as tattooists (Krutak 2014a:30–35).
16. Carpenter (2011:112, fig. 25); Krutak (1998:82, plates 9, 11; 2014a:49, 52); Wardwell (1986:plates 25, 65, 118).
17. Hawkes (1916:107) also illustrated an old Inuit man from Ungava, Canada, with tattooed fluke tails at the corners of his mouth.
18. For examples of prehistoric Old Bering Sea/Okvik objects that have tattoos crossing the bridge of the nose, see Wardwell (1986:47, plates 26, 63, 67).
19. Inuk filmmaker Alethea Arnaquq-Baril interviewed many Inuit elders for her 2010 documentary *Tunniit: Retracing the Lines of Inuit Tattoos*. She recalled the elders telling her: " 'Your tattoos stay with your soul after you die,' so when you pass on you can recognize your family based on the tattoos [they] carried into the afterlife." (Krutak 2014a:28)
20. Iñupiaq elder Jack Ningealook from Shishmaref, Alaska, remembered from his childhood that the shamans "were the only ones that had dolls . . . [i]f the medicine man dies, then they cut off the head of the doll" (Fair 1982:46).

19

A Long Sleep

REAWAKENING TATTOO TRADITIONS IN ALASKA

Lars Krutak

Across the Arctic, the practice of tattooing has been invariably performed by female technicians for over 3,000 years (Krutak 2014a). Typically, expert tattooers were respected women. Their extensive training as skin seamstresses (of parkas, pants, boots, hide boat-covers, etc.) facilitated the need for precision when stitching or pricking human skin for tattoos.

Skin-stitching was the predominant method of tattooing among the Inuit of the Canadian Arctic. However, hand-poking has been documented for St. Lawrence Island, Alaska (Geist 1927–1934c:n.p.), and the Central Inuit region of Canada (Birket-Smith 1945:46, fig. 16; Mathiassen 1928:201, fig. 159). A few historic tattooing instruments from the Central Inuit region of Canada as well as from East Greenland (e.g., the Ammassalik) exist today in museum collections (e.g., American Museum of Natural History, 60/4891 A; Musée du Quai Branly, 71.1930.12.38; Neuchâtel Museum of Ethnography, VI.60). Interestingly, the ethnographic record is strangely silent concerning occurrences of hand-poke tattooing along northern Alaska shores, although the Athabaskan Indian people of Alaska's interior utilized skin-puncturing awls to create tattoos (Osgood 1940:71–73). Despite the paucity of historic evidence for Inuit (Eskimo) hand-poking in Alaska, a prehistoric tattooing-like implement was uncovered in summer 2016 at a Birnirk/early Thule culture house at Cape Espenberg, Alaska (Owen Mason, personal communication, September 14, 2016) (fig. 19.1). This tool, dated to approximately 1100 CE (calibrated), closely resembles historic, in-line hand-poking tattoo tools from East Greenland and the Central Inuit region. The Thule culture is directly ancestral to the

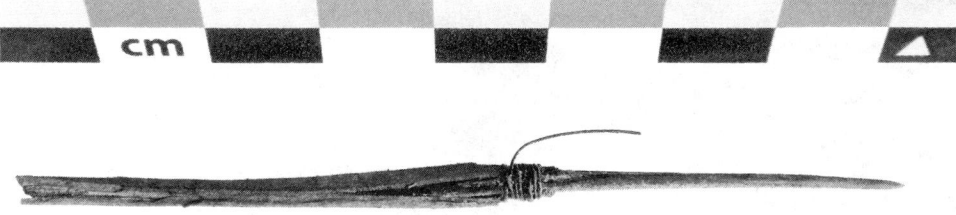

Fig. 19.1. Prehistoric implement, perhaps used for tattooing. Wood handle, baleen lashing, and bone point, L. 8 cm, W. 0.5 cm. This ancient tool, indirectly radiocarbon dated to ca. 1100 CE (calibrated), was uncovered during excavations of a Birnirk/early Thule culture house in 2016 at Cape Espenberg, Alaska. Morphologically speaking (i.e., needle to handle length ratio, overall size), it closely resembles historic in-line hand-poking tattoo tools collected in East Greenland and the Central Inuit region, except for the bone point. If the identification offered is correct, this tattoo tool would represent the oldest known in-line example from the Arctic. Courtesy of Owen Mason (Institute of Arctic, Antarctic and Alpine Research, University of Colorado) and Claire Alix (Université Paris 1, Panthéon Sorbonne). (Inv. Bela 63240 Bela-00143.)

contemporary Iñupiat of northwestern Alaska and the Inuit of Northern Canada (Alix et al. 2015) as well as the Ammassalimniut[1] of East Greenland.

With the arrival of missionaries and government agents in the Northland in the late nineteenth century, Inuit tattooing practices began to fade from view. Traditional religious beliefs and cultural practices were suppressed and children were forcibly removed from their communities to federally operated residential boarding schools in an attempt to assimilate them into the "modern" world. By the turn of the twenty-first century, only a handful of traditionally tattooed elders—all women—remained. Tattooing had not been practiced in some eighty years.

A Contemporary Tattoo Artist

"We have entered a generation of reawakening, we come with energy and eagerness to celebrate and practice our traditions just as our ancestors did so long ago," says contemporary Iñupiaq/Kiowa tattoo artist Marjorie Tahbone. With pigment soaked needles embedded into a hand-poking tool, she methodically plies the wrists of her Yup'ik client Moriah Sallaffie with short pricks, moving back and forth to create ancient designs. Tahbone also applies tattoos through the traditional technique of skin-stitching, which was once practiced across the Arctic (fig. 19.2).

"Stitching hasn't been regularly practiced in Alaska for nearly a century," Tahbone reveals. "When tattooing was still a strong tradition, it was the most skilled seamstresses that performed the tattooing because they would have the straightest lines with the most detail. I figured since I had been sewing since I was four I would naturally pick up the ability to tattoo, and it turns out I did."

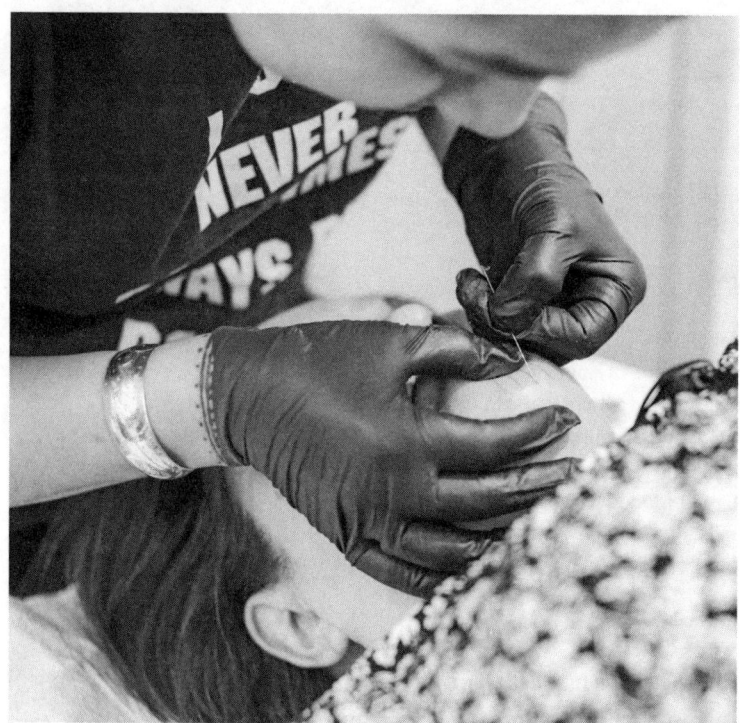

Fig. 19.2. Indigenous tattoo artist Marjorie Tahbone at work in Kugluktuk, Nunavut, Canadian Arctic (2016). Photograph © Little Inuk Photography.

Based in Nome, Alaska, Tahbone is one of only a very few contemporary Native Alaskan artists who have remastered the art of tattooing by hand-poking and skin-stitching. In 2015, she was approached by Filipino-American tattooist Elle Festin (see Krutak, chapter 3, this volume) after he had seen pictures of her facial tattoos on Facebook; those tattoos are hallmarks of womanhood and signify that a person is ready to start a family and be a working member of the community.

"Elle told me, 'You need to become a traditional tattoo artist so you can revitalize something that's been asleep far too long.' So I jumped at the opportunity and flew down to his studio near Los Angeles and learned. At first, I was scared to tattoo because it is permanent and I would be delivering pain to that person. But I realized that this tradition has a purpose, and pain in our culture is part of life. In fact, tattooing helped prepare women for childbirth and other painful experiences in the harsh environment that we lived in."

During Tahbone's visit with Festin, she also received her traditional "birthing tattoos." These are placed on the thighs, and are meant for the next generation (plate 24). "When the child enters this world we want to ensure that the first thing they see is a thing of beauty and they know they are entering a world full of love," Tahbone explains. "My children will enter this world knowing they are loved and already have a strong identity."

After Tahbone received instruction, she began practicing tattooing on her family members. She has completed many more tattoos at cultural events and conferences in Alaska and Nunavut (Canada), and also back home in Nome.

Tahbone's client Moriah Sallafie feels that reviving traditional tattooing practices among Native Alaskans is significant, not only because it bolsters a sense of cultural pride but also because it is healing deep wounds inflicted upon Indigenous communities by outsiders.

Sallafie says, "We have suffered so many traumas as a result of colonization and assimilation. The government and missionaries left absolutely no stone unturned when it came to dismantling our cultures and communities. We have lost so much and in that sense we have so much left to learn. It's both heartbreaking and exciting at the same time. Bringing back practices like skin-stitching helps us heal individually and as a whole."

Tattooing is also a way of reclaiming one's Native identity, Tahbone exclaims. "My goal has always been to strengthen our cultural identity. Because of our recent history of assimilation into Western society, we as Inuit have lost a significant part of ourselves. As a result, our people suffer from abuse, alcoholism, and suicide. Now, when someone receives a traditional tattoo, it heals, it reminds them who they are, where they come from and the strength our people have. The tattoo makes a powerful statement that we are still here and will continue to live and thrive in this world."

Technically speaking, plying human skin with needle and thread is a tedious undertaking and requires much skill and patience. When asked what was the hardest part of being a traditional tattooist, Tahbone replied: "I learned patience from [traditional] skin-sewing and worked hard to create tight, perfect stitches. I knew if I made a mistake, though, I could take the stitch out and redo it. But with tattooing I am unable to do that. As a result, I have to put extra energy and patience into each stitch to make sure my lines are straight, and that makes it difficult. I also find it hard to design the tattoos because I believe in doing original work, but I also need to honor the unique patterns and designs our ancestors left for us. Inuit have been tattooing for thousands of years, and it is difficult to learn and understand all of the meanings and patterns. So I try to build from what I know and what knowledge I gather from elders and through study."

For Tahbone, however, working as a tattoo artist also comes with certain cultural responsibilities. These obligations are self-imposed, but she is committed to tattooing in the most respectful manner possible.

"Tattooing is so much more than lines on skin, because our tattoos have deep cultural meanings related to clans, families, spiritual beliefs, ceremonies, and legends," she says. "My biggest challenge practicing tattooing today is trying to learn a tradition that is so very sacred in a respectful way that does no harm to our people. Cultural appropriation is something that is constantly on my mind and I am trying to remain aware of our cultural values and our Inuit way of life as I stitch and poke the skin."

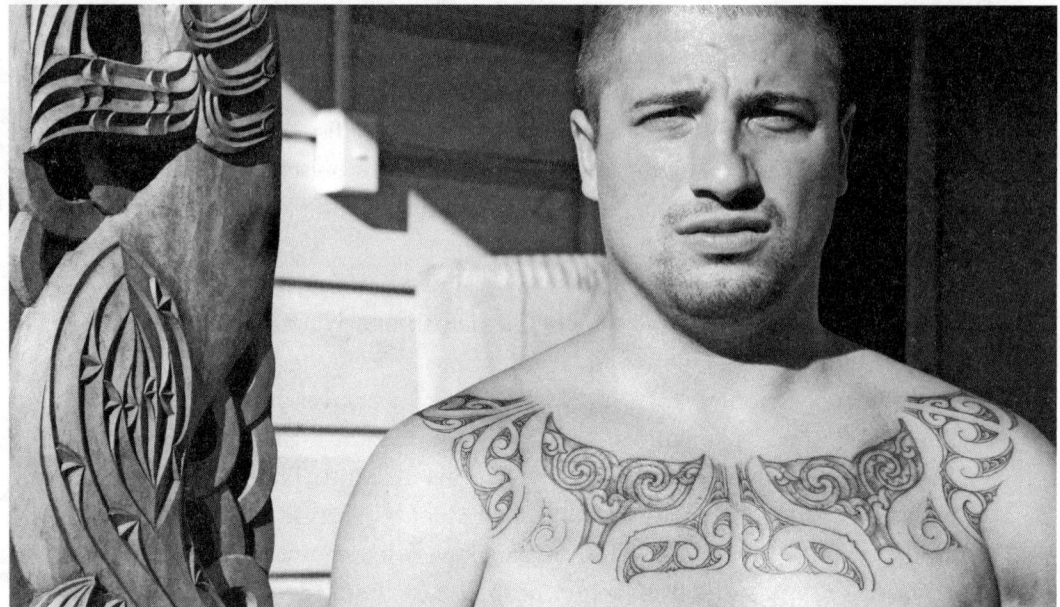

Fig. 19.3. Qaiyaan Harcharek (Iñupiaq) displaying his whale fluke tattoos in Aotearoa, New Zealand (2016). Photograph courtesy of Qaiyaan Harcharek.

"Tattooing illustrates our traditions, spiritual beliefs, communities, and our legends," Tahbone says. "Because it has been so long since tattooing was practiced, there is limited knowledge about it. That makes it challenging to learn and teach others about this tradition, especially in a way that is respectful to our culture and way of life. I have comfort knowing that my ancestors are with me and that I must always be aware of our cultural values so that I can stay on a path that is respectful, encouraging, and healing."

Tahbone continued, "I have learned so much on my journey of being a young, emerging traditional tattoo artist. This is a beautiful tradition and I am excited to learn more about it, and I feel honored to be helping with the revitalization of Inuit tattoos. I want to thank all of the elders who have taken time to teach and explain things to me. I also want to thank my community here in Nome and my family, who have given me a strong foundation and the strength to continue to do what I am doing with traditional tattooing."

An Iñupiaq Whaleman

Five hundred and twenty miles to the north of Nome, Qaiyaan Harcharek is preparing for the whaling season in Barrow, Alaska. Descended from a long line of Iñupiaq whalers, he has chest tattoos that reflect a heritage in which they traditionally served as tally marks counting the number of whales a hunter harpooned (fig. 19.3). In fact, Harcharek's great-great grandfather Amayun (see Krutak, chapter 18, this volume) was similarly tattooed and his hard-earned body markings, consisting of a band of seven whale flukes, were documented by Smithsonian ethnologist John Murdoch (1892) in his book *Ethnological Results of the Point Barrow Expedition*.

Harcharek has been blessed nine times as a harpooner (*kapuqti*) (fig. 19.4) and wears five large tattooed flukes around his neck to honor these accomplishments and the whales that gave themselves to him. The marks also pay tribute to Amayun.

"I harpooned my first whales in 2003 and 2004, and I knew I wanted whales' tails tattooed on me. Around that time I was troubled because I felt part of me was missing. I wasn't a fluent speaker of my language, our tattooing culture had vanished, and so too had many of our traditional beliefs and religious practices. I had a lot of resentment and anger toward the church and their religion, because they attempted to strip us of our language and traditional beliefs, and I highly resented that. I felt a deep emptiness in my soul or *inua* because of this, so I decided to embark on a quest of cultural rediscovery to fill this void of emptiness. I knew receiving a traditional *kakiniq* (tattoo) would help, but there was no one here who could give it to me. So I had to put this idea on hold until I found someone."

Harcharek later attended the University of Alaska to study anthropology and the Iñupiaq language. During his time in Fairbanks, he also traveled to Aotearoa, New Zealand, with a group of Iñupiat elders to investigate cultural and linguistic revitalization efforts among the Maori. Here he met a master wood carver named Mitchell Hughes who offered to tattoo him.

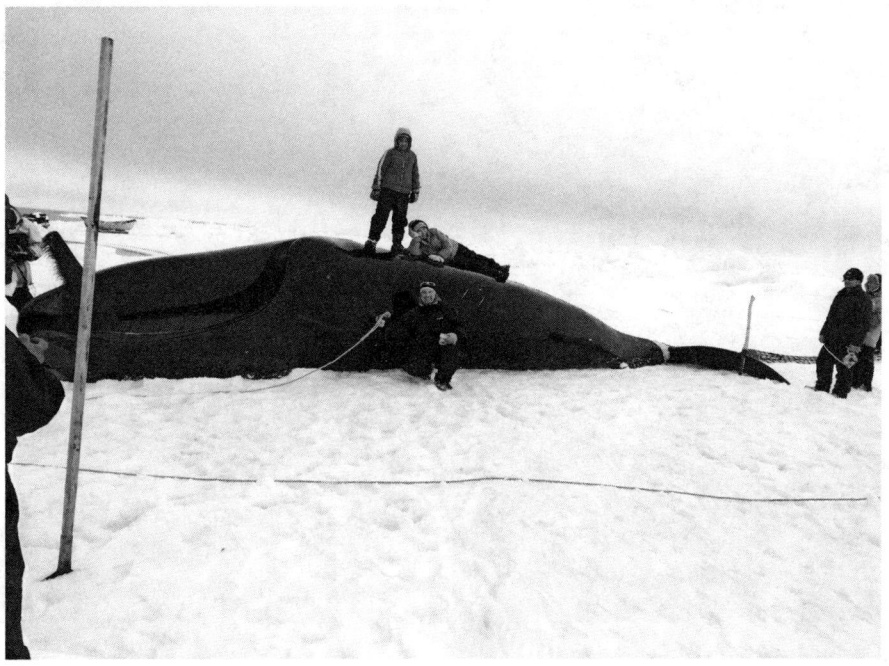

Fig. 19.4. Bowhead whale harpooned by Qaiyaan Harcharek (Iñupiaq) at Barrow, Alaska (April 2016). Photograph courtesy of Qaiyaan Harcharek.

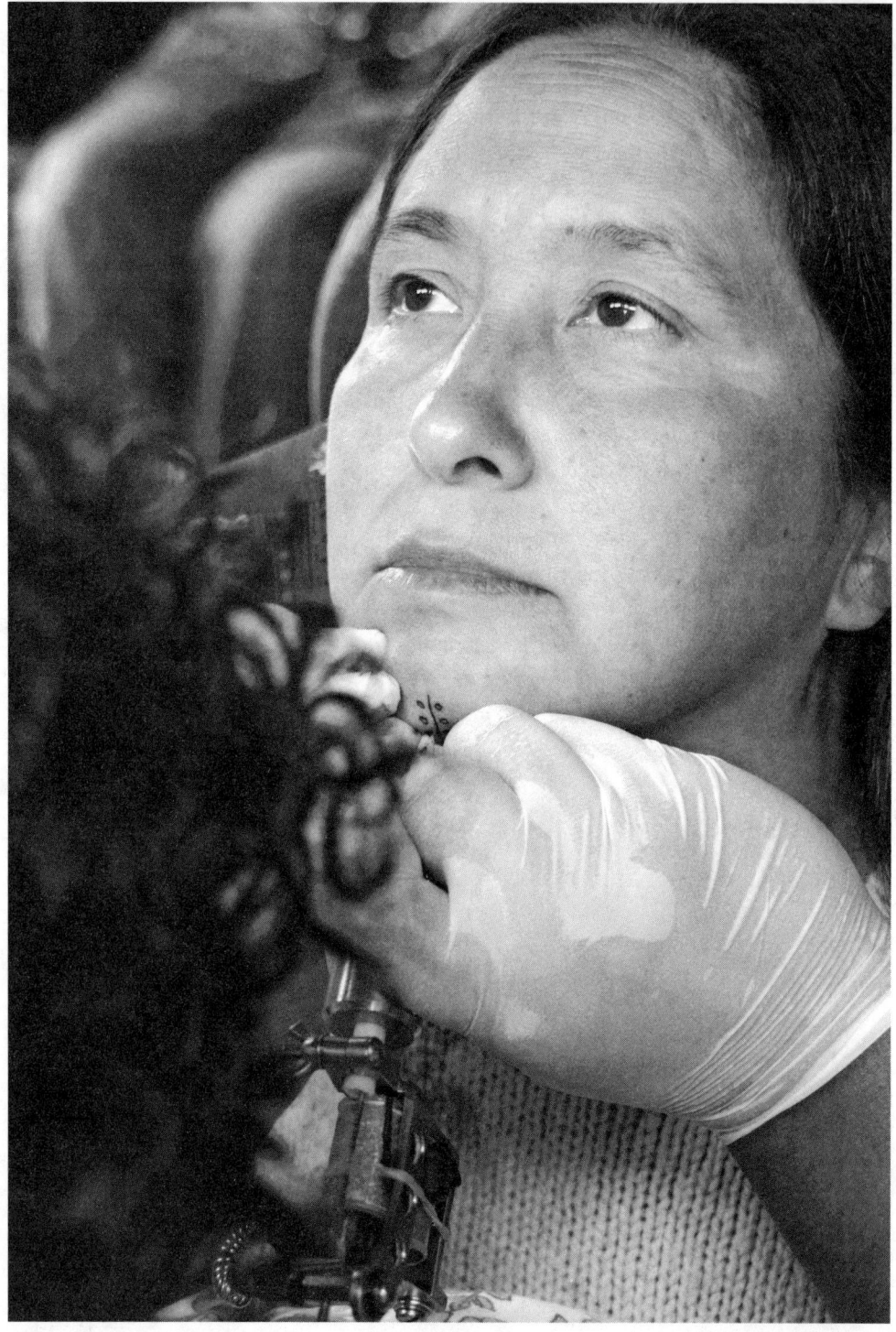

Fig. 19.5. Jana Harcharek receiving her chin tattoo (*tavluġun*) from Maori tattoo artist Mitchell Hughes (2006). Photograph courtesy of Qaiyaan Harcharek.

"I shared my story with Mitch. He wanted to incorporate several Maori design concepts into my tattoo because they were particularly relevant to my personal story. These elements represent growth, the spiral of life and abundance from the ocean, and were incorporated into the two whale flukes I first received."

Harcharek's mother Jana accompanied him to Aotearoa (fig. 19.5). Inspired by the facial tattoo worn by her late grandmother, she asked Hughes to ink a subtle blue stripe encompassed by six small circles on her chin, "to foster pride in who we are in our identity as Iñupiaq people."

Harcharek revisited Aotearoa after subsequent successful whale hunts, adding to his tattooed tally. His wife Jamie was also tattooed by Hughes during the family's past visit to New Zealand, and she bears her very own chin tattoo (*tavluġun*). "The lines on her chin represent the number of whales I harpooned since we have been together, and another line symbolizes the birth of our daughter Aaġluaq. She is being raised with this knowledge and will receive her *tavluġun* once she comes of age."

Since their last trip to see Hughes, four more whales have given themselves to Harcharek. He expects to travel to Aotearoa in the near future to honor their spirits, his ancestors, and family through the receipt of additional tattoos.

Note

1 The inhabitants of Ammassalik also practiced skin-stitching (Holm 1914:29; Thalbitzer 1914:608).

REFERENCES

Agre, Daniela
2011 *The Tumulus of Golyamata Mogila near the Villages of Malomirovo and Zlatinitsa.* Avalon, Sofia.
2015 Cat. 59 Premier ensemble d'appliques et d'accessoires de harnachement [Catalog 59: first set of ornaments and harness accessories]. In *L'épopée des rois thraces: Des guerres médiques aux invasions celtes, 479–278 av. J.-C.: Découvertes archéologiques en Bulgarie* [The epic of the Thracian kings: The Persian wars to the Celtic invasions, 479 BC–278 AD: Archaeological finds in Bulgaria], ed. Jean-Luc Martinez, Alexandre Baralis, Néguine Mathieux, Totko Stoyanov, and Milena Tonkova, 98–99. Somogy éditions d'art, Paris.

Airvaux, Jean
2001 *L'art préhistorique du Poitou-Charentes: Sculptures et gravures des temps glaciaires* [Prehistoric art of Poitou-Charentes: Ice age sculptures and engravings]. La Maison des roches, Paris.

Alejo-Hila, Ma. Corazon A., Mitzie Marie Aguilar-Reyes, and Anita B. Feleo
2008 *Barong: Garment of Honor, Garment of Identity.* EN Barong, Quezon City.

Alekseev, Andrey Yu, Nikolai A. Bokovenko, S. S. Vasiliev, V. A. Dergachev, Ganna I. Zaitseva, N. N. Kovaliukh, G. Cook, J. van der Plicht, G. Possnert, A. A. Sementsov, E. Marian Scott, and Konstantin V. Chugunov (eds.)
2005 *Evrazia v skifskuju epokhu: radiouglerodnaya i arkheologicheskaja khronologia* [Eurasia in Scythian time: Radiocarbon and archaeological chronology]. THESA, Saint Petersburg.

Alix, Claire, Owen K. Mason, Nancy H. Bigelow, Shelby L. Anderson, Jeffrey Rasic, and John F. Hoffecker
2015 Archéologie du Cap Espenberg où la question du Birnirk et de l'origine du Thulé dans le nord-ouest de l'Alaska [Archeology of Cape Espenberg and the question of Birnirk and the origin of Thule in Northwestern Alaska]. *Archéologie boréale* [Boreal archeology] 41:13–19.

Allen, Melinda
2014 Marquesan Colonisation Chronologies and Post-Colonisation Interaction: Implications for Hawaiian Origins and the "Marquesan Homeland" Hypothesis. *Journal of Pacific Archaeology* 5(2):1–17.

Allen, Tricia
2006 *Tattoo Traditions of Hawai'i.* Mutual Publications, Honolulu, Hawai'i.

Alvrus, Annalisa, David Wright, and Charles F. Merbs
2001 Examination of Tattoos on Mummified Tissue Using Infra-Red Reflectography. *Journal of Archaeological Science* 28(4):395–400.

Ambrose, Wal
2007 The Implements of Lapita Ceramic Stamped Ornamentation. In *Oceanic Explorations: Lapita and Western Pacific Settlement*, ed. Stuart Bedford, Christophe Sand, and S. P. Connaughton, 213–21. Terra Australis 26, ANU E Press, Canberra.
2012 Oceanic Tattooing and the Implied Lapita Ceramic Connection. *Journal of Pacific Archaeology* 3(1):1–21.

Anales del Museo Nacional de Antropología
- 1998 *Nosotros: Numero 5* [Us: Issue 5]. Edición dirigida y coordinada por Concha Mora Postigo. Ministerio de Educacion, Dirección General de Bellas Artes y de Conservación y Restauración de Bienes Culturales, Madrid.

Anderson, Atholl
- 2014 Ancient Origins, 3000 B.C.–A.D. 1300. In *Tangata Whenua, an Illustrated History,* ed. Atholl Anderson, J. Binney, A. Harris, 16–41. Bridget Williams Books, Wellington.

Anderson, Atholl, John Chappell, Michael Gagan, and Richard Grove
- 2006 Prehistoric Maritime Migration in the Pacific Islands: An Hypothesis of ENSO Forcing. *The Holocene* 16:1–6.

Anderson, Atholl, and Rod Wallace
- 1993 The Chronology of Mount Camel Archaic Site, Northland, New Zealand. *New Zealand Journal of Archaeology* 15:5–16.

Anderson, Atholl, and Yosihiko Sinoto
- 2002 New Radiocarbon Ages of Colonization Sites in East Polynesia. *Asian Perspectives* 41(2):242–57.

Anderson, David A.
- 2011 Evidence for Early Ritual Activity in the Predynastic Settlement at el-Mahâsna. In *Egypt at Its Origins 3: Proceedings of the Third Iternational Conference "Origins of the State, Predynastic and Early Dynastic Egypt." London, 27 July–1 August, 2008,* ed. Renée Friedman and Peter N. Fiske, 3–29. Orientalia Lovaniensia Analecta 205, Peeters, Leuven.

Anderson, H. Dewey, and Walter C. Eells
- 1935 *Alaska Natives: A Survey of Their Sociological and Educational Status.* Stanford University Press, Stanford, California.

Angel, Gemma
- 2012 The Tattoo Collectors: Inscribing Criminality in Late Nineteenth-Century France. *Bildwelten des Wissens* [Visual Worlds of Knowledge] 9(1):2–38. Akademie Verlag, Berlin.
- 2013 In the Skin: An Ethnographic-Historical Approach to a Museum Collection of Preserved Tattoos. PhD dissertation, History of Art Department, University College, London.
- 2015 Roses and Daggers: Expressions of Emotional Pain and Devotion in Nineteenth-Century Tattoos. In *Probing the Skin. Cultural Representations of Our Contact Zone,* ed. Caroline Rosenthal and Dirk Vanderbeke, 211–38. Cambridge Scholars Publishing, Newcastle upon Tyne.

Anonymous
- 1887 *Catálogo de la Exposición General de las Islas Filipinas 1887* [Catalog of the general exposition of the Philippine Islands 1887]. Ricardo Fé, Madrid.

Antoine, Daniel, and Janet Ambers
- 2014 The Scientific Analysis of Human Remains from the British Museum Collection: Research Potential and Examples from the Nile Valley. In *Regarding the Dead: Human Remains in the British Museum,* ed. Alexandra Fletcher, Daniel Antoine, and J. D. Hill, 20–30. British Museum Press, London.

Apangalook, John
- 1985 Traditional Sacrificial Ceremonies. In *Sivuqam Nangaghnegha: Sivanllemta Ungipaqellghat* [Lore of St. Lawrence Island: Echoes of our Eskimo elders], vol. 1: Gambell, ed. Anders Apassingok, Willis Walunga, and Edward Tennant, 204–9. Bering Strait School District, Unalakleet, Alaska.

Apassingok, Anders, Willis Walunga, and Edward Tennant (eds.)
- 1985 *Sivuqam Nangaghnegha: Sivanllemta Ungipaqellghat* [Lore of St. Lawrence Island: Echoes of our Eskimo elders], vol. 1: Gambell. Bering Strait School District, Unalakleet, Alaska.

Arbore Popescu, Grigore, Yuri Piotrovskii, and Andrey Alekseev (eds.)
2001   *Siberia: Gli uomini dei fiumi ghiacciati* [Siberia: The men of the frozen rivers]. Trieste Scuderie del Castello di Miramare, 5 Marzo–29 luglio 2001, Milano.

Argent, Gala
2013   Inked: Human-Horse Apprenticeship, Tattoos, and Time in the Pazyryk World. *Society & Animals* 21:178–93.

Armelagos, George J.
1969   Disease in Ancient Nubia. *Science* 163(3864):255–59.

Aromin, Federico
1985   Preservation of Kabayan Mummies. Report on file, National Museum of the Philippines, Manila.

Aruz, Joan, Ann Farkas, Andrei Alekseev, and Elena Korolkova (eds.)
2000   *The Golden Deer of Eurasia: Scythian and Sarmatian Treasures from the Russian Steppes.* The State Hermitage and Metropolitan Museum of Art, Saint Petersburg and New York.

Atakuman, Çiğdem
2015   From Monuments to Miniatures: Emergence of Stamps and Related Image-Bearing Objects during the Neolithic. *Cambridge Archaeological Journal* 25(4):759–88.

Atanasova, Ilinka
2011   Anthropomorphic Cult Figurines from the Eneolithic Sanctuary Near v. Spančevo in the Kočani Region. In *The Golden Fifth Millennium: Thrace and Its Neighbour Areas in the Chalcolithic,* ed. Yavor Boyadzhiev and Stoilka Terzijska-Ignatova, 225–37. Proceedings of the International Symposium in Pazardzhik, Yundola, 26–30 October 2009. NIAM-BAS, Sofia.

Audoin, Frédérique, and Hugues Plisson
1982   Les ocres et leurs témoins au Paléolithique en France: Enquête et expériences sur leur validité archéologique [Ochres and their associated evidence during the French paleolithic: Investigation and experiments on their archaeological validity]. *Cahiers du Centre de Recherches Préhistoriques de Paris* [Handbooks of the Paris Center for Prehistoric Research] 8:33–80.

Aufderheide, Arthur C.
2003   *The Scientific Study of Mummies.* Cambridge University Press, Cambridge.

Aufderheide, Arthur C. (ed.)
2009   *Overmodeled Skulls.* Feline Press, Gainesville, Florida.

Avon, S. L., and R. E. Wood
2005   Porcine Skin as an In Vivo Model for Ageing of Human Bite Marks. *The Journal of Forensic Odonto-Stomatology* 23(2):30–39.

Bacus, Elisabeth
2002   The Archaeology of the Philippine Archipelago. In *Southeast Asia: From Prehistory to History,* ed. I. Glover and P. Bellwood, 25–281. Routledge-Curzon, London.

Baduel, Nathalie
2008   Tegumentary Paint and Cosmetic Palettes in Predynastic Egypt: Impact of Those Artefacts on the Birth of the Monarchy. In *Egypt at its Origins 2. Proceedings of the International Conference "Origins of the State. Predynastic and Early Dynastic Egypt," Toulouse (France), 5–8 September 2005,* ed. Béatrix Midant-Reynes and Yann Tristant, 1057–1090. Orientalia Lovaniensia Analecta 172, Peeters, Leuven.

Bagamaspad, Anavic, and Zenaida Hamada-Pawid
1985   *A Peoples' History of Benguet Province.* Provincial Government of Benguet, Benguet.

Bailey, Douglass W.
1994   Reading Prehistoric Figurines as Individuals. *World Archaeology* 25(3):321–31.

1999   What is a Tell? Settlement in Fifth Millennium Bulgaria. In *Making Places in the Prehistoric World: Themes in Settlement Archaeology*, ed. Joanna Bruck and Melissa Goodman, 94–111. University College of London Press, London.

2005   *Prehistoric Figurines: Representation and Corporeality in the Neolithic*. Oxon and Routledge, New York and London.

2010   The Figurines of Old Europe. In *The Lost World of Old Europe: The Danube Valley, 5000–3500 BC*, ed. David W. Anthony, 113–28. Princeton University Press, Princeton and Oxford.

Baretto, Grace

2002   *Research among the Mummies in Kabayan*. Report on file, National Museum of the Philippines, Manila.

Barkova, Ludmila

2014   *Fantasticheskie zveri na tatuirovkakh altaiskogo vozhdja: 250 istorij pro Ermitazh: 'Sobranje pestrykh glav. . .'* [Fantastic animals in the tattoos of the Altai chieftain: 250 Stories about The Hermitage]. V 5 knigakh [In 5 books. Book] III:98–101. Saint Petersburg.

Barkova, Ludmila, and Ilia Gokhman

2001   Eschjo raz o mumijah cheloveka iz Pazyrykskikh kurganov [One more time about the human mummies from the Pazyryk mounds]. *Archeologicheski Sbornik Gosudarstvennogo Ermitazha* [Archaeological collection of articles of the State Hermitage] 35:78–90. Saint Petersburg.

Barkova, Ludmila L., and Svetlana V. Pankova

2005   Tatuirovki na mumiyakh iz bolshikh Pazirikskikh kurganov (novie materiali) [Tattoos on mummies from the large Pazyryk kurgans: New materials]. *Arkheologia, etnographia i antro* [Archaeology, ethnography and anthropology of Eurasia] 2(22):48–59. Institute of Archaeology and Ethnology, Novosibirsk.

2006   Tatuirovki na mumijakh iz Pazyrykskikh kurganov v infrakrasnykh luchakh [Tattoos on the mummies from the Pazyryk burial mounds in the Infrared rays]. *Vestnik istorii, literatuty, iskusstva* [Bulletin of history, literature and art]. Tom 3:31–42. Moscow.

Beardsley, Felicia

1996   Bone Tool Technology on Easter Island. *Rapa Nui Journal* 10(4):77–80.

Beckett, Ronald G.

2013   Report AA100391. Accelerator Mass Spectrometry Laboratory, University of Arizona, Tucson.

Beckett, Ronald G., Ulla Lohmann, and Josh Bernstein

2011   A Field Report on the Mummification Practices of the Anga of Koke Village, Central Highlands, Papua New Guinea. *Yearbook of Mummy Studies* 1:11–17.

Bedford, Stuart

2015   Going Beyond the Known World 3000 Years Ago: Lapita Exploration and Colonisation of Remote Oceania. In *The Lapita Cultural Complex in Time and Space: Expansion Routes, Chronologies and Typologies*, ed. Christophe Sand, Scarlett Chiu, and Nicholas Hogg, 25–47. Archeologia Pasifika 4, Institut d'archéologie de la Nouvelle-Calédonie et du Pacifique, Nouméa, New Caledonia.

Benecke, Norbert

2001   Die Tierwelt Thrakiens im Mittelholozän (ca. 6000–2000 v. Chr.): Anthropogene und Natürliche Komponenten [The wildlife of Thrace in the mid-Holocene (ca. 6000–2000 BC): Anthropogenic and natural components]. In *Beiträge zur Archäologie und Prähistorischen Anthropologie, Band III*. [Contributions to archaeology and prehistoric anthropology, vol. III], eds. Eberhard May and Norbert Benecke, 29–38. Wais & Partner, Stuttgart.

Benecke, Norbert, Svend Hansen, and Dirk Nowacki
2013 Pietrele in the Lower Danube Region: Integrating Archaeological, Faunal and Environmental Investigations. *Documenta Praehistorica* 40:175–93.

Berchon, Ernest
1869 *Histoire Medicale du Tatouage* [Medical history of tattoos]. Baillère, Paris.

Berciu, Dumitru
1971 *Das Thrako-Getische Fürstengrab von Agighiol in Rumänien* [The Thraco-Getic prince's grave of Agighiol in Romania]. Gruyter, Berlin.

Bertholon, Lucien
1904 Origines néolithique et mycénienne des tatouages des indigènes du nord de l'Afrique [Neolithic and Mycenaean Origins of Indigenous North African Tattooing]. *Archives d'Anthropologie criminelle, de médecine légale et de psychologie normale et pathologique* [Archives of criminal anthropology, forensic medicine and normal and pathological psychology] (19):756–86

Best, Elsdon
1904 The Uhi-Maori, or Native Tattooing Instruments. *Journal of the Polynesian Society* 13:166–72.

Beyer, H. Otley
1947 Outline Review of Philippine Archaeology by Islands and Provinces. Bureau of Printing, Manila.

Bezu, Judith van
2013 De Tatoeage als Erfgoed: Een Onderzoek naar Aspecten die van Belang zijn bij het Verzamelen van Getatoeeerde Huiden ten Behoeve van Museumcollecties [The Tattoo as Heritage: A study on the Issues of Collecting Tattooed Skins for Museum Collections]. Bachelor's thesis, Reinwardt Academy, Amsterdam.

Bianchi, Robert S.
1988 Tattoo in Ancient Egypt. In *Marks of Civilization: Artistic Transformation of the Human Body*, ed. Arnold Rubin, 21–28. University of California, Los Angeles.

Birket-Smith, Kaj
1945 Ethnographical Collections from the Northwest Passage. Translated by W. E. Calvert. *Report of the Fifth Thule Expedition, 1921–24*, vol. 6(2). Gyldendalske Boghandel, Nordisk Forlag, Copenhagen.

Blassi, Lincoln
1985 Remembrance Rituals for Our Forefathers. In *Sivuqam Nangaghnegha: Sivanllemta Ungipaqellghat* [*Lore of St. Lawrence Island: Echoes of Our Eskimo Elders*], vol. 1: Gambell, ed. Anders Apassingok, Willis Walunga, and Edward Tennant, 242–45. Bering Strait School District, Unalakleet, Alaska.

Blust, Robert
2011 The Problem of Doubletting in Austronesian Languages. *Oceanic Linguistics* 50(2):399–57.

Blust, Robert, and Stephen Trussel
2012 *The Austronesian Comparative Dictionary.* www.trussel2.com/ACD/, accessed April 4, 2012.

Boghian, Dumitru D.
2010 Les Marquages Corporels Chez les Communautés Néolithiques et Énéolithiques Carpato Danubiennes (I) [Body markings in the Neolithic and Eneolithic communities of the danubian Carpathians, vol. 1]. *Codrul Cosminului* 16(1):5–20.

Boghian, Dumitru D., Sergiu-Constantin Enear, and Ciprian-Cătălin Lazanu
2014 The Anthropomorphic Plastic of Cucuteni A3 Site from Tăcuta (Vaslui County). In *Anthropomorphism and Symbolic Behavior in the Neolithic and Copper Age Communities of South-Eastern Europe*, ed. Constantin-Emil Ursu and Stanislav Țerna, 415–34. K. A. Romstorfer, Suceava.

Bogoras, Waldemar

1901 Notes on the Asiatic Eskimo. W. Bogoras Papers, MssCol 328, Box 131-F-4, Fldr. E 1.1. New York Public Library, New York.

1904–1909 *The Chukchee*. 3 vols. The Jesup North Pacific Expedition, vol. 7, parts 1–3, ed. Franz Boas. Memoirs of the American Museum of Natural History, vol. 11. Brill, Leiden.

1913 *The Eskimo of Siberia*. The Jesup North Pacific Expedition, vol. 8, part 3, ed. Franz Boas. Memoirs of the American Museum of Natural History, vol. 12. Brill, Leiden.

Bonin, "Jolicoeur" Charles

1887 *Voyage au Canada, dans le nord de l'Amerique Septentrionale, depuis l'an 1751–1761, par J.C.B.* [Trip to Canada, to the north of Dutch America, during the years 1751–1761 by J.C.B.]. Abbe H. R. Casgrain, Quebec.

Bosinski, Gerhard, Francesco D'errico, and Petra Schiller

2001 *Die gravierten Frauendarstellungen von Gönnersdorf* [The engraved depictions of women from Gönnersdorf]. F. Steiner, Stuttgart.

Bossu, Jean Bernard

1768 *Nouveaux Voyages aux Indes Occidentales* [New journeys to the West Indies]. vol. II. Chez Le Jay, Paris.

Boudreaux, Edmond A.

2005 The Archaeology of Town Creek: Chronology, Community Patterns, and Leadership at a Mississippian Town. PhD dissertation, Department of Anthropology, University of North Carolina at Chapel Hill.

Boyadzhiev, Kamen

2011 Development and Distribution of Close Combat Weapons in Bulgarian Chalcolithic. In *Festschrift for Marion Lichardus-Itten* [Essays in honor of Marion Lichardus-Itten], ed. Vassil Nikolov, Krum Bacvarov, and Maria Gurova, 265–82. Studia Praehistorica, 14. National Institute of Archaeology and Museum, BAS, Sofia.

Bréhard, Stéphanie, and Adrian Bălăşescu

2012 What's Behind the Tell Phenomenon? An Archaeozoological Approach of Eneolithic Sites in Romania. *Journal of Archaeological Science* 39(10):3167–83.

Bréhard, Stéphanie, Valentin Radu, and Alexis Martin

2014 Food Supply Strategies in the Romanian Eneolithic: Sheep/Goat Husbandry and Fishing Activities from Hârşova Tell and Borduşani-Popină (5th Millennium B.C.). *European Journal of Archaeology* 17(3):407–33.

Breuil, Henri

1907 Étude sur les œuvres d'art de Laugerie Basse [A study of the works of art from Laugerie Basse]. *L'Anthropologie* [Anthropology] 18:10–36.

Brewster, Adolph B.

1922 *The Hill Tribes of Fiji*. J. B. Lipincott Company, Philadelphia.

Brilot, Madeline (ed.)

2004 *Tatu-Tattoo!* Musees Royaux d'Art et d'Histoire, Brussels.

Brunton, Guy, and Gertrude Caton-Thompson

1928 *The Badarian Civlization and the Predynastic Remains near Badari*. Egyptian Research Account and British School of Archaeology in Egypt, London.

Buc, Natacha

2011 Experimental Series and Use-Wear in Bone Tools. *Journal of Archaeological Science* 38:546–57.

Budge, E. A. Wallis

1920 *By Nile and Tigris: A Narrative of Journeys in Egypt and Mesopotamia on Behalf of the British Museum Between the Years 1886 and 1913*. John Murray, London.

Bunker, Emma
1992   Significant Changes in Iconography and Technology among Ancient China's Northwestern Pastoral Neighbors from the Fourth to the First Century B.C. *Bulletin of the Asia Institute* 6:99–115.

Burchett, George and Peter Leighton
1958   *Memoirs of a Tattooist.* Crown Publishers, New York and Norwich.

Buswell, James O., III
1972   Florida Seminole Religious Ritual: Resistance and Change. PhD dissertation, Department of Anthropology, Saint Louis University, St. Louis, Missouri.

Byrd, Julia C.
2011   Archaic Bone Tools in the St. Johns River Basin, Florida: Microwear and Manufacture Traces. Master's thesis, Department of Anthropology, Florida State University, Tallahassee.

Byrne, Denis
2007   *Surface Collection: Archaeological Travels in Southeast Asia.* AltaMira Press, Lantham, Maryland.

Caneva, Isabella (ed.)
1988   *El Geili: The History of a Middle Nile Environment 7000 BC–AD 1500.* BAR International Series 424, Oxford.

Cantwell, John C.
1902   *Report of the U.S. Steamer Nunivak on the Yukon River Station, Alaska, 1899–1901.* U.S. Government Printing Office, Washington, DC.

Caplan, Jane
1997   Speaking Scars: The Tattoo in Popular Practice and Medico-Legal Debate in Nineteenth-Century Europe. *History Workshop Journal* 44:106–42.

Capron, Louis
1953   *The Medicine Bundles of the Florida Seminole and the Green Corn Dance.* Anthropological Papers, No. 35. Bureau of American Ethnology Bulletin 151, 155–210. U.S. Government Printing Office, Washington, DC.

Cardin, Matt
2014   *Mummies Around the World: An Encyclopedia of Mummies in History, Religion, and Popular Culture.* ABC Clio, Santa Barbara, California.

Carpenter, Edmund
2011   *Upside Down: Arctic Realities.* Menil Foundation and Yale University Press, Houston and New Haven.

Casal, Gabriel
1998   *Kasaysayan, the Story of the Filipino People: The Earliest Filipinos*, vol 2. Asia Publishing Company, Manila, Philippines, and Pleasantville, New York.

Casson, Lionel and Ivan Venedikov
1977   *The Thracians*, vol.1. *Bulletin of the Metropolitan Museum of Art* 35. Metropolitan Museum of Art, New York.

Chamay, Jacques (ed.)
1993   *L'art des peuples italiques, 3000 à 300 avant J.-C.* [Art of the Italian peoples, 3000 to 300 BC]. *Collections suisses exhibition* [Swiss collections exhibition], Genève, Musée Rath, 6 nov. 1993–13 février 1994 [Geneva, Rath Museum, November 6,1993–February 13, 1994]; Paris, Mona Bismarck Foundation, 1 mars–30 avril 1994. Hellas et Roma and Electa Napoli, Geneva and Naples.

Chamay, Jacques, and Chantal Courtois (eds.)
- 2002 *L'art premier des Iapyges: Céramique antique d'Italie méridionale* [Tribal art of the Yapigeans: Antique ceramics of southern Italy]. Exposition, Genève, Musée d'art et d'histoire, 22 octobre 2002–19 juin 2003; Paris, Mona Bismarck Foundation, 5 février–5 avril 2003 [Exhibition, Geneva, Museum of Art and History, October 22, 2002–June 19, 2003; Paris, Mona Bismarck Foundation, February 5–April 5, 2003. Hellas et Roma 11, Electa Napoli, Naples.

Chaussonnet, Valérie
- 1989 Needles and Animals: Women's Magic. In *Crossroads of Continents: Cultures of Siberia and Alaska,* ed. William W. Fitzhugh and Aron Crowell, 209–26. Smithsonian Institution Press, Washington, DC.

Cheremisin, Dmitry V.
- 2008 *Iskusstvo zverinogo stilja v pogrebalnykh kompleksah rjadovogo naselenija pazyrykskoj kultury* [Art of the animal style in sepulchral complexes of the ordinary people of the Pazyryk culture]. Institute of Archaeology and Ethnology, Novosibirsk.

Cheynier, André
- 1931 Pointes à piquer [Puncturing pointed tools]. *Bulletin de la Société préhistorique française* [Bulletin of the French prehistoric society] 28(11):486–88.

Chikisheva, Tatjana N.
- 2003 Paleodemograficheskaja kharakteristika naselenija pazyrykskoi kuljtury [Paleodemographic characteristic of the Pazyryk culture population]. In *Naselenie Gornogo Ataja v epokhu rannego zheleznogo veka kak etnokuljturny phenomen: proiskhozhdenie, genezis, istoricheskie sudjby (po dannym arkheologii, antropologii, genetiki)* [Population of the Altai Mountains in the time of the early Iron Age as ethnocultural phenomena: Emergence, genesis, historical destinies (according to archaeological, anthropological, genetic data)], 73–82. Institute of Archaeology and Ethnology, Novosibirsk.

Chirino, Pedro
- 1969 *Relación de las Islas Filipinas* [The Philippines in 1600]. Historical Conservation Society XV, translated by R. Echevarria. Historical Conservation Society, Manila.

Churcher, Charles S.
- 1984 Zoological Study of the Ivory Knife Handle from Abu Zaidan. In *Predynastic and Archaic Egypt in the Brooklyn Museum*, ed. Winifred Needler, 152–68. Wilbour Monographs 9. Brooklyn Museum, Brooklyn.

Clark, Geoffrey
- 2014 Micronesia. In *The Cambridge World Prehistory, vol. 1: Africa, South and Southeast Asia, and the Pacific*, ed. Colin Renfrew and Paul Bahn, 614–21. Cambridge University Press, New York.

Coe, Joffre L.
- 1952 The Cultural Sequence of the North Carolina Piedmont. In *Archaeology of the Eastern United States*, ed. James B. Griffin, 301–11. University of Chicago Press, Chicago.
- 1995 *Town Creek Indian Mound: A Native American Legacy*. University of North Carolina Press, Chapel Hill.

Collins, Henry B.
- n.d. St. Lawrence Island Notes on Miscellaneous Ethnological Data . . . Field Notes from the H. B. Collins Collection, Box 108. National Anthropological Archives, Smithsonian Institution, Suitland, Maryland.
- 1929 *Prehistoric Art of the Alaskan Eskimo*. Smithsonian Miscellaneous Collections 81, no. 14. Smithsonian Institution, Washington, DC.
- 1930 Notebook A. Field Notes from the H. B. Collins Collection, Box 45, folder 83. National Anthropological Archives, Smithsonian Institution, Suitland, Maryland.

1937 *Archeology of St. Lawrence Island, Alaska.* Smithsonian Miscellaneous Collections 96, no. 1. Smithsonian Institution, Washington, DC.

1961 Eskimo Cultures. In *Encyclopedia of World Art*, vol. 5, 1–28. McGraw-Hill, New York.

Comşa, Eugen

1994 Le Tatouage chez les Communautés de la Culture Gumelniţa [Tattoo in the communities of the Gumelniţa culture]. *Dacia* 38–39:441–44.

Conard, Nicholas J.

2009 A Female Figurine from the Basal Aurignacian of Hohle Fels Cave in Southwestern Germany. *Nature* 459(7244):248–52.

Conard, Nicholas J., and Harald Floss

2001 Une statuette en ivoire de 30,000 ans B.P. trouvée au Hohle Fels près de Schelklingen, Baden-Württemberg, Allemagne [An ivory statuette from 30,000 years B.P. found at Hohle Fels near Schelklingen, Baden-Württemberg, Germany]. *PALEO: Revue d'archéologie préhistorique* [PALEO: Journal of prehistoric archaeology] 13:241–44.

Connell, Charlie

2013 Save Your Own Skin. *Inked Magazine*, December 9, 2013. www.inkedmag.com/save-your-own-skin/

Conrad, Lawrence A.

1991 The Middle Mississippian Cultures of the Central Illinois River Valley. In *Cahokia and the Hinterlands: Middle Mississippian Cultures of the Midwest*, ed. Thomas E. Emerson and R. Barry Lewis, 119–56. University of Illinois Press, Chicago.

Craig, Austin, and Conrado Benitez

1916 *Philippine Progress Prior to 1898.* Philippine Education Co., Manila.

Crawfurd, John

1856 *A Descriptive Dictionary of the Indian Islands and Adjacent Countries.* Bradbury and Evans, London.

Crowell, Aron L.

2009 Sea Mammals in Art, Ceremony, and Belief: Knowledge Shared by Yupik and Iñupiaq Elders. In *Gifts from the Ancestors: Ancient Ivories of Bering Strait,* ed. William W. Fitzhugh, Julie Hollowell, and Aron L. Crowell, 206–25. Princeton University Art Museum and Yale University Press, Princeton and New Haven.

Daguillon, Dr.

1895 Contribution a l'étude du tatouage chez les aliénés [Contribution to the study of tattooing among the insane]. In *Archives d'anthropologie criminelle* [Archives of criminal anthropology], 175–99.

D'Alleva, Anne

2005 Christian Skins: Tatau and the Evangelization of the Society Islands and Samoa. In *Tattoo. Bodies, Art and Exchange in the Pacific and the West*, ed. Nicholas Thomas, Anna Cole, and Bronwen Douglas, 90–119. Reaktion Books, London.

Davidson, Deborah (ed.)

2017 *The Tattoo Project: Commemorative Tattoos, Visual Culture, and the Digital Archive.* Canadian Scholars' Press, Toronto.

Davidson, Janet M.

2012 Intrusion, Integration and Innovation on Small and Not-So-Small Islands with Particular Reference to Samoa. *Archaeology in Oceania* 47:1–13.

Davis, Simon

2015 Human Pelts: The Art of Preserving Tattooed Skin after Death. Vice Media LLC, June 30, 2015: www.vice.com/read/the-art-of-preserving-tattooed-skin-after-death-629.

Dawson, Warren R., and P.H.K. Gray

   1968   *Catalogue of Egyptian Antiquities in the British Museum. I: Mummies and Human Remains.* British Museum, London.

Déchelette, Joseph

   1907   La peinture corporelle et le tatouage [Body painting and tattooing]. *Revue archéologique* [Journal of archaeology] 9:38–50.

   1908   *Manuel d'archéologie préhistorique celtique et gallo-romaine* 1 [Handbook of Celtic and Gallo-Roman prehistoric archaeology 1]. Picard, Paris.

Decker, Wolfgang, and Michael Herb

   1994   *Bildatlas zum Sport im alten Agypten* [Picture atlas for sport in ancient Egypt], 2 vols. E. J. Brill, Leiden.

Dee, Michael, David Wengrow, Andrew Shortland, Alice Stevenson, Fiona Brock, Linus Girdland Flink, and Christopher Bronk Ramsey

   2013   An Absolute Chronology for Early Egypt Using Radiocarbon Dating and Bayesian Statistical Modelling. *Proceedings of the Royal Society A: Mathematical, Physical, and Engineering Sciences* 469(2159):20130395.

Deffarge, René, Pierre Laurent, and Denise de Sonneville-Bordes

   1975   Art mobilier du Magdalénien supérieur de l'Abri Morin à Pessac-sur-Dordogne (Gironde) [Portable art of the upper Magdalenian at the Morin Rock-Shelter in Pessac-sur-Dordogne (Gironde)]. *Gallia préhistoire* [Gallia prehistory] 18(1):1–64.

Delarue, Jacques, and Robert Giraud

   1999 [1950]   *Le Tatouages du "Milieu"* [*The tattoo milieu*]. L'Oiseau de Minerve, Paris.

Demello, Margot

   2007   *Encyclopedia of Body Adornment.* Greenwood Press, Westport, Connecticut.

Densmore, Frances

   1928   Use of Plants by the Chippewa Indians. *Forty-fourth Annual Report of the Bureau of American Ethnology,* 281–97. U.S. Government Printing Office, Washington DC.

d'Errico, Francesco, and Lucinda Backwell

   2009   Assessing the Function of Early Hominin Bone Tools. *Journal of Archaeological Science* 36:1764–73.

d'Errico, Francesco, Michèle Julien, Despina Liolios, Marian Vanhaeren, and Dominique Baffier

   2003   Many Awls in our Argument: Bone Tool Manufacture and Use in the Châtelperronian and Aurignacian Levels of the Grotte du Renne at Arcy-sur-Cure. In *The Chronology of the Aurignacian and of the Transitional Technocomplexes: Dating, Stratigraphies, and Cultural Implications,* ed. João Zilhão and Francesco d'Errico, 247–70. Istituto Português de Arqueologia, Lisbon.

d'Errico, Francesco, Martina Laznickova-Galetova, and Duncan Caldwell

   2011   Identification of a Possible Engraved Venus from Předmostí, Czech Republic. *Journal of Archaeological Science* 38(3):672–83.

Derry, Douglas E.

   1942   Mummification II: Methods Practised at Different Periods. *Annales de Service des Antiquités de l'Égypte* 41:240–70.

Deter-Wolf, Aaron

   2009   Needle in a Haystack: Examining the Methods and Materials of Prehistoric Tattooing in the Southeast. Paper presented at the 66th annual meeting of the Southeastern Archaeological Conference, Mobile, Alabama.

   2013a   The Material Culture and Middle Stone Age Origins of Ancient Tattooing. In *Tattoos and Body Modifications in Antiquity: Proceedings of the Sessions at the Annual Meetings of the European Association of Archaeologists in The Hague and Oslo, 2010/11,* ed. Philippe Della

Casa and Constanze Witt, 15–26. Zurich Studies in Archaeology 9. Chronos-Verlag, Zurich.

2013b Needle in a Haystack: Examining the Archaeological Evidence for Prehistoric Tattooing. In *Drawing with Great Needles: Ancient Tattoo Traditions of North America*, ed. Aaron Deter-Wolf and Carol Diaz-Granados, 43–72. University of Texas Press, Austin.

Deter-Wolf, Aaron, and Carol Diaz-Granados (eds.)

2013 *Drawing with Great Needles: Ancient Tattoo Traditions of North America*. University of Texas Press, Austin.

Deter-Wolf, Aaron, and Tanya M. Peres

2013 Flint, Bone, and Thorns: Using Ethnohistorical Data, Experimental Archaeology, and Microscopy to Examine Ancient Tattooing in Eastern North America. In *Tattoos and Body Modifications in Antiquity: Proceedings of the Sessions at the Annual Meetings of the European Association of Archaeologists in The Hague and Oslo, 2010/11*, ed. Philippe Della Casa and Constanze Witt, 35–48. Zurich Studies in Archaeology 9. Chronos-Verlag, Zurich.

Deter-Wolf, Aaron, Benoît Robitaille, Lars Krutak, and Sébastien Galliot

2016 The World's Oldest Tattoos. *Journal of Archaeological Science: Reports* 5:19–24.

Deutsch, Anthony

2013 Dutch Entrepreneur to Preserve Tattoos of the Dead. Reuters News Agency, December 26, 2013: www.reuters.com/article/us-dutch-tattoo-art-idUSBRE9BP03F20131226

Dias, Jorge, and Margot Dias

1964 *Os Macondes de Moçambique* [The Makonde of Mozambique], 4 vols. Centro de Estudios de Antropologia Cultural, Lisbon.

Dimitrova, Diana

2015 *The Tomb of King Seuthes III in Golyama Kosmatka Tumulus*, translated by Nikolina Guiosheva. Arros, Sofia.

Dimova, Bela

2014 Royal Bodies, Invisible Victims: Gender in the Funerary Record of Late Iron Age and Early Hellenistic Thrace. In *Fingerprinting the Iron Age: Approaches to Identity in the European Iron Age: Integrating South-Eastern Europe into the Debate*, ed. Cătălin Nicolae Popa and Simon Stoddart, 33–46. Oxbow Books, Oxford and Philadelphia.

Domaradzki, Mieczyslaw

1994 Trakiiskoto Izkustvo Prez Kusnozhelyaznata Epoha [Thracian art in late Iron Age]. *Problemi na Izkustvoto* [Problems of art] (4):46–48.

Domaradzki, Mieczyslaw (ed.)

1990 *Trakiiska Kultura v Rodopite I Gornite Porechiya Na Rekite Maritsa, Mesta I Struma* [Thracian culture in the Rhodopes and the Upper Catchement of the Maritsa, Mesta, and Struma Rivers]. AIM-BAS, Historical Museum Smolyan, Smolyan.

Dougherty, Sean P., and Renée Friedman

2008 Sacred or Mundane: Scalping and Decapitation at Predynastic Hierakonpolis. In *Egypt at its Origins 2. Proceedings of the International Conference "Origins of the State. Predynastic and Early Dynastic Egypt," Toulouse (France), 5–8 September 2005*, ed. Béatrix Midant-Reynes and Yann Tristant, 311–38. Orientalia Lovaniensia Analecta 172, Peeters, Leuven.

Dougherty, Sean P., and Anna Pieri

2015 Making a List, Checking It Twice: Body Count at HK27C. *Nekhen News* 27:23.

Draşovean, Florin, and Dragomir Popovici

2008 *Neolithische Kunst in Rumänien: Dieses Buch erschien aus Anlass der Ausstellung 'Steinzeitkunst. [Neolithic art in Romania: On the occasion of the exhibition of Stone Age Art]. Frühe Kulturen aus Rumänien' im Historischen Museum Olten, vom 3. Juni bis 5. Oktober 2008, erste Etappe einer internationalen Tournee, die in Bukarest endet* [The historical museum of Olten, June 3–October 5, 2008]. Ed. Manuela Wullschleger. Arte'm, Naples.

Duff, Roger S.
1956   *The Moa-Hunter Period of Maori Culture*. Government Printer, Wellington.

Duhard, Jean-Pierre
1996   *Réalisme de l'image masculine paléolithique* [Realism of male representations in paleolithic art]. Jérôme Millon, Grenoble.

Dumlao, Artemio
2013   Probe Launched over Benguet's Stolen Mummies. *The Phillipine Star*, January 10, 2013: www.philstar.com/nation/2013/01/10/895422/probe-launched-over-benguets-stolen-mummies.

Dumont de Montigny, Jean-François Benjamin
1753   *Mémoires Historiques sur la Louisiane* [Historic memories of Louisiana], vol. 1. C. J. B. Bauche, Paris.

Durham, Mary E.
1929   *Some Tribal Origins, Laws and Customs of the Balkans*. Macmillan Co., New York.

Dzhanfezova, Tanya
2003   Neolithic Pintaderas in Bulgaria (Typology and Comments on Their Ornamentation). In *Early Symbolic Systems for Communication in Southeast Europe*, ed. Lolita Nikolova, 97–108. BAR IS, 1139. Archaeopress, Oxford.

Eastaugh, Nicholas, Valentine Walsh, Tracey Chaplin, and Ruth Siddall (eds.)
2004   *Pigment Compendium: A Dictionary of Historical Pigments*. Elsevier Butterworth-Heinemann, Oxford.

El Globo
1887   *Exposición de Filipinas: Colección de artículos publicados en El Globo* [Philippines exposition: A collection of articles published in the Globe]. Salgado de Trigo, Madrid.

Emory, Kenneth P.
1946   Hawaiian Tattooing. *Occasional Papers of the B. P. Bishop Museum* 18:235–69.

Fahmy, Ahmed Gamal-El-Din
2005   Missing Plant Macro Remains as Indicators of Plant Exploitation in Predynastic Egypt. *Journal of Vegetation History and Archaeobotany* 14:287–94.

Fair, Susan W.
1982   Eskimo Dolls. In *Eskimo Dolls*, ed. Suzie Jones, 45–71. Alaska State Council on the Arts, Anchorage.

Faylona, Pamela
2002   *Kabayan Mummies*. National Museum of the Philippines, Manila.

Fellmann, Berthold
1978   Zur Deutung Frühgriechischer Körperornamente [On the meaning of early Greek body ornaments]. *Jahrbuch des Deutschen Archäologischen Instituts* [Yearbook of the German Archeological Institute] 93:1–29.

Feng, Qu
2013   The Legacy of Shamans? Structural and Cognitive Perspectives of Prehistoric Symbolism in the Bering Strait Region. PhD dissertation, University of Alaska Department of Anthropology, Fairbanks, Alaska.

Ferdon, Edwin H.
1961   The Ceremonial Site of Orongo. In *Archaeology of Easter Island: Reports of the Norwegian Archaeological Expedition to Easter Island and the East Pacific*, ed. Thor Heyerdahl and Edwin Ferdon, 221–55. George Allen & Unwin, London.

Fienup-Riordan, Ann
1995   *Boundaries and Passages: Rule and Ritual in Yup'ik Eskimo Oral Tradition*. University of Oklahoma Press, Norman.

1996 *Agayuliyararput: Our Way of Making Prayer. The Living Tradition of Yup'ik Masks*. University of Washington Press, Seattle.

Firth, Cecil M.

1927 *The Archaeological Survey of Nubia: Report for 1910–11*. National Printing Department, Cairo.

Firth, Raymond

1936 Tattooing in Tikopia. *Man* 36:173–77.

Fitzhugh, William W.

2009a Stone Shamans and Flying Deer of Northern Mongolia: Deer Goddess of Siberia or Chimera of the Steppe? *Arctic Anthropology* 46(1–2):72–88.

2009b Notes on Art Styles, Cultures, and Chronology. In *Gifts from the Ancestors: Ancient Ivories of Bering Strait*, ed. William W. Fitzhugh, Julie Hollowell, and Aron L. Crowell, 88–93. Princeton University Art Museum and Yale University Press, Princeton and New Haven.

2010 The Mongolian Deer Stone-Khirigsuur Complex: Dating and Organization of a Late Bronze Age Menagerie. In *Current Archaeological Research in Mongolia*, ed. Jan Bemmann, Hermann Parzinger, Ernst Pohl, and Damdinsuren Tseveendorzh, 183–99. Vor- und Frühgeschichtliche Archäologie, Rheinische Friedrich-Wilhelms-Universitat, Bonn.

Fitzhugh, William W., and Aron L. Crowell

2009 Ancestors and Ivories: Ancient Art of Bering Strait. In *Gifts from the Ancestors: Ancient Ivories of Bering Strait*, ed. William W. Fitzhugh, Julie Hollowell, and Aron L. Crowell, 18–41. Princeton University Art Museum and Yale University Press, Princeton and New Haven.

Fitzhugh, William W., and Aron L. Crowell (eds.)

1988 *Crossroad of Continents: Cultures of Siberia and Alaska*. Smithsonian Institution Press, Washington, DC.

Fitzhugh, William W., Julie Hollowell, and Aron L. Crowell (eds.)

2009 *Gifts from the Ancestors: Ancient Ivories of Bering Strait*. Princeton University Art Museum and Yale University Press, Princeton and New Haven.

Fletcher, Joann

2005 The Decorated Body in Ancient Egypt: Hairstyles, Cosmetics and Tattoos. In *The Clothed Body in the Ancient World*, ed. Liz Cleland, Mary Harlow, and Lloyd Llewellyn-Jones, 2–13. Oxbow Books, Oxford.

Fouquet, Daniel M.

1898 Le Tatouage Médical en Égypte: dans l'antiquité et à l'époque actuelle [The Medical Tattoo in Egypt in Antiquity and in Modern Times]. *Archives d'Anthropologie Criminelle de Criminologie et de Psychologie Normale et Pathologique* [Archives of criminal anthropology and of normal and pathological psychology] 13:270–79.

France, Anatole

1901 *L'Affaire Crainquebille* [The Crainquebille affair]. Édouard Pelletan, Paris.

Friedman, Renée F.

2001 Nubians at Hierakonpolis: Excavations in the Nubian Cemeteries. *Sudan & Nubia* 5:29–38.

2003 A Basket of Delights: The 2003 Excavations at HK43. *Nekhen News* 15:15–9.

2004 Excavation of the C-Group Cemetery at HK27C. *Sudan & Nubia* 8:47–51.

2007 The C-Group Cemetery at Locality HK27C: Results of the 2007 Season. *Sudan & Nubia* 11:57–62.

2016 Yet More Tattoos! *Nekhen News* 28:26–27.

Friedman, Renée F., and Janet Ambers

2016 Painted Ladies of the Predynastic Era. *Newsletter of the Department of Egypt and Sudan, British Museum* 3:12–13.

Friedman, Renée F., and Joel Paulson
2013 More Tattoos! *Nekhen News* 25:26.

Furey, Louise
1990 The Artefact Collection from Whitipirorua (T12/16), Coromandel Peninsula. *Records of the Auckland Institute and Museum* 27:19–60.
1996 *Oruarangi. The Archaeology and Material Culture of a Hauraki Pa.* Bulletin of the Auckland Institute and Museum 17, Auckland.
2002 *Houhora. A Fourteenth Century Village in Northland.* Bulletin of the Auckland Museum 19, Auckland.

Garong, Ame, Shozo Mihara, Franciso Datar, Wilfredo Ronquillo, and Hiroko Koike
2010 Carbon and Nitrogen Stable Isotope Analysis Using Human Bones and Hair from Philippine Burial Sites. *Bulletin of the Graduate School of Social and Cultural Studies, Kyushu University* 16:25–43.
2012 Kabayan Mummies Research: Timbac Rockshelters 1–2, Timbac, Pacso, Kabayan, Benguet. Preliminary Report on file, National Museum of the Philippines, Manila.

Gates St-Pierre, Christian
2007 Bone Awls of the St. Lawrence Iroquoians: A Microwear Analysis. In *Bones as Tools: Current Methods and Interpretations in Worked Bone Studies*, ed. Christian Gates St-Pierre and Renee B. Walker, 107–18. BAR International Series, Oxford.
2010 Iroquoian Bone Artefacts: Characteristics and Problems. In *Ancient and Modern Bone Artefacts from America to Russia: Cultural, Technological and Functional Signature*, ed. Alexandra Legrand-Pineau, Isabelle Sidéra, Natacha Buc, Eva David, and Vivian Scheinsohn, 71–85. BAR International Series 2136, Archaeopress, Oxford.
2017 Needles and Bodies: A Microwear Analysis of Experimental Bone Tattooing Implements. Paper presented at the 82nd Annual Meeting of the Society for American Archaeology, Vancouver, Canada.

Gates St-Pierre, Christian, and Renee B. Walker
2007 Introduction. In *Bones as Tools: Current Methods and Interpretations in Worked Bone Studies*, ed. Christian Gates St-Pierre and Renee B. Walker, 1–7. BAR International Series, Oxford.

Gaydarska, Bisserka, John Chapman, and Ilka Angelova
2005 On the Tell and Off the Tell: The Fired Clay Figurines from Omurtag. In *Scripta praehistoria: Miscellanea in honorem nonagenarii magistri Mircea Petrescu-Dîmboviţa oblate*, ed. Victor Spinei, 341–85. Trinitas, Iași.

Geist, Otto W.
1927–34a St. Lawrence Island Ethnology, Skin Canoe Worship and Sacrifice. Field Notes from the Otto Geist Papers, Box 3, Fldr. 61. Alaska and Polar Regions Archives, University of Alaska, Fairbanks.
1927–34b Sacrifice to the Dead. Field Notes from the Otto Geist Papers, Box 3, Fldr. 58. Alaska and Polar Regions Archives, University of Alaska, Fairbanks.
1927–34c Tattooing. Field Notes from the Otto Geist Papers, Box 3, Fldr. 62. Alaska and Polar Regions Archives, University of Alaska, Fairbanks.

Geist, Otto W., and Frohlich G. Rainey
1936 *Archaeological Excavations at Kukulik, St. Lawrence Island, Alaska.* Miscellaneous Publications of the University of Alaska 2. Washington, DC.

Gell, Alfred
1993 *Wrapped in Images: Tattooing in Polynesia.* Clarendon Press, Oxford.

Georgieva, Rumyana
2003 The Early Iron Age Pottery from Southwestern Bulgaria and the "Tsepina" Phenomenon. In *Pyraichmes*, ed. Dragi Mitrevski, 159–96. National Museum, Kumanovo.

Gerlach, Craig S., and Owen K. Mason
    1992   Calibrated Radiocarbon Dates and Cultural Interaction in the Western Arctic. *Arctic Anthropology* 29(1):54–81.

Gilbert, Steve
    2000a   Ancient History. In *Tattoo History: A Sourcebook*, ed. Steve Gilbert, 10–19. Juno Books, New York.
    2000b   Confessions of a Tattoo Addict. In *Tattoo History: A Source Book*, ed. Steve Gilbert, 8–9. Juno Books, New York.

Gilbert, William H., Jr.
    1943   *The Eastern Cherokees*. Anthropological Papers No. 23, Bureau of American Ethnology Bulletin 133, 169–413, plates 13–17. U.S. Government Printing Office, Washington, DC.

Gillis, Rosalind, Stéphanie Bréhard, and Adrian Bălăşescu
    2013   Sophisticated Cattle Dairy Husbandry at Borduşani-Popină (Romania, Fifth Millennium B.C.): The Evidence from Complementary Analysis of Mortality Profiles and Stable Isotopes. *World Archaeology* 45(3):447–72.

Goodman, Claire Garber
    1984   *Copper Artifacts in Late Eastern Woodlands Prehistory*, ed. Anne-Marie Cantrell. Center for American Archaeology at Northwestern University, Evanston, Illinois.

Gordon, George B.
    1906   Notes on the Western Eskimo. *Transactions of the Department of Archaeology, Free Museum of Science and Art* 2(1):69–101. University of Pennsylvania, Philadelphia.

Graff, Gwenola
    2009   *Les peintures sur vases de Naqada I–Naqada II: Nouvelle approche sémiologique de l'iconographie prédynastique* [The paintings on vases of Naqada I–Naqada II: New semiotic approach to dynastic iconography]. Egyptian Prehistory Monograph 6. Leuven University Press, Leuven, Belgium.

Graven, Jean
    1960   Le Tatouage et son Importance en Criminologie, IIeme Partie [The tattoo and Its importance in criminology, 2nd party]. *Revue Internationale de Criminologie et du Police Technique* [International journal of criminology and police technique] 14:83–104.

Graves-Brown, Carolyn
    2010   *Dancing for Hathor: Women in Ancient Egypt*. Bloomsbury, London.

Gros, Stephane
    2012   *La part manquante: Echanges et pouvoirs chez les drung du Yunnan, Chine* [The missing share: Exchange and power among the drung of Yunnan, China]. Société d'ethnologie, Nanterre.

Gryaznov, Mikhail P.
    1983   O monumentaljnom iskusstve na zare skifo-sibirskih kuljtur v stepnoj Azii [About monumental art at the dawn of the Scytho-Siberian cultures in steppe Asia]. In *Archeologicheski Sbornik Gosudarstvennogo Ermitazha, Vypusk 25* [Archaeological collection of articles of the State Hermitage, 25], ed. Boris Piotrovsky, 76–82. Saint Petersburg.

Guise, R. E.
    1899   On the Tribes Inhabiting the Mouth of the Wanigela River, New Guinea. *Journal of the Anthropological Institute of Britain and Ireland* 28(3–4):205–19.

Hambly, Wilfrid D.
    1925   *The History of Tattooing*. Whitherby, London.

Hančar, Franz
    1952   The Eurasian Animal Style and the Altai Complex. *Artibus Asiae* 15(1/2):171–94.

Handy, E. S. Craighill, and Willowdean C. Handy

1924 *Samoan House Building, Cooking, and Tattooing*. Bernice P. Bishop Museum Bulletin 15. Honolulu, Hawai'i.

Handy, Willowdean C.

1922 *Tattooing in the Marquesas*. B. P. Bishop Museum Bulletin 1. Honolulu.

Hänsel, Bernhard

1976 *Beiträge zur Regionalen und Chronologischen Gliederung der Älteren Hallstattzeit an der Unteren Donau* [Contributions to the regional and chronological outline of the older Hallstatt period and the lower Danube]. Beiträge zur Ur-Und Frühgeschichtlichen Archäologie des Mittelmeer-Kulturraumes [Contributions to the prehistory and archaeology of the protohistoric Mediterranean cultural area] 16–17. Habelt, Bonn.

Hansen, Svend

2007 *Bilder Vom Menschen Der Steinzeit: Untersuchungen Zur Anthropomorphen Plastik Der Jungsteinzeit Und Kupferzeit in Südosteuropa* [Pictures of Stone Age man: Investigations of anthropomorphic sculpture in the Neolithic and Copper Age in Southeastern Europe], Archäologie in Eurasien, Band 20 [Archaeology in Eurasia, vol. 20]. Philip von Zabern, Mainz.

2011 Figurines in Pietrele: Copper Age Ideology. *Documenta Praehistorica* 117–29.

2015 Pietrele: A Lakeside Settlement, 5200–4250 B.C. In *Neolithic and Copper Age between the Carpathians and the Aegean Sea. Chronologies and Technologies from the 6th to 4th Millennium B.C.* International Workshop Budapest 2012, ed. Svend Hansen, Pál Raczky, Alexandra Anders, and Agathe Reingruber, 273–93. Archäologie in Eurasien, 31. Bonn.

Hansen, Svend, Meda Toderaş, and Agathe Reingruber

2008 Der Kupferzeitliche Siedlungshügel Măgura Gorgana Bei Pietrele in Der Walachei: Ergebnisse Der Ausgrabungen Im Sommer 2007 [The Copper Age hill settlement of Măgura Gorgana at Pietrele, Wallachia: Results of the summer 2007 excavations]. *Eurasia Antiqua* [Ancient Eurasia] 14:1–83.

Hansen, Svend, Meda Toderaş, Agathe Reingruber, Ivan Gatsov, Christina Georgescu, Jochen Görsdorf, and Tim Hoppe

2007 Pietrele, Măgura Gorgana: Ergebnisse der Ausgrabungen im Sommer 2006 [Pietrele, Măgura Gorgana: Results of the summer 2006 excavations]. *Eurasia Antiqua* [Ancient Eurasia] 13:43–112.

Hansen, Svend, Meda Toderas, Agathe Reingruber, Jürgen Wunderlich, and Norbert Benecke

2012 Pietrele an der Unteren Donau. Bericht über die Ausgrabungen und geomorphologischen Untersuchungen im Sommer 2011 [Pietrele on the Lower Danube: Report on excavations and geomorphological investigations in summer 2011]. *Eurasia Antiqua* [Ancient Eurasia] 18:1–68.

Hardy, Don Ed

1987 Remains to be Seen. *TattooTime* no. 4:74–78.

Harley, Rosamund Drusilla

1982 *Artists' Pigments c.1600–1835: A Study in English Documentary Sources*. Butterworth Scientific, London.

Harn, Alan

1980 *The Prehistory of Dickson Mounds: The Dickson Excavation*. Illinois State Museum Report of Investigations 35, Dickson Mounds Museum Anthropological Studies. Illinois State Museum, Springfield.

2013 Tattooing Kits (Dickson Mounds Report excerpt). Unpublished manuscript on file, Illinois State Museums (ISM) at Dickson Mounds Museum in Lewistown, Illinois.

Harrington, Marc R.
1913 A Visit to the Otoe Indians. *The Museum Journal, University of Pennsylvania* 4(3):107–13.

Hartog, François
1988 *The Mirror of Herodotus: The Representation of the Other in the Writing of History*, translated by Janet Lloyd. University of California Press, Berkeley, Los Angeles, and London.

Hawkes, Ernest W.
1914 *The Dance Festivals of the Alaskan Eskimo.* Anthropological Publications of the University Museum, University of Pennsylvania 6(2).
1916 *The Labrador Eskimo.* Canada Department of Mines. Geological Survey Memoir 91, Anthropological Series 14. Commission géologique du Canada, Ottawa.

Hendrickx, Stan
2002 Bovines in Egyptian Predynastic and Early Dynastic Iconography. In *Droughts, Food and Culture: Ecological Change and Food Security in Africa's Later Prehistory*, ed. Fekri A. Hassan, 275–318. Plenum, New York, and London.

Hendrickx, Stan, Heiko Riemer, Frank Förster, and John C. Darnell
2009 Late Predynastic/Early Dynastic Rock Art Scenes of Barbary Sheep Hunting from Egypt's Western Desert. From Capturing Wild Animals to the Women of the "Acacia House." In *Desert Animals in the Eastern Sahara: Status, Economic Significance and Cultural Reflection in Antiquity*, ed. Heiko Riemer, Frank Förster, Michael Herb, and Nadja Pöllath, 189–244. Proceedings of an international ACACIA workshop held at the University of Cologne, Germany, December 14–15, 2007. Heinrich-Barth Institut, Cologne.

Hendrix, Elizabeth A.
2003 Painted Early Cycladic Figures: An Exploration of Context and Meaning. *Hesperia* 72(4):405–46.

Hermann, Aymeric, Robert Bollt, and Eric Conte
2015 The Atiahara Site Revisited: An Early Coastal Settlement in Tubuai (Austral Islands, French Polynesia). *Archaeology in Oceania* 50:1–14.

Hiekisch, Carl
1879 *Die Tungusen: Eine Ethnologische Monographie* [The tungus: An ethnological monograph]. Buchdruckerei der Kaiserlichen Akademie der Wissenschaften, St. Petersburg.

Hilger, Mary Inez
1992 [1951] *Chippewa Child Life and Its Cultural Background.* Minnesota Historical Society Press, St. Paul.

Hiroa, Te Rangi (Peter H. Buck)
1927 *Material Culture of the Cook Islands, Aitutaki.* Memoirs of the Board of Maori Ethnological Research, vol. 1. Honolulu, Hawai'i.
1930 *Samoan Material Culture.* Bernice P. Bishop Museum Bulletin 75. Honolulu, Hawai'i.

Hollowell, Julie
2009 Ancient Ivories in a Global World. In *Gifts from the Ancestors: Ancient Ivories of Bering Strait*, ed. William W. Fitzhugh, Julie Hollowell, and Aron L. Crowell, 252–89. Princeton University Art Museum and Yale University Press, Princeton and New Haven.

Holm, Gustav F.
1914 Ethnological Sketch of the Angmagsalik Eskimo. *Meddelelser om Grønland* 39(1):3–147, Copenhagen.

Hornblower, George D.
1929 Predynastic Figures of Women and Their Successors. *The Journal of Egyptian Archaeology* 15:29–47.

Howard, James H.
1990 *Oklahoma Seminoles: Medicines, Magic and Religion.* University of Oklahoma Press, Norman.

Hrdlička, Aleš

1930   Anthropological Survey in Alaska. In *Forty-Sixth Annual Report of the Bureau of American Ethnology for the Years 1928–1929*, 19–347. Washington, DC.

Hudson, Charles

1976   *The Southeastern Indians*. University of Tennessee Press, Knoxville.

Hughes, Charles C.

1959   Translation of I. K. Voblov's "Eskimo Ceremonies." *Anthropological Papers of the University of Alaska* 7(2):71–90.

1984   Saint Lawrence Island Eskimo. In *Handbook of North American Indians*, vol. 5, *Arctic*, ed. David Damas, 254–77. Smithsonian Institution Press, Washington, DC.

Hughes, Charles C., and Jane M. Hughes

1960   *An Eskimo Village in the Modern World*. Cornell University Press, Ithaca, New York.

Igualdo, Lolito

1989   The Social World of the Kankana-eys. PhD dissertation. Department of Education, Baguio Central University, Baguio City, Philippines.

Ingalls, Teresa

2011   The Use of Bird Bone Picks in Hawaiian Tattooing. Paper presented at the 17th Annual Meeting of the European Association of Archaeologists, Oslo, Norway.

Ivanova, Mariya

2008   Tells, Invasion Theories, and Warfare in Fifth Millennium B.C. North-Eastern Bulgaria. In *War and Sacrifice: Studies in the Archaeology of Conflict*, ed. Tony Pollard and Iain Banks, 33–48. Brill, Leiden.

Ivantchik, Askold

2011   The Funeral of Scythian Kings: The Historical Reality and the Description of Herodotus (4, 71–72). In *The Barbarians of Ancient Europe: Realities and Interactions*, ed. Larissa Bonfante, 71–106. Cambridge University Press, Cambridge.

Iwe, Karina

2013   Tattoos from Mummies of the Pazyryk Culture. In *Tattoos and Body Modifications in Antiquity: Proceedings of the Sessions at the Annual Meetings of the European Association of Archaeologist in The Hague and Oslo, 2010/11*, ed. Philippe Della Casa and Constanze Witt, 89–95. Zurich Studies in Archaeology 9. Chronos-Verlag, Zurich.

Jacobsen, Esther

1993   *The Deer Goddess of Ancient Siberia: A Study in the Ecology of Belief*. E. J. Brill, Leiden and New York.

2006   The Filippovka Deer: Inquiry into Their North Asian Sources and Symbolic Significance. In *The Golden Deer of Eurasia: Perspectives on the Steppe Nomads of the Ancient World*, ed. Joan Aruz, Ann Farkas, and Elisabetta Valtz Fino, 182–95. Metropolitan Museum of Art and Yale University Press, New York and New Haven.

Jacomb, Chris, Richard Holdaway, Morten Allentoft, Michael Bunce, Charlotte Oskam, Richard Walter, and Emma Brooks

2014   High-Precision Dating and Ancient DNA Profiling of Moa (Aves: Dinornithiformes) Eggshell Documents a Complex Feature at Wairau Bar and Refines the Chronology of New Zealand Settlement by Polynesians. *Journal of Archaeological Science* 50:24–30.

Jettmar, Karl

1994   Body-painting and the Roots of the Scytho-Siberian Animal Style. In *The Archaeology of the Steppes: Methods and Strategies*. Papers from the International Symposium held in Naples 9–12 November 1992, ed. Bruno Genito, 3–15. Naples.

Jochelson, Waldemar
1908 *The Koryak*, 2 vols. The Jesup North Pacific Expedition 6, ed. Franz Boas. Memoirs of the American Museum of Natural History 10. Brill, Leiden.

Jolles, Carol Z.
2002 *Faith, Food, and Family in a Yupik Whaling Community*. University of Washington Press, Seattle.

Jolley, Fletcher III
1978 Sharpened Bone Splinters from Eastern Arkansas: An Archeological Occurrence of Scarifiers? *Central States Archaeological Journal* 25(1):20–32.

Johnston-Saint, Peter
1929 Johnston-Saint Reports, Jan–Nov 1929. Archives and Manuscripts of the Wellcome Library, London, WA/HMM/RP/Jst/B.4 Box 10.

Judd, Tony
2009 *Rock Art of the Eastern Desert of Egypt: Content, Comparisons, Dating and Significance*. BAR International series 2008, British Archaeological Reports Publishing, Oxford.

Kaeppler, Adrienne L.
1978a *Artificial Curiosities: An Exposition of Native Manufactures Collected on the Three Pacific Voyages of Captain James Cook*, R .N. Bishop Museum Press, Honolulu.
1978b Exchange Patterns in Goods and Spouses: Fiji, Tonga and Samoa. *Mankind* 11:246–52.

Kalchev, Petar
2005 *Neolithic Dwellings Stara Zagora Town: Exhibition Catalogue*. Regional Historical Museum Stara Zagora, Bulgaria.

Kapel, Hans, N. Kromann, F. Mikkelsen, and E. Løytved Rosenløv
1991 Tattooing. In *The Greenland Mummies*, ed. Jens Peder Hart Hansen, Jørgen Meldgaard, and Jørgen Nordqvist, 102–15. McGill-Queen's University Press, Montreal and Kingston.

Karadzhinov, Ivaylo
2013 Originality and Influences in the Zoomorphic Bronze Plastic Art from the Early Iron Age (10th–6th centuries B.C.): A Stag Figurine from the Area of Sevlievo. In *Memoriam of the Academician D. P. Dimitrov*, ed. Kostadin Rabadzhiev, Hristo Popov, Margarit Damyanov, and Veselka Katsarova, 75–86. NAIM-BAS, Sofia University, Bulgaria.

Keim, Charles J.
1969 *Aghvook, White Eskimo: Otto Geist and Alaskan Archaeology*. University of Alaska Press, Fairbanks.

Keimer, Ludwig
1948 *Remarques sur le Tatouage dans l'Égypte Ancienne* [Notes on tattooing in ancient Egypt]. Memoires Presentés à l'Institut D'Égypte, vol. 53. L'institut Français d'Archéologie Orientale, Cairo.

Keith, Gabriel Pawid, and Emma Baban Keith
1981 *Kabayan Mummies: A Glimpse of Benguet*. Hilltop Printing Press, Baguio City.

Keyser, Christine, Caroline Bouakaze, Eric Crubézy, Valery G. Nikolaev, Daniel Montagnon, Tatiana Reis, and Bertrand Ludes
2009 Ancient DNA Provides New Insights into the History of South Siberian Kurgan People. *Human Genetics* 126(3):395–410.

Khazanov, Anatoly M.
1963 Religiozno-magicheskoe ponimanie zerkal u sarmatov [Magico-religious concepts of mirrors among the Sarmatians]. *Sovetskaya etnographia* [Soviet ethnography] 4:89–96.

Kimball, Larry R., Thomas R. Whyte, and Gary D. Crites
2010 The Biltmore Mound and Hopewellian Mound Use in the Southern Appalachians. *Southeastern Archaeology* 29(1):44–58.

Kind, Claus-Joachim, Nicole Ebinger-Rist, Sibylle Wolf, Thomas Beutelspacher, and Kurt Wehreberger
- 2014 The Smile of the Lion Man: Recent Excavations in Stadel Cave (Baden-Württemberg, southwestern Germany) and the Restoration of the Famous Upper Palaeolithic Figurine. *Quartär* 61:129–45.

Kirch, Patrick V.
- 1985 *Feathered Gods and Fishhooks: An Introduction to Hawaiian Archaeology and Prehistory.* University of Hawai'i Press, Honolulu.
- 1997 *The Lapita People: Ancestors of the Oceanic World.* Blackwell Publishers, Oxford.
- 2000 *On the Road of the Winds: An Archaeological History of the Pacific Islands Before European Contact.* University of California Press, Berkeley.
- 2011 When Did the Polynesians Settle Hawai'i? A Review of 150 Years of Scholarly Inquiry and a Tentative Answer. *Hawaiian Archaeology* 12:3–26.

Kirch, Patrick V., David W. Steadman, Virginia L. Buttler, Jon Hather, and Marshall I. Weisler
- 1995 Prehistory and Human Ecology in Eastern Polynesia: Excavations at Tangatatau Rockshelter, Mangaia, Cook Islands. *Archaeology in Oceania* 30:47–65.

Kirch, Patrick V., and Douglas E. Yen
- 1982 *Tikopia: The Prehistory and Ecology of a Polynesian Outlier.* Bernice P. Bishop Museum Bulletin 238. Bernice P. Bishop Museum, Honolulu.

Kleinschmidt, Theodor
- 1984 Theodor Kleinschmidt's Notes on the Hill Tribes of Viti Levu, 1877–1878. *Domodomo* 2(4):146–90.

Kononenko, Nina
- 2012 Middle and Late Holocene Skin-Working Tools in Melanesia: Tattooing and Scarification? *Archaeology in Oceania* 47:14–28.

Kononenko, Nina, and Robin Torrence
- 2009 Tattooing in Melanesia: Local Invention or Lapita Introduction? *Antiquity* 83(320): Project Gallery: http://antiquity.ac.uk/projgall/kononenko/.

Kononenko, Nina, Robin Torrence, and Peter Sheppard
- 2016 Detecting Early Tattooing in the Pacific Region through Experimental Use-Wear and Residue Analyses of Obsidian Tools. *Journal of Archaeological Science: Reports* 8:147–63.

Korolkova, Elena F.
- 2006 Zveriny stil Evrazii. Iskusstvo plemen Nizhnego Povolzhja i Priuralja v skifskuju epokhu (VII-IV vv. do n.e.) [Animal style of Eurasia: Art of the tribes of lower Volga and south Ural region in the Scythian time (7th to 4th centuries BC)]. *Problemy stilja I etnokuljturnoi prinadlezhnosti* [Problems of style and ethnocultural affiliation]. Saint Petersburg.

Kost, Catrin
- 2014 *The Practice of Imagery in the Northern Chinese Steppe (5th to 1st centuries BCE).* Bonn Contributions to Asian Archaeology 6. Vor und Frühgeschichtliche Archäologie, Rheinische Friedrich Wilhelms Universität, Bonn.

Kovalev, Alexey A.
- 1999 O svjazjakh naselenija Sayano-Altaja i Ordosa v V-III vekakh do n.e [About connections between Sayan-Altai and Ordos populations in 5th to 3rd centuries BC]. *Itogy izuchenija skifskoy epokhi Altaja I sopredelnikh territorii* [Results of studying the Scythian epoch in Altai and adjacent regions], 75–82. Barnaul, Russia.

Kozeltsov, Vladislav L., and Juriy A. Romakov
- 2000 Novyi sposob sokhranenija chelovecheskih mumii [New method of preservation of human mummies]. *Arkheologia, etnographia i antropologia Evrazii* [Archaeology, ethnography and

anthropology of Eurasia] 4:103–6. Institute of Archaeology and Ethnology, Novosibirsk, Russia.

Krauß, Raiko, Gerwulf Schneider, and Malgorzata Daszkiewicz

2014 *Ovčarovo-Gorata. Eine Frühneolithische Siedlung in Nordostbulgarien* [Ovčarovo-Gorata: An early neolithic settlement in northeast Bulgaria]. Habelt, Bonn.

Krupnik, Igor, and Michael Chlenov

2013 *Yupik Transitions: Change and Survival at Bering Strait, 1900–1960*. University of Alaska Press, Fairbanks.

Kruta, Venceslas

1992 *L'Europe des origines: La Protohistoire 6000–500 avant J.-C.* [The beginnings of Europe: Protohistory 6000–500 BC]. Gallimard, Paris.

Krutak, Lars

1998 One Stitch at a Time: Ivalu and Sivuqaq Tattoo. Master's thesis, University of Alaska, Department of Anthropology, Fairbanks.

1999 St. Lawrence Island Joint-Tattooing: Spiritual/Medicinal Functions and Intercontinental Possibilities. *Études/Inuit/Studies* 23(1–2):229–52.

2007 *The Tattooing Arts of Tribal Women*. Bennett & Bloom, London.

2009 Of Human Skin and Ivory Spirits: Tattooing and Carving in Bering Strait. In *Gifts from the Ancestors: Ancient Ivories of Bering Strait*, ed. William F. Fitzhugh, Julie Hollowell, and Aron L. Crowell, 190–203. Princeton University Art Museum and Yale University Press, Princeton and New Haven.

2010 *Kalinga Tattoo: Ancient and Modern Expressions of the Tribal*. Edition Reuss, Aschaffenburg, Germany.

2012 *Magical Tattoos and Scarification: Spiritual Skin*. Edition Reuss, Aschaffenburg, Germany.

2013a Spiritual Journey Tattoo & Tribal Gallery: Whispers of the Ancestors. *Tattoo Savage* 122:76–83.

2013b The Power to Cure: A Brief History of Therapeutic Tattooing. In *Tattoos and Body Modifications in Antiquity: Proceedings of the Sessions at the EAA Annual Meetings in The Hague and Oslo, 2010/11*, ed. Philippe Della Casa and Constanze Witt, 27–34. Zurich Studies in Archaeology 9. Chronos-Verlag, Zurich.

2013c Die Tattoos der Managalase-Stammes auf Papua-Neuguinea [The tattoos of the Managalase tribe of Papua New Guinea]. *TätowierMagazin* [Tattoo magazine] 1:118–22.

2013d Tattoos, Totem Marks, and War Clubs: Projecting Power through Visual Symbolism in Northern Woodlands Culture. In *Drawing with Great Needles: Ancient Tattoo Traditions of North America*, ed. Aaron Deter-Wolf and Carol Diaz-Granados, 195–30. University of Texas Press, Austin.

2014a *Tattoo Traditions of Native North America: Ancient and Contemporary Expressions of Identity*. LM Publishers, Arnhem, Netherlands.

2014b Whispers of the Ancestors: Tribal Tattoos of the Philippines. In *TATTOO* (Exhibition catalogue, Musée du quai Branly, Paris, May 6, 2014–October 18, 2015), ed. Sébastien Galliot, Pascal Bagot, and Anne & Julien, 193–98. Actes Sud and Musée du quai Branly, Arles and Paris.

2014c The Bold and the Beautiful: Women's Tattoos of Coastal Papua New Guinea. *Ink Fashion* 8:16–23.

2015 Elle Festin. In *The World Atlas of Tattoo*, ed. Anna F. Friedman, 68–71. Yale University Press, New Haven and London.

Kunter, Manfred

1971 Zur Geschichte der Tatauierung und Körperbemalung in Europa [The history of tattooing and body painting in Europe]. *Paideuma* 17:1–20.

Kutschera, Walter, Robin Golser, and Alfred Priller

2000 Radiocarbon Dating of Equipment from the Iceman. In *The Iceman and His Natural Environment*, ed. Sigmar Bortenschlager and Klaus Oeggl, 1–9. *The Man in the Ice 4.* Springer, Vienna.

Kyzlassow, Leonid

1971 Das Grabmal am Jenissei [Tomb on the Yenesei]. *Ideen des Exakten Wissens* [Ideas of exact knowledge] 8:517–22. Stuttgart.

Kyzlasov, Leonid R., and Svetlana V. Pankova

2004 Tatuirovki drevnej mumii iz Khakasii (rubezh nashei ery) [Tattoos on a mummy from Khakasia (turn of the Christian era)]. *Soobshenija Gosuderstvennogo Ermitazha* [Reports of the State Hermitage] LXII:61–67. St. Petersburg.

Lacassagne, Alexandre

1881a Recherches sur les Tatouages et principalement du tatouage chez les criminels [Research on tattoos and especially those of criminals]. *Annales d'Hygiene et de medicine legale* [Annals of hygiene and lawful medicine], 3rd Series, 5(4):289–304.

1881b *Les Tatouages: Etude anthropologique et medico legale* [The tattoo: Anthropological and forensic study]. Bailliere, Paris.

Lacassagne, Alexandre, and Emile Magitot

1881 *Du Tatouage: Recherches anthropologiques et médico-légales* [The tattoo: Anthropological and forensic study]. Extrait du dictionnaire encyclopédique des sciences médicales [Extract from the encyclopaedic dictionary of medical sciences], 1–66. Paris.

La Flesche, Francis

1921 The Osage Tribe: Rite of the Chiefs, Sayings of the Ancient Men. In *Thirty-Sixth Annual Report of the Bureau of American Ethnology, 1914–1915*, 37–640. Smithsonian Institution, U.S. Government Printing Office, Washington, DC.

1930 The Osage Tribe: Rite of the Wa-xo'Be. In *Forty-Fifth Annual Report of the Bureau of American Ethnology, 1927–1928*, 523–833. Smithsonian Institution, U.S. Government Printing Office, Washington, DC.

Landes, Ruth

1937 *Ojibwe Sociology*. Columbia University Contributions to Sociology, vol. 29. Columbia University Press, New York.

Lartet, Édouard, Henry Christy, and Thomas Rupert Janes

1875 *Reliquiae Aquitanicae, Being Contributions to the Archaeology and Palaeontology of Périgord and the Adjoining Provinces of Southern France*. Williams, London.

Latyshev, Vasyly V.

1947a Izvestija drevnikh pisatelej o Skifii I Kavkaze [Reports of ancient writers about Scythia and the Caucuses]. *Vestnik drevney istorii* [Bulletin of ancient history] XIX(1):253–316.

1947b Izvestija drevnikh pisatelej o Skifii I Kavkaze [Reports of ancient writers about Scythia and the Caucuses]. *Vestnik drevney istorii* [Bulletin of ancient history] XX(2):249–332.

Laukien, Michael

2000 Die traditionellen tätowierungen der Katholiken Bosnien [The traditional tattooing of the Bosnian Catholics]. *TätowierMagazin* [Tattoo Magazine] 12:92–97.

Lavker, Robert M., Gang Dong, Peishu Zheng, and George F. Murphy

1991 Hairless Micropig Skin: A Novel Model for Studies of Cutaneous Biology. *American Journal of Pathology* 138(3):687–97.

Lavker, Robert M., and Tung-Tien Sun

1982 Heterogeneity in Epidermal Basal Keratinocytes: Morphological and Functional Correlations. *Science* 215:1239–41.

Law, Gary
1972 Archaeology at Harataonga Bay, Great Barrier Island. *Records of the Auckland Institute and Museum* 9:81–123.

Lawson, John
1709 *A New Voyage to Carolina, Containing the Exact Description and Natural History of that Country, together with the Present State Thereof*. Electronic edition: http://docsouth.unc.edu/nc/lawson/menu.html.

Le Page du Pratz, Antoine Simone
1947 [1758] *The History of Louisiana or of the Western Parts of Virginia and Carolina*. Pelican Press, New Orleans.

Leach, B. Foss
1979 Excavations in the Washpool Valley, Palliser Bay. In *Prehistoric Man in Palliser Bay*, ed. B. Foss Leach and Helen M. Leach, 67–136. Bulletin of the National Museum of New Zealand 21, Wellington.

Leahy, Anne
1974 Excavations at Hot Water Beach (N44/69), Coromandel Peninsula. *Records of the Auckland Institute and Museum* 11:23–76.

Legrand, Alexandra, and Isabelle Sidéra
2007 Methods, Means, and Results when Studying European Bone Industries. In *Bones as Tools: Current Methods and Interpretations in Worked Bone Studies*, ed. Christian Gates St-Pierre and Renee B. Walker, 67–79. BAR International Series, Oxford.

Leighton, Alexander H., and Charles C. Hughes
1955 Notes on Eskimo Patterns of Suicide. *Southwestern Journal of Anthropology* 11(4):327–38.

LeMoine, Genevieve M.
1997 *Use-Wear Analysis on Bone and Antler Tools of the Mackenzie Inuit*. BAR International Series 679. British Archaeological Reports, Oxford.

Letyagin, Andrey Ju., Andrey A. Savelov, and Natalia V. Polosmak
2014 High Field Magnetic Resonance Imaging of a Mummy from Ak-Alakha-3 Mound 1, Ukok Plateau, Gorny Altai: Findings and Interpretations. *Archaeology, Ethnology and Anthropology of Eurasia* 4(60):83–91.

Li, X.
2010 Interaction of Cultures in Turfan Hollow and Adjacent Regions in the Bronze–Early Iron Age. In *Di san jie Tulufan xue ji Ou Ya you mu min zu de qi yuan yu qian xi guo ji xue shu yan tao hui lun wen ji* [Journal of Turfan studies: Essays of the third international conference on Turfan studies. The origin and migrations of Eurasian nomadic people], 3–20.

Lichter, Clemens
2011 Neolithic Stamps and the Neolithization Process. A Fresh Look at an Old Issue. In *Beginnings–New Research in the Appearance of the Neolithic between Northwest Anatolia and the Carpathian Basin: Papers of the International Workshop 8–9 April 2009, Istanbul, organized by Dan Ciobotaru, Barbara Horejs, and Raiko Krauss*, ed. Raiko Krauß, 35–44. Menschen, Kulturen, Traditionen; Forschungscluster 1: Von Der Sesshaftigkeit Zur Komplexen Gesellschaft: Siedlung, Wirtschaft, Umwelt [People, cultures, traditions; Research cluster 1: From sedentariness to the complex society: Settlement, economy, environment]. Verlag Marie Leidorf, Rahden, Westfalen, Prussia.

Linn, Angela J., and Molly Lee
1999 Intimates and Effigies: Dolls and Human Figurines in Alaska Native Cultures. In *Not Just a Pretty Face: Dolls and Human Figurines in Alaska Native Cultures*, ed. Molly Lee, 3–48. University of Alaska Museum, Fairbanks.

Liu, Yu, Jun-ying Chen, Hai-tao Shang, Chang-e Liu, Yong Wang, Rong Niu, Jun Wu, and Hong Wei
    2010   Light Microscopic, Electron Microscopic, and Immunohistochemical Comparison of Bama Minipig (*Sus scrofa domestica*) and Human Skin. *Comparative Medicine* 60(2):142–48.

Lodder, Matt
    2011   The Myths of Modern Primitivism. *European Journal of American Culture* 30(2):99–111.

Long, John
    1791   *Voyages and Travels of an Indian Interpreter and Trader*. Printed for the author, London.

Lüning, Jens (ed.)
    2005   *Die Bandkeramiker: Erste Steinzeitbauern in Deutschland; Bilder Einer Ausstellung Beim Hessentag in Heppenheim, Bergstrasse im Juni 2004* [Linear pottery: The first Stone Age farmers in Germany; Pictures at an exhibition at Hessentag in Heppenheim, Mountain Road, June 2004]. Verlag Marie Leidorf, Rahden, Germany.

MacIver, David R., and C. Leonard Woolley
    1909   *Areika*. Eckley B. Coxe Junior Expedition to Nubia, vol. 1. Publications of the Egyptian Department of the University Museum, University of Pennsylvania, Philadelphia.

MacLeod, William C.
    1938   Self-Sacrifice in Mortuary and Non-Mortuary Ritual in North America. *Anthropos* 33:349–400.

Makkay, János
    1984   *Early Stamp Seals in South-East Europe*. Akadémiai Kiadó, Budapest.

Malakhov, Vladislav V., Anatoly A. Vlasov, Izabella A. Ovsjannikova, Ludmila M. Pljasova, Inna L. Kraevskaja, Sergey V. Tzybulja, and Vladimir G. Stepanov
    2000   Veshestvenny sostav nakhodok iz "zamerzshikh" zakhoronenii pazyrykskoi kuljtury. *Fenomen altaiskih mumii* [The material composition of the finds from the "frozen" burials of the Pazyryk culture. In Phenomena of the Altai mummies], 162–75. Russian Academy of Sciences, Siberian Branch, Institute of Archaeology and Ethnography, Institute of Archaeology and Ethnology, Novosibirsk.

Mallory, James P., and Victor H. Mair
    2000   *The Tarim Mummies: Ancient China and the Mystery of the Earliest Peoples from the West*. Thames & Hudson, London.

Mangos, Therese, and John Utanga
    2011   *Patterns of the Past: Tattoo Revival in the Cook Islands*. Punarua Productions, Auckland.

Mantu, Cornelia-Magda, Gheorghe Dumitroaia, and Aris Tsaravopoulos Aris (eds.)
    1997   *Cucuteni: The Last Great Chalcolithic Civilization of Europe*, translated by Bogdan Stefanescu. Athena Publishing, Bucharest.

Marangou, Christina
    1992   *ΕΙΔΟΛΙΑ: Figurines et Miniatures du Néolithique Récent et du Bronze Ancien en Grèce* [Idol: Figurines and miniatures from the late Neolithic period and Bronze Age in Greece], vol. 576. British Archaeological Reports. Archaeopress, Oxford.

Marazov, Ivan
    1980   *Nakolennikat ot Vratsa* [Vratsa greave]. Bulgarski hudozhnik. Sofia, Bulgaria.
    2010   *Paradnite Nakolennitsi v Drevna Trakia* [Parade greaves in ancient Thrace]. Cultural Heritage Studies 2. New Bulgarian University, Sofia.
    2011   Philomele's Tongue: Reading the Pictorial Text of the Thracian Mythology. In *The Barbarians of Ancient Europe: Realities and Interactions*, ed. Larissa Bonfante, 132–89. Cambridge University Press, Cambridge.

Marche, Alfred
    1970 [1887]   *Luçon et Palaouan: Six Années de Voyages aux Philippines* [Luzon and Palawan: Six years of journeys in the Philippines]. Librairie Hachette, Paris.

Mason, Owen K.
    1998   The Contest Between the Ipiutak, Old Bering Sea, and Birnirk Polities and the Origin of Whaling during the First Millennium A.D. along Bering Strait. *Journal of Anthropological Archaeology* 17:240–325.

Massi, Agnese, Mauro Coltorti, Francesco d'Errico, Margherita Mussi, and Daniela Zampetti
    1997   La Venere di Tolentino e i Pionieri della Ricerca Archeologica [The Venus of Tolentino and the pioneers of archaeological research]. *Origini: Preistoria e Protostoria delle Civiltà Antiche* [Origins: Prehistory and proto-history of antique civilization] 21:23–65.

Mathiassen, Therkel
    1928   Material Culture of the Iglulik Eskimos. *Report of the Fifth Thule Expedition, 1921–24*, vol. 6(1). Gyldendalske Boghandel, Nordisk Forlag, Copenhagen.

Maxim-Alaiba, R.
    1987   Le Complexe de Culte de La Phase Cecuteni A3 de Dumești (Dép. Vaslui) [The cult complex phase of cecuteni A3 dumesti (dep. Vaslui)]. In *La Civilisation de Cucuteni en Contexte Europeen. Session Scientifique Dédiée au Centenaire des Premieres Découvertes de Cucuteni* [Civilization Cucuteni: The European context. Scientific session dedicated to the centenary of the first discoveries at Cucuteni] (Iași–Piatra Neamț, 24–28 Septembrie 1984), 269–86. Bibliotheca Archaeologica Iassiensis 1. Université, Al. I. Cuza, Iași.

Mayor, Adrienne
    2014   *The Amazons: Lives and Legends of Warrior Women Across the Ancient World.* Princeton and Oxford, Princeton University Press.

Mazierski, Dave
    2014   Stephen Goltra Gilbert (1931–2014). https://bmc.med.utoronto.ca/bmc/stephen-goltra-gilbert-1931-2014, accessed January 14, 2016.

McGovern-Wilson, Richard, Brian Allingham, Peter Bristow, and Ian Smith
    1996   Other Artefacts. In *Shag River Mouth: The Archaeology of an Early Southern Maori Village*, ed. Atholl Anderson, Brian Allingham, Ian Smith, 161–81. ANH Publications, Canberra, Australia.

McIntyre, Chuna
    2005   Quiet and Reserved Splendor: Central Yup'ik Eskimo Fancy Garments of Kuskokwim Bay, Bering Sea. In *Arctic Clothing*, ed. J.C.H. King, Birgit Pauksztat, and Robert Storrie, 37–41. McGill-Queens University Press, Montreal.

Meldgaard, Jorgen
    1960   *Eskimo Sculpture.* Clarkson N. Potter, New York.

Merino, Florentino S.
    1989   *The Kabayan Mummies and the Bendiyan Canao.* Self-published.
    1999   The Mummies of Kabayan. *Proceedings of the Series of Seminar-Workshops and Exhibit on Oral and Local History* 3:92–94. National Historical Institute, Manila.

Métraux, Alfred
    1971   *Ethnology of Easter Island.* Bernice P. Bishop Museum Bulletin 160. Honolulu, Hawai'i.

Meurer, Georg
    1996   *Nubier in Ägypten bis zum Beginn des Neuen Reichs: Zur Bedeutung der Stele Berlin 14753* [Nubians in Egypt until the beginning of the New Kingdom: The importance of Berlin Stele 14753]. Abhandlungen des Deutschen Archäologischen Instituts, Kairo, Ägyptologische Reihe 13, Berlin.

Meyer, Hans
    1885   Die Igorrotten, Appendix. *Eine Weltreise: Plaudereien au seiner zweijahrigen Erdumsegung* [The Igorot, appendix. A journey around the world: Stories from circumnavigating the world for two years], 299–301. Verlag der Bibliographischen Instituts, Leipzig.

Meyer, W., R. Schwarz, and K. Neurand
1978 The Skin of Domestic Mammals as a Model for Human Skin, with Special Reference to the Domestic Pig. *Current Problems in Dermatology* 7:39–52.

Middendorf, Alexander von
1875 *Reise in den äussersten Norden und Osten Sibiriens* [Travel in the extreme north and eastern Siberia]. Band IV. Buchdruckerei der Kaiserlichen Akademie der Wissenschaften, Saint Petersburg.

Mills, William C.
1904 *Exploration of the Gartner Mound and Village Site*. Fred J. Heer, Columbus. Reprint from the Ohio Archaeological and Historical Quarterly XIII(2).

Mitkova, Rositsa
2005 Za Edin Znak Ot Kusnoeneolitnata Ornamentika [About a sign of the Late Eneolithic ornamentics]. In *Kulturnite Tekstove Na Minaloto: Nositeli, Simvoli I Idei* [Cultural texts from the past: Carriers, symbols and ideas], 7–20. *In honorem* Prof. Popkonstantinov. Sofia.

Molle, Guillaume, and Eric Conte
2013 Approche techno-typologique des peignes à tatouer en nacre polynésiens. Un moyen d'appréhender la pensée technique [A techno-typological approach to Polynesian mother-of-pearl tattooing combs: A way of understanding technical thinking]. *Journal de la Société des Océanistes* [Journal of the society of oceanists] 136:209–26.

Molodin Vyacheslav I.
2000 Kulturno-istoricheskaya kharakteristika pogrebalnogo kompleksa kurgana No. 3 pamyatnika Verkh-Kaldzsin II [Cultural-historical characteristics of the funeral site Kurgan 3 at Verkh-Kaldzsin II]. *Fenomen altaiskhih mumii* [Phenomena of the Altai mummies], 86–119. Russian Academy of Sciences, Siberian Branch, Institute of Archaeology and Ethnography, Institute of Archaeology and Ethnology, Novosibirsk.

Molodin, Vjacheslav I., Hermann Parzinger, and Tzevendorzh Damdinsuren
2012 *Zamerzshie pogrebaljnyje komplexy pazyrykskoi kuljtury na juzhnykh sklonakh Sailjugema (Mongoljski Altai)* [Frozen burial complexes of the Pazyryk culture on the southern slopes of Sailjugem (Mongolian Altai)]. Triumph Print, Moscow.

Molodin, Vjacheslav I., and Natalia V. Polosmak
2005 Die Tätowierung bei der antiken Bevölkerung Siberiens [The tattooing of the ancient population of Siberia]. *Mitteilungen der Anthropologischen Gesellschaft in Wien* [Communications of the anthropological society in Vienna] 134/135:95–114.

Montagna, William, and Jeung S. Yun
1964 The Skin of the Domestic Pig. *Journal of Investigative Dermatology* 42:11–21.

Mooney, James
1896 The Ghost-Dance Religion and the Sioux Outbreak of 1890. *Fourteenth Annual Report of the Bureau of Ethnology*, 653–1110. U.S. Government Printing Office, Washington, DC.
1902 Myths of the Cherokee. *Nineteenth Annual Report of the Bureau of American Ethnology, 1897–98*. U.S. Government Printing Office, Washington, DC.

Moore, Riley
1912 Riley Moore Materials on St. Lawrence Island, Sacrifice or Ock kuh sah'took. In Aleš Hrdlička Papers, Box 97. National Anthropological Archives, Smithsonian Institution, Suitland, Maryland.

Morgan, Louis
1912 *The Modern Tattooist*. Courier, Berkeley, California.

Morris, Ellen F.
2011 Paddle Dolls and Performance. *Journal of the American Research Center in Egypt* 46:71–103.

Morse, Dan F.

1960 The Southern Cult: The Crable Site, Fulton County, Illinois. *Central States Archaeological Journal* 7(4):124–34.

Morse, Dan F., Phyllis A. Morse, and Merril Emmons

1961 The Southern Cult: The Emmons Site, Fulton County, Illinois. *Central States Archaeological Journal* 8(4):124–40.

Morse, Phyllis A., and Dan F. Morse

1990 The Zebree Site: An Emerged Early Mississippian Expression in Northeastern Arkansas. In *The Mississippian Emergence*, ed. Bruce D. Smith, 51–66. University of Alabama Press, Tuscaloosa.

Moss, Claude Russel

1920 *Kankanaey Ceremonies*. University of California Press, Berkeley.

Müller, Michael

2012 Die Statuetten. Die Verteilung der anthropomorphem Plastik auf dem Siedlungshügel [The statuettes: The distribution of anthropomorphic plastic on the mound]. In *Pietrele an der Unteren Donau. Bericht über die Ausgrabungen und geomorphologischen Untersuchungen im Sommer 2001* [Pietrele on the lower Danube. Report on the excavations and geomorphological studies, summer 2011], ed. Svend Hansen, Meda Toderaş, and Agathe Reingruber, 40–47. Eurasia Antiqua. DAI, Eurasia, Berlin.

Murdoch, John

1892 Ethnological Results of the Point Barrow Expedition. In *Ninth Annual Report of the Bureau of American Ethnology for the Years 1887–1888*, 19–441. Washington, DC.

Murphy, Jane M.

1964 Psychotherapeutic Aspects of Shamanism on St. Lawrence Island, Alaska. In *Magic, Faith, and Healing: Studies in Primitive Psychiatry Today*, ed. Ari Kiev, 53–83. The Free Press, New York.

Museum of Xinjiang Uygur Autonomous Region and Xinjiang Institute of Archaeology

2001 *Sanpula in Xinjiang of China: Revelation and Study of Ancient Khotan Civilization*. Xinjiang Peoples Publishing House, Urumqi.

Nancke-Krogh, Søren

1969 Kunsten på Kroppen [Art on the body]. *Skalk* 4:10–15.

Nanoglou, Stratos

2015 A Miniature World: Models and Figurines in South-East Europe. In *The Oxford Handbook of Neolithic Europe*, ed. Chris Fowler, Jan Harding, and Daniela Hofmann, 621–37. Oxford University Press, Oxford.

Nava, Maria Luisa

1980 *Stele Daunie I* [Daunian stelae 1]. G. C. Sansoni, Florence, Italy.

Naville, Edouard

1914 *The Cemeteries of Abydos I, 1909–1910*. Egypt Exploration Fund, London.

Nelson, Edward W.

1899 The Eskimo about Bering Strait. In *Eighteenth Annual Report of the Bureau of American Ethnology for the Years 1896–1897*, 3–518. Smithsonian Institution, Washington, DC.

Nikolov, Vassil

1989 La scène de culte d'Ovtcharovo [The Ovtcharovo cult scene]. *Dossiers Histoire et Archéologie* [Records of history and archaeology files] 137:68–71.

Nordström, Hans-Ake

1972 *Neolithic and A-Group Sites*. The Scandinavian Joint Expedition to Sudanese Nubia, vol. 3. Scandinavian University Books, Stockholm.

2002   The Nubian A-Group: Women and Copper Awls. In *A Tribute to Excellence: Studies Offered in Honor of Enrö Gaál, Ulrich Luft, Lászlo Török,* ed. Tamás Bács, 361–72. Studia Aegyptiaca XVII, Budapest.

Nørgaard, Heide

2011   Der Nichtmetallene Schmuck aus Pietrele [Non-metal jewelry from Pietrele]. *In Die Kupferzeitliche Siedlung Pietrele an Der Unteren Donau: Bericht Über Die Ausgrabungen Und Geomorphologischen Untersuchungen Im Sommer 2010* [The Copper Age settlement at Pietrele on the lower Danube: Report on the excavations and geomorphological studies, summer 2010], ed. Svend Hansen, 99–113. Eurasia Antiqua 17. Zabern, Darmstadt.

Norman, Camilla

2011a   The Tribal Tattooing of Daunian Women. *European Journal of Archaeology* 14:133–57.

2011b   Weaving, Gift and Wedding: A Local Identity for the Daunian Stelae. In *Communicating Identity in Italic Iron Age Communities,* ed. Margarita Gleba and Helle W. Horsnaes, 33–49. Oxbow Books, Oxford and Oakville.

Obermaier, Hugo

1912   *Der Mensch der Vorzeit* [Prehistoric man]. Allgemein Verlags Gesellschaft, Berlin.

Osgood, Cornelius

1940   Ingalik Material Culture. *Yale University Publications in Anthropology* 22.

Oxford English Dictionary

2016   Scarify, v.1. OED Online. September 2016. Oxford University Press, accessed December 6, 2016.

Pabst, Maria Anna, Ilse Letofksy-Pabst, Elisabeth Bock, Maximilian Moser, Leopold Dorfer, Eduard Egarter-Vigl, and Ferdinand Hofer

2009   The Tattoos of the Tyrolean Iceman: A Light Microscopical, Ultrastructural and Element Analytical Study. *Journal of Archaeological Science* 36(10):2335–41.

Pabst, Maria Anna, Ilse Letofksy-Pabst, Maximilian Moser, Konrad Spindler, Elisabeth Bock, Peter Wilhelm, Leopold Dorfer, Jochen B. Geigl, Martina Auer, Michael R. Speicher, and Ferdinand Hofer

2010   Different Staining Substances Were Used in Decorative and Therapeutic Tattoos in a 1,000-Year-Old Peruvian Mummy. *Journal of Archaeological Science* 37(12):3256–62.

Pales, Léon

1946   Les Mutilations Tégumentaires en Afrique Noire [Integumental mutilation in North Africa]. *Journal de la Société des Africanistes* [Journal of the society of Africanists] 16(1):1–8.

Pales, Léon, and Marie Tassin de Saint Péreuse

1976   *Les Gravures de la Marche* [The La Marche engravings], vol. 2. *Les Humains* [The humans]. Ophrys, Gap, France.

Palmer, J. B.

1958   Tattoo in Transition: A Post-European Maori Tattooing Kit. *Journal of the Polynesian Society* 67:387–93.

Pankova, Svetlana V.

2013   One More Culture with Ancient Tattoo Tradition in Southern Siberia: Tattoos on a Mummy from the Oglakhty Burial Ground, 3rd to 4th centuries A.D. In *Tattoos and Body Modifications in Antiquity: Proceedings of the Sessions at the Annual Meetings of the European Association of Archaeologist in The Hague and Oslo, 2010/11,* ed. Philippe Della Casa and Constanze Witt, 75–88. Zurich Studies in Archaeology 9. Chronos-Verlag, Zurich.

Pankova, Svetlana V., Sergey S. Vasiliev, Valentin A. Dergachev, and Ganna I. Zaitseva

2010   Radiocarbon Dating of Oglakhty Grave Using a Wiggle Matching Method. *Archaeology, Ethnology and Anthropology of Eurasia* 38(2):46–56.

Parkitny, Jens U.
2010   *Chin Women of Burma and Their Facial Tattoos: A Portrait*. Staatliches Museum für Völkerkunde, Munich.

Patch, Diana C.
2011   *Dawn of Egyptian Art*. Metropolitan Museum of Art, New York.

Paulson, Joel
2012   The Lady in InfraRed. *Nekhen News* 24:25.

Peck, William H., and John Ross
1978   *Egyptian Drawings*. E. P. Dutton, New York.

Pendergrast, Mick
2000   Tikopian Tattoo. *Bulletin of the Auckland Museum* 18. Auckland.

Péquart, Marthe, and Saint-Just Péquart
1962   Grotte du Mas d'Azil (Ariège): Une Nouvelle Galerie Magdalénienne [The Mas d'Azil cave: A new Magdalenian gallery]. *Annales de Paléontologie* 48:167–256, 197–286.

Peralta, Jesus, and A. M. Legaspi
1968   A Preliminary Report on the Timbac Cave Mummies, Benguet. Manuscript on file, National Museum of the Philippines, Manila.

Peres, Tanya M., and Aaron Deter-Wolf
2016   Reinterpreting the Use of Garfish (Family Lepisosteidae) in the Archaeological Record of the American Southeast. In *People with Animals: Perspectives and Studies in Ethnozooarchaeology*, ed. L. Broderick, 103–14. Oxbow Books, Oxford.

Peréz, Angel
1988 [1902]   *Igorots: Geographic and Ethnographic Study of Stone Districts of Northern Luzon*, translated by Enriqueta Fox et al. Cordillera Studies Center Monograph 02. Cordillera Studies Center, University of the Philippines Baguio, Baguio City.

Perez, Ursula G.
1979   The Ibaloys of Benguet and Their Material Customs. *Mountain State Agricultural College Research Journal* 4–5.

Perino, Gregory H.
1968   The Pete Klunk Mound Group, Calhoun County, Illinois: The Archaic and Hopewell Occupation, in *Hopewell and Woodland Site Archaeology in Illinois,* ed. James A. Brown, 9–124. Illinois Archaeological Survey Bulletin No. 6.

Petrić, Mario
1973   Običaj tatauiranja kod balkanskih naroda: Karakteristike, uloga i porijeklo [Tattooing custom of the Balkan peoples: Characteristics, role and origin]. Doktorska disertacija, Univerzitet u Sarajevu, Filozofski fakultet, Sarajevu. [PhD dissertation, University of Sarajevo, Department of Philosophy, Sarajevo].
1976   O pitanju porijekla običaja tatauiranja kod balkanskih naroda [On the issue of tattoo origins in the Balkan nations]. *Glasnik Etnografskog Muzeja u Beogradu* [Ethnographic Museum of Belgrade] 39–40:219–37.

Petrie, William Flinders Matthew
1896   *Naqada and Ballas*. British School of Archaeology in Egypt and Egyptian Research Account 1, Bernard Quaritch, London.

Philippine Daily Inquirer
2004   Stolen Mummies to be Returned to Kabayan Caves. February 13, 2004, A8.

Picpican, Isikias
2000   A Cultural and Historical Treatise: Understanding the Benguet Mummies. *SLU Research Journal* 31(2):319–74.

2003 *The Igorot Mummies: A Socio-Cultural and Historical Treatise*. Rex Bookstore, Quezon City, Philippines.

Pieri, Anna, and Daniel Antoine

2014 A Tattooed Trio at HK27C. *Nekhen News* 26:28–29.

Pierrat, Jérôme, and Éric Guillon

2004 *Le tatouage à Biribi: Les vrais, les durs, les tatoués* [The Biribi tattoo: The real, the hard, the tattooed]. Éditions Larivière, Clichy.

Piette, Édouard

1895 La station de Brassempouy et les statuettes humaines de la période glyptique [The Brassempouy settlement and the human statuettes of the Glyptic period]. *L'Anthropologie* [Anthropology] 6(2):129–51; plates I–VI.

Pinch, Geraldine

1993 *Votive Offerings to Hathor*. Griffith Institute, Oxford.

Piotrovsky, Boris, Ljudmila L. Barkova, and Maria P. Zavitukhina (eds.)

1978 *Frozen Tombs: The Culture and Art of the Ancient Tribes of Siberia*. British Museum Press, London.

Polhemus, Richard R.

1998 Activity Organization in Mississippian Households: A Case Study from the Loy Site in East Tennessee. PhD dissertation, Department of Anthropology, University of Tennessee, Knoxville.

Polosmak, Natalia V.

1994a The Ak-Alakh: "Frozen Grave" Barrow. *Ancient Civilizations from Scythia to Siberia*, vol. I, 3:346–54. Leiden.

1994b A Mummy Unearthed from the Pastures of Heaven. *National Geographic* 4:80–103.

1998 Pazyrykskie analogii v mogilakh Sinjiana [Pazyryk analogies in the graves of Xinjiang]. *Problemy archeologii, etnografii, antropologii Sibiri i sopredelnykh territorij* [Problems of archaeology, ethnology, anthropology of Siberia and adjacent areas] IV:337–43. Institute of Archaeology and Ethnology, Novosibirsk.

2000 Tatuirovki u paziriktsev [Pazryk tattoos]. *Arkheologia, etnographia i antropologia Evrazii* [Archaeology, ethnography and anthropology of Eurasia] 4:95–102.

2001 *Vsadniki Ukoka* [Riders of Ukok]. Institute of Archaeology and Ethnology, Novosibirsk.

Polosmak, Natalia V., and Ludmila L. Barkova

2005 *Kostium i tekstil' pazyryktsev Altaia (IV–III vv. do n.e.)* [Costume and textiles of the Pazyryks of Altai (IV–III centuries BCE)]. Institute of Archaeology and Ethnology, Novosibirsk.

Poon, Kelvin W. C.

2008 *In Situ* Chemical Analysis of Tattooing Inks and Pigments: Modern Organic and Traditional Pigments in Ancient Mummified Remains. PhD dissertation, Center for Forensic Science, University of Western Australia, Perth.

Poon, Kelvin W. C., and Terry I. Quickenden

2006 A Review of Tattooing in Ancient Egypt. *The Bulletin of the Australian Centre for Egyptology* 17:123–36.

Popov, Hristo

2015 Settlements. In *A Companion to Ancient Thrace*, ed. Julia Valeva, Emil Nankov, and Denver Graninger, 107–25. John Wiley & Sons, Chichester, England.

Poulsen, Jens

1987 *Early Tongan Prehistory*. Terra Australis 12. Research School of Pacific Studies. Australian National University, Canberra.

Pozzi, Enrico

2004 *Les magdaléniens: Art, civilisations, modes de vie, environnements* [The Magdalenians: art, civilization, lifeways, and environments], translated by Danielle Depracter and Sandra De La Torre. Jérôme Millon, Grenoble.

Prickett, Nigel

1990 Archaeological Excavations at Raupa: The 1987 Season. *Records of the Auckland Institute and Museum* 27:73–153.

Pshenichnuk, Anatoly

2012 *Filippovka: Nekropoli kochevoi znati IV c. B.C. na Uzhnom Urale* [Filippovka: Necropolis of the nomadic elite of the 4th century BC in the southern Urals]. Ufa Science IIYAL, Ufa.

Purdy, D. W.

1896 *Tattooing: How to Tattoo, What to Use, and How to Use Them*. Self-published pamphlet, London.

Rabadzhiev, Kostadin

2015 Cat. 305–06 Appliques. In *L'épopée des rois thraces : Des guerres médiques aux invasions celtes, 479–278 av. J.-C. : Découvertes archéologiques en Bulgarie* [Catalog 305–06, Ornaments: In The epic of the Thracian kings: The Persian wars to the Celtic invasions, 479 BC–278 AD: Archaeological finds in Bulgaria], ed. Jean-Luc Martinez, Alexandre Baralis, Néguine Mathieux, Totko Stoyanov, and Milena Tonkova, 348–49. Somogy éditions d'art, Paris.

Raczky, Pál, Alexandra Anders, and László Bartosiewicz

2011 The Enclosure System of Polgár-Csöszhalom and Its Interpretation. In *Sozialarchäologische Perspektiven: Gesellschaftlicher Wandel 5000–1500 v. Chr. Zwischen Atlantik Und Kaukasus; Internationale Tagung 15–18. Oktober 2007, Kiel* [Social archaeological perspectives: Social change 5000–1500 BC between the Atlantic and the Caucasus. International Conference 15–18 October 2007, Kiel], ed. Svend Hansen and Johannes Müller, 57–59. Archäologie in Eurasien 24. Phillip von Zabern, Berlin.

Radu, Valentin, Dragomir Nicolae Popovici, Cătălina Cernea, Ioan Cernău, and Adrian Bălășescu

2016 Harvesting Molluscs in the Eneolithic: A Study of Freshwater Bivalve Accumulations from the Tell Settlements of Borduşani-Popină and Hârşova (Romania, 5th Millennium B.C.). *Environmental Archaeology* 4:1–17.

Ratzel, Friedrich

1896 *The History of Mankind* (vol. I). The Macmillan Co., London and New York.

Raudot, Antoine-Denis

1904 [1709] Lettre XXIVe: Des Sauvages et des Sauvagesses et de Leur Habillement et de la Manière de se Piquer [XXIVth letter: Of male and female savages, their dress and the manner in which they puncture themselves]. In *Relation par Lettres de l'Amérique Septentrionalle (Années 1709 et 1710)* [Epistolary accounts of Northern America (in the years 1709–1710)], ed. Camille de Rochemonteix, 63–65. Letouzey et Ané, Paris.

Raue, Dietrich

2014 Elephantine und Nubien vom 4–2. Jt. v. Chr. [Elephantine and Nubia from the 4th–2nd millennia BC]. PhD dissertation, Institute of Egyptology, University of Leipzig, Germany.

Reed, Carrie E.

2000 Early Chinese Tattoo. *Sino-Platonic Papers* 103:1–52.

Reingruber, Agathe

2011 Soziale Differenzierung in Pietrele [Social differentiation in Pietrele]. In *Sozialarchäologische Perspektiven: Gesellschaftlicher Wandel 5000–1500 v. Chr. Zwischen Atlantik und Kaukasus* [Social archaeological perspectives: Social change 5000–1500 BC between the Atlantic and the Caucasus]. *International Conference 15–18 October 2007, Kiel*, ed. Svend Hansen and Johannes Müller. Archäologie in Eurasien 24. Phillip von Zabern, Berlin.

2012 Copper-Age House Inventories from Pietrele: Preliminary Results from Pottery Analysis. In *Tells: Social and Environmental Space. Proceedings of the International Workshop "Socio-Environmental Dynamics over the Last 12,000 Years: The Creation of Landscapes 2 (14–18 March 2011)," in Kiel*, vol. 3, ed. Robert Hofmann, Fevzi-Kemal Moetz, and Johannes Müller, 139–52. Universitätsforschungen Zur Prähistorischen Archäologie, 207. Habelt, Bonn.

2014 The Wealth of the Tells: Complex Settlement Patterns and Specialisations in the West Pontic Area between 4600 and 4250 calB.C. In *Western Anatolia before Troy: Proto-Urbanisation in the 4th Millennium B.C.? Proceedings of the International Symposium Held at the Kunsthistorisches Museum Wien, Vienna, Austria, 21–24 November, 2012*, ed. Barbara Horejs and Mathias Mehofer, 217–43. Austrian Academy of Sciences, Vienna.

Reingruber, Agathe, Svend Hansen, and Meda Toderaş

2010 Monumental Living: Pietrele Near the Lower Danube River in the 5th Millennium B.C. In *Landscapes and Human Development: The Contribution of European Archaeology. Proceedings of the International Workshop "Socio-Environmental Dynamics over the Last 12,000 Years: The Creation of Landscapes (1–4 April 2009)," in Kiel*, ed. Hans-Rudolf Bork, 171–81. Universitätsforschungen Zur Prähistorischen Archäologie 191. Habelt, Bonn.

Reinold, Jacques

2000 *Archéologie au Soudan: Les civilisations de Nubie* [Archaeology in Sudan: The civilizations of Nubia]. Editions Errace, Paris.

Reisner, George A.

1923 *Excavations at Kerma (Parts I–III)*. Harvard African Studies, vol. 5, Cambridge, Massachusetts.

Reiter, Jon

2012 *King of Tattooists: George Burchett*. Solid State, Milwaukee.

Reith, Timothy M., Terry Hunt, Carl Lipo, and Janet M. Wilmshurst

2011 The 13th Century Polynesian Colonization of Hawai'i Island. *Journal of Archaeological Science* 38:2740–49.

Renaut, Luc

2004a Marquage corporel et signation religieuse dans l'antiquité (thèse de doctorat) [Body marking and religious signation in antiquity.] PhD dissertation. École Pratique des Hautes Études, Paris.

2004b Les tatouages d'Ötzi et la petite chirurgie traditionnelle [Ötzi's tattoos and traditional minor surgery]. *L'Anthropologie* [Anthropology] 108:69–105.

2008 Die Tradition der weiblichen Tätowierung seit dem Altertum: Schönheit, Liebesspiel und soziale Wertschätzung [Female tattooing in ancient and traditional societies: Beauty, sexuality and social value]. In *Der schöne Körper: Mode und Kosmetik in Kunst und Gesellschaft* [The Beautiful Body: Fashion and Cosmetics in Art and Society], ed. Annette Geiger, 91–112. Böhlau Verlag, Cologne.

2009 Recherches sur le henné antique [Research on henna in the ancient world]. *Journal of Near Eastern Studies* 63(3):193–212.

2011 Mains peintes et menton brûlé: La parure tatouée des femmes thraces [Painted hands and burned chins: The tattooed adornment of Thracian women]. In *Parures et artifices, le corps exposé dans l'antiquité Gréco-Romaine* [Adornment and artifice: The exposed body in Graeco-Roman antiquity], ed. Lydie Bodiou, Florence Gherchanoc, Valérie Huet, and Véronique Mehl, 191–216. L'Harmattan, Paris.

2014 Tattooing in Antiquity. In *TATTOO* (Exhibition catalogue, Musée du quai Branly, Paris, May 6, 2014–October 18, 2015), ed. Sébastien Galliot, Pascal Bagot, and Anne & Julien, 22–26. Actes Sud and Musée du quai Branly, Arles and Paris.

Renfrew, Colin, Marija Gimbutas, and Ernestine S. Elster

1986 *Excavations at Sitagroi: A Prehistoric Village in Northeast Greece.* University of California Press, Los Angeles.

Robitaille, Benoît

2007 A Preliminary Typology of Perpendicularly Hafted Bone Tipped Tattooing Instruments: Toward a Technological History of Oceanic Tattooing. In *Bones as Tools: Current Methods and Interpretations in Worked Bone Studies,* ed. Christian Gates St-Pierre and Renee B. Walker, 159–74. British Archaeological Reports International Series 1622. Archaeopress, Oxford.

Robley, Horatio

1987 *Moko, or Maori Tattooing.* Southern Reprints, Papakura, New Zealand.

Roehrig, Catharine

2015 Two Tattooed Women from Thebes. *Bulletin of the Egyptological Seminar* 19:527–36.

Rolett, Barry, and Eric Conte

1995 Renewed Investigation of the Ha'atuatua Dune (Nukuhiva, Marquesas Islands): A Key Site in Polynesian Prehistory. *Journal of the Polynesian Society* 104:195–228.

Rollefson, Gary O.

2008 Charming Lives: Human and Animal Figurines in the Late Epipaleolithic and Early Neolithic Periods in the Greater Levant and Eastern Anatolia. In *The Neolithic Demographic Transition and its Consequences,* ed. Jean-Pierre Bocquet-Appel and Ofer Bar-Yosef, 387–416. Springer, Dordrecht and London.

Roth, H. Ling

1905 Tatu in the Society Islands. *Journal of the Royal Anthropological Society* 35(2):283–94.

1906 Tonga Islanders' Skin-Marking. *Man* 3–4:6–9.

Rovillos, Raymundo

2005 Paglikha at Paglalarawan sa Pagkakakilanlang Tinguian [Creation and representation of Tinguian identity (1823–1904)]. PhD dissertation, Department of History, University of the Philippines, Diliman.

Rubino, Carl Galvez

2000 *Ilocano Dictionary and Grammar (Ilocano-English, English-Ilocano).* University of Hawai'i Press, Honolulu.

Rudenko, Sergei I.

1949 Tatuirovka aziatskikh eskimosov [Tattoo of the Asiatic Eskimos]. *Sovetskaya etnographia* [Soviet ethnography] 1:149–54.

1953 *Kultura naseleniya Gornogo Altaya v skifskoe vremya* [The culture of the population of the high Altai in Scythian times]. Izd. Akademii Nauk, Moscow-Leningrad.

1970 *Frozen Tombs of Siberia: The Pazyryk Burials of Iron Age Horsemen.* University of California Press, Berkeley.

Ruffer, Marc A.

1921 *Studies in the Palaeopathology of Egypt.* University of Chicago Press, Chicago.

Ryan, Dawn

1970 Rural and Urban Villages: A Bi-Local Social System in Papua. PhD dissertation, University of Hawai'i, Honolulu.

Saint-Périer, René de

1932 Deux figures humaines gravées de la grotte d'Isturitz [Two engraved human figures from the Isturitz cave]. *Comptes rendus des séances de l'Académie des Inscriptions et Belles-Lettres* [Report on the sessions of the académie des inscriptions et belles-lettres] 76(1):41–44.

Salcedo, Cecilio G.

1980 Brief Report on the Kabayan Mummies. Manuscript on file, National Museum of the Philippines, Manila.

Salman, Michael

2001 *The Embarrassment of Slavery: Controversies over Bondage and Nationalism in the American Colonial Philippines*. University of California Press, Los Angeles.

Salomon, Hélène

2009 Les matières colorantes au début du Paléolithique supérieur: sources, transformations et fonctions (thèse de doctorat) [Origins, transformations, and functions of coloring material during the early upper Paleolithic.] PhD dissertation. Université Bordeaux 1, Bordeaux.

Salvador-Amores, Analyn

2002 *Batek*: Traditional Tattoos and Identities in Contemporary Kalinga, North Luzon Philippines. *Humanities Diliman* 3(1):105–42.

2010–2011 Ibaloy Tattoo Interviews. Unpublished Field Notes. Baguio City, Philippines.

2011 *Batok* (Traditional Tattoos) in Diaspora: The Reinvention of a Globally Mediated Kalinga Identity. *Southeast Asian Research* 19(2):293–318.

2013 *Tapping Ink, Tattooing Identities: Tradition and Modernity in Contemporary Kalinga Society, North Luzon, Philippines*. University of the Philippines Press, Quezon City.

Samadelli, Marco, Marcello Melis, Matteo Miccoli, Eduard Egarter Vigl, and Albert R. Zink

2015 Complete Mapping of the Tattoos of the 5300-year-old Tyrolean Iceman. *Journal of Cultural Heritage* 16(5):753–58.

Sánchez Gómez, Luis Angel

2003 *Un Imperio en La Vitrina: El Colonialismo Español en el Pacifico y la Exposicion de Filipinas de 1887* [The imperial showcase: Spanish colonialism in the Pacific and Philippine Exhibition of 1887]. Colección Tierra Nueva e Cielo Nuevo, Ministerio de Ciencia y Tecnologia, Madrid.

Sand, Christophe

2015 Comparing Lapita Pottery Forms in the Southwestern Pacific: A Case-Study. In *The Lapita Cultural Complex in Time and Space: Expansion Routes, Chronologies and Typologies*, ed. Christophe Sand, Scarlett Chiu, and Nicholas Hogg, 125–71. Archeologia Pasifika 4, Institut d'archéologie de la Nouvelle-Calédonie et du Pacifique, Nouméa, New Caledonia.

Sand, Christophe, and Stuart Bedford

2010 Lapita: Archaeological Signature of the First Austronesian Settlement of the Southwest Pacific. In *Lapita: Ancêstres Océaniens, Oceanic Ancestors*, ed. Christophe Sand and Stuart Bedford, 14–27. Somogy Editions d'Art and Musée du Quai Branly, Paris.

Santure, Sharron K., and Duane Esarey

1990 Analysis of Artifacts from the Oneota Mortuary Component. In *Archaeological Investigations at the Morton Village and Norris Farms 36 Cemetery*, ed. Sharron K. Santure, Alan D. Harn, and Duane Esarey, 75–110. Illinois State Museum Report of Investigations No. 45. Illinois State Museum, Springfield.

Saul, Jamie D.

2006 *The Naga of Burma: Their Festivals, Customs and Way of Life*. Orchid Press, Bangkok.

Säve-Söderbergh, Torgny

1989 *Middle Nubian Sites*. The Scandinavian Joint Expedition to Sudanese Nubia, vol. 4, Uppsala, Sweden.

Savinov, Dmitrii G.

1994 *Olennye kamni v kulture kochevnikov Evrazii* [Deer stones in the culture of Eurasian nomads]. Saint Petersburg.

Sawyer, Frederic Henry Read

1900 *The Inhabitants of the Philippines*. Charles Scribner's Sons, New York.

Schadenberg, Alexander

1975 [1887]   Berlage zur Kentniss de Banao-Leute und der Guinaanen. Gran Cordillera Central, Insel Luzon, Philippinen [The Banao people and the Guinaangs, Gran Cordillera Central, Luzon Island, Philippines]. In *German Travelers in the Cordillera (1860–1890)*, translated and annotated by William H. Scott, 81–96. Filipiniana Book Guild, Manila.

Schier, Wolfram (ed.)

2005   *Masken-Menschen-Rituale. Alltag und Kult vor 7000 Jahren in der prähistorischen Siedlung von Uivar, Rumänien (Katalog zur Sonderausstellung, Martin-von-Wagner-Museum der Universität Würzburg)* [Masks-Men-Rituals: Everyday life and cult 7,000 years ago in the prehistoric settlement of Uivar, Romania (Exhibition catalogue, Martin von Wagner Museum, University of Würzburg)]. April 21–July 10, 2005. Lehrstuhl für Vor- und Frühgeschichtliche Archäologie: Institut für Altertumswissenschaften der Universität, Würzburg.

Schorta, Regula

2001   A Group of Central Asian Woolen Textiles in the Abbeg-Stiftung Collection. In *Fabulous Creatures from the Desert Sands: Central Asian Woolen Textiles from the Second Century BC to the Second Century AD*, ed. Dominik Keller and Regula Schorta, 79–114. Riggisberger Berichte 10, Abbeg-Stiftung, Riggisberg.

Schuster, Carl

1970   Pendants in the Form of Inverted Human Figures from Paleolithic to Modern Times. *Proceedings of the 7th International Congress of Anthropological and Ethnological Sciences* 7:105–17.

Schuster, Carl, and Edmund S. Carpenter

1996   *Patterns that Connect: Social Symbolism in Ancient and Tribal Art.* Harry N. Abrams, New York.

Scott, William H.

1974   *The Discovery of the Igorots: Spanish Contacts with the Pagans of Northern Luzon.* New Day Publishers, Quezon City, Philippines.

1975   *German Travelers in the Cordillera*, ed., translated, and annotated by William H. Scott. Filipiniana Book Guild, Manila.

1994   *Barangay: Sixteenth-Century Philippine Culture and Society.* Ateneo de Manila University Press, Quezon City.

Semper, Carl

1975 [1862]   Reisen durch die nordlichen Provinzen der Insel Luzon [Travel through the northern provinces of Luzon]. *Zeitchrift fur Allgemeine Erdkunde* [Journal of general ethnography] 13:81–96. In *German Travelers in the Cordillera,* ed., translated, and annotated by William H. Scott. Filipiniana Book Guild, Manila.

Shaw, Ian, and Paul Nicholson

2008   *The British Museum Dictionary of Ancient Egypt.* British Museum Press, London.

Sheehan, Dezna C., and Barbara B. Hrapchak

1980   *Theory and Practice of Histotechnology.* C. V. Mosby, St. Louis, Missouri.

Shulga, Petr I.

2010   *Xinjiang v VIII-III vv. do n.e. (Pograbalnye komplexy, khronologia I periodizatsija).* [Xinjiang in the VIII–III centuries B.C. (Sepulchral complexes, chronology, and periodization)]. Barnaul, Russia.

Silook, Paul

n.d.   Information on Whaling Charms. Manuscript on file. Alaska and Polar Regions Archives, University of Alaska, Fairbanks.

1917   Tattooing; and Tattooing of a Man. Daniel S. Neuman Papers, MS 162, Box 1, Fldrs. 6 and 10. Alaska State Library, Juneau.

1940 Life Story of Paul Silook. Dorothea Leighton Collection, Box 3, Fldr. 66. Alaska and Polar Regions Archives, University of Alaska, Fairbanks.

Silook, Susie

2009 Gifts from My Ancestors. In *Gifts from the Ancestors: Ancient Ivories of Bering Strait*, ed. William F. Fitzhugh, Julie Hollowell, and Aron L. Crowell, 290–95. Princeton University Art Museum and Yale University Press, Princeton and New Haven.

Sinopoli, Carla M., and Lars Fogelin (eds.)

1998 Imperial Imaginings: The Dean C. Worcester Photograph Collection of the Philippines, 1890–1913. Digital image collection. University of Michigan Museum of Anthropology, Ann Arbor.

Sinoto, Yosihiko H.

1970 An Archaeologically Based Assessment of the Marquesas as a Dispersal Center in East Polynesia. In *Studies in Oceanic Culture History*, vol. 1, ed. Roger C. Green and Marion Kelly, 105–32. Pacific Anthropological Records 11, Department of Anthropology, Bishop Museum, Honolulu.

Skeates, Robin

2007 Neolithic Stamps: Cultural Patterns, Processes, and Potencies. *Cambridge Archaeological Journal* 17(2):183–98.

Skinner, Alanson B.

1921 *Material Culture of the Menomini*. Indian Notes and Monographs, vol. 20, ed. F. W. Hodge. Museum of the American Indian, Heye Foundation, New York.

1926 Ethnology of the Ioway Indians. *Bulletin of the Public Museum of the City of Milwaukee* 5(4):181–352.

Skinner, Lucy, and Christine Rogge

2016 Matriarchs, Red Leather, and Polka-Dots: More Leather from HK27C. *Nekhen News* 28:22–23.

Skinner, Lucy, and Andre Veldmeijer

2015 Skin Deep: The Beautiful Leather of the Nubians at Hierakonpolis. *Nekhen News* 27:19–21.

Slavchev, Vladimir, Kalin Dimitrov, and Marion Etze

2015 Die Komplexe 2, 3 und 15 Mit Gesichtsdarstellungen Aus Dem Kupferzeitlichen Gräberfeld von Varna [Complexes 2, 3 and 15 with face images from the Copper Age cemetery of Varna]. In *Der Schwarzmeerraum Vom Neolithikum Bis in Die Früheisenzeit (6000–600 v. Chr.)* [The Black Sea area from the Neolithic to the early Iron Age (6000–600 BC)]. Kulturelle Interferenzen in Der Zirkumpontischen Zone und Kontakte mit Ihren Nachbargebieten. Humboldt-Kolleg Varna, Bulgarien [Cultural Interference in the Circum-Pontic zone and contacts with neighboring areas. Humboldt College, Varna, Bulgaria], 16–20 May 2012, ed. Vasil Nikolov and Wolfram Schier, 400–25, Prähistorische Archäologie in Südosteuropa. Rahden, Westf.

Sljusarenko, Igor

2011 Datirovanije skifskikh drevnostei Evrazii: sovremennye tendenzii, dostizhenija, problemy, perspektivy [Dating of the Scythian antiquities of Eurasia: Modern trends, achievements, problems, perspectives]. In *"TERRA SCYTHICA": Materialy mezhdunarodnogo simpoziuma "Terra Scythica" (17–23. Avgust 2011, Denisova Peshera, Altai)* [Materials of the international symposium 'terra scythica' (17–23 August 2011, Denisova Cave, Altai)], 239–51, ed. Vjačeslav I. Molodin and Svend Hansen. Verlag des Instituts fuer Archaeologie und Ethnographie der SA RAW, Novosibirsk.

Smeaton, Winifred

1937 Tattooing Among the Arabs of Iraq. *American Anthropologist* 39:53–61.

Smith, Anita
2002 *An Archaeology of West Polynesian Prehistory.* Terra Australis 18. Pandanus Books, Australian National University, Canberra.

Smith, George S., and M. Robert Zimmerman
1975 Tattooing Found on a 1600-Year-Old Frozen Mummified Body from St. Lawrence Island, Alaska. *American Antiquity* 40:433–37.

Smith, Grafton Elliot
1923 *The Egyptians and Their Influence upon the Civilization of Europe.* Harper, London.

Smith, Huron Herbert
1923 *Ethnobotany of the Menomini Indians.* Bulletin of the Public Museum of the City of Milwaukee, vol. 4, no. 1.

Speck, Frank G.
1909 *Ethnology of the Yuchi Indians.* Anthropological Publications of the University Museum, vol. I. no. 1. University of Pennsylvania, Philadelphia.

Steere, Benjamin A.
2013 Swift Creek Paddle Designs as Tattoos. In *Drawing with Great Needles: Ancient Tattoo Traditions of North America*, ed. Aaron Deter-Wolf and Carol Diaz-Granados, 73–94. University of Texas Press, Austin.

Steindorff, Georg
1935 *Aniba*, vol. I. J. H. Augustin, Glückstadt.

Steinen, Karl von den
1925 *Die Marquesaner und Ihre Kunst,* Band 1*, Tatauierung* [The Marquesans and their art, vol. 1, tattooing]. Dietrich Reimer, Berlin.

Stevenson, Alice
2017 Predynastic Egyptian Figurines. In *The Oxford Handbook of Prehistoric Figurines,* ed. Timothy Insoll. Oxford University Press, Oxford.

Steward, Samuel
1990 *Bad Boys and Tough Tattoo: A Social History of the Tattoo with Gangs, Sailors, and Street-Corner Punks, 1950–1965.* Harrington Park Press, New York and London.

Streit, C.
1935 Unbewegliche Körperzier in Vorgeschichtlicher Zeit. 5. Plastiken (Schluß) [Immovable body trim in prehistoric time. 5. sculptures (conclusion)]. *Anthropos* 30(5/6):681–706.

Strezewski, Michael
2003 Mississippian Period Mortuary Practices in the Central Illinois River Valley: A Region-Wide Survey and Analysis. PhD dissertation, Department of Anthropology, Indiana University, Bloomington.

Strouhal, Eugen
1992 *Life of the Ancient Egyptians.* University of Oklahoma Press, Norman.

Struve, Vasily V.
1968 *Etjudy po istorii Severnogo Prichernomorja, Kavkaza i Sredney Asii* [Essays on the history of the northern Black Sea region, Caucuses, and middle Asia]. Leningrad.

Sturtevant, William C.
1955 The Mikasuki Seminole: Medical Beliefs and Practices. PhD dissertation, Department of Anthropology, Yale University, New Haven.

Summerfield, Artur, François Meurens, and Meret E. Ricklin
2015 The Immunology of the Porcine Skin and its Value as a Model for Human Skin. *Molecular Immunology* 66(1):14–21.

Swanton, John R.

1928 Social Organization and Social Usages of the Indians of the Creek Confederacy. In *Forty-Second Annual Report of the Bureau of American Ethnology, 1924–1925,* 23–472. U.S. Government Printing Office, Washington, DC.

Taborin, Yvette

2004 *Langage sans parole: La parure aux temps préhistoriques* [Language without words: Adornment in prehistoric times]. La Maison des roches, Paris.

Tallgren, Aarne M.

1937 The South Siberian Cemetery of Oglakhty from the Han period. *Eurasia Septentrionalis Antiqua* 11:69–90. Helsinki.

Tardieu, Auguste Ambroise

1855 *Étude médico-légale sur le tatouage considéré comme signe d'identité* [Forensic study on tattooing as considered a sign of identity]. J. B. Baillière, Paris.

Tassie, Geoffry J.

2003 Identifying the Practice of Tattooing in Ancient Egypt and Nubia. *Papers from the Institute of Archaeology* 14:85–101.

Taviel de Andrade, Enrique

1887 *Historia de la Exposicion de las Filipinas en Madrid en el Año de 1887* [History of the Philippines exposition in Madrid in the year 1887]. Imprenta de Ulpiano Gomez y Perez, Manila.

Te Awekotuku, Ngahuia

2007 *Mau Moko: The World of Maori Tattoo.* Viking, Auckland.

Tein, Tassan S.

1994 Shamans of the Siberian Eskimos. *Arctic Anthropology* 31(1):117–25.

Teleaga, Emilian

2010 Die Prunkgräber aus Agighiol und Vraca [The magnificent tombs from Agighiol and Vraca]. In *Amazonen: Geheimnisvolle Kriegerinnen* [Amazons: Mysterious warriors], ed. Renate Rolle and Sabrina Busse, 78–85. Edition Minerva, Speyer.

Teodossiev, Nikola

2015 Cat. 238 Appliques de harnachement et mors. *In L'épopée des rois thraces: Des guerres médiques aux invasions celtes, 479—278 av. J.-C.: Découvertes archéologiques en Bulgarie* [Catalog 238 Harness Ornaments. In The epic of the Thracian kings: The Persian wars to the Celtic invasions, 479 BC–278 AD: Archaeological finds in Bulgaria], ed. Jean-Luc Martinez, Alexandre Baralis, Néguine Mathieux, Totko Stoyanov, and Milena Tonkova, 276–77. Somogy éditions d'art, Paris.

Teploukhov, Sergei A.

1929 Opyt classificazii drevnih metallicheskih kuljtur Minusinskogo kraja (v kratkom izlozhenii) [Classification of the ancient metal cultures of the Minusinsk region (in brief)]. In *Materialy po etnographii,* Tom 4, vypusk 2, 41–62 [Materials on Etnography 4(2):41–62]. Leningrad.

Tep Tok

2015 *Tep Tok.* Documentary film. 59 min. Sunameke Productions, Darwin.

Țerna, S. V.

2013 The Distribution of Clay Figurines in the Neolithic and Copper Age Necropolis of Durankulak (North-Eastern Bulgaria): A Case Study. *Stratum Plus Journal* (2).

Thalbitzer, William

1914 Ethnographical Collections from East Greenland (Angmagsalik and Nualik) made by G. Holm, G. Amdrup, and J. Petersem and described by W. Thalbitzer. The Ammasalik Eskimo 1(7). *Meddelelser om Grønland* 39(1):319–755. Copenhagen.

Thiel, Barbara

1988 Austronesian Origins and Expansion: The Philippine Archaeological Data. *Asian Perspectives: The Journal of Asia and the Pacific* 26:119–29.

Thomas, Nicholas

2005 Introduction. In *Tattoo: Bodies, Art and Exchange in the Pacific and the West*, ed. Nicholas Thomas, Anna Cole, and Bronwen Douglas, 7–29. Reaktion Books, London.

Thompson, Laura

1940 *The Fijian Frontier*. Institute of Pacific Relations, San Francisco.

Todorova, Henrieta

1978 *The Eneolithic Period in Bulgaria in the Fifth Millennium B.C.* BAR International Series 49. Oxford.

1980 Klasifikatsiya I Chislovoy Kod Plastiki Neolita, Eneolita I Bronzovoy Epohi [Classification and numeric coding of Neolithic, Eneolithic, and Bronze Age figurines from Bulgaria]. *Studia Praehistorica* 3:43–64.

1982 *Kupferzeitliche Siedlungen in Nordostbulgarien* [Copper Age settlements in northeast Bulgaria], ed. Hermann Müller-Karpe. Materialien zur Allgemeinen und Vergleichenden Archäologie 13. C. H. Beck, Munich.

1986 *Kamenno-Mednata Epoha v Bulgaria* (Peto Hilyadoletie Predi Novata Era) [Eneolithic in Bulgaria (fifth millennium BCE)]. Nauka i izkustvo, Sofia.

Todorova, Henrieta, and Ivan Vajsov

2001 *Der kupferzeitliche Schmuck Bulgariens*, vol. 6 [The Copper Age jewelry of Bulgaria, vol. 6]. Prähistorische Bronzefunde XX. Franz Steiner, Stuttgart.

Tooley, Angela M. J.

1989 Middle Kingdom Burial Customs: A Study of Wooden Models and Related Materials, vol. I, PhD dissertation, University of Liverpool. (In press) Notes on Type 1

2017 Truncated Figurines: The Ramesseum Ladies. In *Company of Images: Modeling the Imaginary World of Middle Kingdom Egypt (2000–1550 B.C.)*, ed. Gianluca Miniaci, Marilina Betro, and Stephen Quirke, 421-56. Orientalia Lovaniensia Analecta 262, Peeters, Leuven.

Torbov, Nartsis

2005 *Mogilanskata Mogila Vav Vratsa* [Mogilanska mound in Vratsa]. Mayobo, Vratsa.

Truhelka, Ćiro

1896 Die Tätowirung bei den Katholiken Bosniens und der Hercegovina. *Wissenschaftliche Mitteilungen aus Bosniens und der Herzegowina* [Tattooing among Catholics of Bosnia-Herzegovina. Scientific releases from Bosnia and Herzegovina] 4:493–508.

Tsiafakis, Despoina

2015 Thracian Tattoos. In *Bodies in Transition: Dissolving the Boundaries of Embodied Knowledge*, ed. Dietrich Boschung, Alan Shapiro, and Frank Wascheck, 89–118. Morphomata 23. Wilhelm Fink, Paderborn.

Tubbs, Ryan M.

2013 Ethnic Identity and Diet in the Central Illinois River Valley. PhD dissertation, Department of Anthropology, Michigan State University, Lansing.

Turalija, Tea

2011 Traditional Croatian Tattooing in Bosnia and Herzegovina. Unpublished manuscript in possession of author, Kupres, Bosnia.

Ucko, Peter J.

1962 The Interpretation of Prehistoric Anthropomorphic Figurines. *The Journal of the Royal Anthropological Institute of Great Britain and Ireland* 92(1):38–54.

1968 *Anthropomorphic Figurines of Predynastic Egypt and Neolithic Crete with Comparative Material from the Prehistoric Near East and Mainland Greece*. Occasional Paper No. 24, Royal Anthropological Institute, London.

Ucko, Peter J., and H.W.M. Hodges

1963 Some Pre-Dynastic Figurines: Problems of Authenticity. *Journal of the Warburg and Courtland Institutes* 26(3/4):205–22.

Universitaet Tübingen

2015 Fragments of a New Female Figurine from Hohle Fels Cave. *ScienceDaily*, July 22, 2015: www.sciencedaily.com/releases/2015/07/150722081414.htm.

Vadetskaya, Elga B.

2007 Rospisj tashtykskih masok. *Arkcheologia, etnographia i antropologia Evrazii* [Painting of the Tashtyk masks: Archaeology, ethnology, and anthropology of Eurasia] 1:46–56. Institute of Archaeology and Ethnology, Novosibirsk.

2009 *Drevnie maski Yeniseja* [Ancient masks of the Yenisey Valley]. Institut Istorii Material'noj Kul'tury RAN, Krasnoyarsk, Saint Petersburg

Vajsov, Ivan

1998 Studies *in Memoriam* James Harvey Gaul on the Typology of the Anthropomorphic Figurines from Northeastern Bulgaria. In *James Harvey Gaul in Memoriam*, ed. Mark Stefanovich, Henrieta Todorova, and Harald Hauptmann, 107–42. In the Steps of J. H. Gaul, 1. The J. H. Gaul Foundation, Sofia.

2002 Das Grab 982 und die Protobronzezeit in Bulgarien. In *Durankulak, Band II: Die prähistorischen Gräberfelder* [Grave 982 and the Proto Bronze Age in Bulgaria. In Durankulak, vol. 2: The prehistoric cemeteries], ed. Henrieta Todorova, 159–176. Anubis, Sofia.

Vandenbeusch, Marie, and Daniel Antoine

2015 Under Saint Michael's Protection: A Tattoo from Christian Nubia. *Journal of the Canadian Centre for Epigraphic Documents* 1:15–19.

Van der Sanden, Wijnand, and Sabine Eisenbeiss

2006 Imaginary People: Alfred Dieck and the Bog Bodies of Northwest Europe. *Archäologisches Korrespondenzblatt* 36(1):111–122.

van Dinter, Maarten Hesselt

2005 *The World of Tattoo: An Illustrated History*. KIT Publishers, Amsterdam.

Vanhaeren, Marian, and Francesco d'Errico

2011 L'émergence du corps pare [The emergence of the adorned body]. *Civilisations: Revue internationale d'anthropologie et de sciences humaines* [Civilisations: International journal of anthropology and the humanities] 59(2):59–86.

Vanoverbergh, Morice

1929 Dress and Adornment in the Mountain Province of Luzon, Philippine Islands. *Catholic Anthropological Conference Publications* 1(5):181–244.

VanStone, James W.

1959 Carved Human Figures from St. Lawrence Island, Alaska. *Anthropological Papers of the University of Alaska* 2(1):18–29.

Vasileva, Slava

2016 Tattoos of the Thracian Women. In *The Mirror of Time: Female Beauty through the Ages*, ed. Nataliya Ivanova, Petya Andreeva, and Maria Reho, 30. National Institute of Archaeology with Museum, Bulgarian Academy of Sciences, Sofia.

Verger, Stéphane

2008 Notes sur les vêtements féminins complexes figurés sur les stèles dauniennes [Notes on the complex female garments represented on Daunian stelae]. In *Storia e archeologia della Daunia* [History and archaeology of Daunia]. *In ricordo di Marina Mazzei* (atti delle giornate di studio) [In Memory of Marina Mazzei (workshop proceedings)], Foggia, May 19–21, 2005, ed. Giuliano Volpe, Maria Josè Strazulla, and Danilo Leone, 103–132. Edipuglia, Bari.

Vila, André

1967 *Aksha II: Le Cimetière Méroitique d'Aksha* [Aksha II: The Meroitic Cemetery at Aksha]. Librairie Klincksieck, Paris.

Vogelsang-Eastwood, Gillian

1993 *Pharaonic Egyptian Clothing*. E. J. Brill, Leiden.

Voget, Fred W.

1998 The Shoshoni-Crow Sun Dance. University of Oklahoma Press, Norman.

Volkov, Vitaly V.

2002 *Olennye kamni Mongolii* [Deer stones of Mongolia]. Moscow.

Wallace, Antoinette

2013 Native American Tattooing in the Protohistoric Southeast. In *Drawing with Great Needles: Ancient Tattoo Traditions of North America*, ed. Aaron Deter-Wolf and Carol Diaz-Granados, 1–42. University of Texas Press, Austin.

Walter, Philippe

1995 La peinture des femmes préhistoriques [The body painting of prehistoric women]. In *La Dame de Brassempouy: Actes du Colloque de Brassempouy* [The lady of Brassempouy: Proceedings of the Brassempouy Colloquium] July 1994, ed. Henri Delporte, 259–71. Université de Liège, Belgium.

Walter, Richard

1996 What is the East Polynesian "Archaic"? A View from the Cook Islands. In *Oceanic Culture History: Essays in Honour of Roger Green*, ed. Janet Davidson, Geoffrey Irwin, Foss Leach, Andrew Pawley, and Dorothy Brown, 513–29. New Zealand Journal of Archaeology Special Publication, Dunedin.

1998 *Anai'o: The Archaeology of a Fourteenth Century Polynesian Community in the Cook Islands*. New Zealand Archaeological Association Monograph 22. New Zealand Archaeological Association, Auckland.

Wang, Binghua (ed.)

1999 *The Ancient Corpses of Xinjiang: The Peoples of Ancient Xinjiang and Their Culture*. CIP, Urumqi, China.

Wang, Yak Nam, and Joan Sanders.

2005 Skin Model Studies. In *Pressure Ulcer Research: Current and Future Perspectives*, ed. Dan L. Bader, Carlijn V.C. Bouten, Denis Colin, and Cees W. J. Oomens, 263–85. Springer-Verlag, Berlin.

Waraksa, Elizabeth A.

2008 Female Figurines (Pharaonic Period). In *UCLA Encyclopedia of Egyptology*, ed. Willeke Wendrich, 1–6. University of California eScholarship, Los Angeles: http://escholarship.org/uc/item/4dg0d57b.

Wardwell, Allen

1986 *Ancient Eskimo Ivories of the Bering Strait*. Hudson Hills Press, New York.

1992 *Prehistoric Eskimo Ivories*. Daedalus Ancient Art, New York.

1994 *Island Ancestors: Oceanic Art from the Masco Collection*. University of Washington Press, Seattle.

Watson, Traci

2016 Intricate Animal and Flower Tattoos Found on Egyptian Mummy. *Nature News*, May 5, 2016. Nature Publishing Group, London: www.nature.com/news/intricate-animal-and-flower-tattoos-found-on-egyptian-mummy-1.19864.

Weitzner, Bella
1979 *Notes on the Hidatsa Indians Based on Data Recorded by the Late Gilbert L. Wilson.* American Museum of Natural History Anthropological Papers 56(2).

Wernert, Paul
1939 La scarification à l'époque paléolithique [Scarification during the paleolithic]. In *Mélanges de préhistoire et d'anthropologie offerts par ses collègues, Amis et disciples au Professeur Comte H. Begouën* [Papers on prehistory and anthropology offered to Professor Comte H. Begouën by his colleagues, friends, and disciples], 321–35. Édition du Museum, Toulouse.

Weyer, Edward M., Jr.
1932 *The Eskimos: Their Environment and Folkways.* Yale University Press, New Haven.

Whistler, W. Arthur
1991 Polynesian Plant Introductions. In *Islands, Plants, and Polynesians*, ed. Paul A. Cox and Sandra A. Banack, 41–66. Dioscorides Press, Portland, Oregon.
2009 *Plants of the Canoe People: An Ethnobotanical Voyage through Polynesia.* National Tropical Botanical Garden, Kaua'i, Hawai'i.

Wilkes, Charles
1845 *Narrative of the United States Exploring Expedition during the Years 1838–1842.* Lea and Blanchard, Philadelphia, Pennsylvania.

Williams, Bruce
1983 *Excavations Between Abu Simbel and the Sudan Frontier: C-Group, Pan Grave, and Kerma Remains at Adindan Cemeteries T, K, U, and L.* The University of Chicago Oriental Institute Nubian Expedition, vol. 5, Chicago.

Williams, Stephen
1954 An Archeological Study of the Mississippian Culture in Southeast Missouri. PhD dissertation, Department of Anthropology, Yale University, New Haven.

Williams, Thomas, and James Calvert
1859 *Fiji and the Fijians.* D. Appleton and Company, New York.

Wilson, Jeremy J.
2010 Modeling Life through Death in Late Prehistoric West-Central Illinois: An Assessment of Paleodemographic and Paleoepidemiological Variability. PhD dissertation, Department of Anthropology, State University of New York at Binghamton.

Winlock, Herbert E.
1923 The Museum's Excavations at Thebes. *The Metropolitan Museum of Art Bulletin* 18(12), Part 2:11–39.

Winters, Howard D.
1974 Some Unusual Grave Goods from a Mississippi Burial Mound. *Indian Notes* 10(2):34–46.

Wolf, Bill
2015 Figurative Sculpture of the Prehistoric Alaskan Inuit. In *Art of the Arctic: Reflections of the Unseen. Ivories from the Bering Sea*, ed. Donald Ellis, 30–43. Black Dog Publishing, London.

Worcester, Dean C.
1906 The Non-Christian Tribes of Northern Luzon. *The Philippine Journal of Science* 1(8):791–875.

Yabes, Leopoldo
1958 The Ilocano Epic: A Critical Study of the Life of Lam-ang. *Philippine Social Sciences and Humanities Review* 23(2–4):283–338.

Yablonsky, Leonid T.
2009 Novye sensatsionnye nahodki v Filippovke (k diskussionnym voprosam o khronologii pamjatnika, osobennostjah ego pogrebal'nogo obrjada i tipologii) [New sensational finds at Filippovka 1 (to the discussion questions about chronology of the site, its funeral rite,

specificity, and typology)]. *U istokov arkheologii Volgo-Kam'ja (k 150-letiju otkrytija Anan'inskogo mogil'nika)* [At the emergence of the Volga-Kama region's archaeology (to the 150 year anniversary of the Anani'no Cemetery's discovery)], 150–58. Elabuga.

2010 New Excavations of the Early Nomadic Burial Ground at Filippovka (Southern Ural Region, Russia). *American Journal of Archaeology* 114:129–43.

2013 *Zoloto sarmatskikh vozhdeĭ. Ėlitnyĭ nekropol' Filippovka 1 (po materialam raskopok 2004–2009 gg.)* [Gold of the Sarmatian chiefs: The elite necropolis of Filippovka 1 (from excavations during 2004–2009)]. Collection Catalog. Book 1, Moscow.

2014a Glorious Warriors: Discovering the Splendid Nomadic Tribes of Southern Ural Mountains. *World Archaeology* (63):16–20.

2014b Novie nahodki v «tsarskom» kurgane 1 mogilnika Filippovka 1 (predvaritelnoe soobshenie) [New Finds in the "King's" Kurgan 1 at Filippovka 1 Burial Mound]. Trudi IV (XX) *Vserossiiskogo arheologicheskogo s`ezda v Kazani 2014 g. Tom II. Kazan.* [Proceedings of the 4th all-Russian archaeological congress in Kazan (2)], 194–98.

Zidarov, Petar

2007 The Worked Osseous Finds from Pietrele: Raw Material Selection Strategies. In *Pietrele, Magura Gorgana: Ergebnisse der Ausgrabungen im Sommer 2006* [Pietrele, Magura Gorgana: Results of the summer 2006 excavations], ed. Svend Hansen, 81–85. Eurasia Antiqua 13. DAI, Berlin.

2008 Pointed Bone Tools from Magura Gorgana. In *Der Kupferzeitliche Siedlungshügel Măgura Gorgana Bei Pietrele in Der Walachei* [The Copper Age hill settlement of Măgura Gorgana at Pietrele, Wallachia], ed. Svend Hansen, 39–45. Eurasia Antiqua 14. DAI, Berlin.

2009 Tattooing in the Balkan Copper Age: Bone Needles and Mineral Pigments from Pietrele, Romania. In *Saxa Loquuntur:* In Honorem *N. Sirakov*, ed. Ivan Gatsov, 327–30. Avalon, Sofia.

Zimmermann, Konrad

1980 *Tätowierte Thrakerinnen auf griechischen Vasenbildern* [Tattooed Thracian women on Greek vase painting]. Jahrbuch des Deutschen Archäologischen Instituts. Band 95 [Yearbook of the German Archaeological Institute], vol. 95, 163–96. Walter de Gruyter and Co., Berlin.

CONTRIBUTORS

ORLANDO V. ABINION is a curator at the National Museum of the Philippines, Manila.

GEMMA ANGEL is a research fellow at Cornell University Society for the Humanities, Ithaca, New York.

RONALD G. BECKETT is a mummy specialist at the Bioanthropology Research Institute, Quinnipiac University, Hamden, Connecticut.

TARA CLARK is a tattoo enthusiast and collector in Nashville, Tennessee.

COLIN DALE is a tattooist and independent scholar at Skin and Bone Tattoo, Copenhagen.

AARON DETER-WOLF is a prehistoric archaeologist with the Tennessee Division of Archaeology, Nashville, Tennessee, and an adjunct professor in the Department of Sociology and Anthropology at Middle Tennessee State University in Murfreesboro, Tennessee.

RENÉE FRIEDMAN is a research fellow at the Griffith Institute, University of Oxford, England.

LOUISE FUREY is the E. E. Vaile Curator of Archaeology at Auckland War Memorial Museum, Auckland, New Zealand.

LARS KRUTAK is a research associate at the National Museum of Natural History, Smithsonian Institution, Washington, DC.

SVETLANA PANKOVA is senior research fellow and curator of Siberian collections in the Department of Archaeology of Eastern Europe and Siberia, The State Hermitage Museum, St. Petersburg, Russia.

DARIO PIOMBINO-MASCALI is a bioarchaeologist with the Department of Cultural Heritage and Sicilian Identity, Palermo, Italy.

LUC RENAUT is a lecturer in the History of Art at Université Grenoble-Alpes and reseacher at Laboratoire Universitaire Histoire Cultures Italie Europe, Grenoble, France.

BENOÎT ROBITAILLE is an independent scholar in Valcourt, Quebec.

ANALYN SALVADOR-AMORES is an associate professor at the University of the Philippines, Baguio City.

DONG HOON SHIN is an anatomist with the Institute of Forensic Science, Seoul National University College of Medicine, Seoul, South Korea.

ISAAC WALTERS is an educator and independent scholar in Blair, Wisconsin.

LEONID T. YABLONSKY is the former head of the Scytho-Sarmatian Department at the Institute of Archaeology, Russian Academy of Sciences, Moscow, Russia.

PETAR N. ZIDAROV is a PhD candidate in the Department of Early History, at the Institute of Prehistory, Early History, and Medieval Archaeology, Eberhard Karls University, Tübingen, Germany, and a research assistant at the Lab of Archaeometry and Experimental Archaeology, New Bulgarian University, Sofia.

INDEX

A

Abydos (Egypt), 12*map*, 35n11
Achaemenid Empire, 68
Adindan site (Sudan), 12*map*, 33
"Adorant" of Geißenklösterle, 252
Adriatic Sea, 257, 259
Aegean culture, 256, 260
Africa, 4–5, 16, 120*table*, 122, 125–26, 127*fig.*, 129nn17,22, 229, 251, 260
afterlife, 46–47, 99, 227, 270, 272, 284, 285n19
Agighiol site (Romania), 139, 149n4
Aitutaki (Cook Islands), 167
Ak-Alakha-3 site (Russia), 67*map*, 69, 87–88, 215, 216*map*
Akhmim site (Egypt), 12*map*, 13*table*
Aksha site (Sudan), 12*map*, 13*table*
Alaska, xi, 8, 262, 263*map*, 264, 266*fig.*, 268*fig.*, 270, 273, 273*fig.*, 275, 277*fig.*, 278, 278*fig.*, 279, 279*fig.*, 280–82, 285n20, 286–87, 287*fig.*, 288–90, 291*fig.*, plate 22, plate 23, plate 24
Albania, 150, 259
Alberta, 211, 212*fig.*
Aleksandar, Sasha, xi, 6, 154, 157*fig.*, 158, 158*fig.*
Algeria, 120*table*, 125–26
Alps, 103, 145, 260
Altai Mountains, 5, 66–67, 67*fig.*, 68, 96–97, 97n1, 101, 137, 215–16
Amayun (Amaiyuna), 279, 290–91
Ambrose, Wal, xi, 162, 180, 184n, plate 13
Amenemhet I, 13*table*
American Museum of Natural History, 280*fig.*, 286, plate 16
American Southeast, 200

Ammassalik, 286, 293n1
Ammassalimniut (people), 287
amputation, 128n4
Amsterdam Colonial Exposition (1883), 55n14
amulet straps, 263–64, 265*fig.*, 266*fig.*, 273, 279*fig.*, 282
Amunet, 13*table*, 22, 23*fig.*, 24, 31, 36nn14,15
Anai'o site (Cook Islands), 168*fig.*, 184n
Anatolia, 252
ancestors, 8, 38, 54n2, 58–59, 62, 88, 141–42, 188, 210–12, 212*fig.*, 214, 265–66, 269–71, 274, 282, 285n9, 287, 289–90, 293
ancestral spirits, 46–47, 62, 266–67, 269–70, 282, 284, 284n7
Ancient Egypt, 11, 12*map*, 17, 28, 34; Graeco-Roman Period, 13*table*; Middle Kingdom, plate 2; New Kingdom, 11, 13*table*, 32*fig.*, 33; Old Kingdom, 35n13; Predynastic, 5, 11–12, 13*table*, 14–16, 14*fig.*, 15*fig.*, 16*fig.*, 17–18, 18*fig.*, 19, 19*fig.*, 20–22, 26, 35nn4,8,9,13, plate 1
Aningayou, James, 271
anthropomorphic figures: and figurines, 7–8, 17–18, 18*fig.*, 19, 19*fig.*, 20, 20*fig.*, 21, 24–25, 25*fig.*, 26, 31–33, 36n17, 43*fig.*, 140*fig.*, 141, 141*fig.*, 142–43, 143*fig.*, 144–45, 149n9, 243, 245, 245*fig.*, 252, 252*fig.*, 253, 253*fig.*, 254, 254*fig.*, 255, 255*fig.*, 256, 256*fig.*, 257*fig.*, 259–64, 266*fig.*, 268*fig.*, 272–73, 273*fig.*, 274, 275*fig.*, 277*fig.*, 278*fig.*, 279*fig.*, 281–82, 283*fig.*, plate 2, plate 22, plate 23
anvil: as tattoo motif, 123, 124*fig.*
Aotearoa, 290*fig.*, 291, 293

Apeyeka, Polly, 275*fig.*
Appo Anno (mummy), 42, 42*fig.*, 43*fig.*, 50, 51*fig.*, 54n, 55n11
Apulia, 137, 138*fig.*, 257, 259
Aral Sea, 216*map*
Arapaho (people), 202–3, 204*fig.*
Archives de la Préfecture de Police (Paris), 122
Arctic, 4, 7–8, 230, 280, 285n15, 286, 287, 287*fig.*, 288*fig.*
argillite, 220, 221*fig.*
Arku cave site (Philippines), 43
Arnaquq-Baril, Alethea, 281, 285n19
Aroma (people), 185
Arpi site (Italy), 259
Arriesgado, Nick, 50
Asasif site (Egypt), 12*map*, 13*table*, 26
Asia Minor, 68
assimilation, 59, 122, 289
astrology, 60
Astudillo-Ash, Tina, xi, 58, 58*fig.*
Athabaskan (people), 286
Athenaeus, 149n1
Atiahara site (Austral Islands), 168, 169*fig.*, 170–71, 181–83
Atlantic Ocean, 195*map*
Auckland War Memorial Museum, 165
Auki, Ofoi Isoaimo, plate 15
Aurignacian, 252*fig.*
Australia, 13*table*, 61; and Australian, 6, 187
Austral Islands, 168, 169*fig.*, 181–82
Austria-Hungary, 152
Austronesian, 38, 159–60, 162, 165, 183
Ayngaangaawen, 276

B

Badari site (Egypt), 12*map*; and Badarian culture, 18, 18*fig.*
Baguio City, 38*map*, 44, 52
Balfour, Henry, 209n12
Balkan Peninsula, 6, 145, 150, 153, 259
Banao (people), 38–39, 47–48, 54n4

Banat culture, 256*fig.*
Bantilles, Vince, 59*fig.*
barbarians, 68
Bardhosh site (Kosovo), 255*fig.*
Baroa, Ade, xi, 187*fig.*
Barrow, Alaska, 263*map*, 278–79, 290, 291*fig.*, 291, 291*fig.*
basketry: and tattoo motifs, 61
belemnite, 219
Bendis (Thracian goddess), 149n4
Benguet Province (Philippines), 37, 38*fig.*, 39, 41–42, 42*fig.*, 43, 43*fig.*, 44, 44*fig.*, 45, 46*fig.*, 47*fig.*, 48, 48*fig.*, 49, 51, 51*fig.*, 53, 54n4, 55nn8,11,13, 58, 62, plate 3, plate 5
Berber (people), 122, 129n17
Berchon, Ernst, 128n4
Bering Sea, 263, 263*map*, 278*fig.*, 279*fig.*, plate 23
Bering Strait, 8, 262, 263*map*, 264, 267, 269, 270, 277–79, 280*fig.*, 281, 284
Bering Strait Eskimo (people), 280*fig.*
Bertholon, Lucien, 260
Beyer, H. Otley, 42, 54nn2,3
Biloxi (people), 195*map*
bird bone, 167, 173, 175–76, 179, 182, 207, plate 14, plate 17
birds: as tattoo motifs, 16, 26, 50, 69, 72, 73*fig.*, 74, 76*fig.*, 78, 79*fig.*, 81, 81*fig.*, 83, 83*fig.*, 84*fig.*, 87, 106
Birnirk culture, 286, 287*fig.*
Bismarck Archipelago, 160, 161map, 162, 184n2
Black Coyote (*Watonga*), 202–3, 204*fig.*
Blackfoot (people), 202
Black Sea, 68, 96, 216–17
bloodletting, 199, 199*fig.*, 200, 204, 208n3
Blumentritt, Ferdinand, 55n10
boarding schools, 287
body painting, 96, 248, 251, 253, 255, 260
Bogoras, Waldemar, 265, 268–69, 272, 280*fig.*
Bontoc (people), 37, 38*map*, 39, 48, 54nn3,5, 55n14
Bosnia and Herzegovina, 150, 152–53, plate 12

Bosnian Catholics, 150, 152, plate 11, plate 12
Bosnian-Croat iconography, 152–54, 154*fig.*, 157*fig.*, 158*fig.*, 158n4, plate 11, plate 12
Bossu, Jean Bernard, 201
Brassempouy site (France), 245, 245*fig.*, 247–48
Breuil, Henri, 244
"Brides of the Dead": and faience figurines, 24–25, plate 2
British Columbia, 211
British Museum, xi, 12, 14*fig.*, 15*fig.*, 16*fig.*, 19*fig.*, 35n6, 138*fig.*, 244*fig.*, plate 2
Bronze Age, 7, 243
Bulgarian e-Journal of Archaeology, 139
Burchett, George, 109, 118, 128nn5,6
Bureau of American Ethnology, 199
burials, 13*table*, 21–22, 24, 26–27, 34n4, 35n4, 44–45, 54n, 55n11, 64, 66, 68–70, 87–89, 96, 99, 101, 139, 200, 201*fig.*, 207, 215–17, 218*fig.*, 219, 219*fig.*, 220, 221*fig.*, 222*fig.*, 223, 223*fig.*, 224*fig.*, 225*fig.*, 226*fig.*, 227–30, 269, 271, plate 1, plate 19; and coffins, 42–43, 44*fig.*, 45, 55n13, 62, 69, 72, 87; kurgans, 68–69, 71*fig.*, 72, 72*fig.*, 73, 73*fig.*, 74, 74*fig.*, 75*fig.*, 76*fig.*, 77*fig.*, 78*fig.*, 79*fig.*, 80*fig.*, 81*fig.*, 82*fig.*, 83, 83*fig.*, 84, 84*fig.*, 85*fig.*, 86*fig.*, 87–89, 99, 101, 106, 215–17, 218*fig.*, 219, 219*fig.*, 220, 221*fig.*, 222*fig.*, 223*fig.*, 224*fig.*, 225*fig.*, 226*fig.*, 227–29, plate 7, plate 19; tombs, 13*table*, 22, 26–28, 28*fig.*, 29, 29*fig.*, 30, 30*fig.*, 31, 33–34, 36n14, 63, 68, 84, 87–90, 95–96, 98n8, 139, 140*fig.*, 217, 256, 257*fig.*

C

Canada, 7, 61n, 103, 105*fig.*, 195, 204, 210–11, 212*fig.*, 285n17, 286–87, 289
Cape Espenberg site (Alaska), 286, 287*fig.*
Caplan, Jane, 107
Capron, Louis, 203
Carolina Algonquian (people), 195*map*
Caroline Islands, 180, 183
Carpathian Mountains, 68

Caspian Sea, 216*map*
Catawba (people), 195*fig.*, 200
Cayuga (people), 195*fig.*, plate 18
Celts, 107, 261
Central Inuit (people), 286, 287*fig.*
cetaceans: as tattoo motifs, 279, 279*fig.*, 280*fig.*, 281, 285n17, 290*fig.*, 291, 293
charcoal, 117, 159, 198, 228, 244, plate 16
Chasseur à l'aurochs (Laugerie-Basse), 248
Chatham Island, 161*map*, 181
Cherokee (people), 197, 200, plate 17
chert, 22, 199, 199*fig.*, 202, 223, 233–34, 249, plate 20
Chickasaw (people), 195*map*, 197
China, 66, 67*map*, 68–69, 89, 95–96, 99, 117, 120*table*, 159–60, 184, 184n1, 216*map*
Chippewa (people). *See* Ojibwe
Chitimacha (people), 195*map*, 197
Choctaw (people), 195*map*, 197
Chukchi (people), 230, 263*map*, 264, 272, 274, 276, 276*fig.*
Chukotka Peninsula, 262, 263*map*, 264, 270, 274, 284n3
cinnabar, 117, 129n10, plate 8
circus, 55, 120*table*, 123–24, 125*fig.*, 128
collagen, 63–65, plate 6
Collins, Henry B., 264, 274
colonization, 53, 59, 145, 289
Communists, 153
computerized tomography (CT) scanning, 97n3
conquistadores, 39
Cook, Captain James, 159, 164, 167, 170, 171*fig.*, 183
Cook Islands, 161*map*, 162–63, 166–68, 168*fig.*, 170, 181–82, 187
copper, 21, 35, 145; and copperas, 95
Copper Age, 6, 144–45
Cordillera (Philippines), 37, 38*map*, 39, 41, 42, 48–50, 51*fig.*, 54nn1,4, 56
Crawfurd, John, 54n6
Cree (Nêhiyawahk people), 195*fig.*, 197, 205, 211, 212*fig.*

Creek (people). *See* Muscogee

criminology of tattoo, 107, 109, 119–20, 123, 126–27, 129n18

Croatia: and Croatian, 6, 150–51, 153–54, 156*fig.*, 158, 259, plate 12

Croatian Catholics, 150

Cross, Timothy, 59*fig.*

Crow (people), 202

cruciform, 39, 120*table*, 122, 129n19, 138, 144, 149n9, 151, 151*fig.*, 152–53, 154*fig.*, 155*fig.*, 156*fig.*, 157*fig.*, 158, 158*fig.*, 159, 258, 277, plate 11, plate 12

Cucuteni culture, 142, 254, 254*fig.*

culture area concept, 195

cuneiform, 68

Cycladic culture: and figurines, 256, 257*fig.*

D

Daguillon, Dr., 118, 129n20

Danube River, 144–45

Daunians (people), 159, 257, 259; and ceramics, 258, 258*fig.*; and stelae, plate 21

decolonization, 7, 210

deer bone, 235*fig.*, plate 20

"deer stones," 96

Deir el Bahari site (Egypt), 5, 11, 12*map*, 13*table*, 22, 23*fig.*, 24, 26–27, 31, 33, 36n14, 260

Deir el Medina site (Egypt), 12*map*, 13*table*, 34

Delarue, Jacques, 122

Delaware (people), 195*fig.*, 197

Demingoy, Kimo, 59*fig.*

Densmore, Frances, 198–99

Department of Forensic Medicine, Jagiellonian University (Krakow), 128n1

Dickson Mounds site (Illinois), 207, 207fig., 208n

Dieck, Alfred, 261n10

Diomede Islands, 262, 263*map*, 278, 280

DNA studies, 67

dog bone, 176, plate 14

dreams, 202, 274, plate 18

Dumești site (Romania), 142, 254, 254*fig.*

Durankulak site (Bulgaria), 142

Durham, Mary E., 150, 151*fig.*, 152

Dutdutan exposition, 50, 55n15

Džeko, Marica, 153

E

Eastern Woodlands, 7, 193, 195, 195*fig.*, 197–98, 204–5, 208n

East Greenland, 286–87, 287*fig.*

Egypt, 5, 11–12, 12*map*, 13*table*, 14, 17–18, 20–26, 28, 28*fig.*, 29*fig.*, 30*fig.*, 33–34, 35nn7,11, 36n17, 260, plate 1, plate 2

El Globo, 55n9

El Niño, 160

Enay, Bubu, 59*fig.*

En Barong, xii, 52, 52*fig.*, 53

Eskimo (people). *See* Inuit

Ethnological Results of the Point Barrow Expedition (Murdoch), 201

Ethiopia, 229*fig.*

et-Tereif site (Sudan), 12*map*, 13*table*

Eurasian steppe, 103, 215–16, 216*fig.*

Evenki (people), 230

Exposición General de las Islas Filipinas (1887), 39

F

Faber, John, Jr., 196*fig.*

feast of the dead, 270

Feleo, Roberto, 53

felines: as tattoo motifs, 73, 73*fig.*, 74*fig.*, 75*fig.*, 78, 79*fig.*, 82*fig.*, 87–88, 101, 101*fig.*, 126, plate 7

fertility magic, 20, 25–26, 32–33, 129n17, 152, 274–76, 276*fig.*, plate 22, plate 23

Festin, Elle, xi, 57–58, 60*fig.*, 61, 288, plate 24

Festin, Zel, 58, plate 24

figurative designs, 41*fig.*, 45, 47, 89, 250–52, 260

Fiji, 160, 161*map*, 163–65

Filippovka 1 site (Russia), 216, 216map, 217, 218*fig.*, 219*fig.*, 221*fig.*, 222*fig.*, 223*fig.*, 224*fig.*,

225*fig.*, 226*fig.*, 227–28, 230, plate 19
"Fire Mummies." *See* Kabayan mummies
Firth, Cecil, 31
fish: as tattoo motifs, 96, 105, 120*table*
flesh offerings, 202–3
flint. *See* chert
floraforms: as tattoo motifs, 41, 79*fig.*, 83*fig.*, 115, 115*fig.*, 119, 123*fig.*, 126, 129n13, 220, plate 8
Fore-Caucasus region, 216
Foundation for the Art and Science of Tattooing (Netherlands), 6, 130–32, plate 9
Fouquet, Dr., 23
France, Anatole, 120
"Fromain," 122, 123*fig.*, 127, 129n18
Fukushi Collection (Tokyo), 130
funerals. *See* mortuary practices

G

Gaba Gaba village (Papua New Guinea), 186, 187*fig.*, 188
Galban, Michael, xi, 210–12, 214, 214n
galena, 20, 22
Gambell village (St. Lawrence Island), 263*map*, 271, 273–74, 276
Ganondagan Seneca Art and Culture Center, 210, 212
Garcia, Al, 133*fig.*
Garong, Ame, 45, 54n
Gebelein site (Egypt), 5, 12, 12*map*, 13*table*, 14, 14*fig.*, 15, 15*fig.*, 16, 16*fig.*, 17, 19–22, 34, 35n8
Geißenklösterle site (Germany), 252
Geist, Otto W., 267, 269, 273, 273*fig.*, 274, 281, 285n13
Gell, Alfred, 181
geometric designs, 18–19, 32, 39, 41*fig.*, 43, 45, 47, 89, 121*fig.*, 122, 137, 142, 247, 257
Germans, 107
Gilbert, Steve, 5, 34n2, 103, 104, 104*fig.*, 105, 105*fig.*, 106
Godthaab Fjord, 281*fig.*
Golyama Kosmatka site (Bulgaria), 149n4
Golyamo Delchevo site (Bulgaria), 143, 143*fig.*
Gönnersdorf site (Germany), 250, 250*fig.*
Gordon, George B., 278
Graven, Jean, 121
Gravettian, 245*fig.*, 247*fig.*
Gray, Julia Mage'au, xi, 188, 190, 191*fig.*, 192, 192*fig.*, plate 15
Great Plains, 197, 202, 205
Greeks: and vase painting, 96, 259
Green Corn Dance, 203
Greenland Inuit (people), 88, 281, 281*fig.*, 286, 287, 287*fig.*
greywacke, 20, 22, 35n10
"guardians," 197, 273–75, 275*fig.*, 277, 282, 284
Guillon, Eric, 126
Gulf of Mexico, 195, 195*map*
Gutierrez, Bianca, plate 4

H

Ha'atuatua site (Marquesas Islands), 172*fig.*
Hamar (people), 229*fig.*
Hamm, Charles, xii, 132*fig.*, 133, 133*fig.*, 134
hammer: as tattoo motif, 123, 124*fig.*
Hanatekua site (Marquesas Islands), 170, 172*fig.*, 173
hand-poking, 55n18, 61, 108–9, 111, 198, 198*fig.*, 211, 286–87, 287*fig.*, 288
hand-tapping, 49, 51, 55n18, 56, 61
Hane site (Marquesas Islands), 170, 172*fig.*, 173, 182
Harataonga site (New Zealand), 183
Harcharek, Jana, xi, 292*fig.*, 293
Harcharek, Qaiyaan, xi, 290, 290*fig.*, 291, 291*fig.*, 293
Hathor, 22, 23*fig.*, 25
Haudenosaunee (people), 211–12, 214, 214n2
Hawai'i, 161*map*, 174*fig.*
Hawkes, Edward W., 270, 285n17
Hehlenstein-Stadel site (Germany), 252
Hendrix, Elizabeth, 256, 257*fig.*
henna, 261n8

Herodotus, 99–100, 137, 139, 217, 259
Hidatsa (people), 202
Hierakonpolis site (Egypt), 5, 13*table*, 21, 26, 28*fig.*, 29*fig.*, 30, 30*fig.*, 33–34, 34n, plate 1
hiri expeditions, 185–87
Hiri Moale festival, 191, 192*fig.*
Histories (Herodotus), 99
Ho-Chunk (people), 195*map*
Hohle Fels site (Germany), 251–52, 252*fig.*
Holocene, 160
Hot Water Beach site (New Zealand), 183
Houhora site (New Zealand), 170, 176, 176*fig.*, 182
Huahine, 161*map*, 170
Hudson, Charles, 205
Hughes, Mitchell, 291, 292*fig.*, 293
Hula (people), 185, 188, 189*fig.*
human bone, 64, 90, 165, 173, 176, plate 14
Huron (people). *See* Wyandot

I

Iapygian culture, 259, plate 21
Ibaloy (people), 5, 37–38, 38*fig.*, 43, 45–46, 48, 48*fig.*, 49–50, 52–53, 54n2, 55n8, 56–59, 59*fig.*, 62–64
Iceman (mummy). *See* Ötzi
identity, xi, 5, 7, 34, 34n4, 35n11, 50, 52–53, 62, 152–53, 158, 181, 188, 190, 282, 288–89, 293, plate 11
Ifugao (people), 37, 38*map*
Igorot (people), 37, 38–40, 40*fig.*, 41–42, 54n1, 55n10, 62
Ilek River, 217, 230
Îles-du-Vent site (Society Islands), 170, 171*fig.*
Illinois (people), 195*map*, 197
Illyria, 259–60; and Illyrian people, 150, 259
ilustrados, 55n10
Imperial Russian Archaeological Commission, 101
Inawi village (Papua New Guinea), plate 15

India, 184n1, 206, 209n12
Indian Ink: Iroquois and the Art of Tattoos (exhibition), 214n2
Indigenous people on exhibit, 38–41, 55n10
Indo-Europeans, 67, 72, 99
Indonesia, 162
infrared photography, 11–14, 14*fig.*, 15*fig.*, 27, 28*fig.*, 29, 29*fig.*, 30*fig.*, 31, 33–34, 34n3, 68, 70, 71*fig.*, 72, 74*fig.*, 75*fig.*, 76*fig.*, 77*fig.*, 78*fig.*, 80*fig.*, 81*fig.*, 82*fig.*, 83, 83*fig.*, 84, 84*fig.*, 85*fig.*, 86*fig.*, 89, 90*fig.*, 91*fig.*, 92*fig.*, 94, 97, 106
ink. *See* tattooing: pigments
Inked Magazine, 131
insects: as tattoo motifs, 45, 56
Instituto Nacional de Medicina Legal e Ciências Forenses (Lisbon), 128n1
Inuit (people), 230, 281, 285nn10,17,19, 286–87, 287*fig.*, 289–90, plate 23
Iñupiaq (people), 263*map*, 285n20, 287, 290, 290*fig.*, 291, 291*fig.*, 293, plate 24
Ioway (people), 195*map*, 197, 205
Ipet-Tawaret, 26, plate 2
Irian Jaya, 161*map*
Iron Age, 5, 7, 66, 96, 230, 252, 261
Iroquois (people). *See* Haudenosaunee
Iroquois Museum, 214
Isturitz site (France), 248, 248*fig.*, 249, 260
Italy, 61, 103, 249, 249*fig.*, 257, 259, plate 21
Itneg (people), 37–38
ivory: amulets and charms, 273*fig.*, plate 22, plate 23; combs, 22; dolls and doll heads, 8, 272, 273*fig.*, 277*fig.*, 278*fig.*, 282, 285n12, plate 22, plate 23; figures, 262, 266*fig.*, 268*fig.*, 279*fig.*, 282, 283*fig.*, 284, plate 23; fireboards, 272–73; hunting paraphernalia, 264; mammoth, 247*fig.*; needles, 109; sculptural and carving tradition, 264, 277; statuettes, 245*fig.*, 252*fig.*; walrus, 8, 262, 266*fig.*, 268*fig.*, 277*fig.*, 278*fig.*, 279*fig.*, 283*fig.*, plate 22, plate 23

J

jadeite, plate 23
James, Ranu, xi, 188, 191
Japan, 103–4, 109, 114
Jemison, Peter, 212
Jesus, 152
Johnston-Saint, Peter, 108, 119
joint-marking, 13, 272
Jungaria, 96

K

Kabayan mummies, 5, 37, 44, 44*fig.*, 50, 54nn2, 62–63, plate 3, plate 5, plate 6
Kabayan Museum, 44*fig.*, 54n
Ka'cak, 269
Kadada site (Sudan), 12*map*, 20*fig.*
Kafr Hassan Dawood site (Egypt), 12*map*, 21
Kankanaey (people), 37, 38*fig.*, 39, 49, 55n11
Kalinga (people), xi, 5, 37, 49–50, 56–57, 57*fig.*
Kaszas, Dion, xi, 210–11, 212*fig.*, 213*fig.*, 214, 214nn1
Kaua'i, 175
Kazakhstan, 66, 67*map*, 69, 96, 216*map*, 230
Keimer, Ludwig, 19, 23, 23*fig.*, 24, 34n2
Keros Island, 257*fig.*
Khakassia, 70
King Nebhepetre Mentuhotep II, 13*map*, 22
Kiowa (people), 287, plate 24
Kiribati (Gilbert Islands), 162, 180
Kiyaghneq, 267, 269
Kolou, Frank, 188
Kolou, Vali, xi, 189*fig.*
Konyak (people), 209n12
Koroka, Taitá, xi, 190*fig.*
Koryak (people), 264, 273–74
Kosovo, 255, 255*fig.*
Krause, Bryan, 132*fig.*
Kubban site (Sudan), 11, 12*map*, 13*table*, 26, 30–31
Kukulik site (St. Lawrence Island), 266*fig.*, 276, 284n8
Kuna, Marta, 150, 152
"Kunsten på Kroppen" (Nancke-Krogh), 103
Kupres Municipality (Bosnia), 150
Kyzlasov, Leonid, 89

L

Lacassagne, Alexandre, 123, 124, 124*fig.*, 125, 125*fig.*, 126–27, 129n12
La Femme au renne (Laugerie-Basse), 245, 246*fig.*
L'Affaire Crainquebille (France), 120
lakatoi (sea canoes), 185–86
Lakota (people), 202
La Madeleine site (France), 244, 244*fig.*
La Marche site (France), 251, 251*fig.*, 259
Langsdorff, Georg Heinrich von, 171
Lapita culture: and Lapita Cultural Complex, 160, 162–65, 183, plate 13
La Poire (Brassempouy), 245, 245*fig.*, 247–48
l'Archer (Laussel), 247
Laugerie-Basse rock-shelter site (France), 245, 246*fig.*, 248
Laukien, Michael, 153
Laussel site (France), 247
Lejre Archaeological Research Center, 101*fig.*
Le Page du Pratz, Antoine-Simon, 204, 209n11
Lepanto (Philippines), 37, 39, 41
Les Tatouages du "Milieu" (Delarue), 122
Le Tatouage à Biribi (Pierrat and Guillon), 126
Letnitsa treasure (Bulgaria), 139, 140*fig.*
Levant, 252
l'Homme à l'ours (Maz-d'Azil), 248
lightning, 53
limb-souls, 272, 285n10
"Lion Man" of Hehlenstein-Stadel, 252
Lopez, Fray Angel, 45
Louisiana, 204
lozenges, 23–25, 27, 29–31, 253–54, 260
Lumaquin, Jordan, 59*fig.*
Luzon, 5, 37, 38, 38*map*, 39, 41, 43, 49, 54n6, 55n6, 56, 62

M

Macdonald, Sutherland, 118
Macusi, Dada, 50–51, 51*fig.*
Magdalenian, 244*fig.*, 246*fig.*, 248, 248*fig.*, 250*fig.*, 251*fig.*
Mahican (people), 195*map*
Makani'olu Shelter site (Hawai'i), 174*fig.*
Makonde (people), 229*fig.*
malachite, 20
Mallari, Ryan, 58–59, 59*fig.*
Malomirovo site (Bulgaria), 139, 140*fig.*
Managalase (people), 192n1
Mangaia Island, 161*map*, 167, 168*fig.*, 170, 182, 184n
Mangareva, 168
Mangon, Irene, plate 4
Manila, 49, 52, 55n11
Maori (people), 108, 180–81, 203, 211, 291, 292*fig.*, 293
Marche, Antoine-Alfred, 40*fig.*, 41
Mariana Islands, 162
Mark of the Four Waves Tribe, 5, 57, 58*fig.*, 59*fig.*, 60*fig.*, plate 4
Marquesas Islands, 161*map*, 162–63, 166–68, 170, 172*fig.*, 182–83
marrow, 234, 272
Marshall Islands, 161*map*, 162, 180, 183
Masao, Indo, 54n2
Mas d'Azil site (France), 243, 258
masking: and masks, 13*table*, 21, 87, 89–90, 94–95, 142, 268, 285n13
Mauke Island, 161*map*, 167, 168*fig.*
Mazierski, Dave, xi, 5, 103–4, 104*fig.*, 105, 105*fig.*, 106
Mediterranean region, 145, 258, 260, 261n8
Mekeo (people), 185, 188, 191, plate 15
Memoirs of a Tattooist (Burchett), 109, 128n5
Menominee (people), 195*map*, 197–98, 198*fig.*, 199, 205, plate 16
Menominee tattooing instruments, 198, 198*fig.*, 199, 205, plate 16

Meskwaki (people), 195*map*
Meyer, Hans, 39, 41*fig.*, 42, 52*fig.*, 53
Miami (people), 195*map*
Micronesia, 159, 162–63, 180–84, 232
microwear, 6–7, 148, 149n13, 193–94, 207, 207*fig.*, 232–35, 237–39, 240n3
Mihaljevic, Tea, xi, 6, 150–53, plate 12
Mi'kmaq (people), 195*fig.*
Miller, Huron, 212
Mindanao, 56
Minusinsk region, 66, 70, 95
mirrors, 227, 230, plate 19
missionaries: and missionization, 4, 44, 49, 163, 166–67, 180–81, 185, 188, 194, 265, 287, 289
Mississippian period: and Mississippian culture, 197, 200, 207, 207*fig.*, 209n4
Mississippi River, 195, 197, 200
Missouria (people), 195*map*, 205
"mistress of sea animals," 267
"Modern Primitive" movement, 195
Mohawk (people), 195*map*, 197, 210
moko (Maori tattoo), 180, 203, 211
Molodin, Vjacheslav, 69
Mongolia, 66, 67*map*, 69, 87, 89, 96
Mooney, James, 200, 202–3, 204*fig.*
Moore, Riley, 271
mortuary practices, 17, 20, 46, 53, 66, 89–90, 99, 134, 217, 227, 271–72, 285nn11,14
mother's milk, 151, 158n1
Motu (people), 185–86, 187*fig.*, 188, 191, 192*fig.*
Mountain Province (Philippines), 38, 38*map*, 39, 54nn3,4, 55n13
Mount Pulag (Philippines), 46
Mount Santo Tomas (Philippines), 54n3
Mozambique, 229*fig.*
mummification: and mummies, xi, 4–6, 13*table*, 14, 14*fig.*, 15, 15*fig.*, 16, 16*fig.*, 22, 23, 23*fig.*, 35n6, 36n14, 37, 42, 42*fig.*, 43, 43*fig.*, 44, 46*fig.*, 47, 47*fig.*, 51, 51*fig.*, 55n11, 62–66, 69–70, 73*fig.*, 74, 74*fig.*, 75*fig.*, 76*fig.*, 77*fig.*, 78, 78*fig.*, 79*fig.*, 80*fig.*, 81*fig.*, 82*fig.*, 83*fig.*, 84, 84*fig.*,

85fig., 86fig., 87, 89–90, 90fig., 91, 91fig., 92, 92fig., 93, 93fig., 94, 94fig., 95–97, 101, 215, 230, 281fig., plate 3, plate 5, plate 6
Murdoch, John, 279, 291
Muscogee (people), 195map, 197, 200–201
Museo archeologico nazionale di Manfredonia, plate 21
Muséum National d'Histoire Naturelle, 128n1
Myanmar, 184n1, 206, 209n12
mythological animals: as tattoo motifs, 71fig., 72, 83, 85fig., 86fig., 87–89, 101, 106, plate 7, plate 18
mythology, 68, 87, 89, 267–68, 281, 284n3

N

Naga (people), 184n1, 209n12
Nancke-Krogh, Søren, 5, 103
Natchez (people), 195map, 197
National Association for the Preservation of Skin Art (USA), xii, 132fig., 133, 133fig.
National Tattoo Artists Association (Philippines), 55n16
Native Americans, 7, 193, 195, 195map, 197–98, 200–206, 208, 208n, 233, plate 17
Naxos Island, 257fig.
needle. See tattoo: implements
Nekhen site (Egypt). See Hierakonpolis
Nelson, E.W., 275, 278
Neolithic, 18, 20fig., 142, 160, 252–53, 260–61
neo-Pazyryk tattoos, 99, 100fig., 101fig., 102fig., 103, 104fig., 105fig.
Neuchâtel Museum of Ethnography, 286
New Caledonia, 160, 161map
New Guinea, 6, 159–60, 161map, 183, 184n2, 185, 187fig., 189fig., 190fig., 191fig., 192fig., plate 15
New Zealand, 61n, 108, 161map, 162–63, 168, 170, 175–76, 177fig., 178, 178fig., 179fig., 180–84, 187, 191, 203, 290fig., 291, 293, plate 14
Nikaupara site (Cook Islands), 167
Nile Valley, 11, 33–34, 35n10
Ningealook, Jack, 285n20

'Nlaka'pamux (people), 213fig.
Nome (Alaska), 263map, 288–90, plate 24
Nordström, Hans Ake, 35n11
Norman, Camilla, xi, 257–58, plate 21
North America, 7, 193–95, 195map, 202, 210, 232, 233
North Island (New Zealand), 175–76, 178
Nu'alolo Kai site (Hawai'i), 175
Nubia, 5, 11–12, 12map, 13table, 20fig., 21, 24, 26–28, 30–34, 36nn17,21, 260; and A-Group culture, 35n11; C-Group culture, 5, 13table, 25fig., 26, 28fig., 29fig., 30fig., 31–33, 34n, 260; Christian Period, 13table; Meroitic Period, 13table, 21
Nuku Hiva, 161map, 170–71, 173
Nukuoro, 161map, 180
Nunavut, 288fig., 289
Nupok, Florence (Napaaq), 165fig.

O

O'ahu, 174fig.
Obermaier, Hugo, 274, 274fig.
Oceania, 6, 160, 161map, 162, 183–84, 184n2, 199, 206
ochre, 20, 22, 145, 159, 244, 258: red, 146, 148, 200, 228, 243–44, 258, 261nn2,3, plate10; yellow, 228
Oglakhty site (Russia), 66, 67map, 70, 89, 90fig., 91fig., 92fig., 93fig., 94, 94fig., 97, 98n8; Oglakhty mummy, 70, 87, 89, 90fig., 91fig., 92fig., 93fig., 94fig., 94, 95, 98n8
Ojibwe (people), 195map, 197–99, 199fig., 208n3
Okvik/Old Bering Sea culture, 262–64, 267, 268fig., 272–73, 273fig., 278, 278fig., 279fig., 281–82, 284, 285n18, plate 23
Olon-Kurin-Gol-10 site (Mongolia), 67map, 87
Omaha (people), 195map, 197
omen creatures, 45
Oneida (people), 195map
Onondaga (people), 195map, 212
Oozevaseuk, Estelle, 267, 276

Opu, Magaiva Oini, plate 15
Ordaz, Iam, 59*fig.*
Ordos site (China), 89
Orenburg Governor's Museum of Local Lore and History, xi, 218*fig.*, 219*fig.*, 221*fig.*, 222*fig.*, 223*fig.*, 224*fig.*, 225*fig.*, 226*fig.*, plate 19
Orenburg region, 217
ornamentation, 8, 21, 34, 35n13, 53, 139, 142, 145, 220, 232, 253, 259, 263
Orpheus, 137
Oruarangi site (New Zealand), 176, 178–79, 182, plate 14
Osage (people), 195*map*, 197, 205, 206*fig.*
Oshkosh Public Museum, xii, 198, 198*fig.*, 208n
ostracon, 32*fig.*, 33
Ottawa (people), 195*map*
Ottoman Empire: and Turks, 151–52, plate 12
Ötzi (mummy), 4, 15, 102–3, 145, 148, 243, 260–61
Ovcharovo-Gorata site (Bulgaria), 142, 143*fig.*
oyster, 163

P

paddle dolls, 26, plate 2
Palau, 161*map*, 162, 180
Paleo-Eskimo culture, 88, 262, 264, 284
Palicas, Grace, 56
Pallas Athena, 149n4
palmetto, plate 17
Pan Grave culture, 13*table*, 33
Pankova, Svetlana, 5, 105–6
Papua New Guinea, 6, 159–60, 185, 187*fig.*, 188, 189*fig.*, 190, 190*fig.*, 191*fig.*, 192*fig.*, 192n1, plate 15
Parkinson, Sydney, 170
Parța site (Romania), 256, 256*fig.*,
Pazyryk site (Russia), 5, 66, 67*map*, 68–89, 96–97, 97n2,3,5,6, 101, 103–6, 215, 216*map*, 230; and mummies, 5, 69–70, 71*fig.*, 72*fig.*, 73*fig.*, 74*fig.*, 75*fig.*, 76*fig.*, 77*fig.*, 78*fig.*, 79*fig.*, 80*fig.*, 81*fig.*, 82*fig.*, 83*fig.*, 84*fig.*, 85*fig.*, 86*fig.*, 97, 97nn2,3, 101–3, 105–6, 139, 216, plate 7
Peabody Essex Museum, 175
pearl shell, 167–68, 168*fig.*, 169, 169*fig.*, 170–71, 171*fig.*, 172*fig.*, 173, 175, 182–84
Péquart, Marthe, 243
Péquart, Saint-Just, 243
Persians (people), 68, 217
Petersen, Inge-Mette, 100*fig.*
Petrić, Mario, 150
Petrovich, Peter, 100
Phanokles, 149n2
Philippine Daily Inquirer, 55n11
Philippines, 5, 37, 38*map*, 44, 49, 50, 51, 53, 56–61, 62, 162. See also *burik*
Philippine Tattoo Artists Guild (PHILTAG), 50
Picts, 107
Pierrat, Jérôme, 126
Pietrele site (Romania), 6, 143–46, 147*fig.*, 148, 149n13, plate 10
Piette, Édouard, 245, 245*fig.*
"*Pintados*," 51, 56
Pitt Rivers Museum, 165, 209n12
Plains Cree (people), 205
Pohnpei, 180, 183
Polosmak, Natalia, 69
Polyanitsa site (Bulgaria), 143, 143*fig.*
Polynesia, 6, 50, 148, 159–60, 161*map*, 162–63, 165–68, 170, 173, 175, 178, 180–84, 191, 211, 232
Polynesian Outliers, 165–66, 180, 182–83
pomelo thorns, 56, 163
Pontic-Caspian steppe, 216
Port Moresby, 191
Potawatomi (people), 195*map*
Předmostí site (Czech Republic): Venus of Predmost, 247*fig.*
pumice, 178, 178*fig.*
Punuk culture, 262–63, 272, 274, 277*fig.*, 278*fig.*, 278, 281–82, 283*fig.*, 284, plate 22
Purissima, Daniel, 51

Q

Qilakitsoq mummies, 88, 281*fig.*
Qizilchoqa site (China), 67*map*, 96
Quapaw (people), 195*map*, 197

R

Radoš, Anica, 153
Rapa Nui (Easter Island), 161*map*, 162–63, 166, 173, 174*fig.*, 175
Raupa site (New Zealand), 179, 179*fig.*
Reid, Bill, 105–6
reindeer: and antlers, 244, 244*fig.*; meat and fat, 269; bones, 270
Reiter, Jon, 128n5
revitalization movements, 291
rheumatism, 199
Richards, Nata, xi, 188
Rijksmuseum voor Volkenkunde, 55n14
Romania, 6, 139, 142–43, 145, 147*fig.*, 254, 254*fig.*, 255–56, 256*fig.*, plate 10
Rotuma, 161*map*, 166
Rovinj, 154
Rudenko, Sergei, 68, 84, 97n2, 101, 103
Russia, 67*map*, 216*map*, 263*map*, plate 7, plate 19

S

Sac (people), 195*map*
Sagada Igorots, 37
saliva, 117, 129n9, 151
Sallaffie, Moriah, 287
Samoa, 160, 161*map*, 163–64, 164*fig.*, 165, 181–83, 187, 190–91
Samovodene site (Bulgaria), 142
Santa Cruz Islands, 160, 161*map*
Sarmatian culture, 7, 84, 95, 99, 215–17, 219, 227–28, 230
Save My Ink Forever (USA), 6, 134
Savoonga village (St. Lawrence Island), 263*map*
scarification, 7, 20*fig.*, 21, 24, 142, 201–3, 208, 209n7, 229, 229*fig.*, 245, 247–48, 251, 256
Schadenberg, Alexander, 48, 55n14
Science Museum (London), 108, 110*fig.*, 111*fig.*, 112*fig.*, 113*fig.*, 114*fig.*, 115*fig.*, 116*fig.*, 121*fig.*, 123*fig.*, 124*fig.*, 125*fig.*, 127, 127*fig.*, plate 8
scratching (ritual), 7, 148, 193, 200–201, 203, 205–6, 207*fig.*, 208, 208n, plate 17
Scythians (people), 68, 87, 95–96, 99–101, 107, 137, 149n1, 216–17, 220, 227
Scytho-Siberian animal style, 68, 87, 100, 220, 227
seclusion: as ritual, 186
Selkup (people), 230
Seminole (people), 200, 203, plate 17
Semna South site (Sudan), 12*map*, 13*table*
Semper, Carl, 41
Seneca (people), 195map, 197, 210, 212
Serbia, 255
serpents: as tattoo motifs, 41, 41*fig.*, 45–46, 50, 53, 56, 138
Sevlievo site (Bulgaria), 138*fig.*, 139
Seward Peninsula, 262
Shag River site (New Zealand), 176, 183
shamans, 263, 265, 274–75, 277, 281–82, 285n20
Shanpula site (China), 67*map*, 95–96
Shengjindian site (China), 67*map*, 96
Shishmaref, 285n20
Shuvalova, Kiran, 102*fig.*
Sibenik, 153
Siberia, 4–5, 66, 97n2, 137, 216, 230, 262, 264–65, 267, 269, 270, 272–76, 276*fig.*, 279, 280*fig.*, 282, 284nn3,8, 285n9
Siberian Yupik (people), 263*map*, 265, 270, 274, 279, 280*fig.*, 282, 284n3
Siculus, Diodorus, 217
Silook, Paul, 267, 274, 277, 284nn7,8
Šimić, Ljuba, 152–53
Sitagroi site (Greece), 253*fig.*
Sivonjíc, Jela, plate 11
Skinner, Alanson B., 205, plate 16
skin-stitching, 109, 128n3,159, 211, 213*fig.*, 286–88, 288*fig.*, 289, 293n1
slaves, 95, 152

Smith, Grafton Elliot, 31
Smith, Huron, 199
Smithsonian Institution, 206*fig.*, 264, 271, 275, 283*fig.*, 291
Society Islands, 161*map*, 162–63, 167–68, 170–71, 171*fig.*, 173, 181–83
solar symbolism, 39, 41, 45–46, 46*fig.*, 138, 151, 157*fig.*
Solomon Islands, 159, 165, 184n2
soot, 48–49, 87, 95, 117, 151, 158n2, 244, 272, 285n11
souls, 46, 59, 211, 267, 269–70, 272, 281–82, 285nn10,19, 291
South Island (New Zealand), 175–76
spirits, 46–47, 62, 97n3, 197, 265–67, 269–70, 272, 274–77, 282, 284, 284nn4,6,7, 285n9,10, 293
Spiritual Journey Tattoo and Tribal Gallery, 61, plate 24
Stara Zagora site (Bulgaria), 141*fig.*
State Hermitage Museum, xi, 68, 71*fig.*, 80*fig.*, 84*fig.*, 85*fig.*, 86*fig.*, 90*fig.*, 91*fig.*, 92*fig.*, 93*fig.*, 215, plate 7
State Historical Society of North Dakota, 198, 208n
Steward, Samuel, 110
Stieda, Ludwig, 128n1
St. Lawrence Island, 263*map*, plate 22
St. Lawrence Island Yupik (people), 263*map*
Stobaeus, Joannis, 149n2
Strabo, 259
Sulu'ape Sa'a Alaiv'a Petelo, 190
Sun Dance, 202
Susquehannock (people), 195*map*
Sustento, Agit, 51
Swabian Jura Mountains, 252, 252*fig.*

T

Tabuyog, Junjun, 50
Tăcuta site (Romania), 255
Tahbone, Marjorie, xi, 287–88, 288*fig.*, 289–90, plate 24

Tahiti, 159, 171*fig.*, 187
talisman, 37, 47
Tangatatau Rockshelter site (Cook Islands), 167, 168*fig.*, 170, 183
Tardieu, Auguste Ambroise, 119, 129n12
Tarim Basin, 67*map*, 95–97
Tashtyk culture, 5, 67, 89, 94–95, 97
Tato Jim, 103
tattooing: anthropomorphic, 43*fig.*, 46, 275, 275*fig.*, 276, 282; apotropaic, 95, 129n17, 272, 285n11; beading, 110, 110*fig.*, 111, 113; bundles, 111, 144–46, 203, plate 10; ceremonies, 61, 188; circus performers, 120*table*, 123–24, 125*fig.*, 128; days, 152; experimental, 7, 22, 207, 207*fig.*, 232–34, 238, plate 20; fading, 110, 113, 113*fig.*; feathering, 110, 111*fig.*; fertility, 25–26, 32–33, 129n17, 152, 276, 276*fig.*, plate 22; genealogical, 58, 60; hygiene and infection, 22, 50, 128n4, 129n9; implements, 199, 199*fig.*, 233, plate 1, plate 10, plate 13, plate 14, plate 16, plate 17, plate 20; insignias, 119, 120*table*, 123, 124*fig.*, 125, 125*fig.*, 126, 127*fig.*, 129nn14,19; medicinal and therapeutic, 22–23, 34, 89, 103, 122, 145, 197, 199–200, 210, 260–61, 277–78, plate 18; military, 118–19, 120*table*, 122–23, 125–27, 127*fig.*, 129nn17,19; patriotic, 120*table*; pigments, 3, 20–21, 48–49, 55, 63, 70, 87, 95, 103, 108–10, 110*fig.*, 113, 113*fig.*, 115, 117, 129nn9,10,11, 134, 144–46, 148, 150–51, 154, 158–59, 165–66, 178*fig.*, 178–79, 183–84, 198–99, 218*fig.*, 219, 219*fig.*, 220, 223, 226, 226*fig.*, 227–28, 230, 233, 235, 238–39, 244, 256, 272, 287, 293, plate 8, plate 10, plate 16; preserved skin specimens in medical and mortuary collections, 4–5, 107–9, 110*fig.*, 111*fig.*, 112, 112*fig.*, 113*fig.*, 114*fig.*, 115*fig.*, 116*fig.*, 118–19, 120*table*, 121*fig.*, 123, 123*fig.*, 124, 124*fig.*, 125*fig.*, 126, 127*fig.*, 128nn1,8, 130–31, 131*fig.*, 132, 132*fig.*, 133*fig.*, 134, plate 8, plate 9; religious, 8, 37, 53, 119, 120*table*, 152–53, 181, 186, 193, 284, 289–91, plate 11; revivals, 4–7,

57–58, 58*fig.*, 59, 59*fig.*, 60, 60*fig.*, 61, 100*fig.*, 101*fig.*, 102*fig.*, 104*fig.*, 105, 105*fig.*, 106, 153, 153*fig.*, 154, 154*fig.*, 155*fig.*, 156*fig.*, 157*fig.*, 158, 158*fig.*, 187–88, 190–91, 191*fig.*, 192, 192*fig.*, 210–12, 212*fig.*, 213*fig.*, 214, 287–88, 288*fig.*, 289–90, 290*fig.*, 291, 292*fig.*, 293, plate 12; rite of passage: and initiation, 25, 32, 34, 37, 47, 95, 181, 188, 192n1, 197, 214, plate 3; shading, 109, 114, 114*fig.*, 115, 115*fig.*, 116*fig.*, 124, 128n7; skin-stretching, 112; social status, 16, 37, 41, 45, 47, 49, 53, 69, 88, 96, 197, 210, 230, 281; souvenirs, 56, 118, 120*table*, 126; stencils, 78, 112, 151, 217, 218*fig.*, 219*fig.*, 226, 226*fig.*, 228, 230; taboos, 59, 186; tally marks, 278, 278*fig.*, 279–80, 290, 290*fig.*, 291, 293; techniques (*see* hand-poking; hand-tapping; skin-stitching); technology, xi, 3–7, 11, 21–22, 48–51, 55n18, 56, 61, 84, 95, 97n6, 105, 105*fig.*, 108–10, 110*fig.*, 111, 114, 123, 128n3, 144, 146, 148, 149n13, 159, 163–64, 164*fig.*, 165–66, 166*fig.*, 167, 168, 168*fig.*, 169, 169*fig.*, 170–71, 171*fig.*, 172*fig.*, 173–74, 174*fig.*, 175–76, 177*fig.*, 178, 178*fig.*, 179, 179*fig.*, 180–84, 184nn1,5, 190–91, 191*fig.*, 193–94, 198, 198*fig.*, 199, 199*fig.*, 200, 203–6, 206*fig.*, 207, 207*fig.*, 208, 208n3, 209nn4,12, 211, 213*fig.*, 215–17, 218*fig.*, 219, 219*fig.*, 221*fig.*, 222*fig.*, 223*fig.*, 224*fig.*, 225*fig.*, 226, 226*fig.*, 227, 228–35, 235*fig.*, 236, 236*fig.*, 237, 237*fig.*, 238–39, 240n3, 243–44, 286–87, 287*fig.*, 288, 288*fig.*, 289, 292*fig.*, 293n1, plate 1, plate 10, plate 13, plate 14, plate 16, plate 20; tradesmen's, 123–24, 124*fig.*
tebori (Japanese tattoo), 103–5
Tein, Tassan, 270
Tell Hotnitsa site (Bulgaria), 141*fig.*
Tep Tok: Reading Between Our Lines (Gray et al.), 187–88, 190–91, 192n2
terra-cotta, 139, 141*fig.*, 143*fig.*, 254, 255*fig.*, 256, 260
Thebes, 11, 13*table*, 22

The Southeastern Indians (Hudson), 205
Thracian culture, 95–96, 137–38, 138*fig.*, 139, 140*fig.*, 149n1, 259–60
Thule culture, 286, 287*fig.*
Thunderbird, plate 18
Tikopia, 161*map*, 166, 166*fig.*
Timbac rock-shelter site (Philippines), 43, 45–47, 64, plate 3, plate 5, plate 6
Timor-Leste, 183
Timucua (people), 195*map*, 197
To.1 site (Tonga), 162–63, plate 13
tobacco, 282; and smoke, 63–64; wrappers, 151
Toea, Terita Gamoga, 192*fig.*
Tolentino site (Italy), 249, 249*fig.*, 260
Tomochichi (Yamacraw), 196*fig.*
Tonga, 160, 161*map*, 163–65, 181, 183, plate 13
Tongareva, 181
Tongatapu Island (Tonga), 161*map*, 162–64, plate 13
Toodlican, Molly, 213*fig.*
Toolie, Mabel, 276
totemic animals: as tattoo motifs, 89, plate 18
Town Creek site (North Carolina), 201*fig.*
traditional healers, 58, 70, plate 18
Transbaikal region, 89, 96
Truhelka, Ćiro, 150, 152, 154
Tsar Peter the Great, 100
Tuamotu Islands, 166, 181
Tubuai Island, 161*map*, 168, 169*fig.*, 181
Tunniit: Retracing the Lines of Inuit Tattoos (Arnaquq-Baril), 285n19
Turalija, Bosiljka, 153
Turfan Oasis, 96
Tuva, 96
Tuvalu, 161*map*, 165

U

Ukok Plateau, 69, 72, 84, 87–88, 215
Ukraine, 254
Ungava Peninsula, 285n17

ungulates: as tattoo motifs, 17, 19, 69, 71*fig.*, 72, 73*fig.*, 74, 77*fig.*, 78*fig.*, 87, 101*fig.*, 105, 215, plate 7

University of Alaska Museum of the North, xii, 266*fig.*, 273, 273*fig.*
University of British Columbia–Okanagan, 211
Upper Paleolithic, 7, 243–44, 249*fig.*, 259
Ural Mountains, 96, 100, 215, 217, 230
urine, 117, 272, 285n11
use-wear analysis. *See* microwear
Usoe site (Bulgaria), 142, 143*fig.*

V

Vairoronga site (Cook Islands), 167
Vaitoʻotia site (Society Islands), 171*fig.*
van der Helm, Peter, xi, 130–31, 131*fig.*, 132–33, plate 9
Vandeventer site (Illinois), 207
VanStone, James, 274
Vanuatu, 159–60, 161*map*, 162
Venus figurines, 245, 245*fig.*, 247, 247*fig.*, 251–52, 252*fig.*
Verelst, William, 196*fig.*
Verkh-Kaldzhin-2 site (Russia), 67*map*, 69, 88, 215, 216*map*
vermilion, 117, plate 8
Vinča culture, 255, 255*fig.*, 256, 256*fig.*
Virginia Algonquian (people), 195*map*, 197
Visayas, 51
Vogelherd site (Germany), 252
Volga River, 217
von den Steinen, Karl, 173
von Hagens, Gunther, 131
Vratsa site (Bulgaria), 139, 140*fig.*, 149n4

W

Waima (people), 185, 188, 190*fig.*
Wairau Bar site (New Zealand), 175–76, 177*fig.*, 182, 184n
Walters, Isaac, 7

war honors, 197
Washpool site (New Zealand), 183
weapons: as tattoo motifs, 93, 93*fig.*, 94, 94*fig.*, 103, 121*fig.*, 122, 123*fig.*
Wellcome Collection, 5, 108–9, 111–12, 114–15, 116*fig.*, 117–19, 120*table*, 122–23, 123*fig.*, 124, 126–27, 129n17, 130, plate 8; and Sir Henry Wellcome, 108
Wells-Listener, Carla, xi, 211, 212*fig.*, 214n
West Greenland, 281*fig.*, plate 23
Weyer, Edward M., 285n10
Whang-Od, xi, 5, 49, 56, 57*fig.*, 61
White, Alan, xi, plate 18
Whitipirorua site (New Zealand), 183
Wong, Stan, 105
Woodland period, 197, 200
Wyandot (people), 195*map*

X

X-rays, 70, 87
Xinjiang site (China), 89; and region, 67*map*
Xiongnu culture, 99

Y

Yaavgaghsiq, Alice, 275
Yamacraw (people), 195*map*, 196*fig.*
Yanghai site (China), 67*map*, 96
Yap Island, 162
Yenisei River, 67
Yuchi (people), 195*map*, 197, 200
Yuezhi culture, 99
Yugoslavia, 152
Yup'ik (people), 263*map*, 264, 270, 275, 281–82, 287

Z

Zaghunluq site (China), 67*map*, 96
Zagreb, xi, 152, 154*fig.*, 155*fig.*, 156*fig.*
Zele, xi, 6, 152–53, 154*fig.*, 155*fig.*, 156*fig.*
Zlatinitsa site (Bulgaria), 139, 149n4